AF478128

SPANISH
BORDERLANDS
SOURCEBOOKS

Presenting Over Four Hundred and Fifty Scholarly Articles and Source
Materials Documenting Interactions Between Native Americans and
Europeans from California to Florida

Each Volume Edited with an Introduction by a Major Scholar

General Editor
David Hurst Thomas
American Museum of Natural History

A GARLAND SERIES

2

Native American Demography in the Spanish Borderlands

Edited with an Introduction by
Clark Spencer Larsen

GARLAND PUBLISHING, INC.
NEW YORK & LONDON, 1991

Library of Congress Cataloging-in-Publication Data

Native American demography in the Spanish borderlands / edited with an introduction by Clark Spencer Larsen.

p. cm. — (The Spanish borderlands sourcebooks ; 2)

Includes bibliographical references.

ISBN 0-8240-0781-6 (alk. paper)

1. Indians of North America—Population. 2. Indians of North America—Diseases. 3. Indians of North America—History—Sources. 4. Epidemics—United States—History. 5. Spain—Colonies—America. I. Larsen, Clark Spencer. II. Series

E98.P76N38 1991

305.8'97073—dc20   90-22357

CONTENTS

Sources

Aten, Lawrence E.
1983   Population Reconstruction. In his *Indians of the Upper Texas Coast.* Pp. 43–66. New York: Academic Press. Reprinted by permission.

Cook, S. F.
1943   *The Conflict Between the California Indian and White Civilization: I. The Indian versus the Spanish Mission.* Pp. 3-101. Ibero-Americana 21. Berkeley: University of California Press. Reprinted by permission.

Dobyns, Henry F.
1963   Indian Extinction in the Middle Santa Cruz River Valley, Arizona. *New Mexico Historical Review* 38(2):163–181. Reprinted by permission.

1983   An Outline of Florida Epidemiology. In his *Their Number Become Thinned: Native American Population Dynamics in Eastern North America.* Pp. 247–295. Knoxville: University of Tennessee Press. Reprinted by permission.

Ewers, John C.
1973   The Influence of Epidemics on the Indian Populations and Cultures of Texas. *Plains Anthropologist* 18:104–115. Reprinted by permission.

Hann, John H.
1986   Demographic Patterns and Changes in Mid-Seventeenth Century Timucua and Apalachee. *Florida Historical*

Quarterly 64(4):371–392. Reprinted by permission of the
Florida Historical Society.

JACKSON, ROBERT H.

1985   Demographic Change in Northwestern New Spain. *The
Americas* 41(4):462–479. Reprinted by permission of the
Academy of American Franciscan History.

MEISTER, CARY W.

1976   Demographic Consequences of Euro-American Contact
on Selected American Indian Populations and Their
Relationship to the Demographic Transition. *Ethnohistory*
23(2):161–172. Reprinted by permission of the American
Society for Ethnohistory.

MILNER, GEORGE R.

1980   Epidemic Disease in the Postcontact Southeast: A
Reappraisal. *Midcontinental Journal of Archaeology*
5(1):39–56. Reprinted by permission of Kent State
University Press.

PALKOVICH, ANN M.

1985   Historic Population of the Eastern Pueblos: 1540–1910.
Journal of Anthropological Research 41(4):401–426.
Reprinted by permission of the University of New Mexico
Department of Anthropology and the author.

RAMENOFSKY, ANN F.

1987   The Lower Mississippi Valley. In her *Vectors of Death:
The Archaeology of European Contact.* Pp. 42–71.
Albuquerque: University of New Mexico Press. Reprinted
by permission.

REFF, DANIEL T.

1987   Old World Diseases and the Dynamics of Indian and Jesuit
Relations in Northwestern New Spain, 1520–1660. In
Ejidos and Regions of Refuge in Northwestern Mexico, N.
Ross Crumrine, Phil C. Weigand, eds. Pp.85–94.
Anthropological Papers of the University of Arizona,

No. 46. Tucson: University of Arizona Press. Reprinted by
permission of the University of Arizona Press and the
University of Arizona Department of Anthropology.

SCHUETZ, MARDITH KEITHLY
    1980   Demography of the Mission Indians. In *The Indians of the
San Antonio Missions.* Pp. 116–231. unpublished doctoral
dissertation, University of Texas at Austin. Reprinted by
permission of the author.

SMITH, MARVIN T.
    1987   The Demographic Collapse. In his *Archaeology of
Aboriginal Culture Change in the Interior Southeast.* Pp.
54–85. Gainesville: The University of Florida Press.
Reprinted by permission.

INTRODUCTION

Perhaps the most discussed issue regarding the impact of the arrival of Europeans in the New World on native populations is the precipitous decline in population size among the latter. Early historical accounts provide us with numerous observations on the apparent relationship between epidemic diseases and population decline. For example, in the Southeast, one member of the de Soto entrada noted in 1540 that at Cofitachequi (South Carolina side of the Savannah River) "within a league, and halfe a league about this towne, were great townes dispeopled, and overgrowne with grasse, which shewed that they had been long without inhabitants. The Indians said, that two years before there was a plague in that countrie, and that they remooved to other townes" (Elvas 1851; quoted in Milner 1980: this volume). When the same expedition arrived at the town of Talomeco, a chronicler pointed out that "The Castilians found no people in Talomeco because the previous pestilence had been more rigorous and devastating in this town than in any other of the whole province, and the few Indians who had escaped had not yet reclaimed their homes; hence our men paused but a short time in these houses" (Garcilaso 1951; quoted in Milner 1980 this volume).

Most would agree that disease contributed substantially to heavy population losses throughout the period of time encompassing the Spanish occupation of the Borderlands, and the evidence in support of this abounds in the existing historical sources provided in census records and other documentation. In 1657, Governor Rebolledo remarked that in *La Florida*—Timucua and Guale, in particular—few individuals remained alive because of high levels of mortality due to the "sickness of the plague and of small pox" (quoted in Hann 1988: 175).

Population declines were exacerbated by settlement changes that were occasioned by the process of missionization of native populations for many areas of the Borderlands. That is, the Spanish practiced a system of *Reduccion* whereby native populations were concentrated into a limited number of centers (e.g., missions), thus providing control that was more easily maintained than with more dispersed populations (Geiger 1937; Jones 1978). The effects of this nucleation policy were disastrous for the Indians, primarily because conditions were established that were conducive to the maintenance and spread of existing as well as newly introduced infectious diseases (various authors in this volume).

Castillo (1978: 102–103) has succinctly summarized the effects of this settlement change on native California populations: "The mission housing aggregated many people in a relatively small area with bad sanitation and minimal ventilation and heat, providing favorable environment for the spread of contagious diseases.... [As a result,] [t]hree major epidemics occurred.... The first was reported at Mission Santa Clara in 1777 and was said to have been respiratory in nature. In 1802 a pneumonia and diptheria epidemic, almost entirely confined to the young, ravaged the natives from Mission San Carlos to San Luis Obispo. The most devastating malady of this era occurred in 1806 when a measles epidemic decimated native peoples from San Francisco to Santa Barbara. In this catastrophe at least 1,600 natives died and in some missions it was reported that children under 10 years of age were almost completely wiped out."

Why was it, then, that so many Indians died, yet relatively few Europeans succumbed to these maladies? It is unlikely that native populations lacked *inherent* genetic resistance to newly introduced diseases (Newman 1976; Kelley 1988). Europeans had the advantage over native populations in that their experience with Old World pathogens resulted in *acquired* immunities. Kelley (1988) has pointed out, moreover, that native populations lacked knowledge of simple medical attendance for individuals with viral and bacterial diseases, including in particular, rest, warmth, and fluid consumption. He notes that for colonial New England, for example, seventeenth-century Europeans were well aware of the value of these factors in health care of the sick. Native populations were not. Stearn and Stearn (1945; see Aten 1983 this volume) point out that native populations did not quarantine individuals with smallpox, thereby leading to epidemic events of the disease.

Although a host of European-introduced diseases (e.g., smallpox, measles, influenza, the common cold) contributed to population decline in most regions of the Borderlands, other variables must be considered in the interpretation of population decline. Indians associated with missions provided an important source of labor both on the local level and for projects away from the home missions. This labor pool provided the necessary workforce for growing of crops and other subsistence activities. One sixteenth-century governor of Florida noted that "but with all this and the grain from the maize, the labor that they endure in the many cultivations that are given is great, and, if it were not for the help of the Indians that I make them give, and they come from the province of Guale, Antonico, and from other caciques, it would not be possible to be able to sow any grain" (unpublished translation provided by John H. Hann).

The passage presented suggests that Indians were under tremendous pressures to provide food for Europeans. This factor, combined with other labor pressures and abuses almost certainly contributed to declines in some of these regions. Fray Alonso Moral, a thirty-three-year veteran of the Florida missions, noted in 1676 that "All of the natives . . . suffer great servitude, injuries, and vexations from the fact that the governors, lieutenants, and soldiers oblige them to carry loads on their shoulders. . . . And it usually happens that to enhance their own interests they pretend that this work is in Your Majesty's service, without paying them what is just for such intolerable work. And if now and again they give them something for that reason, it is a hoe or an axe or a cheap blanket or some other thing of such slight value to pay for their work, which involves carrying a cargo on their shoulders from the [St. Augustine] fort to the Province of Apalachee, which is eighty leagues distant, and the same to return. . . . And in addition to this, in order to employ them further they detained them in St. Augustine for as long as they wish . . . with very short rations, such as giving them only two pounds of corn a day and giving them for pay, at the most, one real for each day of work, which sum is usually given them in the form of old rubbish of little or no value or utility to them. Add to this the further vexation or injury of being snatched by force from their homes and villages, not only for tasks at the fort but also for work for private citizens, and this in the rigor of winter (when they come naked) or in the middle of summer, which is when they are most occupied in the labor of their crops on which solely depends not only their sustenance and that of their wives and children but also the victuals necessary for the relief of the garrison. . . . Each year from Apalachee alone more than three hundred are brought to the fort at the time of the planting of the corn, carrying their food and the merchandise of the soldiers on their shoulders for more than eighty leagues with the result that some on arrival die and those who survive do not return to their homes because the governor and the other officials detain them in the fort so they may serve them and this without paying them a wage. . . . This is the reason according to the commonly held opinion that they are being annihilated at such a rate" (quotation from Hann 1988: 140–141).

Other factors that contributed to population decline included deaths from confrontations with Spanish military such as those associated with reprisals following native revolts. In the missions of Florida and the Pueblos of the Southwest, many lives were lost in this manner (see Jones 1978; Simmons 1979; Palkovich 1985 this volume).

A decline in dietary quality following the arrival of Europeans also quite likely had a negative effect on native populations. With respect to

Georgia coastal Indians, Jones (1978) has noted that maize was an important component of native diet. Although maize is a relatively reliable food source, over-dependence on it leads to health problems. Both living and past populations emphasizing maize as a dietary focus exhibit evidence of growth disruption and other changes that reflect a reduced quality of life (see Huss-Ashmore et al. 1982; Cohen and Armelagos 1984; Larsen 1987). Although malnutrition alone will not necessarily lead to death, it has a synergistic relationship with infectious disease. Poor nutrition will result in lowering an individual's resistance to infection and depress the cell-mediated immune response (Hoffman-Goetz 1986; Mims 1982).

In order to understand the magnitude of population loss due to disease, physical abuse, malnutrition, and other factors, it is important that population size at initial contact be accurately estimated. A very wide range of estimates has been provided in this regard (see Ubelaker 1988; Thornton 1987; Joralemon 1982), therefore it is difficult to precisely track population size reduction at the time of contact. Dobyns (1966, 1983 this volume) has advocated revising population estimates sharply upward from those figures provided by Mooney (1928), Kroeber (1939), and others. Although Dobyns has quite likely overestimated population size (see, for example, discussions by Henige 1986 and Ubelaker 1988), he has, nevertheless, stimulated much fruitful discussion among historians, anthropologists, and demographers regarding native population size at contact.

Ubelaker (1988) has estimated population size for the major regions of North America, including the Spanish Borderlands. His estimates of population at initial contact compared with nadir figures indicate that in the Borderlands, California was hardest hit by population losses—95 percent reduction. This is followed by the Southeast (71 percent reduction) and the Southwest (65 percent reduction). It is important to note, however, that some areas within these regions saw *complete* population loss. For example, due to a combination of factors—disease, starvation, military force, out-migration, slave-raiding, and piracy—the Guale along the Georgia coast experienced nearly complete extinction as a tribal entity by the late seventeenth century (Jones 1978). On the other hand, other regions did not show steady declines, but rather, showed periodic increases (see Larsen et al. 1990; Meister 1976 this volume; Palkovich 1985 this volume). Despite this variation, however, the overall result for native populations was near extermination.

Since the time of the first chroniclers up to the present day, a voluminous scholarly literature has developed documenting the impact of European contact. Most of this literature is based on historical sources involving the analysis of census records, translations, and other documentation. More recently, however, archaeological studies have demonstrated the potential for understanding the dynamics of postcontact population change. Smith (1987 this volume) has looked at site size, number of sites, and population movement in the interior Southeast and points to possible changes relating to epidemic disease and other factors. Similarly, Ramenofsky (1987 this volume) has examined settlement counts and distribution in the analysis of population change. This analysis suggests that population loss in the lower Mississippi Valley was rapid and began with initial contact, namely at the time of the de Soto entrada in the mid-sixteenth century. This finding is especially important because it indicates that population decline for this region was initiated with first contact and did not arise from the later and more sustained French presence in the region (see also Dobyns 1983; Upham 1986).

Archaeological documentation of population change in the Southwest by Haas and Creamer (1988) is beginning to show a number of important developments regarding the timing of reduction. In particular, in the Chama River drainage of New Mexico, analysis of surface ceramics and tree-ring dates suggests that the majority (80 percent) of villages appear to have been abandoned in the first quarter of the sixteenth century. Although environment may have influenced these changes, Haas and Creamer note that disease and warfare need to be considered in explanation of this large-scale abandonment.

The study of the human skeletal record offers another dimension to our understanding of contact human biology and population dynamics. During the years of growth and development and adulthood, the skeleton is sensitive to the environment in that a variety of factors, including diet, disease, and physical work, leave a cumulative record of life experiences in bones and teeth (reviewed in Huss-Ashmore et al. 1982; Larsen 1987). Thus, the study of human remains can reveal a wealth of information on past populations and their ability or lack of ability to cope with environmental circumstances.

For a number of regions of the Borderlands, biological anthropologists have begun investigating the impact of the arrival of Europeans by examining human skeletal remains from contact period sites. Larsen and co-workers (Larsen 1990; Larsen et al. 1990) have been examining native populations from precontact sites and descendant mission populations from coastal Georgia and Florida. This investigation has revealed a probable decline in quality of life for native populations during later prehistory and in the contact period for this region. For example, there is dental evidence of increased nonspecific physiological stress (Hutchinson and Larsen 1988). Analysis of carbon and nitrogen isotopic ratios in bone collagen revealed an increased emphasis on maize during the contact period (Schoeninger et al. 1990 ; Larsen et al.

1990). Moreover, analysis of skeletal morphology (Ruff and Larsen 1990) and osteoarthritis (Griffen and Larsen 1989) showed an increase in physical demand and work load in the contact period.

Blakely and co-workers (Blakely 1988; Blakely and Detweiler-Blakely 1989) have examined a series of human remains from the King site, a sixteenth-century occupation in northwest Georgia. Study of the human remains from this locality has shown that a number of individuals were killed in a violent encounter with Spanish military, most likely from the de Soto entrada in 1540. The encounter was brief and appears not to have resulted in large-scale death (see also Hutchinson 1990 for another instance of violent encounter with Spaniards). In contrast to the Georgia coast, no clear decline in quality of life is evident in these materials in comparison with precontact populations in the region. The presence of decline in the later Georgia coastal population, but not in the King site population, suggests that the impact of European presence was not fully experienced until more sustained contact later in the seventeenth century (see also discussion in Blakely and Detweiler-Blakely 1989).

Preliminary study of contact period human remains from missions of Texas (Miller 1989) and California (Walker et al. 1989) and Pueblos of the Southwest (Stodder 1989, n.d.) has provided initial findings on lifeway and human health. Miller (1989) and Stodder (1989, n.d.) have both reported increased levels of nonspecific bone infections and other markers of stress in contact period populations. Walker and co-workers (1989) indicate that there was a marked decrease in dietary diversity in California mission populations that they have studied. They note that this may have led to growth retardation in Indians that occupied these missions.

In sum, most evidence for change in demographic profiles, quality of lifeway, and related issues is derived primarily from historical sources. Recent analyses based on archaeological and bioanthropological data are providing important findings.

The purpose of this volume is to reprint scholarly works relating to demography and other aspects of human biology in the Spanish Borderlands. The volume is divided into four geographic regions: Southeast, Texas, Southwest (including northwest Mexico), and California (including Baja and Alta California).

Five works are reprinted representing the Southeast, including chapters from two books that consider the archaeological evidence for population change (Smith 1987; Ramenofsky 1987), excerpts by Dobyns (1983) and Hann (1986) on the respective Timucua and Apalachee tribes of *La Florida*, and a discussion of general aspects of demographic change and epidemic disease by Milner (1980).

Texas is represented by three works. They include a general paper on the influence of epidemics on population size and culture change by Ewers (1973), a chapter from a book on the upper Texas Gulf coast by Aten (1983), and a chapter from an unpublished doctoral dissertation by Schuetz (1980) on demography of the missions of San Antonio.

The Southwest is represented by previously published papers by Palkovich (1985) on population change in the eastern Pueblos, by Dobyns (1963) on northern Piman Indians from the Santa Cruz River Valley, and by Meister (1976) on variability of demographic change. The wealth of data from historical sources in northwest Mexico has been examined in a doctoral dissertation by Reff (1985), the results of which are summarized in a shorter work reprinted here (Reff 1987).

Commencing with groundwork laid by Peveril Meigs III and Sherburne F. Cook in the mid-1930s, scholarship dealing with California has become the most extensive relative to other regions of the Spanish Borderlands (e.g., Meigs 1935; Cook 1935, 1937, 1940, 1943 this volume, 1947, 1976; Cook and Borah 1971–1979; Aschmann 1959). More recently, Jackson and co-workers have continued the tradition of demographic research, building upon the record established by Cook and others (e.g., Jackson 1981a, 1981b, 1981c, 1983a, 1983b, 1984, 1985 this volume, 1986; Stern and Jackson 1988; Langer and Jackson 1988). This volume reprints excerpts from a classic monograph by Cook (1943), and Robert Jackson's volume in *The Spanish Borderlands Sourcebooks* reprints sections of one of Aschmann's (1959). More recent analysis is provided in a publication by Jackson (1985 this volume) on population change in Baja and Alta California. This latter work also presents data on populations in Sonora.

The reader will observe that very little of this volume includes works published by biological anthropologists. This paucity of material reflects the fact that minimal research has been done that uses human remains as a data source (see discussion in Larsen 1990.) However, as pointed out above, biological anthropologists are beginning to examine human remains from contact period sites in order to provide a broader basis for discussion regarding biocultural change and adaptation following the arrival of Europeans in the New World.

Each of these approaches has its biases. Historical sources, for example, can be misleading. For instance, until a decade ago, a consensus had developed regarding Georgia coastal subsistence and settlement pattern. That is, unlike interior Southeast populations, coastal populations practiced shifting cultivation, and were characterized as highly dispersed and mobile (see Larson 1978). Jones (1978) has reexamined the early sources and found them to be distorted representations of what coastal lifeways were really like. Jones notes that in contrast to what Jesuits presented, earlier French records and later records indicate that coastal populations were far less mobile and certainly more dependent upon maize than the Jesuits had implied (see also discussion in Thomas 1987).

Archaeological sources, too, have their limitations. For example, in order to diachronically document population and settlement change, it is essential that chronology be accurate. Ramenofsky (1987 this volume) notes that in the lower Mississippi Valley archaeologists have not developed a single, consistent chronology for the region, especially for late prehistoric and early historic periods. Ramenofsky offers an alternative chronology that "crosses into historical periods but does not prejudge the nature of changes that occur in those periods" (1987 this volume). Other biases in the archaeological record include sampling problems and site identification (Smith 1987 this volume; Ramenofsky 1987).

The human skeletal record is also limited by a number of biases. For example, demographic reconstruction based on age composition of skeletal series is often hampered by cultural and preservation factors (Buikstra and Mielke 1985; Larsen 1987). Many skeletal series are underrepresented in both very young and very old age cohorts, either due to cultural practices and differential treatment, or because the bones of very young and very old individuals are thinner and more susceptible to poor preservation.

Despite these problems, however, the integration of ethnohistorical, archaeological, and biocultural approaches has potential for looking at a wide range of issues, not only for demographic reconstruction, but for understanding patterns of health, dietary change, and lifeway overall.

Biological disruption at contact should not be viewed as simply a matter of population size reduction, but rather, should be understood in the context of the interplay between dietary change, malnutrition, work load, warfare, disease, social change, as well as other factors that contribute to documented population changes, especially as they relate to alterations in fertility (birth rate) and mortality (death rate) profiles. Each of the approaches—ethnohistorical, archaeological, and biocultural—offers a unique perspective that taken in combination holds promise for future study of the consequences of contact.

I wish to thank Winifred Creamer, Anne Fox, Ann L. W. Stodder, Robert H. Jackson, and Daniel T. Reff for providing several works cited or reprinted in this volume.

Clark Spencer Larsen

REFERENCES

ASCHMANN, HOMER

1959   *The Central Desert of Baja California: Demography and Ecology.* Ibero-Americana 42: 133–253, 269–282.

BLAKELY, ROBERT L. (EDITOR)

1988   *The King Site: Continuity and Contact in Sixteenth-Century Georgia.* Athens: University of Georgia Press.

BLAKELY, ROBERT L., AND BETTINA DETWEILER-BLAKELY

1989   The Impact of European Diseases in the Sixteenth-Century Southeast: A Case Study. *Midcontinental Journal of Archaeology* 14: 62–89.

BUIKSTRA, JANE E., AND JAMES H. MIELKE

1985   Demography, Diet, and Health. In *The Analysis of Prehistoric Diets*, Robert I. Gilbert and James H. Mielke, eds. Pp. 359–422. Orlando: Academic Press.

CASTILLO, EDWARD D.

1978   The Impact of Euro-American Exploration and Settlement. In *California*, Robert F. Heizer, ed. Pp. 99-127. Handbook of North American Indians, Vol. 8, William G. Sturtevant, general editor. Washington, D.C.: Smithsonian Institution Press.

COHEN, MARK NATHAN, AND GEORGE J. ARMELAGOS (EDITORS)

1984   *Paleopathology at the Origins of Agriculture.* Orlando: Academic Press.

COOK, SHERBURNE F.

1935   Diseases of the Indians of Lower California in the Eighteenth Century. *Journal of California and Western Medicine* 43: 1–6.

1937   *The Extent and Significance of Disease among the Indians of Baja California from 1697–1773.* Ibero-Americana 12.

1940   *Population Trends among the California Mission Indians.* Ibero-Americana 17.

1947   Survivorship in Aboriginal Populations. *Human Biology* 19: 83–89.

1976   *The Conflict between the California Indian and White Civilization.* Berkeley: University of California Press.

ELVAS, THE GENTLEMAN OF
1851   *The Discovery and Conquest of Terra Florida.* Hakluyt
            Society 9.

GARCILASO DE LA VEGA
1951   *The Florida of the Inca.* Translated by J. G. Varner and J. J.
            Varner. Austin: University of Texas Press.

GEIGER, MAYNARD
1937   *The Franciscan Conquest of Florida (1573–1618).* Studies in
            Hispanic-American History 1. Washington, D.C.: Catholic
            University of America.

GRIFFIN, M.C., AND C. S. LARSEN
1989   Patterns in Osteoarthritis: A Case Study from the South-
            eastern U.S. Atlantic Coast. *American Journal of Physical
            Anthropology* 78: 232.

HAAS, JONATHAN, AND WINIFRED CREAMER
1988   Demography and the Proto-Historic Pueblos of the North-
            ern Rio Grande: A.D. 1450–1680. Paper presented at the
            "Current Research on Late Prehistoric and Early Historic
            New Mexico" conference. New Mexico Archaeological
            Council.

HANN, JOHN H.
1988   *Apalachee: The Land between the Rivers.* Gainesville:
            University of Florida Press.

HENIGE, DAVID
1986   Primary Source by Primary Source: On the Role of Epidem-
            ics in New World Depopulation. *Ethnohistory* 33: 293–312.

HOFFMAN-GOETZ, L.
1986   Malnutrition and Immunological Function with Special
            Reference to Cell-Mediated Immunity. *Yearbook of Physi-
            cal Anthropology* 29: 139–159.

HUSS-ASHMORE, REBECCA, ALAN H. GOODMAN, AND GEORGE J. ARMELAGOS
1982   Nutritional Inference from Paleopathology. In *Advances in
            Archaeological Method and Theory*, Vol. 5, Michael B.
            Schiffer, ed. Pp. 395–473. New York: Academic Press.

HUTCHINSON, DALE L.
1990   Postcontact Biocultural Change and Mortuary Site
            Evidence. In *Columbian Consequences, Volume 2:
            Archaeological and Historical Perspectives on the Spanish
            Borderlands East,* David Hurst Thomas, ed. 61–70
            Washington, D.C.: Smithsonian Institution Press.

HUTCHINSON, DALE L., AND CLARK SPENCER LARSEN

1988   Determination of Stress Episode Duration from Linear Enamel Hypoplasias: A Case Study from St. Catherines Island, Georgia. *Human Biology* 60: 93–110.

JACKSON, ROBERT H.

1981a   Epidemic Disease and Population Decline in the Baja California Missions, 1697–1834. *Southern California Quarterly* 63: 308–346.

1981b   The Last Jesuit Censuses of the Pimeria Alta Missions, 1761 and 1766. *The Kiva* 46: 243–272.

1981c   The 1781–1782 Smallpox Epidemic in the Baja California Missions. *Journal of California and Great Basin Anthropology* 3: 138–143.

1983a   Disease and Demographic Patterns at Santa Cruz Mission, Alta California. *Journal of California and Great Basin Anthropology* 5: 33–57.

1983b   Demographic Patterns in the Missions of Northern Baja California. *Journal of California and Great Basin Anthropology* 5: 131–139.

1984   Demographic Patterns in the Missions of Central Baja California. *Journal of California and Great Basin Anthropology* 6: 91–112.

1986   Patterns of Demographic Change in the Missions of Southern Baja California. *Journal of California and Great Basin Anthropology* 8: 273–279.

JONES, GRANT D.

1978   The Ethnohistory of the Guale Coast through 1684. In *The Anthropology of St. Catherines Island: 1. Natural and Cultural History*, David Hurst Thomas, Grant D. Jones, Roger S. Durham, and Clark Spencer Larsen. Anthropological Papers of the American Museum of Natural History 55 (part 2): 178–210.

JORALEMON, DONALD

1982   New World Population and the Case of Disease. *Journal of Anthropological Research* 38: 109–127.

KELLEY, MARC A.

1988   Ethnohistorical Accounts as a Method of Assessing Viral and Bacterial Spread among New World Inhabitants. Paper presented at the International Congress of Anthropological and Ethnological Sciences, Zagreb.

KROEBER, ALFRED L.
1939   *Cultural and Natural Areas of Native North America.*
            University of California Publications in American Arche-
            ology and Ethnology 38.

LANGER, ERICK D., AND ROBERT H. JACKSON
1988   Colonial and Republican Missions Compared: The Cases
            of Alta California and Southeastern Bolivia. *Comparative
            Studies in Society and History* 30: 286–311.

LARSEN, CLARK SPENCER
1987   Bioarchaeological Interpretations of Subsistence Economy
            and Behavior from Human Skeletal Remains. In *Advances
            in Archaeological Method and Theory*, Vol. 10, Michael B.
            Schiffer, ed. Pp. 339–445. San Diego: Academic Press.

LARSEN, CLARK SPENCER (EDITOR AND CONTRIBUTOR)
1990   *The Archaeology of Mission Santa Catalina de Guale: 2.
            Biocultural Interpretations of a Population in Transition.*
            Anthropological Papers of the American Museum of
            Natural History, No. 68.

LARSEN, CLARK SPENCER, MARGARET J. SCHOENINGER, DALE L. HUTCHINSON,
KATHERINE F. RUSSELL, AND CHRISTOPHER B. RUFF
1990   Beyond Demographic Collapse: Biological Adaptation and
            Change in Native Populations of L*a Florida*. In *Columbian
            Consequences, Volume 2: Archaeological and Historical
            Perspectives on the Spanish Borderlands East*, David Hurst
            Thomas, ed. 409–428 Washington, D.C.: Smithsonian
            Institution Press.

LARSON, LEWIS H., JR.
1978   Historic Guale Indians of the Georgia Coast and the Im-
            pact of the Spanish Mission Effort. In *Tacachale: Essays on
            the Indians of Florida and Southeastern Georgia during the
            Historic Period*, Jerald T. Milanich, ed. Pp. 120–140.
            Gainesville: University of Florida Press.

MEIGS, PEVERIL, III
1935   The *Dominican Mission Frontier of Lower California*.
            Berkeley: University of California Press.

MILLER, ELIZABETH
1989   The Effect of European Contact on the Health of Indig-
            enous Populations in Texas. Paper presented at the
            meetings of the American Association of Physical Anthro-
            pologists, San Diego.

MIMS, C.A.
1982   *The Pathogenesis of Infectious Disease.* London: Academic Press.

MOONEY, JAMES
1928   The Aboriginal Population North of Mexico. *Smithsonian Miscellaneous Collections* 80: 1–40.

NEWMAN, MARSHALL T.
1976   Aboriginal New World Epidemiology and Medical Care, and the Impact of Old World Disease Imports. *American Journal of Physical Anthropology* 45: 667–672.

RUFF, CHRISTOPHER B., AND CLARK SPENCER LARSEN
1990   Postcranial Biomechanical Adaptations to Subsistence Strategy Changes on the Georgia Coast. In *The Archaeology of Mission Santa Catalina de Guale: 2. Biocultural Interpretations of a Population in Transition*, Clark Spencer Larsen, ed. 94–120 Anthropological Papers of the American Museum of Natural History, No. 68.

SCHOENINGER, MARGARET J., NIKOLAAS J. VAN DER MERWE, KATHERINE MOORE, JULIA LEE THORP, AND CLARK SPENCER LARSEN
1990   Decrease in Diet Quality between the Prehistoric and Contact Periods. In *The Archaeology of Mission Santa Catalina de Guale: 2. Biocultural Interpretations of a Population in Transition*, Clark Spencer Larsen, ed. Pp. 78–93. Anthropological Papers of the American Museum of Natural History.

SIMMONS, MARC
1979   History of Pueblo-Spanish Relations to 1821. In *Southwest*, Alfonso Ortiz, ed. Pp. 178–193. *Handbook of North American Indians*, Vol. 8, William G. Sturtevant, general editor. Washington, D.C.: Smithsonian Institution Press.

STEARN, E. WAGNER, AND ALLEN E. STEARN
1945   *The Effect of Smallpox on the Destiny of the Amerindian.* Boston: Bruce Humphries, Inc.

STERN, PETER, AND ROBERT H. JACKSON
1988   Vagabundaje and Settlement Patterns in Colonial North ern Sonora. *The Americas* 44: 461–481.

STODDER, ANN LUCY WIENER
1989   Bioarchaeological Research in the Basin and Range Region. In *Human Adaptations and Cultural Change in the*

Greater Southwest: An Overview of Archaeological Resources in the Basin and Range Province, Alan H. Simmons, Ann Lucy Wiener Stodder, Douglas D. Dykeman, and Patricia A. Hicks, pp. 167–190. U.S. Army Corps of Engineers, Southwestern Division, contract DACW63-84-C-0149.

n.d.   Pueblo Health and Disease in Protohistoric New Mexico. Paper presented at the "Second Conference on Health and Disease in the Prehistoric Southwest," Albuquerque: Maxwell Museum of Anthropology.

THOMAS, DAVID HURST

1987   *The Archaeology of Mission Santa Catalina de Guale: 1. Search and Discovery.* Anthropological Papers of the American Museum of Natural History 63 (part 2).

THORNTON, RUSSELL

1987   *American Indian Holocaust and Survival: A Population History Since 1492.* Norman: University of Oklahoma Press.

UBELAKER, DOUGLAS H.

1988   North American Indian Population Size, A.D. 1500 to 1985. *American Journal of Physical Anthropology* 77: 289–294.

UPHAM, STEADMAN

1986   Smallpox and Climate in the American Southwest. *American Anthropologist* 88: 115–128.

WALKER, PHILLIP L., PATRICIA LAMBERT, AND MICHAEL J. DeNIRO

1989   The Effects of European Contact on the Health of Alta California Indians. In *Columbian Consequences, Volume 1: Archaeological and Historical Perspectives on the Spanish Borderlands West*, David Hurst Thomas, ed. Pp. 349–364. Washington, D.C.: Smithsonian Institution Press.

SOUTHEAST

EPIDEMIC DISEASE IN THE POSTCONTACT SOUTHEAST: A REAPPRAISAL

George R. Milner

ABSTRACT

European-introduced disease has previously been cited as contributing to the major postcontact demographic and cultural transition experienced by many native populations of the New World. The study of postcontact depopulation can make substantial contributions to the refinement of pre-Columbian population estimates, studies of regional cultural history, and analyses focusing on the processes involved in population and culture change. While information concerning the impact of European disease on the native populations in many regions of the Western Hemisphere is available, little is known about the effects of disease on groups in the southeastern portion of the United States. This paper evaluates the scanty ethnohistorical accounts of disease among southeastern Indian groups prior to 1700 by using a disease model developed from the epidemiological literature. A satisfactory correspondence between the disease model and historical accounts suggests strongly that European-introduced crowd infections contributed to population reduction and culture change in the Southeast early in the historic period. This possibility has yet to be evaluated with archaeological material; the manner in which this might be accomplished with data from mortuary contexts is discussed.

Introduction

The devastating effect of European epidemic disease on Native American populations has long been regarded with interest by anthropologists, historians, and demographers. Information on the extent of depopulation and attendant culture change is essential for accurate reconstructions of culture history and pre-Columbian population estimates. Several regions of the Western Hemisphere, the areas encompassed by the civilizations of South and Central America, parts of California, and, to a lesser extent, portions of the American Southwest, Northeast, and Plains have been the subjects of analyses relying primarily on documentary data. Preliminary estimates of regional population decline attributable to epidemic disease are available for these areas (Cook 1940, 1976a, 1976b; Cook and Borah 1971, 1974; Denevan 1976; Dobyns 1966, 1977; and others). Disease-

Mid-Continental Journal of Archaeology, Vol. 5, No. 1
0146-1109/80/0051-0002 $00.90/0

induced depopulation in the southeastern portion of the United States, however, has not been systematically investigated.

Adequate recording of epidemic disease and its impact on the Indian population of the Southeast does not occur until the eighteenth century; however, a major demographic and cultural transformation prior to 1700 is indicated by archaeological research and by the few existing early historic accounts. When De Soto traversed the Southeast in 1539–1543, the Spanish encountered areas of high population density and complex socio-cultural systems (Brain, Toth, Rodriguez-Buckingham 1974; Swanton 1939). European penetration of the interior was infrequent, brief and geographically restricted for more than a hundred years following the famed De Soto Entrada. By 1700, English and French adventurers, traders, missionaries, and soldiers had entered this region in numbers, and many wrote of their encounters with the Indians. Accounts dating from this period describe areas of low population density. Although a number of continuities in artifact style and site organization were present, socio-cultural systems very different from those encountered previously by De Soto were described (Waring 1968; Willey 1966). The Natchez, who occupied portions of the Lower Mississippi Valley in the early eighteenth century, were one of the few groups that remained as an example of the elaborate and complex sociocultural systems so vividly described by the De Soto chroniclers. Because the early ethnohistorical record for the Southeast is both incomplete and primarily restricted to areas surrounding the European coastal settlements, archaeological studies are necessary to document and explain the extent of population reduction and culture change prior to 1700.

Archaeologists generally acknowledge that epidemic disease was an important factor in the sixteenth- and seventeenth-century cultural and demographic transition (Griffin 1967; Phillips, Ford, and Griffin 1951; Swanton 1946; Willey 1966); systematic analyses of this suggested relationship, however, have yet to be initiated. Ford and Willey did suggest in 1941 that the elaborate, ritualistic Southern Cult artifacts and motifs were part of a messianic reaction to contact with Europeans and their diseases, but this proposition was soon discredited by demonstrating an extended time depth for Southern Cult items (Krieger 1945; Lewis and Kneberg 1946; Waring 1968; Waring and Holder 1945). Unfortunately, since the 1940s archaeological interest in epidemic disease has languished. This neglect is somewhat surprising because the study of epidemic disease is clearly relevant to our understanding of the processes of native population and culture change in the Southeast.

This paper will demonstrate that the study of epidemic disease in prehistory is a fruitful area for future research. A disease model, based on epidemiological theory and modern medical studies, is developed in the following pages as a general framework for the analysis of postcontact southeastern epidemics. Points of correspondence between the disease model and ethnohistorical accounts are considered after a discussion of documented epidemic disease episodes in the sixteenth and seventeenth centuries. Finally, this paper will discuss the manner in which mortuary site material may reflect the existence of epidemic disease in societies for which there are no extant written records.

The Epidemic Disease Model

The settlement pattern described by De Soto's chroniclers was one of discrete territorial units comprised of towns and villages varying in size, and arranged in a hierarchical order of political and presumably economic significance (Biedma 1851; Elvas 1851; Garcilaso 1951). These territorial units were frequently separated by natural barriers, including almost impassable swamps or tracts of unoccupied land. The extent of communication between territorial units is unknown, but perennial raiding and the widespread activity of traders are mentioned in the De Soto narratives. Unfortunately, complete contemporaneous records concerning the impact of epidemic disease on these sociocultural systems are unavailable. The ramifying effects of epidemic disease will only be appreciated through the combined use of epidemic disease models, the scanty ethnohistorical literature, and archaeological data sets.

The diseases discussed here are those known as acute crowd infections: measles, smallpox, influenza, and others. Acute crowd infections share several characteristics which require a large host population for disease maintenance (Black 1966, 1975; Burnet and White 1972; Cockburn 1963, 1971). Such diseases are largely restricted to one species, do not form host/pathogen commensual states, do not remain viable for an extended period outside the host, and the surviving host develops an immunity to subsequent infection with the pathogen. For the disease to be maintained in a host community, sufficient new susceptibles must be added continually through birth or migration. The overall disease pattern is one of low incidence punctuated by periodic episodes, or epidemics, of higher than usual morbidity among the susceptible segment of the population. A pathogen-specific minimum host community size is necessary for the persistence of the disease. In populations below this threshold, the input of new susceptibles is inadequate to support the disease indefinitely. For instance, Black (1966) estimates that a minimum of 200,000 persons are necessary to maintain measles, and his analysis of insular host communities demonstrates that the disease disappeared periodically in populations of half a million or less. When introduced to a small, isolated community, an acute crowd infection will run its course and eventually die out. After a disease-free interval, the same illness may be reintroduced and the next cohort of susceptibles infected. In host communities where all individuals are potential susceptibles, or "virgin-soil" populations, the introduction of an acute crowd infection is potentially devastating. Morbidity is widespread, and the entire population may succumb to the disease within a short period.

The spread of a disease through a susceptible host population is approximated by the Reed-Frost epidemic model (Figs. 1, 2). Extensive treatments of the mathematical bases and applicability of this epidemic model can be found in Fox (1971), Frost (1976), Lilienfeld (1976), and Sartwell (1976). Here the model is used solely for illustrative purposes.

The Reed-Frost model is a deterministic model in which the number of new cases (C_{i+1}), that is, the number of individuals acquiring the disease, can be computed for successive intervals given an initial set of values:

(1)   the probability that two individuals will achieve adequate contact for disease transmission (p);

(2)   the number of susceptibles in the previous interval (S_i);

(3)   the number of cases in the previous interval (C_i).

The intervals can be thought to approximate the disease-specific incubation period from exposure to the development of disease symptomology. The contact rate (p) equals the number of persons with whom an individual has had sufficient contact to permit disease transmission (K), divided by ($N-1$), the number of potential contacts an individual can make in a population size N. Factors which affect host susceptibility to any particular disease, including pathogen virulence, mode of transmission, and the host's health state, are subsumed in the contact rate (p). The resulting formulae are:

$$C_{i+1} = (1 - (1 - p)^{C_t}) S_i$$
$$p = \frac{K}{(N-1)}$$

In Fig. 1, the following arbitrary initial values were specified for the following variables: $N = 200$; $K = 5$; and $C_i = 2$. All members of the population are considered potential susceptibles. The initial precipitous rise in cases, shown by line A, is followed by a steep drop which ultimately reaches zero. At this point, no additional individuals contract the disease and the pathogen disappears from the host population. The cumulative number of cases and the susceptibles remaining in the population at each interval are indicated in Fig. 1 as lines B and C. Disease spread in somewhat larger populations is shown in Fig. 2. New cases per interval for population sizes (N) of 200, 500 and 1000 are indicated by lines A, B and C.

Figures 1 and 2 graphically illustrate the unchecked, rapid spread of disease among a susceptible host population. The initial values are arbitrary, but are not unreasonable. A change in the initial set of values will produce different results, but the general curve characteristics remain unchanged. It is important to note that within a short period of time the disease can spread from only a few cases to infect a large portion of the susceptible population.

Where quarantine methods are nonexistent or ineffectual, disease spread is facilitated by intergroup contact. People may travel to visit sick kinsmen or flee the foci of infection to seek refuge in neighboring settlements. Both patterns of contact were recently implicated in the rapid spread of measles among the Yanomamo, a South American tribal group (Centerwall 1968; Neel et al. 1970). When contact occurs during the initial or peak phases of the epidemic cycle, rapid dissemination of the disease among neighboring social units is virtually ensured.

Mortality tends to increase markedly when acute crowd infections are introduced to virgin-soil populations (Dobyns 1966, 1977; Neel et al. 1970). The debilitating effects of disease tend to be aggravated by inadequate care or abandonment of the sick. In addition, essential child care, including nursing, may suffer when parents become severely ill (Centerwall 1968; Neel et al. 1970). Neel et al. (1970) consider much of the excess mortality experienced by contact groups to be a result of widespread social disintegration, despondency, and ineffectual health care. These researchers suggest that a genetically based, inherent susceptibility to the European acute crowd infections need not be assumed to account for the staggering mortality experienced by contact groups in the Western Hemisphere and elsewhere.

The Ethnohistoric Evidence For Population Reduction

Prior to 1700, most direct European contact with southeastern Indians was restricted to coastal exploration and settlements, occasional shipwrecks, and limited incursions into the Gulf Coastal Plain and Piedmont region of the Atlantic Coast states. The many attempts at exploration and settlement are not treated in depth here; discussion is restricted to accounts of disease among the native inhabitants of the region.

The chroniclers of the De Soto expedition were apparently the first Europeans to record the presence of epidemic disease among the Indians of the Southeast. In 1540, De Soto's expedition arrived at Cofitachequi, probably located on the South Carolina side of the Savannah River near the fall line (Swanton 1939). Elvas (1851:51–57) reports that: "Within a league, and halfe a league about this towne, were great townes dispeopled, and overgrowne with grasse, which shewed that they had been long without inhabitants. The Indians said, that two years before there was a plague in that countrie, and that they remooved to other townes."

After visiting Cofitachequi, the Spaniards traveled to the nearby abandoned town of Talomeco to loot the charnel structure. Garcilaso (1951:315) describes the effect of disease on the inhabitants: "The Castilians found no people in Talomeco because the previous pestilence had been more rigorous and devastating in this town than in any other of the whole province, and the few Indians who had escaped had not yet reclaimed their homes; hence our men paused but a short time in these houses before proceeding to the temple." Garcilaso (1951:325) also writes of "four large houses" in the town "filled with the bodies of people who had died of the pestilence."

During their stay in Cofitachequi, the explorers found items of Spanish manufacture stored in the charnel structure. The various De Soto chroniclers and Swanton (1939) believe these were obtained from Ayllon's abortive attempt in 1526 to settle the South Carolina coast. Clearly, even at this early date European influence outdistanced direct contact between the two peoples.

Twenty years later, an expedition commanded by De Luna disembarked at Pensacola Bay to establish a settlement and explore the interior (Priestley 1928). The expedition soon failed, largely because of food shortages. The Spanish expected to find *La Florida* a land of plenty, where abundant stored foodstuffs could readily be obtained in large Indian towns. In contrast to De Soto's earlier experience, supplies were not found by the De Luna explorers in quantities sufficient to support a large expedition. In a desperate attempt to secure much needed food, an expedition was sent to find Coosa, a large town and province lavishly described by the survivors of the De Soto expedition. On arriving at the town, the Spanish found only eight small clusters of structures, and not enough food to avert starvation. In a letter addressed to De Luna in 1560, the Viceroy attempted to explain the lack of food (Priestley 1928, II:149): "I think it has been because you have not reached the country which Soto traveled through, and the Indians had time to gather and hide the food." Swanton (1939), however, in an extensive review of the early Spanish accounts, maintains that the De Luna expedition reached the Coosa discovered by De Soto. The apparent discrepancy is suggestive of demographic and cultural change in the twenty-year interval between the two Spanish explorations.

Indisputable examples of epidemic disease ravaging the Spanish Florida Indian population can be found in later writings. Sir Frances Drake introduced a disease, possibly typhus, among the Indians of the St. Augustine area during his 1585 punitive expedition against Spanish colonies (Crosby 1972). Thirty years later a Spanish missionary reports that half of the converted Indians died of disease during the four years prior to 1617; 8000 remained alive at the time of the missionary's writing (Swanton 1922). Epidemics among the Indians in the Spanish possessions were also recorded in or immediately prior to the years 1659 and 1672 (Swanton 1922). When the French explored Mobile Bay in 1699, evidence of abandoned coastal villages was abundant, and no Indians were encountered. This is in marked contrast with the 40 inhabited settlements along the shore previously reported by Pineda who discovered the bay in 1519 (Swanton 1935).

Little is known about disease occurrence in the Mississippi River Valley. St. Cosme, a missionary writing in 1699, arrived just after a smallpox epidemic swept throughout one of the Quapaw villages in Arkansas (St. Cosme 1861: 72). "It is not a month since they got over the small pox which carried off the greatest part of them. There is nothing to be seen in the village but graves. There were two (groups) together there and we estimated that there were not a hundred men; all the children and a great part of the women were dead." The Quapaw, however, were possibly recent arrivals in what was by 1700 a markedly depopulated region. The earlier inhabitants of this region visited by the De Soto expedition may have been represented at the end of the seventeenth century by a number of small groups aggregated along the Yazoo River. Phillips, Ford, and Griffin (1951) describe the Yazoo Basin as a "refuge area" occupied by groups once larger but considerably reduced in numbers by European disease and conflict with the Quapaw and Chickasaw.

Perhaps significant is the early eighteenth-century observation by Du Pratz (1972:292) that the "nations" of Louisiana were once "both numerous and populous" but at the time of his writing were "thinned and diminished." According to Du Pratz, several groups had been destroyed outright while other formerly discrete nations had coalesced. Du Pratz discusses the Natchez at length, and notes that they were no longer the very large and powerful nation described in their traditions. Du Pratz attributes the Natchez population reduction to the sacrifice of numerous victims at the death of their leaders. Elsewhere, however, he remarks that diseases had a devastating impact on all the native inhabitants of Louisiana.

> Two distempers, that are not very fatal in other parts of the world, make dreadful ravages among them; I mean the small-pox and a cold, which baffle all the art of their physicians, who in other respects are very skilful. When a nation is attacked by the small-pox, it quickly makes great havock; for as a whole family is crowded into a small hut, . . . the distemper, if it seizes one, is quickly communicated to all. The aged die in consequence of their advanced years and the bad quality of their food; and the young, if they are not strictly watched, destroy themselves, from an abhorrence of the blotches in their skin. If they can but escape from their hut, they run out and bathe themselves in the river, which is certain death in that distemper. . . . Colds, which are very common in the winter, likewise destroy great numbers of the natives. (Du Pratz 1972:291–292)

European diseases undoubtedly contributed much to the depopulation of Louisiana. Population reduction was accompanied by change in a variety of cultural practices. "Although all the people of Louisiana have nearly the same usages and customs, yet as any nation is more or less populous, it has proportionally more or fewer ceremonies. Thus when the French first arrived in the colony, several nations kept up the eternal fire, and observed other religious ceremonies, which they have now disused, since their numbers have been greatly diminished" (Du Pratz 1972:333).

The English colonial efforts on the Atlantic Coast were no less destructive to the indigenous native population. Thomas Harriot accompanied Sir Walter Raleigh to Roanoke Island in 1585 and wrote of a malady afflicting the Indians surrounding the settlement:

> . . . within a few dayes after our departure from euerie such towne, the people began to die very fast, and many in short space; in some townes about twentie, in some fourtie, in some sixtie, & in one sixe score, which in trueth was very manie in respect of their numbers. . . . The disease also so strange, that they neither knew what it was, nor how to cure it, the like by report of the oldest men in the countrey neuer happened before, time out of mind. . . . there was no man of ours knowne to die, or that was specially sick . . . . (De Bry 1966: 28–29)

John Smith, writing of the early seventeenth-century explorers of Virginia and New England (1966:229), regarded epidemic disease as a providential phenomenon wholly beneficial to the colonists: " . . . God had laid this Country open for vs, and slaine the most part of the inhabitants by ciuill warres and a mortall disease, for where I had seene one hundred or two hundred Saluages, there is scarce ten to be found, and yet not any one of them (the European explorers) touched with any sicknesse but one poore French man that died."

Smallpox was introduced to the Virginia Indians by a sailor in 1667 who disembarked with the disease with devastating impact (Duffy 1953). Between the years 1696 and 1698 another smallpox epidemic spread from the Virginia and Carolina colonies to infect neighboring Indian groups (Duffy 1953; Stearn and Stearn 1945). The devastating impact of seventeenth-century disease on the aboriginal Virginia and Carolina population led Lawson to write in 1709 (Lawson 1966:223–224):

> The Small-Pox has been fatal to them; they do not often escape, when they are seiz'd with that Distemper, which is a contrary Fever to what they ever knew. Most certain, it had never visited *America*, before the Discovery thereof by the Christians. Their running into the Water, in the Extremity of this Disease, strikes it in, and kills all that use it. Now they are become a little wiser; but formerly it destroy'd whole Towns, without leaving one *Indian* alive in the Village. . . . The Small-Pox and Rum have made such a Destruction amongst them, that, on good grounds, I do believe, there is not the sixth Savage living within two hundred Miles of all our Settlements, as there were fifty Years ago.

Discussion

The sixteenth- and seventeenth-century accounts cited above acquire more than anecdotal historical significance when reinterpreted in light of the disease model. The southeastern Indians were apparently unfamiliar with the many epidemic diseases reported by the Europeans. Significantly, Europeans were less severely affected, and a number of the outbreaks among Indian groups occurred immediately after visits by colonists. The available evidence strongly supports the conclusion that acute crowd infections were repeatedly introduced by Europeans to the southeastern region.

Morbidity attributable to the European diseases was high; the majority, if not all, of the inhabitants in infected towns or villages rapidly became ill. The mortality rate was correspondingly high, and specific age groups, in particular the infants and children, suffered disproportionately. While seventeenth-century European commentaries on health care are of questionable value, given their faulty concepts of disease etiology, remarks on the Indian reaction to infection leave little doubt that the effects of disease were exacerbated by ineffectual and inappropriate care.

The spread of disease was to some extent geographically circumscribed, and appears to correspond to the Indian sociopolitical units in existence at the time of infection. Towns, villages, and possibly such larger integrative entities as territorial units did not suffer to the same extent in each epidemic. This suggests that the pattern of disease spread was largely determined by the degree of interpersonal contact between members of various social groupings. Intersettlement spread of disease within any given region was undoubtedly ensured by the documented flight from infection foci. Disease spread between larger territorial units was probably opportunistic, depending on the degree of amicable and antagonistic social contact between contiguous, semi-isolated areas and contact through the widely traveled traders.

Many initial infection foci are documented among the various southeastern Indian groups, and each epidemic eventually terminated for want of sufficient new susceptibles. Pandemics sweeping the entire Southeast might have occurred, but the usual pattern was perhaps one of exogenous disease introduction and restricted geographical spread closely corresponding to a socially heterogeneous landscape. Black (1966) reaches a similar conclusion in his analysis of the minimum host community size required for measles to persist without reintroduction.

The Europeans wrote little about the immediate impact of epidemic disease on the southeastern Indian social systems. The high morbidity and mortality undoubtedly had direct, catastrophic effects on the performance of subsistence activities. Depending on the extent to which food procurement and distribution were disrupted, famine could eventually result, compounding the detrimental effects of infectious disease. Long-term effects attributable to an insufficient labor force, including specialists, probably necessitated societal reorganization and coalescence of formerly discrete groups in order to remain as viable social and economic entities.

Clearly, the accumulated evidence suggests that epidemic disease may have had an effect as devastating to the southeastern peoples and cultures as elsewhere in the Western Hemisphere. Until archaeological data is marshalled to evaluate the impact of southeastern epidemics, however, discussions of disease as an important agent in processes of change remain little more than unsubstantiated, although perhaps intuitively pleasing, "just-so stories." Archaeologists, including Phillips, Ford, and Griffin (1951), have suggested that discontinuities in early historic regional archaeological sequences may be the result of epidemic disease introduced by Europeans. Mortuary site material is a data set particularly well suited for analyses of epidemic disease in archaeological contexts. This data set should exhibit some, or all, of the characteristics discussed below when derived from sites which experience rapid, epidemic disease-induced depopulation.

Mortuary customs are generally regarded as reflecting the characteristics, achieved and ascribed, which accrue to an individual throughout a life cycle. Biological characteristics, such as age, sex and obvious deforming pathology, plus socially important aspects of the deceased, including status position or social group affiliation, are recognized by most cultures in funerary ritual or material grave attributes (Binford 1972; Saxe 1970). In addition, in many groups the treatment of the dead is influenced by the circumstances surrounding death. Customarily this is restricted to unusual events, including death by disease. Modifications in the material and ceremonial aspects of funerary activity reflecting the peculiar circumstances of death may actually supersede the mortuary treatment awarded had the individual died from a culturally perceived "natural" death.

Binford (1972) has suggested that the victims of mass disasters, including epidemics, might be treated by the remaining members of the society as a corporate unit. The mortuary treatment of numerous persons as an aggregate who would normally be differentiated by various individual biological and social characteristics signifies the extraordinary manner of death. Presumably the interment of numerous individuals in a single facility also functions as an energy-saving device. In such situations it is likely that the remains of many individuals are interred in single mortuary facilities. The mass burial of numerous individuals in a common grave or the interment of several individuals in graves usually restricted to single burials would be a conspicuous feature of the archaeological record. Corporate treatment of epidemic victims was probably witnessed by the De Soto expedition at Talomeco (Garcilaso 1951).

Certainly, all multiple interments do not represent the remains of mass disaster victims. For example, the numerous Cahokia Mound 72 skeletons in common graves probably represent sacrificial, rather than epidemic, disease victims (Fowler 1974). Though the interpretation of any single example is admittedly difficult, such problems can be resolved by examining the archaeological context from which the skeletal series is derived. The burial of numerous individuals in single mortuary facilities may well represent an abrupt shift in interment mode. In addition, it is possible that classes of individuals formerly distinguished by mortuary-related paraphernalia were undifferentiated when buried with other epidemic victims. It scarcely needs repeating that changes in mortuary practices are not solely attributable to the occupation of a region or site by new peoples. Synchronic and diachronic mortuary variability is a result of many factors, including the particular problem posed by the disposal of numerous epidemic victims within a relatively short period of time.

The archaeological analysis of mortuary practices is admirably complemented by the study of prehistoric skeletal series. Unfortunately, acute crowd infections do not involve hard tissue in a manner permitting differential diagnosis. Several acute contagious diseases contribute to transient long bone growth arrest with the subsequent formation of radio-paque Harris lines and a localized interruption of ameloblast activity during tooth development resulting in enamel hypoplasia (Garn et al. 1968; Sweeney et al. 1969). These hard tissue defects are, however, only nonspecific markers of stress experienced by the surviving host during ontogeny since a number of diverse etiological agents have been implicated in their formation.

Analyses of the age and sex structure of mortuary samples may be more instructive in the context considered here than are studies of gross bone and tooth morphology. Many acute communicable diseases cause a disproportionate mortality among the very young and old (Burnet and White 1972). When morbidity is high among the entire social unit, adequate child care necessary for satisfying basic nutritive requirements may not be available. This compounds the effect of infectious disease in these dependent age classes, and mortality increases precipitously, as St. Cosme (1861) noted among the Quapaw. In addition, Burnet and White (1972) indicate that for several acute communicable diseases there is some evidence for a third peak in mortality involving the adolescent and young adult age categories of virgin-soil populations. This increase in mortality possibly results from an excessive immunological response elicited in the nonimmune individuals of these age categories upon contracting the disease.

The age groups disproportionately represented in epidemic mortuary series would, therefore, be the very young, the old, and perhaps to a lesser extent adolescents and young adults. In those extreme cases where all members of a community die within a short period, the age and sex characteristics of the mortuary series would approximate the demographic structure of a living population. If the skeletal series examined by the archaeologist was the result of a repeat infection with the same disease, the sample would be truncated somewhere in the upper age ranges. Only individuals born after the preceding epidemic would be infected and find their way into the mortuary series examined; the older individuals, survivors of the previous epidemic, would have already acquired immunity to the disease.

13

The demographic configuration of mortuary samples believed to be the result of past epidemic disease episodes can be compared with model life tables developed by various researchers for anthropological populations (Acsadi and Nemeskeri 1970; Weiss 1973) or with other series derived from the same or neighboring sites. Inferences based on comparative studies, however, should be evaluated cautiously because small sample sizes can compromise the results (Moore et al. 1975). Nevertheless, Ubelaker's (1974) analysis of two Late Woodland Maryland ossuaries amply demonstrates the potential of paleodemographic study for the refinement of pre-Columbian population estimates.

Conclusion

Although the study of postcontact Native American depopulation has in recent years received increasing attention by researchers in a variety of fields, the southeastern portion of the United States has been largely neglected. The scanty historical documentation for the period between the initial exploration of the interior and substantial European settlement, trading and missionizing efforts beyond the coast has undoubtedly contributed to the lack of population-oriented research. The documentation available for depopulation in the Southeast prior to 1700 constitutes a valuable resource, but one that is impressionistic, limited in quantity and primarily restricted to the vicinity of coastal settlements. These accounts, however, take on added significance when considered in reference to the epidemic disease model presented here. The satisfactory correspondence between the model and early narratives strongly suggests that European-introduced disease played a significant role in cultural and population change prior to 1700. Archaeological material must be used to test this proposition, and a research strategy integrating cultural and biological data derived from mortuary contexts is advocated.

Acknowledgments

I would like to thank the following individuals who read various drafts of this paper and contributed many valuable suggestions: James A. Brown, Jane E. Buikstra, John E. Kelly, Carolyn McElrath, James W. Porter, Ann Palkovich. Guy Prentice prepared the graphs and Joyce Williams typed the final manuscript. The major part of this paper was prepared while I was supported by a National Science Foundation Graduate Fellowship at Northwestern University.

Department of Anthropology
FAI-270 Archaeological Project
University of Illinois - Urbana

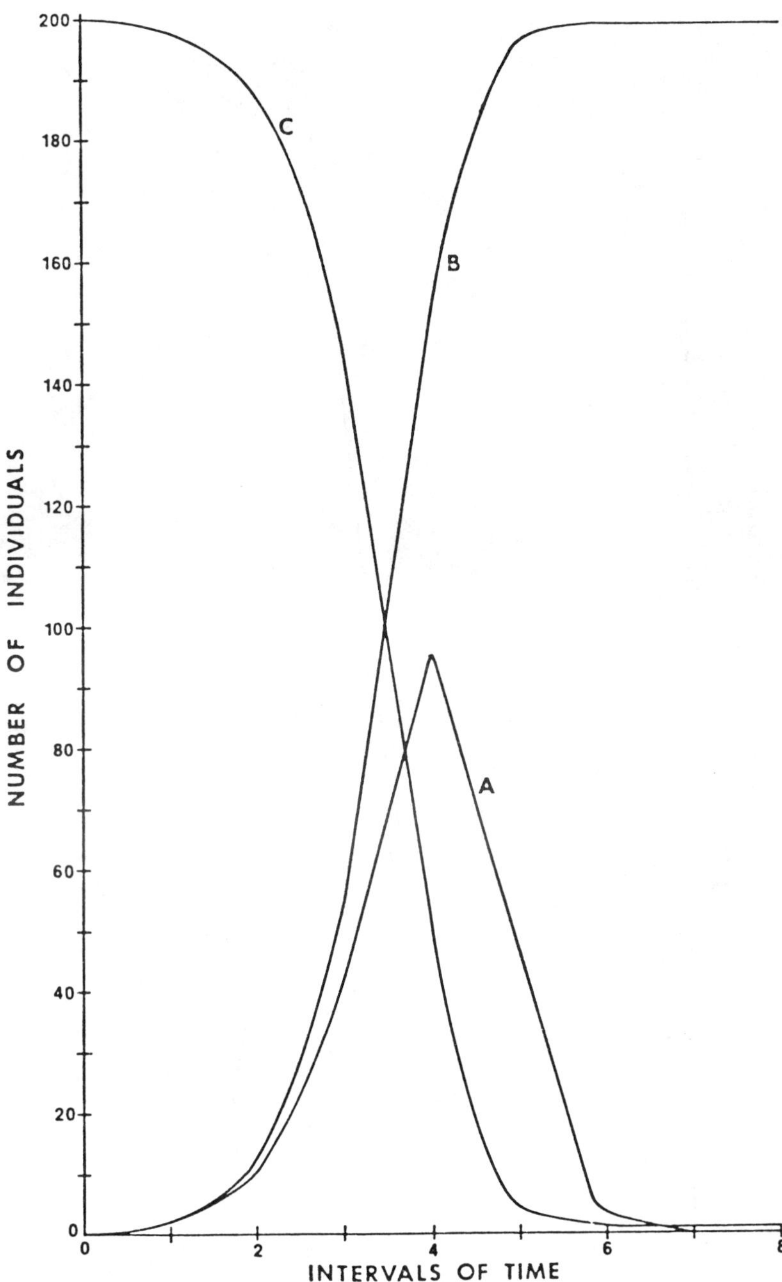

Fig. 1. The course of a hypothetical epidemic disease in a small population ($N =$ 200) from introduction to eventual disappearance is described by the number of new cases developing at sequential intervals (A), the cumulative number of cases (B), and the number of susceptibles remaining in the population (C).

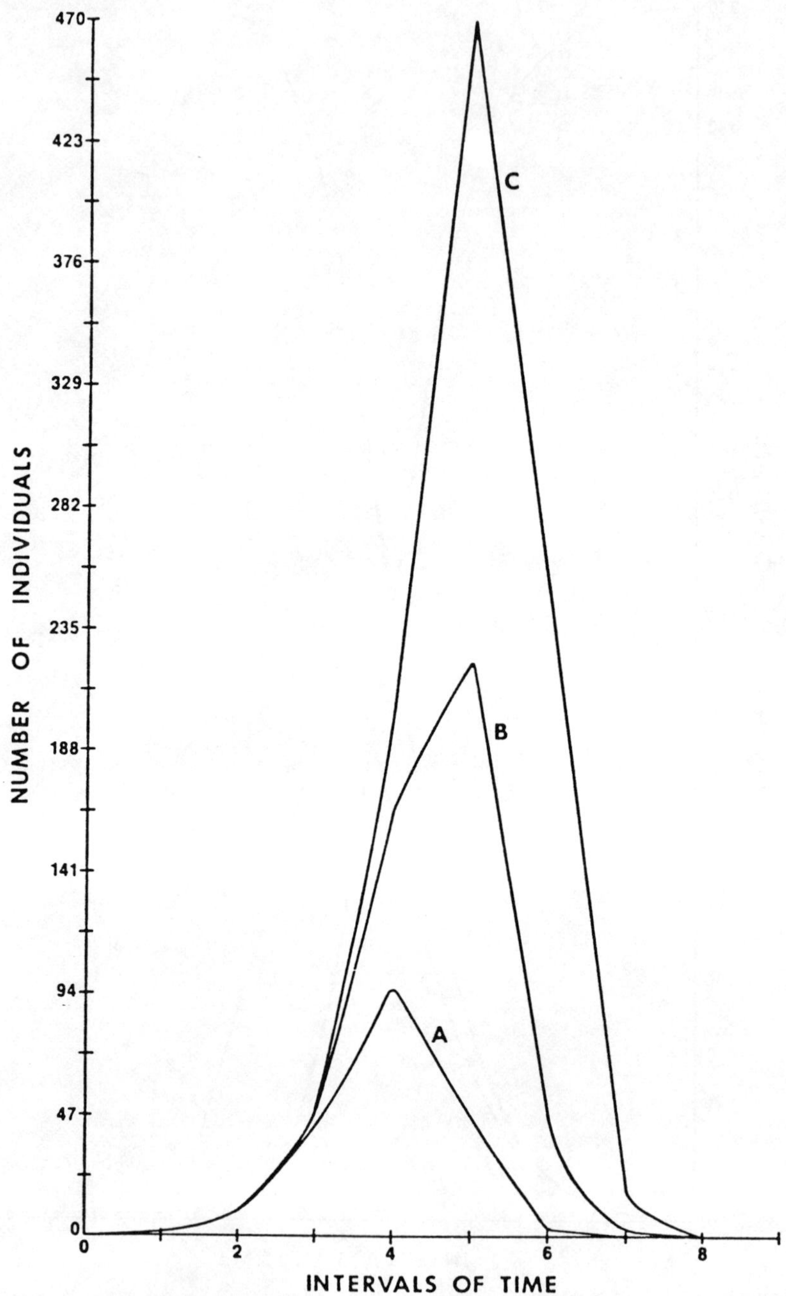

Fig. 2.   The number of new cases developing at each interval are plotted for small populations of size 200 (*A*), 500 (*B*), and 1,000 (*C*).

References

Acsadi, G., and J. Nemeskeri
1970 *History of human life span and mortality*. Akademiai Kiado, Budapest.

Biedma, L. H. D.
1851 A relation of what took place during the expedition of Captain Soto. Translated by W. B. Rye. *Hakluyt Society*, Vol. 9.

Binford, L. R.
1972 Mortuary practices: their study and their potential. In *An archaeological perspective*, edited by L. R. Binford, pp. 208–243. Seminar Press, N.Y.

Black, F. L.
1966 Measles endemicity in insular populations: critical community size and its evolutionary implication. *Journal of Theoretical Biology* **11**:207–211.
1975 Infectious diseases in primitive societies. *Science* **187**:515–518.

Brain, J. P., A. Toth, and A. Rodriguez-Buckingham
1974 Ethnohistoric archaeology and the De Soto Entrada into the Lower Mississippi Valley. *The conference on historic site archaeology papers, 1972*, edited by S. South, 7:232–289.

Burnet M., and D. O. White
1972 *Natural history of infectious disease*, 4th ed. Cambridge University Press, London.

Centerwall, W. R.
1968 A recent experience with measles in a "virgin-soil" population. In *Biomedical challenges presented by the American Indian*, pp. 77–80. *Pan American Health Organization, Scientific Publication* 165.

Cockburn, A.
1963 *The evolution and eradication of infectious disease*. Johns Hopkins University Press, Baltimore.
1971 Infectious diseases in ancient populations. *Current Anthropology*, **12**:45–54.

Cook, S. F.
1940 Population trends among the California mission Indians. *Ibero-Americana*, Vol. 17.
1976a *The Indian population of New England in the seventeenth century*. University of California Press, Berkeley.
1976b *The population of the California Indians, 1769–1970*. University of California Press, Berkeley.

Cook, S. F., and W. Borah
1971 *Essays in population history: Mexico and the Caribbean, volume 1*. University of California Press, Berkeley.
1974 *Essays in population history: Mexico and the Caribbean, volume 2*. University of California Press, Berkeley.

Crosby, A. W.
1972 *The Columbian exchange: biological and cultural consequences of 1492*. Greenwood Press, Westport.

De Bry, T.
  1966   *Thomas Hariot's Virginia*. University Microfilms International, Ann Arbor.

Denevan, W. M. (ed.)
  1976   *The native population of the Americas in 1492*. University of Wisconsin Press, Madison.

Dobyns, H. F.
  1966   Estimating aboriginal American population: an appraisal of techniques with a new hemispheric estimate. *Current Anthropology* 7:395–416.

  1977   *Native American historical demography: a critical bibliography*. Indiana University Press, Bloomington.

Duffy, J.
  1953   *Epidemics in colonial America*. Louisiana State University Press, Baton Rouge.

Du Pratz, L. P.
  1972   *The history of Louisiana*. Claitor's Publishing Division, Baton Rouge.

Elvas
  1851   The discovery and conquest of Terra Florida. Translated by R. Hakluyt. *Hakluyt Society*, Vol. 9.

Ford, J. A., and G. R. Willey
  1941   An interpretation of the prehistory of the Eastern United States. *American Anthropologist* 43:325–363.

Fowler, M. L.
  1974   *Cahokia: ancient capital of the Midwest*. Addison-Wesley Module in Anthropology, Number 48, pp. 3–38.

Fox, J. P., L. Elveback, W. Scott, L. Gatewood, and E. Ackerman
  1971   Herd immunity: basic concept and relevance to public health immunization practices. *American Journal of Epidemiology* 94:179–189.

Frost, W. H.
  1976   Some concepts of epidemics in general. *American Journal of Epidemiology* 103:141–151.

Garcilaso, V.
  1951   *The Florida of the Inca*. Translated by J. G. Varner and J. J. Varner. University of Texas Press, Austin.

Garn, S. M., F. N. Silverman, K. P. Hertzog, and C. G. Rohmann
  1968   Lines and bands of increased density. *Medical Radiography and Photography* 44:58–89.

Griffin, J. B.
  1967   Eastern North American archaeology: a summary. *Science* 156:175–191.

Krieger, A. D.
  1945   An inquiry into supposed Mexican influence on a prehistoric "cult" in the Southern United States. *American Anthropologist* 47:483–515.

Lawson, J.
  1966   *A new voyage to Carolina.* University Microfilms International, Ann Arbor.
Lewis, T. M. N., and M. Kneberg
  1946   *Hiwassee Island.* University of Tennessee Press, Knoxville.
Lilienfeld, A. M.
  1976   *Foundations of epidemiology.* Oxford University Press, New York.
Moore, J. A., A. C. Swedlund, and G. J. Armelagos
  1975   The use of life tables in paleodemography. In *Population studies in archaeology and biological anthropology: a symposium,* edited by A. C. Swedlund. *Society for American Archaeology, Memoir* 30:57–70.
Neel, J. V., W. R. Centerwall, N. A. Chagnon, and H. L. Casey
  1970   Notes on the effects of measles and measles vaccine in a virgin-soil population of South American Indians. *American Journal of Epidemiology* 91:418–429.
Phillips, P., J. A. Ford, and J. B. Griffin
  1951   Archaeological survey in the lower Mississippi alluvial valley, 1940–1947. *Papers of the Peabody Museum of Archaeology and Ethnology,* Vol. 25.
Priestley, H. J. (ed.)
  1928   *The Luna Papers,* 2 vols. Florida State Historical Society, Deland.
Sartwell, P. E.
  1976   Memoir on the Reed-Frost epidemic theory. *American Journal of Epidemiology* 103:138–140.
Saxe, A. A.
  1970   *Social dimensions of mortuary practice.* Unpublished Ph.D. dissertation, University of Michigan, Ann Arbor.
Smith, J.
  1966   *The general historie of Virginia, New England, and the Summer Isles.* University Microfilms International, Ann Arbor.
St. Cosme, J. F. B.
  1861   Letter to the Bishop of Quebec. In *Early voyages up and down the Mississippi,* edited by L. C. Shea. Joel Munsell, Albany.
Stearn, E. W. and A. E. Stearn
  1945   *The effect of smallpox on the destiny of the Amerindian.* Bruce Humphries Inc., Boston.
Swanton, J. R.
  1922   Early history of the Creek Indians and their neighbors. *Bureau of American Ethnology, Bulletin* 73.
  1935   Notes on the cultural province of the Southeast. *American Anthropologist* 37:373–385.
  1939   Final report of the United States De Soto expedition commission. Chairman. *76th Congress, 1st Session: House Document* 71.
  1946   The Indians of the Southeastern United States. *Bureau of American Ethnology, Bulletin* 137.
Sweeney, E. A., J. Cabbrera, J. Urrutia, and L. Matta
  1969   Factors associated with linear hypoplasia of human deciduous incisors. *Journal of Dental Research* 48:1275–1279.

Ubelaker, D. H.
   1974   Reconstruction of demographic profiles from ossuary skeletal samples. *Smithsonian Contributions to Anthropology*, 18.
Waring, A. J.
   1968   The southern cult and Muskhogean ceremonial. In *The Waring Papers*, edited by S. Williams. *Papers of the Peabody Museum of Archaeology and Ethnology*, Vol. 58.
Waring, A. J., and P. Holder
   1945   A prehistoric ceremonial complex in the southeastern United States. *American Anthropologist* 47:1–34.
Weiss, K. M.
   1973   Demographic models for anthropology. *Society for American Archaeology, Memoir* 27.
Willey, G. R.
   1966   *An introduction to American archaeology, volume one: North and Middle America.* Prentice-Hall Inc., Englewood Cliffs.

4

The Demographic Collapse

ANTHROPOLOGISTS and historians have long recognized that early European explorers introduced European and African diseases to the New World (Crosby 1972; Fish and Fish 1979; Hudson 1980; Milner 1980; Dobyns 1983). Native Americans had no natural immunity to these new diseases, and death rates soared. What in the Old World had become survivable childhood diseases, such as measles, in the New World became plagues, literally exterminating populations of New World natives. For example, the Arawaks of Santo Domingo numbered an estimated 1 million in 1492, but by 1548 only about 500 survived, according to Oviedo (Crosby 1972:45).

While historical accounts of the effects of European diseases have long existed, it is only recently that their devastating effects have been analyzed. Research by Henry Dobyns in particular has made us aware of the massive destruction of the epidemics (Dobyns 1963, 1966, 1983). Carl Sauer (1971), Alfred Crosby (1972), Suzanne Fish and Paul Fish (1979), Charles Hudson (1980), George Milner (1980), and Ann Ramenofsky (1982) have further described the process in the southeastern United States.

Historical background

What is the history of epidemic disease in the Southeast? We still do not really know, but the ethnohistorical literature provides some clues. It is, of course, possible that the first explorers who visited the Southeast introduced diseases. A single sick European could easily infect a vulnerable aboriginal group It is well documented that one car-

54

rier of smallpox who served with Cortés's conquering army was responsible for a massive epidemic in Mexico (Crosby 1972:48–49).

Ponce de León has been credited as the first European to "discover" the southeastern United States. After he explored the coast of Florida in 1513, he returned in 1521 with two hundred colonists and their livestock and horses and landed somewhere in Florida, probably at Charlotte Harbor. Indian attacks forced the colonists to retreat. Significantly, many of the colonists fell ill from an unidentified disease, which the Indians possibly also contracted (Hudson 1980).

Pedro de Salazar visited one of the barrier islands of the Atlantic coast sometime between 1514 and 1516 and contacted Indians (Hoffman 1980). In 1516, Diego Miruelo is believed to have traded with the Florida Indians for gold somewhere on the Gulf, and in 1517 Francisco Hernández de Córdova visited the same harbor previously visited by Ponce de León. In 1519, Alonzo Álvarez de Piñeda coasted the entire Gulf of Mexico from southern Florida to Panuco. He stopped at a great river, believed to be Mobile Bay, where he noted some forty villages (Swanton 1946:35). It is not known if these voyagers spread any disease, but it certainly is possible.

In 1521, Lucas Vázquez de Ayllón sent a slave-raiding expedition to the Atlantic coast; it captured several Indians. In 1526, Ayllón himself traveled to the Atlantic coast in a colonizing venture, but the colonists became ill and many died, including Ayllón. It appears likely that the Ayllón colony also was responsible for the introduction of European disease (Hudson 1980), as shall be seen later.

Pánfilo de Narváez attempted to settle Florida in 1528, but his attempts failed and a few survivors reached Mexico. Again there is specific mention of disease among Spaniards of this expedition (Fish and Fish 1979:31).

From the accounts of the de Soto expedition of 1539–43, it is clear that epidemic disease had preceded the expedition to the interior. The chroniclers of the de Soto expedition note that there had been an epidemic at Talomeco on the South Carolina fall line. According to Garcilaso, hundreds of bodies were stacked up in four of the houses. Elvas reports that several towns were depopulated and survivors had moved to other towns (in Milner 1980:43–44). Hudson notes that in the mortuary temple de Soto's men discovered European items that they believed to have come from the Ayllón colony (Hudson 1980).

In 1559, Tristan de Luna attempted to found a colony on the Gulf coast, probably at Pensacola Bay. With his food supply failing, he sent a contingent of troops inland to Coosa. Swanton (1939) and Charles

Hudson (Hudson et al. 1985) maintain that the Luna expedition reached the same Coosa town site as de Soto. If they did, it had changed: Instead of a powerful chiefdom, seven small villages are mentioned (Priestley 1928). Milner (1980:44) maintains that the discrepancy is due to demographic collapse. While generally agreeing, Hudson (1980) notes that the evidence is not as clear as he wished.

Later coastal colonizing attempts by the French and Spaniards in Florida and South Carolina in the 1560s culminated in the founding of St. Augustine and Santa Elena (Bennett 1975; Lyon 1976). Coastal mission stations were soon set up and the expeditions of Juan Pardo were sent into the interior in 1566–68, retracing a segment of the de Soto expedition from the Carolina fall line into eastern Tennessee (DePratter et al. 1983). Spanish missions were established as far north as Chesapeake Bay (Lewis and Loomie 1953). Again, opportunities for the spread of disease were many.

Once Europeans were firmly entrenched in the Southeast, historical documentation of European disease epidemics was more frequent and more reliable. In 1585, Sir Francis Drake's men contracted a highly contagious fever in the Cape Verde Islands, which Crosby believes was typhus, and they brought it to Florida when they attacked St. Augustine (Crosby 1972:40). Indians in the St. Augustine region died rapidly.

The English colony at Roanoke Island in 1587 left an impressive account of the effects of European disease on the local Indians. Thomas Hariot noted that "within a few days after our departure from everies such townes, that people began to die very fast, and many in short space" (in Crosby 1972:40; Fish and Fish 1979:32).

Later English accounts in Virginia and the Carolinas document further epidemics, John Smith in early seventeenth-century Virginia noted that for every one to two hundred Indians previously observed, only about ten remained. Smallpox epidemics are recorded for 1667 and 1696–98 (Milner 1980:46). John Lawson wrote in 1709 that smallpox had destroyed entire towns without leaving even one survivor. He estimated that only one-sixth as many Indians remained in the area as had been there fifty years earlier (in Milner 1980:46).

Spanish missionaries also dutifully recorded reduction of population due to disease in seventeenth-century Florida–Georgia. In a 1617 report, they noted that half of the missionized Indians had died in the preceding four years. Other epidemics were noted for 1659 and 1672 (Swanton 1922; Milner 1980:44). Henry Dobyns has docu-

Table 4.1. Disease epidemics in Florida, 1512–1672

Date	Disease	Probability	Mortality
1513–14	Malaria (?)	Likely	Unknown
1519–24	Smallpox	Nearly certain	50–75%
1528	Measles or typhoid	Nearly certain	About 50%
1535–39	Unidentified	Documented	High
1545–48	Bubonic plague	Nearly certain	About 12.5%
1549	Typhus	Very probably	Perhaps 10%
1550	Mumps	Possible	Unknown
1559	Influenza	Nearly certain	About 20%
1564–70	Unidentified and endemic syphilis	Documented	Severe
1585–86	Unidentified	Documented	Severe
1586	Vectored fever	Probable	15–20%
1596	Measles	Documented	About 25%
1613–17	Bubonic plague	Documented	50%
1649	Yellow fever	Documented	About 33%
1653–	Smallpox	Documented	Unknown
1659	Measles	Documented	Unknown
1672	Influenza (?)	Documented	Unknown

SOURCE: After Dobyns 1983: tables 25, 27.

mented European disease epidemics in Florida (1983); his findings are summarized in table 4.1.

Clearly there was ample opportunity for the spread of epidemic disease during the early historic period. Certainly epidemics raged in coastal areas, but did they enter the interior in general and the present study area in particular? The evidence from de Soto and the Luna expeditions suggests that they did, although Milner suggests that disease epidemics were largely geographically circumscribed within Indian sociopolitical units (1980:47). Certainly de Soto's chroniclers report evidence of disease only in the provinces of Cofitachiqui and Chalaque (Hudson et al. 1984:73).

On the other hand, it is entirely possible that pandemics swept the Southeast, a fact that Milner (1980) and Hudson (1980) consider. Henry Dobyns makes a strong case for pandemics sweeping coastal North America and suggests they spread inland as well (1983:24–25, 319). Looking at analogous situations elsewhere proves interesting.

Crosby notes that a 1518–19 smallpox epidemic in Santo Domingo could have spread to the continent before Cortés's invasion of Mexico. Smallpox has been reported in the written records of the

Maya themselves during the second decade of the sixteenth century (Crosby 1972:48).

In Peru there is good evidence that European disease preceded the Spaniards. The Inca Huayna Capac appears to have been killed, along with many of his subjects, in an epidemic, probably smallpox, in the province of Quito before Europeans landed in Peru (Crosby 1972: 51–52). It is clear that Huayna Capac had heard of the Europeans. Crosby notes, "Such is the communicability of smallpox and the other disruptive fevers than any Indian who received news of the Spaniards could also have easily received the infection of the European diseases" (1972:51). It thus seems safe to infer that Indians of the southeastern United States probably underwent multiple epidemics during the sixteenth century. Ann Ramenofsky (1982) and Henry Dobyns (1983) have argued that European disease epidemics often preceded direct European contact in North America, and Mary Helms's model (1979) of chiefly trade in Panama supports the idea that long-distance movements by traders probably ensured the rapid spread of disease vectors even across sociopolitical units.

Given the strong arguments amassed by Dobyns and Ramenofsky and the historically documented pattern of rapid spread of disease in other parts of the New World, I assume here that disease rapidly spread inland in the southeastern United States.

Documented effects of disease

Depopulation was clearly the major effect of European disease epidemics recorded in historic sources. Figures from Santo Domingo (cited previously) are no doubt representative. Henry Dobyns (1966) cites historical evidence from several New World locales to arrive at an overall depopulation ratio of 20 to 1—that is, for every twenty people in the New World in 1492, at the low point of any group's population (the times vary) only one remained. Smallpox, one of the worse killers, has a mortality rate among populations with no natural immunity of about 30 percent (Crosby 1972:44). Hudson suggests that introduced diseases such as smallpox, measles, and influenza may have killed up to 90 percent of the population (1980). Considering John Lawson's remarks that entire villages were destroyed, even that figure may not have been high enough in some areas.

In addition to depopulation, epidemic disease had many effects on the survivors. They may have been weakened enough to die later of starvation (Crosby 1972:47; Fish and Fish 1979:32), especially if everyone was sick at critical times of planting or harvest and subsistence activities were thus interrupted.

Social and political relations were also affected by epidemic disease. Crosby discusses the effects of disease on the Aztec power structure (1972:54). As the leaders were struck down by disease, the processes of government were disrupted and conquest by the Europeans was assured. Milner notes that the long-term effects of disease "attributable to an insufficient labor force, including specialists, probably necessitated societal reorganization and coalescence of formerly discrete groups in order to remain as viable social and economic entities" (1980:47). Such population movements are well documented. In such a reorganization in Amazonia during the twentieth century, surviving Sabane "have joined forces with survivors of other Nambikwara groups, so an amalgam social unit may eventually survive" (Dobyns 1966:413). Banding together of survivors then was one response to epidemics. Another was flight, the best account of which is that of the Gentleman of Elvas. Discussing the effects of disease on the province of Cofitachiqui in piedmont South Carolina just east of the study area, Elvas reported that plague survivors removed to other towns (Smith 1968:63; Milner 1980:43). Clark Wissler (in Dobyns 1966:441) reports a shift in tribal territory following a 1780 epidemic that swept western North America, a shift resulting from differential survival. The Cakchiquel Mayas of Guatemala, in their own record of an epidemic of 1520–21, noted that half of the people fled (Crosby 1972:58). Dobyns discusses simplification of social systems and settlement shifts as a response to disease (1983:313–28).

Perhaps the most serious effect of epidemic disease is an overall loss of elements of culture. Charles Hudson (1980) cites Akiga, a Tiv, who told of depopulation so swift and so devastating that ancestral traditions were lost. Hudson suggests that such was the case in the Southeast: "We can be sure that our understanding of southeastern Indian knowledge, philosophy, religion, and art symbolism is the merest fragment of what existed at the time of de Soto's *entrada*." Bruce Trigger (1976:601) similarly suggests the loss of much traditional religious lore among the Huron following the epidemics of the 1630s. The loss of religious and genealogical lore to a traditional aboriginal group must not be underestimated: It is an important factor in culture change, and it surely paves the way for acculturation. Hudson (1980) further suggests that a heavy loss of life in the chiefly lineage "would probably have led to the segmentation of chiefdoms into several smaller, less centralized social entities."

The historical record documents several results of epidemic European diseases that can be expected to have occurred in the southeastern United States: massive depopulation, population movement, social and political reorganization, and loss of many elements of culture.

Archaeological parameters

It is clear from historical accounts and work by ethnologists and ethnohistorians that European epidemic disease had a devastating effect on the New World, but few anthropologists have made an effort to correlate these historically known phenomena with the archaeological record. Can archaeological data be used to fit the model of drastic population decline? Some of the hypotheses offered in the remainder of this chapter can be tested with available data; others will require further research.

Skeletal remains might seem to hold the most obvious evidence of the effects of European-introduced epidemic diseases. Those diseases, however, were usually quick killers in newly contacted populations and left little evidence on bones (Milner 1980:49). Bones of survivors may show the formation of Harris lines or enamel hypoplasia, but these are simply markers of stress and cannot be correlated positively with specific diseases (Milner 1980:49). Such stress markers might also be associated with famine—which may or may not be a secondary result of epidemic disease (Fish and Fish 1979:32; Milner 1980:47).

Hudson (1980) suggests that the first epidemics may have been so devastating that no one was left to bury the bodies. The historical accounts of epidemic disease suggest that a few people always survive; however, it is possible to believe that sometimes bodies were left exposed before burial. In such a case, several pieces of evidence could be hypothesized for the archaeological record. Bones left exposed might show gnawing marks from dogs or rodents, but, to my knowledge, no such marks have been reported in the literature. Only disarticulated or partially disarticulated remains might be available for later burial; portions of the body might have been removed by scavengers. Recent research by David Mathews on the King site skeletal series indicates that there is evidence of gnawed bones. Seckinger (1975:67) notes missing skeletal elements, but it is not clear whether lack of preservation, delayed burial, or some other factor is to blame.

Burial at a later date might take the form of a "mass" burial (i.e., more than two bodies) (Milner 1980:48). Milner cautions that, because mass burial may be the result of other factors such as retainer sacrifice, the context of mass graves must be considered carefully. Mass burial was not common in the prehistoric Southeast; however, at the sixteenth-century King site a mass grave was found that would appear to be a strong candidate for a postepidemic burial. The Period A and D Toqua site excavated by Richard Polhemus for the University of Tennessee's Tellico Reservoir project contained three mass burials of three, five, and seven individuals, again suggesting European disease (Richard Polhemus, personal communication). Other evidence of depopulation at Toqua will be considered below. Mass burial grave features should be encountered on other early sites when they are excavated.

Milner suggests that "multiple" burials (i.e., exactly two bodies) could also be expected to result from European disease epidemics (see fig. 4.1). There is historical documentation that multiple burial can be the result of European epidemic disease. Describing the Arkansas in 1698, St. Cosme noted, "Not a month had elapsed since they had rid themselves of smallpox, which had carried off most of them. In the village are now nothing but graves, in which they were buried two together, and we estimated that not a hundred men were left" (Kellogg 1917, quoted in Philips et al. 1951:410).

There does appear to be a rapid increase in multiple burials in the study area during the sixteenth century (Periods A and B). Again, the King site provides the best documented examples: 9 of 210 burials at the site were multiple burials (Hally 1975; Seckinger 1977).

In eastern Tennessee, Lewis and Kneberg note, multiple burials were numerous on sites of the Mouse Creek culture: "In numerous instances two bodies had been interred at the same time, one directly superimposed above the other, usually both individuals being of the same sex. There is little likelihood that the second body was placed in the grave at a later time than the first since the bones were in actual contact and often without the slightest trace of soil between the points of contact" (1941:8). Both the Ledford Island and Rymer sites, which have been assigned to Period A, are Mouse Creek sites, as is Upper Hampton Place, which is from Period B.

Available data on mass and multiple burials are summarized in

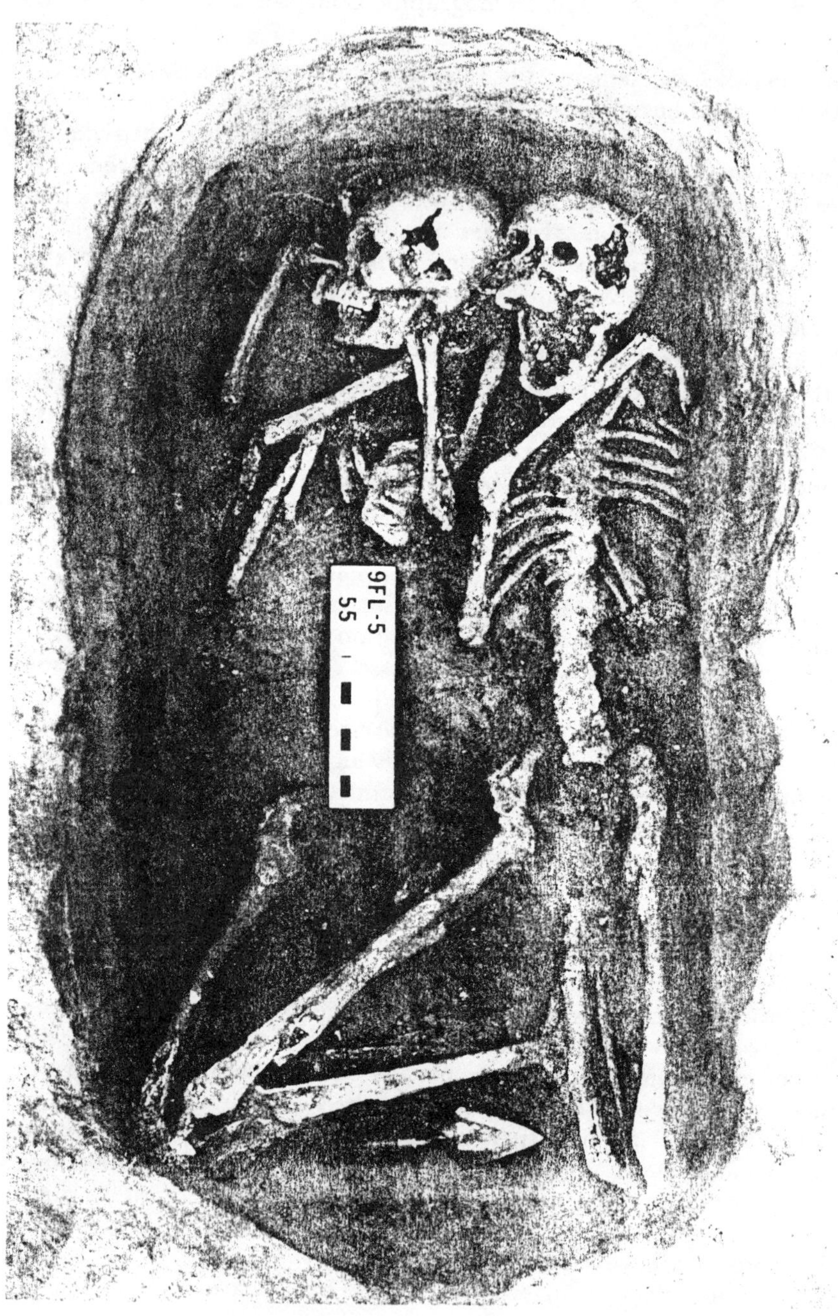

Figure 4.1. Multiple burial, King site.

table 4.2. Unfortunately, there are biases in these data. Several of the sites have long, prehistoric occupations; if these burials measure the frequency and extent of European disease epidemics, then earlier prehistoric individual graves dilute the findings. It is also possible that victims of particularly horrible epidemics may have been disposed of in some other fashion than the normal village burial.

The King site, occupied for less than fifty years (Hally 1982), probably all within Period A (1525–65) (including a possible prehistoric founding), provides probably the best data for the evaluation of European disease epidemics. While only 6 percent of the graves were mass or multiple burials, these graves account for at least 15.5 percent of the people. This percentage may not seem high when up to 90 percent may have been affected by an epidemic disease, but it must be remembered that there is no reason to expect that all victims received multiple or mass burial.

Data from Period B (1565–1600) are hard to find. While site 1Ce308 has a high frequency of mass and multiple burials, its low sample size makes the figure suspect. A better sample from Upper Hampton Place suggests that disease became less a problem in the late sixteenth century after Spanish exploration was over. Clearly, more data are needed.

Period C (1600–30) again shows evidence of mass and multiple burials. Both Bradford Ferry and Tomotley appear to be single component sites, and they have fairly large samples of burials. Again, the interpretation may be put forward that disease was a problem in the early seventeenth century, precisely the period that sees a tremendous influx in European goods. Ramenofsky (1982:257) noted that smallpox virus can be transmitted in a dry state on objects; thus anyone coming into contact with European goods could be exposed to smallpox.

Period D (1630–70) appears to be relatively disease-free, judging from the lower frequency of mass and multiple burials. Clearly more data are needed for all these periods. It is possible that mass and multiple burials are not directly associated with European epidemics but are the result of another event.

Recent reanalysis of the King site skeletal series under the direction of Robert Blakely of Georgia State University has produced another interpretation of mass and multiple burials. At least one person in each mass or multiple burial appears to have been the victim of a battle with Europeans, probably from the de Soto expedition. The

Table 4.2. Frequency of mass and multiple burials

Site	Number of burials	Number of mass graves	Number of multiple graves	Mass plus multiple (percent)	Reference
Period A (1525–65)					
King	213	4	9	6.1	Hally 1975
Ledford Island	459	6	16	4.8	McClung Museum notes
Rymer	168	0	6	3.6	McClung Museum notes
Toqua[a]	433	3	6	2.1	Richard Polhemus, pers. comm.
Citico 40Mr7[a]	194	0	0	0.0	Richard Polhemus, pers. comm.
Citico 40Ha65[a]	106	0	1	0.9	Moore 1915
Period B (1565–1600)					
1Ce308	14	1	0	7.1	Little and Curren 1981
Upper Hampton	56	0	1	1.8	McClung Museum notes
DeArmond Village[a]	52	0	0	0.0	McClung Museum notes
Period C (1600–1630)					
Bradford Ferry	47	1	1	4.3	DeJarnette et al. 1973; Appendix 1
Tomotley	92	1	7	8.7	Guthe and Bristline 1978
Hampton Place	31	0	0	0.0	Moore 1915
Period D (1630–70)					
1Ms100	74	1	1	2.7	Webb and Wilder 1951
1Ms32	68	0	0	0.0	Webb and Wilder 1951
1Ms91 Unit 1	56	0	1	1.8	Webb and Wilder 1951
Cooper Farm	25	0	0	0.0	Lindsey 1964; Battles 1969, 1972; Humbard and Humbard 1965

a. Includes prehistoric component.

types of wounds and their locations on the body indicate that the trauma was inflicted by metal weapons in a manner consistent with warfare in medieval Europe (Mathews 1984). However, only some of these wounds were fatal; many healed (Blakely, personal communication).

One of the goals of this skeletal reanalysis was to look for evidence of epidemic disease. Robert Blakely (personal communication) states, "In theory at least there is room for both European disease and trauma among King's decedents. However, Koener's and my exhaustive search for epidemic disease at the site has failed to turn up any evidence for Spanish-introduced diseases. The bones show no lesions indicative of smallpox, typhus, measles, etc. (Statements to the contrary notwithstanding, these diseases do occasionally produce skeletal symptoms.) Concerning demographic structuring, one would anticipate elevated mortality in the 4- to 18-year-old age category as a result of European diseases. (The reason is that such diseases, again contrary to oft-stated opinion, do not preferentially affect the aged and very young; under lack of immunity conditions, morbidity shows no favorites. Therefore, the typically healthiest segment of the sample should show the greatest mortality in contrast to nondiseased populations.) King actually evidences lowered mortality in that age group when compared with prehistoric samples. . . . The bottom line is that there is no direct or indirect evidence that European diseases visited the King site. That does not, of course, mean that they were absent."

The King site data are thus inconclusive. Apparently, some of the multiple-burial decedents were casualties of warfare, perhaps a European-Indian confrontation; some whose wounds healed clearly died well after the trauma. Others exhibit no wounds and may have been disease victims. The fact that some "battle victims" were interred in multiple graves confirms that such a mode of burial was not reserved for epidemic disease victims. Yet multiple burials occur from central Tennessee to central Alabama. Certainly, de Soto did not eliminate such a large quantity of natives. Aboriginal warfare is, of course, a possibility, but an interpretation encompassing all explanations is also feasible. Perhaps multiple and mass burials were used for victims of either war or disease.

Urn burial and bundle burial may also reflect the presence of European disease epidemics. These secondary forms may have been adopted when there were not enough healthy individuals to bury the victims of epidemic diseases promptly and more conventionally.

Urn burial has a long history; it definitely occurs in the study area in the prehistoric period. It was common for children during the

Early Dyar phase (about 1450–1500) in the Oconee River drainage (Smith 1981). By the time of European contact, urn burial was no longer practiced in the Oconee area, but it became important along the western margin of the study area at precisely the period under discussion. The Alabama River phase, located along the margins of the Alabama River and up the Black Warrior drainage, used urn burial as a common treatment of the dead (Sheldon 1974). European trade goods are found in urn burials occasionally, allowing a dating to Period C (Curren 1982:107). There is little doubt that the Alabama River phase was primarily a seventeenth-century phenomenon.

A similar practice (without the pottery vessels) is reflected in the bundle burials of the Tennessee River area. The best reported series of bundle burials comes from the Hiwassee Island site (Lewis and Kneberg 1946:150–51). Lewis and Kneberg date all Hiwassee Island burials with trade goods to the early eighteenth century, but the trade materials illustrated in their plates 86–88 appear to date from the period 1650–1700, or Period D and later. The brass discs, lugged hoes, seal top spoon, brass tubular beads, and some of the glass beads seem to be diagnostic of the seventeenth century. Lewis and Kneberg report European objects with both flexed and bundle burials. The flexed burials seem to date to Period D, the bundle burials slightly later but perhaps still in the terminal portion of Period D. That the urn reburials of the Alabama River and the bundle reburials of the Tennessee River reflect seventeenth-century responses to European disease epidemics is a hypothesis worth pursuing.

What other evidence for early European contact might be expected from burial analysis? Perhaps the most obvious would be the burial of a European. Such a find would not be unexpected, given the number of people who died on the de Soto and Luna expeditions. Burials of mixed European (or African) and Indian genetic types should also be expected on sites of the early historic period. To date, no such burials have been found (or recognized) within the study area, but one has been recognized from the Georgia coast (Zahler 1976:27–28, 50–51) and another from the early seventeenth-century Neutral Iroquois Grimsby site in Canada (Kenyon 1977, 1982:39). Most of the skeletal series from sites of the early historic period have not been analyzed by physical anthropologists.

Another analysis of burial data for indications of European disease involves looking at population curves for large skeletal series. Such analysis has been advocated by Milner (1980) and Hudson (1980).

Since disease is hardest on the very young and very old, these age groups would be represented disproportionately in an epidemic mortuary series. There is even some evidence that adolescents and young adults would also be affected to a greater degree than the remainder of the population (Milner 1980:49). Such analysis requires a large skeletal series. To date only the King site sample of 213 burials has been analyzed; it showed an unusual population curve suggestive of European epidemic disease (Hally 1975:34; Tally 1975). However, reanalysis by Gary Funkhouser (1978) disputed Tally's conclusions. The major reanalysis of the King site skeletal series currently being conducted by Robert Blakely should help resolve the dispute. He notes (personal communication) that the population curve is unusual, but it does not seem to indicate epidemic disease.

While analysis of burials might offer the best opportunity for studying the effects of European disease, it is clear that these data have not been developed to any extent. Fortunately, other archaeological parameters enable us to seek out the effects of European epidemic disease and depopulation over time. These include site size, number of sites, and population movement (Hassan 1981; Ramenofsky 1982).

The idea that sites would become smaller and fewer over time as population is reduced is obvious, but measuring such changes must be done cautiously. It is clear from the ethnohistorical literature that much population movement was taking place during the late part of the early historic period. The effects of such movements and the banding together of refugee groups must be taken into consideration. A model of the expected changes in settlement might be expressed as follows.

In the period around initial contact (including the pre—de Soto interior), populations would be expected to decline rapidly (Ramenofsky 1982). New sites established during this period by people fleeing disease areas might be considerably smaller and for at least a limited time should grow smaller and smaller. When town populations reach a certain low limit, population movement and the possible regrouping of populations could be expected to take place. Milner (1980:47) has noted that long-term effects of European epidemic disease and ensuing famine would lead to an insufficient labor force, including specialists, and would probably necessitate the reorganization of society and the coalescence of formerly discrete groups in order to remain viable social and economic entities (see also Dobyns 1983:303). Thus there should be a detectable population movement and a decrease in the number of sites through time. It now remains to determine appropriate archaeological measurements of this hypothesized process.

Site size

Site size is a recognized parameter of population size (Hassan 1981: 66–72; Ramenofsky 1982). Certainly site size can be simply measured, but a number of factors must be considered. A village's size can fluctuate over time, growing larger or smaller and varying with many factors other than European disease. Since we are interested not in the extent of a site but in its population, the best approach would be to count the number of houses in a site and multiply that number by an estimated family size (Hassan 1981:72). Another estimate that can be made from the archaeological record is to measure the floor area of domestic structures and estimate the population using Raoul Naroll's figure of one person per ten square meters of floor area (1962). For purposes of comparison, Naroll's is probably the most accurate means of estimating population, but it requires extensive archaeological excavations to determine the number of houses present on a site contemporaneously and their dimensions. Such data are available only for the King site (table 4.3) and only for approximately one-half of it. Assuming the unexcavated half to mirror the excavated half (Hally 1975), we can estimate a population (rounded) of three hundred for the King site, which has a habitation area of 138,300 square feet (calculated from figures in Hally 1975), not including the central open plaza. This method yields a figure of 461 square feet of habitation area per person in the village overall. It could be argued that this figure reflects a normal proximic situation for this specific archaeological culture (Barnett phase) or this ethnohistorically known province (Coosa). Making this assumption, it will be possible to estimate populations for a number of other sites when site size and sacred precinct size (plaza and mound area) are known. The estimated population will equal the total site size minus the plaza size (which equals the habitation area) divided by the constant 461 square feet per person. Table 4.4 presents such data for sites believed to be closely related politically to the King site.

A cruder measurement, but useful when sacred precinct area is unknown, is the overall area of site per person. Again, using the King site data as the base (220,800 divided by 300), we calculate one person to about 736 square feet of total site area. This cruder figure will allow us to measure additional sites (table 4.4). This estimate is considered less diagnostic because the relationship of habitation area to sacred

Table 4.3. King site structure data

Structure number	Dimensions (in feet)	Area (in m²)	Total population (at 1 per 10 m²)
1	32×32	95.13	9
2	27×29	72.74	7
3	20×22	40.88	4
4	18×18	30.10	3
5[a]	24×27	60.20	6
6	25×25	58.06	5
7	21×22	42.92	4
8	27×26	65.22	6
9	24×24	53.51	5
10[a]	26×30	72.46	[7]
11	26×21	50.73	5
12	26×26[b]	62.80	6
13	30×31	86.40	8
14	27×29	72.74	7
15	29×31	83.52	8
16[c]	21×20.5	39.99	
17[c]	49.5×49	225.3	
18	21×20	39.02	3
19	21×23	44.87	4
20	21×23	44.87	4
21	30.5×30	85.01	8
22	25×24	55.74	5
23	29×31	83.52	8
24	32.5×27	81.52	8
25	24×30	66.89	6
26	27×27	67.73	6
27	31×31.5	90.72	9
28	21×21	40.97	4
			148

a. Only structure 5 or 10 occupied at same time.
b. Incomplete excavation.
c. Not a domestic structure.

precinct area is not known and may not be linear. Politically important towns may have had a proportionally larger sacred precinct than did sites farther down the hierarchy.

While there are few data for comparison, the two Period A sites, Etowah and Little Egypt (probably the towns of Itaba and Coosa, respectively), that have long prehistoric occupations and multiple mounds are larger than sites that probably originated during the historic period, such as the King site. It is possible that the King site

Table 4.4. Site size and population data: Coosa province

Site	Site size (sq. ft.)	Sacred precinct	Habitation area	Habitation population[a]	Site area population[b]	Reference
Period A (1525–65)						
King	220,800	82,500	138,300	300	300	Hally 1975, 1982
Little Egypt	600,000[c]	126,400	473,600	1,027	815	Hally 1980:8
Etowah	2,265,120[c]	295,425	1,969,695	4,273	3,078	Larson 1972
Audubon Acres	152,460[d]	–	–	–	207	Evans, Hood, Lautzenheiser 1981
Ogeltree Island	200,000	–	–	–	272	Alabama site files
Citico 40Mr7	111,000	3,200	107,800	234	151	Richard Polhemus, pers. comm.
Rymer	210,000	–	–	–	285	McClung Museum files
Toqua	180,000[c, e]	26,250	153,750	334	245	Richard Polhemus, pers. comm.
Brown Farm	390,000	–	–	–	530	Appendix I
Period B (1565–1600)						
Upper Hampton	476,000	–	–	–	647	McClung Museum files
DeArmond (village)	315,000[c]	–	–	–	428	McClung Museum files
Period C (1600–1630)						
Bradford Ferry	70,000	–	–	–	95	DeJarnette et al. 1973
Tomotley	135,000[c]	–	–	–	183	Guthe and Bristline 1978
Period D (1630–70)						
1Ms100	45,000	–	–	–	61	Webb and Wilder 1951
1Ms32	264,000	–	–	–	359	Webb and Wilder 1951
After Period D						
Woods Island	180,000	–	–	–	245	Morrell 1965

a. At one per 461 square feet.   b. At one per 736 square feet.   c. Prehistoric occupation present; size of historic component unknown.
d. 3.5 acres.   e. Latest.

simply is lower in a hierarchy of sites, but other sites occupied during the historic period, such as Audubon Acres and Ogeltree Island, are of similar size. Data are not available to permit determining whether these sites originated during the early historic period or had long occupations. With current data we can only suggest a trend toward smaller sites. Later sites, such as the Period C Bradford Ferry site, are considerably smaller.

Some sites do not appear to fit the hypothesized pattern. The exact culture history of the Upper Hampton Place site is not known. It may or may not have a long prehistoric component. Its long, thin settlement area may indicate a transition to the dispersed settlement type discussed below, but the site does have a series of palisade ditches. Its large population estimate (table 4.4) remains anomalous. The De-Armond village site definitely has a long prehistoric occupation, so the total site size may not have any bearing on the area occupied in Period B. The site size for Citico, 40Mr7, seems too small for a mound center (its reported size is the best estimate available: Richard Polhemus, personal communication). There is some archaeological evidence that Citico was first occupied in Period A, so perhaps the small size reflects early epidemics. Finally, 1Ms32 appears to be a large site with a high population; but it is a dispersed linear settlement, and there is no reason to believe it was as densely populated as the earlier palisaded towns (see discussion below).

The Toqua site deserves special mention, since it was excavated carefully during the University of Tennessee's Tellico Reservoir project (Schroedl and Polhemus 1977; Richard Polhemus, personal communication). This Dallas mound center was occupied from around 1215 to 1620 (based on radiocarbon dates from mound A) and was carefully fortified by palisades. Interestingly enough, the size of the site shrank during its life span. The earliest village covered some 420,000 square feet with houses neatly dispersed. Later the occupied area shrank to 210,000 square feet, and houses were densely packed into the fortified area. This reorganization of the settlement took place between 1350 and the sixteenth century. Then (perhaps 1580–1600, according to Polhemus) the fortified area shrank again, to 180,000 square feet; in this area are all the burials containing European trade goods (both Periods A and D). All three mass burials excavated were within this last palisade, strengthening the argument that they represent victims of European disease epidemics. Mound B is excluded by this last palisade. It should be noted, however, that two of the six multiple burials fall outside of this latest palisade line. The overall impression is that, after the initial reorganization of Toqua settlement into a densely nucleated town of the size of the King site, there was further shrinkage perhaps due to disease (the mass burial evidence). Clearly the site was on the decline, because mound B was abandoned. The evidence from trade goods, both types and scarcity, suggests that Toqua was abandoned in the sixteenth century. The Period D occupation probably signals the arrival of the Cherokee in the valley during the last quarter of the seventeenth century.

Number of sites

Another obvious measure of depopulation would be a decrease over time in the number of sites occupied. Interestingly, the number of sites occupied at one time is not considered by Hassan (1981) as a measure of population, probably because he does not adopt a regional approach. Ramenofsky (1982), to the contrary, does consider settlement counts as a method of measuring population decline. If only a small area is looked at with this measurement in mind, then it must be strongly considered that population movement (migration) could be an explanation for any observed decrease in the number of sites. If areas as large as the study area are considered as a whole, then the effects of migration should be minimized. Ramenofsky advocates such a regional approach. Table 4.5 presents data by drainage system and as totals for the western study area (Coosa and Tennessee River drainages). In both of these drainages, there is a decrease in the number of sites from Period A to Period B followed by a stabilization or increase from Period B to C and a subsequent decrease to Period D. There is no evidence that populations were living in small hamlets or farmsteads in the Tennessee Valley either in the late prehistoric or early historic periods (Richard Polhemus, personal communication). The data in table 4.5 might be interpreted as follows: major European disease epidemics reduced populations during Period A; by Period C,

Table 4.5. Decrease in number of sites in western study area

	Period A 1525–65	Period B 1565–1600	Period C 1600–1630	Period D 1630–70
Coosa River drainage	9	7	6	2
Tennessee River drainage	12	8	10	8
Miscellaneous drainages	–	1	–	1
Totals	21	16	16	11

populations were stabilizing or even growing to some extent; by Period D, the number of sites again diminished, perhaps reflecting the beginning of population consolidation and the beginning of the Creek Confederacy, as well as renewed contact with Europeans.

The Wallace Reservoir provides additional data. Few Wallace Reservoir sites have produced European trade goods, primarily due to lack of extensive excavations. Nonetheless, a detailed ceramic chronology has been established (Smith 1981), and radiocarbon determinations and some European trade goods provide tight chronological controls.

Explorations in the Wallace Reservoir have located approximately 800 Mississippian sites (Rudolph and Blanton 1980:14), ranging in size from large towns to small special-purpose sites, an unusually large sample. The largest site (229,273 square feet), the Dyar mound and village, was occupied from approximately A.D. 1000 to 1550 (Smith 1981) and is the type site for the Dyar phase, an archaeological construct overlapping the period of early Spanish exploration. The Dyar site may well be the Cofaqui of the de Soto chronicles, as discussed previously. It shows gradual decline and abandonment during the sixteenth century, suggesting the effect of European disease (Smith 1981:256).

The subsequent indigenously developed occupation of the reservoir is the Bell phase. The largest known site of the Bell phase (65,340 square feet), Joe Bell, 9Mg28, is the type site for the phase (Williams 1981). The Bell site has produced European trade materials and radiocarbon determinations (Williams 1981) that date it to Period C. Comparing the largest sites, we observe a reduction in site size from the Dyar phase to the Bell phase, which suggests drastic population decline.

To study more closely the effects of disease on the Wallace Reservoir area, a large sample of sites was investigated for data on the number and size of components of the Late Dyar and Bell phases. This sample consisted of four transects, which were selected to cross the reservoir area in specified ecological niches. Both broad alluvial valley uplands and narrow valley shoals areas were selected as sample strata (Siegel n.d.). Within these strata, 253 Lamar period components were recognized (see appendix 2 for ceramic dating methodology): 101 were Late Dyar phase components (sixteenth century) and 63 were Bell phase components (seventeenth century). Since the durations of these phases are for all practical purposes identical (a minimum of fifty years and a maximum of one hundred years by current estimates

[Smith 1981; Williams 1983; Gary Shapiro, personal communication]), these two phases will be considered directly equivalent temporal units. Differences between the settlement of these two phases can be attributed to the effects of European disease or migration. Since no heavy Bell phase occupation is known outside the Wallace Reservoir area, the migration explanation appears unlikely.

Are there differences between the settlement of the two phases? It is obvious that numbers of sites decreased dramatically from 101 to 63, but what about site area? In order to test for differences in site area, it was necessary to remove multicomponent sites from consideration since the size of each individual component was not calculated by Wallace Mitigation Survey personnel. Indeed, such identification would have been impossible, since the phase designations utilized here were developed in the laboratory after the survey was completed. The removal of multicomponent sites results in a sample consisting of 38 Bell phase sites and 80 Late Dyar phase sites. Site area had been calculated in the field (David J. Hally, personal communication), and these figures were compared with a T test (SPSS = X Release 2.0). A two-tailed test was used on the hypothesis that mean site size for each phase was equal. Even though the mean site size for the Bell phase was only 4,648.4 square meters compared to 6,807 square meters for the earlier Late Dyar phase, the T test indicated that these sizes were not significantly different (T = 1.08; DF = 116; significant only at 0.285 level). How is this lack of difference to be interpreted?

The largest single component site of the Late Dyar phase in the transects covered 61,286 square meters, the largest Bell phase site 42,394 square meters. There were fifteen Late Dyar phase sites with areas over 10,000 square meters compared to only five Bell phase sites of this size, indicating that the larger sites were dropping out of the settlement hierarchy (at least few large sites were established during the Bell phase).

Nonetheless the T test indicates that mean site size is not significantly different in the two phases. The likely explanation is that both phases have large numbers of smaller sites that are about the same size. While there is a great decrease in numbers of sites, it is apparent that an attempt was made to maintain certain site size units for economic or social reasons or both. The Bell phase survivors of epidemic disease probably regrouped into basic socioeconomic units that were approximately the same size as units of the Late Dyar phase. Thus site size remained roughly constant, but numbers of sites decreased dramatically. This interpretation fits the historically expected processes described by Milner (1980:47) discussed earlier. Dobyns also discusses the notion of a culturally defined model of a proper settlement size (1983:303). Ramenofsky (1982:267) notes that "Residential instability and/or village reduction coupled with amalgamation processes which occur when the population of villages falls below a threshold necessary for defense and maintenance are attempts to maintain adaptations that developed when the population base was much larger." This process is hypothesized as the best explanation of the Wallace Reservoir data.

Population movement

Another historically documented effect of European disease is population movement. Two types are mentioned in the documents: rapid flight from areas of epidemic disease and slower movements brought about as tribal balances of power shift with changing demography.

As we understand the earliest Spanish explorers, there is not much evidence of rapid flight from sites in the study area because of disease. While the de Soto narratives mention the abandonment of Talomeco just east of the study area, interpretations of the routes of de Soto, Luna, and Pardo by Charles Hudson and his associates (DePratter et al. 1983, 1985; Hudson et al. 1984, 1985) indicate that the later Luna and Pardo expeditions visited the same towns as de Soto. It is possible that these towns were abandoned for short periods and then subsequently reoccupied, but this premise would be difficult to demonstrate archaeologically.

What can be demonstrated, at least in some portions of the study area, are gradual population movements. It is assumed that these movements were the result of European disease since a great deal of residential stability can be demonstrated in the study area prehistorically. Some major mound centers were occupied for hundreds of years (see chapter 5 and table 5.1). It is possible, of course, that other factors caused population movements.

The Coosa River drainage provides the best evidence for gradual population movement. It is an area in which intensive archaeological research has taken place (Morrell 1964, 1965; Wauchope 1966; DeJarnette et al. 1973; Smith 1977; Little and Curren 1981; Curren et al. 1982; and data gathered from several private collectors), and it can comfortably be assumed that there is a good sample of the archaeological sites of the early historic period—perhaps even all of them of village size. Smaller sites do not appear to characterize the settlement hierarchy of the area. I earlier demonstrated (1977) that the area of

Table 4.6. European disease and Coosa River settlement

| Coosa River sequence | | Documented Florida epidemics (after Dobyns 1983:270, 285) | |
Site	Estimated date	Date	Disease
King	1540–70[a]	1535–39	Unidentified
		1564–70	Unidentified and syphilis
Ce308	1570–90		
		1585–86	Unidentified
Terrapin Creek	1590–1600		
		1596	Measles
Bradford Ferry	1600–1630	1613–17	Bubonic plague
Cooper Farm	1630–70	1649	Yellow fever
		1653	Smallpox
		1672	Influenza
Woods Island	1670–1700	1686	Unidentified (typhus?)
		1716	Unidentified

a. Luna apparently found natives in the same location as Desoto, so movement after 1560 is suggested.

the Upper Coosa drainage in the present state of Georgia appears to have been totally abandoned during the sixteenth century (Periods A and B). Since that time, more data have been collected, but the conclusion remains much the same. Figure 4.2 presents data on changes in settlement for the Coosa River area north of the present Childersburg, Alabama. It is believed to be the area of the sixteenth-century province of Coosa known from the de Soto narratives (DePratter et al. 1985; Hudson et al. 1985).

With the exception of the Ogeltree Island site, all sites demonstrably within Period A are located along the upper reaches of the Coosa River drainage system in present Georgia.

Sites that fall within Period B are all downstream in present Alabama; no sites of Period B are known from northwestern Georgia (with the possible exception of the Little Egypt site), suggesting that the area was abandoned before the seventeenth century and not subsequently occupied until much later. In a concentration of sites of Periods B and C in the Weiss Reservoir area of Cherokee County, Alabama, excavations show that the sites did not have late prehistoric components but had relatively short occupations during the early historic period (DeJarnette et al. 1973; Smith 1977). There is another concentration of Periods B and C sites along creek drainages in Talladega County, Alabama, south of Ogeltree Island. This area is probably the province of Talisi mentioned in the de Soto narratives (Hudson et al. 1985). Several Period D sites are known from the Gadsden, Alabama, area, such as the Cooper Farm site. Finally, the Woods Island site (around 1670–1700) is located slightly farther south of the Gadsden cluster.

These distributional data indicate the gradual movement of a cluster of sites (the Coosa Province) down the Coosa River Valley. If we consider Ogeltree Island and sites southward as a separate cluster (the province of Talisi), then we have seven Period A sites in Georgia, two Period B sites in northeastern Alabama, four Period C sites in Alabama (probably only three of which are contemporary—the Terrapin Creek site was probably abandoned early in Period C), and two Period D sites farther south, with the post–early historic period Woods Island site located still farther south. The eighteenth-century location of the town of Coosa is the Childersburg site (DeJarnette and Hansen 1960) located still farther south. The sixteenth-century site of the main town of Coosa is believed to be the Little Egypt site (DePratter et al. 1985; Hudson et al. 1985), the site farthest north. It thus appears that the core of the chiefdom of Coosa shrank from a minimum of five towns to one or two towns and constantly moved southward during the period 1540–1740.

Dobyns has suggested (1983:313–27) that major European epidemics may have been responsible for settlement shifts among aboriginal populations. He illustrates his suggestion by comparing a sequence of historic Seneca Iroquois sites developed from archaeological seriation by Charles Wray and Harry Schoff (1953) with a list of documented and probable epidemics that he has found through analysis of historical records. There is a strong correlation between the archaeologists' estimated dates of occupation and the known occurrences of epidemic disease, suggesting to Dobyns that sites were abandoned because of specific epidemics. How do the epidemics documented by Dobyns match the occupation dates of archaeological sites in our study area?

To test the hypothesis that epidemics resulted in the abandonment of certain sites known archaeologically, the tightly clustered sites on the Coosa River drainage near the present Georgia-Alabama border have been chosen to compare with the epidemics in Florida documented by Dobyns (1983:270, 285). Since he strongly argues that most of these were pandemics, it does not seem unreasonable to compare the interior sites to the Florida epidemics. Table 4.6 compares the site sequence presented in chapter 3 with documented epidemics.

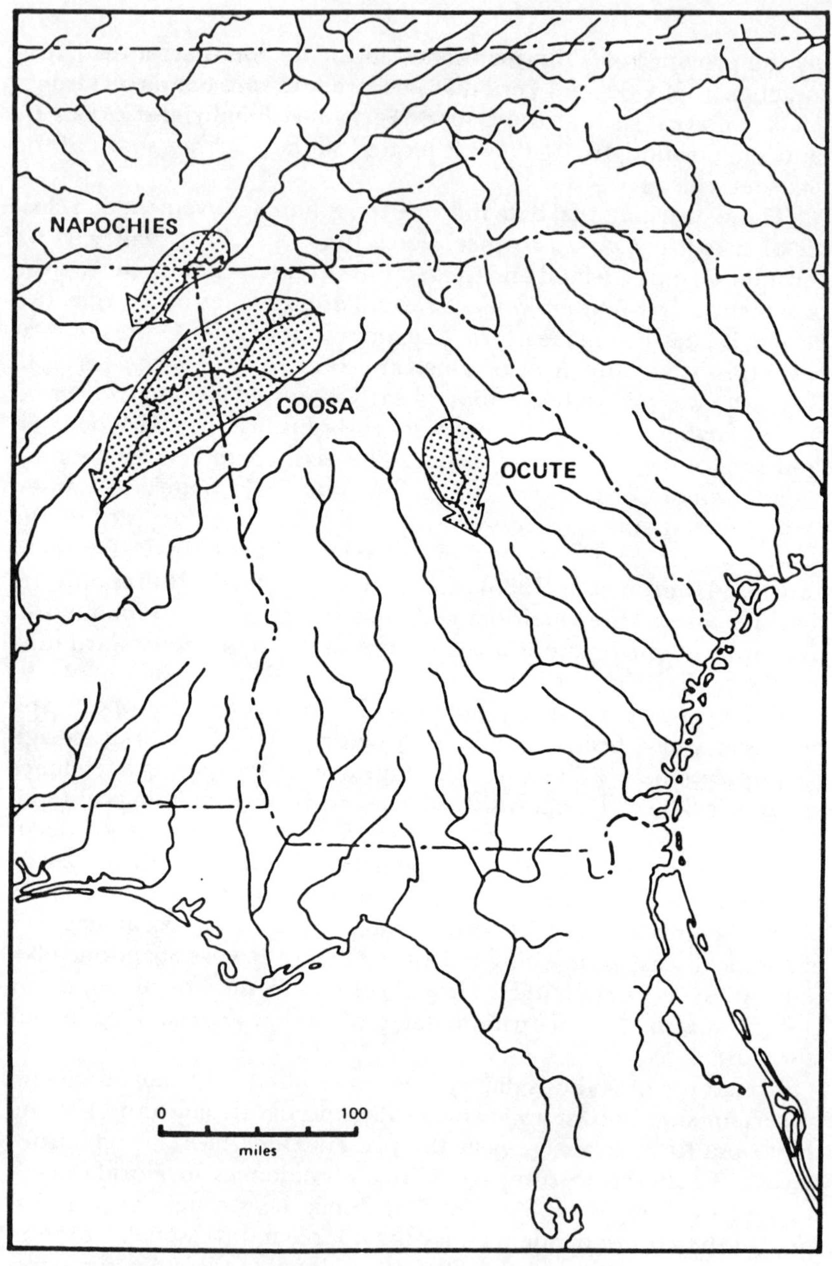

Figure 4.2. Suggested population movements.

(Dobyns also lists possible epidemics, but this application considers only those definitely documented.)

Just as Dobyns found with the Seneca, there appears to be a high correspondence between some settlement shifts and specific occurrences of epidemic disease. The King site, known to have had short occupation (suggested at 1540–70), and perhaps identified in the de Soto (1540) and Luna (1560) documents as the town of Piachi (Hudson et al. 1985), is such a case. Dobyns documents an epidemic of unknown disease during the period 1535–39, just before de Soto, the same epidemic that hit the province of Cofitachiqui in South Carolina. It appears highly likely that the King site was founded just after this epidemic but before the appearance of de Soto in 1540. Similarly, another epidemic of unknown disease of 1564–70 suggested by Dobyns may account for the abandonment of the site and perhaps for the occupation at site 1Ce308 to the south. Again, a documented epidemic of 1585–86 closely matches the estimate of 1590 suggested for the end of the occupation at 1Ce308 and the beginning of the historic component at the Terrapin Creek site, some eleven miles downstream. A 1596 measles epidemic may account for the abandonment of Terrapin Creek and the subsequent movement to the Bradford Ferry site, again closely matching the estimate of 1600.

No documented epidemic closely matches the 1630 estimate for the end of the occupation at Bradford Ferry. Dobyns does list an occurrence of plague in New Mexico in 1630 and a measles outbreak in New England in 1633 (1983:315), but he has no documented evidence of these diseases in Florida. The archaeological evidence, however, suggests that there was a further southward population shift on the Coosa River at this time to the Cooper Farm site. Finally, the estimated abandonment of the Cooper Farm site around 1670 is closely matched by a documented influenza outbreak in 1672.

There seems to have been a high correspondence between diseases and settlement shift in the Coosa area. Only the abandonment of the Bradford Ferry site has not been correlated with a documented epidemic. Obviously the Coosa River area requires further study. Analysis of large skeletal populations might add to the archaeological and historical evidence for settlement shift due to disease. It should also be noted that Dobyns does document other epidemics that do not correlate with Coosa River settlement shifts, so clearly there were factors in addition to disease that caused population shifts.

Population movement can be seen in the Oconee River drainage (fig. 4.2). During the precontact part of the sixteenth century, a powerful chiefdom consisting of three multiple mound sites, two single mound sites, and numerous smaller sites, occupied the Oconee Valley for some sixty miles north to south (Smith and Kowalewski 1980). This is the archaeological Dyar phase and the historically known province of Ocute (Smith 1981) mentioned in the de Soto narratives.

The subsequent Bell phase began about 1600 and lasted until around 1675. European trade material recovered from two sites in the Wallace Reservoir, located approximately in the center of the province, places them in Period C. Several additional sites have produced nondiagnostic European goods. Bell phase sites are small villages or smaller special-purpose sites, and none has mounds (Williams 1983:54).

While downstream movement cannot be clearly demonstrated for the Oconee drainage from the available data, it is apparent that the large mound centers were abandoned. No European artifacts were recovered from relatively extensive excavations at the Dyar mound site, nor were any ceramics characteristic of the Bell phase (Smith 1981). Recent test excavations at the Scull Shoals mound group (Williams 1984; personal communication) recovered one spherical navy blue bead, a type that was in use from Period A through Period D. Some historic occupation is noted for Scull Shoals, but the scarcity of Bell phase ceramics (Williams 1984) argues that the occupation was probably terminated by 1600.

The only known eighteenth-century site on the Oconee drainage is the Oconee Old Town site located near the fall line near Milledgeville, Georgia. Research was carried out at this site by A. R. Kelly with a W.P.A. crew. To date, no report has been made of the findings, but the collections are stored at the Southeastern Archaeological Center in Tallahassee, Florida. This material has been inspected by Mark Williams, who reports that the ceramics are not like the Bell phase material but consist of brushed types typical of those from the Ocmulgee and Chattahoochee drainages (Williams 1983 and personal communication).

John Swanton (1922:179–81; 1946:165) has described the known history of the Oconee. In 1602 the Timucua missionary Pareja mentions that the Ocony were three days' journey from San Pedro (Cumberland Island). In a letter dated April 8, 1608, Ibarra says that the chief of Oconee was marching against the province of Tama. Swanton states that this reference could refer to either of two Oconee groups: one in Florida or one on the Oconee River in Georgia. It is probably a reference to the latter, as the Tama of interior Georgia are no doubt the Altamaha of the de Soto narratives (Swanton 1946:208). Other references to the Oconee noted by Swanton include a 1655 reference to a mission station called Santiago de Ocone, which Swanton places near Jekyll Island, relatively close to the mouth of the Oconee River–Altamaha River drainage system. Ambiguity arises from the fact that there was also an Oconee mission among the Apalachee Indians of Florida in 1680 and from Swanton's interpretations that it had been there as early as 1655. There are references to Oconee Old Town near Milledgevilie around the turn of the eighteenth century. Their later movements into Florida do not concern us here.

Swanton's interpretations of Oconee movements are as follows: they were probably on the Chattahoochee River until 1695, when they moved over to the Oconee Old Town Site on the Oconee River near Milledgeville, Georgia. After the Yamassee War, they moved back to the Chattahoochee (Swanton 1946:165).

Another interpretation is offered here. There are references to the province of Ocute in 1540 and 1596 in which Altamaha or Tama are connected. In the 1602 and 1608 references noted by Swanton, the Oconee are also closely tied to the Tama. I suggest that the sixteenth-century province of Ocute became known as Oconee during the seventeenth century. An early English reference (1690) to Chief Altamaha, a powerful Yamassee head man (Wright 1981:158), suggests that the earlier Spanish province of Altamaha became the Yamasee of the English. From this viewpoint, there was population continuity along the piedmont Oconee drainage between the de Soto expedition and the Yamassee War. The Oconee drainage was heavily populated during the sixteenth century (Dyar phase), but its population declined during the seventeenth century (Bell phase). It seems more prudent to show continuity between the groups.

What is suggested, in short, is that because of European-introduced disease, the huge province of Ocute, with its allied town of Altamaha described in the de Soto narratives, shrank into one town, Oconee Old Town, by about 1700. While Williams (1983:440) has correctly pointed out an apparent ceramic discontinuity, an alternative explanation of that phenomenon will be offered in chapter 7. The location of Oconee Old Town at the fall line ecotone and adjacent to the Lower Creek trading path (Goff 1953), which led to Charles Towne, was no accident.

The Tennessee River drainage system settlement distribution is far more complex. It is perhaps most profitably looked at in small segments (figs. 3.1).

The area around Chattanooga, Tennessee, is identified with the Napochies of the Luna narratives of 1560 (DePratter et al. 1985). Current archaeological and historical evidence suggests the following interpretation of population movements. Of sites producing European trade goods, both Citico and Audubon Acres were occupied during the sixteenth century. Audubon Acres appears to have Period A material only, while Citico has at least some Period B material (a few blue beads) and iron chisels that could date to Period A, B, or even C. The overall scarcity of trade goods, and the nature of what there is, suggests placing Citico in Period A to early B. The Citico site is a major mound center; it has produced Southern Cult material (Hatch 1976). The Audubon Acres site is a village (Evans et al. 1981) located up South Chickamauga Creek. It is likely that the sites are contemporaneous, although Citico undoubtedly had a longer occupation. According to the Luna narratives, the first Napochie village was located two leagues from the great river, and another was located on the banks of the river itself. These Napochie villages have been identified with the Audubon Acres and Citico sites (DePratter et al. 1985). Current archaeological evidence, admittedly weak, suggests that Audubon Acres was abandoned before Citico. This view makes sense if European epidemics struck the Napochies and they fell back to their old capital of Citico. The Citico site itself was probably abandoned by 1600. Two Period C sites (1600–1630) are known from this area and no doubt represent later villages of the Napochies. These are Williams Island and Hampton Place (Smith 1976). While these sites may be contemporaneous, the wider variety of trade material at Hampton Place suggests that it is the most recent site in the area, but it does not appear to contain a distinctive assemblage of type D. What happened to the Napochies after 1630? They probably migrated downstream to the big bend of the Tennessee River in Alabama, settling at the Period D sites 1Ms32 and 1Ms91 and finally 1Ms100 late in the seventeenth century (fig. 3.1).

The situation in the Hiwassee River drainage is not as clear. There are two Period A sites, Rymer and Ledford Island, in the middle reaches of the river and a component from Period D on Hiwassee Island at the mouth of the river. Sites of the intermediate Periods B and C are unknown for that drainage, the closest being DeArmond (B) and Upper Hampton Place (B) located on the Tennessee River to the northeast. Data to tie all these sites into one sociopolitical group are not available at this time. The suggested population movement based on dating of sites with European goods is from the Hiwassee River northward to the Tennessee River and then downstream to Hiwassee Island at the junction of the Tennessee and Hiwassee rivers (fig. 3.1). Subsequent early eighteenth-century components are known from upstream in the Hiwassee River drainage, so there was apparently an upstream movement near the turn of the century. These hypothesized movements require further archaeological demonstration. The sites must be shown to be closely related in aboriginal culture.

The Little Tennessee River drainage also presents a complex situation. The Great Tellico site, located up the Tellico River, apparently was occupied from the prehistoric period through Periods A, B, and C. It was also an important eighteenth-century Cherokee site. Although it is known only from surface collections and amateur excavations, the considerable amount of information on Great Tellico available suggests that it was occupied continuously from the early sixteenth through the late eighteenth centuries.

Along the Little Tennessee River proper, there is a great concentration of sixteenth-century European trade goods (Period A) on four sites (Brain 1975; Smith 1976; Polhemus 1982). The mound centers Toqua, Citico, and McMurry were abandoned apparently at this early period, also probably because of disease. No sites with a definite Period B component are recognized in the archaeological record (although Citico may have been occupied), but again there is a cluster of Period B sites located to the northeast on the Tennessee–French Broad river drainage. While at first glance this distribution suggests a movement from the Little Tennessee River to the larger river paralleling the hypothesized movement from the Hiwassee, it should be noted that all three sites (Stratton, Brakebill, and McMahon) have mounds and at least some have long-term occupations in the prehistoric period (especially McMahon, which had a long, documented shell gorget sequence [see Kneberg 1959]). The prehistoric occupation suggests that these sites were not newly settled during the early historic period unless it was a reoccupation of an old town site.

Period C components do occur on sites on the Little Tennessee River proper, including Bussell Island, Tomotley, and perhaps Tallassee. This last site continued to be occupied into Period D. It is thus possible that the Little Tennessee was abandoned during Period B, or right after the Spanish *entradas* of the sixteenth century. The four sites with Period A components are reduced to three sites of Period C and three sites of Period D, again suggesting population decline; however, it is possible that a sampling bias was introduced by only using sites that have produced European goods. The sudden florescence of period D trade goods at sites such as Toqua, Citico, and Tallassee may reflect the entrance of the Cherokee into the Little Tennessee Valley. Specific data indicating European disease in the area have been discussed above in conjunction with the Toqua site.

Some data have been collected on historic occupations on the Clinch, Holston, and Nolichucky rivers (see fig. 3.1), but they do not allow discussions of population movements. The cluster of sites on the Nolichucky River may represent the Chiscas of the de Soto narratives (DePratter et al. 1983).

DePratter et al. (1983, 1985) have identified the Chiaha of the de Soto and Pardo relations with the archaeological site of Zimmerman's Island. Limited archaeological research was conducted on this site before it was inundated by reservoir construction. No European artifacts were found, but aboriginal materials, especially shell gorgets demonstrating a sixteenth-century occupation, were recovered (Kneberg 1959). While we do not have the archaeological data necessary to document the timing of the demise of this Chiaha site, it is interesting to note that they had settled among the Lower Creeks on the Ocmulgee River by 1713, and in 1715 they moved to the Chattahoochee River with the Creek towns (Swanton 1946:115–16). While we cannot prove that there were not two different groups with the same name, it appears likely that the Chiaha fled northern Tennessee sometime in the seventeenth century, possibly to escape other Indian groups armed with firearms from Virginia or the Great Lakes area.

Discussion

Archaeological evidence for depopulation in the study area is not particularly strong. Both mass and multiple burials from the early historic period have been found, but we cannot demonstrate that they were not also present in the prehistoric period. Unfortunately, most of the Period A and many of the Period B sites in the study area also have prehistoric components, and it is thus impossible to contrast clearly protohistoric sites with early historic sites. Indeed, they are frequently the same site, and it is impossible to assign all burials to one component or the other. It can be suggested that mass and multiple burials indicate the occurrence of epidemics, but it cannot be proved at this time.

Evidence from population curves might be suggestive; but to date such analysis has been carried out only on the King site skeletal series, and results from the several analyses are conflicting. It must be conceded that population curves suggestive of epidemics could be the result of famine or other causes.

Indirect measures of depopulation have proven only slightly more useful. There does seem to have been a trend during the early historic period toward a decrease in site size, but data are available for only a few sites. A larger sample of site sizes is needed. While it can be argued that most sites of the early historic period from the Tennessee and Coosa drainages are known, a more intensive survey would generate more confidence in the assertion. The locating of additional sites might severely alter the argument presented here.

Population movements can be documented within the study area, and historical evidence suggests such movements may result from reactions to epidemics. But certainly other events may account for population displacements, among them ecological disasters or warfare.

Carmack and Weeks (1981) point out that archaeological and ethnohistorical data often conflict. While we accept the view of Dobyns and Ramenofsky that southeastern Indian societies underwent drastic depopulation following the introduction of European diseases, the archaeological evidence of epidemics that can be assembled at this time is admittedly weak. But the political breakdown that resulted from this depopulation can be more fully documented. This breakdown of the political structure of the aboriginal Southeast is the subject of chapter 5.

References Cited

Battles, Mrs. Richard E.
1969   One foot in a grave. Journal of Alabama Archaeology 15:35-38.
1972   Copper and lithic artifacts. Journal of Alabama Archaeology 18:32-35.
Bennett, Charles, trans.
1975   [1586] Three voyages by René Laudonnière (1586). Gainesville: University Press of
        Florida.
Brain, Jeffrey P.
1975   Artifacts of the adelantado. The Conference on Historic Site Archaeology Papers 1973
        8:129-38.
Carmack, Robert, and John Weeks
1981   The archaeology and ethnohistory of Utatlan: A conjunctive approach. American Antiquity
        46:323-41.
Crosby, Alfred W., Jr.
1972   The Columbian exchange. Westport, Conn.: Greenwood Press.
Curren, Cailup
1982   The Alabama River phase: a review. In Archaeology in Southwestern Alabama: A collection
        of papers, ed. Cailup Curren, 103-14. Camden, Ala.: Alabama Tombigbee Regional
        Commission.
Curren, Cailup, Keith Little, and George Lankford
1982   The route of the expedition of Hernando de Soto through Alabama. Revised draft of paper
        presented at the Southeastern Archaeological Conference. Asheville, North Carolina, 1981.
DeJarnette, David L. and Asael T. Hansen
1960   The archaeology of the Childersburg site, Alabama. Florida State University Notes in
        Anthropology 4. Tallahassee.
DeJarnette, David L., Edward Kurjack, and Bennie Keel
1973   Archaeological investigations of the Weiss Reservoir of the Coosa River in Alabama.
        Journal of Alabama Archaeology 19.1-201.
DePratter, Chester, Charles Hudson, and Marvin Smith
1983   The route of Juan Pardo's explorations in the interior Southeast. 1566-1568. Florida
        Historical Quarterly 62:125-58.
1985   The DeSoto expedition: From Chiaha to Mabila. In Alabama and the borderlands, from
        prehistory to statehood, ed. Reid Badger and Lawrence Clayton, pp. 108-27. Tuscaloosa:
        University of Alabama Press.
Dobyns, Henry F.
1963   An outline of Andean epidemic history to 1720. Bulletin of the History of Medicine 37:493-
        515.
1966   Estimating aboriginal American population: An appraisal of techniques with a new
        hemispheric estimate. Current Anthropology 7:395-416.
1983   Their number become thinned. Knoxville: University of Tennessee Press.
Evans, E. Raymond, Victor Hood, and Loretta Lautzenheiser
1981   Preliminary excavations on the Audubon Acres site (40Ha84), Hamilton County,
        Tennessee. Typescript, Department of Anthropology, University of Tennessee,
        Chattanooga.
Fish, Suzanne, and Paul Fish
1979   Historic demography and ethnographic analogy. Early Georgia 7:29-43.
Funkhouser, Gary
1978   Paleodemography of the King site. Master's thesis, University of Georgia.
Goff, John H.
1953   Some major Indian trading paths across the Georgia piedmont. Georgia Mineral
        Newsletter 6.

1

Guthe, Alfred, and Marian Bristline
    1978   Excavations at Tomotley, 1973-74, and the Tuskeegee Area: Two Reports. University of
            Tennessee Department of Anthropology Report of Investigations, no. 24.
Hally, David J.
    1975   Archaeological investigation of the King site, Floyd County, Georgia. Report submitted to
            the National Endowment for the Humanities. Department of Anthropology, University of
            Georgia. Photocopy.
    1980   Archaeological investigation of the Little Egypt site (9Mu102), Murray County, Georgia,
            1970-72 season. Submitted to the Heritage Conservation and Recreation Service, U.S.
            Department of the Interior.
    1982   Archaeological investigations at the King site, Floyd County, Georgia. National Geographic
            Society Research Reports 14:303-9.
Hassan, Fekri A.
    1981   Demographic archaeology. New York: Academic Press.
Hatch, James W.
    1976   The Citico site (40Ha65): A synthesis. Tennessee Archaeologist 1:75-103.
Helms, Mary W.
    1979   Ancient Panama. Austin: University of Texas Press.
Hoffman, Paul E.
    1980   A new voyage of North American discovery: Pedro de Salazar's voyage to the Island of
            Giants. Florida Historical Quarterly 38:415-26.
Hudson, Charles M.
    1980   An unknown South: The world of sixteenth-century southeastern Indians. Paper presented
            at the Chancellor's Symposium, University of Mississippi.
Hudson, Charles M., M. T. Smith, and C. B. DePratter
    1984   The route of the de Soto expedition from Apalachee to Chiaha. Southeastern Archaeology
            3:65-77.
Hudson, C., M. Smith, D. Hally, R. Polhemus, and C. DePratter
    1985   Coosa: A chiefdom in the sixteenth-century southeastern United States. American
            Antiquity 50:723-37.
Humbard, Richard, and John Humbard
    1965   Burial caches. Journal of Alabama Archaeology 11:133-42.
Kenyon, Walter A.
    1977   Some bones of contention: The Neutral Indian burial site at Grimsby. Rotunda 10(3):4-13.
    1982   The Grimsby site. Toronto: Royal Ontario Museum.
Kneberg, Madeline
    1959   Engraved shell gorgets and their associations. Tennessee Archaeologist 15:1-39.
Larson, Lewis H.
    1972   Functional considerations of warfare in the Southeast during the Mississippi period.
            American Antiquity 37:383-92.
Lewis, Clifford, and Albert Loomie
    1953   The Spanish Jesuit mission in Virginia, 1570-1572. Chapel Hill: University of North Carolina
            Press.
Lewis, T. M. N., and Madeline Kneberg
    1941   The prehistory of the Chickamauga Basin in Tennessee: A preview. Tennessee
            Anthropological Papers 1. Knoxville: Division of Anthropology, University of Tennessee.
    1946   Hiwassee Island. Knoxville: University of Tennessee Press.
Lindsey, Mrs. E. M.
    1964   Cooper Farm salvage project. Journal of Alabama Archaeology 10: 22-29.
Little, Keith, and Cailup B. Curren, Jr.
    1981   Site 1Ce308: A protohistoric site on the Upper Coosa River in Alabama. Journal of
            Alabama Archaeology 27:117-24.
Lyon, Eugene
    1976   The enterprise of Florida. Gainesville: University Presses of Florida.

2

Mathews, Davis S.
    1984   The King site battle victims: The discovery of De Soto in Georgia. Paper presented at the
            annual meeting of the Southern Anthropological Society, Atlanta.
Milner, George G.
    1980   Epidemic disease in the postcontact Southeast: A reappraisal. _Midcontinental Journal of
            Archaeology_ 5:39-56.
Moore, Clarence B.
    1915   Aboriginal sites on Tennessee River. _Journal of the Academy of Natural Sciences of
            Philadelphia_ 16:169-427.
Morrell, I. Ross
    1964   Two historic island sites in the Coosa River. _Florida Anthropologist_ 17:75-76.
    1965   _The Woods Island site in southeastern acculturation, 1625-1800_. Florida State University
            Notes in Anthropology, no. 11.
Naroll, Raoul
    1962   Floor area and settlement populations. _American Antiquity_ 27:587-89.
Phillips, Philip, James A. Ford, and James B. Griffin
    1951   _Archaeological survey in the Lower Mississippi alluvial valley, 1940-1947_. Papers of the
            Peabody Museum of American Archaeology and Ethnology 25. Cambridge, Mass.:
            Harvard University Press.
Polhemus, Richard
    1982   The early historic period in the East Tennessee Valley. Typescript in possession of the
            writer.
Priestley, Herbert I.
    1928   _The Luna papers: Documents relating to the expedition of Don Tristan de Luna y Arellano
            for the conquest of La Florida in 1559-1561_. 2 vols. Florida State Historical Society
            Publication no. 8. DeLand, Florida.
Ramenofsky, Ann F.
    1982   The archaeology of population collapse: Native American response to the introduction of
            infectious disease. Ph.D. diss., University of Washington. Ann Arbor, Mich.: University
            Microfilms.
Rudolph, James, and Dennis Blanton
    1980   A discussion of Mississippian settlement in the Georgia piedmont. _Early Georgia_ 8:14-36.
Sauer, Carl Ortwin
    1971   _Sixteenth-century North America_. Berkeley: University of California Press.
Seckinger, Ernest W.
    1975   Preliminary report on the social dimensions of the King site mortuary practices.
            Southeastern Archaeological Conference Bulletin 18:67-73.
    1977   Social complexity during the Mississippian period in Northwest Georgia. Master's thesis,
            University of Georgia.
Sheldon, Craig T., Jr.
    1974   The Mississippian-historic transition in central Alabama. Ph.D. diss., University of Oregon.
            Ann Arbor, Mich.: University Microfilms.
Siegel, Charles
    n.d.   Producing a sampling scheme for the Wallace project subsurface survey. Department of
            Anthropology, University of Georgia. Typescript.
Smith, Buckingham
    1968   _Narratives of De Soto_. Gainesville, Fla.: Palmetto Books.
Smith, Marvin T.
    1976   The route of De Soto through Tennessee, Georgia, and Alabama: The evidence from
            material culture. _Early Georgia_ 4:27-48.
    1977   The early historic period (1540-1670) on the Upper Coosa River drainage of Alabama and
            Georgia. _The Conference on Historic Site Archaeology Papers 1976_ 11:151-67.
    1981   _Archaeological investigations at the Dyar site, 9Ge5_. Wallace Reservoir Project
            Contribution no. 11. Department of Anthropology, University of Georgia.

Smith, Marvin T., and Steve A. Kowalewski
    1980   Tentative identification of a prehistoric "province" in piedmont Georgia. <u>Early Georgia</u> 8:1-13.
Swanton, John R.
    1922   <u>Early history of the Creek Indians and their neighbors</u>. Bureau of American Ethnology Bulletin 73. Washington, D.C.
    1939   <u>Final report of the United States De Soto Expedition Commission</u>. House Document 71, 76th Cong., 1st sess., Washington, D.C.
    1946   <u>Indians of the Southeast</u>. Bureau of American Ethnology Bulletin 137. Washington, D.C.
Tally, Lucy
    1975   Preliminary demographic analysis of the King site burial population. <u>Southeastern Archaeological Conference Bulletin</u> 18:74-75.
Trigger, Bruce G.
    1976   <u>The children of Aataensic</u>. 2 vols. Montreal: McGill-Queens University Press.
Wauchope, Robert
    1966   <u>Archaeological survey of Northern Georgia</u>. Society for American Archaeology Memoir no. 21. Washington, D.C.
Webb, William S., and Charles Wilder
    1951   <u>An archaeological survey of Guntersville Basin on the Tennessee River in Northern Alabama</u>. Lexington: University of Kentucky Press.
Williams, John Mark
    1981   <u>Archaeological investigations at the Joe Bell site, 9Mg28</u>. Wallace Reservoir Contributions, no. 18. Department of Anthropology, University of Georgia.
    1983   The Joe Bell site: Seventeenth-century lifeways on the Oconee River. Ph.D. diss., University of Georgia. Ann Arbor, Mich.: University Microfilms.
    1984   <u>Archaeological excavations at Scull Shoals Mounds, Georgia</u>. Cultural Resources Report no. 6. U.S. Department of Agriculture, Forest Service Southern Region.
Wray, Charles F., and Harry L. Schoff
    1953   A preliminary report on the Seneca sequence in western New York, 1550-1687. <u>Pennsylvania Archaeologist</u> 23:53-63.
Wright, J. Leitch, Jr.
    1981   <u>The only land they knew</u>. New York: The Free Press.
Zahler, James W., Jr.
    1976   A morphological analysis of a protohistoric-historic skeletal population from St. Simons Island, Georgia. Master's thesis, University of Florida.

4

DEMOGRAPHIC PATTERNS AND CHANGES IN MID-SEVENTEENTH CENTURY TIMUCUA AND APALACHEE

by JOHN H. HANN

SURPRISINGLY little is known about the village patterns of northern Florida's natives prior to their missionization or about the settlement policy followed by the friars during the formation of the Florida mission chains. This is particularly true for the inland missions of Potano, Utina, Ustaca, and Apalachee. There is no evidence that the Florida Franciscans followed the "reduction"[1] approach of their Jesuit contemporaries in the South American mission provinces of Guaira, Itatin, Tape and Paraguay, whose people had a material culture roughly similar to that of North Florida's missionized tribes.[2] Thus, it is generally assumed that the friars adapted their mission organization in Florida to the aboriginal settlement pattern, setting up their mission centers in a principal village of the district. From there the friars went out to catechise the natives in nearby subordinate villages, which became known as visitas, rather than insisting that those natives move to the mission center, which was called a doctrina.[3] Only after the establishment of these missions, when most of the natives of the mission zone had already been Christianized, are there indications that some of the Indians did change their domicile at the instigation of the Spaniards. But in those cases the moves were inspired by secular rather than reli-

---

John H. Hann is historic site specialist at the San Luis Archaeological and Historic Site, Division of Archives, History and Records Management, Department of State, Tallahassee. He was formerly professor of Latin American history at Florida State University.

1. The "reduction" system was the concentration of scattered, often seasonally, nomadic native populations at mission centers located usually at sites chosen by the priests, at which the natives were expected to live year-round.
2. These missions spread over much of the Parana-Paraguay Basin of what is today southern and southwestern Brazil, Paraguay, and northeastern Argentina.
3. Visitas, however, were not always subordinate villages. And once the people of a visita had been Christianized, they were expected to come to the doctrina for Sunday mass when those visitas were reasonably close to the center.

[371]

gious authorities. One parallel, however, to the Jesuit's policy in the South American interior was the Franciscans' attempt at mid-century to isolate their charges in Apalachee from contact with any Spaniards other than themselves by excluding soldiers and settlers from that province.

In contrast to the prevailing paucity of information on settlement patterns, the record of Governor Diego de Rebolledo's 1657 visitation of Apalachee and Timucua provides information on this topic. Although that visitation record has been mined extensively during the last two decades for two dissertations and for a number of journal articles, a valuable aspect of that document's contents has not yet received much attention.[4] This is its depiction of the settlement pattern in the two provinces and its indication of drastic decline and dislocation in western Timucua's population.

For Apalachee the village distribution pattern reflected in this 1657 document, and in other later ones, mirrors the less well defined one presented in the De Soto chronicles. The pattern is one of a considerable number of more or less autonomous principal villages surrounded by subordinate or satellite villages, hamlets, and individual farmsteads scattered through the countryside.[5] Among the Timucuans, by contrast, many villages and their chiefs were united under a regional tribal chief who enjoyed considerable authority throughout the area.[6] In the 1650s a friar referred to these Timucuan tribal chiefs as having been like emperors and absolute lords when they were pagans.[7]

<hr>

4. Fred Lamar Pearson, Jr., "Spanish-Indian Relations in Florida: A Study of Two Visitas, 1657-1678" (Ph.D. dissertation, University of Alabama, 1968); Robert Allen Matter, "The Spanish Missions of Florida, the Friars Versus the Governors in the 'Golden Age', 1606-1690" (Ph.D. dissertation, University of Washington, 1972).
5. A caution is in order. There is no categorical description of the Apalachees political organization either during the De Soto intrusion or during the mission era such as there is for other groups in the southeast. In using such scintilla as is available, these limitations must be considered.
6. Jerald T. Milanich, "The Western Timucua: Patterns of Acculturation and Change," in Jerald T. Milanich and Samuel Proctor: *Tacachale, Essays on the Indians of Florida and Southeastern Georgia during the Historical Period* (Gainesville, 1978), 67.
7. Fray Juan Gómez de Engraba to Fray Francisco Martínez, March 13, 1657, Archivo General de Indias, Seville (hereinafter AGI) 54-5-10, in the Woodbury Lowery Collection (hereinafter WLC) mf. reel III. Most of the material cited from this collection was viewed on the microfilm copy held by the Florida State University, which is contained in four reels in contrast to the

But soon after the establishment of the missions, Timucuan political organization became decentralized as the tribal level organization declined in importance or disappeared entirely.[8] For extraordinary situations some vestige of that tradition appears to have survived until the 1650s. The same friar who characterized the Timucuan tribal chiefs as having been absolute lords in pagan times and who seemingly implied that they had largely lost that position also noted that during the 1656 revolt, "while being Christian, they still recognized him as such an absolute lord, and as a result many other chiefs and leading-men and vassals followed him."[9] This tribal leader was the Utinan chief of San Martín de Ayaocuto. In 1607 another friar had described him as the chief of more than twenty villages.[10]

The 1657 visitation record identifies twenty-nine western Timucuan villages and thirty-four or thirty-five Apalachee villages.[11] The completeness of that listing for western Timucua remains an unknown, as the assembling of the Timucuan chiefs took place soon after the 1656 rebellion during which eleven chiefs were hanged and a number of villages depopulated. And for Timucua there is no pre-rebellion estimate of the total number of either the missions or the native villages for comparison with the figure from 1657. For Apalachee, by contrast, it is evident that the 1657 identification of thirty-four or five separate villages represents most of the forty-some settlements the province was said to contain a decade earlier.[12] And for Apalachee, all the missions mentioned in 1657, along with a number of their satellites, appear on the various subsequent

---

P. K. Yonge Library's copy which is spread over seven reels. Whenever the writer has used transcriptions made from the P. K. Yonge Library's copy, he has changed the reel citation to conform to that of the Florida State University copy.

8. Milanich, "The Western Timucua," 67.
9. Gómez de Engraba to Martínez, March 13, 1657, AGI 54-5-10, WLC, reel III.
10. Luis Gerónimo de Oré, OFM, *The Martyrs of Florida* (1513-1616) trans., Maynard Geiger, OFM (New York, 1936), 114.
11. Diego de Rebolledo, Testimony from the Visitation That Was Made in the Provinces of Apalache and Timucua and Ustaca, 1657, AGI Escribanía de Cámara (hereinafter EC), leg. 155B, Stetson Collection (hereinafter SC). Inasmuch as this document and the pieces appended to it are the major source for this article, the material drawn from it will not be footnoted hereinafter when it is clear that this document is its source, in order to avoid a plethora of repetitious footnotes.
12. Royal Officials of Florida to king, March 18, 1647, AGI 54-5-14/105, SC.

mission lists for the rest of the century, whereas the roster for Timucua shrank steadily.

In Apalachee the governor himself, in the course of the visitation, traveled successively to all ten of the missions then in existence there. The chiefs and the leading-men of the twenty-four satellite villages identified were required to assemble in the principal council house of the mission village under whose jurisdiction they fell.[13] Inasmuch as the governor began the inspection at the western end of the province in Cupaica, it is probable that he had already visited all or most of the missions on the royal road as he traveled westward to reach San Luis and Cupaica.[14] In Timucua, however, Governor Rebolledo did not carry out an inspection of each mission village. Instead he instructed Matheo Luis de Florencia, a Spaniard from San Luis, to visit the Timucuan villages to summon those surviving chiefs who remained loyal and those who had been newly installed to a general visitation to be held by the governor at San Pedro de Potohixiba.[15]

The following Timucuan villages were represented at this meeting together with their respective native leaders.[16]

I- SAN PEDRO DE POTOHIXIBA—Diego Heba, principal chief

   1.   Santa Ana—María Meléndez, chieftainess.

II- CHAMILE AND SAN MARTÍN—Lázaro, principal chief
   1.   Cachipile—Francisco, chief
   2.   Chuaquin—Lorenzo, chief

III- AXAPAJA AND SANTA FÉ—Alonso Pastrana, principal chief
   1.   San Francisco Potano—Domingo, chief

---

13. There probably were more satellite villages than were identified here as the naming of such villages was consequent on the naming of the chief. In the chief's absence the settlement was not named.
14. Such a prior consultation with the native leaders is indicated by the governor's issuance of his regulations to deal with the province's problems and complaints at the completion of the visitation of Cupaica. Usually such regulations were issued only after all the villages had been heard formally.
15. The spelling of native names varies considerably from document to document. In quotations the spelling used by the source will be retained; otherwise a standard spelling based on one commonly found in the documents will be used. Potohiriba was here spelled Potohixiba. The 'x' here and elsewhere could be either an 'r' or a 'j'.
16. Upper case denotes the villages whose chiefs were identified as principal chiefs.

    2.   San Pablo—Francisco Alonso, chief
    3.   San Juan—Juan Bautista, chief

IV- SANTA ELENA DE MACHABA—Pedro Meléndez, principal chief
    1.   San Joseph—Sevastian, chief
    2.   San Lorenço—Dionisio, chief

V- SAN MATHEO—Sevastian, principal chief
    1.   San Francisco—Francisco, chief
    2.   San Miguel—Francisco Alonso, chief
    3.   Santa Lucia—Francisco, chief
    4.   San Diego—Francisco, chief
    5.   Santa Fée—Antonio, chief
    6.   San Pablo—Bernabé, chief
    7.   San Francisco—Francisco, chief
    8.   San Lucas—Lucas, chief
    9.   San Matheo—Santiago, chief

VI- San Agustín [de Urica?]—Domingo, chief[17]

VII- NIHAYCA—Lucia, principal chieftainess

VIII- TARI—No leader in attendance[18]
    1.   San Pedro de Aqualiro—Martín, chief

IX- Santa María—Alexo, chief, and Alonso, leading-man

Analysis of this listing and of the meager content of the visitation record for Timucua and other sources suggests several conclusions and raises many questions. Among the twenty-nine villages, Potohiriba, Potano, Santa Fé de Toloca, Machaba, Chuaquin, Tarihica, and San Matheo have been identified as having participated in the 1656 revolt. Guacara, not mentioned on this list, has also been identified as one of the rebellious settlements. Guacara's absence from the 1657 list, together with its identification as one of the vital communication links still in need of being resurrected at the end of 1659, suggests that by 1657 its people either had taken flight or had been obliterated during the fighting that accompanied the rebellion or during

---

17. The position of this village and its leader, as well as that of Santa María, is anomalous. Neither chief was given the title of principal chief, but neither were they said to belong to another's jurisdiction.

18. Tari was not mentioned during the main general visitation session, but Florencia was instructed to visit Tari to deliver the summons to the general visitation. The chiefs of Aqualiro and Santa María (IX) appear to have arrived late as they were given a separate interview.

the plagues that preceded and followed the revolt. Situated where one of the trails crossed the Suwannee, Guacara would have been particularly exposed to traveller-borne pathogens. San Francisco Potano, Santa Fé, and San Martín were other communication links identified as being in need of resurrection at the end of 1659.[19] Tari's inclusion among those to be summoned to the general visitation seemingly indicates that the village had survived to some degree. But the absence of the leader of the principal village of Tari suggests that the leadership element and many of the people had taken to the woods. If apprehended, Tari's chief would likely have been executed. He had been the first to voice opposition to Governor Rebolledo's orders that would lead to revolt. But it was San Martín's chief who initiated the armed rebellion in protest of the governor's policy when Rebolledo spurned the native leaders' objections to his demand that leading-men, as well as ordinary Indians called to St. Augustine for labor details, should carry seventy-five pounds of corn with them. This seems to indicate that the chief of San Martín still held something of the leadership position attributed to that village's chief in 1607, when he was described as the head chief of twenty Timucuan, i.e. presumably Utinan settlements.[20] However, both this reference to San Martín's chief in 1607 and his role in the 1656 rebellion suggest that in wartime his leadership may have extended beyond Utina. It was this chief's war with Apalachee, which the friars viewed as a hindrance to their work in western Timucua, that moved Fray Martín Prieto to journey to Apalachee's Ivitachuco in 1608 to establish peace between the warring Apalachee and western Timucuans.[21]

The depopulation of San Martín, along with the disappearance of its leadership element is confirmed by the visitation record. The reason for the pairing of Chamile and San Martín on this list was Chief Lázaro Chamile's agreement to move with the inhabitants of his village almost 100 miles to the east to occupy

---

19. Gómez de Engraba to Martínez, March 13, 1657, and April 4, 1657; Domingo de Leturiondo (partial report on the service-record of Captain Juan Francisco de Florencia, January 29, 1671), AGI 54-5-10, WLC, reels III and IV.
20. Gómez de Engraba to Martínez, March 13, 1657, and April 4, 1657, AGI 54-5-10, WLC, reel III; Oré, *The Martyrs*, 114.
21. Oré, *The Martyrs*, 114-16.

the presumably deserted settlement of San Martín. In agreeing to the move, Chief Chamile asked the governor to prohibit any encroachment by other natives on the lands he was leaving behind. He wished to maintain control over them so that his people might hunt and gather fruit there. The visitation record does not make clear whether the people of Chamile's satellite villages of Cachipile and Chuaquin were to accompany him on this migration, but their denomination as satellites would seem to imply that. On the 1655 mission list both had been identified as mission centers under the names San Francisco de Chuaquin and Santa Cruz de Cachipile, located sixty and seventy leagues respectively from St. Augustine. Chamile, presumably, is the San Ildefonso de Chamini of the 1655 list, which also was seventy leagues from St. Augustine. In 1662 some friars noted that most of the transplanted Indians had fled to the woods to live with pagan natives. Observing that some had died there in apostasy, the friars requested that the survivors be returned to their former homes. Though the records do not indicate whether any of Chamile's people did return to their home villages, the lack of any further mention of Chamile, Chuaquin, or Cachipile suggests that they did not.[22]

Nihayca's identity raises some questions. No village name with that spelling appears on any earlier or later mission list or in Swanton's catalogue of Timucuan village names. Pearson's rendering of the name as Nihoica is similar enough to Ajoica to suggest that Nihayca could be Ajoica. This in turn would mean that Ajoica as a mission center goes back beyond the circa-1660 foundation date generally assigned to it.[23]

The Potano region also experienced a desolation similar to that suffered by San Martín. That Arapaja and Santa Fé were being fused in a manner similar to the fusion of Chamile and San Martín is revealed by Chief Pastrana's request for the same rights as Chamile's to the lands he was abandoning. Although Pastrana's prior identification with Arapaja is not clearly delineated, this move also seems to have involved the migration southeastward of an Utinan people who had been living seventy leagues from St. Augustine to a site only thirty leagues distant

---

22. Charles W. Spellman, "The 'Golden Age' of the Florida Missions 1632-1674," *Catholic Historical Review*, LI (October 1963), 355.
23. Pearson, "Spanish Indian Relations," 109; Milanich, "The Western Timucua," 72.

from Spanish Florida's capital. Although San Francisco Potano
had survived the debacle of 1656 and the preceding epidemics,
its decline and/or its punishment is reflected in its reduction to
the status of a village subordinate to the new Utinan principal
chief of Santa Fé.

In an early August 1657 reply to charges by the friars, Governor Rebolledo attested to the sharp decrease in Timucua's
population, noting that the opportunity for conversions and the
number of people needing the services of the friars had diminished both there and in Guale. He observed that very few
Indians were left in either province "because they have been
wiped out with the sickness of the plague and small-pox which
have overtaken them in the past years."[24] He said nothing about
the losses he was responsible for, that resulted from the rebellion and from the flight from Timucua's villages by the survivors
of the fighting. Rebolledo's use of the more remote northern
Utinan villages as a population reservoir from which to replenish the depopulated mission centers on the royal road
suggests that their location may have protected them to some
degree from the worst ravages of the plagues of the 1649-1656
and the 1613-1617 periods or from direct involvement in the
revolt and the subsequent fighting.

Potano continued to decline in population, and Rebolledo's
efforts to revitalize Santa Fé and San Martín failed. On
November 19, 1659, Juan Francisco de Florencia was ordered
to go to Ustaca and to Timucua to repopulate and to resurrect
the places of San Francisco, Santa Fé, and San Martín, as well
as San Juan de Guacara. At this time these villages' depopulation
was attributed to some of the natives having died from an
epidemic and to others having fled to the woods. The resuscitation of these settlements was deemed necessary because they
served as way-stations on the road from St. Augustine to Ustaca
and Apalachee.[25] Inasmuch as none of the four sites designated
for repopulation were in Ustaca, it is reasonable to assume that
Florencia's mandated visit to Ustaca was to obtain colonists for
the deserted sites. This pattern would be repeated on a smaller
scale a generation later in 1678 when the visitador, Domingo de

---

24. Rebolledo (reply to the Franciscan's petition of August 4, 1657), August 5,
    1657 (document appended to Rebolledo's visitation record), AGI; EC, leg.
    155B, folios 40-50, SC.
25. Leturiondo (partial report, January 29, 1671), AGI 54-5-10, WLC, reel IV.

Leturiondo, would recruit another band of Ustacans drawn from Potohiriba, Machaba, and San Matheo for the establishment of an entirely new settlement at Ivitanayo, where it was felt that a way-station was needed.[26]

This documentation of the Spaniards' method of moving about the various branches of the Timucuan polity from the west and north (and particularly toward Potano) offers an additional explanation for the ability of certain villages in this area to hold their own, or even to grow, despite the province's general secular trend toward sharp demographic decline. It provides an explanation as well for the early disappearance of the northernmost Utinan missions. And it supplies documentary corroboration in part for the findings of archeologists who have noted changes in ceramic types for these areas during this time period. Milanich, citing Kathleen Deagan, observed that circa 1660 at the Fig Springs-Santa Catalina-Ajohica site "there was an almost complete replacement of prehistoric pottery types by types of the Leon-Jefferson, historic, wooden paddle-stamped series." The Potano region, Milanich noted, also experienced an intrusion of non-Potano ceramics, one that was more diverse than that at Fig Springs. Archeological research, he commented, indicated that eastern Timucuan and Guale peoples, as well as Apalachee and/or Utina and Yustega, were moving into the area.[27] For the late-seventeenth century the Joaquín de Florencia visitation record documents the presence of significant numbers of Apalachee men in Timucua working as contract laborers. But, inasmuch as they were unaccompanied by women, it is not clear whether their presence would be reflected by a change in ceramic styles.[28]

In this Apalachee migration, some of Florida's hispanicized Indians were following a classic pattern that prevailed elsewhere in Spanish America. The pattern consisted of an evolution from the repartimiento system's sporadic compulsory labor at pre-

---

26. Leturiondo, Inspection of the Provinces of Apalache and Timucua, 1677-1678, AGI, EC, leg. 156B, folios 596-598, SC.
27. Milanich, "The Western Timucua," 75, 79-80.
28. Joaquín de Florencia, General Inspection That the Captain, Joaquín de Florencia Made of the Provinces of Apalache and Timucua, Interim Treasurer of the Fort of St. Augustine of Florida, Judge Commissary and Inspector-general of Them by Title and Nomination of Don Laureano de Torres y Aiala, Knight of the Order of Santiago, Governor and Captain General of the Said *Presidio* and Provinces by His Majesty, November 5, 1694, AGI, EC, leg. 157A, cuaderno 1, folios 44-205, passim, SC.

scribed low wages, to freely undertaken regular long-term contract labor at more attractive wages, as employers sought to compensate for the shrinking of the available labor pool. In time the free contract-laborer would have been converted imperceptibly into a debt-peon in most cases had not the process been interrupted in the first decade of the eighteenth century by the English-inspired attacks that destroyed or dispersed most of Florida's surviving native population.

To date there is no precise indication of the relative impact of Timucua's various troubles on the reduction of the population there during the 1649 to 1659 period. Epidemic disease, hunger, overwork under harsh conditions, rebellion, and flight have all been mentioned as factors responsible for this calamity. But epidemic disease is clearly indicated as a major factor. In mid-1650 the governor reported that "the plague" had afflicted the presidio.[29] That it spread to the natives is suggested by a friar's report that during 1649 and 1650 many of the missionaries had died of the plague.[30] Late in October 1655 Rebolledo reported that since the start of that year there had been "a high mortality rate," resulting from a "series of small-pox plagues which have affected the country for the last ten months. Many have died," he added, "as a result of this and of the trials and hunger which these unfortunate people have suffered." So great was the decrease of the available labor force that the governor found it necessary to suspend his plans for the urgently-needed repair of St. Augustine's fort. He noted that the practice of having the Indians cut the wood and haul it on their shoulders over the considerable distance from the forest had been ruled out.[31] Fifteen months later the governor commented once more on the impact of the recent epidemics. On this occasion he indicated that all three mission provinces had been affected. Noting that there was a loss of population even in Apalachee, he remarked that the loss had been less drastic there than in

29. Benito Ruíz de Salaçar to king, July 14, 1650, AGI 54-5-10, WLC, reel III. This ambiguous term, presidio, could signify either the garrison alone or St. Augustine alone or the entire region under St. Augustine's jurisdiction.
30. Fray Pedro Moreno Ponce de León, memorial, September 7, 1651, AGI 54-5-10, WLC, reel III.
31. Rebolledo to crown, October 24, 1655, AGI 58-2-2/2, North Carolina Collection, xerox copy of translation by Ruth Kuykendall made from P. K. Yonge Library of Florida History's microfilm copy, in the possession of the author.

Guale and Timucua. In the latter two, he observed, very few Indians were left because so many had died off in recent years "with the illnesses of the plague and of small pox."[32] Modern authorities differ as to the nature of the disease the Spaniards spoke of in this instance as "the plague."[33] Still another epidemic struck the natives in the latter 1650s. In 1659 the incoming governor reported that a recent epidemic of measles had killed 10,000 Indians.[34]

Data from Oré's work reveal the extent of Potano's decline in the mere half-century that had passed since Fray Prieto began his formal evangelization in 1607. Prieto mentioned the existence in that year of four Potano towns containing a total of 1,200 people. He gave their names as San Miguel, San Francisco (one and one-half leagues from the former), Santa Ana, and San Buenaventura. Initially the friar resided at San Miguel, visiting San Francisco and Santa Ana each day to offer catechetical instruction. By 1616, however, the convent was at San Francisco Potano, and another mission among the Potano, named Santa Fé de Teleco in Oré's work, had made its appearance.[35] By 1659, few if any Potanans were left in that area.

Several of Rebolledo's remarks during the visitation, coupled with the 1655 mission list, provide insight into the geographical distribution of the Utinan villages, few of which have yet been found by archeologists. Utina's reputed possession of the largest population among the various Timucuan provinces undoubtedly was a reason for the governor's turning to it for people to resurrect the above-mentioned depopulated villages.[36] But probably no less important in Spanish eyes was the unsuitability for Spanish purposes of the 1657 locations of a number of the Utinan villages. As one of his pretexts for not holding a regular

---

32. Rebolledo, reply to the Franciscans' petition, August 5, 1657, AGI, EC, leg. 155B, folio 43, SC.

33. John R. Swanton, *Early History of the Creek Indians and Their Neighbors* (Washington, D.C., 1922), 338; Amy Bushnell, "The Menéndez-Marquez Cattle Barony at La Chua and the Determinants of Economic Expansion in 17th Century Florida," *The Florida Historical Quarterly*, LVI (April 1978), 419; Henry F. Dobyns, *Their Number Become Thinned, Native American Population Dynamics in Eastern North America* (Knoxville, 1983), 279-80.

34. Alonso de Aranguiz y Cotes to king, November 1, 1659, AGI 58-2-2/4, SC.

35. Oré, *The Martyrs*, 112-14.

36. Milanich, "The Western Timucua," 69-70; Manuel Serrano y Sanz, *Documentos históricos de la Florida y la Luisiana, siglos XVI al XVIII* (Madrid, 1912), 132-33; B. Calvin Jones, conversation, June, 1985.

visitation in Timucua, Rebolledo remarked that the places in Timucua were "far apart from one another along crosswise paths, and not along the royal road," scattered in such a fashion that the personal visitation of all of them would put a serious drain on his time. This awkward dispersion for Spanish communications purposes is corroborated in the distances from St. Augustine given for the twelve inland Timucuan missions mentioned on the 1655 list. Classified by province they are the following:

UTINA	1-San Martín de Ayaocuto thirty-four leagues 2-Santa Cruz de Tarica fifty-four leagues 3-San Agustín de Urica sixty leagues 4-San Francisco de Chuaquin sixty leagues 5-Santa Cruz de Cachipili seventy leagues 6-San Ildefonso de Chamini seventy leagues 7-Santa María de los Angeles de Arapaja seventy leagues
USTACA	8-San Pedro y San Pablo de Poturiba sixty leagues 9-Santa Elena de Machaba sixty-four leagues 10-San Miguel de Asile seventy-five leagues
POTANO	11-San Francisco Potano twenty-five leagues 12-Santa Fé de Toloco thirty leagues

Although Utina was east of Ustaca and thus, supposedly, closer to St. Augustine, three of its seven listed missions are farther away than two out of the three Ustacan villages mentioned. An additional two Utinan settlements, at sixty leagues from St. Augustine, are at the same distance from that center as is Ustaca's Poturiba. Inasmuch as the Santa Fé River is considered to be Utina's southern limit, this phenomenon can only be accounted for by angling a number of those villages off to the north somewhere along an arc swinging from the vicinity of present-day Moultrie and Tifton, Georgia, through the area just south of the Altamaha River. That Utina reached deep into southern Georgia is suggested as well by Father Oré's 1616 itinerary for his visitation of the Franciscan convents then in existence. From Santa Cruz de Tarihica, Oré recounted, "he determined to take a shortcut that was arduous by entering a desert and unpopulated district for fifty leagues in order to go to the convent of Santa Isabel de Utinahica . . . [and on the way] he passed through some towns inhabited by pagan Indians . . . [and] arrived at Tarraco . . . [whose Indians] formed a fairly large district. Continuing our journey, we arrived at three or four small towns containing pagans." Before he reached Utinahica he traveled an unspecified, but likely considerable distance further, crossing various rivers too deep to ford. From Utinahica he descended to the land of Guale in canoes by a river that he described as larger than the Tagus.[37]

This "splendid isolation" of the more northern Utinan settlements may have preserved them and the villages north of them along the Oconee from the ravages of the earlier epidemics. But when those who migrated from these remoter villages at the governor's behest began to perish soon after in the measles epidemic of the late 1650s, the surviving migrants likely fled to the woods as Juan Francisco de Florencia and the friars reported.

These are the points that are indicated or that can be inferred from the Timucua visitation record and the few other documents cited. Records suggest a massive depopulation as a result of the death or flight of the original inhabitants of a number of Timucuan villages, particularly those living inland near St. Augustine, and those of northern Utina. The records also indicate a significant shift in Utina's population southward and eastward, and the rapid disappearance (from the mission scene at least) of most of this migrant population.

Archeologists have found changes in the pottery types at these sites that coincide with these demographic developments recorded in the documents. They have suggested that they are reflective in part of a movement into these areas from Apalachee, Ustaca, or Utina. But, in addition to these migrants from within the Spanish ecumene, they have suggested that these changes in ceramic types (which they describe as originating with central Georgia Muskhogean speakers), indicate that there was "some sort of population movement of Creeks into" these areas of northern Florida "during the middle of the seventeenth century."[38] The present writer is unaware of any

---

37. Oré, *The Martyrs,* 129-30.
38. Milanich, "The Western Timucua," 75.

documentary record for the intrusion of Creeks into these areas at so early a date. Indeed such an intrusion might seem to be ruled out by Rebolledo's remark that the drastic decline of the Timucuan population removed the need for as many friars as were then in Timucua. He suggested that this surplus might be better employed by being sent westward to launch the Christianization of the Apalachicolas (Creeks) and Chacatos. Had pagan Creeks been moving into the abandoned or depopulated Timucuan settlements, their evangelization would seem to have provided ample work for the friars and, accordingly, the governor would have been unlikely to advance such a proposal. The movement southward and eastward of the Utinans from the northernmost settlements, followed by the influx of Ustacans, seems to offer an adequate explanation that is solidly documented. The inhabitants of these northern Utinan villages would have been one of the "Florida" groups most ideally situated for receiving influences from that central Georgia area in the vicinty of Macon and for carrying them southward and eastward.

No definitive conclusions are presently possible in this matter. As Milanich noted, "The question of whether or not the adoption of Georgian pottery styles by Florida Indians represents diffusion of techniques or actual population mixing remains unanswered." The subject, he concluded, is one that needs more research.[39] B. Calvin Jones stated the problem most succinctly, observing that not enough is known about Utina ceramics to make a judgment concerning their nature either prior to or during the mission era. Baptizing Springs, he noted, is the only Utina mission site that has been explored to any significant degree. Lana Jill Loucks, who worked at that site, described its ceramic assemblage as predominantly Leon-Jefferson.[40] In his limited surface collecting at the Guacara site, Jones found a heavy Leon-Jefferson representation in it. Before solid judgments can be made as to the provenience of Leon-Jefferson type ceramics from sites such as Baptizing Springs or those in Potano, Jones concluded, a closer analysis of all the ceramics is

---

39. Ibid.
40. Jones, conversation, 1985; Lana Jill Loucks, "Political and Economic Interactions between Spaniards and Indians: Archaeological and Ethnohistorical Perspectives of the Mission System in Florida" (Ph.D. dissertation, University of Florida, 1979), 302.

needed in order to identify traits within the widely diffused Leon-Jefferson ceramic complex that might distinguish the Leon-Jefferson-type ceramics found in Ustaca or Utina or Potano from the better-known Apalachee variety for which the style is named.[41]

Study of the 1657 visitation record and other documents of the period indicates that for Timucua the 1655 mission list is anything but a complete enumeration of the mission villages in existence at that date. It omitted the Guacara mission, which was in existence as early as 1616 and vital enough to take part in the revolt in 1656. The 1655 list also omitted San Matheo. The latter's identification in 1657 as having nine daughter-villages, all bearing saints' names, suggests that it had been a mission center for some time. This brings into question the practice of using absence from the 1655 list as a criterion for concluding that a mission was founded only after that date, as has been done, for example, with reference to both Santa Catalina and Ajoica.[42]

For Apalachee, by contrast, the 1655 enumeration omitted only one of the pre-existing missions, San Antonio de Bacuqua. But the 1657 listing of the Apalachee missions is no less valuable for that than the one for Timucua, because it also lists most of the satellite villages under the jurisdiction of each mission center and, for the first time, it provides the native name of each of the Apalachee missions. The following is the data on the Apalachee settlements and on their leaders as recorded by Governor Rebolledo in the course of his visitation of each of those missions.

I-   SAN DAMIÁN DE CUPAICA—Baltasar, principal chief
        1-Nicapana—Bentura, chief
        2-Faltassa—Martín, chief
        3-San Cosme—Bentura, chief
        4-San Lucas—Lucas, chief

---

41. Jones, conversation, June, 1985.
42. These two sites are commonly identified conjointly as Santa Catalina de Ajoica (or Ajohica). By 1678 the two villages' people had indeed been merged as the surviving people of Ajoica moved to Santa Catalina, but prior to this the two settlements were distinct.

II-   SANTA MARÍA DE BACUCUA—Alonso, principal
         chief[43]
         1-Guaco—Martín, chief
III-   SAN PEDRO DE PATALI—Baltasar, principal chief
         1-Ajamano—Francisco, chief
         2-Talpahique—Alonso, chief
IV-   SAN LUIS DE XINAYCA[44]—Francisco Luis, principal
         chief
             Antonio García, its captain and cousin of the chief
             Antonio de Ynija, a leading man
             Pedro García, a leading man
         1-Abaslaco—Gerónimo, chief
         2-San Francisco—Francisco, chief
V-   SAN JUAN DE ASPALAGA—Alonso, principal chief
         1-Pansacola—Manuel, chief
         2-Sabe—Xpobal [Christobal], chief
         3-Jipe—Santiago, heir to the chieftainship
VI-   SAN MARTÍN DE THOMOLE—Antonio, the *hinija*,[45]
         representing the absent principal chief
         1-Ciban—Bernardo, chief
         2-San Diego—Diego, chief
         3-Samoche—Bernardo, chief
VII-   SAN JOSEPH DE OCUYA—Benito Ruiz, principal
         chief
         1-Sabacola—Gaspar, chief
         2-Ajapaxca—Santiago, chief
         3-Chali—Jerónimo, chief
VIII-   SAN FRANCISCO DE OCONE—Francisco Martín,
         principal chief
         1-San Miguel—Alonso Martín, chief
IX-   SANTA MARÍA DE AYUBALE—Martín, principal
         chief, and Alonso, a leading man and brother of the
         chief
         1-Cutachuba—Adrián, a leading man

---

43. Elsewhere the name was always given as San Antonio de Bacuqua.
44. Subsequently in this visitation record the name was given as San Luis de
    Nixaxipa.
45. This title, usually spelled *inija*, was given to the native official second-in-
    command to the chief.

X-   SAN LORENÇO DE YBITACHUCO—Don Luis
      Ybitachucu, principal chief
          Lourenço Moreno, captain of the place
          Francisco and Santiago, leading men
          1-San Juan—Andrés, chief and uncle of Don Luis
          2-San Pablo—Pedro Muñoz, chief
          3-San Nicolás—Thomás, chief
          4-Ayapasca—Fabian, chief

XI-   SAN MIGUEL DE AZILE[46]—Gaspar, principal chief
      and uncle of Ybitachuco's Don Luis
          Lucas, identified as a chief, but no village mentioned
          Juan de Medina, principal heir to Lucas
          Lázaro, a leading man and father of the chief of Sabe

The Apalachee list requires little comment as the settlement pattern that it reflects does not appear to have altered much over the remaining half-century that these missions endured. No subsequent mission list furnishes as detailed a catalogue of the satellite villages. However, the mid-1670s Ball-game Manuscript states that each main village had three or four smaller satellite villages attached to it, and, using San Luis as an example, named its three satellites as San Francisco, San Bernardo, and San Agustín. One of the latter two is probably the Abaslaco mentioned by Rebolledo as there is evidence for Abaslaco's continued existence into the 1690s. A 1680s reference indicates that San Luis then had four subordinate villages.[47] For Aspalaga, the 1677-1678 visitation record identifies Culcuti as an additional satellite beyond those mentioned in 1657. On a later list a fifth satellite village, named San Pedro, is noted for Cupaica, and a 1657 letter written from there by a soldier also mentions a San Pedro. Cupaica's Nicopana and Faltassa reappear in 1677 as a consequence of a dispute over the chieftainship of the latter. Tomole's Samoche and San Diego also reappear in the Ball-game Manuscript. The same diffuse settlement pattern was depicted for Apalachee as late as October 1702, somewhat ob-

---

46. Normally Asile was considered to be a part of Ustaca. It is not clear why Rebolledo recorded it as being "of the jurisdiction of Apalachee."
47. Leturiondo, Inspection . . . 1677-1678; Florencia, General Inspection, November 5, 1694; Vi Ventura, testimony by, 1686; AGI, EC, leg. 156B, folio 575; EC, leg. 157A, cuaderno I, folios 71-73; EC, leg. 156C, pieza 25 (E. 20), folio 67, SC.

liquely, in a remark by the governor's deputy that "The villages of this province are very insecure as they are widely scattered, as the individual houses are likewise, inasmuch as the villages are distributed over a radius of three or four leagues."[48]

The additional villages mentioned after 1657 bring the total of named Apalachee villages during the mission era to forty, just short of the forty-plus spoken of as existing in the 1640s. The 1657 listing, accordingly, would seem to be incomplete. It is probable that San Luis's four satellites of the 1680s and the satellites of other villages mentioned later already existed in 1657, as there seems to be a general correlation between the populations given for the missions in 1675 and 1689 and the number of satellites they were recorded as having.[49] Ayubale, with only one noted in 1657, is an exception. That suggests the possibility that one or more satellites of this sizeable mission were omitted on the 1657 list, probably because their leaders did not appear for the visitation.[50] Recent archeological research has revealed the existence of two presumably temporally distinct missions for Patale on sites that were little more than three miles apart.[51] Patale's usual name of San Pedro y *San Pablo* de Patale suggests the possibility of a separate village of San Pablo. This was the case for Apalachee's other twin-patron mission, Cupaica. In 1657 it was identified only as San Damián de Cupaica, and San Cosme was named as a subordinate village. Ustaca's twin-patron site of Potohiriba had two temporally distinct mission centers.[52] It is possible that either of Patale's subordinate villages, Ajamano and Talpahique, could also have borne the name San Pablo, but the early abandonment of one of the Patale sites seems to rule that out. To date no documentary evidence has

---

48. Leturiondo, Inspection . . . 1677-1678; Manuel Solana to Governor Joseph de Zúñiga y Cerda, October 22, 1702; AGI, EC, leg. 156B, folios 546-49, 555-56, 579; and 58-2-8, SC.
49. Pablo de Hita Salazar to queen, August 24, 1675; Bishop Diego Ebelino de Compostela to king, September 28, 1689; AGI 58-1-26/38 and 54-3-2/9, SC.
50. In 1675 it had about 800 inhabitants, and in 1689, it was the third largest mission, surpassed only by Cupaica and San Luis.
51. Jones, conversation, May 1985; Rochelle Marrinan, conversation, 1985. One of these sites has been explored sufficiently to indicate that it dates from the early mission period and that its existence as a mission site was short-lived. The other site has not been explored sufficiently to permit conclusions about the time of its occupation with such precision.
52. Andrés García, *Autos* Made Officially against Santiago, Native to the Village of San Pedro, 1695, AGI, EC, leg. 157A, cuaderno I, folios 177-78, SC.

surfaced concerning the reason for the early abandonment of that site. Indeed, the only such evidence for the move is a reference in the year 1700 to the rancher Marcos Delgado's having moved his existing ranch, that lay between Bacuqua and Patale, to a chicasa[53] of Patale in response to the complaints of the natives of those two missions that the cattle from his Bacuqua ranch of Our Lady of the Rosary were destroying their crops.[54]

This use of the lands of abandoned native villages was not unusual. In 1699 another Apalachee rancher, Diego Ximénez, moved his enterprise to a chicasa of Cupaica.[55] During the 1678 visitation of Utina's Santa Catalina, Lucas, the chief of Ajoica, reported that "he had entered an agreement with Nicolás Suárez so that he might place a cattle ranch between the two (Ajoica and Santa Catalina) on the former site of Ajoica, which is depopulated."[56] And it is this writer's opinion that the original site of Delgado's ranch was probably the former site of the village of Bacuqua. In 1657 Bacuqua's chief received permission to move his village because the site's soil and firewood were exhausted. On reading this passage, the recollection that Delgado gave Bacuqua as his place of residence on a 1693 sales contract triggered the thought that an abandoned native village and its surrounding farmlands would make an ideal ranch site with their abundance of cleared land and nearby water source and that the high airy location of the typical Apalachee village would be attractive as a ranch headquarters.[57] It is known that Delgado's residence was on the ranch and not in the 1693-era village of Bacuqua. In 1695, on agreeing to move his ranch, Delgado asked to be allowed to keep his residence at the former ranch site.[58]

There is evidence in the 1657 visitation record that some of the rebellious elements from Ustaca had sought refuge in

---

53. It is the Apalachee word for the site of an abandoned village and for the surrounding lands that belonged to the settlement.
54. Manuel Jacomé de Fuentes, testimony of, December 21, 1700 (residencia of Governor Laureano de Torres y Ayala, 1700), AGI, EC, leg. 157A, microfilm roll 27P in the residencia series, P. K. Yonge Library of Florida History.
55. Ibid.
56. Leturiondo, Inspection . . . 1677-1678, AGI, EC, leg. 156B, folios 602-04.
57. Marcos Delgado, bill of sale by, 1693, in Irving Leonard, trans., *Spanish Approach to Pensacola, 1689-1693* (Albuquerque, 1939), 254, fn. 3.
58. Florencia, General Inspection, November 5, 1694, AGI, EC, leg. 157A, cuaderno I, folios 77-79, SC.

Apalachee and had attempted to foment revolt there. On completing his visitation of Apalachee with the session at Asile, Rebolledo issued a proclamation that the Timucuans and Ustacans who were then living in Apalachee were to return to their home village within fifteen days, unless they had been domiciled in that province for two years or more. The penalty for men caught in non-compliance of this order was 100 lashes and four years at forced labor. The women also were to receive 100 lashes and would be remanded to serve at the fort at St. Augustine. The record gave no indication of the number of Timucuans thought to be present in Apalachee as refugees from the governor's brutal repression of the rebels.

This proclamation is probably one of the sources of the oft-repeated misconception that Apalachee participated in the 1656 Timucuan revolt. Most of the secondary sources that mention the revolt speak of it as having spread to Apalachee in 1656 or in 1657.[59] This writer, however, is unaware of any primary sources to indicate that the revolt actually spread to Apalachee. On the contrary, a number of such sources state the opposite. The soldiers in Apalachee whom the governor commissioned to investigate the rumors of impending trouble there reported that those rumors were precisely that, characterizing them as merely inventions of the priests, designed to thwart the governor's plans to expand the military's presence there. One soldier observed, "This is the sum total of the uprising in Apalachee, because I do not find any other one," while another soldier, playing down even the threat of revolt, attributed the rumors to "Timucuan gossips who have assumed that Apalachee wishes to revolt because they asked it to."[60] In August 1657 the governor himself, writing to report his having twenty-six of the Apalachee leaders as house guests, affirmed unequivocally that their loyalty was the principal reason that Apalachee had not participated in the

---

59. Among the scholars who have worked with the primary sources for this period, Amy Bushnell is the only one whom this author is aware of who has avoided this pitfall.
60. Adrián de Canisaxes y Ossoxio to Rebolledo, May 8, 1657, and May 21, 1657; Pedro de la Puerta to Rebolledo, July 12, 1657; Antonio de Santucha to Rebolledo, July 18, 1657, AGI, EC, leg. 155B, no. 18, folios 50-57 in microfilm roll 27-G of the residencia series, P. K. Yonge Library of Florida History. These documents are among those appended to the Rebolledo visitation record.

recent revolt in Timucua.[61] Although misinterpretation of some of the earlier heated remarks of the more voluble of the friars appears to have been a major source of the misconception, the absence of revolt in Apalachee at this time is reflected equally clearly in a 1664 collective note to the king by a number of the friars.[62] Doubtless there was unrest, but it does not seem to have passed beyond a threat of revolt. And possibly the threat consisted of little more than the friars' perception that there was such a threat.

In addition to the already noted request for the moving of the site of Bacuqua in 1657, there is evidence that during the preceding year San Luis's chief had moved his village to be where the soldiers were.[63] More directly expressed is the revelation of the continuity between that chief's 1657 mission village of San Luis and the native village of Anhayca Apalachee appropriated by Hernando de Soto for his winter quarters in 1539. The triad of Anhayca-Iviahica-Iniahico by which the De Soto chroniclers identified this village is similar enough to the Xinayca-Nixaxipa of 1657 to suggest that the earlier renditions are garbled versions of the latter as perceived by sixteenth-century Spanish ears unaccustomed to the Florida natives' tongues. A half century earlier an even more recognizable variant of Anhayca was similarly linked with one of Apalachee's leading chiefs. In 1608 Fray Prieto recorded that the Apalachee leaders assembled at Ivitachuco to meet him delegated the chief of Inihayca to go to St. Augustine to give obedience to the governor in their name. Noting this resemblance, Father Geiger observed that "Inihayca is probably the Anhayca Apalache mentioned by the Gentleman of Elvas."[64] The survival of these names from the early sixteenth century into the mission era in association with the head village of San Luis suggests that San Luis de Xinayca of 1657 represented the same corporate entity as De Sotos's Anhayca, though the two probably did not occupy the same physical site. It is possible, however, that the Spanish came to

61. Rebolledo reply to the Franciscans' petition, August 5, 1657, AGI, EC, leg. 155B, no. 18, folios 40-50, in microfilm roll 27-G of the residencia series, P. K. Yonge Library of Florida History.
62. Franciscan Friars to king, June 16, 1664, AGI 58-1-35, WLC, reel IV.
63. Canisaxes y Ossoxio to Rebolledo, May 8, 1657, and May 21, 1657, AGI, EC, leg. 155B, no. 18, folios 50-54, microfilm roll 27-G of the residencia series, P. K. Yonge Library of Florida History.
64. Oré, *The Martyrs*, 117, 122, fn. 13.

the San Luis site because of its' historic associations as much as its' strategic qualities.

In conclusion, the 1657 visitation record and the other pertinent documents from the era give no indication that Apalachee was experiencing the calamitous demographic dislocation and decline that was manifest in Timucua. Whereas this trend would continue for Timucua, as the number of its missions shrank with each successive listing, one additional Apalachee mission was to emerge by the mid-1670s along with several other missions inhabited by non-Apalachees. Moreover, all the Apalachee missions existing in 1657 were to survive till the eve of the province's destruction in 1704.

Why there is so sharp a difference is a subject that needs further research. Similarly, the presence of non-western Timucuans and non-Timucuans in western Timucua merits further documentary research. While the Spaniards meticulously noted the presence of non-Apalachees in Apalachee territory, to this writer's knowledge, no one has cited documentary evidence that the Spaniards similarly identified the non-locals from coastal Timucua, and Guale, and Creek territory whose presence there archeologists have detected.

In view of the magnitude of Timucua's demographic disaster and dislocation, Father Spellman's remark concerning Timucua's troubles during this period is particularly apropos. He observed that this period of the mid-seventeenth century that has so often been hailed as the beginning of the missions' "Golden Age" was anything but that for Timucua.[65] In June 1657 the Council of the Indies was of a similar mind in recommending the immediate removal and imprisonment of Governor Rebolledo for "the cruelty and inhumanity" of his repression of the revolt that "his own actions had precipitated," and for having created a situation that seemed to threaten the total loss of the Florida missions whose natives' "conversion and conservation had cost so much wealth and effort."[66]

---

65. Spellman, "The 'Golden Age'," 355.
66. Council of the Indies, Order for Governor Rebolledo's Removal and Imprisonment, WLC, reel III. As reproduced by Lowery, this document bears the heading "In the council on May 29," and the closing note, "Madrid, twelfth of June of sixteen hundred and fifty seven."

An Outline of Florida Epidemiology

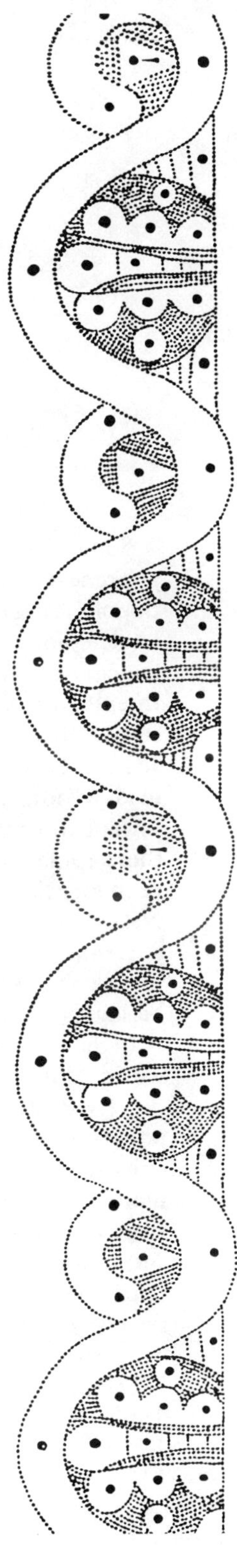

Some scholars of Florida's Native Americans have demonstrated an awareness that Old World diseases greatly thinned the area's aboriginal population. No one seems to have identified, however, nearly all of the lethal epidemics that occurred or the Old World diseases that became endemic on the peninsula. Archaeologists have tended to focus on only three seventeenth-century epidemic episodes. Briefly reporting that state archaeologists had located four Apalachee and Yustega mission sites, B. Calvin Jones stated that epidemics had taken a toll in 1613 – 1617, in 1649 – 1650, and in 1672.[1] Jerald T. Milanich also wrote that epidemics "swept through the Timucua" on the same three occasions.[2] Two of these epidemic episodes, those beginning in 1613 and 1672, had already been mentioned by an ethnohistorian of the Southeast.[3] Actually, the Native American peoples of Florida suffered perhaps eight major epidemic episodes during the protohistoric half century from A.D. 1512 to 1562. Native American numbers did not merely become thinned; biological disaster struck the inhabitants of the peninsula.

In the course of analyzing the impact of plagues on the peoples of the world, William H. McNeill pointed out that historians have seriously neglected disease in explaining human events.[4] So have anthropologists. McNeill called for a broad reinterpretation of history explicitly taking disease and epidemics into account; I will undertake to illuminate only one small area. This analysis points to evidence suggestive of seaborne commerce, message transmission, personnel transfers, and supply shipments between Caribbean islands and continental Colonial New Spain and Florida frequent enough to maintain Florida in the same epidemic region as the colonized area of the Spanish empire between 1512 and 1763.

The procedure in this analysis is simple. I identify episodes of epidemic diseases in Florida, examine the documentary record of New

248

Spain and the West Indian colonies, to discover whether the epidemic in Florida was apparently transmitted from the European-colonized areas, and also seek alternative sources of contagion in the documentary record. In this essay, the general summary of major epidemics presented in the initial essay is particularized to a specific portion of North America. I also amplify the record of lethal epidemics in this smaller region. Each disease is diagnosed as best it can be at this time, given the available clues.

NOTES

1. B.C. Jones, "Spanish Mission Site," 1972, p. 1.
2. Milanich, *Excavations*, 1972, p. 58.
3. Swanton, *Early History*, 1922, p. 338.
4. McNeill, *Plagues and Peoples*, 1976, p. 4.

SECTION ONE
The Protohistoric Period, 1512-1562

Certain Spanish maps indicate that explorers discovered and charted at least the southern portion of the peninsula of Florida in about A.D. 1500.[1] Documented European exploration on land began several years later, in 1513. Then French Huguenots set up a temporary settlement in 1564. Ousting the Huguenots, the Spaniards settled the first permanent town in North America at St. Augustine in 1565. Florida was, of course, inhabited by several Native American chiefdoms. They were subject to indirect transmission of Old World pathogens from the time the Spaniards conquered insular Native Americans and settled on Hispaniola and Puerto Rico. They became especially vulnerable after Spaniards colonized Cuba, because its people and the South Florida Calusa seem to have kept up regular communication. Florida's natives were also subject to direct transatlantic transmission of lethal Old World diseases from the time European ships were wrecked along the peninsular coast, and survivors were held captive by Native American chiefs. The documentary record of such biological contacts between Europeans and Native Americans, while scant, is analyzable. Consequently, the label "protohistoric" applies to the period from about 1512 to 1562, when a continuous documented record of European colonization and intermittent contact with Native Americans began. The Columbian Exchange of diseases and human genes flourished during that protohistoric period. While it is doubtful whether historians will ever be able to reconstruct the entire record of microbial invasion of Florida's Native American population prior to 1563, enough clues are available to permit the identification of some major epidemic episodes that struck Florida's Native Americans before 1565.

The brief French colonization in north Florida provided a comparative wealth of information about several Timucuan-speaking peoples. The French observer most important to the present analysis arrived at the mouth of the St. Johns River from France on June 22, 1564.[2] He was Jacques Le Moyne de Morgues. This artist observed the Saturiwa chiefdom and other Timucuans until Spanish forces overwhelmed French Fort Caroline on September 20, 1565.[3] Le Moyne painted a number of scenes showing Timucuans in a variety of roles, including contacts with Frenchmen. Moreover, Le Moyne wrote specific comments on the natives in addition to his narrative of events in the French

250

colony. The available engravings and text provide significant information about the transmission of diseases to the Native Americans in Florida during the protohistoric period and their cultural changes to attempt to cope with those biological invasions.

One of Le Moyne's forty-three paintings shows Timucuan transvestites, termed "hermaphrodites" by Le Moyne, carrying the bodies of dead Timucua to a burial ground. De Bry's engraving of pairs of transvestites carrying bodies on European-style litters with a handle in each hand does not agree with Le Moyne's textual description. Le Moyne wrote that the transvestites fastened hide thongs to the ends of poles and supported these with their heads. The very use of a woven-reed mat-and-pole litter, however supported, suggests that a cultural change had occurred during protohistoric times. It was not common among North American peoples for bodies to be carried to interment on woven reed mats that transvestites supported by poles. Usually relatives buried their dead, or members of a paired moiety spared relatives from the sad task.

At the end of his text, Le Moyne added a single sentence of great significance. He wrote that the "hermaphrodites" looked after "those who have contagious diseases; they take the sick on their shoulders to places selected for the purpose and feed and care for them until they are well again."[4] The engraving shows in the upper left background two transvestites carrying presumably sick adults on their backs. The implications of this engraving and text appear not to have been realized by historians or archaeologists writing about the Timucua.

1. The first inference to be drawn from Le Moyne's record, brief though it may be, is that cultural change had occurred.

a. The Timucua had learned to identify at least some contagious— Old World—diseases.

b. They had also learned the concept and instituted the practice of isolating patients—placing them in quarantine—and of providing them with nursing care to aid their recovery.

c. Moreover, the Timucua assigned a specific group in the population to this risky task. High-risk nursing it was, inasmuch as truly contagious diseases would have been contracted by transvestite nurses oftener than by any other component of the population.

The Timucuan therapy Le Moyne recorded in 1564 was truly astonishing behavior for a Native American group. When the first smallpox pandemic struck the New World peoples in 1520, Native Americans lacked any cultural pattern for dealing with the contagious diseases that had evolved in the Old World. They lacked any cultural behavior identifiable as nursing. Indeed, Native American religious beliefs and practices of ritual purification dictated taking sweat baths, which increased Native American mortality from febrile, eruptive diseases such as smallpox, measles, and chickenpox. Spanish observers of Nahuatl behavior commented on the negative consequences of sweat bathing.[5] Yet Le Moyne apparently did not paint or mention a sweat lodge—a very significant omission. Almost certainly Le Moyne would have seen a sweat lodge if the Timucua had still used them regularly in 1564, and Le Moyne would almost surely have painted one; the sweat lodge was an exotic building in which practices strange to Europeans were carried out.

Instead, Le Moyne painted another scene showing Timucua utilizing the heat of fires, and the smoke of burning leaves, including tobacco, to treat patients. The scene is entirely in the open air, but patients lie on what de Bry engraved to look rather like cots. Le Moyne wrote that the Timucua built what he called "a bench long enough and wide enough for the sick person, and he is laid upon it, either on his back or on his stomach," depending on the illness. One part of a treatment that Le Moyne evidently observed and remembered consisted of burning "seeds" on hot coals placed under the face of the patient on his stomach. "This is to act as a purge, expelling the poison from the body and thus curing the disease," according to Le Moyne.[6]

Le Moyne's two sets of descriptions of Timucuan curing are not entirely mutually consistent. One painting shows men, women, and children surrounding patients being treated while lying on "cots." No transvestites are in evidence. The difference conceivably lay in Timucuan perception of contagion, so that the shamanistic treatment described dealt with what the Timucua did not regard as contagious diseases. Le Moyne specifically stated that "venereal disease is common among them, and they have several natural remedies for it." Thus it is possible that the scene portrayed Timucuan treatment of one venereal disease, among other ailments.

If Le Moyne's painting did depict Timucuan treatment of syphilis, then it provides very significant evidence of the epidemiology of that disease. Syphilis is caused by a relatively fragile spirochete that cannot survive fresh air or sunlight. It flourishes only within the body, in the bloodstream. That is why syphilis is a venereal disease—the most frequent mode of transmission is contact between penis and vagina, where the tender spirochete is protected. There is, however, an additional mode of transmission—the direct blood-to-blood transfer of spirochetes, which can and does occur in modern medical practice. First, a syphilitic pregnant woman can transmit the spirochete to her fetus. Then, too, the afflicted woman can transmit the spirochete to an attending physician during delivery, should she hemorrhage, and should the physician happen to cut a hand through a rubber glove, so that the spirochete-carrying blood flows over the cut. Finally, a nurse who handles syringes used for injecting syphilitic patients can become infected if a spirochete-contaminated needle comes in contact with an open cut.

The point of this summary is that Le Moyne depicted and described a nearly perfect mechanism for transmitting the spirochete from sick patients to well men and women. That is, Le Moyne wrote that "cutting the skin of his forehead with a sharp shell, they suck the blood with their own mouths, spitting it out into an earthen jar or a gourd. Women who are nursing or are pregnant come and drink this blood."[7] As a result any shaman who happened to have a cut or sore in his mouth and sucked blood from a syphilitic patient could contract the disease. Moreover, a woman who promptly drank the extracted blood could also contract syphilis if she had any cut in her mouth or any gum disease. The pregnant woman could then transmit the disease transplacentally to her growing child. It is thus quite probable that Le Moyne recorded major evidence as to why the Timucuan population declined with even greater rapidity than most North American native groups. Timucuan treatment provided a second direct blood-to-blood mode for transmitting syphilis to pregnant and nursing women, precisely the most vulnerable individuals, demographically speaking.

2. The second inference to be drawn from Le Moyne's pictures is that Old World contagious diseases had long since invaded the Native Americans of Florida. The Timucuan cultural change in life-support provision recorded by Le Moyne in 1564—1565 could have come about only through reinforcement by repeated epidemic episodes prior to that time. More will be said on this point below.

3. The concentration of evident European therapeutic traits present among the Timucuans by 1564 implies the origin of both contagious diseases and cultural knowledge of their treatment. The numerous Spaniards shipwrecked on the shores of southern Florida for some twenty years prior to 1564, many of whom were rescued and held captive by the Calusa, clearly are implicated. A high proportion of the Spanish ships wrecked off Florida had sailed more or less directly there from the port of Vera Cruz with New Spain's and Peruvian bullion shipments. Consequently, the wrecked ships had not been at sea long enough for whatever contagious diseases passengers might have been suffering to run their course before the shipwrecked survivors were rescued by the Calusa. Calusa covetousness for European goods, which kept them alert for wrecked vessels, and the basic humanitarian instinct that led

them to rescue survivors (even if some were later sacrificed to chiefdom deities), inevitably exposed the Calusa and the other peoples of Florida with whom they traded to Old World contagious diseases.

The shipwrecked Spaniards held among the Calusa would have known European techniques for nursing patients with various diseases. The European life-support techniques Le Moyne noted among the Timucua in 1564 indicate that the captive Spaniards did in fact nurse Calusa patients with some, and perhaps marked, success. The observant Native Americans copied European nursing techniques. On the record, these included (1) patient isolation, (2) assigning semioutcasts as nurses, whether slaves among the Calusa or transvestites among the Timucua, (3) the provision of life-support services, and (4) a termination of sweatbathing.

It bears emphasis that such new cultural practices were too complex to have been learned during a single epidemic episode, nor would they have been transmitted from the South Florida Calusa to the northeast Florida Saturiwa in a short period of time. Le Moyne's 1564 observations among the Saturiwans indicate, therefore, that the peoples of Florida were repeatedly attacked by Old World pathogens prior to 1564. Shipwrecked Spaniards transmitted some if not all of those pathogens to the Florida Native Americans. Shipwrecked Spaniards among the Calusa also evidently taught the natives, intentionally or not, how to nurse patients with contagious diseases. The scarcity of accounts by rescued Spanish captives and the laconic nature of the few that survive from Florida no doubt mean that all of the diseases that shipwrecked Spaniards transmitted to the Calusa will never be identified. Some probable epidemics can nonetheless be listed.

1513 – 1514

The first epidemic of Old World disease may have swept through the native peoples of Florida in 1513–1514. Most historians of early sixteenth-century New World epidemiology have viewed the smallpox transmitted to Mesoamericans in 1520 after the outbreak on Hispaniola in late 1518 as the initial continental pandemic.[8] There is, however, rather extraordinary evidence that an earlier episode affected the natives of Florida.

During the early and middle sixteenth century, Spaniards, Cuban natives, and at least the ruling elite of the peoples of Florida all sought there a "River Jordan." There was, needless to say, no river named "Jordan" in Florida until Spaniards applied that biblical term to one stream in Apalachee and to another in Guale country. Actually, the searchers sought not a river bearing that name but one possessing the miraculous curative powers that many Christians attribute to the River Jordan in the Christian Holy Land. Many an otherwise staid Protestant pilgrim returns home bearing a vial of Jordan River water, at least hoping that it may be good for the ills of the flesh. Sixteenth-century Spaniards tended to be fanatical true believers in Christianity at the end of 700 years of warfare against Islam. They were credulous believers in miraculous cures of disease wrought by divine providence. The European pilgrimage to the Spanish shrine of St. James Major still flourished at the time—a pilgrimage that mobilized many people seeking cures to earthly ills as well as a future state of grace.[9] Moreover, those Spaniards were frustrated because in spite of repeated Christian Crusades to the Holy Land, Islamic military prowess continued to interdict Christian access to the miraculous waters of the Palestinian River Jordan. The search for a River Jordan in Florida can be understood only within that historic frame of reference of Christian belief and behavior.

The Florida River Jordan that people talked about, wrote the one-time Calusa captive Diego de Escalante Fontaneda, was "a superstition of the Indians of Cuba"[10] and did not exist. Escalante also reported that "anciently," from his perspective (he wrote in about 1575), many Cuban natives landed at Calusa ports to seek the miraculous river. Chief Sunquene, father of Calusa Headchief Carlos whom the Spaniards found in power in the 1560s, halted the searchers and formed them into an enduring Cuban settlement in his domain.[11] This apparently constituted the very first recorded historic settlement of Cuban refugees in South Florida.

Writing a generation or more after the Cuban migration, Escalante seems to have fallen into an error all too common among later ethnographers. He assumed an interethnic contact phenomenon to have been an aboriginal Native American trait. As indicated earlier, Native Americans had no need for miraculous cures until Old World diseases began to decimate them. They certainly could not refer to any stream as the River Jordan until they had learned something about Christianity. On the face of the facts, few as they are, what Escalante recorded was a Native American millenarian movement couched in terms that clearly reflected Christian teaching. Having somehow heard from Spaniards about the Holy Land River Jordan's miracloous reputation for curing, Cuban Native Americans paddled their canoes to Florida to seek waters "which did good work, even to the turning of aged men and women back to their youth."[12] The parallel with late nineteenth-century Ghost Dance Movement belief that the dead would be restored to life and game renewed by proper ritual is clear.[13] The natives of Cuba had come under such psychological stress that they sought a millennial solution to their problems. Their quest was primarily for curative waters. Unfortunately, historians picked up Escalante's probably ridiculing aside, "even to the turning of aged men and women back to their youth" and transformed it into a fictitious "Fountain of Youth."

One can also attribute part of the cause of a millenarian movement among Cuban natives to acute deprivation under harsh Spanish Colonial exploitation[14] if this series of events occurred in 1512–1523, for the Spaniards launched their conquest of that island in 1511.[15] During that conquest, Spanish leaders reportedly broke their pledges of peace to Native Americans who greeted them hospitably with gifts of food. Bartolomé de las Casas witnessed one Spanish massacre of 3,000 such men, women, and children.[16] Las Casas wrote that 70,000 Cuban natives perished in Spanish mines during a three- to four-month period.[17] Such an attrition rate indicates that contagious disease ran rampant, apart from Spanish treatment of Native American laborers that was wasteful rather than conservative.

On the other hand, the Florida natives who joined the millenarian search for a Jordan River were not yet subject to Colonial rule. Consequently, deprivation under Colonial exploitation cannot account for their participation. Yet "the kings and caciques of Florida" gathered information about the miraculous waters and joined the search for them, according to Escalante. "So earnestly did they engage in the pursuit, that there remained not a river nor a brook in all Florida, not even lakes and ponds, in which they did not bathe."[18] The peoples of Florida must have had a powerful motivation for seeking curative waters. The obvious explanation for the behavior of the Cubans and the Florida ruling elite is that all suffered from a serious, lethal, contagious epidemic of an Old World disease to which neither Native American population possessed any immunity. Waves of Native American refugees from Spanish Conquest may have transmitted disease to their hosts beyond the area under Colonial control. A chief known as Hatuey fled Hispaniola with many of "his people." They found temporary refuge on Cuba before the Spaniards invaded that island in 1511. Hatuey had his followers dance before a basket full of gold and jewels on the premise that this was the Spanish deity, believing that such an offering might alter the distressing course of events—certainly a religious innovation of a millenarian nature. The Spaniards captured Hatuey, however, and burned him at the stake in Cuba.[19]

Surprisingly, there is a record of direct carriage of disease to the natives of Cuba in 1512. "Certain" Europeans sailing along the Cuban coasts "left" with a chief who was already known by a Spanish name, "a certeyne poore maryner beinge diseased." That mariner soon recovered his health. He learned enough of the local language to communicate with the Cuban natives. He evidently became both a mercenary and a free-lance, nonclerical, Mariolatrous missionary. On the one hand, "he was oftentymes the kynges Lieuetenaunt in his warres ageynst other princes his bortherers." On the other hand, he wore a picture of the Virgin Mary and persuaded the chief whom he served to build a chapel and altar and to begin to pray there in memorized Spanish words. Accounts carried to credulous intellectuals in Spain described Mary performing miracles in a battlefield contest of champions.[20] Vain about their military prowess, Europeans typically went into details about battles but neglected other aspects of culture.

Native Americans viewed events very differently, as William McNeill noted. They viewed epidemic disease as divine punishment for human transgressions. During early sixteenth-century epidemic episodes, they watched adult Europeans stay healthy or recover from pathogens that killed their relatives in demoralizing numbers. They concluded, therefore, that the God about whom Christians talked in fact possessed greater power than their own.[21]

The rapid conversion of the leader of one Cuban chiefdom by a sailor put ashore while ill who recovered and then preached the miraculous powers of the Virgin appears suspiciously like the action of a chief who had just watched great numbers of his people perish from the disease that the sailor survived. The recovered lay preacher could have been the European Christian source of Cuban knowledge about the Christian concept of the River Jordan's waters as miraculously curative.

The extremely rapid decline in Native American numbers on the island of Hispaniola, where Spaniards first colonized New World territory, attests to early transatlantic transmission of Old World diseases. S.F. Cook and W.W. Borah calculated from available information about population that these numbers fell from 3,770,000 in 1496 to only 92,300 in 1508, then to 61,600 in 1509 and 65,800 in 1510, and to only 26,700 in 1512 and 27,800 in 1514, with a mere 15,600 remaining in 1518.[22] Not only the gross depopulation but also the age structure of the population attests to catastrophically disproportionate mortality among children. During the latter half of 1514, Rodrigo de Albuquerque carried out a *repartimiento*, or assignment of Native Americans for work and payment of tribute. He counted adults and in some places enumerated children and the aged.[23] Cook and Borah located 279 statements of children and found a ratio of only 141 children per 1,000 adults. That is an extraordinarily small proportion[24] and could have resulted only from disproportionately high child mortality unless Hispaniola natives were successfully hiding their children from Spanish authorities. If they hid their offspring, the question arises, who cared for them?

The dearth of children does not support Sauer's interpretation that Spanish disruption of native economic and social organization caused the precipitous decline.[25] Old World diseases are surely implicated. Cook and Borah pointed out that Columbus made his first voyage with sick men, a large proportion of Colonial Spaniards were ill at any given moment, and the Spaniards suffered steady mortality.[26]

The kind of psychological shock that mortality on the scale suffered by the aborigines of Hispaniola caused certainly could generate a millenarian response among Cubans similarly afflicted. At least one Spaniard heard natives talk about the quest for miraculous water in Florida and joined the quest. "It is a cause for merriment," scoffed Escalante, "that Juan Ponz de León went to Florida to find the River Jordan."[27] Anyone attempting to determine an epidemic chronology for the native peoples of Florida must be grateful that the conqueror of the island of San Juan de Puerto Rico did join in the quest. Juan Ponce de León sailed to Florida twice. He made his initial trip in 1513, apparently exploring at least part of the Atlantic Coast of the peninsula. He returned in 1521, when the Calusa stoutly resisted his landing. The Calusa so severely wounded Ponce de León that he sailed to Havana, where he died from his wound, probably from infection. The conditions of intergroup contact during Ponce's 1521 voyage were not very propitious for transmission of disease.

Tempting though it might be to attribute the millenarian search for miraculous curing waters to the smallpox epidemic that reached Cuba in 1519, Ponce actually became part of the quest in 1513. Peter Martyr d'Anglería mentioned the supposedly miraculous waters in his Decade 2, which was published in 1515–1516.[28] What remains in doubt is the diagnosis of the disease that stressed the peoples of Florida.

Whatever the disease that swept through the Native Americans of the Caribbean islands and sent Cubans to Florida seeking miraculously curative waters, it seems to have reached the Isthmus of Panamá. The Spaniards were still learning how to colonize the New World. Consequently, they sometimes failed to carry with them provisions sufficient to sustain them until they could raise their own food or could obtain it from Native Americans whom they conquered. Such was the situation among hundreds of Spanish colonists on the Isthmus in 1514. As a result, 700 Spaniards perished during one month from starvation and from an unidentified disease. The contagion probably spread from the Europeans to the Native American population. From 1514 to 1530, 2 million Native Americans died in the isthmus region, according to a Colonial historian who was himself present during the period of highest mortality and who buried a wife and son there.[29]

1519 SMALLPOX

The most lethal Old World disease to decimate Native American populations lacking any immunity or resistance to European and African pathogens was smallpox. Spanish ships appear to have transported persons with active cases of smallpox to the Caribbean islands in 1518. Smallpox broke out on the island of Hispaniola in December. By early January 1519, royal officials reported to the crown that one-third of the natives had died and that the epidemic continued.[30] By May 20, 1519, colonial officials on Hispaniola estimated that more than half of the Native American population was dead.[31] The epidemic had spread to the natives of Puerto Rico by the end of 1518,[32] and by mid-1519 it was sweeping through the natives of Cuba.[33] It was from Cuba that Pánfilo de Narváez sailed to the continent with a soldier suffering from smallpox that he transmitted to the Native Americans of Central Mexico.[34]

Cuba may have been the source of transmission of this epidemic disease to Florida, across the relatively narrow stretch of ocean between the island and the Florida cape. The likelihood of such transmission lay in the frequency with which oceangoing Calusa canoeists visited Cuba to trade. During his 1513 voyage, Ponce de León engaged the Calusa, who fought from double-hulled canoes.[35] Such watercraft clearly possessed considerable seagoing capacity. The Calusa traded with Bahama Islanders and with the aboriginal sixteenth-century Colonial inhabitants of Cuba.[36] The flight of Cuban natives to Calusa territory early in the sixteenth century attests both to their ability to cross the ocean between the island and Florida and to their having learned something about Florida during previous contacts. As late as the mid-eighteenth century, visits to Havana by Calusa leaders were frequent.[37]

No doubt European commodities as well as the strange behavior of colonials in Havana attracted Calusa chiefs and traders during Colonial times. The watercraft technology that the Calusa used to reach Cuba and to return was evidently aboriginal, judging from archaeological recovery of Key Marco toy double-hulled canoes.[38] Consequently, if Calusa traders visited Cuba during 1519 and 1520 when the great smallpox pandemic raged there, they almost certainly contracted the disease and transmitted it to their relatives in Florida.

New Spain might also have been a source of transmission of smallpox to Florida, via a continental-margin canoe trade route. When smallpox spread through the Central Mexican empires and kingdoms and northward, Native American traders traveled by canoe on the protected waters sheltered by the barrier islands from civilized coastal ports in Mesoamerica to North America. Documentary evidence of that aboriginal trading pattern and its survival was provided to an extent by a cleric who survived a shipwreck on the Gulf Coast. The event has usually been dated as occurring in 1553,[39] but almost surely Marcos de Mena was aboard the 1554 treasure fleet. He struggled for some distance along the coast toward Pánuco. Native American canoe traders found the lone Spaniard wandering dazed along the shore and invited him to ride in their canoe. They returned Mena to the coast of New Spain, within easy walking distance of the Colonial settlement of Tampico. Wise in the ways of colonials, the Native American textile traders declined to accompany the grateful lay brother into the Spanish town.[40]

Their reluctance to expose themselves to Spanish official action indicates that a possibly still very large aboriginal-style trade in religious goods illegal and immoral in Spanish eyes flourished along what is now called the intracoastal waterway, invisible to and unknown to Spanish authorities. The rapidity of canoe travel from Mesoamerica to Native American coastal settlements on the water route east to Florida made transmission of smallpox by the crews of seagoing canoes feasible in 1520.

1528 GASTROINTESTINAL INFECTION

The Native American population of Florida was again threatened by Old World contagion no later than 1528 through 1530. In 1528, a major pestilence attacked Cuba's surviving Native American population, prompting a militant nativistic movement against the Spaniards in October 1529.[41] An estimated third of that island's Native Americans perished.[42] The Spanish dominant group "suffered" from a general shortage of subservient ethnic-group labor.[43] The Calusa propensity for visiting Cuba by canoe fostered transmission of this disease to the Native Americans of Florida.

An official with the Pánfilo de Narváez expedition of 1528 to Florida, Alvar Núñez Cabeza de Vaca, became one of its few survivors and the principal chronicler. When the expedition's members attempted to build rafts and sail around the Gulf of Mexico Coast to New Spain, large numbers were wrecked on Galveston Island. There many of the

Spaniards died. Some probably perished from starvation, some possibly from scurvy, a vitamin deficiency ailment but not an infectious one. On the other hand, one or more carriers among the Spaniards survived long enough to transmit a deadly infection to the island-dwelling Native Americans who succored the Europeans. Núñez recorded that half of the economically specialized islanders perished.[44] Núñez described their ailment as a stomach sickness. He reported that the Native Americans believed that their uninvited European guests had killed those who died. They were biologically correct.

The islanders were economically specialized, collecting shellfish and fish in the estuary and trading marine products for vegetable produce collected by inland groups. A waterborne germ or virus is therefore probably implicated in the Native American epidemic, and consequently the disease was probably self-limiting and did not spread beyond the Galveston Islanders. John C. Ewers suggested that cholera might have been the cause of the 1528 insular mortality.[45] Medical historians date the worldwide spread of cholera to the nineteenth century,[46] however, so typhoid fever seems a more likely culprit.

A more epidemic disease than typhoid fever may have been abroad in Cuba for members of the 1528 Narváez expedition to carry with them to peninsular Florida and the Gulf Coast. It is possible that the epidemic disease that further depopulated Cuba in 1528–1530 was the measles that a Spaniard carried to New Spain and to Central America in 1530. In Cuba, the disease was labeled smallpox,[47] but smallpox could not have caused such a high mortality so soon after the 1518–1520 episode; only one-third of the people reportedly survived in 1528. *Viruelas* meant no more, apparently, than "red-rash-producing disease with high fever and appreciable mortality." Thus either measles or typhoid fever could have been the disease.

What spread widely through New Spain and Peru during 1530 and 1531 was, however, identified as measles.[48] Spanish settlement in Honduras,[49] Nicaragua,[50] and Panamá,[51] generated documentary record of a rapid spread of the measles pandemic through the Native American populations of all of Central America. Measles should not have caused high mortality among Spaniards, who presumably had had childhood cases and had gained immunity. Yet members of the Narváez expedition were sick in significant numbers at least while they were in the territory of the Apalachee chiefdom before they embarked on their ill-fated rafting venture. Having traveled north and then west from their landing on Florida's west, or Gulf, coast, Narváez's men rested for nearly a month at Apalachee. Then they spent more than a week moving to Aute near the Gulf Coast. A contingent began to build rafts. The expedition's leader and many men remained at the near-coast town of Aute, where Native Americans killed ten men, and more than forty died from disease. Apparently six others had earlier succumbed to disease. The expedition suffered a mortality rate of 153 per 1,000 even before it embarked on its hastily built rafts. Most interaction between Native Americans and Spaniards was hostile, which tended to limit opportunities for the invaders to transmit their ailment(s) to the native peoples in Florida.

One point should be clarified. The forty Spaniards who died from illness at Aute did not perish from scurvy. The Spaniards found abundant unharvested crops of maize, beans, and squash in the fields around Aute, and the fresh foods would have eliminated any scurvy that might have existed among the invaders.[52] The pathogen killed adult Europeans at a 15 percent rate, a fact suggestive of typhoid fever, scarlet fever, or plague rather than smallpox, measles, or chickenpox. Núñez Cabeza de Vaca emphasized a disordered stomach as a symptom, making typhoid a likely diagnosis.

At least one additional possible mode of transmission to Native Americans of the 1528 infection running through the Narváez expedition bears mentioning. One man whom Narváez ordered to sail to Cuba for supplies and to return carried out the commander's orders. When the brigantine returned to Charlotte Harbor, the disaffected local Calusa chief managed to capture four Spaniards who went ashore. He held three captive for several days before having them tortured and killed during a ceremonial. The chief's wife and daughters pled for the life of the fourth Spanish captive, then just eighteen years of age, and he was spared.[53] Thus the Calusa were exposed to four possible Old World pathogen carriers for a period of several days and kept one enslaved for a year and a half.

The young Spanish captive, Juan Ortiz, then escaped to the town of teenaged Chief Mocozo.[54] That Townchief sent him to Fernando de Soto when the expeditionary leader landed on the Calusa coast of Florida in 1539.[55] Ortiz could have transmitted whatever contagion assaulted Cuba in 1528–1530 if he had a mild case when he returned to South Florida. If he was a typhoid carrier, Ortiz could have transmitted that disease to both Calusa and Mocozo.

1535–1538

In 1540, members of Fernando de Soto's marauding party marched into Cofitachique, a Creek settlement north of the Savannah River in modern South Carolina. De Soto's men found an abundance of what they regarded as poor-quality freshwater pearls. The Native Americans wore these pearls as bracelets and necklaces. They also bedecked the bodies of their dead leaders with pearls and stored them in chests. De Soto and his men carried off mortuary gift pearls without Native American hindrance; de Soto himself claimed the chest full of pearls. Many of these precious stones came from one or more settlements near Cofitachique Town that were completely abandoned in 1540. The various Spanish accounts of the expedition's visit to Cofitachique agreed that the abandoned towns had been depopulated by a terrible pestilence one or two years earlier.[56] That dating appears to have been reliable, inasmuch as members of de Soto's expedition provisioned themselves with dried maize from the intact maize cribs in the town that had survived the epidemic and from another town subject to the ruling family.[57] While pearls and even wooden chests holding them would have persisted for a number of years, maize would not have remained edible for many years without house and crib maintenance in the moist southeastern climate.

The distance between Central Mexico and Florida and the Savannah River was so great that an epidemic under way in southern New Spain in 1539 likely could not have spread to Native Americans on the Atlantic Coast that year. A "plague" occurred in Central Mexico in 1538,[58] reportedly smallpox,[59] causing a red rash. The mechanism of transmission by canoe trader still operated then, so that rapid seaborne transmission was possible. There is little doubt that the Creeks were significantly depopulated, implying that the Timucua and probably other Florida Native Americans were also. If canoe traders did not transmit the contagion raging in Central Mexico to the Floridians in 1539, then the epidemic disease transmitted earlier to the Central Mexicans evidently spread overland from tribe to tribe. Evidence that such an overland spread of infectious disease occurred along Native American inland trade routes is found in the narrative of Alvar Núñez Cabeza de Vaca.

In 1534, Núñez and his fellow survivors of the Narváez expedition began to travel westward across Texas toward New Spain. Núñez and the Moor gained freedom of movement by becoming curing shamans. The frequency with which they performed cures, or convinced Native Americans of their shamanistic relationship to the supernatural, indicates that one or more epidemics originating in Colonial New Spain had spread northward and eastward through Texas tribal peoples.[60] In 1535, Núñez and his companions crossed from Texas to Sinaloa. Sickness broke out among the hundreds of Native Americans accompanying them. They halted their march; more than 300 Native Americans fell ill. Many of them died.[61] Whatever killed Núñez's companions may have been the disease that reached the Creeks on the Atlantic Coast, perhaps in 1536, 1537, 1538, or 1539, depopulating entire settlements. That disease may be inferred to have spread to the peoples of Florida.

1545–1548 BUBONIC PLAGUE

In New Spain, the third massive historic pandemic struck native Americans in 1545. The disease recurred until 1548. This ailment was called *cocoliztli* in Nahuatl, and it spread widely, causing its greatest mortality in coastal peoples.[62] Patients suffered from high fever and bled from the nose, a frequent sequel of high fever. Mendieta placed Tlaxcalan mortality alone at 150,000 persons.[63] One historian estimated that five-sixths of the Native Americans died, a suspiciously high mortality rate.[64]

Hans Zinsser suspected that typhus was the disease.[65] On the other hand, the Bishop of Mexico, Fray Juan de Zumárraga, founded a hospital to treat either syphilis or bubonic plague patients in 1545 or 1546.[66] Such Colonial hospitals often were founded when an epidemic made clear the need for them. A plague diagnosis is consistent with the fact that in the central Andes, llamas suffered from the pestilence that struck people there in 1546.[67] Llamas are cameloids, so are presumably able to serve as an animal reservoir for flea-vectored bubonic plague.[68] The epidemic was termed *gucumatz* in Mayan. In Guatemala, the epidemic was termed in Spanish *peste*, which refers specifically to plague, although it also means "epidemic" in a general sense. In Totonicapán in that province, it lasted from 1541 to 1545,[69] although it ran from 1545 to 1548 in most of Mesoamerica.

The persistence of the intracoastal waterway Mesoamerican canoe trade into at least the following decade implies that the 1545–1548 bubonic plague epidemic in Mesoamerica could have been quickly transmitted to Florida by canoe crews. If the plague did not come to Florida quickly via canoe, it almost certainly came slowly overland.

A third possible mode of rapid transmission of plague, specific and general, from New Spain to Florida either began in 1545 or assumed significant proportions at that date. This was direct Spanish shipboard transmission via treasure fleet vessels that wrecked on the Keys or peninsula, some of whose passengers and crew members were saved by the Calusa. No doubt some of the rats that inevitably infested the ships also survived the wrecks and could have carried plague-vector fleas ashore to seek food and shelter in Native American dwellings and storehouses. At least one Spanish ship was wrecked on the Florida coast in 1545. A survivor who was shipwrecked twenty years prior to his rescue was ransomed from Native American hands by Pedro Menéndez de Avilés in 1565.[70] The year before, the French Huguenot René Laudonnière persuaded Florida chiefs to send to Fort Caroline two captive shipwrecked Spaniards. They told him that they had been aboard one of three ships wrecked on the Keys fifteen years earlier, or in 1549.[71] The possibility of ship transmission of disease to Florida arose when Peru and New Spain began shipping silver from the great strikes made in 1545 at Andean Potosí[72] and in 1546 at Zacatecas.[73]

1549 TYPHUS

Spaniards possibly directly transmitted one of the fever-producing diseases, perhaps "ship's typhus," to the Calusa in 1549. The *Santa Maria de la Encina* sailed from Vera Cruz early in the year, bound for Florida. The ship's pilot, Juan de Arana, found that portion of Florida then known to the Spaniards. On May 30, Dominican priest Luís Cancer de Barbastro landed on the shore near the Bay of Espiritu Santo (Charlotte Harbor). Father Diego de Toloso, or Peñalosa, a lay brother named Fuentes, and a Native American woman the Spaniards knew as "Magdalena" accompanied Cancer. The Spaniards gave presents to the first Native Americans they met, sat in a hut for a while talking to Calusa spokesmen through the interpreter, and returned to the ship for more gifts.[74] A sailor went ashore with Tolosa, Fuentes, and Magdalena.

When Cancer returned to land, his companions had disappeared. After a week's sailing along the coast, the ship spent another week entering the bay, and Cancer continued to seek the missing people. Magdalena, whom the Spaniards had brought along as an interpreter, appeared at nearly every landing, having shed her Colonial clothing. Incredibly, on June 23 a Spaniard named Juan Muñoz paddled out to the ship in a canoe. He identified himself as a member of de Soto's marauders who had been captured ten years before and enslaved. He reported that the Calusa had killed the priest and lay brother and had enslaved the sailor.[75] Cancer nonetheless went ashore on June 26, and the Calusa clubbed him to death on a mound near his landing place. The ship then returned to New Spain, and with good reason. Most of its crew was too ill with a fever to work the craft. Moreover, it was running low on water and had exhausted its store of unspoiled provisions.[76]

In other words, both Magdalena and the sailor who was enslaved could have carried ashore typhus-vectoring lice to transmit to the Florida native population. The Calusa might even have been attacked by lice from the bodies of the two slain priests and lay brother.

The Spanish plan to employ Magdalena as an interpreter is epidemiologically significant not only for the 1549 incident but also for earlier epidemics. Although she came from Cuba to Florida, once ashore among the Calusa, she assured the Spaniards that the natives belonged to "her tribe" and spoke "her" language. If Magdalena was a Calusa, at least one other Spanish ship had visited the same coast and had captured people to take to Cuba as slaves. Evidently that slaving expedition occurred long enough before 1549 for the Florida woman to acquire the reasonable fluency in Spanish that she would have needed before Cancer and his companions could consider her a suitable interpreter. If the Florida warriors managed to capture any of the slavers who were ill or were carriers of Old World pathogens, they ran the risk of another ailment besides enslavement.

If Magdalena had not been captured in Florida, she had evidently been enslaved during a Calusa canoe voyage visit to Cuba, an instance of overseas contact that exposed the Calusa to nearly every disease that Europeans transmitted to the natives of that island. If such was the case, the presence of a woman on a Calusa voyage to Cuba indicates that such trips were made rather routinely and by numbers of Calusa.

If Magdalena was a native of Cuba, then her "tribesmen" must have been the refugee Cubans whom Headchief Carlos's father settled in his territory when they came seeking the magically curative effects of a putative Jordan River. Otherwise, the Calusa must have spoken the same language as one or more aboriginal groups of Cuba. All the interpretations that can be placed on the peregrinations and reported statements of Magdalena indicate so frequent contact by such large numbers of individuals passing between Calusa and Cuba that epidemic transmission of infectious disease to the Calusa is very highly probable.

1550 MUMPS

Mumps are not often regarded as a lethal disease in modern times, but they were in Tacuba and elsewhere in New Spain in 1550.[77] There is a possibility that the infection was transmitted to Florida by Native American canoe traders.

The direct evidence for transmission of bubonic plague in 1545–1548, of typhus in 1549, or of mumps in 1550 from Spanish Colonial areas to

Florida's Native Americans is scant. Indirect evidence, on the other hand, is convincing. This evidence consists of a wholesale depopulation of the Southeast, accompanied by a collapse of the aboriginal way of life, between 1542 and 1559. When de Soto's marauders marched around the Southeast for three years, they everywhere found large Native American settlements. The expedition's chroniclers repeatedly commented on the populous horticultural districts along main river valleys and around the capital towns of native chiefdoms. Here and there the raiders encountered groups temporarily short of horticultural supplies, as in the Cofitachique chiefdom, where the flight of people from a frightening epidemic during the planting season of 1539 had causd them to miss a year's production. Yet the aboriginal way of life persisted over a broad expanse of territory.

Powerful chiefs reclined under canopies on large state canoes or were carried on litters on land by lower-class retainers. Some theocratic heads of chiefdoms declined even to meet Spaniards face to face, delegating that no doubt unpleasant task to "talking chiefs." The population of many native towns was large enough to impress the marauders, many of whom should not have been easily impressed, as they were veterans of the conquest of Tawantinsuyu or the Triple Alliance. The fact that de Soto's large task force successfully lived from supplies given to it by some Native American chiefs and seized from the storehouses of others attested to the continued functioning of traditional ways of life and successful food production despite pre-1539 depopulation by invading Old World diseases.

By the time Tristán de Luna attempted to colonize the Gulf Coast at Pensacola in 1559, that situation had very dramatically changed. Only twenty years after de Soto's rampage through the Southeast began, the Native American way of life his men saw had for the most part collapsed. A few chiefdoms, such as the Natchez on the lower Mississippi River and the Timucuan chiefdoms and the Calusa in South Florida, still functioned with something resembling the splendor and commodity abundance that they had known before 1539–1542. Search as he might, however, de Luna could not find Native American food supplies to seize to sustain his colonists. His followers almost certainly themselves transmitted epidemic disease to Native Americans that may well have interrupted planting in 1559, as had the 1539 episode among the Cofitachique.

The general collapse of the good society that Native Americans had known for centuries in the brief period of twenty years indicates that demographic catastrophe struck the peoples of the Southeast between 1542 and 1559. The scope of that disaster cannot be attributed to the loss of a single summer's harvest in 1559. Areas that were heavily populated in 1539–1542 appeared virtually depopulated by 1559–1560. Archaeologists have found many large "prehistoric" sites that were occupied until approximately the 1542–1559 interval, as best they can be dated, and were then abruptly abandoned.[78] I conclude that invading Old World diseases led to rapid depopulation and a collapse of food production because of demoralization and loss of manpower coupled with major disruptions of traditional social organization.

The dense pre-Columbian population of Florida and the rest of the Southeast culture area had been thinned even before de Soto's marauders devastated the region in 1539–1542. That much is clear from the expedition's chroniclers' descriptions of the state of the Cofitachique chiefdom in 1540. Consequently, there can be little doubt that the aboriginal cultural patterns had already been weakened. The depredations of de Soto's marauders contributed to weakening the chiefdoms even more by selective homicide against ruling elite lineages. The simultaneous enslavement of large numbers of human carriers and concubines may have offset the high mortality de Soto's men caused among the native elites. Removal of the numerous concubines de Soto's men seized for their licentious binge apparently was on a scale sufficient to depress significantly the birth rate in a number of towns in succeeding years.

To attribute the subsequent collapse of the aboriginal way of life in the bulk of the Southeastern culture area chiefdoms to the de Soto expedition's depredations would be, however, to accord it too much impact. The final blows to the aboriginal way of life occurred after 1542 and after the departure of the survivors of the de Soto expedition to New Spain. The bubonic plague pandemic of the late 1540s was clearly one of the culprits. The disease peaked in central New Spain in 1545, but it was present and caused significant mortality for several years. It must be assumed that the disease either spread through the Southeast overland through the Southwest and across the southern Great Plains or was transmitted by canoe traders via the major waterways. If plague recurred during the planting season of two or three summers in succession, it could have caused frightened Native Americans to flee from permanent towns that had become infested with plague-bearing rats. Like the Cofitachique people in 1539, they would have failed to plant. While their food stores would carry them through one year without a harvest, it is extremely doubtful whether food stored under the already disrupted conditions prior to 1545 would have carried very many town populations for two years without harvests, much less three. Moreover, starvation could have become truly massive if bubonic plague had been spread by hordes of invading rats that consumed stored dried foods and soiled what they did not eat. Starvation added to epidemic disease mortality would account for the demographic and cultural collapse that clearly occurred.

1559 INFLUENZA

One of the Old World diseases particularly likely to have been transmitted from Native American to Native American well beyond the populations under European Colonial rule was influenza. A major worldwide influenza pandemic struck Native Americans in Florida in 1559. The contagion was directly transmitted by sea by colonists aboard thirteen sailing vessels that left Vera Cruz on June 11, 1559. The ships carried approximately 1,500 individuals—soldiers, their wives and children, servants, Black slaves, "and a number of Florida Indians who had come to Mexico with the escaped Spaniards" and had returned. There were also 240 horses on the ships, a significant detail if the specific virus happened to be transmitted by horses.[79] This was the de Luna colony that landed near modern Pensacola. The Native Americans from Florida who returned there with the de Luna expedition provided an ideal mechanism for spreading influenza widely among Native Americans as they returned to their homes or acted as interpreters and cultural brokers between the Spanish colonists and Native Americans.

Pandemic influenza had broken out in Europe in 1556. It recurred off and on until 1560 and caused "serious demographic consequences" on both sides of the Atlantic. In England, where a number of people had begun to try to count the population, an estimated one-fifth perished.[80] The epidemic struck Spanish troops fighting Muslims in Algeria in 1558,[81] having begun in Madrid in 1557.[82] Influenza began to kill Mayan-speaking Native Americans in Guatemala a week after Easter in 1559.[83] Thus the epidemic was well under way before the de Luna expedition left Vera Cruz early in June. That the colonists carried the disease with them is indicated in the serious illness of 800 settlers who stayed at the place the Spaniards called Nanipacna, an eighty-house Native American settlement that had been abandoned when the colonists reached it.[84] The influenza virus spread also to the South American viceroyalty of Peru, causing heavy mortality in the capital city of Lima. The Spanish responded strongly, founding a new charity nursing order and a hospital.[85]

The geographic explorations by components of the de Luna colony, and frequent face-to-face contacts between those Spaniards and the

Apalachee and other tribes, made virtually certain the transmission of influenza to the natives of Florida. Intertribal trade on the peninsula and canoe trade between Florida Native Americans and Spaniards at Havana would then probably have spread the virus to all of the peninsular ethnic groups. Patients ill with influenza would have responded better when given nursing care (such as that which Le Moyne described Saturiwan tranvestites as providing in 1564), so the 1559 epidemic episode was no doubt a major experience reinforcing the new cultural pattern learned from Spanish captives. The virus was probably about as lethal among Florida Native Americans as among Englishmen.

SUMMARY

This section has examined evidence for the transmission of epidemic diseases to the Native American population of Florida during the protohistoric period from about A.D. 1512 to 1562. Available clues suggest that pathogens causing eight serious epidemics in Colonial populations could rather easily have been transmitted from New Spain and/or Cuba to the Calusa and Timucua (see table 25). Significantly, at least six different diseases are known to have been present in Cuba and/or New Spain for continental overland or seaborne ship and/or canoe transmission to Florida. These were (1) smallpox in 1519, (2) perhaps typhoid fever in 1528, or measles in 1528 – 1531, (3) bubonic plague in 1545 – 1548, (4) typhus in 1549, (5) mumps in 1550, and (6) influenza in 1559. Only the 1513 – 1514 disease—although it was most likely malaria—and the decimating pestilence of 1535 – 1539 remain unidentified. The significance of

TABLE 25
Possible and Documented Epidemic Disease Episodes
among Native Americans of Florida, 1512—1562

Date	Disease	Probability	Mortality
1513—1514	Malaria (?)	likely	unknown
1519—1524	Smallpox	nearly certain	50—75%
1528	Measles or typhoid fever	nearly certain	about 50%
1535—1539	Unidentified	documented	high
1545—1548	Bubonic plague	nearly certain	about 12.5%
1549	Typhus	very probable	perhaps 10%
1550	Mumps	possible	unknown
1559	Influenza	nearly certain	about 20%

the diversity of pathogens attacking Florida's Native Americans in 1512–1562 is that survivors of one epidemic gained no immunity to the next disease. Thus each pathogen could achieve maximal mortality.

French observation of disease conditions among the Timucua in 1564 made clear that venereal disease(s) was endemic at that time. Consequently, each of the epidemic episodes of a major pathogen would result in higher mortality than would have occurred in a population free from endemic ailments. Evidence from protohistoric times strongly suggests that Florida's native peoples were decimated during that period by assaults from a succession of contagious Old World diseases. Yet the functioning authoritarian political structure of the Timucuan chiefdoms reported in the 1560s suggests that Florida's peoples may have suffered less depopulation during preceding decades than did inhabitants of chiefdoms elsewhere in the Southeast.

NOTES

1. True, "Some Early Maps," 1954, pp. 77–80.

2. Lorant, ed., *New World*, 1946, p. 36.

3. Ibid., 30.

4. Ibid., 69.

5. Díaz del Castillo, *Discovery and Conquest*, 1908 (1956), 293–94.

6. Lorant, ed., *New World*, 1946, p. 75.

7. Ibid., 75.

8. Dobyns, "Outline," 1963, p. 494.

9. Rousell, *Les Pèlerinages*, 1954, pp. 37, 47, 163, etc.

10. B. Smith, trans., *Letter and Memoir*, 1854, p. 17; True, ed., *Memoir*, 1944, 1945, p. 28.

11. B. Smith, trans., *Letter and Memoir*, 1854, p. 17; French, comp., *Historical Collections*, 1875, p. 253; True, ed., *Memoir*, 1944, 1945, p. 29.

12. B. Smith, trans., *Letter and Memoir*, 1854, p. 17; French, comp., *Historical Collections*, 1875, p. 253; True, ed., *Memoir*, 1944, 1945, p. 29.

13. Mooney, "Ghost Dance Religion," 1896, pp. 777–83.

14. C.O. Sauer, *Early Spanish Main*, 1966, pp. 202–204, argued that Spanish demands disrupted Native American socio-organization and demoralized the people.

15. Las Casas, *Devastation*, 1974, p. 53.

16. Ibid., 55–56.

17. Ibid., 57.

18. Smith, trans., *Letter and Memoir*, 1854, p. 17; True, ed., *Memoir*, 1944, 1945, p. 29. French (*Historical Collections*, 1875, p. 253) translated the Spanish: "So eager were they in their search, that they did not pass a river, a brook, a lake, or even a swamp, without bathing in it; and even to this day, they have not ceased to look for it."

19. Las Casas, *Devastation*, 1974, pp. 54–55.

20. Anghiera, *Decades*, 1555 (1966), 73–74.

21. McNeill, *Plagues and Peoples*, 1976, pp. 207–208.

22. Cook and Borah, *Essays*, 1971, vol. I, p. 401.

23. Ibid., 380.

24. Ibid., 383.

25. C.O. Sauer, *Early Spanish Main*, 1966, pp. 202–204.

26. Cook and Borah, *Essays*, 1971, vol. I, pp. 409–10. A majority of the Spaniards attempting to colonize the Caribbean coast of South America during the initial decade of the sixteenth century died from disease or in battle with Native Americans (Andagoya, *Narrative*, 1865, p. 4).

27. Smith, trans., *Letter and Memoir*, 1854, p. 18; True, ed., *Memoir*, 1944, 1945, p. 19. French (*Historical Collections*, 1875, p. 254) put it: "It seems incredible that Juan Ponce de León should have gone to Florida to look for such a river."

28. True, ed., *Memoir*, 1944, 1945, p. 46, n. 21E. Anghiera, *Decades*, 1555 (1966), 86–87 (book 10, decade 2) said many wise or fortunate courtiers in Spain believed in the existence of a spring that "maketh owld men younge ageyne." The real New World presented so many strange things to Europeans that many of them credulously believed rumors and tales of quite unreal phenomena.

29. Crosby, *Columbian Exchange*, 1972, p. 50. In 1514, Pedro Arías de Avila arrived at Darién at the end of July with 1,500 men fresh from Spain. Vasco Núñez de Balboa led some 450 men already there. This colonial population of about 1,950 men lost 700 who "died of sickness and hunger" in a single month (Andagoya, *Narrative*, 1865, pp. 2, 4, 6). Thus almost 36 percent of the colonists perished in that lethal month. Seawater had damaged the flour and other stores that Arías's ships had brought from Spain. Consequently some Spaniards who were unable to change their food habits probably did starve, and others probably died from scurvy for lack of Vitamin C that abounded in tropical fruits on the Isthmus. Andagoya (*Narrative*, 1865, p. 6) attributed at least some illness to the ecology of the Darién outpost. Its environs were "woody covered with swamps." The environment was hospitable to mosquitoes, in other words. So malaria brought by earlier Spanish pioneers may have been the disease that ran rampant in 1512–14.

30. Dobyns, "Outline," 1963, p. 494. Pacheco and Cárdenas, eds., *Colección*, 1864, vol. I, p. 367. B. Smith, comp., *Colección*, 1857, p. 44.

31. Pacheco and Cárdenas, eds., *Colección*, 1864, vol. I, p. 370.

32. Ibid., vol. I, p. 368. B. Smith, comp., *Colección*, 1857, p. 45.

33. Wright, *Early History of Cuba*, 1916, pp. 86–87.

34. Herrera y Tordesillas, *Historia General*, 1945, vol. III, pp. 274–75; Clavijero, *Historia Antigua*, 1944, vol. II, p. 232; *Desertazioni Sulla Terra* 1781, p. 282; Sahagun, *Historia de las Cosas*, 1955, pp. 61–62; Díaz del Castillo, *Discovery and Conquest*, 1908 (1956), 293–94; Steck, *Motolinia's History*, 1951, pp. 87–88; Mendieta, *Historia*, 1945, p. 173.

35. C.M. Lewis, "Calusa," 1978, p. 20.

36. Ibid., 21.

37. Sturtevant, "Last," 1978, pp. 78, 142.

38. Gilliland, *Material Culture*, 1975, pp. 55, 123, 126.

39. Lowery, *Spanish Settlements*, 1905 (1959), vol. I, p. 352; Kerrigan, trans., *Barcia's Chronological History*, 1951, pp. 30–32.

40. Lowery, *Spanish Settlements*, 1905, vol. I, p. 353; Kerrigan, trans., *Barcia's Chronological History*, 1951, p. 32.

41. Wright, *Early History*, 1916, pp. 136–37.

42. Guerra y Sánchez, *Historia*, 1952, vol. I, p. 230.

43. Wright, *Early History*, 1916, p. 201.

44. Bandelier, trans., *Journey*, 1904 (1922), 64; Davenport, trans., "Expedition," 1924, p. 230. The *Relación* specified that "the Indians took sick with a disease of the stomach of which half of their people soon died" (n. 2). Fernandez de Oviedo (*Historia general*, 1959, vol. IV, p. 295) clearly stated: "An illness of the stomach struck the natives of the land from which half of them died."

45. Ewers, "Influence of Epidemics," 1973, p. 108.

46. May, *Ecology*, 1958, pp. 38–43.

47. Wright, *Early History*, 1916, p. 136; Guerra y Sánchez, *Historia*, 1952, vol. I, p. 230.

48. McNeill, *Plagues and Peoples*, 1976, p. 209; Dobyns, "Outline," 1963, pp. 497–99; Mendieta, *Historia*, 1945, p. 174; Steck, *Motolinia's History*, 1951, p. 88.

49. Chamberlain, *Conquest and Colonization*, 1953, p. 28.

50. Porras Barranechea, *Cartas*, 1959, p. 46.

51. Ibid., 24, 26.

52. Hallenbeck, *Alvar Núñez Cabeza de Vaca*, 1940, p. 44, discussed the 40 deaths from sickness and 10 casualties at Aute while the task force threw the rafts together, also provisions found at Aute (42).

53. Varner and Varner, trans., *Florida*, 1962, pp. 62–63. The Gentleman of Elvas reported that only two men landed and that the natives slew one on the spot (Robertson, trans., *True Relation*, 1933, vol. II, p. 40).

54. Varner and Varner, trans., *Florida*, 1962, pp. 70–71; Robertson, trans., *True Relation*, 1933, vol. II, pp. 42–44.

55. Varner and Varner, trans., *Florida*, 1962, pp. 76, 79; Robertson, *True Relation*, 1933, vol. II, pp. 45–46.

56. C.O. Sauer, *Sixteenth Century North America*, 1971, p. 167. De la Vega reported that six negotiators who met de Soto outside Cofitachique explained that there was a food shortage because people fled their town without planting during the "great pestilence" that had struck all towns in the chiefdom just one year before (Varner and Varner, trans., *Florida*, 1962, p. 298.

57. C.O. Sauer, *Sixteenth Century North America*, 1971, p. 302; Varner and Varner, trans., *Florida*, 1962, pp. 300, 325–26.

58. Gerhard, *Guide*, 1972, p. 23.

59. Gibson, *Aztecs*, 1964, p. 448.

60. Translator Bandelier (*Journey*, 1904 [1922], 204–208) mentions cures in 1534–35.

61. C.O. Sauer, *Sixteenth Century North America*, 1971, p. 302; Bandelier, trans., *Journey*, 1904 (1922), 147–49.

62. Gerhard, *Guide*, 1972, p. 23; Bancroft (*Native Races*, 1875, vol. I, p. 639), on the contrary, located the greatest havoc "in the interior, on the central plateau, and in the coldest and most arid regions, the lowlands of the coast being nearly . . . free from its effects."

63. Mendieta, *Historia*, 1945, p. 174.

64. Bancroft, *History*, vol. II, 1886, p. 553.

65. Zinsser, *Rats, Lice*, 1934, p. 256.

66. García, *El Clero*, 1907, p. 103.

67. Polo T., "Apuntes," 1913, p. 56.

68. Dobyns, "Outline," 1963, p. 513.

69. Veblen, "Native Population Decline," 1977, p. 497.

70. True, ed., *Memoir*, 1944, 1945, p. 12; Connor, trans., *Colonial Records*, 1925, vol. I, pp. 34–35. Menéndez reported other Spaniards had spent 15 and 18 years as captives, dating their wrecks to 1547 and 1550, partly still within the 1545–48 period of epidemic bubonic plague in New Spain.

71. Laudonnière, *Three Voyages*, 1975, pp. 109–10.

72. Dobyns and Doughty, *Peru*, 1976, p. 86.

73. Powell, *Soldiers, Indians*, 1952, pp. 10–12. The "rush" to Zacatecas came in 1549.

74. Gannon, *Cross*, 1965, pp. 10–11; O'Daniel, *Dominicans*, 1930, pp. 61–63; B. Smith, comp., *Colección*, 1857, p. 193–95.

75. Gannon, *Cross*, 1965, p. 14; O'Daniel, *Dominicans*, 1930, pp. 64–65; B. Smith, comp., *Colección*, 1857, p. 196.

76. Gannon, *Cross*, 1965, p. 14; O'Daniel, *Dominicans*, 1930, pp. 66–67; B. Smith, comp., *Colección*, 1857, p. 199; "los mas de ellos estavan con calenturas" (p. 201).

77. Gerhard, *Guide*, 1972, p. 23.

78. Milner, "Epidemic Disease," 1980, pp. 39–56.

79. Lowery, *Spanish Settlements*, 1905 (1959), vol. I, p. 359.

80. McNeill, *Plagues and Peoples*, 1976, p. 209.

81. Alegre, *Historia*, Tome I, Libros 1–3, 1956, vol. I, p. 51.

82. McBryde, "Influenza," 1940, p. 297.

83. Ibid., 294, 300.

84. Lowery, *Spanish Settlements*, 1905 (1959), 368–69; Priestley, *Luna Papers*, 1928, p. 103.

85. Cobo, *Fundación*, 1956, vol. II, p. 447.

The Colonial Period, 1562–1763

The historic, or Colonial, period in Florida, when literate Europeans recorded a fairly continuous, if ethnocentric, set of observations of Native American life, opened with the arrival of French Huguenot colonists in 1562. The type of documentation available altered dramatically with Jacques Le Moyne's arrival in 1564. Because Le Moyne's forty-three paintings depicted a wide range of Timucuan activities—two of them often represented within one painting—Le Moyne's record actually documented events of which he was apparently not conscious. Europeans tended to view Native Americans as unchanged by the Columbian Exchange, a cultural and biological process of which they were only marginally conscious in the 1560s, especially if the Europeans thought themselves the "first White men" to have come into contact with particular Native Americans. European observers lacked, moreover, any earlier record of observations against which they could compare their own so as to become conscious of changes among the Native Americans they saw.[1]

1564–1570

In this situation, Jacques Le Moyne actually painted and wrote evidence of a major epidemic of infectious disease among the Saturiwa Timucuan chiefdom in 1564–1565 without consciously recognizing it. The evidence for Timucuan cultural change in providing European-style nursing and life support for persons sick with Old World contagions has already been discussed in the last chapter. What should be recognized at this point is that Le Moyne could not have painted transvestites carrying sick adults off to special nursing locations and could not have written that transvestites performed this function for those ill from contagion in Timucua society *unless an episode of epidemic Old World disease had swept through the Saturiwa during the period when Le Moyne was at Fort Caroline (or among the Utina serving as a mercenary) to observe the behavior an epidemic elicited.* Had an epidemic episode not occurred between Le Moyne's arrival on June 22, 1564, and the Spanish capture of Fort Caroline on September 20, 1565, Le Moyne simply could not have learned about epidemic-period behavior by Timucuan transvestites.

275

Actually, the epidemic episode among the Timucuans can be otherwise dated to 1564. When Spanish Jesuits attempted to found missions among the Powhatan Confederacy Native Americans in 1570, they reported that the area had been "chastised . . . with six years of famine and death, which has brought it about that there is much less population than usual."[2] The Jesuit historian Francisco X. Alegre added a year, writing that "for seven years that people had been continually belabored by an epidemic."[3] He probably inadvertently changed "six" into "seven." Thus the Spanish Colonial record indicates that the epidemic spread widely among Atlantic coastal native populations.

The source of infection appears to have been Central Mexico. The several-year-long epidemic on the Atlantic Coast of North America most likely resulted from a variety of diseases that spread through Native American groups in a series, for "various" diseases reached epidemic proportions in the Valley of Mexico during 1563 and 1564.[4] The central Mexican mortality and consequent Indoamerican depopulation prompted a personal inspector for the Spanish crown to increase tributes so as to compensate Spaniards for the thinned number of tribute payers.[5]

1586 DOUBLE JEOPARDY

Late in May 1586 direct transmission of epidemic disease from English privateers to Native Americans living at and near St. Augustine may have occurred. The log of the *Primrose*, one of the ships in the war fleet led by Francis Drake, recorded: "The wilde people at first comminge of our men died verie fast and said amongest themselues, It was the Englisshe God that made them die so faste."[6] The complements of Drake's ships did, in fact, carry with them a deadly contagion. Drake had sailed hurriedly from Plymouth on September 14, 1585. He put into Santiago in the Cape Verde Islands on November 17 to finish fitting for a long voyage and quartered many of his 2,300 men in the deserted town for ten days. "There was adjoining to their greatest church an hospital, with as brave rooms in it, and in as goodly order as any man can devise; we found about 20 sick persons, all negroes, lying of very foul and frightful diseases. In this hospital we took all the bells out of the steeple and brought them away with us."[7] Members of Drake's forces visiting the Black patients in the church hospital may have contracted one or more acute fevers from them. The work force removing the bells may also have caught the disease(s), and men quartered in the vacant houses of the port town may have contracted a disease transmitted by insect vectors in the houses.

Drake sailed again on November 29, and two days later epidemic disease broke out on board his ships.[8] The fleet made its New World landfall at Dominica and traded with the Indoamericans there. The contagion may have spread to them. The English war fleet sailed on to capture the city of Santo Domingo, Spain's oldest New World settlement and a wealthy one. Then Drake occupied the city of Cartagena on the northern coast of South America for six weeks, transmitting the infection his men carried to the Colonial population of South America. By that time, Drake's forces were so diminished and the survivors of the disease so weakened that he sailed for England. His fleet stopped off on its way home to capture St. Augustine, having lost some 750 men. Three-fourths of Drake's casualties were caused by the Cape Verde Island fever, which caused victims to break out with a rash of small spots as well as to suffer from a burning fever.[9] In other words, Drake's men carried an infection aboard ship that had caused a mortality greater than 25 percent among adult Englishmen and had an incubation period of one week, so that his sailors and troops could well have infected the Native Americans about St. Augustine.

On the other hand, the possibility remains that the Florida Native Americans came down with some other infectious disease from which they began by coincidence to die when the English invaders appeared. The log already cited recorded that Drake's fleet arrived at St. Augustine on May 27 and sailed on June 2. That was time enough for a disease with a week-long incubation period to break out as the Englishmen were about to depart. Yet the author of the log wrote that the "wild people" died very fast when the invaders first arrived. Thus the identity of the source of contagion remains unsure, but the ship's log did undoubtedly record a serious epidemic episode.

The epidemic that seamen with Drake witnessed at St. Augustine may well have originated among English colonists at Roanoke. Slightly more than 100 Englishmen in Raleigh's colony suffered no mortality, but Thomas Hariot's report makes clear that they transmitted at least two epidemic diseases to the Native Americans with whom they came into contact. In one dramatic passage, Hariot wrote that a few days after the Englishmen visited hostile settlements, 20 Native Americans died in some, 40 in others, 60 in some, and in one 120 perished, "which in truth was very many in respect to their numbers." The disease was strange to the natives, so that they knew neither how to cure it nor even what it was.[10] Whatever this contagious disease may have been, it appears likely to have been the cause of the epidemic episode from which Native Americans began to die at St. Augustine just when Drake's fleet occupied that Spanish outpost. If Drake's personnel then transmitted the Cape Verde Island affliction from which it suffered to the Timucua, the Florida native American peoples were ravaged by two epidemic episodes in short succession.

1596

A new royal governor, Gonzalo Méndez de Canzo, arrived at St. Augustine on June 2, 1597. Initially, at least, Méndez de Canzo wrote with some enthusiasm about a hospital then under construction in the Florida outpost. He reported that hospital care had kept "many" soldiers, Indians, and Blacks from dying the previous summer.[11] The disease that struck St. Augustine and neighboring Native Americans could have been the measles that was epidemic in Central Mexico in 1595.[12]

Another possibility is that the disease that felled Spaniards, Native Americans, and Blacks in St. Augustine during the summer of 1596 was bubonic plague. Plague appeared in London during the autumn of 1592 and reached its peak there during the summer of 1593.[13] In 1592 and 1593, *cocoliztli* as well as measles was epidemic in Central Mexico[14] and the Mixtec country and along the Pacific Coast.[15] In frontier Sinaloa, however, the 1592–1593 episode was labeled "a most violent pestilence of smallpox and measles."[16] Almost no one among the frontier tribes escaped the contagion. "Repulsive crusts" covered some sick people from head to foot. Others suffered as the skin peeled from their hands and feet. Burning with fever, people fled their homes. Mortality in the Sinaloa frontier area ran 25 percent among Christian converts, 1,000 of the first 4,000 baptized persons perishing.[17] This biological disaster triggered a Native American nativistic movement during which traditionalists slew the Jesuit missionary Gonzalo de Tapia.

Thus, published descriptions of later sixteenth-century Colonial Florida document epidemic disease episodes there at least thrice, in 1564–1570, in 1586, and in 1596. Those were years of fundamentally proprietary governance of the colony when missionary activity was just beginning.

1613–1617 BUBONIC PLAGUE

During the seventeenth century, epidemic mortality began, as Jones and Milanich recognized, when an epidemic struck Colonial Florida in 1613. At least half of the Christianized Native American population perished within a four-year period.[18] Franciscan missionaries reported to the king that half the natives converted to Christianity died of "plague and other contagious diseases." They used the Spanish term for plague, although such usage is not a conclusive diagnosis because, as I noted above, Spaniards also used the term to mean "epidemic." Other evidence supports the specific identification. Central Mexico was afflicted in 1613 by the disease *cocoliztli*.[19]

If *cocoliztli* meant in 1613 what it had meant in 1545, then this disease was, according to the analysis presented above, bubonic plague. That diagnosis is more consistent with the pattern of mortality distributed over four years among missionized Native Americans than a smallpox etiology. Smallpox, transmitted from person to person, spreads to all susceptible individuals in a residential population very quickly. Bubonic plague, transmitted by a flea vector from an animal reservoir (usually rats but on occasion other rodents), does not typically spread in a linear pattern to all susceptible persons in a residential population. Rather, plague typically is transmitted seemingly at random and does take a few years to spread to all of the susceptible individuals.

Franciscan missionaries then in Florida wrote to the crown at the beginning of January in 1617 that during the previous four years, half of the Native Americans there had perished of repeated episodes of epidemics and contagious diseases. The Franciscans claimed that more than 8,000 Christian converts had survived and many heathens. There were still no missions among the Apalachees, the South Carolina tribes, or the Calusa.[20]

1649 YELLOW FEVER

As Jones and Milanich noted, an infectious epidemic struck Spanish Colonial Florida in 1649. It differed from most earlier epidemics in that the pathogen killed Spaniards as well as Native Americans. Officials, such as the provincial governor, two treasury officers, and two company commanders, and many missionaries died. The contagion was directly transmitted by ship's personnel from Havana, where more than one-third of the population had died of the disease.[21] Four successive royal prosecuting attorneys died in Havana in quick succession.[22] This was an epidemic not of a domesticated European disease but of African yellow fever that broke out in Mérida and Campeche, Yucatan; San Juan de Puerto Rico; and Havana, Cuba, in 1648.[23] The population of the Caribbean ports panicked.

Yellow fever could not invade the peoples of the New World until its mosquito vector, *Aedes aegypti*, survived a transatlantic voyage and found a niche in which it could survive. It seems surprising that the mosquito had not hitchhiked across the ocean earlier, inasmuch as it is "domesticated," that is, it breeds in water in a container such as a cistern, water cask, or gourd.[24] The destination of the initial successful transatlantic crossing apparently was Barbados, where the mosquito found a fine ecological niche. Yellow fever was epidemic on that English-ruled island by September 1647.[25] By January 1648 the disease had spread to San Juan de Puerto Rico because of movements of troops and prisoners. Florida became part of its Caribbean and Gulf habitat. It recurred among the presidential troops in 1649[26] and 1650.[27] Because the disease was new, neither Europeans nor Native Americans possessed any immunity to it nor indeed any effective treatment for it.

1653 SMALLPOX

Florida's Governor Diego de Robelledo, who took office in 1655, reported that Spanish inhabitants had smallpox, as did many Native Americans, and that the Blacks had all died.[28] Settlements of the Timucuan-speaking peoples were significantly depopulated by this epidemic and during an uprising against Spanish colonial exploitation that it precipitated as well as by subsequent suppression.[29] The millenarian response to epidemic stress that began early in the sixteenth century continued among surviving Florida Native Americans.

1659 MEASLES

A lethal measles epidemic followed the earlier smallpox episode and consequent Native-American-Spanish war in Florida. The provincial governor who took office on February 20 in 1659, Alonso de Aranguiz y Cotes, reported to Spain on November 1 of that year his bad luck: following his arrival more than 10,000 Native Americans had died from the highly contagious measles.[30] Gov. Aranguiz y Cotes arrived by ship from Havana, where he had been delayed for some time. Again, the chronicle of epidemics in New Spain does not indicate that measles was epidemic there at the time. Transmission may have been transatlantic. Native Americans living near Montreal, in French Canada, "were dying . . . like flies" in 1659,[31] a circumstance that suggests direct transatlantic transmission followed by a spread among Native Americans along the Atlantic Coast.

1672

As Jones and Milanich noted, an unidentified epidemic assaulted north Florida's Native Americans again in 1672.[32] Three years later, an official enumeration of both converted and unconverted Native Americans showed that only 10,766 remained under Colonial rule. Only 13 percent of them were presumably Timucuan-speakers.[33] Overland transmission of the 1672 disease from northern New Spain appears to be a possibility. In the previous year, 1671, the Pueblo peoples of New Mexico suffered from "a great pestilence" that caused high mortality among both people and cattle.[34] Probably, therefore, influenza is implicated.

1675

In mid-1675, Capt. Juan Fernandez de Florencia wrote a report on the missions of the Apalachee and Timucua areas of Spanish Florida. Fernandez was the deputy governor in charge of the Apalachee Province and held the military rank of captain. He listed some twenty-seven mission or related populations that ranged in numbers from 40 at a St. Johns River ferry on the road to St. Augustine, to 1,400 in San Luís, the Apalachee provincial capital. The Guale and Timucuan missions were already nearly depopulated. Those among the Apalachee still had hundreds of residents. Fernandez ended with a key statement: "I have not taken a census and they die daily."[35]

No doubt Fernandez meant his statement that Native Americans died daily to be understood somewhat figuratively. Still, it is indicative of an epidemic in progress, even if Fernandez merely supposed that Native Americans died frequently, for only one-third of the settlements he reported had more than 365 inhabitants. In other words, taking his statement at face value, if the normal death rate was one person daily, two-thirds of the settlements he listed could not have survived another year (see table 26).

Of twenty-six settlements reported by Fernandez, sixteen would have disappeared entirely in less than one year with a death rate of one person per day! None of the settlements he listed could have survived such a death rate for four years. Even if Fernandez exaggerated, his remark identified the summer of 1675 as a period of pestilence and heightened mortality. Possibly smallpox was transmitted overland from northern New Spain via the Coahuiltecan tribes of south Texas.[36] Perhaps there was a direct transmission from Cuba or from Spain itself.

Table 26

Apalache-Guale-Timucua Settlements in 1675,
in Rank Order of Population Size

Settlement	Population	Years of Survival[a]
San Luís	1,400	3.8
San Lorenzo Ybitachuco	1,200	3.3
San Damián Acpayca	900	2.5
San Joseph Ocuya	900	2.5
Concepción Ayabale	800	2.2
San Juan Azpalaga	800	2.2
San Martín Tomole	700	1.9
San Pedro Patale	500	1.4
San Carlos	400	1.1
Candelaria	300	0.8
Asunción de Nuestra Señora	300	0.8
San Matheo	300	0.8
Santa Elena Machava	300	0.8
San Pedro	300	0.8
San Francisco Oconí	200	0.55
San Antonio Bacuqua	120	0.33
Santa Fé	110	0.30
San Nicolás Tolentino	100	0.27
San Juan Guacara	80	0.22
Santa Cruz Taragica	80	0.22
Santa Catholina	60	0.16
San Francisco	60	0.16
Santa Cruz Ytuchafun	60	0.16
Natividad de Nuestra Gracia	40	0.11
San Miguel Asile	40	0.11
Ferry	40	0.11

[a]Assuming a death rate of one person daily.
Source: Boyd, "Enumeration," 1948, pp. 184–87.

1686 FEVER

There is record of illness in 1686 among Gulf Coast inhabitants of Colonial Florida and probably among adjacent Native Americans. Marcos Delgado set out from Apalachee on August 28, 1686, with twelve soldiers and twenty Apalachee auxiliaries. He visited villages of the Creeks with the goal of reaching the Mobile. In mid-September, the expedition's commander reported to the provincial governor that he and half of the soldiers and Apalachee auxiliaries "fell ill with a fever." Delgado wrote that he himself was twice attacked by fever.[37] It seems possible that both the Mestizo soldiers and Apalachee auxiliaries suffered from malaria and that repeated acute attacks occurred as a consequence of physical exertion on the march. On the other hand, it also seems possible that the travelers contracted some contagious disease of which fever was one symptom as they left Apalachee territory, so that they fell ill in the midst of the Creek villages. Typhus could well have been the culprit. That disease was reported as epidemic in Guatemala in 1686[38] and could have been widespread throughout Spanish North America.

1716

The British campaigns of 1702 – 1704 during the War of the Spanish Succession ended the Spanish mission system in northern Florida. South Carolina militia burned some settlements, captured thousands of Timucuans, and marched them off to slavery in South Carolina.[39] Even after the collapse of Christian convert population during the war, serious illness continued to assault the handful of surviving Native Americans. In 1716, Diego Peña led a scouting party from St. Augustine westward through the former Timucuan and Apalachee missions. Peña left the post on August 4, and five days later he encamped "because three Indians were sick."[40]

The illness may have been some chronic ailment to which Native Americans living in or near St. Augustine were subject, aggravated by the rigors of an overland journey. When Peña returned to St. Augustine in early November, Colonial officials turned out to receive him and the independent Native American leaders accompanying him. The governor himself did not greet the chiefs at the town gate but awaited them in the palace because of his own recent illness.[41] In other words, there was probably an endemic, chronic ailment such as malaria that affected both Native Americans and relatively transient inhabitants such as the royal governor.

1727

The extant historical literature appears to contain some confusion about the process of the Columbian Exchange in and around St. Augustine between 1725 and 1729. William Neill referred to an epidemic that struck there in 1726.[42] J.T. Milanich referred to a pestilence that struck the St. Augustine Timucuan town between September 1 and October 5 in 1728.[43] Historian Theodore Corbett referred to an unidentified epidemic that began in "the Indian suburbs and spread to St. Augustine" during 1727.[44]

Original sources include a letter dated September 1, 1727, that Gov. Antonio de Benavides wrote to the king, transmitting a copy of his enumeration of 1,021 Native Americans of various tribal antecedents living in sixteen ethnic settlements. Benavides stated in his cover letter that after he had carried out his inspection of the Native American rancherías, 166 recently converted native Christians had died in an epidemic,[45] a crude death rate of 163 per 1,000 people.

It is quite possible that both measles and smallpox spread to the Florida Native Americans during these years, causing lower death rates than in earlier years because some people were already immune as a result of prior infections. Smallpox reportedly spread to the missionized Native Americans of Sonora in northwestern New Spain in January of 1724.[46] The geographic extension of the epidemic episode is indicated by the death of the reigning Spanish monarch, young Luís I, from smallpox that same year.[47]

Measles is implicated inasmuch as that disease was epidemic in New Spain, and especially in Mexico City during 1727 and 1728, in January of which year the episode ended.[48] Farther south in Guatemala, measles caused epidemic mortality in 1725–1728.[49] Thus measles may have spread northward close on the heels of a widespread although perhaps sporadically distributed smallpox epidemic.

TIMUCUAN EXTINCTION

Spanish officials evacuated Florida in accord with the 1763 Treaty of Paris. British troops landed and occupied the province. The Spaniards took with them nearly all their civilian population, including a few hundred surviving Christian Native Americans. They settled the latter near Veracruz on the fever-wracked coast of New Spain.[50] A few Calusa may have remained in South Florida, never having converted to Christianity. Lower Creek towns becoming known as Seminoles, from Spanish *cimarrón* ("wild"), occupied most of the peninsula, whatever the European notions of sovereignty. In other words, by 1763, the Timucuan-speaking peoples were virtually extinct in Florida, and the Calusa may have been nearly so.

SUMMARY

At least a dozen epidemic disease episodes are known to have occurred among Florida's Native Americans from 1564 to 1727 and are listed in table 27. I have identified episodes of yellow fever, plague, measles, and smallpox and have indicated their probable or possible modes of transmission to the peninsular population. Perhaps the most important finding is that more than a third of the epidemic disease agents appear to have been transmitted directly across the Atlantic Ocean by passengers and/or crewmen on sailing ships. These are (1) the 1586 Cape Verde infectious fever that Drake's fleet carried and possibly transmitted at St. Augustine; (2) another contagion brought the previous year by English colonists on Roanoke Island; (3) the 1649 yellow fever epidemic that followed the initial 1647 transport of mosquito vector and pathogen across the Atlantic; (4) the 1654 smallpox epidemic that may have been carried across the Atlantic by Swedes or colonists other than Spaniards; and (5) the 1659 measles epidemic.

Four other Florida epidemic diseases may have been transmitted from New Spain, but the available documentation does not clearly indicate such transmission. These are (1) the 1564–1570 series of epidemic episodes occurring simultaneously in Central Mexico and in Florida and the Atlantic Coast of North America; (2) the 1613–1617 bubonic plague that spread north along the Atlantic Coast through the New England tribes; (3) the 1672 epidemic, possibly influenza spread in part by domestic animal hosts across the continent from the northern

TABLE 27

Documented and Possible Epidemic Disease Episodes
Among Native Americans of Colonial Florida, 1564–1727

Date	Disease	Probability	Mortality
1564—1570	Unidentified + endemic syphilis	documented	severe
1585—1586	Unidentified	documented	severe
1586	Vectored fever	probable	15—20%
1596	Measles	documented	about 25%
1613—1617	Bubonic plague	documented	50%
1649	Yellow fever	documented	about 33%
1653—	Smallpox	documented	unknown
1659	Measles	documented	unknown
1672	Influenza (?)	documented	unknown
1675	Unidentified	probable	unknown
1686	Unidentified (typhus ?)	documented	unknown
1716	Perhaps chronic	documented	unknown
1726±	Smallpox (?)	nearly certain	unknown
1727 or 1728	Measles (?)	nearly certain	16%

frontier of New Spain; and (4) probably epidemic smallpox, which could have come straight from Spain as well as from New Spain in 1724 or 1725, followed very quickly by measles spreading northward from Central America.

At least five and probably seven infectious epidemics struck the Native Americans surviving in Florida during the seventeenth century, instead of the three usually mentioned. The five differed from each other in the most lethal pattern. First came bubonic plague in 1613–1617. After a long interval possibly indicating that very few Native Americans survived in Florida, yellow fever arrived in 1649, followed in rapid succession by smallpox in 1653, measles in 1659, and probably influenza in 1672. Then came an unidentified contagion in 1675 and perhaps typhus in 1686. Each epidemic found large numbers of susceptible victims because the diseases differed. Earlier diseases conferred no immunity to later ones. Native Americans must have died in great numbers in Florida during the later seventeenth century, but particularly during the sequence of yellow fever (1649), smallpox (1653), and measles (1659). Moreover, other documents still in Spanish archives may record additional epidemic episodes.

The expanded outline of epidemic disease among Florida's native peoples during the seventeenth century still does not mean that the seventeenth century was as lethal as the sixteenth in terms of total mortality. During that initial century Old World pathogens invaded the Florida natives when they had reached their population maximum, in 1513–1514, 1519, 1528–1531, 1535–1538, 1545, 1549, perhaps 1550, 1559, 1564–1570, 1586 (two waves), and finally 1596. That was a total of one dozen epidemic episodes, half of them virtually certain. Given the lethalness of the smallpox, bubonic plague, measles, and other pathogens involved in "virgin soil" pandemics, the native population could not but have fallen rapidly during the entire sixteenth century. Consequently, there simply were not nearly so many Native Americans left to die during the seventeenth century.

A schematic reconstruction of the depopulation trend among Native Americans in Florida appears in figure 3. This chart is even more empirical and schematic than those drawn by S.F. Cook and Woodrow Borah to graph the population trend in Central Mexico during the same period.[51] Whereas Cook and Borah analyzed numbers derived from enumerations or estimates based upon records of tribute payments, figure 3, representing a different approach, presents a trend based only on best-documented epidemic disease episodes and mortality known for the various diseases involved in other Native American populations if not reported from Florida. Figure 3 intentionally emphasizes decisive

FIGURE 3
Schematic Reconstruction of Approximate
Depopulation Trend of Florida Native Americans, 1519–1617

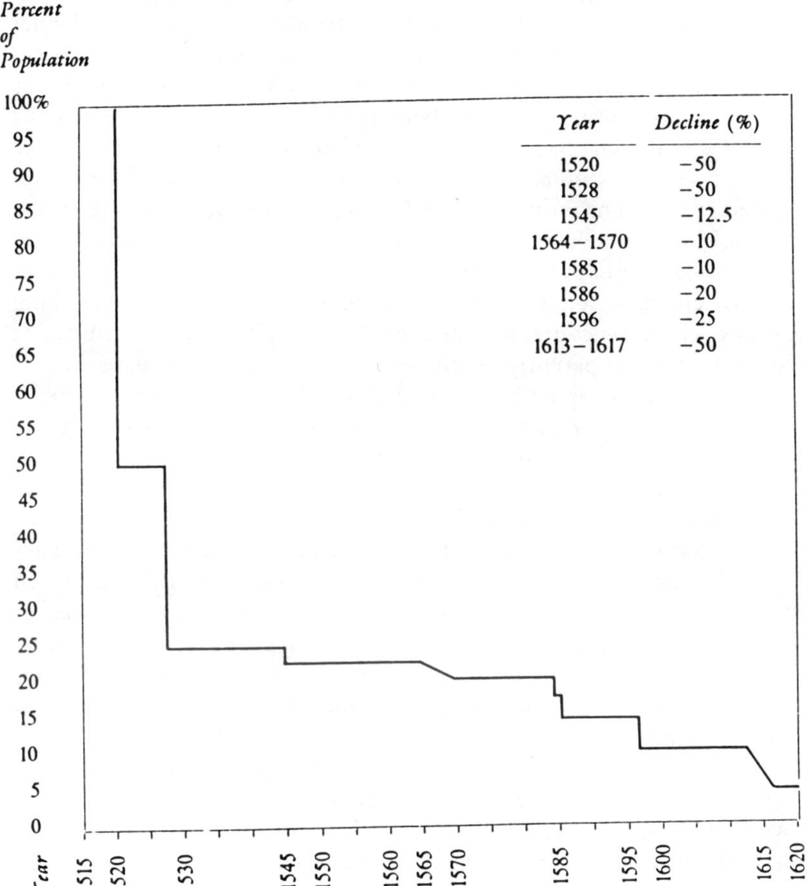

demographic events of a kind unknown during the nineteenth or twentieth century since demography emerged as a science.

This schematic reconstruction ignores the 1513–1514 episode as unquantifiable and starts from the 1517–1519 population. The 1519 smallpox pandemic is shown as killing only half of the people. Then the population is shown as precisely in balance until each of the next epidemics struck. This is a conservative procedure, inasmuch as sequelae of smallpox and other diseases and new endemic ailments elsewhere caused Native American numbers to fall even between epidemic episodes. The 1528 episode is attributed to measles, with another 50 percent loss in population. The 1545 bubonic plague pandemic is assigned 12.5 percent mortality based on a loss of 800,000 of 6,300,000 Central Mexicans. The 1564–1570 episode is attributed an arbitrary 10 percent loss, perhaps an underestimate of mortality in view of the presence of endemic venereal disease among at least Timucuan-speaking groups. The more contagious disease that Raleigh's spies transmitted at Roanoke that apparently reached the Saturiwan Timucuans just as Drake's forces occupied St. Augustine is assigned a 10 percent mortality. That may also be an underestimate, in view of Thomas Hariot's description of village mortality farther north. The vectored fever Drake's men picked up in the Cape Verde Islands is assumed to have been transmitted to the Florida natives. The mortality rate is approximately that which his forces suffered. The end-of-the-century measles epidemic is calculated at 25 percent mortality, although this could well have been considerably higher if there had in fact been no measles in Florida since 1528 or so. The 50 percent mortality Franciscan missionaries reported occurred among Christian converts between 1613 and 1617 during that bubonic plague epidemic is taken to have afflicted non-Christians as well.

This schematic reconstruction omits the 1559 influenza epidemic, which almost certainly caused significant mortality among Florida natives, and other diseases. Nevertheless, it suggests that it is reasonable to think that the 1617 Native American population of Florida was on the order of 5 percent of the size of the 1517 population. It should be emphasized that this schematic chart shows no actual population figures. The figure is presented to stress the conclusion that Florida's Native American population decreased precipitously from at least 1519 and then rapidly until 1617.[52] This demographic trend affected social behavior and cultural patterns in fundamental ways. The demographic losses combined with psychological shock and cosmological confusion to cause the collapse of aboriginal Southeastern cultures. That collapse followed the biological invasion of probably malaria in 1513–1514, smallpox in 1519, measles in 1528, bubonic plage in 1545, and influenza in 1559. The demographic disaster was maximum because none of these pathogens conferred any immunity to any of the subsequent invaders. Consequently every one decimated a completely susceptible population.

NOTES

1. Sixteenth-century observers thought in terms of an inaccurate normative theory of cultural change, like many twentieth-century anthropologists (Steward, "Theory and Application," 1955, pp. 295–96).

2. Lewis and Loomie, *Spanish Jesuit Mission*, 1953, pp. 85, 89.

3. Alegre, *Historia*, 1956, vol. I, p. 77.

4. Gerhard, *Guide*, 1972, p. 23.

5. Mendieta, *Historia*, 1945, p. 174.

6. Quinn, ed., *Roanoke Voyages*, 1955, vol. I, p. 306; J.S. Corbett, "Discourse and Description," 1898, p. 26.

7. Ibid., 9.

8. Ibid., 12. "We had not been two days at sea but there fell a great sickness amongst our men, not in one ship alone but in all the whole fleet." Creighton, *History*, 1891, vol. I, pp. 585–86; Dobyns, "Outline," 1963, p. 504.

9. J.S. Corbett, "Discourse and Description," 1898, p. 52; Creighton, *History*, 1891, vol. I, pp. 587–88; Dobyns, "Outline," 1963, p. 504.

10. C.O. Sauer, *Sixteenth Century North America*, 1971, p. 303; Jennings, *Invasion*, 1975, p. 23; Quinn, ed., *Roanoke Voyages*, 1955, vol. I, p. 378; Crosby, *Columbian Exchange*, 1972, pp. 40–41; Lorant, ed., *New World*, 1946, p. 272.

11. Geiger, *Franciscan Conquest*, 1937, vol. I, p. 77.

12. Beals, "Acculturation," 1967, p. 461; Gibson, *Aztecs*, 1964, p. 449; Mendieta, *Historia*, 1945, p. 174.

13. Creighton, *History*, 1891, vol. I, p. 351.

14. Gibson, *Aztecs*, 1964, p. 449.

15. Gerhard, *Guide*, 1972, p. 23.

16. C.O. Sauer, *Aboriginal Population*, 1935, p. 11.

17. Karns, *Unknown Arizona*, 1954, p. 277.

18. Bushnell, "Menéndez Cattle Barony," 1978, p. 416; Swanton, *Early History*, 1922, p. 338.

19. Gibson, *Aztecs*, 1964, p. 449.

20. Pareja, et al., Oficio, 17 de enero de 1617.

21. Bushnell, "Menéndez Cattle Barony," 1978, p. 419; Ruíz de Salazar, Oficio, 14 de julio de 1650.

22. Silverio Sainza, *Cuba*, 1972, p. 300.

23. Schendel, Alvarez Amezquita, and Bustamante, *Medicine*, 1969, p. 107; McNeill, *Plagues and Peoples*, 1976, p. 213; Brau, *La colonización*, 1907, p. 455; Alegre, *Historia*, 1959, Tomo III, pp. 137–38.

24. McNeill, *Plagues and Peoples*, 1976, p. 213.

25. Creighton, *History*, 1891, vol. I, pp. 620–21.

26. Moreno Ponce de León, Memorial, 7 de setiembre de 1651.

27. Ruíz de Salazar, Oficio, 14 de julio de 1650.

28. Chatelain, *Defenses*, 1941, p. 56.

29. Swanton, *Early History*, 1922, p. 338.

30. Bushnell, "Menéndez Cattle Barony," 1978, p. 420; Aranguíz y Cotes, 1 de noviembre de 1659.

31. Campbell, *Pioneer Laymen*, 1915, vol. I, p. 213.

32. Bushnell, "Menéndez Cattle Barony," 1978, p. 425; Swanton, *Early History*, 1922, p. 338.

33. Bushnell, "Menéndez Cattle Barony," 1978, p. 425.

34. Hackett, ed., *Historical Documents*, 1937, vol. III, pp. 17, 302.

35. Boyd, "Enumeration," 1948, p. 188.

36. Ewers, "Influence of Epidemics," 1973, p. 108; Bolton, ed., *Spanish Exploration*, 1908, p. 298 (refers to perhaps an earlier episode); Sheridan and Naylor, *Rarámuri*, 1979, p. 37.

37. Boyd, trans., "Expedition," 1937, pp. 5–6, 14–16.

38. Veblen, "Native Population Decline," 1977, p. 498.

39. Boyd, Smith, and Griffin, *Here They Once Stood*, 1951, pp. 36–95.

40. Boyd, "Diego Peña's Expedition," 1949, p. 13.

41. Ibid., 11.

42. Neill, "Indian and Spanish Site," 1968, p. 112.

43. Milanich, "Western Timucua," 1978, p. 73; following Geiger, *Biographical Dictionary*, 1940, p. 136.

44. T.G. Corbett, "Population Structure," 1976, p. 275.

45. Benavides, a S. M. dando cuenta de haber hecho la visita a los indios, 1 de setiembre de 1727.

46. Campos, Libro de Bautismos, no. 1, p. 45.

47. Chapman, *History*, 1918, pp. 377–78.

48. Gibson, *Aztecs*, 1964, p. 450.

49. Veblen, "Native Population Decline," 1977, p. 498.

50. Gold, "Settlement," 1965, pp. 567–76; *Borderland Empires*, 1969.

51. Cook and Borah, *Essays*, 1971, p. 83, etc.

52. If figures are fitted to the demographic trend line reconstructed in figure 3, earlier estimates of Florida Native American population can be checked for mutual consistency with the new estimates. The 1562–68 estimate of total population in table 23 based on a multiple of 5.5 persons per warrior is here revised upward to 155,000 individuals. Population estimates and mortality estimates appear in table 28.

Estimates of the Timucuan-Speaking Population, 1517–1620

Reconstructing the historic epidemiology of a population is an important first step—albeit merely initial—toward that accurate interpretation of historic events for which William McNeill eloquently argued. In the New World, reconstructing an approximate depopulation trend such as that presented in figure 3 becomes a second and methodologically significant step toward accurate demographic analysis, for figure 3 describes decisive demographic events affecting real people in real time. The curve in figure 3 shows the magnitude of declines of population during actual pandemic or epidemic episodes. It does not disguise such decisive demographic events by mathematical manipulations.[1] Another analytical step permits the estimation of Native American numbers at several specific time periods, which may then be compared with earlier estimates of Florida population reached using different techniques.

This next analytical step is taken in figure 4. The figures in figure 4 are population estimates instead of the proportions employed in figure 3. The numerical starting point for figure 4 population estimates is a 1564 Timucuan-speaking total population rounded to 150,000 persons. This basic figure is derived from table 23; it is the population estimated from warrior counts for the chiefdoms, allowing two warriors per lineage and 5.5 per counted mobilized warrior. From that base figure, figure 4 relates population estimates to nine decisive demographic events, the earlier epidemics of 1520–1524, 1531–1533, 1545–1548, and 1559, and the later ones of 1564–1570, 1585, 1596, and 1613–1619. This is almost the ten counts that S.F. Cook and Woodrow Borah regarded as "optimal" for historic demographic analysis[2] over a comparable period of time.

The depopulation trend line shown in figure 4 implies that Timucuan population totaled about 150,000 persons for only about five years, between 1559 and 1564. Figure 4 differs from figure 3 in that the 1559 influenza epidemic has been estimated to have produced a 5 percent mortality and to have significantly disrupted horticultural activity during the summer of 1559. This change in reconstructing the depopulation trend has been introduced to help to account for the observed collapse of Southeastern aboriginal chiefdoms between the departure of the de Soto expedition in 1543 and the arrival of the de Luna colonists in 1559 and their inland explorations in 1560.

291

FIGURE 4

Estimate of Timucuan-Speaking Population from
A.D. 1515 to 1620 Based on Reconstructed Depopulation Trend

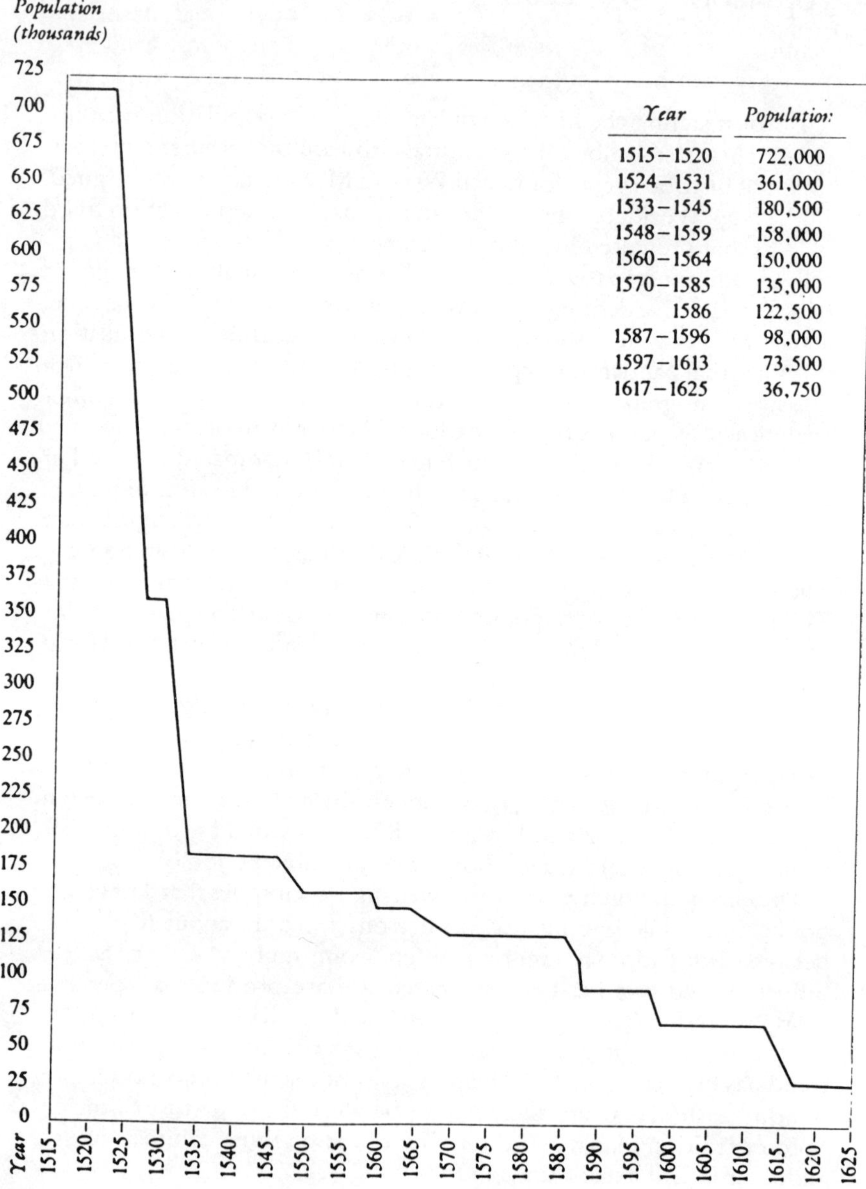

Year	Population:
1515–1520	722,000
1524–1531	361,000
1533–1545	180,500
1548–1559	158,000
1560–1564	150,000
1570–1585	135,000
1586	122,500
1587–1596	98,000
1597–1613	73,500
1617–1625	36,750

In other words, it is now assumed that the influenza pandemic had to contribute to that collapse along with the bubonic plague pandemic of 1545–1548 and the delayed impact of earlier pandemic diseases and the massive mortality they caused. The probable 12.5 percent mortality of the plague pandemic is regarded as an insufficient although necessary condition for the collapse of the Southeastern chiefdoms. Influenza mortality, and more importantly illness that demoralized people and kept them from planting in 1559 and further weakened the already seriously undermined authority of aboriginal theocratic leaders, are hypothesized as the final, sufficient conditions producing the collapse of the chiefdoms during the very period when the de Luna colony tried and failed to settle the Gulf Coast relying on Native American surplus food production. The estimated populations at various dates are summarized in table 28.

There are, of course, alternative explanations for the collapse of the Southeastern chiefdoms between 1543 and 1559. some of them have already been mentioned: surely selective execution of ruling elites by de Soto's marauders so weakened traditional authority as to hasten its disintegration. It is also possible that the bubonic plague caused mortality nearer the 50 percent that Franciscan missionaries reported for the 1613–1617 Florida plague epidemic than the 12.5 percent estimated on the basis of reported 1545–1548 mortality and total population in Central Mexico.

The depopulation trend reconstructed in figure 4 suggests that Timucuan speakers numbered about 158,000 between 1549 and 1559. The reconstructed trend indicates that perhaps 180,500 Timucuan speakers lived between 1533 and 1545 to suffer the depredations of de Soto's

TABLE 28
Estimated Timucuan Population Trend, 1517—1620

Chronology	Event	Mortality	Surviving Population
1517	—	—	722,000
1519—1524	Smallpox pandemic	361,000 (50%)	361,000
1528—1533	Measles pandemic	180,500 (50%)	180,500
1545—1548	Bubonic plague pandemic	22,500 (12.5%)	158,000
1559	Influenza pandemic	8,000 (5%)	150,000
1564—1570	Unidentified epidemic	15,000 (10%)	135,000
1585	Unidentified epidemic	13,500 (10%)	121,500
1586	Cape Verde Island fever	24,300 (20%)	97,200
1596	Measles (?) epidemic	24,300 (25%)	72,900
1613—1617	Bubonic plague	36,450 (50%)	36,450

marauders. Actually, a few thousand more should be added to the 1533–1539 estimate to allow for the direct casualties inflicted by de Soto's men. Before that, the reconstructed trend suggests that there were some 361,000 Timucuan-speakers between 1525 and 1528 and that there had been about 722,000 of them prior to 1519. The last figure can be compared with the estimate of 749,407 people who could have consumed 500 grams of meat daily in aboriginal Florida, according to an earlier estimate (table 19). Even if the Calusa numbered 100,000 and the Apalachee another 100,000, a Florida total population of 922,000 individuals would have been within the environmental human-life-sustaining capacity of the area. The differences between estimates reached on quite different bases are so large as to dismay a modern demographer accustomed to dealing only with modern census enumerations. Still, they are mutually consistent enough to suggest to the historic demographer that they lie within the correct order of magnitude.[3] The mutual consistency is also great enough to indicate that previously published estimates of the number of aboriginal Native Americans in Florida have definitely not been of the correct order of magnitude.

The methodological reasons for the gross underestimates of aboriginal population previously published appear from the depopulation trend reconstructed in figure 4. Historians and anthropologists have typically based their estimates of "aboriginal" numbers on population reports from the seventeenth century. As the figure 4 depopulation trend indicates, Colonial Florida began the seventeenth century with perhaps 70,000 to 75,000 Timucuan-speakers. Most of them had never been counted, however, because the Franciscan missionary program was then just beginning to expand inland beyond the Atlantic coastal chiefdoms. By the time the Christian conversion program achieved any significant amount of success, the Timucuan-speaking population had been halved by the bubonic plague (between 1613 and 1617). If there were about 36,750 Timucuan-speakers left alive in 1618, then the 8,000 the Franciscans claimed as converts amounted to some 21.77 percent of the total. Inasmuch as the missionaries never reached some chiefdoms, their conversion rate was considerably higher among the Saturiwa, Potano, Yustega, and Utina among whom they did work. In other words, the earlier published estimates of total Florida or Timucuan aboriginal population are quite consistent with post-1617 numbers indicated by the figure 4 depopulation trend. Previously published estimates of Florida's aboriginal population all suffered from the same basic methodological defect. They treated seventeenth-century Colonial population counts as reflecting numbers before the Columbian

Exchange. They failed to take into account the sixteenth-century epidemiology of Florida's Native Americans, so they ignored a whole series of decisive demographic events that caused wholesale human mortality. Thus the authors of these estimates postulated quite erroneously low figures for pre-Columbian or early sixteenth-century Native American population magnitudes.

NOTES

1. By drawing graph lines from population count to count, through time, Cook and Borah (*Essays*, 1971, pp. 80 – 81; fig. 1 and 2) effectively mask the decisive impact of epidemic mortality. By converting population counts into their logarithms, Cook and Borah (p. 84, fig. 3; p. 86, fig. 4; p. 88, fig. 5) even more effectively masked the jerkiness that characterized the process of Native American depopulation in Central Mexico. It is possible for a historic demographer to distort reality in the attempt to placate modern demographers by employing inappropriate statistical techniques. The methodological truth is that because modern demographers have not had to analyze populations suffering massive mortality but not enumerated, they have had little occasion to develop tools for such analyses.

2. Cook and Borah, *Essays*, 1971, vol. I, pp. 78 – 79.

3. The difference between the estimated human sustenance capacity of Florida's annual protein supply of 749,407 and 922,000 is about 172,593 persons. That is about 18.7 percent, about three times larger than the 5.8 percent error that Cook and Borah (*Essays*, 1971, vol. I, pp. 74 – 75) characterized as "entirely satisfactory" when studying sixteenth- and seventeenth-century populations.

 *Four*

Archaeological Test Cases

We have become so accustomed to rely upon the testimony of word-written records that we lose sight of the fact that words are but thought symbols, ideaphones, and ideagraphs, and that written records may be erroneous and incomplete while material objects may convey clearer meanings by which a much more accurate knowledge may be gained (Parker 1907:467).

LOWER MISSISSIPPI VALLEY

The archaeological sample used in this analysis is a linear area, approximately 600 km long, that extends from Memphis, Tennessee south to Iberville Parish, Louisiana (Figure 6). Besides Quaternary-Age surfaces of the Natchez Bluffs the sample is restricted to Holocene floodplain surfaces and near surfaces of the St. Francis Lowlands, Yazoo Basin, and Taensa Basin. In addition to the Mississippi River, a number of major drainages flow through the area in a general north-south direction.

The area is one of low elevation, characterized by older ridges, swales, abandoned meander belts, oxbow lakes, active natural levees, and backwater swamps (Fisk 1944; Saucier 1974). Levee developments are extensive along drainages, channeling the direction of normal tributary flow parallel to the main channel of the Mississippi. Because flooding has always been a persistent problem in this section of the valley, most of the human habitation throughout the Holocene has occurred along the levees, which are topographic high areas of the landscape.

Historical Aboriginal Population

Documentation of aboriginal populations within the study area began with the

42

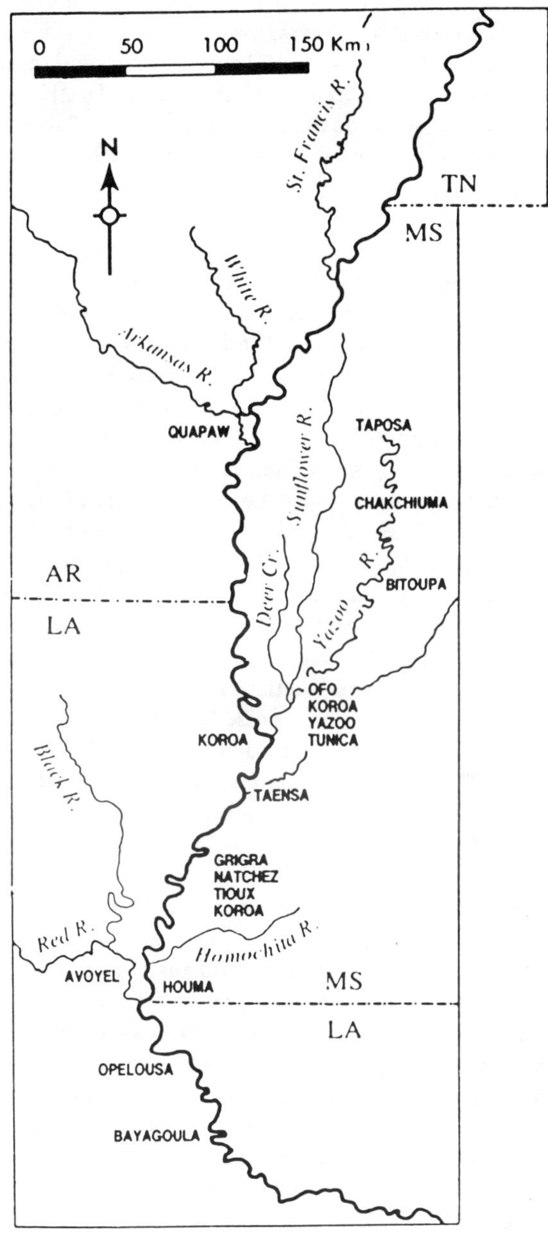

Figure 6. Study Area, Lower Mississippi Valley

De Soto *entrada* in the spring of 1541, when he spent approximately six weeks in the valley before moving west into Texas (Swanton 1939). The French period in the Lower Mississippi Valley began in 1673 with the explorations of Marquette and Jolliet (Shea 1903). The explorations of La Salle and Tonti in 1682 (Kellogg 1917) marked the beginning of consistent documentation of aboriginal groups. Although French settlement along the coast dated to 1699 (Biloxi Bay), permanent French settlements in the Valley occurred roughly a decade later (Swanton 1911).

Aboriginal populations did not persist long after the beginning of European colonization and settlement. Some groups disappeared completely, and even those who survived seemed to have been quite unstable (I. Brown 1985; Davis 1984; Giardino 1984; Swanton 1911). Abandoment, relocation, or amalgamation were frequent descriptions. As a consequence of their early disappearance, anthropologists have based their knowledge of aboriginal groups largely on Spanish and French documents. Swanton (1911, 1928) was responsible for synthesizing and analyzing the major French sources.

For the lower valley, Swanton places the ethnographic present in 1699, the date coincident with the Biloxi colony. According to his map (1911), in 1699 at least eighteen tribal groups were located along the Mississippi between the Yazoo Basin and New Orleans (Figure 6). North of the Yazoo, the valley was largely unoccupied except for the Chickasaw, who lived inland, and north of the study area, on the east side of the river. Although total tribal count could easily give the impression of a sizable population in the valley, this is not the case. Some groups identified in Figure 6 have passed into history only as a name; and the largest population, the Natchez, had no more than 1500 warriors (Swanton 1911). The Natchez War in 1730 marked the terminus of aboriginal systems and the final dispersion of Natchez, as well as other groups.

Significance of the Test Case

The archaeological analysis from the Lower Mississippi Valley is the first systematic test of Dobyns's sixteenth-century disease hypothesis. Since Dobyns (1983) bases his arguments on historical analyses from Florida, a study from the Southeast is crucial for confirming or disconfirming his position. If the lower valley record supports Dobyns's position, the case in favor of the general hypothesis is greatly strengthened. Although evidence for a seventeenth-century collapse does not necessarily exclude disease as causal, the case is simply not as strong. Since sustained European presence began in the late seventeenth century, other variables, including warfare and stress, could be contributing to trends in population; thus, regardless of outcome, the lower valley test is crucial to the general issue.

In addition, the test may help clarify archaeological treatment of the contact period in the lower valley. Although archaeologists interested in this region have entertained discussions of disease and population collapse, there are logical contradictions that make it difficult to determine the timing and nature of demographic change. Before presenting specific hypotheses to be tested, traditional approaches must be discussed.

Lower valley archaeologists have defined De Soto's arrival in 1541 (Bourne 1904) as the beginning of history, but these contacts were irregular and short-lived. As a consequence they were

> a false dawn. . . . These were not enduring affairs, and contact was soon broken, so that the area again receded into the realm of the unknown until European contact was reestablished and the historic period truly begun at the conclusion of the seventeenth century (Williams and Brain 1983:381).

Several cascading consequences have followed from this perspective. The 132 years that separate Spanish from French contact are a vague and largely undifferentiated interim, defined as the protohistoric (Morse and Morse 1983). Significant aboriginal change from Europeans was a late seventeenth-century process that began with French colonization, settlement, and documentation (Brain 1980; Brown 1985; Morse and Morse 1983; Phillips 1970; Williams 1980; Williams and Brain 1983).

Beginning with Collins (1927) and Ford (1936, 1961), the direct historical approach has guided the location and identification of archaeological sites (Brain 1975a, 1980; Hudson et al. 1985; Klinger 1975–77; Morse 1981). Ian Brown's recent work (1985) in the Natchez area is a good example. Although he tested and analyzed a number of deposits from later time periods, the final sample was weighted in favor of the protohistoric. "Sites were chosen on the basis of having protohistoric/historic materials"(1985:188). While it is reasonably certain that most of the sites from the French period are known (Brain 1970, 1973, 1975b, 1980; Brown 1975, 1979, 1985; Ford 1936, 1961; Neitzel 1965), the same statement cannot be made for prehistoric sites or even those occupied in 1541.

Furthermore, the use of the direct historical approach has led to a reliance on documents to reconstruct historic and prehistoric systems (Davis 1984; Ford and Willey 1941; Morse and Morse 1983). According to Griffin:

> The Mississippi Period was in full bloom at the time of the De Soto *entrada* into the Southeast, and at the time of other intermittent Spanish and French contacts in this area. We can, therefore, utilize with considerable confidence the information obtained from these chronicles and from the late seventeenth and eighteenth century European explorers . . . for the reconstruction of the social structure as it existed in the Mississippi Period in the Southeast (1952:362).

The Natchez are most significant in this regard. Because the Natchez persisted longer than many other, perhaps smaller, groups, there are a number of quite good eighteenth-century descriptions of their culture (Le Page du Pratz 1975; Swanton 1911). In addition, because the Natchez social system was seemingly based on ranks, it has become incorporated into the chiefdom model (Service 1962). This model has been used to describe ranked societies in the Southeast in both prehistoric and historical periods. (Davis 1984; Gibson 1973, 1980; Steponaitis 1978). The question of whether the Natchez system is a relevant analogue depends on whether the system was stable when first described. There has been some debate on this issue.

Among the Natchez, the primary class division was between nobility and Stinkards or commoners. Nobility, in turn, was comprised of three hierarchical classes: Suns, Nobles and Honored (Swanton 1911). While Suns provided the political and religious leaders—Tatooed Serpent and Great Sun—Stinkards made tribute payments to the nobility. A form of redistribution was accomplished through feasts, which occurred at regular intervals.

Although classes were permanent, marriage patterns were exogamous, creating an asymetrical structure in favor of nobility. Descriptions of the structure point to a progressive loss of commoners, which would have completely undermined the structure of the chiefdom.

Swanton (1911) thought the asymetrical structure was a social curiosity. When Hart reanalyzed the structure, he found it to be a "biological impossibility" (1943:374), headed toward a crisis if not a total collapse. Quimby (1946) was more generous in his analysis. He suggested that the Natchez practice of absorbing other native people into the social system at the rank of Stinkard compensated for loss of Stinkards through marriage. Given this practice, he concluded that the structure could persist for seven generations. Brain rooted Natchez classes in the prehistory of the Lower Mississippi Valley but suggested that exogamous marriages and the asymetrical structure were "adjustments to a new situation" (1971:221) that postdated De Soto. A grossly reduced population forced Natchez to absorb outsiders into their system with exogamous marriages providing the integrating mechanism. Despite differences in interpretation, it is clear that eighteenth-century Natchez social structure was in a state of flux quite possibly due to earlier population loss.

While assuming continuity, there are extensive discussions of discontinuity. Brain (1978:358) has suggested that during the French period "the great aboriginal climax witnessed by De Soto had passed, and the cultural inventory of the indigenous tribes was a poor reflection." Phillips's archaeological and historical research is primarily responsible for this perspective. (Phillips, Ford, and Griffin 1951). After comparing Spanish and French documents, Phillips concludes that aboriginal populations and cultural adaptations of the French period

. . . are almost revolutionary in their nature and extent. They are not only in excess of the normal development; changes that might take place in a century and a half, but they are in the wrong direction, regressive rather than developmental (Phillips, Ford, and Griffin 1951:419).

According to Phillips, attrition of population was the most dramatic aboriginal change. Sometime between 1541 and 1682, Phillips estimated a population loss "amounting to at least eighty percent" (Phillips, Ford, and Griffin 1951:419). As population fell precipitously, settlement structure and political institutions also changed. By the late seventeenth century, there were not only fewer settlements, but those that persisted were infrequently associated with mounds. Simultaneously, complex political structures (chiefdoms) described in the De Soto chronicles gave way to decentralization and political equality of cultural units.

Since Phillips's convincing interpretations, other archaeologists (for example, Brain 1978, 1980; Ford 1961; Morse and Morse 1983) have adopted a perspective that recognizes significant disruptions of aboriginal population. There is no consensus, however, regarding either the timing or cause of the disruption. While some researchers (for example, Brain 1978; Williams and Brain 1983) think that the population decline began prior to De Soto, Ford (1961), like Phillips, placed its onset sometime between the Spanish and French periods.

The vagueness in terms of time is also expressed in terms of causes of the loss. As early as 1911, Swanton argued that the Natchez decline was due to both warfare and disease:

What actually did destroy, or very nearly decimate the Natchez nation was the attrition of numberless encounters with other Indians, losses in the swamp from sickness and exposure, and epidemics which would have reduced them in any event, with or without warfare (1911:248).

Phillips's perspective is somewhat different (Phillips, Ford, and Griffin 1951) from Swanton's. He placed the origin of disease contact, especially that of smallpox, as a phenomenon of the French period. If disease was a late introduction, then warfare caused the massive loss of population. Since, during the eighteenth century, the Chickasaw were relatively intact and were frequently described as the "Iroquois of the South, the villains responsible for every calamity" (Phillips, Ford, and Griffin 1951:420). Phillips, therefore, suggests that the Chickasaw caused the catastrophic decline.

Milner (1980) and Brain (1980) disagree with Phillips. Milner suggests that disease played a significant role in the decline of southeastern aboriginal populations prior to the French period. Brain (1980) makes an even stronger point, stating that disease was the earliest European introduction and was responsible for massive depopulation episodes prior to sustained European presence:

> The European had many advantages over native aborigines of North America. One advantage, unknown to the participants at the time, was a biological constitution that withstood the new environment with relatively little stress and at the same time contributed diseases which were virulent, epidemic, and all too often fatal to the Indian. Thus, during the protohistoric period, before most Indians had even seen a white man, vast populations were wiped out, and any social, political, or other developments (and these were considerable as De Soto found at great expense) that might have withstood some of the European threat were lost with them. The European then, found only "inferior" cultures when he finally came to exploit and colonize North America (1980:270).

To recapitulate, the test case is significant for two specific reasons: It considers Dobyns's hypothesis in a region where the hypothesis was developed initially, and it may help resolve some of the ambiguities that pervade archaeological treatment of the record of European contact in the lower valley. While archaeologists recognize that the De Soto *entrada* ushered in history in the Lower Mississippi Valley, they equate European contact and its attendant changes with sustained European presence which began with French exploration in the late seventeenth century. This perspective allows archaeologists to make extensive use of documentary evidence. The question is whether such evidence describes populations essentially unaltered by Europeans or in the process of adjusting to catastrophic decline from disease. Only by separating archaeology and history and assessing the archaeological record of population collapse can this question be answered.

If the De Soto *entrada* was, indeed, a "false dawn," archaeological analyses should demonstrate stability of population until French colonization and settlement. If, on the other hand, the De Soto *entrada* marks the terminus of aboriginal population size and distribution, then significant changes in the nature and distribution of settlements ought to precede the late seventeenth century. Moreover, the timing of the collapse has implications for its cause. If the collapse predates sustained European presence in the valley, then Dobyns's idea about infectious disease is most likely correct. If the collapse occurs during the French period, then a combination of factors including both warfare and disease are probably responsible.

I frame alternative views into two hypotheses for testing against archaeological and historical records:

Hypothesis 1 (H1) states: Although European contact begins with De Soto in the lower valley, aboriginal collapse dates to the late seventeenth century and thus coincides with French colonization and settlement. The cause of the decline is a combination of factors including warfare and disease.

Hypothesis 2 (H2) states: Aboriginal collapse is a sixteenth-century event that occurs simultaneously with the earliest documentation in the lower valley. By the time of French colonization, aboriginal populations are drastically reduced. The timing of the event implicates infectious disease as causal in the collapse.

Late Mississippi Period Chronologies

As employed in this work, *Mississippi* refers to the period, and *Mississippian* refers to one cultural tradition of the Lower Mississippi Valley during that period. There are several integrative schemes for the Late Mississippi period in the Lower Mississippi Valley (Table 9), largely developed from analysis of ceramics. Because ceramics have been the primary basis for ordering the record, different theories of classification (Hill and Evans 1972) have affected final outcomes. The works of Ford and Phillips offer major contrasts. Ford was the primary temporal architect of the first Lower Valley Survey (Phillips, Ford and Griffin 1951); all other integrative schemes (Phillips 1970; Willey and Phillips 1958) basically modified Ford's early work.

Ford's interest was primarily chronological, extracting time from space and form. He defined ceramic types accordingly, and ordered archaeological units

Table 9   Late Mississippi Period Chronologies, Lower Mississippi Valley

TIME (A.D.)	PHILLIPS, FORD & GRIFFIN (1951) PERIODS	PHILLIPS (1970) YAZOO BASIN PHASES	WILLIAMS & BRAIN (1983) YAZOO BASIN PHASES	MORSE & MORSE (1983) MIDDLE MISSISSIPPI PHASES	BROWN (1985) NATCHEZ BLUFFS PHASES	RAMENOFSKY PERIODS
1800						
1700						III
1600	A	RUSSELL	RUSSELL	QUAPAW	NATCHEZ	
1500			WASP LAKE	NODENA/PARKIN KENT/WALLS	EMERALD	II
1400		DEER CREEK/ LAKE GEORGE/ WASP LAKE	LAKE GEORGE		FOSTER	I
1300	B		WINTERVILLE			
1200					ANNA	
1100						
1000						

through seriations (Ford 1954, 1962; Phillips, Ford and Griffin 1951). Phillips (1958, 1970), on the other hand, had both cultural and temporal interests. Although his pottery types were basically a reworking of Ford's types, his search for a finer resolution of the record led to the use of types and varieties. Temporocultural units, phases, were established through cumulative frequency curves of ceramics, spatial discontinuities and radiocarbon dates.

Differences are readily apparent. In Ford's order, the Late Mississippi period, A-B, crosses the historic baseline and continues until French settlement. During the Late Mississippi period, the Morses suggest there are a number of phases in the St. Francis Lowlands. At least two of these phases, Kent (House 1984) and Parkin (Morse 1981), cross the De Soto border. In the most recent chronology for the Yazoo Basin, Williams and Brain (1983) separate the Wasp Lake phase as part of the protohistoric or Spanish Period phase. I. Brown's Emerald phase (1985) occupies a similar temporal position in the Natchez Bluffs area.

Although specific sequences may be correct for each area, there is no way to determine which sequence is correct for the whole region. Chronologies of Phillips, Ford, and Griffin and of the Morses, though derived from different epistomologies, do not segregate the sixteenth century. To employ their units would mean that I could not investigate the hypothesis of a sixteenth-century collapse. While Williams, Brain, and Brown separate out the sixteenth century, it cannot be assumed *a priori* that their orders apply to the entire study area. Further, since their orders treat the protohistoric temporal unit as a continuation of earlier prehistoric traditions, they are assuming some degree of continuity through the sixteenth century. Such an assumption is not possible in this work. The creation of another chronology for the entire region that has no assumptions about stability or change is a reasonable alternative.

Although disputing the temporal divisions of the latest period, archaeologists generally agree that during the Late Mississippi period the Mississippian and Plaquemine traditions were present in the lower valley. Vicksburg, Mississippi is a convenient boundary between these two: the Mississippian tradition extended north from the upper part of the Yazoo Basin, while the Plaquemine tradition extended from the southern part of the Yazoo Basin to the coast.

The Mississippian tradition of the Late Mississippi period is composed of numerous and areally distinct phases (Brain 1978; Morse and Morse 1983; Phillips 1970; Williams and Brain 1983). Subsistence was based on maize agriculture, and sedentary settlements were associated with large platform mounds. In some areas, population lived in large, fortified settlements, such as those at Nodena (Morse 1973) and Powers (Price 1978). In other areas, such as Natchez, population was more dispersed (I. Brown 1985; House 1984).

Ceramics, one of the hallmarks of the Late Mississippi period, showed a variety of forms and styles. Subglobular jars with straight or slightly outcurved rims and lug handles, and simple bowls with round bases and curved sides continued from the Early Mississippi period. New forms, including bottles, and effigy bowls or jars, miniature vessels, ladles, discs, discoidals, and rattles were added. Decorative techniques included engraving, incising, and punctating, as well as monochrome or polychrome painting. Motifs occurred on the body, rim, and lip of vessels and included types such as Parkin Punctated, Barton Incised, Leland Incised, Rhodes Incised, Kent Incised, Ranch Incised, Avenue Polychrome and Bell Plain (Phillips 1970; Phillips, Ford, and Griffin 1951).

Mississippi period traits, not specifically limited to the Late Mississippi period, included shell tempered ceramics, willow leaf or half willow leaf projectile points with flat bases, thumbnail scrapers, and square button style beads (Morse and Morse 1983; Phillips, Ford, and Griffin 1951; Williams 1980).

The settlement pattern of some phases may have been hierarchically organized, but this was not a consistent feature of all phases. In the St. Francis Lowlands, Klinger (1975–1977) and Morse (1981) have suggested two different types of settlement hierarchies to account for settlement distribution during the Late Mississippi period. Klinger's model included five settlement types that ranged from specialized ceremonial centers (Parkin) to farmsteads of less than half a hectare. Morse's model, similar to that proposed by Flannery for the Formative in Mesoamerica, included four settlement types. The Parkin site was the major ceremonial center and occupied a strategic location during the Parkin phase. Small centers were removed from Parkin at regular intervals, and in between these centers were villages of two hectares or less. Based on a survey of the area, Morse suggested that there were no isolated farmsteads during the phase. In contrast to both Morse and Klinger, House (1984) suggested that the settlement pattern of the Kent phase was not hierarchically organized. If House is correct, then the variability between adjacent areas was, indeed, impressive.

In addition to a variable settlement pattern, archaeologists (Brain 1978; Brown and Brain 1983; Morse and Morse 1983; Phillips, Ford and Griffin 1951) have suggested that the distribution of population may have changed during the latest prehistoric period. Populations were relocating into fewer but larger settlements away from the main channel of the Mississippi.

Although Quimby (1951) was the first to define traits of the Plaquemine tradition, it had been known for some time in the archaeology of the Lower Mississippi Valley (Griffin 1946a). Like Mississippian, Plaquemine was associated with platform mounds; and settlements may have been organized into some sort of hierarchy. Also, like Mississippian, ceramics were one of best documented features of the tradition. Plaquemine ceramics were clay- or grog-tempered, and included such types as Addis Plain (Baytown Plain var. Addis), Evansville Punctated, Plaquemine Brushed, L'eau Noire Incised, Medora Incised, Fatherland Incised (Leland Incised var. Fatherland), Coles Creek Incised, Manchac Incised (Mazique Incised var. Manchac) (Phillips 1970;

Quimby 1951). Incision was a very common decorative technique in Plaquemine ceramics, and motifs included whorls, swastikas, and geometric designs applied to the body, lip, and rim of a wide variety of vessel shapes. Dominant vessel forms were carinated bowls, beakers, and jars with slightly constricted necks and outflaring rims.

Archaeologists have viewed the Plaquemine tradition as an indigenous lower valley culture that developed out of Coles Creek with the addition of Mississippian traits. Brain (1978), in fact, defined Plaquemine as a "Mississippianized Coles Creek." Beck (1981) has recently challenged this opinion, suggesting that Plaquemine was not a stylistically separate tradition, but a generalized subsistence strategy associated with sedentary settlements. Based on significant statistical correlations between site location and soil types, she contended that the change from a generalized to specialized, or maize-based, subsistence, did not occur until sometime after 1400.

In summary, although there is no consistently applied chronology of the Late Mississippi period for the entire study area, archaeologists generally agree that from roughly A.D. 1400 to 1700, Mississippian and Plaquemine traditions were present in the lower alluvial valley. They defined Mississippian by its stylistic motifs of shell tempered ceramics. Population distribution was variable, ranging from large, fortified and nucleated settlements to dispersed farmsteads. Many settlements were associated with platform mounds. Plaquemine, also defined by sedentary settlements and platform mounds, was distinct from Mississippian tradition because of clay- or grog-tempered ceramics.

Alternative Chronology

I have developed a new chronology (Table 9) that crosses into historical periods but does not prejudge the nature of changes that occur in those periods. Instead, I shall compare demographic indicators of population between temporal units to define whether or not populations catastrophically declined in the sixteenth century.

I employed radiocarbon assays, occurrence seriations of pottery and analysis of European trade goods, to assign sixty-six components to one of my three chronological periods. (See Appendix A for detailed discussion of orders). Radiocarbon dates were of limited utility in developing the chronology. Since only three of sixty-six components had absolute dates (Appendix A, Table 57), I placed greatest weight on the two relative methods.

Forty-nine components were ordered in one of the occurrence seriations; these were largely a reanalysis of Ford's seriations (Phillips, Ford, and Griffin 1951). After subdividing the region into five areas defined by Ford—St. Francis Lowlands, Memphis, Lower Arkansas, Upper Sunflower, and Yazoo Basin (Appendix A, Figure 18)—I employed Mississippi period types defined by Phillips, Ford, and Griffin.

Seventeen components had European material, but I had to limit my temporal analysis to sixteen, because the specific composition of the European assemblage from Haynes Bluff has not been reported. Of the seventeen components, five were also ordered by one of the seriations. Based on a new classification of European material, I analyzed European assemblages qualitatively because counts of individual European items were inconsistently reported in the literature. Finally, I employed dates from documents to determine whether archaeological assignments of components were consistent with the designations from the historical record.

To counteract the imprecision in the temporal dimension, I created minimum, mean, and maximum estimates of each period (Table 10) to bracket period durations. This control afforded three different temporal measures against which changes in settlement counts could be judged. Since settlement counts were the only demographic indicator available in this part of the valley, the control was of some importance.

Table 10   Length of Archaeological Periods in the Lower Mississippi Valley

	Period Length (A.D.)			Period Duration (Years)		
Period	Minimum	Mean	Maximum	Minimum	Mean	Maximum
III	1700–1730	1700–1750	1700–1764	30	50	64
II	1541–1673	1541–1682	1541–1699	132	141	158
I	1500–1540	1400–1540	1000–1540	40	140	540

Period I is the terminal prehistoric time unit in this chronology (Table 11). Based on seriations, I assigned forty-nine components to this period. Although there are twenty-four dates for the period, only two components with absolute dates (Upper Nodena and Lake George) are ordered by one of the seriations. In all three temporal models, the terminal date of Period I is 1540, immediately before De Soto's entry into the region, but origin dates vary. For the minimum estimate, I employed Morse's origin date (1500) for the Parkin phase (1981). Phillips's 1970 origin date for the Late Mississippi period is employed in the mean estimate (1400) and for the maximum estimate, Phillips' 1970 date for the Mississippi period is used (1000). While certain pottery types (for example, Neeley's Ferry Plain, Bell Plain, Barton Incised, and Parkin Punctated) occur throughout the period, other pottery types (for example, Owens Punctated, Avenue Polychrome, Rhodes Incised, Ranch Incised, Kent Incised, and Vernon Paul Applique) are more spatially restricted and have shorter durations. No European material is reported for the period.

Period II, coincides with Spanish and French exploration of the Lower Mississippi Valley, and begins with the De Soto *entrada* of 1541. The minimum

Table 11   Characteristics of Chronological Periods in the Lower Mississippi Valley

PERIOD I

Radiocarbon Dates:	27 (See Appendix A, Table 57)
Minimum Time Range:	A.D. 1500–1540
Mean Time Range:	A.D. 1400–1540
Maximum Time Range:	A.D. 1000–1540
Ceramics:	Shell tempered types including Neeley's Ferry Plain, Bell Plain, Barton Incised, Parkin Punctated, Kent Incised, Rhodes Incised, Ranch Incised, Vernon Paul Applique, Avenue Polychrome, Owens Punctated.
European Trade:	Absent
Components:	49 identified by seriations (Appendix A, Tables 56, 61–66)

PERIOD II

Radiocarbon Dates:	0
Minimum Time Range:	A.D. 1541–1673
Mean Time Range:	A.D. 1541–1682
Maximum Time Range:	A.D. 1541–1699
European Trade:	Present; Clarksdale Bells, Glass Trade Beads.
Components: (n = 10)	Satartia, Clay Hill, Parkin, Wallace, Menard, Oliver, Clarksdale, Haynes Bluff, Rice, Dead Oak.

PERIOD III

Radiocarbon Dates:	0
Minimum Time Range:	A.D. 1700–1730
Mean Time Range:	A.D. 1700–1750
Maximum Time Range:	A.D. 1700–1764
Ceramics:	Not well known.
European Trade:	All classes of European function present.
Components: (n = 7)	Lockgard, Portland, Fatherland, Bayou Goula, Trudeau, Greenfield, Thoroughbred

estimate of period duration covers the time between the exploration of De Soto and that of Marquette and Jolliet (1541–1673). While the mean estimate extends from the De Soto baseline to the first La Salle exploration (1541–1682), the maximum estimate lasts until the beginning of French colonization (1541–1699). During this period, limited quantities of European materials, "Clarksdale" bells and glass trade beads, are found. Pottery is not well reported. Ten components, four of which are ordered by seriations, are assigned to Period II.

Period III coincides with French colonization and settlement and is represented by seven components. European products from this period are fundamentally different from those of Period II. All types of metal products as well as European crockery, glass bottles, and quantities of trade beads are present in aboriginal assemblages. Although period duration varies from thirty to sixty-four years, all three temporal models employ the same origin date, A.D. 1700. The minimum estimate (1700–1730) terminates with the Natchez War; the mean estimate (1700–1750) terminates in the middle of the century, and the maximum estimate (1700–1764) terminates with the abandonment of the Tunica settlement of Trudeau.

This chronology is superficially similar to some other chronologies in that my Period II occupies the same temporal position as I. Brown's (1985) Emerald phase and Williams and Brain's (1983) Wasp Lake phase. Although it would be convenient to treat the new unit as the protohistoric expression of the Late Mississippi period, I choose not to do so because of the use of either term implies a kind of continuity with earlier expressions that may not be justified. If examination of the record reveals catastrophic change in population beginning with Period III, then these attributions are justified. If, however, catastrophic population loss is an event of Period II, then terms that imply continuity in population or culture must be seriously questioned.

To recapitulate, Period I marks the terminus of the aboriginal prehistoric record, ending just before De Soto enters the valley. Period II, the first historical period, begins with the De Soto *entrada* and continues through French exploration of the region. While European material is not reported for any Period I site, European bells and glass trade beads are present at Period II sites. Period III dates to the eighteenth century and coincides with French settlement in the valley. The aboriginal assemblages of European material from Period III are functionally more diversified than those from Period II. Finally, the empirical evidence suggests that European contact begins during Period II. Whether this catastrophic decline begins with Period II will be determined by analysis of aboriginal population.

Analysis of Population Change

Settlement counts (S_c), the most biased of archaeological estimators, are the only archaeological measure of population available in the Lower Mississippi Valley. I cannot, therefore, employ archaeological formulas of population developed in Chapter 3 to estimate population change in the region. I limit analysis to consideration of S_c and to changing distributions of settlements. Although I attempt to make use of counts to assess hypotheses regarding the initiation of collapse, biases implicit in the measurement of S_c are expected to produce ambiguous results (see Appendix A, Table 70 for settlement list).

SETTLEMENT COUNTS (S_c) Table 12 summarizes changes in S_c across temporal units. Actual counts in column 2 (n = 66) are higher than those summarized on Table 6. This difference is because some settlements have multiple occupations. Presented in subsequent columns are counts normalized to a standard period duration.

Table 12   Lower Mississippi Valley Settlement Counts and [$S_c/(T/100)$]

| Raw | | Adjusted Counts [$S_c/(T/100)$] | | | | | |
Period	Counts	Minimum	S_c	Mean	S_c	Maximum	S_c
III	7	0.3	23.3	0.5	14.0	0.6	11.6
II	10	1.3	7.5	1.4	7.1	1.6	6.3
I	49	0.4	123.0	1.4	35.0	5.4	9.1

The actual mathematics of adjusting counts are straight forward. A minimum estimate of a period duration of 200 is normalized to 2 when 200 is divided by the temporal term 100. This figure is then divided into the actual settlement count for that period. For instance, a settlement count of 10 becomes a normalized count of 5 in the above example.

Despite differences in the temporal dimension, [$S_c/(T/100)$] shows similar changes in direction. (See Figure 7 for graphical display of settlement trends.) Between Periods I and II, counts precipitously decrease, followed by a slight increase between Periods II and III. Before evaluating these trends, biases due to archaeological sampling and residental instability must be considered.

As described previously, prehistoric and historic records have not been sampled equally. The importance of ethnohistory, archaeological reliance on the direct historical approach, and judgmental sampling of the prehistoric

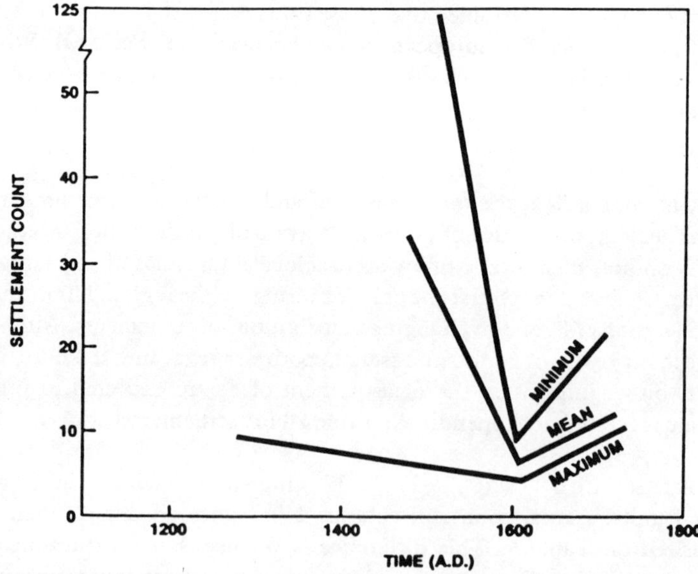

Figure 7. [$S_c/(T/100)$] Measured against Estimates of Period Duration

record have skewed archaeological knowledge in favor of historic periods. Consequently, archaeologists are more likely to have identified a larger fraction of aboriginal settlements occupied during Periods II and III than those of Period I. This known bias should inflate historic counts relative to prehistoric counts.

The question of residential instability needs to be considered. Although there is considerable evidence that groups were abandoning and relocating villages by the late seventeenth century, the onset of this pattern is not reliably placed in time. I. Brown's recent work in the Natchez Bluff area (1982, 1985), however, suggests a pre-French origin.

Relying heavily on historical documents, I. Brown (1985) explicitly attempted to locate specific settlements that the Grigra and other groups occupied during the late seventeenth and early eighteenth centuries. These attempts were unsuccessful, not because the documents were in error regarding the locations of settlements, but because Brown assumed continuity of occupation throughout the temporal period. I. Brown (1985) stated that his assumption was wrong and suggested that other populations had settled and abandoned the Natchez area before the eighteenth-century settlements of the Grigra.

The pattern of abandonment and relocation is well established by the late seventeenth century, the end of Period II. In 1682, La Salle recorded four Quapaw villages at the mouth of the Arkansas River. Between 1690 and 1700, two of these villages were abandoned, one had moved downriver, and a new hybrid community was founded (Kellogg 1917). Between 1698 and 1700, the Tunica resided in the Yazoo Basin. Between 1706 and 1731, they migrated downriver, and either settled with or replaced the Houma at one of the latter's villages. After 1731, the Tunica established residence at Trudeau, located at the mouth of the Red River (Brain 1975b). Between 1699 and 1706, three different groups were living with the Bayagoula (Quimby 1957), and between 1720 and 1730, remnants of the populations of Yazoo, and Tioux were absorbed by the Natchez.

These data suggest that from the latter part of Period II through Period III aboriginal populations of the Lower Mississippi Valley were continually shifting residences. Even though the origin of the movement cannot be identified, it seems probable that French exploration does not mark the origin of the pattern, but rather, the documentation of a preexisting pattern.

The effects of archaeological emphasis on historic period settlements and instability of population should lead to a situation in which S_c steadily increases during Periods II and III. Since between Period I and II counts decrease rather than increase and since the pattern of change is comparable in all temporal models, it is reasonable to assume that the change represents catastrophic population loss that begins with Spanish contact. The question is whether the suggested increase between Periods II and III represents a demographic recovery or is a reflection of sampling and cultural bias. As described below, available information suggests that the increase in counts is a function of bias, not of population increase.

Of the seven Period III settlements, five were new communities (Portland, Lockgard, Trudeau, Greenfield, Thoroughbred) with founding dates ranging from 1708 to 1731. The two other communities (Fatherland and Bayou Goula) were continuations of settlements from earlier periods; amalgamation of smaller remnant groups in part explained the survival of both. None of the seven communities persisted for the maximum duration of Period III (1700–1764). By 1764, Trudeau was the only surviving community, but Trudeau was not founded until 1731.

In summary, the decrease in $[S_c/(T/100)]$ between Periods I and II suggests a precipitous population decline that predates French settlement of the valley. While Period III counts suggest a population increase, counts cannot be taken at face value. In fact, while settlement counts are increasing, population may be declining.

SETTLEMENT DISTRIBUTION   Changes in the distribution of settlements across the three temporal periods demonstrate progressive downriver movement. In Period I, all counties on both sides of the Mississippi River from Memphis through the Yazoo Basin are occupied (Figure 8A). During Period II, populations abandon the area north of the southern end of the Yazoo Basin; and northern settlements that persist are spatially discontinuous (Figure 8B). By Period III, except for two new settlements at the mouth of the Yazoo River, the northern part of the valley is unoccupied (Figure 8C). Population has migrated south, clustering into settlements in the vicinity of Fatherland and Bayou Goula.

CONCLUSIONS   I expected archaeological analysis of population change in the Lower Mississippi Valley to produce ambiguous results regarding the initiation of aboriginal collapse. Settlement counts were the only archaeological measure of population, and counts were extremely biased in favor of the historic periods. Despite these problems, data were not ambiguous, and conclusions were, in fact, strengthened because the initial direction of change so completely contradicted expectations.

As demonstrated by the changes in settlement counts, aboriginal collapse did not begin with sustained French presence in the valley, but rather with the De Soto *entrada* more than 150 years earlier. Consequently, I conclude that the beginning of European contact also marks the onset of aboriginal population loss. Several important consequences follow from this conclusion.

Although the De Soto chronicles may describe pristine populations, French documents do not. The latter are important descriptions of populations in the process of adapting to new environmental conditions, especially catastrophic reduction of people. As suggested by Phillips (Phillips, Ford and Griffin 1951), a comparison of Spanish and French sources may prove very fruitful in determining the nature and direction of these changes.

Furthermore, since the loss predates sustained European presence, infectious disease is causal. This conclusion, in turn, supports Dobyns's hypothesis of the sixteenth century as the disease century in the Southeast.

There are, however, several problems with the archaeological data. While I have argued that the normalized increase in settlement counts of the eighteenth century, Period III, is a function of sampling bias rather than of recovery of population, the archaeological record is insufficient for indicating how population is behaving relative to the increase in counts. Fortunately, there are eighteenth-century census records for aboriginal populations; and these records can be analyzed to determine whether or not the loss, beginning with the De Soto *entrada*, continues into the period of French settlement.

Lower Mississippi Valley History, 1541–1764

In this section, I shall review European exploration and colonization, aboriginal settlement counts and relocation, and aboriginal population estimates. Following these discussions, I shall consider epidemic history of the Southeast.

EUROPEAN EXPLORATION AND COLONIZATION   Spain was the first European nation to explore and to attempt colonization of the Southeast in general. The primary motive in these ventures was the acquisition of wealth. Since native populations had largely disappeared from the Spanish West Indies by 1510, trafficking in aboriginal human populations was the earliest southeastern resource to be exploited (Sauer 1971) (Table 13). Attempts at colonization began shortly thereafter; in 1526, Lucas Vasquez de Ayllon with about 500 settlers established a colony near Winyah Bay, South Carolina. Within six months, the colony had failed; and the 150 survivors returned to the West Indies (Hudson 1976).

The Panifilo de Navaez and Cabeza de Vaca expedition (1527–1536) was the first major Spanish attempt at inland exploration from the west coast of Florida. The party, including 400 men and some 150 horses, explored north from Tampa Bay. Indian resistance was so great that the party never traveled farther inland than northwest Florida. Survivors were forced back to the coast where barges were built in hopes of following the Gulf coast to Mexico. While traveling west, the expedition made a brief foray up the Mississippi delta; and by 1528, ninety survivors, including Cabeza de Vaca, had reached Galveston Bay. For the next six years, survivors lived among native populations in east Texas; by 1536, only four of the original 400 were still alive (Fernandez 1975; Sauer 1971).

The De Soto *entrada*, initially comprised of approximately 600 men, 4 or 5 women, 200 horses and 2500 swine (Swanton 1939), was not only the first

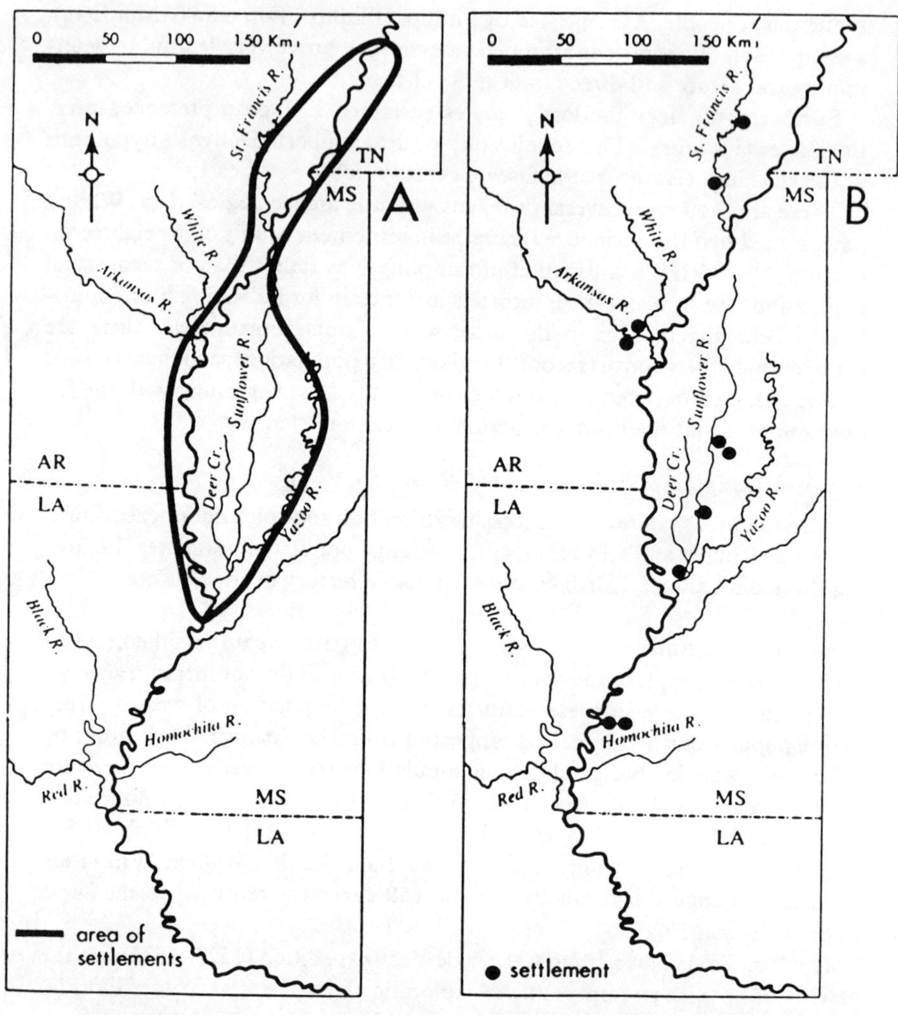

successful inland exploration of much of the Southeast, but also recorded the
first contact in the Lower Mississippi Valley. During the four-year journey
(1539–1543), the party traveled a circuitous route through parts of west Florida, the Carolinas, Tennessee, Alabama, Louisiana, Mississippi, Arkansas, and
Texas (Hudson et al. 1985; Swanton 1939). In May 1541, they reached the
Lower Mississippi Valley, somewhere between the Yazoo and Sunflower drainages. After approximately six weeks, they pushed into Arkansas and then
turned south crossing into Louisiana before reaching Texas. Four narratives by
the Gentleman of Elvas, Hernandez de Biedma, Rodrigo Ranjel (Bourne 1904),

148

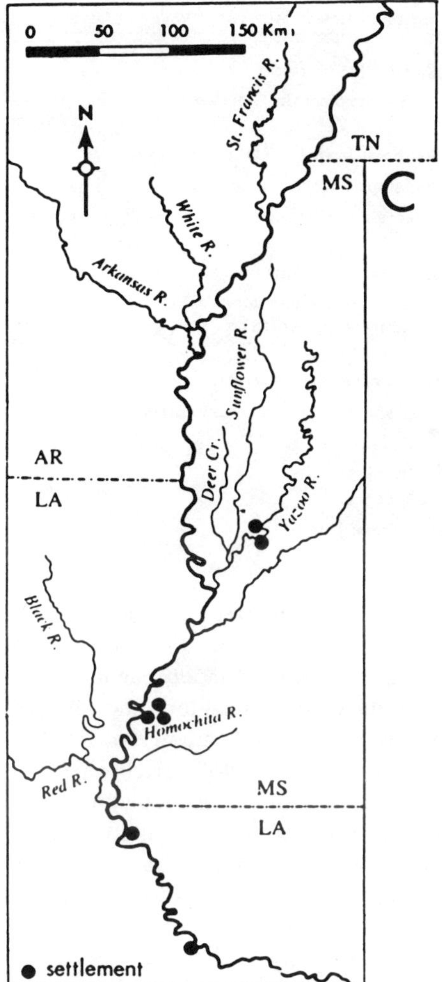

Figure 8. Distribution through Time of Settlements in the Lower Mississippi Valley

and Garcilaso de la Vega, El Inca (Varner and Varner 1951) described the expedition. According to Bourne (1904) and Swanton (1939), the first three chroniclers were the most reliable sources since they were part of the expedition. El Inca was not part of the exploration, and his account was based on the account of a participant made forty years after the event.

Between the De Soto *entrada* and 1673, there were no recorded contacts of Lower Mississippi Valley populations. In that year, Marquette and Jolliet traveled down the Mississippi as far south as the Arkansas River. Although extensive notes were made, many were later lost (Nasatir 1952; Shea 1903). The

Table 13   Some Historical Events in the Southeast and Lower Mississippi Valley

1510	Spanish begin slave raids along east coast of Florida.
1527–1536	Panifilo de Navaez and Cabeza de Vaca explore the Gulf Coast from Florida to east Texas.
1539–1543	De Soto *entrada* explores the Southeast from Florida to east Texas.
1541	De Soto reaches the Lower Mississippi Valley.
1673	Father Marquette and Jolliet explore the Mississippi from its headwaters to the Arkansas River.
1679–1682	La Salle explores the Mississippi as far as its delta.
1686, 1687–1691, 1698–1699	Tonti makes three expeditions in the Lower Mississippi Valley. In 1686 he establishes a small trading post near Osotouy on the Arkansas River. In 1698, he guides French Jesuits into the valley.
1699	Iberville establishes the first French colony at Biloxi Bay.
1698–1710	French religious efforts (Recollets and Jesuits) begin among populations of the Lower Mississippi Valley.
1718	Bienville establishes New Orleans.
1718	French establish Fort Rosalie at Natchez.
1719	Fort St. Pierre established on the Yazoo River.

La Salle and Tonti expedition followed the initial French exploration by roughly ten years (Shea 1903). Their exploration had lasting effects in terms of French control of Louisiana: In the wake of their journey, independent French traders (*Coureurs de Bois*) began exploiting the region. Small forts and colonies such as La Salle's colony in east Texas founded in 1695 (Joutel 1906; Kellogg 1917) and Tonti's fort on the Arkansas River founded 1686 (Kellogg 1917) sprang up. Jesuit missionaries took up residence with native populations.

The push toward permanent French colonies in the Lower Mississippi Valley was triggered by France's desire to expand her empire in America, to increase her revenues, and to curtail British expansion from the rapidly developing colonies along the Atlantic seaboard. To these ends, Iberville established the first colony at Biloxi Bay in 1699. Although the colony persisted, existence was precarious. Given France's financial difficulties in the early eighteenth century, funds and raw materials were always in short supply. Although the colony aimed at self-sufficiency, the low population density and lack of farmers prevented attainment of that goal. Near starvation conditions prevailed more often than not (Giraud 1974).

Gradually, the situation began to change. Between 1715 and 1720, New Orleans was established and military forts began to spring up. French military requested assignment in Louisiana, and the colonial population also began to increase (Giraud 1974; Nasatir 1952). The development came too late. By 1740, French colonies had been pushed south of the Illinois River, and by 1763, France had lost her American empire.

The sequence of events of the early contact period in the Lower Mississippi Valley suggests that archaeological conclusions regarding the loss of aboriginal populations may be correct. Direct interaction with Europeans began in 1541. Although French settlement was established in the early eighteenth century, colonies did not gain a secure foothold until after 1720. As seen in the archaeological record, initial population loss may have predated French settlement by several hundred years.

ABORIGINAL CENSUS COUNTS   As described previously, Phillips (Phillips, Ford, and Griffin 1951) argued that population loss was the most dramatic aboriginal change he could identify in the archaeological and historical records of the Lower Mississippi Valley. This archaeological analysis supported Phillips's position and pointed to an initial catastrophic loss that began in the second half of the sixteenth century and continued through French colonization. By the time France had lost her political position in North America, native populations and cultural systems of the Lower Mississippi Valley were essentially extinct.

Although there were no aboriginal census counts contained in the De Soto chronicles from the Lower Mississippi Valley, the impression one receives from these narratives was that of a sizable population. The impression is entirely consistent with the known archaeological record from 1540. Between the Yazoo Basin and the St. Francis Lowlands, the region was densely populated and divided into four provinces: Quizqui, Aquixo, Casque, and Pacaha (Bourne 1904; Swanton 1939). Aquixo was the smallest province, consisting of only a single town. All other provinces were composed of two or three major towns. While building *piraguas* for the crossing of the Mississippi, Spaniards observed the warrior potential of Pacaha: ". . . about seven thousand warriors . . . with more than two hundred canoes" (Ranjel in Bourne 1904:2:137) traveled onto the river and showered the Spaniards with arrows. When the attack failed to drive the intruders away, the natives themselves withdrew.

The earliest French records described an aboriginal population of the valley that was quite different. In 1682, La Salle and Tonti encountered no resident groups between the St. Francis Lowlands and the Yazoo Basin. The Quapaw were their first aboriginal contacts, and this group lived in four villages at the mouth of the Arkansas River (Kellogg 1917; Shea 1903). Although below the Quapaw, La Salle encountered aboriginal groups such as the Taensa, Natchez, and Bayagoula, the distribution of population was not continuous.

Changes in population density or distribution match the pattern of warrior estimates summarized in Table 14. Except for the Natchez who were actively absorbing smaller remnant populations, initial estimates were low and continued to decrease throughout the eighteenth century.

Variability in Natchez estimates between 1686 and 1722 cannot possibly reflect intrinsic population growth. Although a temporal interval of 36 years is

Table 14   Warrior Counts of Some Aboriginal Groups in the Lower
Mississippi Valley[a]

Year	Natchez	Taensa	Tunica	Bayagoula	Houma	Yazoo
1682		700				
1686	1500					
1699				200–250	350	
1700		300				
1715	4000					
1716	800					
1721	2000					
1722	600					
1729	700					
1730	500					40[c]
1731	200–300					
1735	180					
1739				90–100[c]	90–100[d]	
1758			60		60[d]	15[f]
1764	150[b]					
1784					25[d]	12[f]
1799	50[b]					
1805			25			

[a]After Swanton 1911.
[b]With Creek.
[c]Includes Houma and Acolapissa.
[d]Includes Bayagoula and Houma.
[e]Includes Koroa.
[f]Includes Ofo.

longer than a generation, the period is still too brief to allow for a population
increase of 166% followed by a decrease of 50%. Consequently, the pattern in
the Natchez estimates must be reflecting cultural practices or observer biases.
For instance, the 1715 estimate was made shortly before Ft. Rosalie was
established at Natchez and may have served to justify the establishment of the
post.

Besides showing continuing loss of population, estimates are of interest for
demonstrating amalgamation processes. All Yazoo counts and most of those for
the Houma and Bayagoula include several other groups. Although not indicated
in the table, counts for the Yazoo and Tioux are part of Natchez counts for the
period 1720–1730.

In addition to recorded depopulation trends, there are more general descriptions of population loss during the eighteenth century. In 1704, De La Vente
wrote:

The Natchez . . . assure us that they came here to the number of more than
5,000. The other ones say that many centuries ago they were, some 3,000,

others 2,000, others a thousand, and all that is reduced now to a very moderate number. What is certain is that our people in the six years in which they have been descending the river, know certainly that the number has diminished a third, so true is it that it seems God wishes to make them give place to others (from Swanton 1911:39).

Charlevoix also described aboriginal population loss, attributing the cessation of mound-building activity to the disappearance of people:

The greatest part of the Nations of Louisiana, had formerly their temples as well as the Natchez . . . But the temple of the Natchez is the only one subsisting at present, and is held in great veneration by all the savages inhabiting this vast continent, the decrease in whose numbers is as considerable, and has been, still more sudden, then that of the people of Canada, without it being possible to assign the true reason of this event. Whole nations have entirely disappeared within the space of forty years at most; and those who still remain, are not more than the shadow of what they were, when M. De Salle discovered this country (Charlevoix 1977 [1761]:256).

Finally, census counts are invaluable for pointing out that Period III settlement counts $[S_c/(T/100)]$ are, indeed, biased. While I argued that the increase in Period III counts did not represent a genuine population increase, I was unable to determine whether population was stable or declining. This question can now be addressed. Although settlement counts show an increase, population is declining. Consequently, any attempt to measure prehistoric aboriginal changes in population from historic counts of settlements must be viewed with considerable suspicion.

In summary, then, comparison of Spanish and French sources indicate that at the time De Soto entered the Lower Mississippi Valley, large and dense populations were divided into a number of polities. Following De Soto, populations declined, and the decline continued through the French period. Amalgamation processes were a response to decline.

ABORIGINAL SETTLEMENT HISTORY   From the beginning of consistent documentation, aboriginal populations were in such a state of flux that it is difficult to trace relocations of particular groups or to identify a uniform pattern of movement among all groups. The process of abandonment of the north part of the region continued into the eighteenth century. By 1720, remnant groups were clustered into few villages at the Homochito River or farther south.

Table 15 summarizes what can be gleaned from historical sources. Because these data are in dramatic contrast to the settlement counts and density of Period I, they, like warrior estimates and archaeological trends in population,

Table 15   Village Counts, Lower Mississippi Valley[a]

| | | Ethnic Group | | |
Year	Natchez	Taensa	Quapaw[b]	Tunica	Bayagoula
1686	9	8–9	4		1*
1699		1–7	3	1*	
1706		Abandonment following		1*	Abandonment following
1710		war with Houma			war with Taensa
1720	5				
1731	Abandonment			1*	
1764					Abandonment

[a]Except for Quapaw, all village counts taken from Swanton 1911.
[b]Shea 1903; Kellogg 1917.
*Settlement relocated.

support the argument that catastrophic population loss preceded French settlement. As a consequence, French documents describe the terminus of aboriginal sequences. Moreover, historic records contain descriptions of population instability and offer a number of insights into adaptive strategies that were emerging in response to drastically changed demographic structures.

Of the five groups it is likely that the Bayagoula, Natchez, and Taensa were present in the valley before 1680. Natchez and Bayagoula employed a strategy of amalgamation to survive. They remained in the same area and persisted by absorbing remnants into their ranks. Tunica migrated into the valley after 1680; their survival depended on relocation rather than amalgamation (Brain 1975b, 1980).

The Quapaw strategy is difficult to define largely because there is no agreement about the identity or origin of this ethnic unit (Hoffman 1983). Linguistic affiliation of the Quapaw with Siouan speakers suggests that the group entered the valley after 1680. At the same time, archaeological material from the Lower Arkansas Valley suggests the presence of some group(s) in this area prior to 1650 (Morse and Morse 1983). The question is whether the historically defined Quapaw were a postdisease amalgamation who took up residence in a recently abandoned area or whether they were autochthons of the area who developed other survival strategies.

It seems that residential instability and/or village reduction coupled with amalgamation processes were adaptive responses to new selective pressures. (See Dobyns 1983 for a similar discussion.) When village population fell below a threshold necessary for defense and maintenance, mobility or amalgamation developed as attempts to correct the situation. Although the cause(s) of these responses were obviously complex, population loss was clearly a significant factor. In the end, all such attempts were short-lived since population levels never stabilized.

EPIDEMIC HISTORY My brief historical summary has been quite consistent with archaeologically defined trends in population. The collapse began in the late sixteenth century and continued until aboriginal group sizes were too small to sustain previous cultural adaptations. Had the historical record demonstrated trends of stability or increase in population, the hypothesis of collapse would have been less convincing. Since this was not the case, it is appropriate to consider the epidemic disease record from the Southeast.

Although there are very few direct references to disease outbreaks in the sixteenth and seventeenth-century documents from the lower valley, a considerable body of historical data suggests that the disease contact began in the sixteenth century.

The earliest and only direct documentary evidence of the consequences of disease contact are contained in the De Soto chronicles. Upon reaching Cofitachequi, located on the South Carolina side of the Savannah River or at the headwaters of the Santee River, both Elvas and Biedma described the consequences of some disease on this seemingly impressive town:

> About this place, from half a league to a league off, were large vacant towns grown up in grass that appeared as if no people had lived in them for a long time. The Indians said that two years before, there had been a pest in the land, and that the inhabitants had moved away to other towns (Elvas in Bourne 1904:1:66).

There is some disagreement regarding the timing of this event. At the Cofitachequi temple, Spaniards found "two wood axes of Castilian make, a rosary of jet beads, and some false pearls . . . all of which we supposed they got in exchange, made with those who followed Licentiate Ayllon" (Biedma in Bourne 1904:II:13–14). Although the Spaniards did not see a link between the disease outbreak and trade goods, I think it likely that the two products were simultaneous introductions, diffusing from the Ayllon colony in 1526.

Although Dobyns (1983:262–264) cited the above description, he placed the origin of the epidemic between 1535 and 1538. (See Table 16.) Because maize was still present in the abandoned towns and because the southeastern climate did not facilitate long-term preservation of organics, Dobyns suggested that the epidemic diffused from Mexico shortly before De Soto began his exploration.

Without a finer temporal resolution of the archaeological record, there is no way to resolve the timing of the epidemic episode. It is clear, however, that

Table 16   Known or Probable Epidemics in Florida
and the Lower Mississippi Valley

Lower Mississippi Valley	Florida (Dobyns 1983)
	1513
	1519–1524
	1528
	1535–1538
	1545–1548
	1549
	1550
	1559
	1564–1570
	1585–1586
	1586
	1596
	1613–1617
	1649
	1653
	1659
	1672
	1675
	1686
1698	
	1716
1718–1734	1726–1728

disease affected southeastern aboriginal populations prior to De Soto's exploration.

One sixteenth-century reference to disease is slim evidence to argue for a century of decimation. The lack of direct historical evidence does not mean, however, that native populations did not experience the ravages of such infections as smallpox or malaria simultaneously or sequentially. Sixteenth-century Europeans were unaware of their microbial imports. Further, since parasites that erupt in disease have incubation periods prior to the expression of illness, it is possible that explorers simply did not observe the consequences of microbial introductions. Another possibility is that disease introductions, independent of European presence, diffused like spatial waves.

Spatial diffusion is Dobyns's point of departure. Table 16 summarizes Dobyns's known or suspected epidemics of peninsular Florida. With the exception of the 1535 date, Dobyns thinks all disease episodes prior to 1596 were the result of diffusion from Cuba (Wright 1970) or Mexico (Gerhard 1972) or both. Seventeenth-century epidemics were a different matter. Since documents were a common feature in seventeenth-century Florida, direct historical observations were the sources for epidemic episodes identified by Dobyns.

The question raised by examining Table 16 is whether some or all of Dobyns's reconstructed epidemics for sixteenth-century Florida are applicable to other parts of the Southeast. Without independent evidence, Dobyns's synthesis stands as plausible speculation. When judged by the archaeological record from the Southeast, the synthesis becomes highly probable.

My population analysis from the lower valley was dramatic support of catastrophic population loss that dated to the late sixteenth and early seventeenth century. The magnitude of the loss suggested disease. Caddoan populations in east Texas seem to have experienced a similar and equally dramatic attrition at approximately the same time (Perttula 1984; Perttula and Ramenofsky 1981). Smith (1984), working in the interior Southeast, has also suggested a population collapse of Coosa Chiefdoms during the sixteenth century.

The timing and similarity of demographic events from different areas suggests not only that a single cause is responsible but that the decline postdates De Soto. Given that Dobyns suggests that twelve epidemics spread to Florida before 1600, disease is most likely, if diffusion pathways from outside the continent and across the Southeast can be demonstrated.

Fortunately, mechanisms of spread between the Caribbean or Mexico and the Southeast as well as throughout the Southeast are not difficult to infer. Dobyns (1983:247–289) has provided ample evidence of sixteenth-century contact between European centers outside the continent and the peninsula of Florida. Travel by boat was frequent, and parasites spread as people moved.

Within the Southeast, stylistic similarities across large areas such as the Pensacola complex of the Gulf Coast (Davis 1984; Knight 1984) suggest that southeastern groups were not isolated. Interaction, expressed as a veneer of style overlying regionally distinct systems, was a common feature during later periods. Although stylistic sharing does not necessarily imply disease sharing, it does suggest that pathways existed by which infectious parasites could have diffused from Europeans to uncontacted groups.

In summary, the archaeological record provided the necessary support for Dobyns's hypothesis of a sixteenth-century collapse throughout the Southeast. If the record had been limited to one region or if archaeological styles had suggested isolation, the case in support of sixteenth century disease would have been much weaker. Consequently, although I cannot stipulate specific diseases or precise times of epidemics, I can state that, in light of current evidence, the sixteenth-century is the disease century in the Southeast.

A consequence of consistent documentation is a much improved record of epidemic events. The seventeenth and eighteenth-century documents from the lower valley show that disease and population loss continued after French contact.

St. Cosme was one of the French missionaries whom Tonti guided down the Mississippi. In 1698, he described the consequences of smallpox among the Quapaw:

> We were deeply afflicted by finding this nation of the Arkansas, formerly so numerous, entirely destroyed by disease. Not a month has elapsed since they had rid themselves of smallpox, which had carried off most of them. In the villages are now nothing but graves, in which they were buried two together, and we estimated that not a hundred men were left. All of the children had died, and a great many women (Kellogg 1917:359).

One of the most complete descriptions of native experience of Old World diseases was that of Le Page du Pratz, who lived with the Natchez from 1718 until 1734. Among the Natchez, du Pratz found that both smallpox and colds were particularly devastating:

> Two distempers, that are not very fatal in other parts of the world, make dreadful ravages among them; I mean smallpox and a cold, which baffle all the arts of their physicians, who in other respects are very skillful. When a nation is attacked by the smallpox, it quickly makes great havoc; for as a whole family is crowded into a small hut, which has no communications with the external air, but a door about two feet wide and four feet high, the distemper, if it seizes one, is quickly communicated to all. The aged die in consequence of their advanced years, and the bad quality of their food; and the young, if they are not strictly watched, destroy themselves, from an abhorrence of the blotches on their skin. . . .
>
> Colds, which are very common in winter, likewise destroy great numbers of the natives. In that season they keep fires in their huts day and night; and as there is no other opening but the door, the air within the hut is kept excessively warm without any free circulation; so that when they have occasion to go out, the cold seizes them, and the consequences of it are almost always fatal (Le Page du Pratz 1975 [1758]:305–306).

The discussion of epidemic history has emphasized several points. Disease contact in the lower valley began in the sixteenth century. Some of these contacts may have been the result of direct interactions with Europeans; others were the result of diffusion. In either case, as the archaeological record demonstrated, the attrition in population was catastrophic. Finally, the process of population loss from infectious diseases that preceded colonization continued after the onset of French settlement.

Summary and Conclusions

I presented two hypotheses to account for the European contact record in the Lower Mississippi Valley. The first proposed that while the De Soto *entrada* marked the origin of European contact in the valley, the onset of aboriginal collapse was a later phenemenon, not tied to the initial contact. Either warfare or disease could have caused the collapse. The second hypothesis suggested that the onset of aboriginal decline occurred in the sixteenth century. The timing and magnitude of the loss implicated infectious disease as the primary factor in the change. I stated that resolution of these issues would clarify previous interpretations of the contact record and effectively test the Cook-Dobyns model.

The independent evaluation of both archaeological and historical records supported the second hypothesis: Catastrophic population loss began in the sixteenth century. Based on this evidence, several conclusions are warranted: The De Soto *entrada* was not a "false dawn" in the Lower Mississippi Valley, but marked the beginning of both European contact and the onset of aboriginal population loss; the beginning of history and aboriginal population change were simultaneous events. French records described reduced populations in the process of adjusting to a drastically changed population structure.

Besides offering a new interpretation of the contact period, this analysis has been exceptionally useful in other regards. Despite biases present in the archaeological record, conclusions were not ambiguous. The southeastern test case, thus, supported the position argued first by Cook and most recently by Dobyns. Disease was the earliest European introduction, drastically changing aboriginal demographic profiles and cultural systems long before consistent documentation. Consequently, archaeology, not history, must be the primary basis for developing descriptions of "pristine" aboriginal systems.

Of equal importance has been the demonstration of biases in the historic archaeological record. Although archaeological settlement counts from the eighteenth century suggested that aboriginal populations were increasing, counts were biased by sampling practices and residential instability of native groups. While counts showed an increase, population was, in fact, decreasing. If archaeologists ever want to employ settlement counts for population research more specific than those considered herein, the record must be sampled systematically.

CENTRAL NEW YORK

As used in this analysis, central New York is a roughly oval area that includes a number of major drainage systems as well as the Finger Lakes (Figure 9). The area is bounded on the west by an arbitrary line that crosses the Genessee River; on the eastern edge, the confluence of Schoharie Creek with the Mohawk River

References

Beck, C.
  1981   Prehistoric Settlement Patterns in the Lower Mississippi Valley during the Late Mississippi
          Period (A.D. 1200-1600). Paper presented at the 46th Annual Meeting of the Society for
          American Archaeology, San Diego.
Bourne, E.G.
  1904   Narratives of the Career of Hernando De Soto. 2 vols. A. S. Barnes, New York.
Brain, J.P.
  1970   The Tunica Treasure. Peabody Museum Bulletin 2. Cambridge.
  1971   The Natchez Paradox. Ethnology 10:215-222.
  1973   Trudeau, an Eighteenth-Century Tunica Village. Peabody Museum Bulletin 3. Cambridge.
  1975a   Artifacts of the Adelantado. Conference on Historic Site Archaeology Papers, 1973 5:129-
          138.
  1975b   The Archaeology of the Tunica: Trail on the Yazoo. Peabody Museum, Harvard University,
          Cambridge. Ms. in possession of author.
  1978   Late Prehistoric Settlement Patterning in the Yazoo Basin and Natchez Bluffs Regions of
          the Lower Mississippi Valley. In Mississippian Settlement Patterns, edited by B. D. Smith,
          pp. 331-368. Academic Press, New York.
  1980   Tunica Treasure. Peabody Museum of Archaeology and Ethnology Papers 71. Cambridge.
Brown, B. Mc.
  1985   Floor Area and Population: A World-Wide Cross Cultural Study. Ms. submitted to American
          Antiquity.
Brown, I. W.
  1975   Excavations at Ft. St. Pierre. Conference on Historic Site Archaeology Papers, 1974 9:60-
          85.
  1979   Functional Group Changes and Acculturation: A Case Study of the French and the Indian
          in the Lower Mississippi Valley. Midcontinental Journal of Archaeology 4:147-165.
  1982   An Archaeological Study of Culture Contact and Change in the Natchez Bluffs Region. In
          La Salle and his Legacy, edited by P. K. Galloway, pp. 176-193. University Press of
          Mississippi, Jackson.
  1985   Natchez Indian Archaeology: Culture Change and Stability in the Lower Mississippi Valley.
          Mississippi Department of Archives and History, Archaeological Report 15. Jackson.
Brown, I. W., and J. P. Brain
  1983   Archaeology of the Natchez Bluffs Region, Mississippi: Hypothesized Cultural and
          Environmental Factors Influencing Local Population Movements. Southeastern
          Archaeological Conference, Bulletin 20:38-49.
Charlevoix, P. F. X. de
  1977   Charlevoix's Louisiana: Selections from the History and the Journal [1761], edited by
          Charles E. O'Neill. Louisiana State University Press for Louisiana American Revolution
          Bicentennial Commission, Baton Rouge.
Collins, H. B.
  1927   Potsherds from Choctaw Village Sites in Mississippi. Journal of the Washington Academy
          of Sciences 17:259-263.
Davis, D. D.
  1984   Protohistoric Cultural Interaction along the Northern Gulf Coast. In Perspectives on Gulf
          Coast Prehistory, edited by D. D. Davis, pp. 216-231. Ripley P. Bullen Monographs in
          Anthropology and History 5. Florida State Museum, Gainesville.
Dobyns, H.
  1983   Their Number Become Thinned. The University of Tennessee Press, Knoxville.
Fernandez, J. B.
  1975   Alvar Nunez Cabesa de Vaca, the Forgotten Chronicler. Ediciones Universal, Miami.

1

Fisk, H. N.
  1944   Geological Investigation of the Alluvial Valley of the Lower Mississippi Valley. U.S. Army
          Corps of Engineers, Mississippi River Commission, Publication 52. Vicksburg.
Ford, J. A.
  1936   Analysis of Indian Village Site Collections from Louisiana and Mississippi. Department of
          Conservation, Louisiana Geological Survey, Anthropological Study 2. New Orleans.
  1954   The Type Concept Revisited. American Anthropologist 56:42-53.
  1961   Menard Site: The Quapaw Village of Osotouy on the Arkansas River. American Museum of
          Natural History, Anthropological Papers 48(2). New York.
  1962   A Quantitative Method for Deriving Cultural Chronology. Pan American Union, Technical
          Manual 1.
Ford, J. A., and G. R. Willey
  1941   An Interpretation of the Prehistory of the Eastern United States. American Anthropologist
          43:325-363.
Gerhard, P.
  1972   A Guide to the Historical Geography of New Spain. Cambridge University Press,
          Cambridge.
Giardino, M. J.
  1984   Documenting Evidence for the Location of Historic Indian Villages in the Mississippi Delta.
          In Perspectives on Gulf Coast Prehistory, edited by D. D. Davis, pp. 232-257. Ripley P.
          Bullen Monographs in Anthropology and History 5. Florida State Museum, Gainesville.
Gibson, J. L.
  1973   Social Systems at Poverty Point: An Analysis of Intersite and Intrasite Variability.
          Unpublished Ph.D. dissertation, Department of Anthropology, Southern Methodist
          University, Dallas.
Giraud, M.
  1974   The History of French Louisiana, vol. 1. The Reign of Louis XIV, 1698-1715, translated by
          J. C. Lambert. Louisiana State University Press, Baton Rouge.
Griffin, J. B.
  1946a   Cultural Changes and Continuity in Eastern United States. In Man in Northeastern North
          America, edited by F. Johnson, pp. 37-95. Robert S. Peabody Foundation for Archaeology,
          Papers 3. Andover.
  1952   Culture Periods in the Eastern United States. In Archaeology of the Eastern United States,
          edited by J. B. Griffin, pp. 352-370. University of Chicago Press, Chicago.
Hart, C. W. M.
  1943   A Reconstruction of Natchez Social Structure. American Anthropologist 45:379-386.
Hill, J. N. and R. K. Evans
  1972   A Model for Classification and Typology. In Models in Archaeology, edited by D. Clarke,
          pp. 231-273. Methuen, London.
Hoffman, M. P.
  1983   Protohistory of the Lower and Central Arkansas River Valley in Arkansas. Paper presented
          at the Mid-South Archaeological Conference, Memphis.
House, J.
  1984   Kent Phase Investigations in Eastern Arkansas. Paper presented at the 41st Annual
          Meeting of the Southeastern Archaeological Conference, Pensacola.
Hudson, C.
  1976   The Southeastern Indians. The University of Tennessee press, Knoxville.
Hudson, C., M. Smith, D. Hally, R. Polhemus, and C. DePratter
  1985   Coosa: A Chiefdom in the Sixteenth-Century Southeastern United States. American
          Antiquity 50:723-737.
Joutel, H.
  1906   Joutel's Journals of La Salle's Last Voyage, 1684-1687 [1713]. Joseph McDonough,
          Albany.
Kellogg, L. (editor)
  1917   Early Narratives of the Northwest, 1634-1699. Charles Scribner's Sons, New York.

2

Klinger, T.
1975-   Parkin Archeology: A Report on the 1966 Field School Test Excavations at the Parkin Site.
1977   The Arkansas Archeologist 16-18:45-80.
Knight, V. J.
1984   Late Prehistoric Adaptations in the Mobile Bay Region. In Perspectives on Gulf Coast
         Prehistory, edited by D. D. Davis, pp. 198-215. Ripley P. Bullen Monographs in
         Anthropology and History 5. Florida State Museum, Gainesville.
Le Page du Pratz, A. S.
1975   The History of Louisiana [1758], edited by J. G. Tregle. Reprint, Louisiana State University
         Press for Louisiana American Revolution Bicentennial Commission, Baton Rouge.
Milner, G. R.
1980   Epidemic Disease in the Post-Contact Southeast: A Reappraisal. Midcontinental Journal of
         Archaeology 5:39-56.
Morse, D. F. (editor)
1973   Nodena: An Account of 75 Years of Archeological Investigation in Southeast Mississippi
         County, Arkansas. Arkansas Archeological Survey, Research Series 4. Fayetteville.
Morse, D. F., and P. A. Morse
1983   Archaeology of the Central Mississippi Valley. Academic Press, New York.
Morse, P. A.
1981   Parkin: The 1978-1979 Archeological Investigations of a Cross County, Arkansas Site.
         Arkansas Archeological Survey, Research Series 13. Fayetteville.
Nasatir, A. P.
1952   Before Lewis and Clark: Documents illustrating the History of the Missouri, 1785-1804. 2
         vols. St. Louis Historical Documents Foundation, St. Louis.
Neitzel, R. S.
1965   Archaeology of the Fatherland Site, the Grand Village of the Natchez. American Museum
         of Natural History, Anthropological Papers 51(1). New York.
Parker, A. C.
1907   Excavations in an Erie Village and Burial Site at Ripley, Chautaugua County, New York.
         New York State Museum, Bulletin 117:459-554. Albany.
Perttula, T. K.
1984   The Early Historic Period in the Caddoan Area. Paper presented at the 49th Annual
         Meeting of the Society for American Archaeology, Portland.
Perttula, T. K., and A. F. Ramenofsky
1981   An Archaeological Model of Caddoan Culture Change: The Historic Period. Southeastern
         Archaeological Conference, Bulletin 24:13-15.
Phillips, P.
1958   Application of the Wheat-Gifford-Wasley Taxonomy to Eastern Ceramics. American
         Antiquity 24:117-125.
1970   Archaeological Survey in the Lower Yazoo Basin, Mississippi, 1949-1955. Peabody
         Museum of Archaeology and Ethnology, Papers 60 (parts I and II). Cambridge.
Phillips, P., J. A. Ford, and J. B. Griffin
1951   Archaeological Survey in the Lower Mississippi Alluvial Valley, 1940-1947. Peabody
         Museum of Archaeology and Ethnology, Papers 25. Cambridge.
Price, J. E.
1978   The Settlement Pattern of the Powers Phase. In Mississippian Settlement Patterns, edited
         by B. D. Smith, pp. 201-231. Academic Press, New York.
Quimby, G. I.
1946   Natchez Social Structure as an Instrument of Assimilation. American Anthropologist
         48:134-137.
1951   The Medora Site, Western Baton Rouge Parish, Louisiana. Field Museum of Natural
         History, Anthropological Series 24(2). Chicago.
1957   The Bayou Goula Site, Iberville Parish, Louisiana. Fieldiana: Anthropology 47(2). Chicago.

3

Saucier, R. T.
    1974   <u>Quaternary Geology of the Lower Mississippi Valley</u>. Arkansas Archeological Survey, Research Series 6. Fayetteville.

Sauer, C. O.
    1971   <u>Sixteenth-Century North America: The Land and the People as Seen by Europeans</u>. University of California Press, Berkeley.

Service, E. R.
    1962   <u>Primitive Social Organization: An Evolutionary Perspective</u>. Random House, New York.

Shea, J. D. G.
    1903   <u>Discovery and Exploration of the Mississippi Valley: The original Narratives of Marquette, Allouez, Membre, Hennepin, and Anastase Doway</u>. 2nd ed. Joseph McDonough, Albany.

Smith, M. T.
    1984   <u>Depopulation and Culture Change in the Early Historic Period Interior Southeast</u>. Unpublished Ph.D. dissertation, Department of Anthropology. University of Florida, Gainesville.

Steponaitis, V. P.
    1978   Locational Theory and Complex Chiefdoms: A Mississippian Example. In <u>Mississippian Settlement Patterns</u>, edited by B. D. Smith, pp. 417-453. Academic Press, New York.

Swanton, J. R.
    1911   <u>Indian Tribes of the Lower Mississippi Valley and Adjacent Coast of the Gulf of Mexico</u>. Bureau of American Ethnology, Bulletin 43. Washington, D.C.
    1928   <u>Aboriginal Cultures of the Southeast</u>. Forty-second Annual Report of the Bureau of American Ethnology, 1924. Washington, D.C.
    1939   <u>Final Report of the United States De Soto Expedition Commission</u> 76th Congress, 1st Session, H.R. 71. Washington, D.C.

Varner, J., and J. Varner
    1951   <u>The Florida of the Inca</u>. Univrsity of Texas Press, Austin.

Willey, G. R., and P. Phillips
    1958   <u>Method and Theory in American Archaeology</u>. University of Chicago Press, Chicago.

Williams, S.
    1980   Armorel: A Very Late Phase in the Lower Mississippi Valley. <u>Southeastern Archaeological Conference Bulletin</u> 22:105-110.

Williams S. and J. P. Brain
    1984   <u>Excavations at the Lake George Site Yazoo County, Mississippi, 1958-1960</u>. Peabody Museum of Archaeology and Ethnology Papers 74. Cambridge.

Wright, I. A.
    1970   <u>The Early History of Cuba 1492-1586</u> [1916]. Octagon Books, New York.

4

TEXAS

THE INFLUENCE OF EPIDEMICS
ON THE INDIAN POPULATIONS AND CULTURES OF TEXAS

by

John C. Ewers

ABSTRACT

Historic records indicate that Indian tribes residing in Texas prior to 1820 suffered no fewer than 30 epidemics during the period of white contact prior to 1890. The cumulative effect of successive epidemics was a major factor in the extinction of some of these tribes, and in continued population decreases among the others. Most probably these epidemics also caused significant cultural changes among the Indians who survived them in such varied aspects of life as warfare, political and social organization, and religious beliefs and practices.

That Europeans introduced epidemic diseases into the Americas which drastically reduced the numbers of Indians during the historic period is a fact well known to both historians and anthropologists. But the long range effects of successive epidemics on the populations of particular tribes have not been sufficiently studied, and the effects of these epidemics on the beliefs and customs of the Indians who survived them have been little considered by scholars.

Texas provides a fertile field for studying the influences of epidemics on neighboring tribes of different cultures over an extended period. Nowhere else in the American West did tribes of so many cultures live in such close proximity in the historic period. In Texas alone, buffalo-hunting nomads of the plains met not only horticultural tribes of the plains and woodlands, but also hunter-gatherers of the southwestern deserts and fishermen of the Gulf Coast.

Furthermore, there is a rich and lengthy record of Indian-White contacts in Texas dating back to Cabeza de Vaca's first meeting with Indians on the Gulf Coast in 1528. Most Indian tribes were removed from Texas during the 1850s, but we can follow them to their new homes in present Oklahoma and New Mexico, and continue to study epidemics among them and the possible effects of epidemics on their

numbers and life-ways to the end of the frontier period in 1890.

Texas was also a region of extensive tribal movements during the historic period. There were movements into this region from both north and east before 1820, and out of it before 1860. For purposes of this study let us consider as Indians of Texas those tribes who resided wholly or partially within the area of the present State prior to 1820 — with the exception of those portions of woodland tribes who entered East Texas from the east before 1820 (all of whom, save the Alabama-Coushatta, moved on to present Oklahoma or Mexico before 1860), and the Tigua of the El Paso area, who were Puebloan in culture.

The tribes with whom we shall be concerned, and their relative locations prior to 1820, are shown on the map (Fig. 1).

Any attempt to determine the effects of epidemics on the populations of these tribes must face the difficult problem of estimating their populations at a relatively early date. This is a fascinating numbers game in which a high degree of certainty is impossible because of the general lack of precise contemporary population figures. No actual census of the Indian tribes of the Indian Territory (Oklahoma) was undertaken until 1875, at which time a count of all the men, women, and children of each tribe was needed as a basis for establishing ration rolls. Before that time tribal populations were estimated. James Mooney has reminded us that the first Kiowa census of 1875 yielded a figure almost 50% *less* than an *estimate* of that tribe's population made only two years earlier (Mooney 1898:235).

Before 1875, estimates usually were calculated by formulae — by counting or estimating the number of warriors; or the number of lodges; or

104

Figure 1. Indian tribes of Texas considered in this paper.

the number of families in a tribe; and then multiplying by certain arbitrary factors to arrive at a total tribal population. Not only were the numbers of warriors, lodges, or families usually set down in round numbers, but different estimators employed different factors in their multiplication. Obviously, the man who multiplied the number of warriors by five obtained a tribal total 25% greater than the one who used four for his factor.

Mooney estimated that the Kiowa averaged "6 or 7 souls to a tipi," but he recognized that this ratio "varied greatly with different tribes" (Mooney 1898:236). It also must have varied in the same tribes at different periods, say, before and after a serious and fatal epidemic. On the other hand, Newcomb and Field recently estimated only 10 to 11 occupants in a two-family grass lodge among the horticultural Wichita (Bell, Jelks and Newcomb 1967:340). Whether one estimates 5 or 7 individuals to a family can make a difference of nearly 40% in one's total population for a tribe.

In view of the difficulties in evaluating early estimates of Indian populations, it is not surprising that most anthropologists have relied upon the figures cited in James Mooney's posthumously published study, *The Aboriginal Population of*

105

167

America North of Mexico (Mooney 1928). Because Mooney's industry was enormous, his knowledge of Indians and of the literature was great, and his integrity was beyond question, this study of Indian population became the classic work in its field. Nevertheless, A. L. Kroeber, who carefully reviewed Mooney's estimates for the entire North American continent, concluded that "the best of Mooney's estimates can hardly pretend to be nearer than 10 per cent of the probable truth, and some may be 50 per cent or more from it" (Kroeber 1939:133-134).

Mooney's earliest population figures for the Indian tribes of Texas with whom we are concerned in this study are cited in Table 1 — not because they are accurate in any absolute sense, but because they comprise the best single set of figures now available. Mooney's estimates, of course, are *not truly aboriginal*. He did not deem it possible to estimate the populations of the tribes of south and east Texas before 1690, or of the tribes farther north (who were not even known to whites in 1690) until 1780. Making allowance for the fact that Mooney did not try to distinguish the Coahuiltecan tribes of Texas from those south of the Rio Grande, and he made no separate estimates for the northern and southern divisions of the Cheyenne and Arapaho, of whom only the southern ones lived on the Texas frontier, Mooney's estimates yield a relatively early population for the tribes of Texas (as I have designated them) of about 42,000, a little less than the 1960 population of the town of Brownsville, Texas.

Some of Mooney's tribal estimates now appear too high, and others too low. Kroeber considered Mooney's estimate of Coahuiltecan population far too high; Swanton reduced Mooney's estimate for the Caddoan tribes of East Texas by 500, and he thought Mooney's estimate for the Karankawan tribes "decidedly too high" (Kroeber 1939:133, 158; Swanton 1942:25; Swanton 1952:321).

On the other hand, Newcomb and Field's study of the population of the tribes of the Wichita group suggests that Mooney may have greatly underestimated their numbers in 1690 (Bell, Jelks, and Newcomb 1967:347-349). Mooney's figure for the Lipan Apache is also far below the missionaries' estimates of Lipan population in the mid-18th century (Tunnell and Newcomb 1969:150). I believe Mooney's estimate of 7,000 for the Comanche in 1780 should be increased by at least 50%.[1]

TABLE 1. THE DEPOPULATION OF THE INDIAN TRIBES OF TEXAS

Tribe or Group of Related Tribes	Linguistic Stock	Mooney Est. for 1690	Mooney Est. for 1780	Census for 1890	Per Cent Reduction
Karankawan tribes	Karankawan	2,800		Extinct	100%
Akokisa	Atakapan	500		Extinct	100%
Bidai	Atakapan	500		Extinct	100%
Coahuiltecan tribes	Coahuiltecan	7,500*		Extinct	100%
Tonkawan tribes	Tonkawan	1,600		56	97%
Caddoan tribes of East Texas	Caddoan	8,500		536	94%
Wichita group of tribes	Caddoan	3,200		358	89%
Kichai	Caddoan	500		66	87%
Lipan Apache	Athapascan	500		60**	88%
Mescalero Apache	Athapascan	700		473	32%
Kiowa-Apache	Athapascan		300+	326	+9%
Comanche	Shoshonean	7,000		1,598	77%
Kiowa	Kiowa-Tanoan		2,000	1,140	43%
▪Arapaho	Algonquian		3,000 }	5,630	13%
▪Cheyenne	Algonquian		3,500 }		

* Coahuiltecan tribes in Texas estimated at one-half Mooney's total for these tribes in Mexico and Texas.

** Includes 20 Lipan among Tonkawa and 40 among Mescalero Apache in 1890.

+ Yet Mooney (1898:253) states: "They have probably never numbered much over three hundred and fifty."

▪ All figures for Cheyenne and Arapaho include both Northern and Southern divisions, although only the Southern ones lived on the frontiers of Texas.

106

On the whole, Mooney's estimates for the Indian tribes of Texas appear to be conservative. He may have erred more grievously in underestimating some of the more populous tribes than in overestimating some of the smaller ones. A total population for the tribes considered of at least 50,000 might not be excessive.

By 1890 census figures for these same tribes indicate that their total populations had declined to 12,243, or less than 25% of Mooney's "aboriginal" total for these tribes (Table 1, columns 5-6). Before 1890 the Karankawan, Atakapan, and Coahuiltecan tribes had become extinct. The Caddoan and Tonkawan tribes, as well as the Lipan Apache and Comanche, appear to have suffered reductions of more than 75%. Only the Kiowa, Kiowa-Apache, Mescalero Apache, Arapaho, and Cheyenne appear to have been reduced by less than 50%.[2] It is noteworthy that, with the exception of the Mescalero Apache, all of the last group of tribes had limited contacts with whites prior to 1790, and none of them were missionized during the Spanish Period (Fig. 1).

Epidemics certainly were not the sole cause of this radical reduction of more than 75% in the population of these tribes during the period prior to 1890. Intertribal warfare and wars with Spaniards, Mexicans, Texans, and citizens of the United States also took their toll. Overindulgence in liquor on the part of Indians living near white settlements also contributed to this decrease, as did venereal disease, malnutrition, and starvation. Nevertheless, Mooney's contention that epidemics were *the major cause* of marked population decrease among the tribes of North America prior to 1900 appears to have been true of the Indians of Texas.

Mooney listed but five "great epidemics" in Plains Indian history which decimated some or all of the tribes of Texas: an unidentified disease reported to have killed 3000 Caddoans in East Texas in 1691; widespread smallpox epidemics in 1778, 1801, and during the late 1830's; and a widespread cholera epidemic in 1849 (Mooney 1928:12-13). Yet I found references to no less than *thirty* epidemics which appeared among one or more of the tribes of Texas (as I define them) between 1528 and 1890. There was still another one in 1892 (Table 2). Even this may not be a complete record. The absence of references to any epidemic among these Indians during the 146-year-period 1528-1674 may reflect our paucity of information more accurately than it does their state of health, or freedom from epidemics.

Contemporary writers did not identify the diseases involved in a number of the epidemics of the pre-1800 period. However, Dr. Pat Nixon, a San Antonio physician who reviewed the literature on these early epidemics, suggested the diseases on the basis of the symptoms described (Nixon 1946:8-15). Throughout the entire period, smallpox was the most common cause of epidemics.

There were smallpox epidemics in 1674-5, 1688-9, 1739, about 1746, 1750, 1759, 1763, 1766, 1778, 1801-02, 1816, 1839-40, 1861-2, and 1864. Although the Indians of present Oklahoma were vaccinated against smallpox in 1865, an epidemic of this disease occurred among the Mescalero Apache in New Mexico in 1877. Yet another smallpox epidemic was averted among the Mescalero during the winter of 1882-1883, when timely vaccination enabled these Indians to escape "without a single case of smallpox" (11th U.S. Census Office, Census of 1890:403).

Next to smallpox, measles and cholera appear to have been the most deadly, although epidemics of malaria, whooping cough, and influenza also took their tolls of Indian lives.

The frequency of epidemics within a tribe must be regarded as a very important factor in the progressive decline of Indian population, for it inhibited the recovery and growth of tribal populations. The French biologist, Jean Louis Berlandier, who explored Texas in 1828 and subsequent years, reported that smallpox occurred among the Indian tribes "every sixteen years, making great ravages for a year at a time" (Berlandier 1969:84). He was not precisely accurate in defining the interval between epidemics, but the record is clear that there was a smallpox epidemic among one or more of the tribes of Texas at least once each generation from 1739 to 1877. Losses in these epidemics must have been high among children and teenagers who never lived to reproduce. Older people (including women beyond child-bearing age), who gained immunity by exposure to previous epidemics, presumably survived.

Data on mortality from epidemics are fragmentary, and some of the most precise figures may be exaggerations. Mooney discounted the Kiowa tradition that they had lost half their number in the cholera epidemic of 1849 (Mooney 1898:164). Yet the Cheyenne told of a similar loss, and Comanche mortality must also have been high in the 1849 epidemic (Grinnell

TABLE 2. A CHRONOLOGY OF KNOWN EPIDEMICS
AMONG THE INDIANS OF TEXAS, 1528-1892

Date	Disease	Tribes Infected	Mortality	References
1528	Cholera?	Karankawan tribes	One-half local band, possibly much more widespread	Cabeza de Vaca in Bandelier 1964: 63-4; Nixon 1946:32
1674-5	Smallpox	Coahuiltecan tribes	Widespread north and south of Rio Grande	Bosque in Bolton 1916:298; Castaneda 1936, Vol. I:225; Nixon 1946:53
1688-9	Smallpox	La Salle's Fort, St. Louis	French definitely, Karankawans?	Massanet and De Leon in Bolton 1916:395, 403; Nixon 1946:54
1691	?	Caddoan tribes of East Texas	Estimated 3,000	Father Casanas 1927:294, 303. Mooney 1928:12; Swanton 1942:17
1706	Smallpox	Coahuiltecan tribes in the Rio Grande Missions	Mission Indians almost wiped out	Tunnell and Newcomb 1969:147
1718	?	Caddoan tribes of East Texas	Nearly 100 baptisms in articulo mortis	Father Espinosa in Nixon 1946:46
1739	Smallpox and measles	The five San Antonio Missions	Missions almost depopulated by death and desertion	Castaneda 1936, Vol. III: 71; Nixon 1946:10, 54
ante 1746	Smallpox & measles	Tonkawan & Atakapan tribes	Epidemics prevented any population increase, 1734-1746	Bustillo in Bolton 1914b:334; Nixon 1946:54
1750	Smallpox	San Xavier Missions, Tonkawan and Atakapan tribes	40 at mission	Bolton 1915:223; Nixon 1946:54; Tunnell and Newcomb 1969:151
1751	?	San Antonio Missions	Epidemic "ravaged" the mission Indians	Father Dolores in Bolton 1915:303
1753	Malaria or dysentery?	San Xavier Missions, Tonkawan & Atakapan tribes	"a mortal sickness"	Nixon 1946:44-45
1759	Smallpox	At Nacogdoches (East Texas)	?	Nixon 1946:54
1759	Measles	Caddoan tribes of East Texas	"took its toll of lives"	Nixon 1946:11
1763	?	The San Antonio Missions	"half the population died"	Bolton 1908:304; Nixon 1946:10-1
1763-4	Smallpox	San Lorenzo de la Santa Cruz Mission. Lipan Apache	"devastating scourge"	Castaneda 1936, Vol. IV:179; Nixon 1946:11, 54; Tunnell & Newcomb 1969:171.
1766	Smallpox & or measles	Karankawan tribes	"a devastating scourge"	Castaneda 1936, Vol. IV:200; Nixon 1946:11, 54
1777-1778	Cholera or bubonic plague?	Widespread among East Texas Caddoans, Wichita, Tonkawan, & Atakapan tribes	mortality very high	De Mezieres in Bolton 1914A, Vol II:189, 231-2, 250, 257, 274, 311, 313; Nixon 1946:11
1778	Smallpox	Widespread in Texas and beyond its borders	mortality high	Stearn and Stearn 1945:46, 48; Mooney 1928:12; Nixon 1946:44, 46, 54
1801 1802	Smallpox	Widespread among Texas tribes, especially on Red River	high among the Caddoan tribes	Sibley 1832:721-2; Mooney 1898:168; Mooney 1928:12; Stearn and Stearn 1945:75
1803	Measles	Caddoan tribes of East Texas	Considerable	Sibley 1832:721-2
1816	Smallpox	Caddo, Wichita, Comanche, Kiowa, Kiowa-Apache	Including estimated "4,000 Comanche"	Trimble in Morse 1822:259; Mooney 1898:168; Stearn and Stearn 1945:86
1839-40	Smallpox	Kiowa, Kiowa-Apache Comanche	killed "great number in each tribe"	Mooney 1898:172, 274; Mooney 1928:12; Stearn & Stearn 1945.86
1849	Cholera	Widespread in Southern Plains. Kiowa, Kiowa-Apache, Cheyenne, Comanche	killed "half the Cheyenne"; less than half Kiowa; possibly more Comanche	Mooney 1898:173, 290-291; Mooney 1928:12; Grinnell 1962, Vol. II:164-5; Wallace & Hoebel 1952:298; Fitzpatrick in An. Rept. Com. Ind. Aff. 1850:52

108

Date	Disease	Tribes Infected	Mortality	References
1861-2	Smallpox	Kiowa, Kiowa-Apache, Comanche, Cheyenne & Arapaho	"terrible ravages especially among the Arapaho"	An. Rept. Com. Ind. Aff. 1862:131; Mooney 1898:176, 311
1864	Smallpox	Wichita and Caddo	"fatal in many cases"	An. Rept. Com. Ind. Aff. 1864:319
Note: Tribes of the present Oklahoma region were vaccinated against smallpox in 1865				
1867	Cholera	Wichita and Caddo	"18 deaths in 5 days among Wichita," "47 Caddo victims"	An. Rept. Comm. Ind. Aff. 1867: 322
1877	Smallpox	Mescalero Apache	carried off "a considerable number"	An. Rept. Com. Ind. Aff. 1877:157
1877	Measles & fever	Kiowa, Kiowa-Apache Cheyenne, Arapaho	Killed 136 Cheyenne & 83 Arapaho children; Kiowa losses heavy but not enumerated	An. Rept. Com. Ind. Aff. 1877:85; Mooney 1898:218, 341-342
1882	Whooping cough & malarial fever	Kiowa, Kiowa-Apache, Comanche, Wichita	"malarial fever fatal in number of cases"	An. Rept. Com. Ind. Aff. 1883:70; Mooney 1898:219
1889-1890	Influenza	Cheyenne & Arapaho	"fatal in large number of cases"	An. Rept. Com. Ind. Aff. 1890:177; 182: Rept. of Indians Taxed & Not Taxed 1894:543
1892	Measles, influenza & whooping cough	Kiowa, Kiowa-Apache Comanche, Wichita, and Caddo	"deaths chiefly among infants and children; Kiowa loss nearly 15% of pop.; Cheyenne & Arapaho "mortality very light"	An. Rept. Com. Ind. Aff. 1892:374, 377, 386, 388; Mooney 1898:223, 235, 362-3

1962, Vol. II:164; Annual Rept. Comm. Ind. Aff. 1849:51-52). Comanche mortality in the 1816 smallpox epidemic was estimated at 4000 (Morse 1822:260).

There appears to be no record of any tribe in Texas having suffered as severe a population loss from a single epidemic as did the Mandan of the Upper Missouri River during the smallpox epidemic of 1837, which reduced that tribe from about 1600 to less than 140 — a loss of more than 90% (Hayden 1862:433-434). Nor were epidemics the sole cause of the extinction of any of the Texas tribes who became extinct before 1860. Warfare, liquor, malnutrition, and perhaps the absorption of the last remnants into other Indian or Mexican populations, also played parts in the disappearance of those tribes.

How small a tribe could survive and maintain its political and social identity under the conditions of competition with other Indians and whites which prevailed in Texas prior to 1860? There may have been a few cases among the Caddoan tribes of East Texas of remnants of less than 150 persons who managed to maintain their tribal identity for a short time before they combined with one or more related tribes to insure their biological survival — just as the Mandan combined with the Hidatsa and Arikara on the Upper Missouri River following their disastrous losses in the smallpox epidemic of 1837.

The influence epidemics may have had upon the beliefs and customs of those who survived should be of particular interest to the ethnologist.

To what extent could Indians distinguish between the most common epidemic diseases? Nixon was of the opinion that even the Spaniards, who observed and reported epidemics among the Indians of Texas prior to 1800, tended to confuse smallpox and measles (Nixon 1946:53). Keepers of the 19th century Kiowa pictorial calendars designated epidemics of smallpox and measles by the same graphic symbol — the figure of a standing man, clothed only in a breechclout, his head, body, arms, and legs

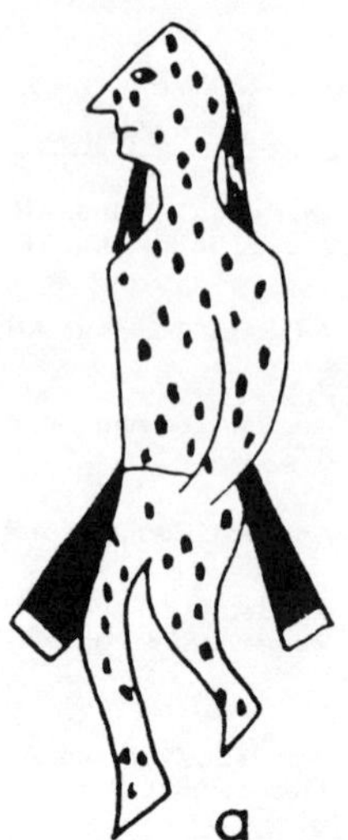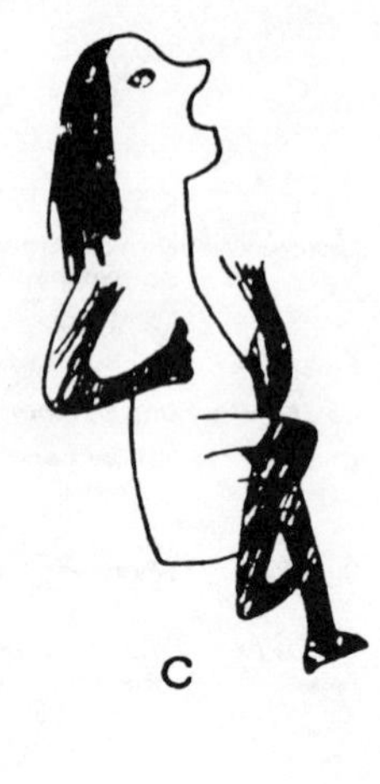

Figure 2. Pictographic representations of epidemics among the Kiowa Indians. *a*, smallpox (winter 1839-40); *b*, measles (summer 1877); and *c*, cholera (summer 1849). After Mooney (1898).

covered with small dots (Fig. 2*a-b*). However, the Kiowa verbally distinguished "hole sickness" (smallpox) from "pimple sickness" (measles). They called the cholera "cramp sickness," and identified the years of cholera epidemics on their calendars by the figure of a man with his legs drawn up in pain (Fig. 2*c*) (Mooney 1898:274, 289, 342, 391-433).

Indian beliefs regarding the causes of epidemics varied. Interestingly enough, the fragmentary records of two of the earliest epidemics indicate that the afflicted Indians initially, and probably correctly, blamed the whites for these plagues. Cabeza de Vaca wrote that the Karankawa *at first* blamed his Spanish party for communicating the epidemic of 1528 to them, "believing we had killed them and holding it to be certain, they agreed among themselves to kill those of us who survived." But one Indian saved the Spaniards' lives by pointing out that if the white men had "so much power" they would not have suffered so many of their own men to perish (Bandelier 1964:64).

Caddoan survivors of the disastrous epidemic of 1691 among the Indians of the East Texas missions at first blamed the high mortality upon the priests' practice of baptizing the stricken Indians during their death throes. But Father Casañas believed that he convinced even the most

hostile Indian medicine men that the priests' attentions had not caused the Indian deaths (Casañas 1927:294, 303).

Other and later Indians attributed epidemics to the angry forces of nature. Morris Opler's conservative Chiracahua Apache informants of the 1920's believed that offenses against the Mountain Spirits caused epidemics, and that earthquakes and eclipses of the sun or moon were warnings of approaching epidemics. Once warned by these signs, the Apache sought to ward off epidemics by performing masked ceremonial dances. One informant told Opler that as recently as 1903, when these Apache lived near Fort Sill, the neighboring Comanche suffered deaths from smallpox. The Apache masked dancers performed for four nights. "And you know," said the Indian, "we never got the smallpox" (Opler 1941:187, 241, 278).

The common practice among the nomadic tribes of scattering once an epidemic struck one of their camps, as well as their avoidance of the locality of the initial outbreak for a considerable time thereafter, must have helped to minimize losses among them. The desertion of the missions by some of the missionized Indians during the epidemic of the 18th century must have had a similar effect. The loyal neophytes who remained with their priests perished, while many of the

110

dispersed apostates survived.

Significantly, the greatest population losses during the 18th century and the early years of the 19th century were suffered by the least mobile tribes. These were the mission Indians and the Caddoan farming tribes. The latter, as well as the Wichita and the tribes of East Texas, lived in compact, semi-permanent villages of multi-family lodges, where conditions were as favorable for the rapid communication of diseases as they were in the mission compounds.

The succession of epidemics must have encouraged a trend in religion toward a greater emphasis upon prayers and ceremonies for protection against sickness and death. This is not to say that they ceased to seek supernatural aid to bring them success in hunting, protection from their enemies, and an abundance of crops (among those who farmed). But their most destructive enemies came to be those unseen ones — epidemics which struck down and killed their women and children, and against which their warriors had no defense. Health magic must not only have grown in importance, but it survived into the Reservation Period after the buffalo were gone and the Indian wars had ended.

At the turn of the century George A. Dorsey was told by an aged Caddo that as a boy he was taught to pray each morning when he returned from his bath, and cast a stick into the family fire, "Grandfather, help me to live and become a good man, and help others to live" (Dorsey 1906:226). One must wonder whether Caddo boys uttered this ardent prayer for life itself in the days before the dread epidemics began to materially lower the life expectancy of children?

Even though traditional curing practices proved ineffective in saving lives of victims of epidemic diseases, Indians persisted in employing them. They may unwittingly have alleviated the patients' sufferings by hastening their deaths. David Burnet described the Comanche treatment of smallpox during the epidemic of 1816:

The patients were strictly confined to their lodges, excluded from the air, and almost suffocated with heat. In many instances while under the maddening influence of the disease, exasperated by a severe paroxysm of symptomatic fever, they would rush to the water and plunge beneath it. The remedy was invariably fatal (Burnet 1851:234).

Even as late as 1892 the Agent for the Cheyenne and Arapaho reported that they treated measles

by subjecting the patient to a severe sweating process, following it with a plunge in the river ... In cases of measles this treatment usually proves fatal (Annual Rept. Comm. Ind. Aff. 1892:374).

Early accounts of the Karankawan and Caddoan tribes of East Texas refer to the common practice of infanticide. It was also the custom of the Caddo to bury a live, nursing infant with its dead mother, and of the Comanche to kill a warrior's wife at his grave (Bandelier 1964:64; Casañas 1927:302-303; Berlandier 1969:96-97; Neighbors 1852:133). These customs do not appear to have survived among these tribes beyond the middle of the 19th century. Why? Did not the continued decline in tribal populations encourage the abandonment of customs so wasteful of human life?

The population decline also may have brought about significant changes in Indian war practices during the 19th century. Eighteenth century accounts indicate that the eating of prisoners, the hideous torture of captives, and the trade of captives as slaves were common among the Indian tribes of Texas. As the 19th century progressed only the Tonkawa continued to practice cannibalism to any extent, and both the torture and sale of captives became less common. Captives became more valuable as adopted members of a family — to replace children, wives, and husbands who had been lost in epidemics — than as human sacrifices or human trade goods.

In 1853 the experienced mountain man and Indian Agent, Thomas Fitzpatrick, observed that Comanche and Apache raids south into Chihuahua and Durango were made to capture Mexican prisoners as well as to "sharpen their appetite for pillage and rapine," and that these raids "tend to keep up the numbers of the tribe." Fitzpatrick found that Mexican captives were "so intermingled amongst these tribes that it is somewhat difficult to distinguish them." At that time the Comanche refused to make any treaty with the United States that would require them to give up any captives. "They stated briefly that they had become a part of the tribe; and that they were identified with them in all their modes of life; and they were the husbands of their daughters and the mothers of their children" (Ann. Rept. Comm. Ind. Aff. 1853:363).

Mooney estimated that during the 1890s "at least one-fourth of the Kiowa had captive blood"

111

173

(Mooney 1898:236).

Even so, the Comanche and Kiowa practice of inducting prisoners into the tribe failed to reverse the continued downward trend in tribal populations during the 19th century. It did, however, result in marked biological changes in the composition of the tribes. In 1931, Marcus Goldstein, a physical anthropologist studying the Comanche, doubted that more than 10% of the members of that tribe at the time were full-bloods (Goldstein 1934:299-300).

Surely the 19th century Comanche and Kiowa were well aware of their dwindling populations, and they became reluctant to have their true numbers known to Whites. The Comanche likewise did not want their numbers counted in 1837 (Smithwick 1900:173). As late as 1890 the Kiowa were "strangely averse to being counted" (U.S. Census Office, 11th Census, 1890:541). In the light of history this aversion to being counted cannot be interpreted as mere superstition: the Comanche and Kiowa were proud peoples who had been much more numerous, and they had no desire to advertise their weakness in numbers.

On the other hand, the declining numbers of tribesmen among the Southern Plains tribes hostile to the United States during the third quarter of the 19th century must have made the Army task of Indian fighting much less difficult than it would have been had they fought these Indians when they were as numerous as they were in 1780, or even before the cholera epidemic of 1849.

Epidemics strongly affected Indian tribal organization — or more properly disorganization and reorganization. Certainly the Karankawan, Atakapan and Coahuiltecan tribes, all of whom were repeated victims of epidemics, suffered the ultimate in social disorganization — extinction. The Lipan Apache lost their political and social autonomy and survived only as minority groups of a few individuals living among friendly Apache tribes in Oklahoma and New Mexico. Remnants of the Tonkawa were preserved from extinction under the protection of the United States Army at Fort Griffin during the waning years of the intertribal wars. The horticultural Caddoans, who numbered nearly thirty tribes before the epidemic of 1691, were reduced to three small tribes, identified as Caddo, Kichai, and Wichita, by the end of the frontier period.

There is need for a thorough study of the processes by which the Caddoans managed to survive, through repeated combinations and reorganizations into fewer and fewer units as their numbers declined. In this process the names of many of the earlier tribes became almost forgotten. But they survived (to a degree) biologically long after they lost their political identity. There are indications of tribal combinations following the deaths of important chiefs and many of their followers during the 18th century epidemics. Why the names of some of these tribes, such as Anadarko, survived, while those of other once equally numerous and prominent tribes disappeared, needs explanation.

Significant changes in social organization also took place among some of the nomadic tribes of the Southern Plains during the 19th century. Grinnell found evidence that the Cheyenne relaxed their tribal taboo against marriage within one's own band *after* the cholera epidemic of 1849 had decimated some of their camps (Grinnell 1962, Vol. I:92-93). During his fieldwork among the Comanche in the 1930's Hoebel found that most Comanche marriages "took place within the band" (Wallace and Hoebel 1952:140). Might not a shift from band exogamy to permissive endogamy have taken place among both Comanche and Cheyenne *after* destructive epidemics, when they needed to strengthen weakened bands by any practical means?

Finally, we may consider briefly the effect the succession of epidemics may have had upon Indian attitudes toward death itself. An observer among the tribes of western Oklahoma in 1890 noted that "with characteristic stoicism an Indian accepts sickness as inevitable, evinces no interest in its cause, and expects no relief" (U. S. Census Office, 11th Census, 1890:541). But by 1890 conditions had changed. Acute smallpox had been brought under control through vaccination, and chronic tuberculosis had become the slower-acting killer of reservation-bound Indians. Might not this passive acceptance of sickness and death also have been historically conditioned?

One finds no indication of this passive acceptance of sickness in the dramatic account of the death of a Cheyenne warrior during the cholera epidemic of 1849, as told by George Bird Grinnell:

Little Old Man ... donned his war-dress, mounted his war horse, and rode through the camp with a lance in his hand, shouting, "If I could see this thing, if I knew where it came from, I would go there and fight it." As he was doing this he was seized with the cramps,

112

fell from his horse, and died in his wife's arms (Grinnell 1962, Vol. II:164-165).

CONCLUSIONS

The cumulative effect of 30 or more epidemics among the Indians of Texas played a major role in the marked decline in population among these tribes during the historic period prior to 1890. Even though our best available set of early population estimates for these tribes, those of James Mooney, cannot be considered exact, comparison of them with 1890 census figures for the surviving tribes clearly indicates both a general population decline and a differential rate of decline among the different tribes. The sedentary, missionized and horticultural tribes suffered the most severe losses. Some of them became extinct; others sacrificed their tribal independence as their numbers decreased but insured their biological survival by combining with other linguistically and culturally related tribes. This practice was most common among the Caddoan tribes of East Texas. The nomadic tribes of the northern periphery appear to have suffered least, due to a combination of factors such as their relative remoteness from Whites until the early years of the 19th century, their common practice of scattering once they learned of the presence of disease among their people, and their very positive efforts to recruit additional tribal members through raiding for captives — both Indian and non-Indian. Yet even these tribes could not maintain their numbers, and as their total populations decreased the non-Indian blood quantum increased among them.

Obviously, they were aware of their decreasing numbers and revealed that awareness in a reluctance to be counted. Obviously too, they tried to prevent further losses as best they could. Their traditional methods of treating the sick proved futile in the cure of infectious diseases such as smallpox and measles. Frequent and fervid appeals for supernatural protection from illness and death proved little more effective in preventing the occurrence of epidemics. They also appear to have taken positive steps to insure survival by abandoning earlier practices which were wasteful of human life. Instead of killing and eating prisoners, or trading them to other tribes outside the area, they adopted them to take the place of their own dead relatives. Infanticide, the burial of a nursing infant with its dead mother, and the sacrifice of a wife upon the death of her husband became obsolete. New political groupings emerged through the merging of remnant tribes. Even among the larger tribes who continued to retain their tribal identity, endogamous taboos may have been relaxed in the extensive band reorganizations necessitated by severe losses in the most disastrous epidemics.

Smallpox, the most destructive of the epidemic diseases, was only brought under control through vaccination shortly before the opening of the reservation period, and before 1890 tuberculosis had replaced the earlier epidemics as a slower-acting killer.

I hope this paper may serve to encourage further studies in a too-long-neglected field. Such studies should not stop with efforts to determine the effects of epidemics upon tribal populations: they should encompass efforts to find the influence of epidemics upon the life ways of those Indians who survived those epidemics.

NOTES

1. Mexican estimates of 20,000 to 30,000 for the Comanche in the early decades of the 19th century may reflect the Mexican authorities' fears of those aggressive Indians more accurately than they do the tribal population. Nevertheless, David Burnet, who knew the Comanche well in 1819, reckoned them at 10,000 to 12,000; and José Francisco Ruíz, who lived for eight years among them prior to 1821, estimated their population at 1000 to 1500 families twelve years after they suffered heavy losses in the smallpox epidemic of 1816 (Burnet 1851:230; Ruíz Manuscript 1828:4).

2. The Kiowa-Apache, Mooney believed, "probably never numbered much over three hundred and fifty" (Mooney 1898:253). Their rather unique ability to retain or enhance their population during the 19th century may have been due to additions from remnants of other Apache tribes, predominantly Lipan.

REFERENCES CITED

Annual Report, Commissioner of Indian Affairs, Washington 1850, 1853, 1862, 1864, 1867, 1877, 1883, 1890, 1892

Bandelier, Fanny, Editor
1964   *The Journey of Alvar Nuñez Cabeza de Vaca.* Chicago.

Bell, R.E., E. B. Jelks, and W. W. Newcomb
1967   A Pilot Study of Wichita Indian Archeology and Ethnohistory (Ms).

113

Berlandier, J. L.
1969   *The Indians of Texas in 1830.* Edited and introduced by J. C. Ewers. Washington.

Bolton, H. E.
1908   The Native Tribes About the East Texas Missions. *Texas State Historical Association Quarterly,* Vol. 11, No. 4.

1914a   *Athanase de Mezieres and the Louisiana-Texas Frontier, 1768-1780.* 2 vols. Cleveland.

1914b   The Founding of the Missions on the San Gabriel River, 1745-1749. *Southwestern Historical Quarterly,* Vol. 17, No. 4.

1915   Texas in the Middle Eighteenth Century. *University of California Publications in History,* Vol. 3.

1916   *Spanish Exploration in the Southwest.* Original Narratives of Early American History. New York.

Burnet, D. G.
1851   The Comanches and Other Tribes of Texas and the Policy to be Pursued Respecting Them. *In:* Henry R. Schoolcraft, *Historical and Statistical Information Respecting the History and Prospects of the Indian Tribes of the United States,* Vol. 1. Philadelphia.

Casañas de Jesus Maria, Fray Francisco
1927   Fray Francisco Casañas de Jesus Maria to the Viceroy of Mexico, August 15, 1691. *Southwestern Historical Quarterly,* Vol. 30, Nos. 3-4.

Castañeda, C. E.

1936   *Our Catholic Heritage in Texas, 1519-1936.* 7 Vols. Austin.

Dorsey, G. A.
1906   Caddo Customs of Childhood. *Journal of American Folk-Lore Society,* Vol. 18.

Goldstein, M. A.
1934   Anthropometry of the Comanches. *American Journal of Physical Anthropology.* Vol. 29.

Grinnell, G. B.
1962   *The Cheyenne Indians, Their History and Ways of Life.* 2 Vols. New York.

Hayden, F. V.
1862   Contributions to the Ethnography and Philology of the Indian Tribes of the Missouri Valley. *Transactions American Philosophical Society,* No. 12.

Kroeber, A. L.
1939   *Cultural and Natural Areas of Native North America.* Berkeley, California.

Mooney, James
1898   Calendar History of the Kiowa Indians. *Seventeenth Annual Report, Bureau of American Ethnology.* Washington.

1928   The Aboriginal Population of America North of Mexico. *Smithsonian Miscellaneous Collections.* Vol. 80, No. 7. Washington.

Morse, Jedidiah
1822   *A Report to the Secretary of War of the United States on Indian Affairs.* New Haven.

Neighbors, R. S.
1852   The Na-u -ni, or Comanches of Texas. *In:* Henry R. Schoolcraft, *Historical and Statistical Information Respecting the History, Condition and Prospects of the Indian Tribes of the United States,* Vol. 2. Philadelphia.

Nixon, P. I.
1946   *The Medical Story of Early Texas, 1528-1853.* Lancaster, Penn.

Opler, M. E.
1941   An Apache Life-Way. The Economic, Social, and Religious Institutions of the Chiricahua Indians. Chicago.

Ruíz, Jose Francisco
1828   Untitled manuscript on several Indian tribes of Texas in Western Americana Collection, The Beinecke Rare Book and Manuscript Library, Yale University, New Haven.

114

Sibley, John
1832   Historical Sketches of the Several
        Indian Tribes in Louisiana, South of
        the Arkansas River, and between the
        Mississippi and River Grande. *Ameri-
        can State Papers, Class II, Indian
        Affairs*, Vol. 1.

Smithwick, Noah
1900   *The Evolution of a State or Recollec-
        tions of Old Texas Days.* Austin.

Stearn, E. W. and A. E. Stearn
1945   *The Effect of Smallpox on the Des-
        tiny of the Amerindian.* Boston.

Swanton, J. R.
1942   Source Material on the History and
        Ethnology of the Caddo Indians.
        *Bureau of American Ethnology, Bul-
        letin* 132. Washington.

1952   The Indian Tribes of North America.
        *Bureau of American Ethnology, Bul-
        letin* 145. Washington.

Tunnell, C. D. and W.W. Newcomb
1969   A Lipan Apache Mission. San Loren-
        zo de la Santa Cruz, 1762-1771.
        Texas Memorial Museum, Bulletin
        14. Austin.

U.S. Census Office, 11th U.S. Census, 1890
1894   Report of Indians Taxed and Indians
        Not Taxed in the United States,
        Washington.

Wallace, Ernest and E. A. Hoebel
1952   The Comanches, Lords of the South
        Plains. Norman, Oklahoma.

Smithsonian Institution
Washington, D. C. 20560
January, 1972

115

CHAPTER 4

Population Reconstruction

Population size and density for given ethnic groups relate intimately to culture history, social integration, cultural ecology—indeed, to a host of historical and processual factors (cf. Dobyns 1966; Hawley 1973; Ubelaker 1975). Therefore, their reconstruction is an important fundamental parameter in the study of culture. However, with regard to the Texas coast, population size and density have never been of particular concern to anthropologists and little more than a footnote has been devoted to them in descriptive summaries of Historic period native groups.

In the analysis of Galveston Bay Area mortuary practices (Aten *et al.* 1976: Chapter 5), population estimates based on the studies of Mooney (1928) and Swanton (1911, 1946, 1952) were used for the first time as an element of analysis (as opposed to description) of this area. The estimate used (i.e., a standing population of about 300 persons in a zone about 30 km wide around Galveston Bay) was little more than a reasonable guess. In light of studies such as those of Jennings (1976) and Dobyns (1966), these estimates now seem highly suspect. Moreover, most estimates of seventeenth-century population used in the current scientific literature are traceable to Mooney and Swanton, but the data they used and their approach to these data are not always clear. In the case of Mooney (1928), the upper Texas coast sources appear to have been heavily based on information supplied by Bolton, augmented by guesses (Ubelaker 1976:278–280). As a result, and in consideration of their importance to clarifying the social context of mortuary practices, as well as investigating the man–land relationships of upper-coast cultures, a review of the original sources of population estimates for the area is undertaken here and new conclusions are drawn.[1]

---

[1] The direction of error in the Harris County Boys School report (Aten *et al.* 1976) was in making too conservative a population estimate. Rectification of that estimate serves to make even more likely the conclusion that archaeologically visible mortuary practices were conducted only in relatively few places and applied to relatively few people.

43

METHODS AND DATA

Of the basic approaches to population reconstruction—ethnohistorical, archaeological, and physical anthropological (Ubelaker 1975)—we will ultimately
need to make use of all three, if for no other reason than to develop independent
checks on the resulting estimates. The ethnohistorical approach at present is the
most practical, and is that to which nearly exclusive attention is devoted in this
study. As a result of the nature of the mortuary practices of the local native
populations on the upper coast (see Aten *et al.* 1976), the physical anthropological approach would uncover no more than a relatively small portion of their
skeletal remains. The archaeological approaches, on the other hand, probably
hold a great deal of promise: small-site studies in conjunction with habitation-
area studies (especially along the lines suggested by Weissner [1974] and Yellen
[1977]) should be fruitful, as should studies of upper coast winter encamp-
ments, winter being the season during which the maximum population aggregates apparently occurred. At present though, principal reliance must be
placed on published historical literature and documents.

The reconstruction attempted here is for the period extending from about
1700 to 1850. The standing population size (whatever it may have been) for the
seventeenth century probably can be taken as the population zenith for the
upper Texas coast, there being no apparent evidence to suggest larger populations earlier. From a reconstruction of this zenith baseline, archaeological research may work either forward or backward in time to study the population
behavior in relation to several factors, for example, technological innovations,
group fissioning and fusion, and settlement pattern changes. One may also
explore the question of functional population size for social groups in this area.
The maximum size estimates obviously have implications for adaptation, resource depletion, and other socioeconomic features. Of equal interest is the
minimum size below which the social system can no longer function. This
feature may be estimated by the population size at which groups began to
merge, as is evident in the late Historic period. It may even be asked whether the
fissioning process that presumably took place much earlier in the prehistory of
the area and the fusioning process that apparently took place at the end of the
existence of the native groups were in any way mirror images of each other.

In carrying out this review of population data, a wide range of the published
literature has been examined for estimates, although some items no doubt were
missed. These data are presented in Table 4.1 in chronological order by ethnic
group and with necessary annotations. For reasons explained in the table, not
all population estimates are used in analysis. For example, a great many Texas
guidebooks and histories of the mid-nineteenth century give population estimates, but here one needs to be cautious. These estimates were frequently
picked up without citation from earlier writers (or so it would appear); others

were written as reminiscences many decades after the observation. Principal reliance here is on eyewitness accounts, on second-hand accounts derived from the reports of an observer, or on accounts that can be supported by independent information.

Since the objective is to examine the time trends of population change through the Historic period, as well as to extrapolate back in time from this baseline, data has been included on the Atakapa, Bidai and Aranama, as well as on the Akokisa and Karankawa. Similarities or differences in their respective trends sheds light on the processes affecting gross population size. Figure 4.1 is a graphic representation of the time trends of data listed in Table 4.1.

A comment is in order at this point about how some of these data were formulated. Many records simply provide figures for numbers of families, or warriors, or men; to translate these estimates into numbers of individuals, all have been multiplied by a factor of 4. The basis for this factor is the average of several estimates of family size or ratios of men/warriors to others in the total society. These other estimates and their sources are given in Table 4.2. Although the ratios are not culturally homogeneous, they are estimates for inhabitants primarily of the upper Texas coast environment living under "primitive" conditions. Aside from the archaeological estimate derived from a much older skeletal population at Harris County Boys School (which has been excluded from the computation), the ratios are remarkably similar. The average of all estimates, except that for the Boys School cemetery, is four persons per family, which we have used to make all family/men/warrior conversions. In the process, it was assumed that there was one warrior per family and that, as used by most early writers on the study area, the terms men and warriors were used interchangeably. Of course, these assumptions may not be correct in every instance, but they reflect the best available information at present. It should be noted here, however, that Mayhall (1939:26) thought a factor of 5 was more realistic, although she did not present data to support her conclusion.

It is necessary to comment on the trends in population size for each native group. The curve in Figure 4.1a, for the Atakapa, is unfortunately very generalized, but its concave shape generally approximates the shape of population curves for the other groups for the same time period. The apparent survivorship of members of this group through the nineteenth century should be considered in light of the fact that in the early nineteenth century, many groups passed out of existence with their few remaining members becoming absorbed into some adjacent group. The recipient groups, under severe pressures themselves, were undoubtedly altered by this fusion process even though they may nominally have retained their former identity. For a brief time, the Karankawa consolidated and enlarged in this way; and the Bidai absorbed some of the Akokisa, as did the Atakapa. The Akokisa and the Karankawa disappeared at an early point in the nineteenth century. The Bidai and the Atakapa, however, seem to have retained their identity as functioning groups for a longer time. Indeed indi-

TABLE 4.1
Population Estimates for Upper Texas Coast Native Groups

Year	Reported estimate of native population	Comments	Population estimate used	Sources
		A. Akokisa		
Post-1830	Extinct(?)	—	0	No references to this group postdating 1830.
1828	40 families	Combined with estimate for Bidai.	<100(?)	Berlandier 1969:139, Footnote 205
1820	300 individuals	—	300	Padilla 1919:51
1820	200–300 individuals	Derived from Padilla (1919).	—	Berlandier 1969:139
1820	(?)	Combined Akokisa and Coco population estimate of 150 individuals; cannot separate.	—	Morse 1822
1778	50 men	—	200	Bolton 1913:347; Faulk 1964:58
1760–1770	80 men	—	320	Sibley 1807:44
Circa 1765	800 individuals	Pacheco claimed to have "reduced" two villages of 400 individuals each; this may be inflated to reflect personal accomplishment. Although not used here, it should not be dismissed altogether; it could be possible.	—	Bolton 1913:347
1764	150 individuals	All located at Orcoquisac; suggests an average of more than 100 per village.	500(?) (5 villages)	Bolton 1913:372
1756	20+ warriors	All located at Canos' village; suggests a total village population of 80 persons, confirms magnitude of 1764 estimate.	400+(?) (5 villages)	Bolton 1913:347
1747	300 families	—	1200	Bolton 1913:346
1721	200–250 individuals	Data from La Harpe and de Bellisle. If this only refers to the single band of de Bellisle, then 5 bands would total about 1000–1250.	200–250 or 1000–1250	Swanton 1946:86

Date	Number	Description	Estimate	Source
1698	1750 individuals	Combined Akokisa, Bidai, Deadose estimate; basis unknown.	—	Swanton 1911:43–45
1690	500 individuals	Basis unknown; not used here.	—	Mooney 1928:13
1650	500 individuals	Basis unknown; not used here.	—	Swanton 1952:199

B. Bidai

Date	Number	Description	Estimate	Source
1854	± 100 individuals	This many removed to Brazos Reserve; some were intermarried with other groups.	100	Sjoberg 1951b:395
1850	± 25 warriors	—	100	Bollaert 1850
Circa 1840	18–25 individuals	—	18–25	Bonnell 1840:139
1828	40 families	Estimate by General Teran.	160	Sanchez 1926:276
Circa 1826	± 500 individuals	Excessively out of phase with other estimates of the period.	—	Grimes cited in Gatschet 1891:39
1820	300 individuals	—	300	Padilla 1919:50
1820	120 individuals	—	120	Morse 1822:373
Circa 1805	100 men	—	400	Sibley 1807:43
1778	100 warriors	Postepidemic.	400	Morfi 1935/1967:105, Footnote 19
1777	200 warriors	Preepidemic.	800	Morfi 1935/1967:105, Footnote 19
1749	239 individuals	Combined Akokisa, Bidai, and Deadose population at San Ildefonso; cannot separate.	—	Bolton 1916:199
1690	500 individuals	Basis unknown; not used here.	—	Mooney 1928:13

C. Atakapa

Date	Number	Description	Estimate	Source
1908	9 individuals	—	9	Swanton 1911:362
1907	25 individuals	Basis unknown but less likely to be a guess than other Mooney data.	25	Mooney 1928
1820	150 individuals	Combined Atakapa plus Coco; cannot separate.	—	Morse 1822:373
1805	50 men	Located near Calcasieu; may approximate a western Atakapa estimate.	200	Sibley 1807:51

(continued)

TABLE 4.1 (*Continued*)

Year	Reported estimate of native population	Comments	Population estimate used	Sources
1779	180 warriors	Minimum estimate; actual number probably larger.	>720	Swanton 1911:43–45
1698	1750 individuals	Apparently based on a linear extrapolation of the annual increment of decline between 1779 and 1805; not used.	—	Swanton 1911:43–45
1650	1500 individuals	Basis unknown; not used here.	—	Mooney 1928:9
		D. Karankawa		
1850	20 warriors	Probably too many but we have no basis to exclude this estimate.	80	Bollaert 1850
1843	40–50 individuals	This estimate appears in several mid-nineteenth-century Texas guidebooks; the ultimate source is unknown.	40–50	Roessler 1883:616
Circa 1840	Not more than 100 individuals	—	50–100(?)	Bonnell 1840:137
Circa 1836	200–250 warriors	Basis unknown; inconsistent with other estimates for the period.	—	Gatschet 1891:15
Circa 1836	3000 warriors	Estimate made as a very rough guess by Oliver; excessively out of phase with other estimates of the period.	—	Gatschet 1891:15
1835	± 50 warriors	In one camp near Refugio; this is an eyewitness account, but was written 50 years after the event; any total estimate from this would be huge for its period; not used.	—	Wilbarger 1889:198
1834	300 warriors	This many warriors reportedly massed at Matagorda; cannot relate this to an estimate of the Karankawa as a group.	—	Muckleroy 1922:230
Circa 1831	40–50 individuals	—	40–50	Holley 1833/1973

Date	Estimate	Notes	Adjusted	Source
Circa 1829	>100 families	Includes only Cocos and Cujanes.	>400	Berlandier 1969
1822	200–300 warriors	Karankawa, including Cokes and Cujanes.	800–1200	Kuykendall 1903:250
1822	± 1000 individuals	Basis unknown.	1000	Roessler 1883:616
1821	100 individuals	Seen at a single camp on Galveston Island; supports other estimates of high population in this period.	—	Wilbarger 1889:199
1820	± 400 individuals	For Cocos only; supports other high estimates for the period.	—	Padilla 1919:51
1820	(?)	Estimated 350 individuals for Karankawa and 150 individuals for Atakapa and Cocos; cannot adjust.	—	Morse 1822:373–374
1819	(?)	La Fitte reportedly fought 300 warriors; tends to support other high estimates.	—	Gracy 1964:41; Gatschet 1891
Circa 1805	500 men	Not clear if this is for all Karankawa groups.	2000(?)	Sibley 1807:45
Circa 1800	600 warriors	May not include Cocos; more or less consistent with previous estimate but sources unknown.	—	Bollaert 1850
Circa 1779	150 men	Unclear whether this is for the entire Karankawa tribe, or just the group of Carancaguases.	600	Morfi 1935/1967:79–80
1751	500 warriors	Excludes the Cocos; based on the 1820 Padilla estimate, we have added 500 individuals to account for the Cocos.	2500	Bolton 1906:115, 128
1690	2800 individuals	Basis unknown; not used.	—	Mooney 1928:13
1685	400 men	Margry's estimate for Bay Saint Louis Karankawa only; probably a very low estimate for the Karankawa tribal group.	>1600	Bolton 1908:274

E. Aranama

Date	Estimate	Notes	Adjusted	Source
1843	Extinct	—	0	Swanton 1952:308
1820	120 individuals	Contemporary estimate.	120	Morse 1822:374
1772	46 warriors	Plus "a goodly number of women and children."	184	Bolton 1914:28, 291; cf. Faulk 1964:58
1690	200 individuals	Basis unknown; not used.	—	Mooney 1928:13

49

TABLE 4.2

Ratios Used on the Upper Texas Coast of the Number of Individuals to the Estimates of Men, Warriors, and Families

Ratio[a]	Basis	Source
1 warrior:4 persons	Karankawa; 100 individuals included 25 warriors.	Bonnell 1840:137
1 family:4 persons	Karankawa; circa 1840	Gatschet 1891:65
1 warrior:3.5 persons	Basis unknown	Swanton 1911:43–45
1 family:4 persons	Akokisa; basis unknown	Bolton 1913:346
1 family:3.7 persons	65 Akokisa, Bidai, and Deadose families totaled 239 individuals.	Bolton 1916:199
1 family:4.9 persons	From census of persons under Spanish control in 1775.	Morfi 1935/1967:103
1 family:3.98 persons	From Akokisa or Coco skeletal data, circa A.D. 1500	Aten *et al.* 1976:90
1 family:6.38 persons	From archaeological skeletal data, circa A.D. 900	Aten *et al.* 1976:90
1 warrior:4 persons	Used by Morfit in 1836 to estimate the native population of Texas.	Muckleroy 1922:241–242

[a] In summary, excluding the 6.38 person estimate, $N = 8$, $\bar{X} = 4.01$ persons, and $s = 0.40$ persons, and including the 6.38 person estimate, $N = 9$, $\bar{X} = 4.27$ persons, and $s = 0.87$ persons.

vidual members have been locatable into the early twentieth century, although their relationship culturally and biologically to the protohistoric Atakapa and Bidai is an arguable matter.

In Figure 4.1b are shown the data for the Bidai. This time trend is very straightforward and shows a sharp decline around A.D. 1775, a leveling off until early in the nineteenth century; further decline nearly to extinction by the 1830's; perhaps a slight recovery of population about the middle of the nineteenth century, and then total extinction.

In Figure 4.1c are the data for the Akokisa. The general form of this curve is similar to that for the Bidai. The record begins with a period of relatively slight decline in the early part of the eighteenth century followed by a sharp decline in the middle of the century; this is followed by a leveling off of the decline, and perhaps even a slight increase up to the first quarter of the nineteenth century, followed by a rapid decline to extinction by some time around 1830. A comment is in order here in the data used for the period of 1721. This was obtained from Swanton (1946) who said the data came from de Bellisle and from La Harpe. I have been unable to locate the source in which this figure is given, but it is absent from Folmer (1940). The number is used since it is represented as a factual accounting, and, presumably, Swanton obtained it from some manuscript source. Although we do show a 200–250 datum (marked with a subscript a), it clearly is out of phase with the later information. The interpretation here is that the estimate reportedly given by de Bellisle was for one village of Akokisa and not for the entire group. If one accepts Orobio's estimate of four or five Akokisa villages in the middle of the eighteenth century, this suggests a minimum population in 1721 of 1000 to 1250 persons, which figure is shown labeled with a subscript b.

In Figure 4.1d are the data for the Karankawa. Again, the general shape of the curve resembles the others just described. In this case, a period of decline in the last half of the eighteenth century is succeeded by a period of even more precipitous decline near to extinction in the first quarter of the nineteenth century. This decline is followed by what may have been a slight population recovery around 1850 followed quickly by extinction.

Several features of these data require some comment. The population estimate for 1685 (subscript c) was explicitly for those Indians living about Bay Saint Louis (Lavaca–Matagorda Bay) and is used here as an estimate only for the Karankawa proper. Points *b* and *d* are not entirely clear as to their referent; d, especially, may only refer to the Karankawa proper (see Table 4.1 for details). In any event, if these points are plotted graphically, as on Figure 4.1, a choice must be made of linking points *a* to *b*, or *a* to *d* to *b*, and so on. In view of the great differences between the sizes of these estimates, the latter alternative seems most unlikely. On the other hand, if one selects the former alternative and then links points *c* and *d*, the two resulting lines are more or less parallel. This solution to the problem is attractive if one assumes that depopulation processes were affecting all of the Karankawa tribal group approximately equally and that a roughly similar relationship would exist between the population of the various constituent tribes of the larger Karankawa group. This assumption could be very risky, but at the moment provides a serviceable explanation of the data.

Finally, in Figure 4.1e are presented the limited data on the Aranama. Here, too, the pattern resembles those for the other groups in that a period of relatively slow decline in the late eighteenth century and early nineteenth century is followed by precipitous decline to extinction.

The nature of the available data is such that the individual graphic displays in Figure 4.1 do not reflect organizations at similar levels of integration. The Louisiana Atakapa, Akokisa, and Bidai are all presumed to be constituents of the major linguistic grouping called Atakapa and are assumed to be at a comparable level of integration to the Coco, Cujane, Guapite, etc., of the Karankawa group. This assumption, of course, follows the interpretations of Bolton and Swanton and is mindful that these are based heavily on "guilt by association." For example, review their treatment of data on the Bidai. The population curve for the Karankawa reflects a more abstract organizational level than do the other curves. There is nothing to be done about this limitation at present other than not to lose sight of it.

Collectively these five population curves all suggest the same, or a similar, situation. That is, a period of apparent relative stability or slow decline in the early eighteenth century is followed by a major, in some cases almost in-

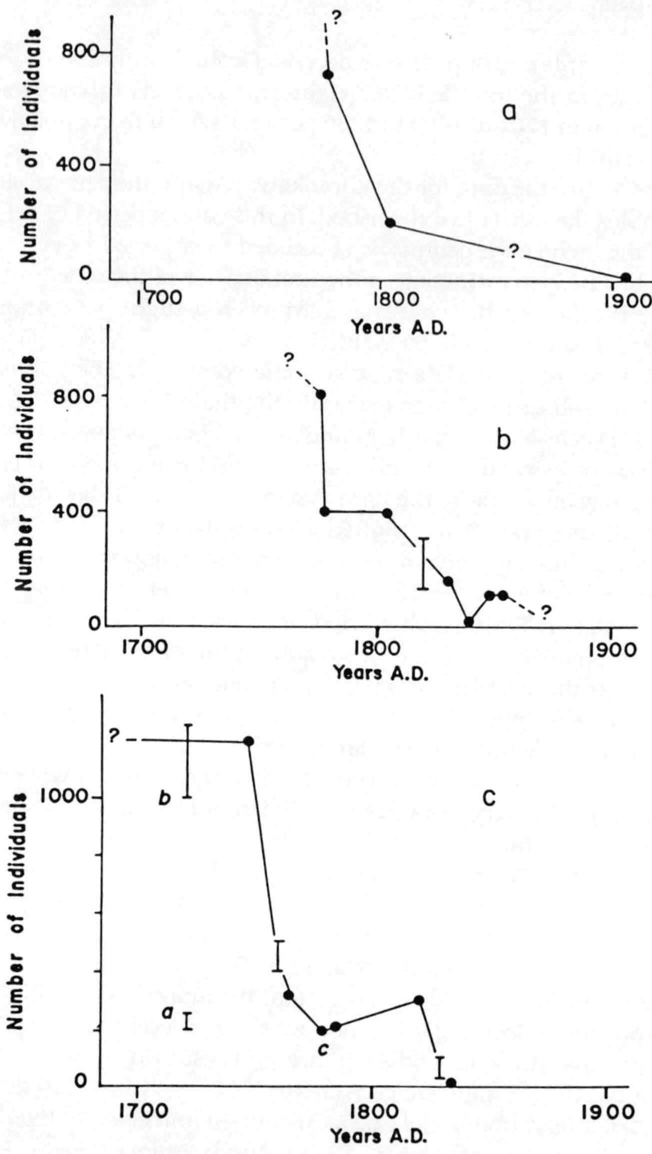

FIGURE 4.1 Population estimates—(a) Atakapa (Louisiana), (b) Bidai, (c) Akokisa, (d) Karankawa, and (e) Aranama—and (f) model of population decline—for upper Texas coast native groups in the eighteenth and nineteenth centuries.

188

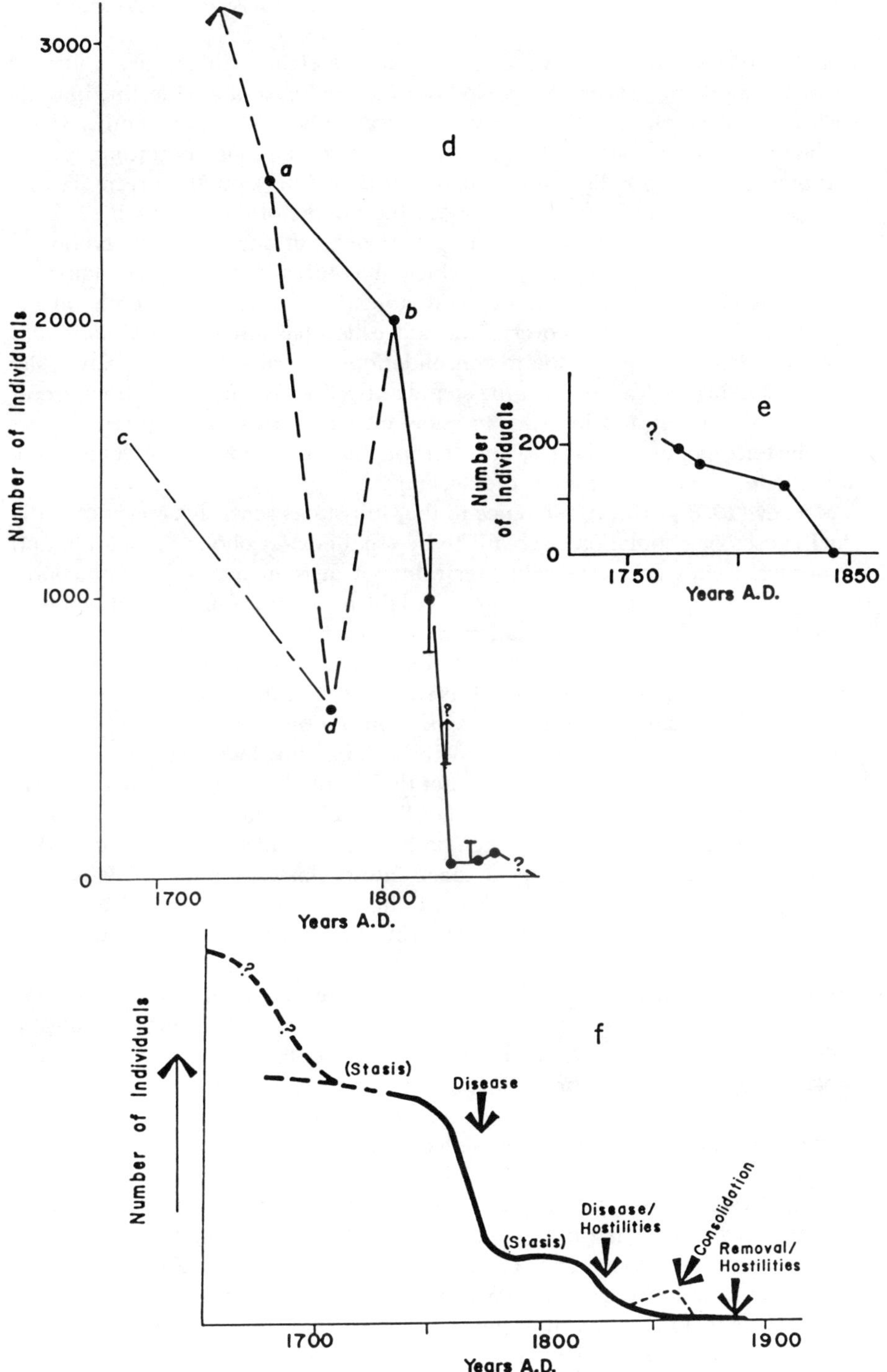

d
Number of Individuals
3000
2000
1000
0
a
b
c
d
?
?
1700
1800
Years A.D.
e
Number of Individuals
200
?
1750
1850
Years A.D.
f
Number of Individuals
?
?
(Stasis)
Disease
(Stasis)
Disease/
Hostilities
Consolidation
Removal/
Hostilities
1700
1800
1900
Years A.D.

189

stantaneous, decline in the third quarter of the eighteenth century, followed either by another stasis or by a period of much reduced rate of decline into the early part of the nineteenth century. This decline is followed by another sharp decline in the first quarter of the century with some groups becoming extinct and others showing a slight and short-lived period of population recovery and then going into extinction, usually about the middle of the century.

These patterns do not reflect a simple model, but one that likely embodies several components (Figure 4.1). Its principal features are twofold: a "stairstep" form in which population size descends to extinction; and, frequently on the last step, a slight rise or recovery. The suggestion has already been made that this latter feature may be due to consolidation of local groups into composite bands. The former feature (i.e., the stepwise decline) has not been discussed at all up to this point and in order to know on what basis to try to reconstruct protohistoric population levels, an attempt must be made to understand the immediate operative factors in the decline.

Mooney (1928:7, 12), in reference to the Gulf states generally, considered the chief causes of population decrease to be smallpox, alcoholic dissipation and demoralization, wars, slave raids, restraints of mission and reservation conditions, and removals to reservations. It might also be presumed that some of these factors, singly or jointly, had some impact on fecundity. Of these causes, there probably are only three major possibilities affecting the upper Texas coast: change in the rate of death through armed conflict, increased death through disease and associated factors, and relocation out of the area.

In general, the period of exploration and colonization by the Spanish was *not* marked by any significant armed conflict that would have resulted in a regular, ongoing death toll as a new component of the area's mortality rate. On the other hand, such conflict did occur between native groups; but since we presume this to have been a feature reaching far back into prehistoric times (cf. Bandelier 1905:74), it is difficult to conclude that this may have introduced any new pressure for population decline into the situation. However, once Anglo colonization of concessions from the Mexican government began in the 1820s, armed conflict (i.e., raiding) became a more common feature of native–European interaction, especially for the Karankawa. It is difficult to estimate whether the resultant death toll was sufficiently large to make a major impact except that by this time the native population had been so reduced that *any* further reduction was probably a serious matter.

The Spanish also made a rather ineffective attempt at establishing a mission system in Texas as part of their program to exercise political control over the area (cf. Kinnaird 1958:172). This effort did involve the relocation of natives from time to time, but rarely seems to have been permanent so far as the coastal groups were concerned. The impact of the missionary effort on population structure is not discernible at present. Later, Indians were relocated to reserves, but only the remnant of the Bidai, among the groups we are interested in, seems to have been affected by this. The third factor, disease, is one for which enough data exist to recognize its major significance in the upper coast demographic history.

IMPACT OF DISEASE

Almost from the moment of Cabeza de Vaca's arrival on the Texas coast in 1528, natives began dying from diseases introduced by Europeans. The serious impact of epidemic diseases is often cited, but usually in a vague way, and no one has attempted to assess quantitatively the role of these diseases in the demography of the upper Texas coast native populations (however, see Ewers 1973 for a nearby example). In recent years, documentary studies have brought the magnitude of this problem more into focus. As a general matter, the population decline in the first century or so of frequent European–Indian contact has usually been in the range of 75–95% in most areas that have been studied (Cook 1973; Dobyns 1966; Jennings 1976; Stearn and Stearn 1945).

In the case of the New England colonies, a 1765 report noted that among the English settlers the mortality rate was about 12–14%. Among native groups, however, mortality rates, even into the nineteenth century, were commonly 55–90%, although this rate varied widely from ±1% to over 95% depending on such factors as type of smallpox, virulence of the virus, and type of care received (Stearn and Stearn 1945:14–15).

Typically, disease struck native populations in two forms (cf. Cook 1973): widespread and lethal epidemics of infectious diseases producing spectacular mortalities in short periods of time, and chronic diseases producing a continuous long-term impact. Cook concluded that the mean annual population decline among New England Indians referable to all types of diseases amounted to about 1.5% of the existing population with 88–100% of the population reduced in the first century of contact (1973:497). In the major study of this issue, Dobyns concluded that a depopulation ratio of 20:1 (i.e., a reduction of 95%) existed about a century or so after the initiation of regular contact (Dobyns 1966:414).

Such high mortalities were not solely a matter of the inability of the native immunity systems to cope with new viruses. More difficult to assess than actual accounts of epidemics and mortality figures are the predisposing causes "such as exposure to weather, malnutrition or outright starvation, bad sanitation, and an all-pervasive feeling of despair," which rendered populations highly vulnerable to disease (Cook 1973:505). Cook goes on to note that to the extent disease resulted in the decline of native populations, this was a medium acting "essentially as the outlet through which many other factors found expression [1973:506]." Evidence of these kinds of factors was not often recorded for the upper Texas coast, but is not totally absent. For example, Wesolowsky and

Malina (in Aten *et al.* 1976) suggested that several systemic factors relating to the settlement pattern resulted in seasonally specific mortality for the prehistoric period. This would seem to indicate the existence of some of the predisposing factors mentioned by Cook. There is also a note on the mental state of the Karankawa in the early nineteenth century: "their continued wars . . . have reduced them to a mere handful, and their spirits have met with a corresponding depression [Bonnell 1840:137]."

There is evidence to indicate that, in general, the type of health care they received contributed significantly to a reduction of the mortality rate among native groups. In an 1898 case among the Pueblo Indians, application of European medical practices reduced smallpox mortality from 74% to 10% (Stearn and Stearn 1945:15). In addition to the nature of health care, a general failure by Native Americans to appreciate the significance of quarantine (even though its use as a control measure was known) also contributed to the enlargement of local smallpox outbreaks to epidemic proportions (Stearn and Stearn 1945:16).

Specific records of epidemics among the native groups of the upper Texas coast are largely absent. There are some lines of evidence, but to place these in any kind of meaningful perspective, it is necessary to reach farther afield for records of chronic and epidemic disease. In order for these to have any significance for the problem of reconstructing upper coast native population sizes, it is necessary to establish that the conditions or the opportunities existed for infection to have occurred (cf. Cook 1973:486; Ewers 1973).

Prior to the first quarter of the eighteenth century, direct European intrusion into the area of the upper Texas coast was very slight. The only known contacts in this early period were Cabeza de Vaca and his shipmates in 1528, La Salle's attempt to establish a colony on Lavaca Bay in 1685, and Alonso de Leon's expedition to drive out La Salle in 1690. There is evidence that both Cabeza de Vaca and La Salle brought infectious diseases with them (Morfi 1935/1967:138; Nixon 1946:32). Around 1720, contacts between the European and the Indian of the upper Texas coast began with the captivity of Simars de Bellisle, the La Harpe expedition to the Texas coast, and the expedition of the Marquis de Aguayo to establish a mission and a presidio at the site of La Salle's fort, and steadily increased in frequency. Although direct records are largely absent, the previously cited 1745 expedition of Orobio y Bazterra discovered evidence of fairly intensive efforts by the French to establish influence among the Indians along the Spanish–French frontier.

Thus, French traders from the Mississippi were reported by the Akokisa to have traveled by ship and overland venturing up the Neches, Trinity, San Jacinto, and Brazos rivers since at least 1738 or 1739 (Bolton 1913:342–344; Castañeda 1939:48). Presumably this means that the Karankawa, Akokisa, Bidai, and western Atakapa, at least, were being reached along the coast by the French in this early time period. Indeed, Blancpain, the Frenchman who was arrested by the Spanish at Orcoquisac in 1754, claimed that he had traded with the Atakapa for more than 25 years (Bolton 1913:348). Blancpain further claimed that until a short time before his arrest at Orcoquisac he had been accompanied "by a considerable party [Bolton 1913:349]." If true, these contacts would have exposed some upper Texas coast Indians to sources of chronic, if not virulent, infectious diseases from Blancpain's and similar parties as early as circa 1725.

It is known, further, that Orobio y Bazterra discovered that the French came to the area annually; that they came in summer, which could mean almost any time between May and October; that the French were not in the area in March; that Blancpain was arrested at Orcoquisac in October; that he had been out trading with the Atakapa for the previous two months; and that there was an implication of trading with the Bidai, as well as the Akokisa (Bolton 1913:342–344). From this it might be concluded that the French trading in the upper Galveston–Trinity Bay area most likely took place in the August–October period to take advantage, among the Akokisa at least, of the probable annual congregation of the bands about the upper end of the bay prior to their return to winter camps (Folmer 1940:217). The significance of this is not only that the opportunities for contact with Europeans existed, but also that these conditions may have optimized the chances for transmission of infectious diseases in the coastal environment.

There also is an account of Frenchmen being lost among the Cujanes in the early 1740s and another party of French being shipwrecked while searching for the first group in 1744 or 1745. It seems to be generally acknowledged that these accounts and especially the capture of Blancpain in 1754 were only the more noticeable aspects of general French and, later, English intrusions on the coast and inland principally for the purposes of the fur trade (Morfi 1935/1967:373).

In any event, these discoveries by Orobio y Bazterra initiated a period of intense Spanish counter-activities that lasted essentially until the abandonment (in 1771) of the mission and presidio at Orcoquisac. Prior to the establishment of these in 1756, Spanish agents acting as traders regularly visited the Akokisa and the Bidai. But, evidently, throughout this period of greater Spanish attention, the French continued to penetrate the area to some extent (Bolton 1913:343–344). For example, in 1759 there were reports of French encampment among the Karankawa on the Brazos River (Bolton 1913:369). More significantly, an incident was reported in which 2 Frenchmen and 100 Louisiana Indians entered the Akokisa country, probably to the east of Orcoquisac. These groups attempted to arouse the natives into attacking and eliminating the Spanish mission and presidio complex at Orcoquisac, but they were repulsed by the Spanish (Bolton 1913:369).

In this same period of the 1750s, the Indians from Bidai and Akokisa villages visited Los Adaes and one Akokisa headman, known as Canos, even visited New Orleans (Bolton 1913:351). Also, in this period of the mid-eighteenth century, the impact of the Spanish mission system was beginning to be felt among the native groups of the upper Texas coast. Coco, Cujane, Karankawa, Bidai, Akokisa, and others entered and left missions throughout Texas and in the process received and transmitted infectious diseases.

Throughout the last half of the eighteenth century, the problem of shipwrecks continued, probably at an accelerating rate. The Karankawa and Akokisa made something of a name for themselves as a result of their habit of plundering such wrecks. In any event, in the 1760s, a band of Acadians was shipwrecked on the central Texas coast and made their way overland back to Louisiana (Bolton 1913:376–377).

By the last quarter of the eighteenth century, the English were regularly penetrating eastern Texas along the coast and inland rivers possibly in preparation for a settlement (Morfi 1935/1967:426). In 1777, an English packet boat carrying bricks and other materials to supply just such a settlement was attacked by Atakapa Indians in the mouth of the Neches River (Morfi 1935/1967:62).

Trading activities became progresssively more intense along the coast into the early nineteenth century. According to Dyer (1917:4), the members of the Lafitte commune on Galveston Island (circa 1817–1821) found it more profitable to dispose of the merchandise they captured by trading it off to the Indians than by selling it to middlemen in New Orleans or Baltimore. In this trade, Lafitte's group operated along all of the Gulf coast from the country of the Aranama on the west to the Mermenteau River of south Louisiana in the east. They entered navigable streams and harbors and included on their rounds some white settlements that were already in existence.

From this evidence it can be concluded that the period of early European–Native American contacts brought abundant opportunities for the transmission of disease. As will be seen shortly, virulent epidemics ravaged the native populations to the east and southwest of the area in the sixteenth and seventeenth centuries. The effect of these epidemics on the upper Texas coast populations would have depended to a large degree on the amount of interaction among the respective local territorial groups. As of 1720, however, there can be no doubt that the opportunity for European transmission of infectious diseases to the native populations of the upper Texas coast was frequent and grew in intensity with the passage of time.

Before reviewing the record for disease outbreaks in the general Texas area, it must be understood that an equally important aspect of the impact of diseases on native populations was the effect of endemic and chronic diseases. These went largely without notice as individual entities against the more spectacular mortalities of the periodic epidemics. Cook (1973:493 ff.) has pointed out that diseases such as tuberculosis, dysentery, pneumonia, influenza, spotted fever, measles, and syphilis (French disease) subjected the native populations of New England to "uninterrupted attrition." There is no reason to believe that the situation in Texas was any different.

There is little information on precisely which diseases were afflicting the coastal populations of Texas; smallpox and measles were certainly present in the area or very nearby (Morfi 1935/1967:307; Bolton, cited in Newcomb 1961:36; Sibley 1807:40). References are also made to yellow fever (Dyer 1917:5;

Gatschet and Swanton 1932:16; Pratt 1954); dysentery (Dyer 1917:107); malaria (Ewers 1973:107; Kinnaird 1958:177); fevers, skin diseases and venereal disease (Morfi 1932:55), and scurvy (Kinnaird 1958:177).

Mention is made of other serious illnesses but their identity remains unclear. Cabeza de Vaca, for example, said "the natives fell sick from the stomach, so that one half of them died [Bandelier 1905:64]." This was suggested to have been cholera by Nixon (1946:32). Sibley (1807:41) noted that around 1790, "a dreadful sickness" struck the Caddos.

In spite of these other records, there is no doubt that periodic smallpox epidemics were the major killer. Smallpox epidemics were recorded in Mexico every 17 or 18 years beginning in 1520 (Stearn and Stearn 1945:42).[2] Within a month of the arrival of Cabeza de Vaca's group, fully half of the population of the native village that had rescued them on the beaches of Malhado had died from a disease that apparently was viral in nature—possibly cholera. Campbell (1977) notes that the populations of the southerly Coahuiltecan groups in northeastern Mexico began to decline as a result of diseases once European settlements were established in the late sixteenth and early seventeenth centuries. Bosque's 1675 expedition through Eagle Pass and into the Edwards County area of west Texas encountered three tribes that were being affected by smallpox (Bolton, cited in Newcomb 1961:36).

When La Salle arrived at Matagorda Bay in February of 1685, he visited a native winter camp containing about 50 huts (Joutel 1962:50). The presence of such a large native village as well as the lack of any mention of disease suggest that the central coast had not yet been affected. However, not long after this, two survivors of La Salle's colony near Lavaca Bay told Alonso de Leon that during the 1688–1689 period more than 100 of the settlers had died from smallpox (Morfi 1935/1967:138). Although one can only speculate about possible effects of this outbreak, the fact that La Salle's colonists did not appear to mingle with the natives may mean that the smallpox did not necessarily spread to them at this time. On the other hand, the fact that this period is synchronous with major epidemics that raged in the eastern United States (Stearn and Stearn 1945:22) is an ominous sign. In 1691, Father Massanet reported an unidentified epidemic disease had spread throughout eastern Texas and Louisiana killing at least 3000 Caddo (Mooney 1928:12; Nixon 1946:4). And in 1698–1699, the whole lower Mississippi Valley was affected by a smallpox epidemic (Stearn and Stearn 1945:33).

In fact, Stearn and Stearn (1945:22) have shown that during the seventeenth and eighteenth centuries, the eastern North American colonies were struck by a continuous series of violent smallpox epidemics, some of which were quite widespread. The dates of these were approximately in the years 1633–1634, 1649, 1666, 1678, 1689, 1702, 1721, 1730, 1752, 1764, and 1778–1779. These

---

[2]The first definite record of smallpox north of Mexico is the 1633–1634 epidemic in the New England colonies (Cook 1973; Stearn and Stearn 1945:20–22).

epidemics became progressively more widespread, as the disease was on its way to becoming endemic to the continent. The most widespread and fatal epidemics occurred in 1747, 1763, and, especially, 1779 (Stearn and Stearn 1945:42); many of these dates coincide with the Texas reports.

Numerous records of native mortality in Texas exist as soon as extensive contact with the Spanish missions began in the period about 1750. An epidemic occurred in San Antonio around 1750 that reduced the numbers of neophytes there (Bolton 1906:122). In 1749, Fray Benito Fernández de Santa Anna went among the Coco on the coast to try to persuade them to return to La Candelaria mission on the San Gabriel River from whence they had recently left; he found them in their homeland suffering from smallpox and measles (Morfi 1935/1967:307). It appears that the Bidai at Mission San Ildefonso were heavily struck by disease in 1749 (Bolton 1915:232). In 1751, a group of 54 Cujane moved to Mission Espíritu Santo de Zuñiga on the Guadalupe River for a period of only 2 ½ months; while there, the missionaries baptized 15 of these natives on their deathbeds (Bolton 1906:126). Disease is not mentioned as the cause but would certainly seem to be indicated for such a high mortality. Finally, we note that by the 1750s, the Coahuiltecan bands on the lower coast had been severely reduced or eliminated by smallpox and measles (Bolton 1914:1, 27).

In 1764, a smallpox outbreak occurred in the Mission Espíritu Santo de Zuñiga at Goliad in which many Indian neophytes and whites died (Mayhall 1939:115, Footnote 142). In 1766, smallpox and measles were reported epidemic among the Karankawa on the Texas coastal islands (Castañeda 1939:179, 220; Nixon 1946:11). In 1767, while at Presidio Nuestra Señora de Loreto, Nicolas de Lafora noted, "There is a strong tendency toward scurvy and a great many people die of it. Few escape malaria in any year [Kinnaird 1958:177]."

In 1778–1779, smallpox raged throughout the east Texas area killing, among others, about half of the Bidai warrior population (Mooney 1928:12; Morfi 1935/1967:105, Footnote 19; Stearn and Stearn 1945:46). Finally, we have the mention by Sibley (1807:41) of "a dreadful sickness" around 1790. Another major epidemic of smallpox occurring in 1801 devastated the remaining native populations on the Plains from the Dakotas to the Gulf of Mexico (Mooney 1928:12; Sibley 1807; Stearn and Stearn 1945:75). Subsequent to this time, smallpox was endemic throughout the North American continent (Stearn and Stearn 1945:77), and Berlandier (1969:84) reported in 1828 that smallpox occurred among the Indians every 16 years.

MAXIMUM POPULATION LEVELS, CIRCA A.D. 1700

As a result of this review it is seen that severe epidemic (and, presumably, chronic) diseases surrounded the upper Texas coast area on all sides almost from the time of first contact in 1528. And while it is exceedingly difficult to evaluate the impact of disease on protohistoric population sizes in the study area, it simply cannot be doubted that Indians of the upper coast suffered severely from the 1720s onward. The inference of major impact is unavoidable and is no different from the experience of the native populations in other areas.

The only mediating factor to be considered seriously as an element working against the establishment of basic conditions for the epidemic spread of disease was the native settlement pattern, especially the scheduling and size of population aggregation. At present, little more can be done than to speculate on the quantitative impact of the more dispersed settlement pattern among the coastal groups as opposed to, say, village agriculturalists. One may confidently draw the further inference that any population level indicated by the data for the mid-eighteenth century period, will be one already depressed, perhaps substantially, from the protohistoric levels. It is difficult, though, to develop specific numbers to express this. The best that may be hoped for at this time is a qualitative model that will serve to advance the issue of estimating sizes of native populations on the upper Texas coast.

The extrapolation methods utilized by Mooney (1928) and Swanton (1911) for the upper coast native groups are not entirely clear. Mooney usually employed an additive approach, sometimes called the "dead-reckoning" method (Ubelaker 1974:2). Swanton's figures are best, although not precisely, replicated by a linear model based on the average rate of decline in the 1779–1805 period. Later, however, Swanton (1952) yielded to Mooney's figures, which were slightly lower. In any event, today we have the benefit of a number of studies of population decline, most of which demonstrate population decay trajectories of a more or less concave form. As described earlier for the Texas coast, local variations may be expected. The best hope at present for developing a model is probably to deduce some reduction factor or rate to apply to their nadir population levels for the Texas groups as was done by Dobyns (1966) and Cook (1973).

A major difficulty with this approach is in deciding on the size of the nadir in a population being steadily reduced to extinction. Practically speaking, and since Dobyns's major thesis is that disease was the main agent of decline (a view with which I agree except possibly for the very latest period when extinction was finally brought about), the nadir should be that lowest level to which population declined primarily due to disease, but from which population survival and recovery would have been possible, all other factors being equal. It is assumed this level is approximated in the Texas data by the break or stasis in the population curves that occurred sometime around 1800 (Figure 4.1). After this stage in the population decline, other factors assumed greater significance than disease and drove the populations down to extinction. Among these factors were Anglo appropriation of Indian lands, failure by the Mexican government to enforce the "Karankawa reserve," genocidal policies of some colonists, and a residual disease component.

A second assumption made for this problem is in reference to the model of population behavior (Figure 4.1f). In light of the data just reviewed on the record of diseases for the area and of the opportunities for transmission to the native populations, it will be assumed that the steplike character of the model back to about 1750 was preceded by at least one more major decrement in the period from 1720 to 1750. Beyond this assumption, each group still must be reviewed separately rather than simply applying a blanket depopulation ratio.

The nadir level for the Akokisa was about 200 individuals and the maximum known population was about 1200 persons in the mid-eighteenth century (Figure 4.1c). A 75% reduction ratio is unlikely since this would result in an original population of 800 persons—less than that observed by several reporters at the period of the 1750s. On the other hand, a 95% reduction ratio would result in an estimate of 4000 persons, which is unattractive only in that there is not a shred of other evidence in its support. For our purposes here, we have simply split the difference and suggest a reduction ratio somewhere in the range of 85–90%. The former rate approximates the highest observed population in the mid-eighteenth century; the latter is speculative but allows for pre-1750 decreases. This latter estimate (about 2000 persons) recalls the claim by Captain Pacheco to have "reduced" (i.e., to mission life) two Akokisa villages of 400 persons each (Bolton 1913:347). This claim usually has been dismissed as boastfulness in a missionary field generally devoid of accomplishment. Also, it is not in accord with the other two contemporaneous estimates (by Orobio y Bazterra and Miranda; see Table 4.1). On the other hand, it is generally agreed that there were five Akokisa villages. If Pacheco's estimate was accurate and reflected the size of all the villages, there would have been a total population estimate similar to that just deduced. Another way to look at this is that even if Pacheco overstated his accomplishment, this does not require that he overstate the actual size of the Akokisa villages. Moreover, Pacheco spent several years in the area, whereas Orobio y Bazterra and Miranda only passed through briefly; as a result there is just as much, if not more, reason to suspect the Orobio y Bazterra and Miranda estimates as to discount the Pacheco estimate.

The Bidai have been approached in a very different manner. Probably because of their less intensive contact with European traders in the mid-eighteenth century, the nadir of the Bidai appears to be about 400 individuals. As a result, to apply the same 85–90% reduction ratio as was done for the Akokisa will result in very high protohistoric population estimates—so high that they seem most unlikely. Instead, the 1749 statement of Father Ganzabal has been recalled to the effect that, if he had the means to support them, he could have added to Mission San Ildefonso *all three* bands of the Bidai and *all five* bands of the Akokisa (Bolton 1915:232). Because of the apparent great similarity between the culture of the Bidai and of the Akokisa, the possibly risky assumption is made that these bands were about equivalent in size and that the Bidai therefore should be roughly ⅗ the size of the Akokisa. This may be an uncertain approach, but it seems more rational than trying to conjure up a reason to adopt a different depopulation ratio for the Bidai than for the Akokisa, es-

TABLE 4.3
Territorial Areas, Protohistoric Population Sizes, and Population Density Estimates

Territorial group	Area[a]		Population estimate (proto-historic) (c. 1700)	Population density[b]		Other population estimates		
	(miles^2)	(km^2)		(per mile^2)	(per km^2)	Mooney (1928)	Swanton (1911)	Swanton (1952)
Atakapa	—	—	1333–2000	—	—	1500	1750	1500
Akokisa	4600	11,900	1333–2000	0.43	0.17	500	—	500
Upper territory	(2800)	(7200)	—	0.71	0.28	—	1750[c]	—
Lower territory	(1800)	(4700)	—	1.11	0.43	—	—	—
Bidai	3500	8900	800–1200	0.34	0.13	500	—	500
Karankawa	5500	14,200	4000–6000	1.09	0.42	2800	—	2800

[a]Rounded off to nearest 100.
[b]For purpose of this table, densities were only calculated for the larger population estimate when a range is given.
[c]Also includes Deadose.

pecially in the absence of any independent verification. The results of these approximations are shown in Table 4.3.

Since it has not been possible to prepare complete maps of the Atakapa territory, making impossible the preparation of population density computations, no special attention is given to population estimates for this group. If the provisional 85–90% reduction ratio derived here is applied, estimates are obtained that are identical to those for the Akokisa. Whether or not this is reasonable cannot now be determined.

The nadir population for the Karankawa tribal group is approximately 2000 persons, but this step in the population curve is not as well defined as it is for some of the other groups. Again, to apply a reduction ratio of 85–90% would result in enormous protohistoric population estimates, which might be correct, but for which there is no independent confirmation. Again, the major factor, as with the Bidai, is probably the relatively lower level of contact intensity with the Europeans in the early eighteenth century. For example, Bolton noted,

> the Karankawan tribes of the coast proved hostile to the French and Spaniards alike, and, while their savage life and inhospitable country offered little to attract the missionary, their small influence over the other groups of natives rendered them relatively useless as a basis for extending Spanish political authority [1908:252].

Here, there are many possibilities, and for reasons solely of internal consistency in this study and as an interim strategy until better data are available, the same reduction ratios will be applied to the Karankawa as were applied to the Bidai. Both the Karankawa and the Bidai appear to have been somewhat less exposed to Europeans in the earlier part of the eighteenth century. In other words, this suggests that the Akokisa, and probably the Atakapa as well, bore the brunt of losses from the transmission of pathogenic organisms, primarily from French traders in the second quarter of the eighteenth century, and as a result were in a more advanced state of reduction at the time of the 1800 stasis that I have adopted as the local population nadir.

POPULATION DENSITIES

Given the preceding reconstructions of territories and population sizes, population density estimates also have been calculated for all native groups but the Atakapa (Table 4.3). These indicate very close similarity between the Karankawa territory, occupying a wholly coastal area, and the coastal part of the Akokisa territory. Moving to the interior, there is a population density gradient that is greatest at the coast and declines as one goes to the interior through the inland winter territory of the Akokisa and on to the territory of the Bidai. We are not interested in quibbling over the absolute magnitude of these numbers. However, as a result of applying similar assumptions to all groups, a measure of internal consistency may have been achieved in postulating population size and territorial area relationships on the upper Texas coast. The previously mentioned agreement between density estimates for the Karankawa and the coastal Akokisa is an encouraging indication of such internal consistency. However, independent verification may be sought by comparison of the upper coast data against (*a*) previous estimates of population densities among hunter–gatherers; (*b*) theoretical models of density gradients; and (*c*) theoretical models of the ratio of actual population density to the potential maximum population density of an area.

Kroeber (1939:171) used Mooney's population estimates, which have been argued here as being too low. Kroeber's estimates for territorial area on the upper coast are much larger than those used here (from Figure 3.1) and their source is unknown. As a result, his estimates of density are lower than those in Table 4.3 by many orders of magnitude and further comparison does not seem useful. Okada (cited in Fried 1967:55) has reported densities ranging from 1.9 persons per km^2 (Andaman Islands) to 0.002 persons per km^2 (Barren Ground of the Canadian Arctic) for egalitarian band level societies. Steward (1955:125) gave estimates of 0.1–0.01 persons per km^2, but did not consider either of the extreme situations cited by Okada. Wobst (1974:170) assembled data on population densities for hunters and gatherers around the world and determined them to range between 0.002–0.8 persons per km^2. Thus the measured population densitites for the upper Texas coast (Table 4.3) are within the middle of the ranges as given by Okada and by Wobst. Unfortunately, this is not a particularly useful comparison except at the grossest level of differentiation from food-producing societies.

A model for comparison of the density gradient going inland from the coastal zone may be constructed with data available in the ecological literature on the primary productivity of various habitats. Fortunately, much of what is needed has already been compiled (Casteel 1972). In Casteel's study, the closest approximation of the habitat transect represented by the coastal Akokisa–Karankawa, inland Akokisa, and Bidai territories are the population densities for tertiary consumers in salt marsh, temperate terrestrial herb, and temperate deciduous forest ecosystems (23.6, 15.5, and 9.3 persons per km^2 respectively). If Casteel's data and the Texas data are normalized by expressing the inland densities as a decimal fraction of the coastal density, the *structure* of the two data sets may be compared. In this comparison, both the coastal Akokisa and the salt marsh ecosystem are set arbitrarily at a value of unity. The remaining values are as follows: (*a*) 0.64 is the inland Akokisa and 0.66 the temperate terrestrial herbs ecosystem; (*b*) 0.34 is the Bidai territory and 0.39 the temperate deciduous forest ecosystem. The congruence between these two data sets is strong evidence that the Texas reconstructions express valid orders of magnitude differences between the several tribal territories.

In addition to examining the structural validity of the population density reconstructions, one also may test whether the relationship is realistic between the magnitudes of the Texas density reconstructions and the potential maximum density levels (assuming consumption of 100% of net primary production) in the same three model habitats used above. Estimates of the amount of net primary production actually used in supporting human food needs range from 0.5–5% (Casteel 1972:21–22). An approximation of this proportion in the Texas situation can be made by determining the ratio between measured densities for the Texas habitat and for the corresponding model habitat. The results range between 2.2 and 2.9%, again confirming that the upper coast population reconstructions are broadly consistent with theoretical expectations and may serve as a starting point for subsistence and other studies requiring population estimates.

References

Aten, Lawrence E., and Charles K. Chandler, Al B. Wesolowsky, and Robert M. Malina
    1976   Excavations at the Harris County Boys School Cemetery: analysis of Galveston Bay area mortuary practices. Texas Archeological Society, Special Publication 3.

Bandelier, Fanny (translator)
    1905   The journey of Alvar Núñez Cabeza de Vaca and his companions from Florida to the Pacific, 1528-1536. New York: Barnes.

Berlandier, Jean Louis
    1969   The Indians of Texas in 1830, edited by John C. Ewers. Washington, D.C.: Smithsonian.

Bollaert, William
    1850   Observations on the Indian tribes in Texas. Journal, Ethnological Society of London 2:262-283.

Bolton, Herbert E.
    1906   The founding of Mission Rosario: a chapter in the history of the Gulf Coast. The Quarterly of the Texas State Historical Association 10(2):113-139.
    1908   The native tribes about the east Texas Missions. The Quarterly of the Texas State Historical Association 11:249-276.
    1913   Spanish activities on the lower Trinity River, 1746-1771. Southwestern Historical Quarterly 15:339-347.
    1914   Athanase de Mézières and the Louisiana-Texas Frontier, 1768-1780. Cleveland: Arthur H. Clarke Co.
    1915   Texas in the middle eighteenth century. University of California Publications in History 3. Berkeley: University of California Press.
    1916   (editor) Spanish exploration in the Southwest, 1542-1706. New York: C. Scribner's Sons.

Bonnell, George W.
    1840   Topographical description of Texas: to which is added an account of the Indian tribes. Austin: Clark, Wing, and Brown.

Campbell, Thomas N.
    1977   Ethnic identities of extinct Coahuiltecan populations: case of the Juanca Indians. Pearce-Sellards Series 26. Austin: Texas Memorial Museum.

Castañeda, Carlos E.
    1939   Our Catholic heritage in Texas, 1519-1936. Austin: Von Boeckman-Jones.

Casteel, Richard W.
    1972   Two static maximum population-density models for hunter-gatherers: a first approximation. World Archaeology 4(1):19-40.

Cook, Sherburne F.
    1973   The significance of disease in the extinction of the New England Indians. Human Biology 45:485-508.

Dobyns, Henry F.
    1966   Estimating aboriginal American population: an appraisal of techniques with a new hemispheric estimate. Current Anthropology 7:395-416.

Dyer, J.O.
    1917   The Lake Charles Atakapas (cannibals): period of 1817-1820. Galveston: privately printed.

Ewers, John C.
    1973   The influence of epidemics on the Indian populations and cultures of Texas. Plains Anthropologist 18(60):104-115.

Faulk, Odie B.
    1964   The last years of Spanish Texas, 1778-1821. The Hague: Mouton.

Folmer, Henri
    1940   De Bellisle on the Texas Coast. Southwestern Historical Quarterly 44:204-231.

1

Fried, Morton H.
    1967   The evolution of political society: an essay in political anthropology. New York: Random House.

Gatschet, Albert S.
    1891   The Karankawa Indians, the coast people of Texas. Archaeological and Ethnological Papers of the Peabody Museum 1(2). Cambridge, Massachusetts.

Gatschet, Albert S., and John R. Swanton
    1932   A dictionary of the Atakapa language: accompanied by text material. Bureau of American Ethnology, Bulletin 108.

Gracy, David B., II
    1964   Jean Lafitte and the Karankawa Indians. East Texas Historical Journal 2(1):40-44.

Hawley, Amos H.
    1973   Ecology and population. Science 179:1196-1201.

Holley, Mary Austin
    1973   Texas: observations, historical, geographical and descriptive. New York: Arno Press. (Reprint of 1833 ed.)

Jennings, Francis
    1976   The invasion of America: Indians, colonialism, and the cant of conquest. New York: W.W. Norton.

Joutel, Henri
    1962   A journal of La Salle's last voyage. New York: Corinth Books.

Kinnaird, Lawrence (editor)
    1958   The frontiers of New Spain. Nicholas de LaFora's description, 1766-1768. Quivera Society Publication 13. Berkeley, California.

Kroeber, A.L.
    1939   Cultural and natural areas of native North America. University of California Publications in American Archaeology and Ethnology 38. Berkeley: University of California Press.

Kuykendall, J.H.
    1903   Reminiscences of early Texans. Texas State Historical Association, Quarterly 6:236-253.

Mayhall, Mildred P.
    1939   The Indians of Texas: the Atakapa, the Karankawa, the Tonkawa. Unpublished Ph.D. dissertation, Department of Anthropology, University of Texas, Austin.

Mooney, James
    1928   The Aboriginal population of America north of Mexico. Smithsonian Miscellaneous Collections 80(7). Washington, D.C., Smithsonian Institution.

Morfi, Fray Juan Agustín de
    1932   Excerpts from the "Memorias" for "The History of the Province of Texas." Prologue, appendix, and notes by Frederick C. Chabot. San Antonio, Texas: privately printed. (Revised by C. E. Castañeda.)
    1967   History of Texas, 1673-1779, translated by C. E. Castañeda. Quivira Society Publications 6. New York: Arno Press. (Originally published in 1935.)

Morse, Jedidiah
    1822   A report to the Secretary of War of the United States, on Indian Affairs, comprising a narrative of a tour performed in the summer of 1820. New Haven: privately printed.

Muckleroy, Anna
    1922   The Indian policy of the Republic of Texas. Southwestern Historical Quarterly 25:229-260.

Newcomb, W. W., Jr.
    1961   The Indians of Texas from prehistoric to modern times. Austin: The University of Texas Press.

Nixon, Pat I.
    1946   The Medical Story of Early Texas, 1528-1853. Lancaster.

Padilla, Juan Antonio
    1919   Texas in 1820, report of the barbarous Indians of the Province of Texas, translated by Mattie Austin Hatcher. Southwestern Historical Quarterly 23:47-68.

2

Pratt, Willis W. (editor)
    1954   Galveston Island: the journal of Francis C. Sheridan, 1839-1840. Austin: University of Texas Press.

Roessler, A.R.
    1883   Antiquities and aborigines of Texas. Smithsonian Institution Annual Report for 1881. Pp. 613-616.

Sanchez, Jose Maria
    1926   A trip to Texas in 1818, translated by Carlos E. Castañeda. Southwestern Historical Quarterly 29:249-288.

Sibley, John
    1807   Historical sketches of the several Indian tribes in Louisiana south of the Arkansa River and between the Mississippi and River Grand. In Travels in the interior parts of America: communicating discoveries made in exploring the Missouri, Red River and Washita by Captains Lewis and Clark, Doctor Sibley, and Mr. Dunbar. London: Richard Phillips.

Sjoberg, Andree F.
    1951b   The Bidai Indians of southeastern Texas. Southwestern Journal of Anthropology 7:391-400.

Stearn, E. Wagner, and Allen E. Stearn
    1945   The effect of smallpox on the destiny of the Amerindian. Boston: Humphries.

Steward, J.H.
    1955   Theory of culture change: the methodology of multilinear evolution. Urbana: University of Illinois Press.

Swanton, John R.
    1911   Indian tribes of the lower Mississippi valley and adjacent coast of the Gulf of Mexico. Bureau of American Ethnology Bulletin 43. Washington D.C. Smithsonian Institution.
    1946   Indians of the southeastern United States. Bureau of American Ethnology Bulletin 137. Washington, D.C.: Smithsonian Institution.
    1952   The Indian tribes of North America. Bureau of American Ethnology Bulletin 145. Washington, D.C.: Smithsonian Institution.

Ubelaker, Douglas H.
    1974   Reconstruction of demographic profile from ossuary skeletal samples. Smithsonian Contributions to Anthropology 18. Washington, D.C.: Smithsonian Institution.
    1976   The sources and methodology for Mooney's estimates of North American Indian populations. In The Native Population of the Americas in 1492, edited by William M. Deneven. Madison: The University of Wisconsin Press. Pp. 243-288.

Weissner, Polly
    1974   A functional estimator of population from floor area. American Antiquity 39:343-350.

Wilbarger, J.W.
    1889   Indian depredations in Texas. Austin: privately printed.

Wobst, H. Martin
    1974   Boundary conditions for Paleolithic social systems: a simulation approach. American Antiquity 39(2):147-178.

Yellen, John E.
    1977   Archaeological approaches to the present: models for reconstructing the past. New York: Academic Press.

3

Chapter 4

DEMOGRAPHY OF THE MISSION INDIANS

Demographic studies of Indians reduced in Spanish missions have been largely restricted to determining aboriginal populations and the rate of mestizaje, or miscegenation.[1] This chapter and the suceeding ones demonstrate that, given comparable data recorded in the entries, a wealth of information can be extracted from the mission registers of baptisms, marriages, and deaths. All entries provide the date and the signature of the officiating priest. The baptismal entries might provide the tribal identity of the individual or his parents, his date of birth, estimated age, or simple identity as párvulo (child) or adulto (adult), the parent's identity, identities of godparents, sometimes his Indian name or the Indian names of his pagan parents. Marriage entries might provide the some kinds of information plus names and identities of any former spouses. Burial entries also provide names of spouses or parents. Because of their status in the pueblos, Indian officials and trade specialists and Spaniards serving in missions were frequently sought as godparents to baptisms or witnesses to marriages, providing us with valuable social data. Marginal notes were often added that were helpful. Some baptismal entries had dates of deaths of those individuals added in the margins, while some burial entries had the deceased's baptismal number.

116

With such data, it is possible to identify families by following the method described below. Some families can be traced through several generations to determine what happened to them. It provides a "control population" of individuals who lived and died in the mission, giving us accurate, rather than estimated, information on such subjects as the average age of first marriages or life span.

This chapter will be found wanting in comparative material. It would be of interest to know whether an estimated mean age of 26.5 years for the San Antonio Indian population was typical of the eighteenth century, or was similar to the Spanish population of the _villa_. Because comparable studies could not be found, recourse was made to the few clues available from such widespread areas as New England, the slave holding states, or Europe.

The small populations with which this study deals are a problem because adequate sampling is needed for statistical validity. However, we proceed on the assumption that a small sample is better than none, This, too, is the reason that certain data are presented in a somewhat unconventional manner. For example, birth and death rates are generally given for 1000 population, but when the population is but a fraction of the basic unit, this is impossible. If one states that in 1720 at Valero there were three births in a population of 290 and in 1745 there were eighteen births in a population of 311, there is no basis for comparison. But if these same figures are presented as 3% and 5.7% of their populations,

then one can readily grasp the significance of the figures. This
is the reason why birth and death rates are presented as percentages of populations.

Nature of the Records Used

The demographic and social histories of the Mission
Indians are developed primarily from the mission registers of
baptisms, marriages, and burials. The originals are in the
Catholic Archives of San Antonio, while microfilm copies are
available in the archives of the Clerk of Bexar County, San Antonio,
Texas.

The only complete registers are those of San Antonio de
Valero. Thus, much of the following data is derived from them,
although the incomplete registers of the other missions do provide
important additional information. The registers were all stored
at the _villa_ church of San Fernando following the secularization
of the missions in 1794. Those that are missing have been presumed
to have been lost during the political upheavals of the early nineteenth century, from disastrous floods of 1815 and 1921, and a fire
in the church in 1828. The discovery of eight missing pages from
the San Fernando Archives which appeared for sale in Europe in
recent years raises the possibility that the missing registers may
not have been destroyed afterall. Of those that remain, many pages
are water-stained and some entries made illegible.

The records from San Antonio de Valero are extant from 1703 through the 1780's. The mission of San Francisco de Solano was founded in Coahuila in 1703. After being moved twice below the border (those moves probably accounting for the gaps in the Solano registers), it was moved to Texas in 1718 and renamed San Antonio de Valero. When Father Buenaventura Olivares moved the mission to the new location, he was accompanied by about seventy Xarames and Siabanes to help in its establishment. Some of these Indians can be traced in both records.

The incomplete registers from the other missions include the marriage records from Nuestra Señora de la Purísima Concepción (1733-1790), baptismal records (1777-1823), marriage records (1778-1822), and burial records (1771-1824) from San José y San Miguel de Aguayo. The late baptisms, marriages, and deaths of Concepción, San Juan de Capistrano, and San Francisco de la Espada are included in the San José registers.

There are counting errors in the various registers, some minimal, others significant. For example, the burial entries from Valero skip from #895 to #1028 with the notation by Father Mariano de Dolores of having adjusted the count. The difference of 133 is obviously from the entries of Solano and the deaths of the Hier-bipiamo which were entered into the first Solano volume. In another case the Valero burial entries skip from #1133 to #10134, but the error was caught after #10143 and the following entry corrected to #1143. Other errors were undetected and are noted below. Any researcher wishing to check the numbers of baptisms or deaths must be cautious of taking entry numbers at face value.

A final note concerning the registers is an observation of under-counts in all three registers. For example, there were baptisms performed _in articulis mortis_ with marginal notes such as "murió luego" or "murió el seis del dicho mes", but no burial entry. Several wives "disappear" from the scene leaving their children and husbands - the only record of their demise being the remarriage of the husband who is identified as the "viudo de ..." Some apostates recorded in the 1772 inventories are unknown in the baptismal records. Lawfully wedded couples who do not appear in the marriage register suddenly appear in the records when their children are baptized. But such failures to record each and every rite performed are probably minimal. Most of the priests were conscientious in keeping records as will become obvious in the following sections.

Methodology Used for the Mission Registers

Each registry entry was recorded on an index card. Valero served as the church for many in the Villa de San Fernando and presidio until about 1739 and even subsequent to the establishment of the _villa_ church, many Spaniards returned to Valero for the important rites of baptism, marriage, and burial. Therefore, because of their numbers, entries for Spaniards were first eliminated, leaving 2,798 cards (1088 burial entries, 1346 baptismal entries, and 364 marriage entries). By putting adult entries in alphabetical

order and entries of children under the father's name, the first
family units began to emerge. Names were not spelled consistently
in the eighteenth century. Given names were sometimes reversed,
i.e., María Ana for Ana María. And in the course of time, some
Indians adopted Spanish surnames to further confound the researcher.
There was a great deal of confusion also on tribal identity, the
earlier ones tending to be the more reliable. An Indian was
identified by the missionaries according to his father's tribe,
but in some cases over the years the priest would recognize him
by his mother's tribe instead. There are several cases in which an
individual was identified by several tribal names, particularly
when coming from what was probably a small tribe absorbed by a
larger one. Or one sometimes came to be identified by the leading
tribe of a confederacy rather than by his own tribe. However, by
cross-checking with all the clues provided in the entries, duplica-
tion was reduced. The last step was to begin recording families
and individuals in a note book by tribal identity. Only then
did it become obvious that "Sinmaiaya" and "Maraquita", the pagan
parents of baptized children, were the same as "Henrique" and "María"
who were baptized at a later date. The case is not isolated.

Although the method is time-consuming, it is the only way
of eliminating inflated numbers of individuals, family units, and
tribal members. For Mission Valero, with its complete registers,
it has the advantage of providing us with a control population for
which actual birth and death dates are known. From this control

population the following answers may be ascertained: the average age of women and men at marriage, the average age of a woman at the birth of her first child, the number of children born to a given woman, the spacing of births, life span, the incidence of deaths resulting from childbirth, evidence of infanticide, and remarriage patterns. As far as the author has been able to determine, this is the first time such a study has been undertaken on a culturally extinct Indian population. There are, therefore, no data with which to compare these findings. Hopefully, future researchers may follow with comparable studies to augment such a small beginning.

The same methodology was used for the downstream missions. Because of the complete marriage records from Concepción, the information from that mission adds much to our understanding of Indian life. The late registers of San José, including entries from the other missions, are less satisfactory in some ways. For example, band identity is seldom included, perhaps because at that late date and because of the racially mixed communities that were growing up around the missions, the _padres_ no longer felt such identification important. In providing us with a social profile of those late colonial communities, however, they extend our knowledge where the Valero record ends. Because of the racial mixture of these communities, elimination of "Spaniards" was impossible. Entries from the downstream missions total 1054 (350 burials, 359 baptisms, and 96 marriages from the combined mission San José

registers, plus 249 marriage entries from Concepción). Combining
the Valero and four downstream mission records makes a total of
3,852 entries.

The basic data derived from the mission registers have
been supplemented through additional sources. The 1772 _Inventar-
ios_ undertaken by the friars from the missionary college of Nuestra
Señora de Guadalupe de Zacatecas when they took charge of those
missions founded by the friars from the college of Santa Cruz de
Querétaro and the censuses undertaken when the missions were secularized in 1794 were helpful in fleshing out the skeletal data
from the registers of the downstream missions. Governmental
statistical reports and censuses from the Béxar and Nacogdoches
Archives and information on land distribution in the early 1800's
contained in the Mission Records (not to be confused with the
mission registers) on file in the Archives of the clerk of Béxar
County augment our information.

The Mission Populations

Table 4:1 shows the populations of the missions from 1720,
when only two missions had been founded, through 1815. Since four
of the missions were under the jurisdiction of the Querétaran
friars and one under the jurisdiction of the Zacatecan, _visitas_
were not undertaken in the same years until the College of Zacatecas took them all over in 1772. Therefore we have few population
totals for the thriving years of mission development. We only know
the total mission populations for 1720, 1740, and 1777 through a

government report, private letters from a missionary, and the inspection of the _Provincias Internas_ undertaken that final year. Actually, were more figures available for those early years that they might be graphed, we would obtain a fluctuating population curve. For example, taking advantage of friction between civil and ecclesiastical authorities, the 230 Indians of Mission Espada are said to have completely abandoned their mission by June of 1736 and the following year all but twenty of San Juan's Indians had fled.[2] In another example, only forty-nine Indians were left at San José following the 1739 epidemic of smallpox and measles, the rest having fled or died.[3] Every epidemic period would have been followed by a slump in population until those who fled had been returned or replaced with new arrivals. Because the death rate exceeded the birth rate until late colonial times there could be no natural increase.

The overall percentage of the native population that was missionized is impossible to ascertain. In discussing the Indian _naciones_ in Chapter 3 the sizes of several _rancherías_ recorded by contemporary observers were noted. If we analyze those that were visited between 1675 and 1709 we obtain a total of 2,445 individuals representing fourteen tribes from Coahuila. Out of five samples, four were _rancherías_ representing more than one tribe. If we were to assume that each tribe were of equal strength - which they were not - we would deduce that a tribe might vary in size from 54 to 293 individuals. The first contemporary estimate of

native populations was that made by Pedro de Rivera on his tour
of inspection of presidios undertaken between 1724 and 1728.
Rivera estimated only 700 Indians left in Nuevo León and "no more
than 815" in Coahuila.[4] It should be noted that at the time of
his visit, Coahuila extended to the Medina-San Antonio Rivers,
thus encompassing what is generally considered Coahuiltecan
range in Texas and the modern state of Coahuila. He did not
estimate the population for the Province of Texas which extended
northeast from the Medina; therefore no Tonkawan groups are considered. Nor did he estimate the population of Tamaulipas, since
its colonization was undertaken after his tour of duty. There is
a dramatic difference between 2,445 (representing only fourteen
tribes) and 815 for the whole of Coahuila. He undertook no actual
census on his trip apparently, but must have relied on estimates
of his presidial commanders. His estimates strike one as too low
at first glance, but may, in truth, have been fairly accurate.
The first consideration is one of time and location. Four of the
five rancherías were visited between 1675 and 1689 and were located
in the Province of Coahuila. The fifth ranchería of Sijames and
their allies, were natives of Coahuila, but were within the
Province of Texas when counted in 1709. The fact is, many tribes,
or segments of tribes native to the Province of Coahuila, moved
into the Province of Texas with Tonkawan groups - perhaps about
1700 (for example, see description of the Ranchería Grande in
Chapter 3). Another consideration is that smallpox epidemics

were taking their toll of Indian populations. Epidemics were recorded in 1674-75 and 1707 (see "The Impact of Diseases" below) prior to Rivera's visit and other outbreaks surely occurred. In summing up the evidence: by Rivera's visit many tribes from the Province of Coahuila had fled to the Province of Texas, their numbers were being reduced by disease, and his estimates may have been based on tribes which had not yet been reduced into missions, since this might be the primary concern of a military man.

The few facts concerning aboriginal populations of the missionized Indians are so scant that the only conclusion we can draw is that they were small - an observation made by Father Vicente Santa María reported in the previous chapter. Another observation can be made, however. It appears reasonable to assert that virtually all the Coahuiltecans became missionized by the end of the eighteenth century. In 1762 the San Antonio missions were working "to complete the reduction" of Borrados, Maraquitas, Pamaques, Piguiques, Manos de Perro, Cocos, and Caranguases (Karankawa).[5] The reduction of Coahuiltecan tribes which had been congregated earlier was complete. A decade later San Antonio de Valero was attempting to bring more Tonkawans and Apaches into its mission. The others were apparently concentrating on a few hold-outs among Coahuiltecans.[6] A population of 10,938 has been estimated by the author for the year 1779 for resident Texas tribes, but excluding Apaches, Comanches, and Pawnees (see Appendix A). Of this number, 890 Indians were located in the five San Antonio missions and those of Espíritu Santo and Rosario, Representing 8.13% of that Indian population. The same ratio of the mission-ized to the non-missionized tribes cannot be extended backward into time, however, because earlier comparative population figures are unavailable and rates of attrition can vary considerably from one group to another. Missionizing among <u>Costeños</u>, primarily Karankawas, was continued by the coastal missions into the nine-teenth century. We should understand, however, that there is no way to determine the percentages of any given tribe that were congregated in any given mission. Most of the Payaya and the members of the Pajalat confederacy were probably reduced at Valero and Concepción, respectively, but some tribes were divided among missions. For example, Pamaques and Piguiques were to be found both at San Juan Capistrano in San Antonio and at San Francisco Vizarrón in Coahuila, or Venados were reduced not only in the same mission in San Antonio, but at San Agustín at Camargo, Tamaulipas as well.

In the light of what were obviously small populations and the numbers of missions established in the northeastern Border-lands, the San Antonio missions drew a respectable percentage of the overall population. It is obvious from Table 4:1 that the missions maintained a fairly stable population through 1772 with a combined population undoubtedly exceeding 1000 from the mid-1740's to the mid-1700's. This nominal stability was due, however,

Table 4:1   POPULATIONS OF SAN ANTONIO MISSIONS   (INDIANS ONLY)

Year	Valero	Concep.	S.Juan	Espada	S.José	Total	Source
1720	290*	--	--	--	227	517	De la Peña[8]
1740	261	120	218	120	95	814	Fernández de Santa Ana[9]
1745	311	207	173	204	--		Ortíz, 1745[10]
1756	328	247	265	200	--		Ortíz, 1756[11]
1757	--	--	--	--	281		Leutenegger-Perry[12]
1762	275	207	203	207	--		Dolores et al.[13]
1768	--	--	--	--	350		Leutenegger-Perry[14]
1772	125	178	198	174	--		Inventarios, Zacatecas[15]
1777	77	140	156	153	183	709	Censu 1777[16]
1783	149	87	99	96	123	554	Census Reports, Texas[17]
1784	147	87	103	98	164	599	Census Reports, Texas[17]
1785	106	94	112	115	190	617	Census Reports, Texas[17]
1786	126	104	110	144	189	673	Census Reports, Texas[17]
1787	68	64	65	81	156	28C	Census, 1787[18]
1789	121	74	80	93	186	554	Census Reports, Texas[19]
1790**	48	47	24	46	104	269	Census Reports, Texas[19]
1790**	82	48	43	66	9C	332	Census Reports, Texas[19]
1791**	48	47	24	46	104	269	Census Reports, Texas[19]
1792**	40	45	29	48	92	213	Census Reports, Texas[19]
1794	--	38	12+	15+	96	--	Mission Records[20]
1805	--	21	21	?	93	--	Census, 1805[21]
1808	--	25	19	24	52	120	Census, 1808[21]
1809	--	21	20	24	55	120	Salcedo Report[22]
1810	--	20	19	26	50	115	Census, 1810[23]
1815	--	16	15	27	49	107	Vallejo[24]

* Includes 50 Hierbipiamo
** See reports from 1790-1792 below for explanation to pop. "decrease"
+ Figures are for adult males only

to continuous recruiting and not to increased birth rates nor decreased death rates as we shall see. After 1772 there is an obvious decline. By 1815 Father Bernardino Vallejo was the only missionary administering to the Indians in the San Antonio area.[7]

Baptisms in the Mission

Data on baptisms comes from the registers of San Francisco Solano and San Antonio de Valero and from the register of San José which dates from 1777 through 1823 and includes some entries from the neighboring three missions. For earlier baptismal data on those lower missions we must rely on other sources.

The baptismal records from San Francisco Solano begin in October of 1703 and end in August of 1716. These entries are recorded in two volumes. Volume 1 includes entries #1 (October 6, 1703) through #336 (June 17, 1708). There follows an unexplained twenty month gap in the record with entry #1 of Volume 11 jumping to March 19, 1710 and ending with entry #27 dated August 22, 1716. There is a second gap of almost two years from the latter date until 1718 when Solano was moved to San Antonio. The Valero entries begin with #28 (1718) in sequence to Volume 11 of Solano. In addition, the baptisms of the Hierbipiamo at Valero were entered into Volume 1 from Solano beginning with #337, in sequence to the Solano records, and ending with #369. The Hierbipiamo and their confederates first came to Valero in 1721, after the founding of both Valero and San José. A third mission was approved for them and has generally been considered to have been founded in 1722 under the name of San Francisco Xavier de Nájera. However, the book of their baptisms clearly states that they had remained at Valero and their entries were therefore recorded at that mission. The baptismal registers for Valero begin in 1718 and end in 1783; the baptismal count is inflated by sixty-seven. Entry #1403 (December 8, 1759) was succeeded by #1460 (May 4, 1760) when Father López took the year 1760 written at the bottom of the page and began his entries with #1460 instead of #1404. A further error was committed when #1470 was followed with #1480. Baptisms performed at Solano and Valero are presented in Table 4:2.

The baptismal register for San José is extant only from September 7, 1777, beginning with entry #832 through September 28, 1823, ending with entry #1211. The entries for the first years are badly scrambled: #833 is dated 1777 while #834 is dated 1780. Furthermore, numbers skip from #835 to #856, but the dates are in sequence. The entries for 1778 through 1781 are in numerical sequence, but dates jump back and forth. One is therefore led to suspect that these entries were copied from other ledgers. It should also be noted that by 1777 San José had a racially mixed population of mission Indians and Indians living outside the mission walls with Spanish, mestizo, and mulato neighbors. The baptismal entries reflect the mixed community and separation of Indians from other races is impossible since few entries record

Table 4:2   BAPTISMS AT SOLANO AND VALERO

Year	No.	Year	No.	Year	No.	Year	No.
1703	14	1726	25	1746	16	1766	6
1704	142	1727	25	1747	48	1767	4
1705	1	1728	67	1748	16	1768	9
1706	73	1729	17	1749	19	1769	4
1707	95	1730	30	1750	19	1770	3
1708	10	1731	16	1751	20	1771	5
1710	3	1732	16	1752	12	1772	2
1711	1	1733	15	1753	14	1773	3
1712	11	1734	14	1754	13	1774	4
1713	9	1735	16	1755	18	1775	1
1715	1	1736	12	1756	12	1776	6
1716	2	1737	14	1757	9	1777	4
1718	1	1738	15	1758	6	1778	2
1719	22	1739	26	1759	17	1779	12
1720	27	1740	33	1760	4	1780	3
1721	12	1741	62	1761	5	1781	3
1722	11	1742	18	1762	4	1782	3
1723	22	1743	46	1763	6	1783	9
1724	14	1744	19	1764	4	Total	1346
1725	14	1745	26	1765	4		

Table 4:3   BAPTISMS AT SAN JOSE

Year	No.	Year	No.	Year	No.
1777	*	1793	1	1809	2
1778	1	1794	6	1810	2
1779	5	1795	16	1811	10
1780	13	1796	7	1812	10
1781	6	1797	6	1813	16
1782	11	1798	6	1814	10
1783	10	1799	3	1815	7
1784	17	1800	5	1816	17
1785	10	1801	6	1817	13
1786	23	1802	4	1818	6
1787	16	1803	3	1819	12
1788	8	1804	1	1820	8
1789	12	1805	1	1821	1
1790	10	1806	5	1822	3
1791	7	1807	2	1823	14
1792	2	1808	3	Total	357

*incomplete year

racial backgrounds at this late date. The record of the San José baptisms is in Table 4:3.

Assuming that a more or less continuous influx of new arrivals, particularly in the early years, might be reflected in the baptismal records and that, therefore, the number of baptisms performed might serve as an indicator of population, the two were plotted together in Figures 4:1 and 4:2 with negative results.

Births at San Antonio de Valero

Table 4:4 records births at San Antonio de Valero by month, year, and sex. The same break-down was attempted for San Francisco Solano, but proved to be fruitless. Baptisms of children estimated ages or identified them only as párvulo or niño. The only patterns which emerge from the Valero table are the larger number of male babies (which we shall consider below) and the obvious low births in the month of May - or fewer conceptions in the month of August. We might speculate that this simply reflects the climate of late summer in Texas, except that such a trend was not limited to the Southwest. Conceptions peaked in the spring and fell to a low in the autumn in Dedham, Massachusetts in the seventeenth century as well.[25] From its founding in 1718 until the last birth recorded, the mean births per year at Valero were 6.93. Three sets of twins were born in those years, or one multiple birth occurred out of every 150. Births are best understood in terms of population for those years

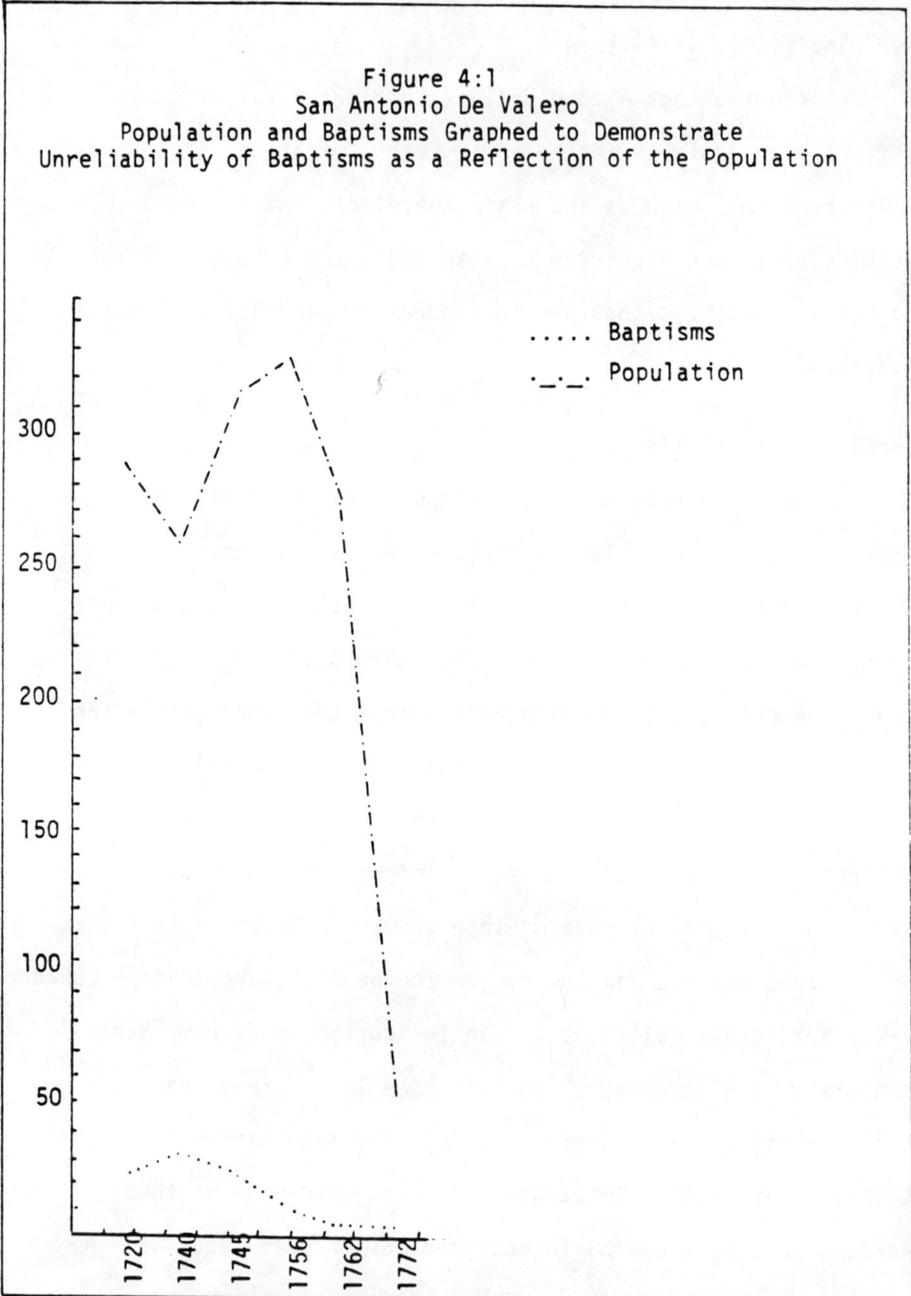

Figure 4:1
San Antonio De Valero
Population and Baptisms Graphed to Demonstrate
Unreliability of Baptisms as a Reflection of the Population
..... Baptisms
._._. Population
300
250
200
150
100
50
1720
1740
1745
1756
1762
1772

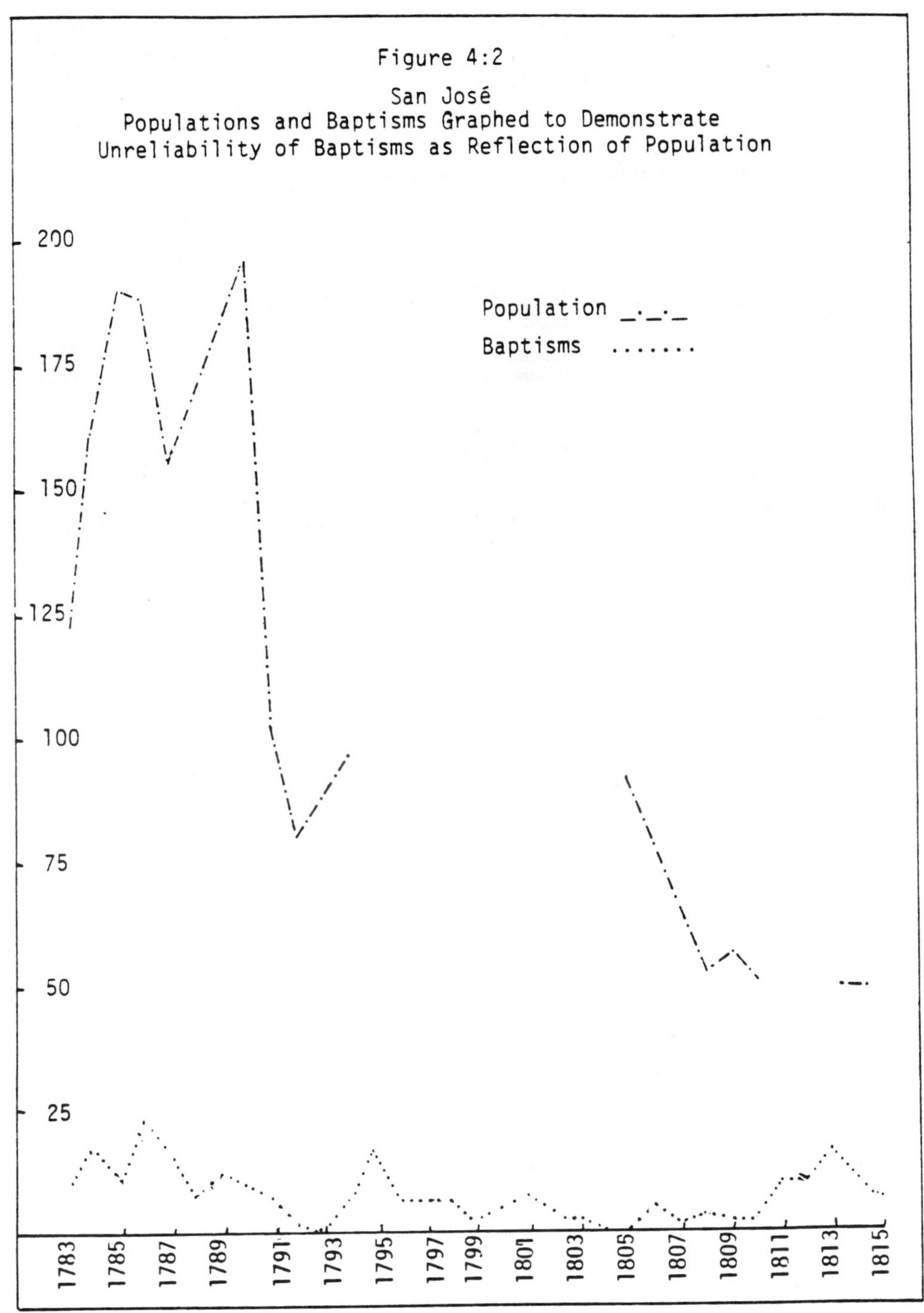

Figure 4:2
San José
Populations and Baptisms Graphed to Demonstrate
Unreliability of Baptisms as Reflection of Population
Population _._._
Baptisms ....
200
175
150
125
100
75
50
25
1783
1785
1787
1789
1791
1793
1795
1797
1799
1801
1803
1805
1807
1809
1811
1813
1815

Table 4:4   BIRTHS BY MONTH, YEAR, AND SEX AT SAN ANTONIO DE VALERO

Year	Jan	Feb	Mar	Apr	May	Jun	Jul	Aug	Sep	Oct	Nov	Dec	?	M	F	Total
1720										1	1	1		2	1	3
1722			1		1		1							1	2	3
1723		1	1	1							2			3	2	5
1724	1		1											2		2
1725			2					2						3	1	4
1726	2	1	1									1		4	1	5
1727		1		2		1		1	2	3		1		6	5	11
1728	4	4	1	1	1	2		1						8	6	14
1729		1								3				4		4*
1730	3	1	2		1	3	1	1				1		6	7	13*
1731	5		3		1		1		1					7	4	11
1732					1		1	1		1	1	2	1	6	2	8
1733			2			1				1	1			2	3	5
1734	2	1		2	1	1	1		1	2		3		8	6	14
1735		1				1		3			1	2		5	3	8
1736	1		1		1					1				1	3	4
1737		1		2		1	3	2	1	1	2			8	5	13
1738	1		2	2	1			2		2	1		2	7	6	13
1739	1	2	3			1			1	3	1			6	6	12
1740			1			1	1	3	2		3	2		11	2	13
1741	2	1					1	3	2	3	1			5	8	13
1742	2			6			2	1		1		1		7	6	13
1743	3	2	2		1	2	1	4		1				12	4	16
1744	2	1		1		2				4	2	4		10	6	16
1745	1		5	2		2		2		3		3		6	12	18
1746	2			1		2	1	1			1	3		8	3	11
1747	2	1	1	2		1	2		4		1	2		8	8	16
1748	2		3	1		2		1	1					5	5	10
1749		1	1	1	1	1	1	1	1		2			7	3	10
1750	3	1	3	1			1							3	6	9

Table 4:4 (continued)

Year	Jan	Feb	Mar	Apr	May	Jun	Jul	Aug	Sep	Oct	Nov	Dec	?	M	F	Total
1751		1	2	1	1	2	2	2		1				6	6	12
1752		1			1		1	1	2	2		1		3	6	9
1753	2	2			2	1	1			1	2			6	6	12
1754							1	2	1			1		3	2	5
1755	1					3	2		2					5	3	8*
1756	1					2	2		2	1	1			4	5	9
1757		1	1			2				1	2	1		4	4	8
1758				1								2		1	2	3
1759					1		1	1	1					1	3	4
1760				1									1	2		2
1761		1							2		1			3	1	4
1762				1				1	2					2	2	4
1763			2					1		1			1	2	3	5
1764		1					1				1			3		3
1765				2			1							2	1	3
1766		1						1							2	2
1767				1	1		1							1	2	3
1768	1			1								2		2	2	4
1769	1		1			1	1							1	3	4
1770				1		1								1	1	2
1771												1	1	2		2
1772							1								1	1
1773				1					1			1		3		3
1774		1						2		1				2	2	4
1775		1												1		1
1776					1	1		1	2		1			4	2	6
1777				1	1				1	1				3	1	4
1778			1											1		1
1779		1			1	1	1		2	2	3	1		5	7	12
1780		1						1		1				1	2	3

Table 4:4 (continued)

Year	Jan	Feb	Mar	Apr	May	Jun	Jul	Aug	Sep	Oct	Nov	Dec	?	M	F	Total
1781		1	1		1									1	2	3
1782								1				1		2		2
1783	1		1						3		1			4	2	6
	46	32	47	36	21	38	35	41	38	42	32	37	6	250	201	451

* Set of twins

for which the latter figures are available. In 1720 births represented 1% of the population, in 1740 4.9%, in 1745 5.7%, in 1756 2.7%, in 1762 1.4%, in 1772 only .8%, in 1777 5.1%, and in 1783 4.0%. An interesting pattern emerges with higher birth rates in the 1740's and late 1770's separated by the nadir of 1772 when it dropped to below 1%.

One observation is not reflected in the birth statistics. Out of 54 births from 1769 to 1783, 21 are either mulato or Indian-mulato. The subject of <u>mestizaje</u> (miscegenation) will be considered below.

Mortality in the Missions

Considerations of mortality are based upon the burial registers from San Francisco Solano and San Antonio de Valero which are more or less intact and the late burial register from San José, beginning in 1781 which includes those from Concepción, San Juan, and Espada from 1805 until 1823.

The first book of burial records for San Francisco Solano begins with entry #1 dated October 8, 1703 and ends with #120 dated July 28, 1708. The records of the Hierbipiamo from San Antonio were entered into this first volume, starting with entry #121 (June 7, 1722) and ending with #131 (August 31, 1729). Inexplicably entry #132, the last in the volume, is dated November 16, 1749. The second volume from Solano jumps to 1710. The date of entry #1 is illegible, but #2 is dated November 26, 1710. The

Solano record is then extant only through #10 (June 8, 1713). The entries from San Antonio de Valero begin with #20 dated April 14, 1721. The final Valero entries are recorded in 1782. There are serious recording errors in the burial registers. Entry #51 is followed by #62 and #267 is followed by #278 although the dates are in sequence in both cases. Conversely #836 should have been #854 which almost cancels out the preceeding inflated figures. More serious, however, is an inflated count of 200 when a page was turned and the entry that should have been recorded as #358 was written as #558. This could have important consequences. For example, upon a visit of inspection, the representative from the mother college would search for the entries of certification from the last inspection and report that so many baptisms, marriages, and burials had been performed since the last inspection. An error of 200 in the count is a significant one to be recorded as history.

The San José records begin with #847, dated January 3, 1781 and are intact and in sequence, except for three or four skipped numbers and two repeated numbers, until entry #1010, which was erroneously recorded as #1110. The sequence from that date (June 14, 1792) follows the error, so that the burial count is inflated by 100. Burial #1286 was misrecorded as #1826 (November 6, 1823) and succeeding entries follow that error - an inflation of 540 for a total error of 640. The priest who recorded the last entry, dated June 20, 1824, however, detected the 540 count error and

corrected his entry to #1297, just one count over. To correct
the earlier error the final count should have been 1177 however.
A side note to the burial entries is that the priests at San José
appear to have begun burying in a cemetery rather than in the
church in 1805, an entry dated 14 of June being the first noted.
And entries from Espada beginning 30 October, 1815 specify burials
in the cemetery of that mission.

Tables 4:5 and 4:6 record deaths at San Francisco Solano-
San Antonio de Valero and San José by month and year. Total
figures which are obviously out of line, such as those for 1707,
1728, 1748, 1751, 1759, 1763, and 1786 indicate serious epidemics.
However a closer look at mortality by monthly break-down provides
clues to the outbreak of less serious illnesses as well. This
subject will be treated later.

For the Indian population of Valero an average of 9.6
deaths per each non-epidemic year is derived over the 61 year span
from 1721 to 1782. The average death rate of the mixed population
at San José over a 43 year span (1781-1824) averages 7.4 deaths
per each non-epidemic year. This dramatic drop is in part indicative of the stabilization of the Indian population in the late
colonial period and, in part, to the mixed population perhaps.

We can obtain an idea of an expectable death rate by
calculating the percentages of deaths in non-epidemic years for
those years for which population figures are available. These
have been tabulated in Table 4:7. The year 1756 is somewhat

Table 4:5   DEATHS BY MONTH AND YEAR, SOLANO AND VALERO

Year	Jan	Feb	Mar	Apr	May	Jun	Jul	Aug	Sep	Oct	Nov	Dec	?	Total
1703													7	7 +
1704	4			3	2	2		3	2	1			1	18
1705	2													2
1706		1		1	2				2		1		5	12
1707	2	3	[illegible]	[illegible]	1	4	1			4	1		5	60
1708	8	3		1	2	2	2							18
1710											1		1	2
1711									2				1	3
1712			1											1
1713			1			3								4
1721				1				1	1					3
1722			1	1	4	6								12
1724	2		1		4			1					1	9
1725		1		1			1	1						4
1727					1	1			1			2		5
1728		2	4	6	2	1	2	4	[illegible]	3				54
1729				1	1	2	2	2		1	3			12
1730	1		5	1	5	2			2	1				17
1731	2			1			3	1						7
1732			1				1	2	1	1	1	1		8
1733	2	2			1	1	2				1			9
1734	3	3	3	1		1				2	1	1		15
1735	1		1	1		1	4		1	1		3	2	15
1736	[illegible]		1						1	[illegible]	[illegible]			27
1737		1			2	1			1		1			6
1738		2						2						4
1739	1	1	[illegible]		2	4		4		3	3	4		35
1740	2	1	1			3	2	1	3		2	2		17
1741	1	2	1		2			1	2	1		4		14
1742	2	2	4	3	2		3	3				1		20

Table 4:5 (continued)

Year	Jan	Feb	Mar	Apr	May	Jun	Jul	Aug	Sep	Oct	Nov	Dec	?	Total
1743		2	1		1	1		3	[illegible]	3		1		23
1744	1	2	1		3							4	3	14
1745	1		2	1		5	2	4	1	3	1	2		22
1746	1	3	3		3	1					2	4	1	18
1747	1	2	1	1		2		1	2	2	3	5	5	25
1748	1	1	2	1				2	[illegible]	[illegible]	5	2	4	50
1749	1	1			1	5	1	1	2	[illegible]	3	1		29
1750	1	2	4	1	2	1	2		1				4	18
1751	1	2		1	1	4	[illegible]			2	1	1	5	41
1752			1	1	2	1		1			1	2	1	10
1753	2	2				1	1			1	4			11
1754		1				1	1	2	1	3	1	2		12
1755	1	1	1		1	6	1	2	1	4	1	1	2	22
1756		2		4	1	4	7	2		5	3			28
1757		2	2	3	1	2	1	2	2			4	8	27 *
1758	1	2		2	2	5	2						8	22 **
1759		3	3				6	3	2	5	4	[illegible]	8	43 ***
1760	1		3		5		1	3		1	1	3		18
1761		1				1	2	1			1	1	2	9
1762			2	1		2	1	1		3	2	1	3	17
1763	6		2		2		[illegible]			1	1	1	4	83
1764							1	2	1	1		1	2	8
1765	1		1	3	1	1		1			1			9
1766		1				1	4	1	5					12
1767	1	1	1	1	1	1	1	1			1	1		9
1768		1	2	2			2	1				1		9
1769	2		2		1	1	4	2				2		14
1770		1	1	1	4			2					2	11
1774		1											9	10 ****
1775								3		1				4

Table 4:5 (continued)

Year	Jan	Feb	Mar	Apr	May	Jun	Jul	Aug	Sep	Oct	Nov	Dec	?	Total
1776				1	1	1		1		1	1			6
1777	1	2	2	1	1		1				1	1	2	12
1778					1		1			1	3	2	5	13
1779													2	2 *****
1780		1						1					1	3
1781													2	2
1782					1								1	2
Total	65	67	95	67	75	83	69	100	126	102	63	68	107	1087
	45	45	50	39	65	65	56	53	28	39	37	50	81	653 ++

+   1703 does not represent a full year

*   one page of 8 entries is missing from the book

**   one page of 8 entries is missing from end of year possibly into 1759

*** one page of 8 entries is missing from March 15 to July 1

**** nine entries are missing between August, 1770 and March 1774

***** two entries are missing from this year

++   totals eliminating epidemic years

Table 4:6   DEATHS BY MONTH AND YEAR, SAN JOSE

Year	Jan	Feb	Mar	Apr	May	Jun	Jul	Aug	Sep	Oct	Nov	Dec	?	Total
1781	6			1		3	3	2	1	2	2			20
1782			1	2	1	1	6		1	3	1			16
1783	2	1			1	1			1					6
1784		1				1						1		3
1785				3	1	1	2	1		2				10
1786		1	1		2			2	[illegible]	[illegible]		3		30
1787				1	1	1		5	1	1	2	5		17
1788	3			4		3		3	1			2		16
1789	1				1	1	1	3	2	3	1			13
1790	2	1	1	1		1	2			1	1	2		12
1791			3			1	1		2			3		10
1792	1	2	1		2	2	2	1			1			12
1793	4	2	2		2	1				1				12
1794				2			1					1		4
1795				1		1	2	1	1	2	1			9
1796				1						1	1			3
1797		2	1	1						1	1	1		7
1798	1		3	2	1							2		9
1799	2		1	1		2								6
1800	2	1	1	1					2			1		8
1801						2	1	2				3		8
1802	2	1		1	3	1	1		1		1			11
1803				1				1		3				5
1804		1	1	1		1						1		5
1805						2								2
1806								1				1		2
1807	1					2								3
1808			2					1						3
1809	1													1
1810								1						1

Table 4:6 (continued)

Year	Jan	Feb	Mar	Apr	May	Jun	Jul	Aug	Sep	Oct	Nov	Dec	?	Total
1811				1										1
1812			1		1									2
1813			1							1	2			4
1814			1	1	1	3	1	1	1			1		10
1815		2							1	2	4	1		10
1816		2	1						1	1	1		1	7 **
1817	1	1					1			1	1			5
1818		3	2			2		1			2	2		12
1819	3		1		4		2	2			1	2		15
1820	1	1		1		2						1		6
1821	1													1
1822														0
1823				1		1		1			4			7
1824	1	3	1			1								6
Total	35	25	26	28	21	37	26	29	26	36	27	33	1	350
	35	24	25	28	19	37	26	27	16	25	27	30	1	320 ++

** illegible

++ totals eliminating epidemic year

Table 4:7   PERCENTAGE OF DEATHS TO POPULATION

Year	Mission	Pop.	Deaths	%	Béxar		
						Pop.	Deaths	%
1740	Valero	261	17	6.5				
1745	Valero	311	22	7.0				
1756	Valero	328	28	8.5				
1762	Valero	275	17	6.1				
1777	Valero	77	12	15.5		1259	63	5.0
1783	San José	123	6	4.8		1509	60	3.9
1784	San José	164	3	1.8		1544	63	4.0
1785	San José	190	10	5.2		1565	49	3.1
1787	San José	156	17	10.8				
1789	San José	186	13	6.9		1648	59	3.5
1790	San José	197	12	6.0				
1809	Combined +	120	1	.8				
1810	Combined +	115	1	.8				
1815	Combined +	107	10	9.3				
		2610	169	6.4		7525	294	3.9
		740	44	5.9*				

+ Four lower missions

* Totals for same five years for which data from Béxar are available for comparative
purposes.

suspect with deaths in July and October which appear a bit high. The deaths for 1787 also appear excessive and Table 4:6 shows us that higher than usual deaths occurred in August and December. The higher numbers for 1814 through 1819 are due, in part, to deaths at the hands of hostile Indians, one victim per year for 1814, 1815, and 1816, three victims in 1818 and five in 1819. For the overall mission population the mean death rate from 1740 through 1815 figures at 6.4% in a non-epidemic year. In the same table, the mean death rate of the mission population with that of the rest of the population is compared for the five years for which data are available from both communities. The figure would appear to indicate higher mortality among Indians, however such a conclusion would be premature. This could only be demonstrated if we had population figures for Béxar during the early colonial period while the mission populations were pure Indian. By the 1780's the mission communities were becoming ethnically mixed and the _villa_ population itself was, in fact, largely mestizo. The figures for Béxar are derived from the statistical reports and censuses and the burial registers of the parochial church in the Villa de San Fernando.

In order to statistically test those years for which the death figures appear high, each suspect year was compared to the remaining total in a Chi Square formula to test for significance. (See Appendix B) For an alpha set at .05 with one degree of freedom a score of 3.84 was required for significance. For an alpha set at .01 with one degree of freedom a score of 6.64 was required. With the alpha set at .05 significance was obtained for all the suspect years (indicated by shading in Tables 4:5 and 4:6) for both Valero and San José except for the year 1743. With the alpha set at .01 significance was obtained for all the years except 1743 and 1736. In addition significance was obtained for the years 1787 and 1788 at San José with alphas set at either .05 or .01. The significance of these years in which abnormally high deaths are noted will be treated below.

It is difficult to make sense of the death rates by months. The totals from non-epidemic years in the tables for Solano-Valero and San José indicate that the missions shared high death rates for June and low death rates for September. But the suggestion that there is a correlation to the season appears doubtful. When the higher mortality figures for May and June at Solano-Valero are compared to the total of the remaining months in a Chi Square formula, significance is obtained when the alpha is set at .05 with one degree of freedom but is insignificant when the alpha is set at .01. Subjecting the figures from San José to the same test we find no significance at an alpha of .05, as we would expect from the fact that May, unlike Solano-Valero, has a low rather than a high rate. When we look at September as having the lowest rate in both missions we obtain significance for Solano-Valero with the alpha set at either .05 or .01, while significance for San José is obtained only when the alpha is set at .05. From the Solano-Valero data we might declare May through August as a high season for deaths, September through November as a low season, and December through February as falling between the extremes, but this could scarcely be explained in terms of weather conditions since the peak period coincides with both the mildest and hottest months in Texas. Furthermore, the data from San José clearly contradicts the other. Finally, we must conclude that the death rate is not correlated to climate.

Figure 4:3 plots the birth and death curves at San Antonio de Valero by years. The birth figures are extracted from the baptismal register. There were only five years in which births exceeded deaths. Epidemic years stand out like so many stalagmitic tombstones over an ever-decreasing birth rate. Figure 4:4 plots birth and death with population curves at the same mission. Population statistics can be seen to disguise a population on its way to extinction.

Factors of Fertility

The fertility rate of a population is dependent upon the number of women of child bearing years in the population, the number who marry, the age at which they marry, and the number of children they bear, particularly female children who themselves are potential mothers.

To determine the mean ages at which young men and women were married for the first time, the Valero sample was first used,

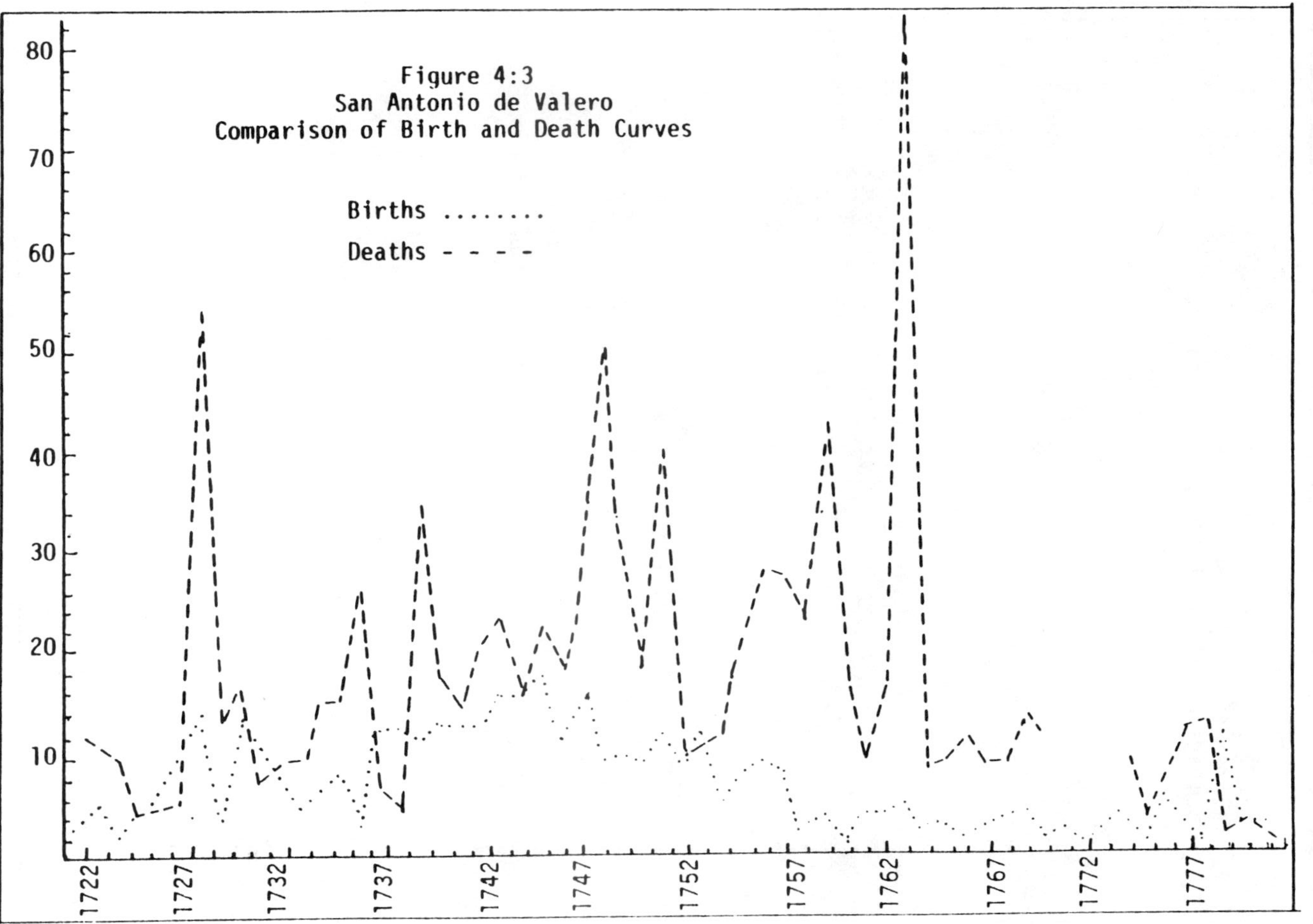
Figure 4:3
San Antonio de Valero
Comparison of Birth and Death Curves
Births ....
Deaths - - - -
80
70
60
50
40
30
20
10
1722
1727
1732
1737
1742
1747
1752
1757
1762
1767
1772
1777

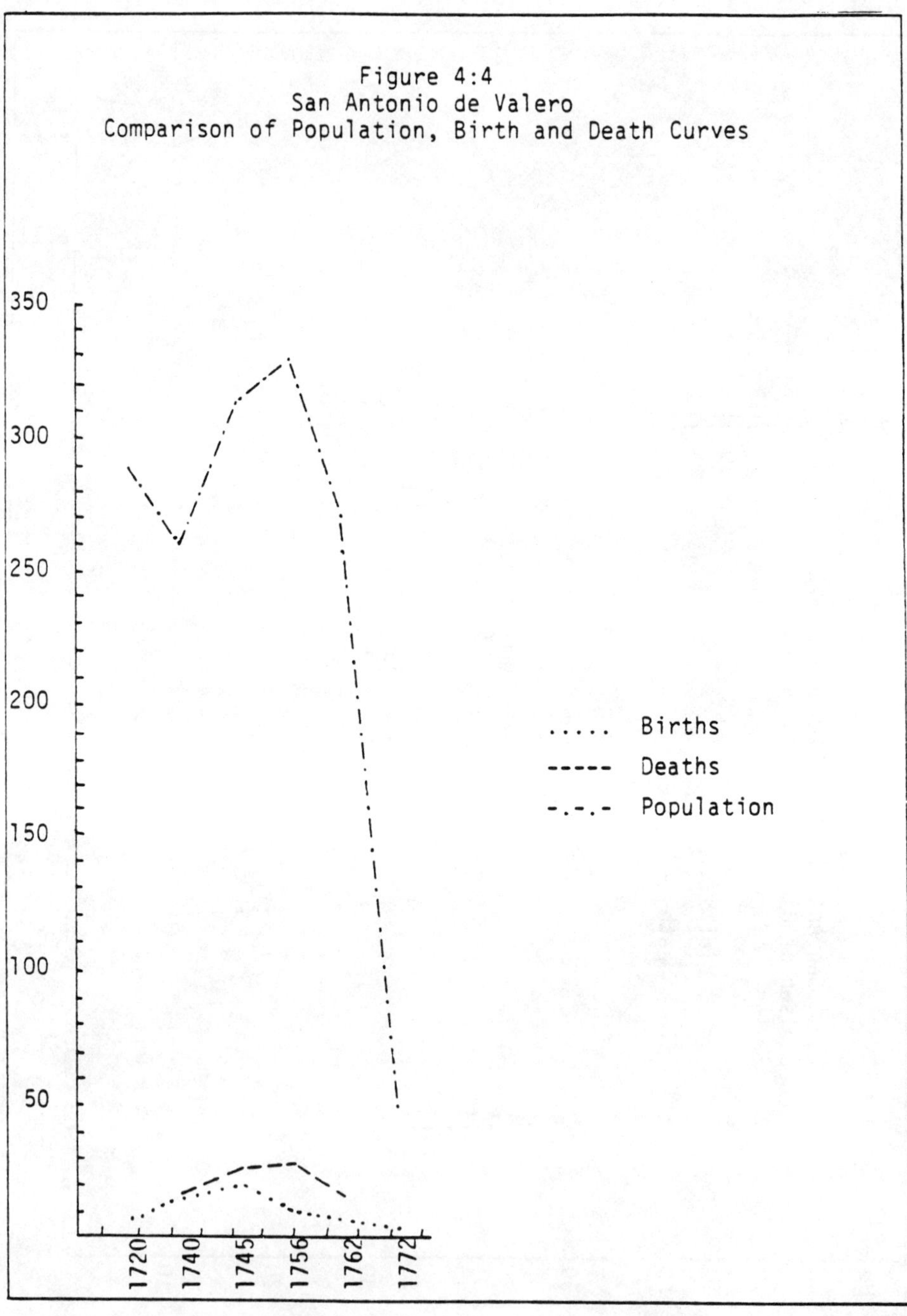

Figure 4:4
San Antonio de Valero
Comparison of Population, Birth and Death Curves
350
300
250
200
150
100
50
..... Births
----- Deaths
-.-.- Population
1720 1740 1745 1756 1762 1772

selecting out the few second generation youths for whom birth and marriage dates were known. The numbers are pathetically small. Three young women married at the age of 12 years. Eleven married at the age of 13 and two married at the age of 14. The mean age of marriage for young women of this population was therefore 12.9 years. Young men married slightly later. One married at 16, two at 17, two at 18, two at 19, three at 20, two at 21, one at 22, and one at 23 for a mean of 19.3 years. This tiny sample can be augmented by ages of young marrieds in the 1772 census taken by the friars of Zacatecas. The numbers extracted here are from very young wives, either without living children or with very small children whose ages can be deducted from their mothers giving us some idea of the age at which each married. Because of their youth we are assuming that these were first marriages. Furthermore, for the same reason, we are assuming that the ages given were reasonably accurate as checking their baptismal entries would have been fairly simple for the priests. The mean estimated age for the marriage of these women is 14.4 years. From the few husbands young enough to represent their first marriage we obtain a mean estimated age of 18.6 years. In comparison with the control population from Valero, the wives would appear to be somewhat older and the men slightly younger. The sample is too small for statistically definitive answers, but is in line with information provided by George Catlin from his travels among various Indian nations in 1823. He reported that girls sometimes married at eleven, but usually from twelve to fourteen years.[26] We can also offer medical evidence that Indian girls matured earlier than their Anglo-Saxon counterparts. Dr. A.B. Holder, a physician attached to the Crow Reservation in the 1890's reported the start of menstruation among Indian girls to be earlier than among Whites with a "mean" of 12.21 to 14.23 years.[27] The women of Spanish America probably married younger than their Anglo-American counterparts. For comparison, the average age of marriage for women was 23 and for men 25 in Dedham, Massachusetts in the seventeenth century while at the same time the average ages in Europe were 25 and 27 respectively.[28]

From the control population at Valero only ten women could be located to determine their age at the birth of their first child. One delivered at 13, four at 14, four at 15, and one at 16 for a mean age of 13.5 years.

In order to determine the effects of childbirth on women a search was made of the Valero records to locate the few women of the second and third generation who lived long enough to bear children. Only two women apparently died in childbirth: Juana de Carabajál, the wife of the Payaya, Manuel "el Cantor," and the Coco María de la Candelária. In the former case the baby was baptized while being born. In the latter case a cesarian section was performed after María died in order to baptize the infant. Another twelve mothers died within days to three to four months after giving birth. The babies inevitably died shortly after the mother, if, indeed, they had not preceeded her. In fact, so few young children survived the deaths of their mothers that we can say that the death of a mother with a child under the age of three just about doomed that child to an early death. There were 33 burials of _párbulos_ recorded (mostly Cocos) without parental identification who are assumed to be orphans.

Although the Valero sample is small it does suggest that childbirth was a contributing cause to the high mortality of young women. Such a fact is biologically predictable among very young mothers. And in an age ignorant of germs and antisepsis, puerperal fever was commonplace. The fact that more men remarried than women (see below) points to a higher mortality rate for women which may well be linked to complications stemming from pregnancy and childbirth. In this vein, it is of some interest that of eleven family units headed by a single parent in 1772, eight were widowers with children under the age of twelve while only three were widows with children.[29]

The next line of investigation was to determine the number of live children - that is, baptized children - born to each woman at Valero. The results are found in Table 4:8. The average number of children born to a woman was 2.45. It might be well to note that the results of Table 4:8 are based upon a larger population of women than the control population of second generation women used above. The count can be considered low. There were women who bore children before missionization and who died in the _monte_

Table 4:8   NUMBER OF CHILDREN BORN TO WOMEN, VALERO

Number of Children	Number of Mothers	Number of Cases	Cumulative Total
1	106	106	106
2	45	90	196
3	35	105	301
4	16	64	365
5	13	65	430
6	7	42	472
7	3	21	493
8	1	8	501
9	2	18	519
10	3	30	549
11	1	11	560
12	1	12	572
	233		

(bush) or remained unidentified in mission records. Also there
must be numerous cases of women who bore children after leaving
the mission. Although the table indicates a number of very fertile women who bore numerous children, infant mortality was
such that few survived childhood. Of the 13 women who bore 5
children, at least 2 survived from one family, at least 3 from
another, single children from two others, and the rest died.
Women who bore 7 children fared a little better. Two of the
seven survived in two families, and three of seven in three
others. Jumping to the really large families we find that three
children may have survived out of nine born to one mother. Three
mothers bore ten children apiece. Of these, three survived into
adulthood in two of the families, while all ten died in the
third. Roque de los Santos, the Xarame Governor of the pueblo,
and his wife, María Antonia, had eleven children, but only one
reached adulthood. And finally, Bentura Medina, an Apion, and
his wife saw only one child of their twelve survive the age of
two. The one son who survived married twice and fathered three
children.

In considering the size of the Indian family we must
first of all remember that the computed average of 2.45 children
is low for the reasons mentioned above. Furthermore, the figure
was derived from reported births - those appearing in the register
of baptisms. We shall see below that abortion and infanticide
were other factors resulting in what appears as a low fertility

rate. Dr. Holder also noted the lower fecundity of Indian women compared to Whites and offered as reasons the custom of couples living apart during the lactation period, the prevalence of prostitution and syphilis, and infanticide.[30] For comparative purposes we find that the average size of the family in Anglo-America during the same period is judged between 5.7 and 6.[31]

The spacing of births is of interest in determining the possibility of birth control practices. Particularly significant are the spacing of births to those women who produced numerous live children. The overwhelming spacing pattern was two years between births in 115 cases. A three year interval was evident in 66 cases, one year in 31 cases, four years in 23 cases, five years in 6 cases, six years in 4 cases, seven years in 2 cases, and one case each for eight, nine, ten, eleven, and thirteen year intervals. It seems quite reasonable to assume some sort of planned birth control, either through abstinance, alternative forms of sexual release to intercourse, or through induced abortion. Father García's confessional points to the practices of homosexuality and heterosexual perversion. Furthermore the question: "when pregnant did you take something to kill the child in your belly?" must have been induced from experience among the Indians.[32] Skeletal fetuses were found in the excavation of the chapel at San Juan and may represent a fairly sizeable component of other local Indian burials as well.[33]

Unnatural Deaths and Various Disorders

Unnatural deaths that occurred in the missions were duly noted by the priests in the _Libros de Entierros_. Most of these were deaths at the hands of hostile Indians and are considered below. Other tragedies had a less theatrical ring. The son of the Payaya Miguel Guerra died from a blow. Another, the son of the Paguache Juan Baptista, also was killed by a blow to the head administered by another youth while "fooling around". The Xarame Manuel died of poisoning from an herb eaten the day before. Antonio Flores died from "mal de corazón" (possibly a heart attack) brought on by an "accident in the river", while Miguel Hernández was felled by a pain in the head (possibly a stroke) which occurred "where they make adobes".

A study of the pathology of a skeletal series recovered from San Juan de Capistrano showed arthritis, osteoporosis, osteitis, and possibly Paget's disease and syphilis affected the population.[34] The 1762 _visita_ report blamed syphilis as a cause of the declining population.[35]

Deaths due to "old age", cold, chills, dysentery, and rabies were noted in the 1820's by a priest at San José who obviously took some interest in the causes of death. Several deaths ascribed to pneumonia and "fevers" were noted in the San Fernando church register for 1812.

Deaths from Hostile Indians

Death at the hands of hostile Indians cannot be considered an important factor in the decline of the mission Indians. Fifteen Valero Indians were killed by Apaches, Comanches, or Cocos from 1718 through 1782. Out of 1088 deaths this represents only 1.3%. Because of their distance from one another and from Béjar, protected both by its larger population and the presidio, the lower missions probably suffered more losses in lives and goods from marauding Indians. Hostile bands quickly capitalized on weakened conditions on the frontier. Towards the end of the eighteenth century the mission populations were greatly reduced. There were not enough able-bodied men to keep up with the work load and to protect the work details also. Nor were there any presidiales to help protect the missions as there had been in the earlier years. Between 1790 and 1819 sixteen people were killed by hostile Apaches or Comanches in the vicinity of the downstream missions. From 199 burials recorded for those years these deaths represent 8.0% of the total. Four of these killed, however, were non-residents of the mission communities and only some of the victims were Indians from the now racially mixed mission communities. Among the Indian victims were a mother and child from Espada killed in 1818, three men from San José killed in the countryside whose remains were found half a year later and buried in 1790, and the governor of Espada, Emeterio Espinosa, who was killed in 1819.

The Impact of Diseases in the Missions

The diseases introduced by the Spaniards were, of course, an important factor in the decline of the Indians as shown in Figure 4:3. Epidemics and outbreaks of lesser ills have been statistically identified above and are indicated in Tables 4:5 and 4:6 as shaded areas in those months in which abnormally high deaths occurred. Some of these can be identified; some we may never learn. The 1707 epidemic at San Francisco Solano was identified from a baptismal entry dated 1708 which recorded that Father Jorge de Puga had died during the epidemic of smallpox the previous year.

The illnesses that took their tolls in 1728 and 1736 are unidentified.

There is a lesson for the historian in the 1739 epidemic. It was identified by Castañeda as a simultaneous outbreak of smallpox and measles. He reported that "in San Antonio de Valero, from more than three hundred only one hundred and eighty-four survived" the scourge.[36] Elsewhere it has been reported that the San Antonio missions were "almost depopulated by death and desertion".[37] These assumptions of a devastating death count for the year apparently rest on a letter written by Father Benito Fernández de Santa Ana to the Father Guardian Pedro del Barco in February of the following year.[38] Under each mission Father Fernández ennumerated the numbers baptized to date, the population following

the epidemic, and notations such as "the rest died". For Valero
the priest noted that "many died" and that following the epidemic
184 people remained. Castañeda's statement is challenged by the
mission register. Yes, many died. We have statistically proven
that something extraordinary occurred in 1739 to account for
35 deaths, but in examining the pattern of deaths for the year we
see that the epidemic probably struck the mission in March and
April and accounted for only thirteen deaths. We cannot make the
error of attributing all deaths for a single year to an epidemic.
Furthermore, if 184 survived and we add the total deaths for the
year, then the population numbered 219 and not more than 300.
Under his report for Capistrano, Fernández wrote "147 have died".
The statement has probably been interpreted as indicating the
number who died in the epidemic, where, in fact, he is giving the
total number of burials from 1731 until 1740. In 1745 Father
Francisco Xavier Ortíz reported the total burials at San Juan at
241.[39] Clearly, if 147 deaths had occurred in one year the difference of ninety-four could not possibly account for the deaths
in a fourteen year period in which the population was sizeable.
The year 1739 is one case in which the effect of an epidemic has
been overestimated and should serve as a warning to use the contemporary data with caution.

   We have seen that, statistically speaking, the twenty-
three deaths in 1743 were not significant. The monthly distributions of the deaths, however, tell us otherwise. Certainly some

extraordinary complaint fell an abnormal number of individuals in September. Contrarily, significance was obtained for the deaths recorded at San José in 1787 and 1788 and yet the monthly distribution for those years does not substantiate the statistical finding. Statistical evidence, too, must be used cautiously: a serious illness could go undetected in a year that otherwise might have had a low death rate were we not looking for a pattern to such an outbreak, or an increased death rate might be due to an increase in population.

The 1748 epidemic is unidentified, but both the 1749 and 1751 epidemics can probably be laid to smallpox. In the Valero register a marginal entry by Father García for the September 6, 1749 baptism of a son of the Sana Torquato (#817) reads "se acabaron las viruelas". Also written in the margin is "murió en 8 de Julio de 1751". The problem is that in 1749 the epidemic did not break out until October, a month after the entry was made. The outbreak in 1751 occurred in July and August. Did García make the note after August in 1751 when the smallpox had finally run its course? Confirmation for an October outbreak of smallpox in 1749 comes from a testimonial of Father Mariano de los Dolores before the presidial captain. Several Apache delegations arrived in San Antonio during the fall of that year requesting that a mission be established for them. The earlier delegations of August 20 and September 24 reported nothing unusual, but the

third delegation which arrived November 29 seeking corn and
tobacco reported an epidemic of smallpox among their people.[40]
Ewers reported smallpox at the San Xavier missions in 1750 adding
to the likelihood of annual occurrences on three successive
years.[41]

An unusual number of deaths occurred in December of 1759,
but affected only a small band of Tancague (Tonkawa) and Yojuan
captives from a chain-gang. All were baptized and died at Valero
during the final days of November and the beginning of December.
It is probable that they were stricken elsewhere and brought to
Valero upon orders of the captain of the presidio.

The most devastating of all was a smallpox epidemic which
struck in August and September of 1763 which all but wiped out the
Cocos and Karankawas at Valero. Forty-six Cocos died and ten out
of seventeen Karankawas, accounting for most of the casualties.
These coastal people had all been baptized at Mission Candelaria
and had come to Valero sometime after their mission had been closed.
One would suspect that they had never been exposed to the disease,
although smallpox was reported in the San Xavier missions in
1750.[42] It is of course possible that they had not been in their
mission at the time of the earlier outbreak. The 1763 epidemic
has been cited elsewhere with the notation that "half the population died" in the San Antonio missions.[43] This is unlikely and
certainly is not true of Valero. The population at Valero in 1762

was 275 and the epidemic accounts for sixty-six deaths, a tragic enough figure without inflating it.

Table 4:6 shows us that 1786 was an epidemic year, but the nature of the disease is undetermined.

In these epidemic years one age group of the population was apt to suffer greater casualties than the other as can be seen in Table 4:9. There is probably no particular significance where adult outnumber child casualties. More adults were victims in 1763 than children for the simple reason that most of the victims were Cocos and Karankawas and there were very few children among these groups. The greater number of adults who fell in 1707 also appears to reflect the greater number of adults in the population. There may be significance in those cases in which child casualties are greater than adult, however, but until the diseases can be identified we cannot be certain that it is not simply a case of a new generation which had not been exposed to the disease before.

In an attempt to determine whether the mission communities suffered greater losses than the combined _villa_ and presidio community of Béjar, the deaths from Valero and San José are compared to those of Béjar in Figures 4:5 and 4:6. Breaks in the graphs are due to gaps in the registers (see Table 4:5). The data for Béjar are derived from two sources. Entries up until 1731 are the non-Indian deaths extracted from the Valero registers. The gap from 1732 through 1743 indicates that the earliest burial register

Table 4:9   MORTALITY OF EPIDEMICS AT SOLANO AND VALERO

Year	Outbreak	Adult Casualties	Child Casualties	Disease
1707	Mar-Apr	26	13	smallpox
1728	Sep-Oct	21	9	?
1736	Jan-Feb Oct-Nov	11	14	?
1739	Mar-Apr	10	3	smallpox measles
1743	Sep	2	9	?
1748	Sep-Oct	12	19	?
1749	Oct	7	6	smallpox
1751	Jul-Aug	18	5	smallpox
1763	Aug-Sep	50	16	smallpox

for the new <u>villa</u> church is lost and no non-Indian burials were registered at Valero. The extant <u>villa</u> register (which starts with #1) was begun in 1744. The few non-Indian burials registered at Valero after 1744 have been added to the <u>villa</u> numbers. In the case of the first graph then we are comparing an essentially mission Indian population at Valero with a mixed population from Béjar made up of socially recognized Spaniards, non-mission Indians, mestizos, and mulattoes. In Figure 4:6 we are comparing two racially mixed communities. Furthermore we should remember that from 1805 through 1824, the San José register included the burials of the other downstream missions.

Both Figures 4:5 and 4:6 illustrate what, except for epidemic peaks, would be a fairly rhythmic alternation of higher and lower points on the graph which reflect the greater number of Valero Indians to the Béjar residents in the earlier years and the steady increase of the Béjar residents over the mission communities from 1763 on. Until 1747, assuming that the missing Béjar entries would have followed the pattern, we see a true correlation between the two communities: the favorable or unfavorable factors that affected one, affected the other and the 1728 epidemic struck both. There is no correlation between 1748 and 1762. The epidemic in 1748 hit the mission Indian community while Béjar had fewer deaths than the year before, while in 1750 deaths in the mission had dropped dramatically as Béjar was experiencing abnormal casualties. Again the 1751 and 1759 peaks for Valero are not

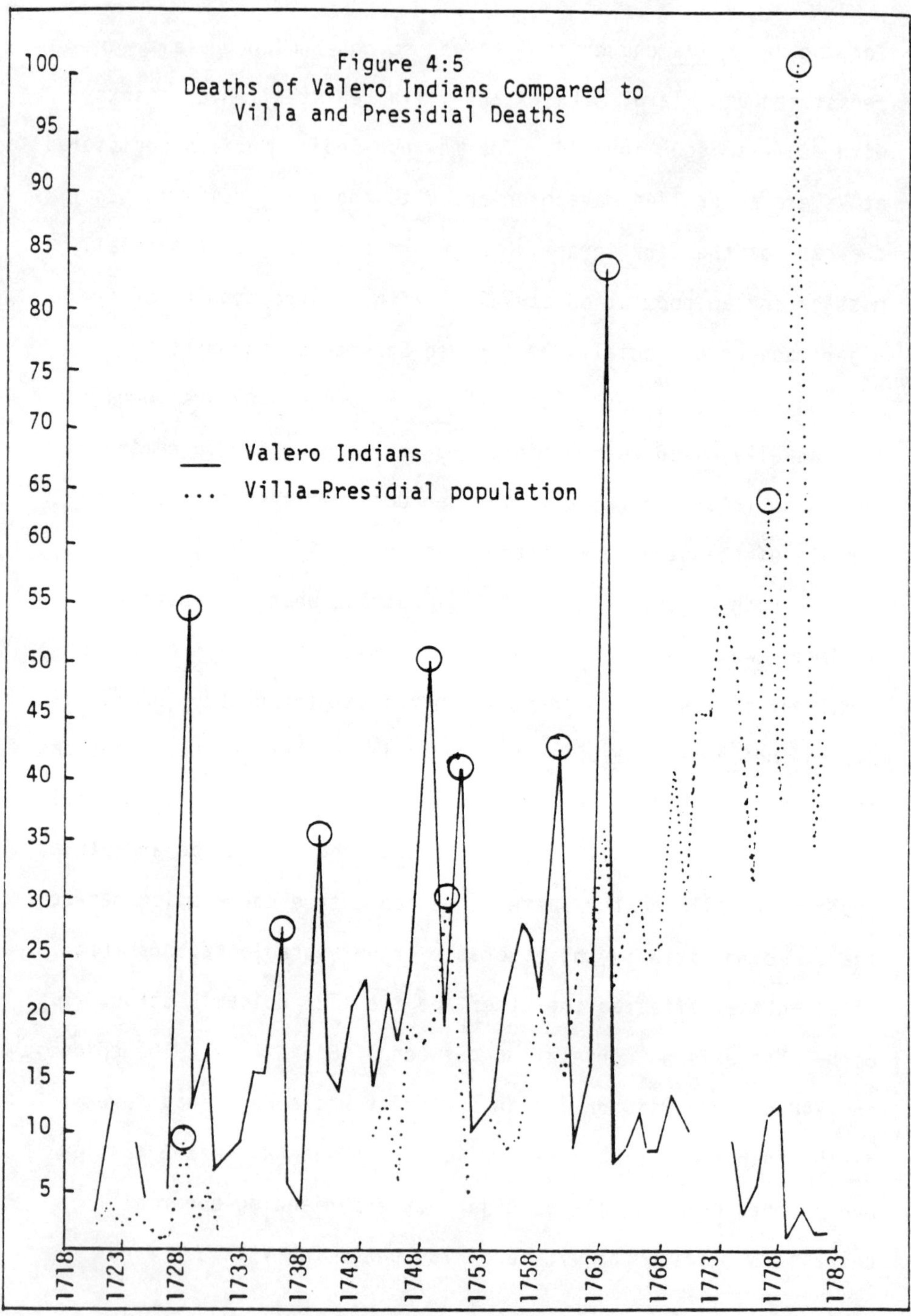

Figure 4:5
Deaths of Valero Indians Compared to
Villa and Presidial Deaths
Valero Indians
Villa-Presidial population

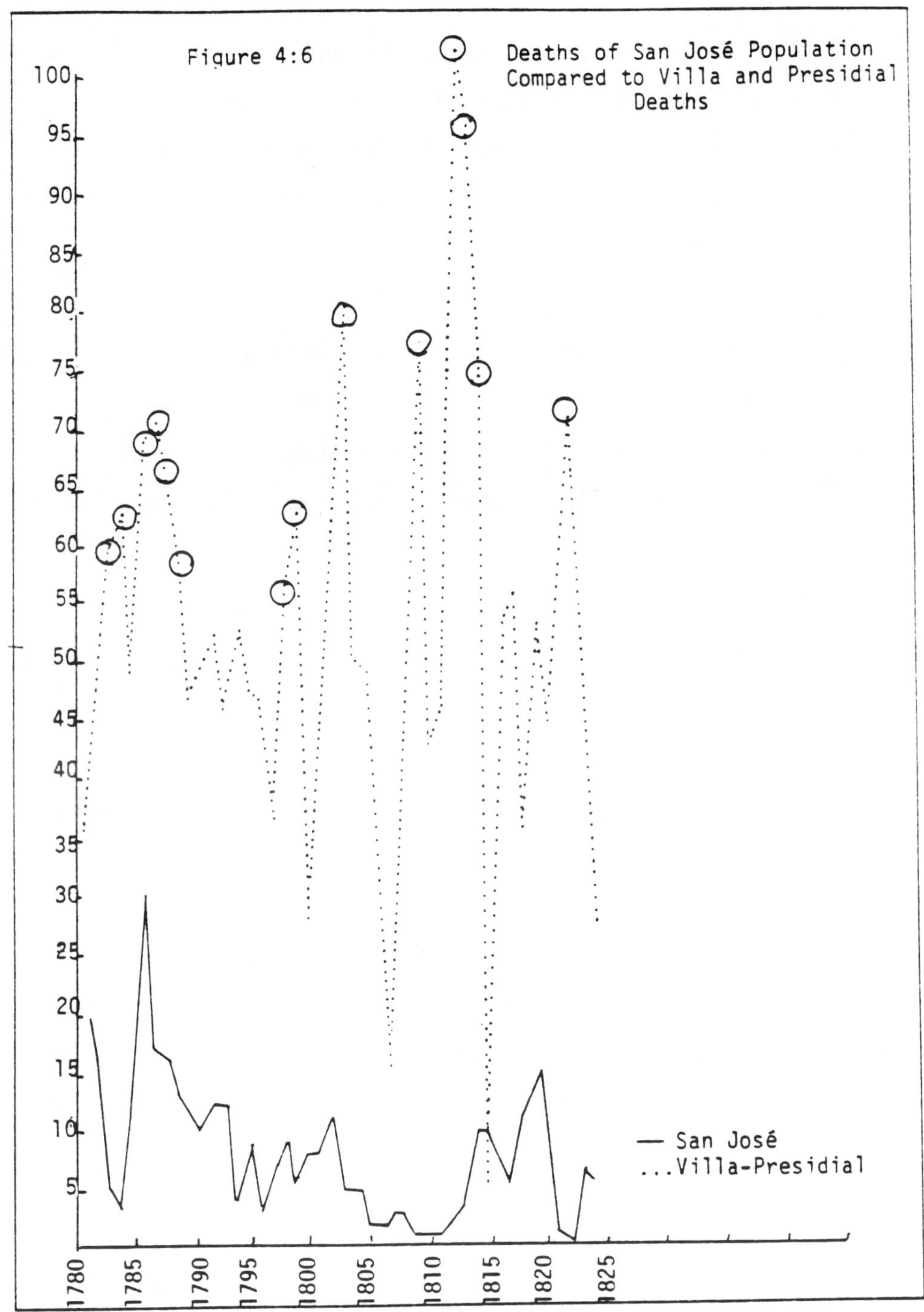

Figure 4:6
Deaths of San José Population
Compared to Villa and Presidial
Deaths
100
95
90
85
80
75
70
65
60
55
50
45
40
35
30
25
20
15
10
5
1780
1785
1790
1795
1800
1805
1810
1815
1820
1825
— San José
...Villa-Presidial

duplicated by Béjar.   With the great smallpox epidemic of 1763 correlation is resumed for a few years. Valero suffered disastrous losses in that year, and, although deaths were up a bit for Béjar, the epidemic had little impact on the community. Contrarily, the epidemics of ˮ77 and 1779 which caused severe casualties at Béjar are not reflected at Valero. The unnamed "cruel epidemic" which struct Béjar, Bucareli, and Nachitoches in 1777 was thought to have run its course until it struck among the Towakanis, Taovayas, and Cadohadachos in northeast Texas, killing more than 300.[44] Ewers ascribes the epidemic to cholera or the bubonic plague and lists smallpox as being widespread in Texas in 1778, but whether it accounted for the peak in Béjar the following year is uncertain.[45]   Except for the 1786 epidemic, and a slight rise in mortality in 1819, which affected both Béjar and San José, there is no correlation as one examines the graph in Figure 6 and, in fact, the two communities are inversely proportional.

The graphs actually provide limited information. We can see that the Valero Indians up until 1763 suffered more deaths than the residents of Béjar, although to what degree this was due to greater vulnerability to diseases is impossible to ascertain without population figures with which we could calculate the death rate for both communities. What is significant is that diseases and illnesses might affect one community without having any noticeable impact upon the other.

Life Span of the Mission Indians

Table 4:10 shows the life spans of a controlled population of 319 from Valero - that is, of individuals for whom actual birth and death dates are known. Out of this number from 1718 to 1783 only fifty survived to reach adulthood (twelve and over in this study). Of those who reached adulthood, fourteen survived into the 20-29 age range and only eight survived into the 30-45 age range. The wrenching statistic is that two-thirds of this population died within the first three years of birth. Another way of stating it is to say that for every one who survived beyond the age of twelve, 6.58 died. The mean age of this population was only 5.57 years.

Within the mission entries there are numerous adults whose ages were estimated at their baptisms or burials, ranging from the forties to over 100. The records would suggest that the Indians aged early and were actually younger than they appeared. At the same time the probable mean age of an Indian population before it was exposed to European diseases was undoubtedly much higher than after missionization.

Other data suggest that the controlled population from Valero does not tell the whole story. When the 1772 census was undertaken by the friars from Zacatecas, they included the ages of those listed. The ages of some of the older people were estimated because Concepción, Capistrano, and Espada had only been located in San Antonio forty-one years and those people had not

Table 4:10   LIFE SPAN, SAN ANTONIO DE VALERO

Years	No.		CT	Years	No.		CT
0-1	126	126	126	17-18	4	72	1012
1-2	57	114	240	18-19	4	76	1088
2-3	28	84	324	10-20	3	60	1148
3-4	11	44	368	21-22	2	44	1192
4-5	18	90	.458	22-23	4	92	1284
5-6	9	54	512	23-24	3	72	1356
6-7	8	56	568	24-25	2	50	1406
7-8	1	8	576	25-26	1	26	1432
9-10	4	40	616	27-28	1	28	1460
10-11	3	33	649	29-30	1	30	1490
11-12	4	48	697	31-32	2	64	1554
12-13	6	78	775	32-33	2	66	1620
13-14	6	84	859	33-34	1	34	1654
14-15	1	15	874	34-35	1	35	1689
15-16	2	32	906	42-43	1	43	1732
16-17	2	34	940	44-45	1	45	1777
					319		

been baptized as recently-born infants whose ages could be verified in the registers. Nevertheless the ages given of the younger portion of the populations are probably fairly accurate. To compute the mean ages of these populations, infants under one year were eliminated from consideration. The mean age of the Indians at Capistrano was 25.7 years. It was 26.1 years at Espada, 26.4 years at Concepción, and 28.0 years at Valero.

How do we reconcile the mean age of 5.5 years for the controlled population of Valero with a mean of 26.5 for the four missions in 1772? There are several considerations that bear on such a discrepancy. We can first of all question how representative the controlled Valero population is of the mission Indians as a whole. The sample is, after all, small and necessarily skewed towards the infant end by the very fact that the most vulnerable portion of the population, the children, were conscientiously baptized first while baptism of the older portion was delayed while they were taking instructions. Numerous others never got around to being baptized. Another consideration is that, assuming Valero to be representative, the European diseases had pretty much exacted their toll of the mission Indians by the mid-1760's. It is likely that the micro-organisms and the Indians had arrived at an accomodation. The virulence of the micro-organisms had been waning since the end of the seventeenth century. We can be sure that the Indians in Texas had been exposed to such

European diseases as smallpox and measles long before any official Spanish colonization had been undertaken. As early as the late sixteenth century illegal slave raids were being conducted among the lower Río Grande tribes by such men as the Governor of Nuevo Leon Luís de Carvajál de la Cueva. Smallpox epidemics are known to have struck tribes in Coahuila in 1674 and 1675 prior to missionization and another in 1707 hit the Río Grande missions.[46] There is abundant evidence from the late seventeenth and early eighteenth centuries that Indians from northeast Texas were penetrating deeply into Spanish settlements below the Río Grande. When De León succeeded in reaching La Salle's Fort St. Louis in 1689 he found that the colonists had been stricken with smallpox and, with the exception of four captives, the remainder massacred by the Indians three months previously. What is significant in these findings by De León is that the ships of the La Salle expedition had sailed from Santo Domingo in 1684. The accounts of the voyage indicate the colonists had picked up diseases before leaving the island which continued wasting many of their numbers, but, clearly, smallpox with its incubation period of ten to twelve days was not one of them or they would all have perished long before arriving at their destination. Therefore the smallpox had to have been transmitted by Texas Indians. In short, perhaps it is not unreasonable to suppose that the Indians had been exposed to such diseases through several generations and that by the mid-eighteenth century their tolerance level had been raised through natural selection while, at the same time, the disease strains were becoming less virulent.

A mean age of 26.5 for the Indian population in 1772 appears resonable in comparing it with data from Anglo-America. In the Virginia Colony the life expectancy for "seasoned adults" (those who had become acclimated to the country) was said to be about 48 or 49.[47] The mean age of the population would be considerably lower than that figure. In 1850 in the slave holding states the average ages for Negroes and Whites at the time of death was 21.4 and 25.5 respectively.[48] Since our Indian population falls somewhere between these two samples we might conclude that the mission Indian population had stabilized by the 1770's and was as healthy as other Europeanized portions of North America. One other bit of evidence comes from Fernand Braudel who wrote that between 1400 and 1800, Europeans died at about the age of twenty on an average.[49]

Infant Mortality

We have seen above that infant mortality was frightfully high in the missions, but so it was elsewhere. T.R.Edmonds estimates that one half of the infants baptized in London between 1770 and 1789 were dead before the age of five. J.R. Brownlee estimated infant mortality between 300 and 400 per 1000 live births for the same city during the same century. And R. Bland found that five of twelve children died before the age of two and seven of ten

before the age of sixteen at Westminster Dispensary in London
between 1774 and 1781.[80] Fernand Braudel reported that between
1400 and 1800, only 58% of the population of Europe and England
reached their fifteenth birthday.[51]

We have determined above that no death pattern can be
correlated to seasonal, or climatic changes. However we can find
a correlation of the death curve with the birth curve when we
shift the death curve by four months (Figure 4:7). Apparently,
the death curve for non-epidemic years simply reflects the high
infant mortality.

Infanticide

The possibility of female infanticide was first suggested
upon tabulating the Valero births and finding that 250 male babies
were baptized to 201 female babies. One hundred and five or six
male births to 100 female births is considered a normal sex ratio.
A 55:45% ratio is high. The possibility again presented itself
upon finding that the number of men who remarried outnumbered the
women. The latter appeared to be scarce in the population. Sixty-
two men married twice as opposed to 40 women. Twelve men married
three times as opposed to seven women. They were about even only
by the fourth marriage with five men and six women taking spouses
again. The pattern was one of older widowers remarrying the few
available women and leaving the younger men out. If female infanticide were a culture trait which missionization had not succeeded

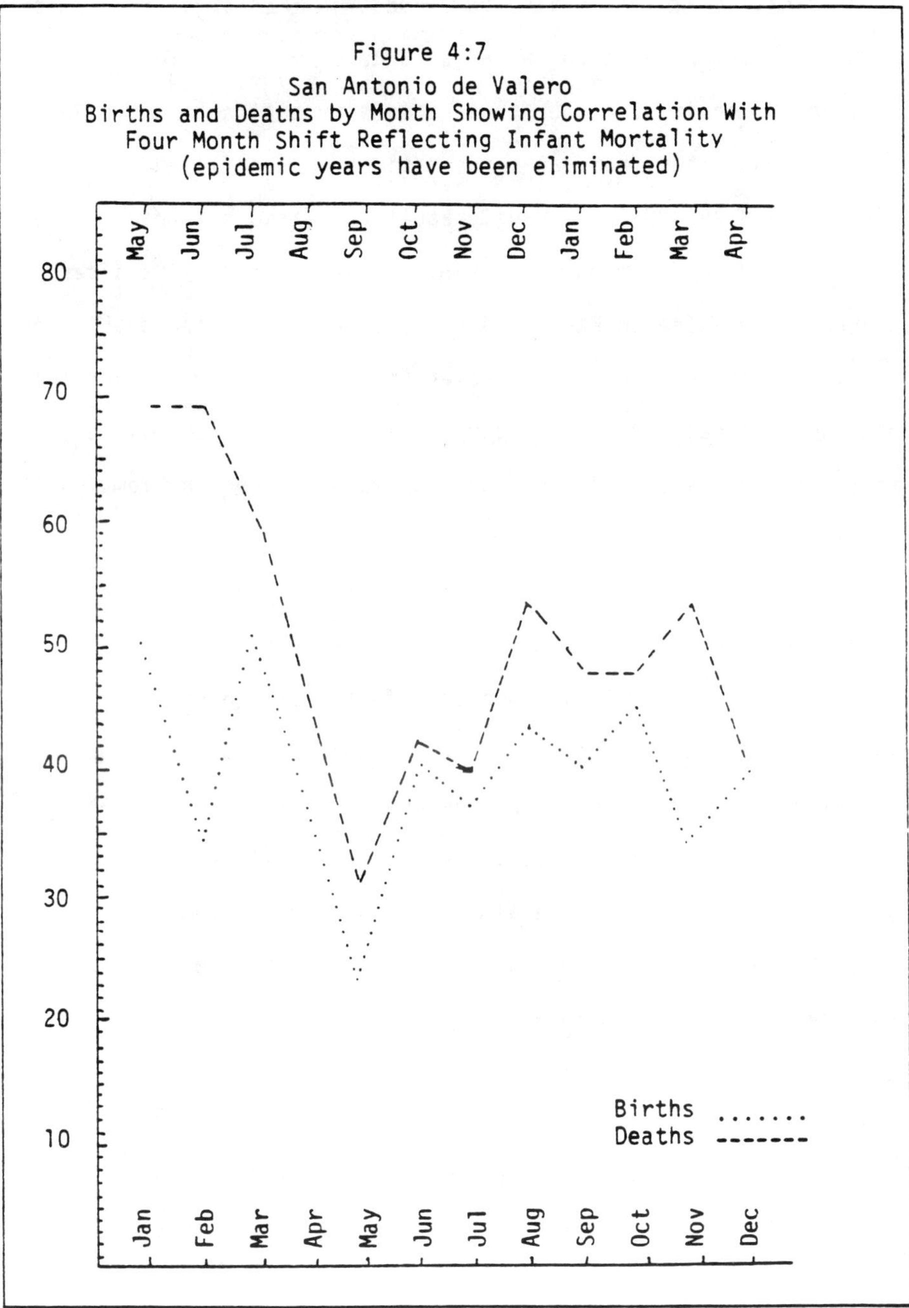

Figure 4:7
San Antonio de Valero
Births and Deaths by Month Showing Correlation With
Four Month Shift Reflecting Infant Mortality
(epidemic years have been eliminated)
May
Jun
Jul
Aug
Sep
Oct
Nov
Dec
Jan
Feb
Mar
Apr
80
70
60
50
40
30
20
10
Jan
Feb
Mar
Apr
May
Jun
Jul
Aug
Sep
Oct
Nov
Dec
Births ....
Deaths -------

in eradicating it should also be evident in the larger population.
A check of the population turned up a total of 833 males and 726
females. Even if we reduce those totals by subtracting the 250
and 201 new births from each, the ratio of men still exceeds that
of women 52% to 48% in a largely adult population in which the
ratio should be reversed. Dr. A.B. Holder wrote in 1892 after
the end of the Indian Wars: "A curious fact of Indian population
statistics is the excess of females in almost all tribes and the
constant increase of this excess. This is due to low female
mortality, since of children born the males exceed the females".[52]
The male-female ratio of the mission Indians is certainly out of
line and the practice of female infanticide would appear to be
confirmed.

The historical evidence of infanticide and reasons for
the practice among the pre-mission Indians have been discussed
in Chapter 3. The survival of the practice into the nineteenth
century by the Karankawa appears evident from Alice Oliver's
observation that there were almost no young girls and few infants
or children among them and Gatchet's comment that he never saw
more than two children to a family.[53] The practice appears to have
been widespread among Indians of the Americas. Dr. Holder considered it to be one cause of the seemingly low fecundity of the
Indians of North America.[54] Furthermore, to bring infanticide
into historical perspective, we need to understand that the

practice was not limited to the "savages" of the New World. A recent study of population statistics considers infanticide to have been prevalent in England and Europe until the last quarter of the nineteenth century when moral censure became severe and when foundling homes were established.[55]

The Distribution of Mission Indian Populations

The census reports undertaken in 1772 listed the people by name, age, ethnic identification, christian or <u>catecumeno</u>, placed them into families or groups of widows, widowers, or orphans, and reported them present or absent from the mission. The information was collected by different priests, however, and the data are not uniform. Data compiled from those reports have been compared with comparable figures from the 1792 census reports and the 1809 Saucedo census in order to determine what changes occurred within the population. (Table 4:11)

Several observations are in order which affect the methodology and would appear to disagree in some particulars with the 1772 reports. The population figures given in Table 4:11 do not coincide in all cases with those given in Table 4:1 which are derived from the same source. The Valero population of 125 (Table 4:1) includes seventy-one apostates who are excluded from Table 4:11 because their ages and statuses are not provided, while eighteen Indians are deducted from Concepción because, as recent arrivals, the same information was not included in that report.

Table 4:11   DISTRIBUTION OF MISSION INDIAN POPULATIONS

In 1772

	Pop.	Adults	Children	Families	Fam.Ind.	Fam.Size	W/W	Singles	Orphans	% Adults	% Children	% Families	% W/W	% Singles	% Orphans
Valero	54	44	10	11	32	2.9	11	11	0	81.4	18.5	59.2	20.3	20.3	0
Concep.	160	131	29	50	122	2.4	27	9	2	81.8	18.1	76.2	16.8	5.6	1.2
Capis.	198	146	52	61	166	2.7	14	8	10	73.7	26.2	83.8	7.0	4.0	5.0
Espada	174	134	40	50	151	3.0	19	3	1	77.0	22.9	86.7	10.9	1.7	.5
Averages						2.7				78.4	21.4	76.4	13.7	7.9	1.6

In 1792

	Pop.	Adults	Children	Families	Fam.Ind.	Fam.Size	W/W	Singles	Orphans	% Adults	% Children	% Families	% W/W	% Singles	% Orphans
Valero	40	24	16	15	36	2.4	1	3	0	60.0	40.0	90.0	2.5	7.5	0
Concep.	45	33	12	15	41	2.7	2	2	0	73.3	26.6	91.1	4.4	4.4	0
Capis.	29	25	4	9	22	2.4	3	4	0	86.2	13.7	75.8	10.3	13.7	0
Espada	48	31	17	11	37	3.3	8	3	0	64.5	35.4	77.0	16.6	6.2	0
S. José	92	68	24	27	78	2.8	9	5	0	73.9	26.0	84.7	9.7	5.4	0
Averages						2.7				71.5	28.3	83.7	8.7	7.4	
Average excluding S.José						2.7				71.0	28.9	83.4	8.4	7.9	
Average excluding Valero						2.8				74.4	25.4	82.1	10.2	7.4	

In 1809

	Pop.	Adults	Children	Families	Fam.Ind.	Fam.Size	W/W	Singles	Orphans	% Adults	% Children	% Families	% W/W	% Singles	% Orphans
Concep.	21	16	5	2	9	4.5	6	6	0	76.1	23.8	42.8	28.5	28.5	0
Capis.	20	16	4	6	16	2.6	2	2	0	80.0	20.0	80.0	10.0	10.0	0
Espada	24	19	5	3	11	3.6	8	5	0	79.1	20.8	45.8	33.3	20.8	0
S. José	55	39	16	11	37	3.3	8	10	0	70.9	29.0	67.2	14.5	18.1	0
Averages						3.5				76.5	23.4	58.9	21.5	19.3	

For this study a family unit may consist of a married couple, with or without children, or at least one parent with a child - sometimes a widowed grandparent constituting part of the family, or even two adults such as a father and grown son. At Espada the category of "widows and widowers" appeared to be a catch-all for singles, because two young men of twelve years and one of thirteen years were included. These have been placed under "singles" in Table 4:11. Widowers, bachelors, and apparently orphans were categorized together at Concepción. If under the age of twenty they are here counted as bachelors. Adults are individuals of twelve and over; children are those under twelve years. There is no census for San José in 1772 and by 1809 Valero no longer had an Indian pueblo. For easier comprehension the statistics have been converted to percentages of the population.

Over the first twenty years the ratio of adults to children dropped. Since the family size remained the same, this points to a drop in infant mortality. There is also a drop in the percentage of widows and widowers in the population in favor of an increase in the percentages of families which also points to a declining mortality rate. Over the remaining seventeen years there is another shift with the adult population increasing again, but these changes are explainable by population movements. By 1809 most of the ladinos (civilized, Spanish speaking Indians), particularly those of the younger generation, had been assimilated into the larger mission communities and Béjar. The few Indians still residing within the missions tended to be an older population with a concomitant number of older, as yet unmarried children and a goodly number of older widows and widowers. What is most significant about the changes is the increase in mean family size from 2.7 to 3.5. These figures are, of course, low because they reflect only the children still residing with parents and not the total number of children born to a family, but the fact that an increase is evident is important to those findings given above that pointed to a stabilization of the Indian population after several generations of severe decline.

Mestizaje (Miscegenation)

The recognized mingling of the races at Valero appears to have been slight until 1774 when an increasing number of mulattoes appeared in the registers as the Indian population was rapidly declining. The mulatta, María Rosa Reyes, married the Apache, Anselmo Cuevas, in 1758. Three of their children possibly survived to become parents themselves. One of their sons, Juan Joseph Cuevas, married María Flores, a mulatta. And the Hierbipian Roque Robles married María Dolores Cuevas. Two of their children may have survived into adulthood. Seven other Indians took mulatta wives in the late years of mission history. María Petra Campa, a Tlascalteca, married a mulatto. The total mulatto count traced from the records is 37 individuals, including eight mulatto families in addition to those who married Indians. The Indians

Margarita, María Getrudis de la Garza Galindo, and María Guadalupe Rodríguez married Spaniards, while the <u>Española,</u> Juana Pérez, and the <u>Francés-Española</u>, Felipa Saró, married Indians. From these cases of <u>mestizaje,</u> possibly twenty-one children survived to become parents themselves and to contribute to the gene pool.

Bartolomé, a mulatto and resident of Concepción, married María Josepha, a Siquipil, in 1738. Bartolomé was such an early resident that he raises the possibility of his having entered the mission with the Pajalat Confederacy. His first wife died before their first anniversary and he took a Tilpacopal wife in 1739. Ysidro Castañeda, another mulatto, married Aqueda Ruiz, a Pachalaque-Orejona, in 1750. Ysidro subsequently took two other Indian wives. Félis Castañeda, apparently the son of Ysidro and Aqueda, married the <u>coyota</u> (Indian-mestizo) María Gertrudis Galván in 1769. This couple had at least two children who survived childhood and married. Félis next married a Pajalache-Apache and took as his third wife the <u>Española</u>, María Trinidad Games. María Gertrudis Galván, prior to her marriage to Castañeda, had been the wife of the Patumaco Bernardino Chagoya. Could we uncover more information on this <u>coyota</u> we would surely find an interesting story. She had earlier served as a maid in the household of Lt. Galván of the Presidio de San Antonio and was probably part Apache. Two other cases of <u>mestizaje</u> can be found in the Concepción registers. Joseph Joachín Pintado, a Siquipil, married the

<u>Española</u>, Brigida Ayala, and Juan Nocolás Flores, a Patumaco, married Ursula, the daughter of a Siquipil father and a mulatta.

Seventeen mulattoes can be identified in the San José registers, but the actual number may have been substantially higher. Without complete records there is no way of determining the number of children produced by these unions at the downstream missions. An inspection of the earliest statistical reports and censuses does augment our information on <u>mestizaje</u> and the racial composition of the various communities of the San Antonio River. With the exception of the Salcedo Report of 1809, the data are derived from the microfilmed "Translations of Statistical and Census Reports of Texas, 1782-1836, and Sources Documenting the Black in Texas, 1603-1803" found at the University of Texas Institute of Texan Cultures at San Antonio. The reports raise numerous questions which are difficult, and some impossible, to explain.[56]

Reports from 1783-1789

The reports from 1783 through 1789 (Tables 4:12-16) are categorized into the Villa de San Fernando and the five mission pueblos. For some years presidial reports are appended. In addition, tables of the racial breakdown of the community are provided. The researcher is frustrated in the attempt to fully understand or to find consistency in the figures. The report for 1783 will illustrate. The population figure given for the

Table 4:12   RACIAL COMPOSITION OF SAN ANTONIO COMMUNITIES, 1783

Indians	Men	Women	Boys	Girls	Total	% of Pop.
M.San José	41	31	26	25	123	
M.San Juan	53	26	13	7	99	
M. Espada	32	28	30	6	96	
M. Concepción	32	29	18	8	87	
M. Valero	49	35	36	29	149	
	207	149	123	75	554	

Villa-Presidio	Men	Women	Boys	Girls	Total	
Spaniard	145	125	246	224	740	
Indian	183	148	26	25	382	
Mestizo	35	25	26	7	93	
Color Quebrado	75	90	94	35	294	
	438	388	392	291	1509	

Combined Pop.					Total	% of Pop.
Spaniard					740	35.8
Combined Indian					936	45.3
Mestizo					93	4.5
Color Quebrado					294	14.2
					2063	

Table 4:13   RACIAL COMPOSITION OF SAN ANTONIO COMMUNITIES, 1784

Indians	Men	Women	Boys	Girls	Total	% Of Pop.
M. San José	60	45	32	27	164	
M. San Juan	54	27	14	8	103	
M. Espada	30	26	33	9	98	
M. Concepción	32	27	18	10	87	
M. Valero	50	36	34	27	147	
	226	161	131	81	599	
Villa-Presidio						
Spaniard	148	136	235	202	721	
Indian	198	185	22	9	414	
Mestizo	46	38	21	12	117	
Color Quebrado	90	93	82	27	292	
	482	452	360	250	1544	
Combined Pop.						
Spaniard					721	33.6
Combined Indian					1013	47.2
Mestizo					117	5.4
Color Quebrado					292	13.6
					2143	

Table 4:14   RACIAL COMPOSITION OF SAN ANTONIO COMMUNITIES, 1785

Indians	Men	Women	Boys	Girls	Total	% of Pop.
M. San José	65	50	44	31	190	
M. San Juan	47	36	10	19	112	
M. Espada	41	29	20	25	115	
M. Concepción	33	30	19	12	94	
M. Valero	36	30	24	16	106	
	222	175	117	103	617	
Villa-Presidio						
Spaniard	187	160	175	170	692	
Indian	214	198	30	15	457	
Mestizo	50	55	23	17	145	
Color Quebrado	83	90	65	33	271	
	534	503	293	235	1565	
Combined Pop.						
Spaniard					592	31.7
Combined Indian					1074	49.2
Mestizo					145	6.6
Color Quebrado					271	12.4
					2182	

Table 4:15   RACIAL COMPOSITION OF SAN ANTONIO COMMUNITIES, 1786

Indians	Men	Women	Boys	Girls	Total	% of Pop.
M. San José	68	47	46	28	189	
M. San Juan	42	38	13	17	110	
M. Espada	49	32	27	36	144	
M. Concepción	31	35	21	17	104	
M. Valero	40	37	28	21	126	
	230	189	135	119	673	
Villa-Presidio						
Spaniard	192	165	180	178	715	
Indian	218	203	37	21	479	
Mestizo	57	60	26	24	167	
Color Quebrado	87	92	72	36	287	
	554	520	315	259	1648	
Combined Pop.						
Spaniard					715	30.8
Combined Indian					1152	49.6
Mestizo					167	7.1
Color Quebrado					287	12.3
					2321	

Table 4:16   RACIAL COMPOSITION OF SAN ANTONIO COMMUNITIES, 1789

Indians	Men	Women	Boys	Girls	Total	% of Pop.
M. San José	70	71	25	20	186	
M. San Juan	28	27	12	13	80	
M. Espada	31	39	13	10	93	
M. Concepción	26	24	14	10	74	
M. Valero	36	36	25	24	121	
	191	197	89	77	554	
Villa-Presidio						
Spaniard	328	218	151	164	861	
Indian	243	214	30	19	506	
Mestizo	83	82	20	18	203	
Color Quebrado	89	114	40	32	275	
	743	628	241	233	1845	
Combined Pop.						
Spaniard					861	35.8
Combined Indian					1060	44.1
Mestizo					203	8.4
Color Quebrado					275	11.4
					2399	

"Jurisdiction of Béxar" is 955. A corrected count of 1227 is given for the "Presidio de San Antonio and the villa de San Fernando" from which we would deduce the population of the presidio to be 272. However, the sum of the racial breakdown is 1509. That total, in turn, is the sum of the population of 955 given for the "Jurisdiction of Béxar" and the population of 554 given for the missions. Therefore, the racial table should include the mission Indians. But such logic is not to be found. Instead, the "Indian" column of the table gives totals lower than the mission populations where, in fact, they should be higher to take into account the sizeable numbers of Indians dispersed through the villa population in addition to the mission Indians. For this study, then, the racial tabulation is assumed to reflect the villa and presidio only. Therefore, in calculating the percentages of each race in the total population, the mission Indians are added to tne villa Indians and to the population total.

In these earlier reports we cannot be sure of the age used to divide adults from children. The individual mission reports for 1790 ennumerated the populations from sixteen years on from which we conclude that those under sixteen were considered as children. However, the 1809 census used twelve years as the dividing line between children and adults, so the question must remain unsettled.

A last observation is that these populations recorded for the missions during the 1780's would appear to count not only those Indians living within the mission walls, but those living outside the walls in the greater mission communities as well. We shall see evidence in a later chapter that by the 1780's many christianized Indians were being absorbed into the non-mission communities. A comparison of the 1789 statistical report with that of 1790 would at first glance suggest a drastic reduction in mission populations were it not for supplemental reports for each mission in 1790 which appear to record those Indians living outside the mission walls as well.

Reports from 1790

Beginning in 1790 the government, perhaps in recognition of the growing complexity of the larger mission communities, changed their census forms (Tables 4:17-18). Since more and more Indians were moving outside the missions, and presumably were self-supporting, these were probably now subject to taxation and the differentiation between mission Indians who were tax exempt, and non-mission Indian would have been called for. Therefore, the populations of each mission presented as before (Table 4:17) appear to reflect only those actually dwelling within the mission walls and explain the apparent drop of those populations from the previous year. Supplementary reports of each mission are categorized by age from sixteen on and by racial distinctions of Spaniard,

Table 4:17   RACIAL COMPOSITION OF SAN ANTONIO COMMUNITIES, 1790

Indians	Men	Women	Boys	Girls	Total	% of Pop.
M. San José	43	42	8	11	104	
M. San Juan	14	10	-	-	24	
M. Espada	15	17	9	5	46	
M. Concepción	20	19	4	4	47	
M. Valero	18	18	8	4	48	
	110	106	29	24	269	

Villa-Presidio(?)

	Men	Women	Boys	Girls	Total	
Spaniard	258	237	146	139	780	
Indian	110	106	29	24	269*	
Mestizo	10	7	8	5	30	
Color Quebrado	106	96	66	56	324	
	484	446	249	224	1403	

Corrected Totals

	Total
Spaniard	847
Mission Indians	601
Color Quebrado	443
	1891+

* Mission Indians instead of villa Indians
+ does not include Indians in villa population

Table 4:18   RACIAL COMPOSITION OF MISSION COMMUNITIES EXCLUDING MISSION INDIANS, 1790

		16-25		25-40		40-50		50-??		
		M	W	M	W	M	W	M	W	Total
M. San José	Spaniard	2	7	1	5	4	2	3	2	26
	Indian	12	12	14	16	20	8	6	5	93
	Mulatto	2	3	4	2	4	3	1	2	21
	Other	2	1	4	1	2	1	2	1	14
										154
M. San Juan	Spaniard	2	3	0	1	0	2	0	0	8
	Indian	8	5	12	5	6	4	2	1	43
	Mulatto	0	0	0	4	0	1	1	0	6
	Other	2	2	1	1	2	1	2	1	12
										69
M. Espada	Spaniard	3	0	0	0	6	5	0	0	14
	Indian	6	10	16	16	8	4	4	2	66
	Mulatto	1	1	1	1	2	1	1	0	8
	Other	1	0	2	1	1	0	1	0	6
										94
M. Concepción	Spaniard	1	0	0	1	1	0	1	0	4
	Indian	11	8	9	8	5	2	3	2	48
	Mulatto	0	1	1	1	1	0	0	0	4
	Other	5	0	0	1	1	1	0	0	8
										64
M. Valero	Spaniard	3	1	2	2	1	2	2	2	15
	Indian	18	8	14	15	17	5	1	4	82
	Mulatto	0	0	1	1	0	1	1	0	4
	Other	2	0	1	2	1	0	0	0	6
										107

Indian, Mulatto and Other castes (mestizo) as shown in Table 4:18. This interpretation of the nature of the two reports appears reasonable if three facts are considered. If the Indian populations, of what are here interpreted as being those residing within and those without the mission walls, are combined and compared with the previous year there is a difference of only forty-seven, while if the population of only those herein regarded as those residing within mission walls is compared to the previous year, there is a difference of 285. A second consideration is that the adults of the supplemental report fail to coincide with the adults of the other 1790 report. The third point to consider is the nature of the supplemental reports themselves. Since they ennumerate only adults of sixteen and over, their primary purpose was probably to serve as a future tax roll - indicative of non-mission Indian status.

There are other difficulties with the 1790 census. A glance at Table 4:17 will show that the figures recorded in the "Indian" column are those of the mission pueblos instead of those of the villa making the total Indian count far short of the reality. Furthermore, the figure of 324 recorded under "color quebrado" exceeds the figure of 182 given for the entire province of Texas. The figure of thirty mestizos is equally suspect.

Since the entire Indian population was apparently not represented in the mission and villa report for 1790, nor, most probably, the other races living around the missions, these have

been added to the 1790 supplemental reports to obtain new totals
presented as "corrected totals" in Table 4:17. Because of the
obvious errors in the mestizo and "color quebrado" categories,
these have been combined. The resultant "corrections" are then
brought into line with the 1789 totals given for Spaniards and the
combined mestizo and "color quebrado" columns. The Indian category is far short, however, as we lack the necessary figures for
the _villa_ Indians. For this reason calculation of racial breakdown of the community in percentages is not presented.

Reports from 1791-1792

Two statistical reports for 1791 have been eliminated because their validity can be seriously questioned. The first is
dated December 16, the second December 31, the date of the others.
Both contain general mission entries without the supplemental
reports of the missions. The first appears to take the figures
from the general 1790 report that gave a total of 269 mission
Indians and simply juggle them slightly to obtain a total of 270.
In addition, the figures given under the "Indian" racial category
have again been obtained by totaling the men, women, and children
of the mission Indians rather than providing data on the Indians
of the _villa_, while the other racial categories are clearly under-
counted. The December 31 report repeats the general mission
Indian population for 1790 exactly. The reporting of 1214
Spaniards, 590 mestizos, and 786 "color quebrado" are completely

out of line with preceeding and succeeding figures. The latter
report presents the combined population of the presidio and
villa as 1509 (the population in 1783 you may note), while the
racial categories add up to 3169!

Bureaucratic "efficiency" expanded in 1792 with more
census reports than ever compiled. One covered the mission communities with a racial breakdown of their populations plus age
and sex categories--the form used in 1790, which did not count
the population under the age of sixteen. For some inexplicable
reason two reports were filed for mission Concepción. One
follows the form of the other missions with the racial breakdown
and clearly states "pueblo de Concepción" while the other speci-
fies "Indians only" and apparently are those Indians living
around, but not in, the mission. Why one mission was singled out
for the 1792 report we cannot guess. It appears not to be a case
of similar reports of the other missions having been lost because
the specifications of "pueblo" and "Indians only" are unique to the
one. Another census included the populations of the Villa de San
Fernando and the missions categorized into "singles", "marrieds",
and "widowers" by sex and age grades from seven years. This one
does not provide the racial composition of the missons, but does
for the _villa_. Additional reports on the mission communities
name mission Indians, servants of the missions, others admitted as
residents, provide ages, the number of children, ethnic origins,
and occupations. Table 4:19 is a composite using data derived from

Table 4:19   RACIAL COMPOSITION OF VILLA AND MISSIONS, 1792

	Span.	Ind.	M.Ind.	Mulatto	Mestizo	Unid.	Total
Villa S.F.	679	289	--	213	121	--	1302*
Valero	9	14	40	9	--	26	98
San José	30	5	92	5	12	10	154
Espada	6	--	48	6	5	32	97
San Juan	10	2	29	19	7	0	67
Concepción	4	--	45	--	1	17	67
	736	310	254	252	146	85	1785
			564				85
% of Pop.	43.4		33.1	14.8	8.5		1700+

* does not include children under seven years of age
+ does not include the presidial population

the <u>villa</u> censuses plus the last mentioned mission censuses. The
table presents as accurate a picture of the composition of Béjar
as we can derive from the uneven sources available. The population
count of the <u>villa</u> is short by the number of children under the age
of seven. The "unidentified" category represents those people admitted as residents to the missions for whom ethnic origins were
not recorded by the author. Their small number would have little
effect on the percentages in any event.

Report from 1809

     The 1809 report (Table 4:20) is based upon the Salcedo
census.[57] The mission populations are divided into Indians and
"Spaniards" renting from the missions. The populations are
further subdivided into married adults, single adults, widows,
widowers, and male and female children to the age of twelve
years.

Reports from 1819-1820

     The last two reports (Table 4:21) recorded prior to
Mexico's independence from Spain in 1821 present population totals
for all of Béjar, no longer recognizing the mission communities
as separate entities nor attempting to differentiate Indians from
mestizos. Furthermore, the age grades now include two categories
under the age of sixteen.

Table 4:20   RACIAL COMPOSITION OF MISSIONS, 1809

		M	W	Boys	Girls	Total
M. San José	Indian	21	18	8	8	55
	"Spaniard"	7	4	2	2	15
						70
M. San Juan	Indian	7	9	2	2	20
	"Spaniard"	16	13	8	9	46
						66
M. Espada	Indian	11	8	3	2	24
	"Spaniard"	33	26	18	16	93
						117
M. Concepción	Indian	7	9	2	3	21
	"Spaniard"	13	8	5	6	32
						53

Table 4:21   RACIAL COMPOSITION OF BEJAR, 1819-1820

Béjar, 1819	0-7		7-16		16-25		25-40		40-50		50-??		Total	% Pop.
	M	W	M	W	M	W	M	W	M	W	M	W		
Spaniard	94	80	97	107	103	123	72	102	37	41	47	41	944	
Ind, Cas, Mes.	56	65	41	65	30	41	52	50	30	31	29	30	520	
Afr. origin	0	0	0	0	2	0	2	2	0	0	1	0	7	
Military Con.														
Span-Europ.	16	21	21	11	42	38	78	32	13	2	4	1	279	
Ind, Cas, Mes.	13	14	7	11	14	13	57	8	5	1	–	–	143	
	179	180	166	194	191	215	261	194	85	75	81	72	1893	
Combined Pop.														
Span-Europ.													1223	64.6
Ind, Cas, Mes.													663	35.0
African													7	.3
Béjar, 1820														
Spaniard	102	108	134	127	73	87	73	144	37	41	47	71	1044	57.50
Ind, Cas, Mes.	74	80	97	90	44	74	55	125	26	40	33	30	768	42.30
African	0	0	0	0	0	0	0	0	1	0	0	0	1	.05
	176	188	231	217	117	161	128	269	64	81	80	101	1813*	

* presumably includes the Military Contingent

Inferences to be Drawn from the Census Reports

In spite of the drawbacks of the colonial census reports, their use can be instructive in revealing the degree to which _mestizaje_ had advanced by the end of the colonial period in San Antonio. The data have been telescoped into Table 4:22 and Figure 4:8.

First, however, we must come to terms with the various identifications used. The earlier reports are categorized by Spaniard, Indian, Mestizo, and "Color Quebrado". Caste-conscious elites of Spanish society provided dozens of terms denoting various degrees of racial admixture - terms which differed in meaning from one country to another. Although _mestizaje_ refers to any racial admixture, the term "mestizo" was restricted to a Spanish-Indian cross. In New Spain, a _castizo_ was a Spanish-mestizo cross, a _lobo_ an Indian-negro cross, and a _coyote_ an Indian-mestizo cross. The generic term "color quebrado" (broken color) included all these latter categories as well as the mulatto, a Spanish-negro cross. The astonishingly few numbers of mestizos and the sizeable numbers of "color quebrado" in the earlier reports provide evidence that the former term was being used in the strict sense of "half-breed" and the latter was being used for all the other Spanish-Indian variations as well as those of varying Negro admixture. The individual reports of the 1790 mission communities use mulatto and "other castes", mulatto apparently being used in the strict sense and "other castes" used

Table 4:22   CHANGING RACIAL COMPOSITION OF SAN ANTONIO
1783-1820

	1783	1784	1785	1786	1789	1792	1819	1820
Spaniard	35.8	33.6	31.7	30.8	35.8	43.4	64.6	57.5
Indian	45.3	47.2	49.2	49.6	44.1	33.1	--	--
Mixed	18.7	19.0	19.0	19.4	19.8	23.3	35.3	42.3

Spaniard	740	721	692	715	861	738	1223	1044
Indian	936	1013	1074	1152	1060	564	--	--
Mixed	387	409	416	454	478	398	670	769
	2063	2143	2182	2321	2399	?	1893	1813

? presidial population and children under age of seven lacking

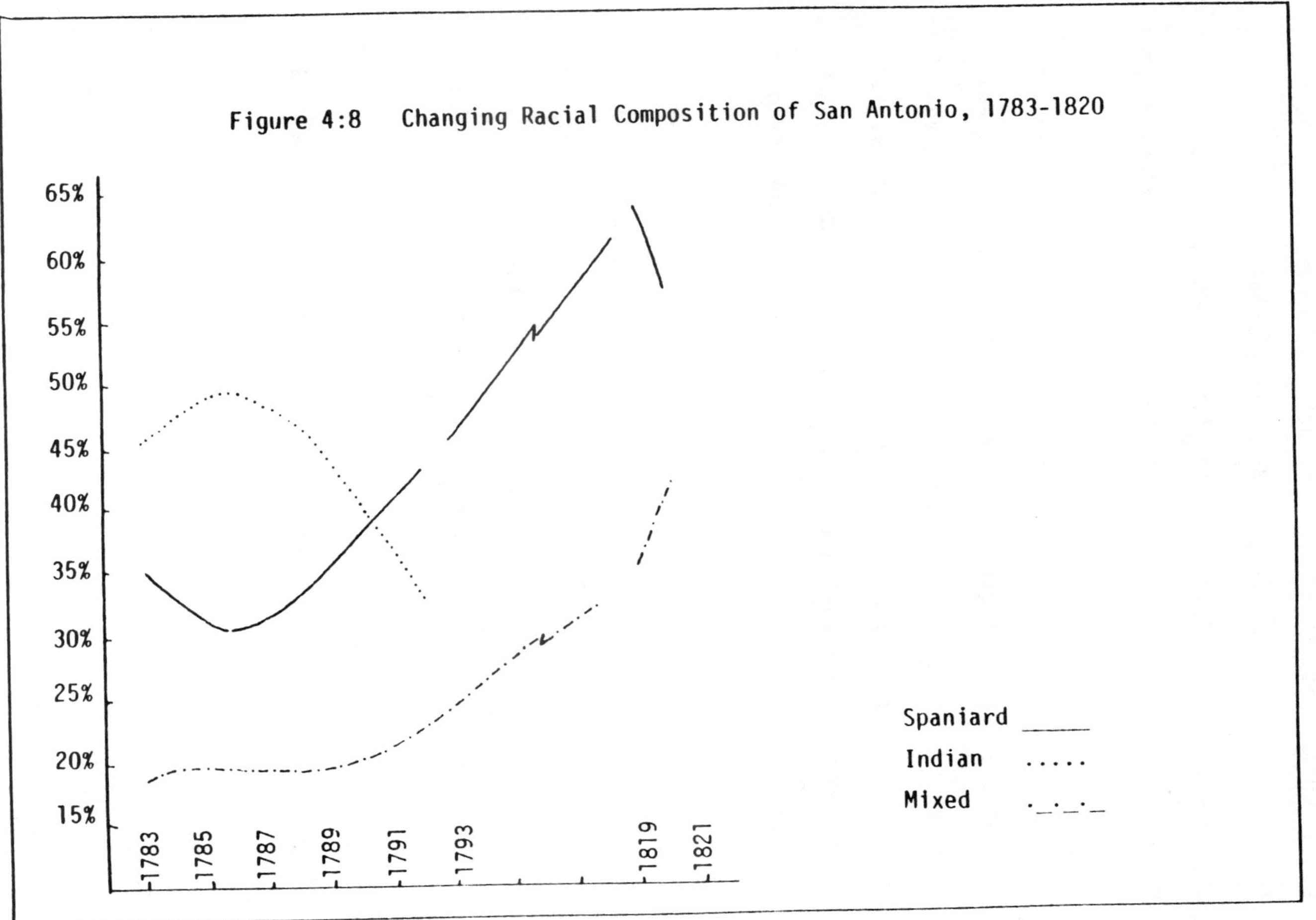

Figure 4:8   Changing Racial Composition of San Antonio, 1783-1820

as the equivalent of "color quebrado". Table 4:19 uses the term
"mestizo" in a generic sense indicating a Spanish-Indian mix of
any degree while "mulatto" is used for any degree of Negro mix.
By 1819 all cases of mestizaje are lumped together except for the
all-but-lost "African origin". One must bear in mind that in
discussing mestizaje as derived from colonial documents we are
not dealing with biological race, but with socially perceived
distinctions of races. Even though "Spaniards" constituted better
than half the population of Béjar in 1820 one does not have to
scratch deeply beneath the surface identification to find that
most are, in truth, a mixture of the three races represented by
the European, the Indian, and the African.

Table 4:22 shows the changing racial composition of San
Antonio over a thirty-seven year period, in both numbers in
and percentages of the population. Figure 4:8 visually presents
the percentages. The Spanish and Indian population curves
(Figure 4:8) are inversely proportional until 1792. From Table
4:22 we can see that the Spanish population was quite stable
through 1786. The divergence in the curves is due to the continued influx of Indians which peaked in 1786. The "mixed" category remained remarkably static until 1790 when it began a steady
climb while the recognized Indian population was rapidly declining.
By 1819 the "Spanish" population had reached its apex at the same
time that the overall population was approaching its nadir during
this thirty-seven year period. By 1820 the "Spanish" and mestizo

curves were within fifteen percentage points of meeting: former
mestizos had become "Spaniards", most of the Indians had become
mestizos, and _mestizaje_ had changed the complexion of the community.

Considerations of Nutrition

We have seen in an earlier chapter that the San Antonio
area harbored an abundance of game animals and edible plants and
even though the mission Indians came to rely on the domestic animals and plants introduced by the missionaries, neither the hunt
nor the old reliance upon gathering were forgotten. Several illustrations should suffice.

Father Morfi recorded in his diary in 1777 that:

The road between villa San Fernando and the downstream
missions is level, well-surfaced, and delightful: for
the greater part it goes along the bank of the San Antonio
River and through a very luxuriant forest of large mes-
quites, walnut, liveoak, pinoak, mulberry, wild grape-
vine, and various other trees and plants; many beautiful
birds inhabit it although we found very few because of the
extreme weather (January). The wild turkeys wander in
flocks of more than 100 and 200. There are squirrels
of different species, the most beautiful are very light
gold with a red belly. On both sides of the road the
crops of the missions are growing, and never in my
life have I seen such a multitude of ducks, geese, and
cranes as those I admired in these fields where the
grain has just been harvested; I do not exaggerate when I
say that they covered the entire prairie. Many ditches
cross these fields, carrying the abundant water of the
river. And they irrigate an immense section of the
country. When they leave them dry to clean them, many
fish of different kinds are caught, and the eels are
especially delicious. . .[58]

On his return trip to Mexico between the San Antonio missions and a distance of forty-six leagues (about 138 miles) to the south, Morfi recorded seeing large herds of deer, mustangs, and antelopes. He also described a hunt.

> When we stopped at 3:00 in the afternoon, the soldiers of the camp had a big rat hunt in the thickets. They ate them with delight, and they also caught a little fox and some rabbits. These rats are almost the size of a small rabbit, of ash gray color, very fine fur, and in all respects very similar to domestic rats; they only have four incisors, large in proportion to the body; they nest at the base of the prickly pears, eat the roots and make their nests with the fragments; the meat is white, very tender, and more tasty than that of the rabbit.[59]

The remains of a sizeable inventory of wild animals were archeologically recovered from San Juan de Capistrano. In addition to bison and deer there were swine, rabbits, hares, bear, coyote (or perhaps domesticated dog), striped skunk, mountain lion, bobcat, opposum, raccoon, alligator, snake, turtle, fish, rat, turkey, and other birds.[60]

Indian women continued to supplement the food issued in the missions with the produce of the land. While gathering fruit on the Medina River in 1737 a party of five women and two boys from mission Espada were attacked by Apaches--the women killed and mutilated, the boys kidnapped.[61] A minister from Mission Concepción wrote (probably in the early 1760's) that the women were accustomed to leaving the missions towards evening "to eat tunas, blackberries, cuacomitos, agaritas, walnuts, camotitos, and other fruits and roots.[62]

Before Governor Alarcón left the San Antonio River in 1719, after having established the Presidio de San Antonio and Mission Valero the previous year, he ordered beans, corn, and other grains as well as grapevines, fig trees, seeds of various fruits, cantaloupe, watermelon, pumpkin, and chili for the frontier community. Hogs and additional cattle, sheep, and goats were also sent for to supplement those brought by the expedition. <u>Acéquias</u> (irrigation ditches) had already been started to assure that the new crops might receive adequate water.[63]

By 1745 the livestock were clearly flourishing. The four missions administered by the Querétaran friars counted 5,215 head of cattle and 3,325 sheep and goats.[64] In 1762 the cattle only numbered 3,987 at the annual roundup, but the count of lesser livestock stood at 12,000 head.[65] In spite of the increasing loss of livestock to Indian raiders as the century wore on, the missions still reported 6,542 head of cattle and 6,016 sheep and goats in 1787.[66] Some swine and poultry were also being raised, but may have been for the exclusive use of the clergy. Espada reported fifty hogs in 1756[67] and poultry houses were inventoried in 1772.[68]

Corn, beans, chili, cantaloupes, and watermelons were grown in all the missions. Carbonized corn cobs, archeologically recovered from Capistrano were found to be similar to several kinds of dent corn grown in central and western Mexico.[69] Scattered accounts provide information on other produce grown in the

mission gardens. The 1762 inspection of the missions specified
that beef, maize, beans, squash, and watermelons were regular
issue.[70] Arandias (sandias?), squash, and sugar cane were listed
for Capistrano in the 1772 inventory.[71] In addition to the
staple crops being grown at San José, Father Morfi mentioned
lentils, sugar cane, sweet potatoes, and peaches sometimes
weighing as much as a pound.[72] The anonymous author of the Concepción "Instructions for the Minister" discussed the difficulty of raising fruit and some vegetables:

> The missionary who has not had experience in raising
> fruit trees should learn to cultivate them, since
> the other missions have them. Once he succeeds, he
> will have the satisfaction of achievement. It is im-
> possible to have any kind of fruit tree with these
> Indians around, because they take the fruit before
> it is ripe. So great is their tendency to steal,
> that in spite of the vigilance of the missionary to
> take care of the nispero trees (native persimmon)
> he cannot stop them from gathering the fruit when it
> begins to ripen. Thus a full harvest of fruit is
> never realized even though the missionary tells the
> Indians that they will get the fruit when it is ripe.
> For the same reason, the tachacual (unidentified) is
> often not cultivated in vegetable gardens where they
> could produce, as the missionary will learn if he
> wishes to cultivate all these plants. When an
> objection is raised concerning the failure here to
> cultivate orchards and gardens as is done at the
> other missions, this can be met by saying that the
> other missions have more docile Indians.[73]

In 1794 Capistrano had forty-seven surcos (furrows)
planted in sugar cane, but most of the "cane of Castile" was
being grown at San José where a sugar mill had been in operation
for many years and where most, if not all, the processing was being
done. The sugar mill was a sizeable industry where piloncillo

(cones of brown sugar) was produced in considerable quantity. The 1794 inventory made at the time of secularization of San José listed 1554 _piloncillo_ molds.[74] Fragments of others were archeologically recovered from Capistrano.

Some wheat was also being raised in the late mission period. The 1772 inventory of Espada mentioned an oven for baking bread for the ministers (tortillas were the usual fare). A flour mill ("un molino para moler trigo") had been constructed at San José and eighty _cargas_ (one carga = 5.15 bushels) of unthreshed wheat were inventoried at Concepción in 1794.[75]

Corn and beans were planted in sufficient quantity not only to maintain each mission community, but also to be used as salaries for mission employees and to be sold. May was considered to be the best time to plant corn, but in years of insufficient harvest to carry them through a full year the corn was sown in February or March.[76] Most years an adequate harvest was probably realized. In 1762 there were 1000 _fanegas_ (one fanega = 1.58 bushels) of maize and 70 _fanegas_ of beans stored at Espada, 800 _fanegas_ of maize and 50 _fanegas_ of beans at Concepción, 1000 and 900 _fanegas_ of maize at Capistrano and Valero respectively and unspecified quantities of beans in the same missions.[77]

The best record of the diet of the Mission Indians is found in the Concepción "Instructions for the Missionary". The anonymous minister wrote that beeves were driven from the ranches into the missions each Saturday to be slaughtered and

issued Sunday morning.   From four to six were slaughtered weekly
in each mission "when there are not many people". One beef went
to the <u>convento</u> (friary) which sounds excessive until one realizes
that it fed not only the priests but, apparently, the sick,
various servants attached to the mission, and numbers of Indian
boys who slept and took most of their meals in the <u>convento</u>. In
summer the <u>fiscal</u> (a native assistant to the missionary) was
charged with seeing that the meat was promptly brought in and
cooked to prevent spoilage. He was also to see that the tallow
and fat were rendered and properly stored.[78]

Corn was issued on Monday, the ration varying with the season and availability. When the supply was abundant married women
were given four <u>almudes</u> (one almud = 6.88 quarts) and widows two
and a half to three <u>almudes</u> of unshelled corn. When scarce the
rations were limited to three and two <u>almudes</u> respectively. Two
<u>almudes</u>, presumably to married women and widows alike, were given
if the corn were shelled. The priest noted that 400 <u>fanegas</u> were
generally needed to maintain the Indians at each mission including
that to be used as salaries or sold.[79]

Cooked beans and squash were given on fast days such as
Lenten Fridays, so that the Indians would not eat meat at home.
Ideally, beans would be issued daily during Lent, but the crop
was seldom sufficient to allow it. Cooked beans and sweet
potatoes, <u>buñuelos</u> (a deep fried pastry sprinkled with sugar) and
other sweets were dispensed on Christmas Eve. A bar of chocolate

was provided for breakfast at Easter, or if unavailable, a whole
or half a _pilonsillo_. _Pilonsillo_ was also used as a special treat
on days when supplies (probably those from Mexico) arrived at
the mission. Each adult received a whole cone, each child a
half. Watermelons and cantaloupes were given out in season.
The feasts of Corpus Christi and the Immaculate Concepción were
special celebrations calling for cooked beef and _pilonsillo_.
If the supply of _polonsillo_ were insufficient, _atole_ or _pinole_
were substituted.[80] The latter drinks were prepared from corn
meal mixed with water and sweetened with sugar, or in the case
of the latter, chocolate or cinnamon.

In spite of the information provided above concerning
the kinds and quantities of food issued to the Indians it is
difficult to estimate actual caloric intake of the population.
Four to six beeves were killed weekly when "there are not many
people", but how many are "not many"? How many mouths was a
married woman to feed with four _almudes_ of corn and why was the
widow given as much as three-quarters as much as the married
woman? Who received and who prepared the rations for widowers
and their children? We have illustrated above the small size
of the nuclear family and even though we are aware that the mean
size is actually a bit low, how many children was each woman
actually feeding from her ration when we consider nursing children
and sons who were actually living in the _convento_?

In order to attempt to determine caloric intake, the first consideration was the size of the population to be used. Although the "Instructions for the Missionary" is undated, the internal evidence suggests a date in the early 1760's. The author of that document identifies the Indians as Pajalache, a generic term that was not in use until 1759 and implicit in the text is the evidence that the Indians had not yet advanced to the state where they were entrusted with positions demanding considerable responsibility. The first Indian _mayordomo_ (majordomo) is identified in 1768 (see Government of the Missions below). The 1762 population of 207 was therefore selected for the calculations.

To determine the amount of meat issued, a weight of 900 pounds per steer with a 40% waste factor was used following the study of the nutrition of California Mission Indians.[81]

To calculate the nutritional value of corn and beans, _fanegas_ and _almudes_ had to be converted to bushels, bushels to estimated weight of each crop, and weight to calories per individual. Weights per bushel and calories per pound were again derived from the California study.

The first approach to calculate the caloric value of corn was on the basis of the weekly issue of that grain and assuming three individuals to a family. This was abandoned when it was found that the number of _fanegas_ that would be required was far in excess of the 400 reported to be adequate to

both maintain the population and to provide extra salaries and
sale as well. The only alternative was to use the 400 _fanega_
figure even though we know it to be more than that actually given
to the Indians.

To calculate the nutrition derived from beans required
some arbitrary decisions. Since beans were issued on fast days
only and the amount was unspecified, we have assumed one ration
per week and have assumed the ration to be the equivalent of
corn in _almudes_. These assumptions may be fairly close to the
mark because they figure to a total of fifty-seven _fanegas_ that
would be needed for a population of 207 per annum. The 1762
visita which was dated in March of that year reported seventy
fanegas of beans stored at Espada, fifty at Concepción, and
unspecified amounts in the other missons.[82] Being early in the
year we might assume that the stored product still represented
the greater quantity of that produced. According to the Concepción "Instructions for the Missionary", beans were planted in
June and the bulk of the harvested crop, which had to be dried,[83]
would not be stored until the fall.

The calculations for these three sources of nutrition are
found in Appendix C. The beef ration would supply 15,300
calories, the corn 4,262, and the beans 804 for a total of 20,366
calories per week per person. The caloric intake from these
products alone may have been adequate. The California study used
an index of 3600 calories per day for a man and 2800 calories for

a woman - or 25,200 and 19,600 calories per week respectively.
This caloric intake is perhaps high. A recent study by the California Medical Association states that only 15 calories per
pound are needed for people leading moderately active lives
that include some exercise.[84] Using their factor, 19,950
calories would be required for a person weighing 190 pounds
and 12,600 calories for one weighing 120 pounds.

The ration of beef (13 pounds per person) was generous.
The corn ration we know to be on the high side, but we must
remember that these foods do not represent the entire diet.
Wild game, fish, other vegetables and grains, domesticated fruits,
and the various gathered fruits, roots, and vegetables supplemented the mission issue. And as for the overall nutritional
intake a balanced diet was probably maintained.   There was certainly sufficient animal protein. Corn is rich in vitamins A and C
and potassium. Beans are rich in minerals. Sweet potatoes,
and both corn and beans have sizeable amounts of niacin, are high
in vitamin A and potassium and have moderate amounts of phosphorus
and calcium. Greens and all the various domestic and wild fruits
enjoyed by the Indians are rich in minerals and vitamins A and C.
Pecans and walnuts also provided minerals and vitamin A. Salt
was stored in the missions and issued upon request. The vast herds
of sheep and goats were generally raised for their wool, but according to the 1762 _visita_ report, mutton was prepared for the sick.
Mutton contains larger amounts of B_1, B_2, and niacin than beef.[85]

Only one small skeletal series recovered from San Juan de Capistrano has been analyzed to date. From that series one possible case of rickets was the only pathology due to dietary insufficiency.[86] The prevalence of dental caries in the same series and a larger sample recovered at a later date by the author should be noted, however.

In conclusion we assume the diet of the mission Indians to have been adequate.

General Health of the Populations and Medical Care

The general health of the Indians of Texas and northeastern Mexico was noteworthy to the Spanish observers.

"A robust health and appreciable wealth of the natural environment brings them to a most advanced age without going through debilitating stages of decreptitude that makes old age odious".[87]

Father Vicente Santa María reported:

One saw bodies so well formed, so robust, and freed (of blemishes) that among them the number of defects is much reduced. Chronic infirmities are extraordinary and if, by chance, they do suffer some (infirmity), they will be of short duration. Through their robustness and agility, 50 or 100 leagues are like 10 or 20 for any other. They find little difference between level ground and the craggiest marches, and to this the better part of them add a height which is common to them and among us would be singular. Ah, if it were possible in practice to join these ends; the errant life of the savages so favorable to human development with the necessity and advantages of civil and societal life![88]

Physical defects would indeed have been rare within the populations because defective infants were not allowed to live. And their physical stamina was pretty well insured by their nomadic existence.

The Spaniards, accustomed to the small stature of the Indians of central Mexico, were first of all impressed by the height of the Indians of their northern frontier. The study of a small skeletal series recovered from San Juan de Capistrano showed males ranging from 5'.5" to 6'.0" and females from 5'.1" to 5'.7" with respective averages of 5'.7" and 5'.4".[89] Of the sample of fifty-three individuals, only about forty-seven were adults, however. The average height for males may well have been somewhat higher. Alice Oliver, who grew up on the Texas coast near a campment of Karankawas remembered; "the men are very tall, magnificently formed, with very slender hands and feet. They were not very dark and many of them had very delicate features, and, without exception, splendid teeth". The women, on the contrary, were "short of stature, stout, and usually disagreeable looking and exceedingly dirty, as were the men".[90] Heights of six feet, or even more, were reported by Catlin as common among males of certain Indian groups inhabiting the Northern Plains, and others marginal to the Plains such as the Osage.

There was probably as much difference in the relative attractiveness between the various Indian bands as there was within the Karankawa. Father José de Solís wrote of the Indians at San José that: "The men are not bad-looking, and the women, except an occasional, coarse-featured one, are graceful and handsome."[91] On the other hand, Henri Joutel, a survivor of La Salle's coastal colony, described the women of the coastal tribes as being singularly ugly.[92] The San Juan skeletal series revealed that that particular population was characterized, generally, by narrow faces and high vaulted crania, but with the head varying from brachycephalic to dolichocephalic while the noses were mesorrhine or leptorrhine.[93] In the absence of comparative material we have no way of knowing whether this sample is typical. Head flattening was reported for the Karankawa in the nineteenth century and the cranium of one individual from San Juan showed evidence of cradleboard deformation.[94]

By European standards the Coahuiltecans were dirty. Father Solís complained: "The Indians (Mission Rosario) are very dirty, and the stench which they emit is enough to turn one's stomach. They are fond of all that is foul and pestiferous, and for this reason delight in the odor of the polecat and eat its flesh".[95] Writing a century later, both Oliver and Gatchet confirmed his observation. Gatchet noted that not only were they very dirty but also their habit of using shark's oil as protection against mosquitos resulted in so horrendous an odor that even horses and cattle fled from them.[96] Mission life presumably corrected this annoyance. Soap was made annually and dispensed by the _fiscal_ to the women on Saturday mornings - the amount determined by the size of the family and the amount of clothing to be washed.[97]

We have examined above the impact of the European-introduced diseases and other infirmities that beset the population. The missionaries were convinced that the Indians were largely responsible for their illnesses because they indulged in harmful foods, refused to shield themselves from the elements, did not take physics or sweat baths, nor medicines - for all of which the slightest infirmity was liable to be grave.[98] In an age in which the nature of diseases and illnesses was unknown, before quarantine was practiced, when antisepsis, anesthesia, pathology, and surgery were all unknown, such procedures would probably have had little effect against the micro-organisms. Medicine, in fact, was pretty well limited to "bleeding" and "sweating", and a barber from the _villa_ or presidio was hired for any bleedings or incisions needed in the missions.[99] The 1762 report mentions the use of "medicines that these lands offer" and others that were brought from Mexico.[100] The 1772 inventories list ceramic and glass medicine vials, but fail to identify the contents. A list of medicines ordered for the military infirmary in 1805 which had been established at the secularized mission of Valero, ennumerates opium, various roots, balsams, salts, ointments, spices, herbs, etc. which may have been representative of those ordered for the frontier.[101] Herbal medicine known to the Indians prior to missionization probably continued to be practiced. A burial entry at San José dated 1787 is for the Indian Mariana Flores who had gone to the presidio "to cure" where she died and was then buried at Valero. The Indians had remedies for wounds. Father Solís wrote: "When they (Indians in Texas) leave on a campaign they carry with them a certain herb. . . with which they stop the flow of blood. For this reason, even if they be wounded, they keep on fighting, for they do not faint from loss of blood".[102] This may have been the same herb called "Yerba del Apache" by Father Santa María who wrote that many presidial soldiers had witnessed a miraculous healing herb known to the Apache who when badly wounded would chew up the herb, swallow half of it and apply the rest to his wounds.[103]

The missionaries felt that the high mortality of infants might be due to harmful foods eaten by the mothers which contaminated their milk.[104] The high mortality of new mothers probably brought on by ignorance of antisepsis and resulting puerpural fever has been noted above. In connection with childbirth it is of some interest that the only evidences for the use of a _partera_ (midwife) are from late San José entries. An unnamed _partera_ baptized an unidentified child who had just been born in 1784. And, again in 1798 an unnamed _partera_ baptized a child in the process of birth who died afterwards.

A final note on eighteenth century medicine is of some interest. An innoculation for smallpox, described by a Turkish

doctor, was first used in the New World during an outbreak of
the disease in Boston in 1721. That first experiment proved the
feasibility of the practice and with the innoculation campaign
undertaken in the same city during the 1729-30 outbreak, statistical proof of the efficacy of the program was collected.[105] The
smallpox innoculation was first used in Latin America during outbreaks of the epidemic during 1779-80 and 1797-98.[106] Its use
on the Texas frontier came a bit later, however. A dissertation
on the treatment of smallpox written by Don Francisco Gil of the
royal monastery of San Lorenzo was sent to the Governor of Texas
in 1786 with the recommendation that the procedure be implemented
on the frontier since its efficacy had proven successful in the
province of Louisiana. The procedure was, however, nothing more
than isolating the victims in a hospital to be located away from
the town and in a healthful place where the winds would not transmit the contagion to neighboring towns or farm estates. In reply,
Governor Domingo Cabello was doubtful of his ability to build
such a hospital because the poverty and ignorance of the people
mitigated against it.[107] From 1803 to 1805 a maritime expedition
from Spain undertook a mass innoculation by traveling with children
innoculated with the virus, extracting fluid from the pustules
on their arms.[108] The innoculation was first used in Béjar the
first of April, 1806. A vial of pus and a paper container of
smallpox scabs had been mailed to Governor Antonio Cordero and he
began the program with the innoculation of twelve children.[109]

Conclusions

The marriage age of Indian women varied from 12.9 to 14.4 years and for men 18.6 to 19.3 years. The distribution of births has no pattern except for the low births in May - or fewer conceptions in August. The average number of children per family at San Antonio de Valero (until 1783) was 2.4. In 1772 and 1792 the mean family size was only 2.7 for all the missions, but by 1809 had increased to 3.5. These averages must be regarded as minimal, however, because they are derived from records of baptisms or from household censuses. In other words, they may not include children born prior to or after missionization, or, for later statistics, children no longer dwelling with parents. The fewer number of women to men in the adult population, female infanticide, the lowered number of girls surviving childhood to become mothers, and the greater mortality of young women due to complications resulting from pregnancy and childbirth all contributed to the low fertility rate in those earlier years.

The average number of births per year at Mission Valero from 1718 to 1783 was 6.93 while the average number of deaths from 1721 to 1782 was 9.6. Between 1740 and 1777 there are five years for which we have population, birth, and death figures available for the same mission. For those five years the average percentage of births to the population was 3.83 while the average percentage of deaths was 7.66. The significance is that deaths outstripped any population gain through births at Valero through 1777. There was no correlation of deaths to season.   Poor nutrition and deaths from the hands of hostile Indians have been ruled out as factors in the decline of the mission Indians. An atrocious child mortality rate, hazards of pregnancy and childbirth for women, and the introduction of European diseases were factors in the early decline of the Indians. The impact of European diseases, however, has probably been overemphasized by historians. The considerations of fertility mentioned above together with the cultural trait of infanticide prevented the population from recovering from the devastation of European diseases during the first half-century of the mission experience.

Numerous signs point to a stabilization of the Indian population by the 1780's. The last epidemic that affected the Indians was in 1785. It appears likely that the Indians had finally developed a greater tolerance to the micro-organisms after several generations of exposure. The mortality rate was dropping. In examining the birth rate in terms of the population of Valero we found that after reaching the nadir in 1772, births showed a dramatic increase just five years later. At Valero, whose figures primarily represent the earlier colonial period (1721-1782), the mean deaths per annum in non-epidemic years, was 9.6. The San José figure, which represents only late colonial times (1781-1824) was 7.4. By 1792 there was an increase in the percentage of children in the population and a decrease in the numbers of widows

and widowers pointing to a declining mortality rate for children
and adults alike. There was an increase in the size of the
family from 2.7 in 1772 and 1792 to 3.5 in 1809. And, finally,
the approximate mean age of the population was 26.5 years, a
figure which is apparently not young for the time.

The census reports point to an increasing amalgamation
of the mission Indians into the larger communities by the 1780's
and an accompanying _mestizaje_ of the better proportion of the
population by the end of the colonial period.

Footnotes to Chapter 4

[1] For examples, see Sherburne F. Cook, The Conflict Between the California Indian and White Civilization (Berkeley and Los Angeles: University of California Press, 1976) or George Kubler, The Indian Caste of Perú, 1795-1940: A Population Study Based Upon Tax Records and Census Reports, Smithsonian Institution, Institute of Social Anthropology, Publication No. 14 (Washington: U.S. Government Printing Office, 1952).

[2] Carlos E. Castañeda, Our Catholic Heritage in Texas, 7 vols. (Austin, Texas: Von Boeckmann-Jones, 1935-1958), Vol. 3, pp.67-71.

[3] Benedict Leutenegger and Carmen Perry, "The Establishment of the Missions and the Work of the Missionary Fathers", in San Antonio in the Eighteenth Century, ed. Frances K. Hendricks (San Antonio, Texas: San Antonio Bicentennial Heritage Committee, 1976), p. 26.

[4] Pedro de Rivera, Diario y Derrotero de lo Caminado Visto y Obcervado en el Discurso de la Visita General de Precidios, situados en las Provincias Ynternas de Nuevo España, 1724-1728 (Mexico: 1945), pp. 125, 131-32.

[5] Fray Mariano Francisco de los Dolores, "Relación del estado en que se hallan todas y cada una de las misiones en el año de 1762" in Documentos para la historia eclesiastica y civil de la Provincia de Texas o Nuevas Philipinas, 1720-1779 (hereafter cited as Documentos), ed. José Porrua Turanzas (Madrid, 1961), p. 268.

[6] "Inventarios, 1772" (Zacatecas Archives: 3 and 4) microfilm copies at Old Spanish Missions Historical Research Library at Mission San José, San Antonio, Texas.

[7] Fray Bernardino Vallejo, "Report of Fr. Bernardino Vallejo" (Nacogdoches Archives, 815:2:11) Texas State Archives, Austin, Texas.

[8] Br. Don Juan Antonio de la Peña, "Derrotero seguida por el Marqués de San Miguel de Aguayo en su viage y expedición a la Provincia de Texas (1720-1722)" in Documentos, p. 20.

[9] Fray Benito Fernández de Santa Ana, "Descripción de las misiones del colegio de la Santa Cruz en el Río Grande, Año de 1770" in Documentos, pp. 307-08.

[10]Fray Francisco Xavier Ortíz, "Visita, 1745" (Celaya Archives, 9: 1265-1284) Microfilm copies at Old Spanish Missions Historical Research Library at Mission San José, San Antonio, Texas.

[11]Fray Francisco Xavier Ortíz, Razon de la visita a las misiones de la Provincia de Texas, 1756, ed. Vargas Rea, Del Fondo Franciscano, Archivo del Museo Paleografiado por el Sr. Raymundo de Luna Olmedo, copy at D.R.T. Library, the Alamo, San Antonio, Texas.

[12]Leutenegger and Perry, op.cit., p. 26.

[13]Fray Mariano Francisco de los Dolores et al., in Documentos, pp. 248-58.

[14]Leutenegger and Perry, op.cit., p. 26.

[15]"Inventarios 1772" op.cit.

[16]"Census, 1777" (from MS in Bibliotéca Nacionál) as Appendix 11 in Juan Augustín Morfi, Viage de Indios y Diario Del Nuevo Mexico, segunda edición con una introdución biobibliográfica y acotaciones por Vito Alessio Robles (México: José Porrua e Hijos, 1935).

[17]"Translations of Statistical and Census Reports of Texas, 1782-1836, and Sources Documenting the Black in Texas, 1603-1803" (microfilm) compiled from various colonial archives in Texas, University of Texas Institute of Texan Cultures at San Antonio, (hereafter cited as Census Reports, Texas).

[18]Census, March, 1787, (Zacatecas 4:5063), op.cit.

[19]Census Reports, Texas, op.cit.

[20]"Ynventarios de los bienes de Temporalidad de las Misiones", Mission Records, Bexar County Archives, Office of the Clerk of Bexar County (hereafter cited as Ynventarios 1794).

[21]Censuses 1805, 1808 (Zacatecas 4), op.cit.

[22]Manuel de Salcedo, "Provincia de los Texas. Padrón general de los quatro misiones" (Guadalajara 414:6034) Archivo General de Indias, Seville.

[23]Census, (1810) Zacatecas 4, op.cit.

[24] Vallejo, op.cit.

[25] Kenneth A. Lockridge, A New England Town: the First Hundred Years. Dedham, Mass. 1636-1736 (New York: W.W. Norton and Co., Inc., 1970), p. 68.

[26] George Catlin, Letters and Notes on the Manners, Customs, and Conditions of North American Indians, 2 vols. (New York: Dover Publications, Inc., 1973), vol. 1, p. 121.

[27] A.B. Holder, "Gynetic Notes Taken Among the American Indians", American Journal of Obstetrics, Vol. 25 (1892).

[28] Lockridge, op.cit., p. 66.

[29] "Inventarios 1772", Zacatecas, op.cit.

[30] Holder, op.cit.

[31] Evarts B. Greene and Virginia D. Harrington, American Population Before the Federal Census of 1790 (New York: Columbia University Press, 1932), p. xxiii.

[32] Fray Bartolomé García, Manual para administrar los santos sacramentos de penitencia, eucharista extreme unción, y matrimonio (México, 1760).

[33] Mardith K. Schuetz, The Dating of the Chapel at San Juan Capistrano, San Antonio, Texas. Texas Historical Commission, Special Reports, no. 12 (Austin, Texas, 1969).

[34] Sherry B. Humphreys, "Human Skeletal Material from San Juan Capistrano Mission" in Mardith K. Schuetz, The History and Archeology of Mission San Juan Capistrano, San Antonio, Texas, 2 vols., State Building Commission Archeological Program, Report No. 11, (Austin, Texas, 1969) pp. 116-124.

[35] Dolores et al, in Documentos, p. 267.

[36] Castañeda, op.cit., p. 71.

[37] John C. Ewers, "The Influence of Epidemics on the Indian Populations and Cultures of Texas", Plains Anthropologist 18-60 (1973), p. 108.

[38] Fernández, op.cit.

[39] Ortíz, in "Visita, 1745", op.cit.

[40]Fray Mariano de los Dolores, "Exposición ante Don Toribio de Urrutia, Capitán Vitalico del Real Presidio de San Antonio de Béjar, de Fray Francisco Mariano de los Dolores" in Documentos eclesiastica y civil, op.cit., p. 179.

[41]Ewers, op.cit.

[42]Ibid.

[43]Ibid.

[44]"Expedición del expresado Teniente Coronel Don Atanacio de Mesieres, 15 Nov., 1778" in Docuementos eclesiastica y civil, op.cit., pp. 425-26.

[45]Ewers, op.cit., pp. 108-109.

[46]Fernando del Bosque, "The Bosque-Larios Expedition" in Herbert Eugene Bolton, Spanish Exploration in the Southwest 1542-1706 (New York: Barnes and Noble, Ind., 1963), p. 298.

[47]Edmund S. Morgan, American Slavery, American Freedom (New York: W.W. Norton and Co., 1975), pp. 160-162.

[48]Eugene D. Genovese, Roll, Jordan, Roll, (New York: Pantheon Books, 1974), p. 521.

[49]Fernand Braudel, Capitalism and Material Life 1400-1800 trans. Miriam Kochan (New York: Harper Colophon Books, 1967), p. 52.

[50]Thomas McKeown, The Modern Rise of Population, (New York and San Francisco: Academic Press, 1976), p. 40.

[51]Braudel, op.cit., p. 45.

[52]Holder, op.cit., p. 46.

[53]Albert S. Gatschet, The Karankawa Indians, Archaeological and Ethnological Papers of the Peabody Museum Harvard University, vol. 1, no. 2 (Cambridge, Mass.: 1891), pp. 17 and 65.

[54]Holder, op.cit., vol. 25.

[55]McKeown, op.cit.

[56]For a discussion of Texas census reports generally, see Alicia V. Tjarks, "Comparative Demographic Analysis of Texas, 1777-1793", Southwestern Historical Quarterly, vol. 77, no. 3 (1974).

[57]Salcedo, op.cit.

[58]Fray Augustín Morfi, "Diary 1777-1778", trans. Virginia Taylor.

[59]Ibid.

[60]Ernst Lundelius, Jr., "Analysis of Non-human Bone Material from San Juan Capistrano Mission" in Mardith K. Schuetz The History and Archeology of Mission San Juan Capistrano, San Antonio, Texas, 2 vols., State Building Commission Archeological Program, Report No. 11 (Austin, Texas, 1969), pp. 110-115.

[61]Castañeda, op.cit., p. 45.

[62]Instructions for the Missionary of Mission Concepción in San Antonio, trans. and annotated by Benedict Leutenegger (San Antonio: Old Spanish Missions Historical Research Library at San José Mission, 1976), p. 49 (hereafter cited as Instructions for the Missionary).

[63]Fray Francisco Céliz, Diary of the Alarcón Expedition into Texas, translated by Fritz Leo Hoffman, Quivira Society Publications 5 (Los Angeles, Calif. Republished by Arno Press, N.Y., 1967), pp. 86-87.

[64]Ortíz, "Visita, 1745", op.cit.

[65]Dolores et al., op.cit.

[66]Census 1787, op.cit.

[67]Ortíz, 1756, op.cit.

[68]"Inventarios 1772, op.cit.

[69]Hugh C. Cutler and Leonard W. Blake, "Analysis of Corn from San Juan Capistrano" in Mardith K. Schuetz, The History and Archeology of Mission San Juan Capistrano, San Antonio, Texas, 2 vols., State Building Commission Archeological Program, Report No. 11 (Austin, Texas, 1969), pp. 107-109.

[70]Dolores et al., op.cit., p. 264.

[71]"Inventarios 1772", op.cit.

[72]Fray Juan Augustín Morfi, History of Texas 1673-1779 (hereafter cited as History), trans. and ed. Carlos Castañeda, Quivera Society Publications, Vol. 6, Part 1 (Albuquerque, 1935; Arno Press 1967), p. 97.

[73]Instructions for the Missionary, op.cit., pp. 53-54.

[74]Inventarios 1794, op.cit.

[75]Inventarios 1772, 1794, op.cit.

[76]Instructions for the Missionary, op.cit., pp. 37-38.

[77]Dolores et al, op.cit., pp. 251-259.

[78]Instructions for the Missionary, op.cit., pp. 46 and 19.

[79]Ibid., pp. 20-21.

[80]Ibid., pp. 23-24.

[81]Sherburne F. Cook, The Conflict Between the California Indians and White Civilization (Berkeley and Los Angeles: University of California Press, 1976), pp. 38-44.

[82]Dolores et al, op.cit., pp. 251-259.

[83]Instructions for the Missionary, op.cit., p. 37.

[84]"Too Fat?", Parade Magazine in Austin (Tex.) American Stateman, (Feb. 18, 1979).

[85]Dolores et al., op.cit., p. 264.

[86]Humphreys, op.cit., p. 119.

[87]Athanacio de Mésières, "Cartas de Don Athanacio de Mésières, October 7, 1779" in Documentos eclesiastica y civil, op.cit., p. 390.

[88]Fray Vicente Santa María, "Relación histórica de la Colonia del Nuevo Santander y Costa del Seno Mexico", Estado general de las fundaciones hechas por Don José de Escandón de la Colonia del Nuevo Santander, Tomo II (México, 1930), pp. 388-389.

[89]Humphreys, op.cit., p. 123.

[90]Gatschet, op.cit., p. 17.

[91]Fray José de Solís, "Diary of 1767", trans Peter Forrestal, Texas Catholic Historical Society (1931), p. 21.

[92]Francis Parkman, La Salle and the Discovery of the Great West: France and England in North America (Boston: Little, Brown, and Company, 1907), p. 381.

93Humphreys, op.cit., p. 123.

94Gatschet, op.cit., pp. 61-62; Humphreys, op.cit., p. 121.

95Solís, op.cit., p. 14.

96Gatschet, op.cit., pp. 17, 61.

97Instructions for the Missionary, op.cit., p. 20.

98Dolores et al., op.cit., p. 267.

99Instructions for the Missionary, op.cit., p. 34.

100Dolores et al., op.cit., p. 265.

101List dated November 18, 1805. (Bexar Archives: 34) also available as transcripts of Texas Medical History, University of Texas, Austin.

102Solís, op.cit., p. 15.

103Santa María, op.cit., pp. 419-420. The wonder drug may have been the trompetilla Bouvardia ternifolia. The plant is also known as "Hierba del Pasmo" or "Hierba del Indio" in some locales. Its distribution is widespread, from Sinaloa and Sonora to Coahuila. Ancient indigenese were said to use the powdered root to stop bleeding. The term "Hierba del Pasmo" is also used for plants belonging to several genera: Baccharis ramulosa (found in northeastern Mexican states), Cordia cylindrostachya (found in western and southern Mexican states), Zexmenia ghies-breghtii (found in Sinaloa and Guerrero), and Waltheria americana (found throughout most of Mexico in warm climates). The latter, known as "Malva de Monte" in Tamaulipas, is used against skin infirmities in that state and to wash wounds in Colima. See Maximino Martínez, Las Plantas Medicinales de México (México: Ediciones Botas, 4th edition, 1959), pp. 452, 499-500 and Maximino Martínez, Catalogo de Nombres Vulgares y Científicos de Plantas Mexicanos (México: Ediciones Botas, 1937).

104Dolores et al., op.cit., p. 268.

105Daniel J. Boorstin, The Americans: The Colonial Experience, 3 vols. (New York: Vintage Books, 1958), Vol. 1, pp. 223-225.

106Nicolás Sanchez-Albornoz, Population of Latin America, trans. W.A.R. Richardson (Berkeley: University of California Press, 1974), pp. 119-120.

[107] Letters dated September 15 and November 5, 1786 (Bexar Archives: 17) op.cit.

[108] Sanchez-Albornoz, op.cit.

[109] Letters dated March 11, April 8, April 19, 1806, (Bexar Archives: 34) op.cit.

SOUTHWEST

HISTORIC POPULATION OF THE EASTERN PUEBLOS: 1540–1910

Ann M. Palkovich

Department of Sociology/Anthropology
George Mason University, Fairfax, VA 22030

Like most North American Indian groups, the Eastern Pueblos of north-central New Mexico historically experienced a reduction in overall population size. Analysis of the available historic population estimates shows dramatic swings in the magnitude and direction of demographic trends. Evaluation of the sources and accuracy of these data suggests that the observed demographic pattern is confounded by enumeration inconsistencies, social disruptions, and a long-established pattern of population shifts in response to inherent environmental instability.

EPIDEMIC DISEASE, WARFARE, and the accompanying disruption of social systems are often cited as major factors that caused the depopulation of Native American Indian groups from the fifteenth through the early twentieth centuries (Aschman 1967; Crosby 1972, 1976; Dobyns 1966; Mooney 1928; Sanchez-Albornoz 1974). Dobyns (1983:310–11) suggests that a coalescing of remnant populations also was a characteristic response to depopulation among these groups, including the Pueblos. Such generalizations require a careful assessment of the context and circumstances of depopulation for each group. However, few detailed analyses have been made of (1) the accuracy of, and the trends reflected by, historic population estimates (Cook and Borah 1971; Ubelaker 1974, 1976); (2) the incidence and patterns of epidemic outbreaks (Aberle, Watkins, and Pitney 1940; Cook 1955, 1973); or (3) the cultural responses to depopulation (Deetz 1967).

This study evaluates the sources and accuracy of available population estimates for the Eastern Pueblos of New Mexico (Ortiz 1979). It also examines the impact of epidemics in light of these population estimates and considers the underlying causes of population movements and resettlement. The resulting analysis suggests that the observed pattern of population fluctuations precedes historic depopulation of Eastern Pueblo populations. Shifting settlement patterns are confounded with overall population size and depopulation trends. Epidemic outbreaks, as well as social disruptions attributable to the Pueblo Revolt of 1680, exacerbated, rather than initiated, dramatic population fluctuations among the Eastern Pueblos.

DEMOGRAPHIC HISTORY OF THE EASTERN PUEBLOS: 1540–1910

Since the time Fray Marcos de Niza first reported the wonders of the Seven Cities of Cibola, numerous explorers, colonizers, and government administrators have counted and commented on the Pueblo people. The sedentary nature

401

of the Pueblos has made the estimation of their population size throughout various historic periods a relatively easy task when compared with nomadic groups such as the Navajos. However, sorting out the details of Pueblo population history is still a complex task.

A number of historians and others have compiled population statistics for the Eastern Pueblos (Bandelier 1890; Hodge 1907–10; Dozier 1970; Simmons 1979; Ortiz 1979). Usually they have briefly discussed Eastern Pueblo population changes, presenting tabulations of available statistics. Unfortunately, little evaluation of these population statistics is presented. Other researchers have worked to make valuable documents available through the translation and publication of early Spanish diaries and government reports (see, in particular, Hammond and Rey 1929, 1938, 1966; Kessell 1979). Such translations are usually accompanied by a discussion of the nature of the documents and the motivations behind the original collection of the data they contain. In addition, isolated documents are reported on or translated by various researchers as they pertain to their particular research (see, for example, Ellis 1964). As a result, it is possible to compile a general survey of Eastern Pueblo population dynamics since the mid-1500s.

Table 1 presents a list of all pueblos noted historically that have total population estimates directly associated with them. With the exception of two years, 1829 and 1874, it is possible to determine the original source of information, usually identifying the actual person who collected the census information. In the majority of cases, it also is possible to locate translations or copies of the original documents, thus making it possible to determine the accuracy of the census information within the context of the original report itself. Accuracy, consistency, and clarity in reporting census figures do not necessarily improve over time. Information varies among observers; thus it is important to consider which individual was taking the census, the conditions under which it was taken, and the reason for taking it. Census information is reviewed by century.

NOTES TO TABLE 1

A) Population estimates for Zuñi and seven Hopi Pueblos combined
B) Jemez by 1626 had already been depopulated by famines and wars
C) Population estimate for Zuñi was probably closer to 3,000, according to the commentaries to Benavides's memorial
D) Population estimates for Santa Clara and San Juan Pueblos combined
E) Population estimates for Nambé and Cuyamunge Pueblos combined
F) Population estimates for Santo Domingo and Cochiti Pueblos combined
G) Population estimates for Galisteo and San Cristobal Pueblos combined
H) Population estimates for Zia and Santa Ana Pueblos combined
I) Population estimates for Sandia and Puaray Pueblos combined
J) Population estimates for Tesuque, Nambé, and Pojoaque Pueblos combined

(*continued on page 406*)

Table 1

HISTORIC POPULATION ESTIMATES FOR THE EASTERN PUEBLOS

	(1) 1539-1541	(2) 1583-1584	(3) 1598-1599	(4) 1621	(5) 1620-1626	(6) 1638	(7) 1664	(8) 1680	(9) 1692	(10) 1706	(11) 1712	(12) 1730	(13) 1749	(14) 1750	(15) 1760	(16) 1776	(17) 1779	(17) 1782	(18) L 1784	(19) 1790	(20) 1794	(21) 1796	(21) 1798	(22) 1799
ABIQUIU																	851		1181	216			176	
ABO							1580	800	[ABANDONED ABOUT 1675]															
ACOMA	200 MEN	6000	3000		2000		600	1500		760		600	960	960	1502	530				820			757	1559 N
ALAMEDA							400	300	[DESTROYED AT TIME OF PUEBLO REVOLT]															
ALAMILLO								300	[DESTROYED BY OTERMIN AFTER REVOLT]															
BELEN																				000			124	
CHILILI							250	500	[ABANDONED ABOUT 1675]															
COCHITI							850 F	300		520		372	521	521	450	486				720	667		505	
CUYAMUNQUE							300 E		[ABANDONED IN 1696]															
GALISTEO							1000 G	800		150	110	188	350	220	255	152		52					189 M	
ISLETA							750	2000					250	421	304	454	352			410			479	
JEMEZ		30,000		6566	3000 B		1860	5000		300		307	574	383	373	345				485			272	1166
LAGUNA										330		400	528	528	600	699			1368	668			802	1559 N
NAMBÉ							300 E	600		300		400 J	350	199	204	183		187		155			178	
PECOS	500 WARRIORS	40,000			2000+		1189	2000	1500	1000		521	1000	300	344	269		84		152			189 M	
PICURIS					2000+		564	3000		300		732 K	400	247	328	223	464		212	254			251	
POJOAQUE											79	400 J		130	99	98		250	368	53			79	
PUARAY							640 T	200	[DESTROYED IN 1711 AND NEVER REBUILT]															
QUARAI							685	600	[ABANDONED ABOUT 1675]															
SAN CRISTOBAL							1000 G		[ABANDONED IN 1696]															
SANDIA							640 T	3000					400	440	291	257			596	304			236	1513
SAN FELIPE							350	600		500		234	400	453	458	406				532			282	
SAN ILDEFONSO							400	800		300		296	354	371	484	387				240			251	
SAN JUAN							993 D	300		340		300	500	261	316	201	1014		1566	260			202	
SAN MARCOS							777	600	[ABANDONED ABOUT 1680]															
SANTA ANA							800 H			340		209	600	353	404	384				356			634	
SANTA CLARA							993 D	300		210		279	272	188	257	229		277	452	134			193	
SANTA CRUZ													580							650	[MEXICANIZED AFTER 1790]			
SANTO DOMINGO					850		850 F	150		240		281	300	300	424	528			608				1483	
TAJIQUE							484	300	[ABANDONED ABOUT 1675 DUE TO APACHE RAIDS]															
TAOS	15,000				2500		600	2000		700		732 K	540	456	505	427	784		578	518			531	782
TESUQUE							170	200		500		400 J	171	171	232	194				138			155	
ZIA		20,000					800 H			500		318	600	481	568	416	580		1035	275			262	
ZUNI	3000-4000 A	20,000			10,000 C		1200	2500		1500		800	2000	824	664	1617	1199		1617	1935			2716	2716
TOTAL	20,000		60,000		40,000														17,153			9453	9732	10,369

Table 1 (Continued)

HISTORIC POPULATION ESTIMATES FOR THE EASTERN PUEBLOS

	(23) 1804	(23) 1805	(24) 1805-1807	(19) 1808	(19) 1809	(25) 1815	(26) 1820	(27) 1820	(27) 1821	(28) 1826	(29) 1829	(30) 1844
ABIQUIU		134	500	122	126				246			
ABO												
ACOMA		731	500	797	816				477			750
ALAMEDA												
ALAMILLO												
BELEN		107		135	133				70	[MEXICANIZED AFTER 1821]		
CHILILI												
COCHITI		656		672	697				339		372	500
CUYAMUNQUE												
GALISTEO				[ABANDONED BY 1805]								
ISLETA		419		471	487				511			450
JEMEZ		264	500	285	297				330			450
LAGUNA		940	250	1007	1022				779			900
NAMBÉ		143		186	133				231			
PECOS		104		132	000	40	58		54	40	[ABANDONED IN 1838 BY 17 REMAINING INDIVIDUALS]	
PICURIS		250		309	313				320			250
POJOAQUE		100	500	83	000				93			200
PUARAY												
QUARAI												
SAN CRISTOBAL												
SANDIA		314	500	358	364				405			400
SAN FELIPE		289	1000	394	405				310			275
SAN ILDEFONSO		175		272	283				527			250
SAN JUAN		194	1000	201	208				232			275
SAN MARCOS												
SANTA ANA		450		535	550				471			300
SANTA CLARA		186		213	220				180			350
SANTA CRUZ				701	720							
SANTO DOMINGO		333	1000						726			750
TAJIQUE												
TAOS		508		527	527				753			
TESUQUE		131	400	156	160				187			
ZIA		254	450	278	286				196			
ZUNI		1470	300	1557	1598				1597			1000-1500
TOTAL	8608	8172						7840	9034			

	(31) 1847	(32) 1849	(33) 1849	(34) 1851	(35) 1852	(36) 1854	(37) 1860	(38) 1863	(39) 1865	(40) 1869	(41) 1871	(42) 1874
ABIQUIU												
ABO												
ACOMA				350		1200	523	499			436	500
ALAMEDA												
ALAMILLO												
BELEN												
CHILILI												
COCHITI				254		800	172	234			243	400
CUYAMUNQUE												
GALISTEO												
ISLETA			600	751		800	440	792			768	1200
JEMEZ		400-500	1918	365		450	650	369			344	800
LAGUNA		800	900	749		800	927	994			927	900
NAMBÉ				111	200	500	103	95			78	100
PECOS												
PICURIS			283	222	100	800	143	125			127	150
POJOAQUE			500	48	48	500	37	32			32	20
PUARAY												
QUARAI												
SAN CRISTOBAL												
SANDIA				241		500	217	200			186	225
SAN FELIPE				411		800	360	430			482	400
SAN ILDEFONSO				139	250	500	154	164			156	570
SAN JUAN			500	568	400	500	341	389			426	350
SAN MARCOS												
SANTA ANA				399		500	316	308			373	500
SANTA CLARA				279	350	600	179	145			189	50
SANTA CRUZ												
SANTO DOMINGO		800		666·		800	261	617	800		735	1000
TAJIQUE												
TAOS	345			361		800	143	369			397	375
TESUQUE				119	250	700	97	102			98	125
ZIA	250			124		450	117	106		110	121	125
ZUNI	2985	1200	1800	1500				1300			1530	1500
TOTAL	10,000			7867		15,300						

Table 1 (Continued)

HISTORIC POPULATION ESTIMATES FOR THE EASTERN PUEBLOS

	(43) 1875	(44) 1876	(45) 1879	(46)° 1880	(47) 1882	(48) 1883	(49) 1884	(50) 1885	(51) 1887	(52) 1889	(53) 1890	(54) 1890	(55) 1891	(56) 1892	(39) 1895	(57) 1898	(58) 1899	(59) 1900	(60) 1901	(61) 1902	(62) 1903	(63) 1904	(64) 1905	(65) 1906	(66) 1910
ABIQUIU																									
ABO																									
ACOMA				582						582	566	597			500		1278	492	650	650		737	739		691
ALAMEDA																									
ALAMILLO																									
BELEN																									
CHILILI																									
COCHITI				271						300	268	285			250		355	198	300		210	217			237
CUYAMUNQUE																									
GALISTEO																									
ISLETA				1081						1037	1059	1007					1000	1021	1120	1135		979	989		956
JEMEZ				401						474	428	483					456	449	450		470	498	500		499
LAGUNA				968						970	1143	963			1100		850	1077		1000		1365	1384		1472
NAMBÉ				66						81	79	86			79		98	80	100		99	100			88
PECOS																									
PICURIS				115						120	100	91													
POJOAQUE				26						18	20	19			20		96	96	125		100	101			104
PUARAY																									
QUARAI																									
SAN CRISTOBAL																									
SANDIA				350						150	140	145			150		77	76	76 p	65		79	74		73
SAN FELIPE				667						501	554	499			550		650	514	550	500		489	475		490
SAN ILDEFONSO				139						189	148	151			148		150	138	250		158	154			123
SAN JUAN			500	408						373	406	374			400		378	379	425		402	419			387
SAN MARCOS																									
SANTA ANA				489						264	253	271					300	228	228 p	223		224	226		211
SANTA CLARA				212						187	225	204			200•		248	221	325		245	251			277
SANTA CRUZ																									
SANTO DOMINGO				1129						930	670	969			690		1015	771	1000		1000	846	1000		817
TAJIQUE																									
TAOS				391						324	409	382					402	414	425			465			517
TESUQUE				99						94	91	102			100		84	80	100		100	86			77
ZIA				58						113	106	110			100		104	114	125		118	116			109
ZUNI				1608					1500	1547	1613	1547			1600	1796	1422	1523	1541	1540	1547		1514	1514	1667
TOTAL	10,000	8400		9060	9060	9240	9200	7762	8337		8278	8285	8120	8536		9494	8961	7883	7790	8259	7124			8926	

(continued from page 402)

K) Population estimates for Picuris and Taos Pueblos combined
L) Ilzarbe did not distinguish the Spanish and Indian portions of the population
M) Population estimates for Pecos and Galisteo Pueblos combined
N) Population estimates for Ácoma and Laguna Pueblos combined
O) Bandelier noted "the figures for Ácoma and Cia [Zia] are hardly correct"
P) Represents the census figure for 1900

REFERENCES FOR TABLE 1

OBSERVER	REFERENCE
1) Castañeda, Explorer	Hodge 1907; Winship 1896
2) Espejo (see Text) Luxan Explorers	Bolton 1916; Hammond and Rey 1929; Hammond and Rey 1966
3) Oñate, Spanish Government Official	Bolton 1916; Hammond and Rey 1938
4) Salmeron, Missionary	Reiter 1938
5) Benavides, Missionary	Hodge, Hammond, and Rey 1945; Benavides 1630
6) Prada, Missionary	Hackett 1937
7) Marquez, Missionary	Scholes 1929
8) Vetancurt, Spanish Government Official	Bandelier 1890
9) Vargas, Spanish Government Official	Espinosa 1940
10) Alvarez, Spanish Government Official	Hackett 1937
11) Annotations to Benavides	Hodge 1907; Hodge, Hammond, and Rey 1945
12) Crespo, Spanish Government Official	Adams 1954
13) Bonilla, Spanish Government Official	Kelly 1940
14) 1750 Spanish Census	Adams 1954
15) Tamaron, Spanish Government Official	Bancroft 1888; Adams 1954
16) Dominguez, Spanish Government Official	Adams and Chavez 1956
17) Anza, Spanish Government Official	A. Thomas 1932
18) Ilzarbe, Spanish Government Official	Bancroft 1888
19) Gigedo, Spanish Government Official	Ward 1868; Bancroft 1888
20) Biblioteca, Spanish Archives	Lange 1959
21) Hezio, Spanish Government Official	Meline 1867
22) Chacon, Spanish Government Official	Meline 1867
23) Alencaster, Spanish Government Official	Meline 1867
24) Pike, Explorer	Coues 1895
25) Spanish Government Official	Chavez 1957
26) Pino, Spanish Government Official	Twitchell 1911–12
27) Celis, Spanish Government Official	Bloom 1913

28) Narbona, Spanish Government Official — Ellis 1964

29) ? — Lange 1959

30) Gregg, Adventurer — Gregg 1844

31) Schoolcraft, U.S. Indian Official — Schoolcraft 1851

32) Simpson, U.S. Indian Agent — Simpson 1850

33) Blummer and Calhoun, U.S. Indian Agents — Abel 1915

34) Merritt, U.S. Indian Agent — Abel 1915

35) Greiner, U.S. Indian Agent — Abel 1915

36) Abert, U.S. Indian Agent — Whipple, Ewbank, and Thomas 1855

37) U.S. Deputy Marshall — Ward 1868

38) Ward, U.S. Indian Agent — Ward 1865

39) Coues, Historian — Coues 1895

40) Colyer, U.S. Indian Agent — Colyer 1869

41) Arny, U.S. Indian Agent — Arny 1872

42) ? — Hodge 1907, 1907–10

43) Thomas, U.S. Indian Agent — B. Thomas 1875

44) Thomas, U.S. Indian Agent — B. Thomas 1876

45) Thomas, U.S. Indian Agent — B. Thomas 1879; Aberle, Watkins, and Pitney 1940

46) Thomas, U.S. Indian Agent — B. Thomas 1881; Lange and Riley 1966

47) Thomas, U.S. Indian Agent — B. Thomas 1882

48) Sanchez, U.S. Indian Agent — Sanchez 1883

49) Sanchez, U.S. Indian Agent — Sanchez 1884

50) Romero, U.S. Indian Agent — Romero 1885

51) Williams, U.S. Indian Agent — Williams 1887

52) McClure, U.S. Indian Agent — McClure 1889

53) 1890 Census — Donaldson 1893; Prince 1890

54) Segura, U.S. Indian Agent — Segura 1890

55) Segura, U.S. Indian Agent — Segura 1891

56) Robertson, U.S. Indian Agent — Robertson 1892

57) Walpole, U.S. Indian Agent — Walpole 1898

58) Walpole, U.S. Indian Agent — Walpole 1899

59) Walpole, U.S. Indian Agent — Walpole 1900

60) Crandall, U.S. Indian Agent — Crandall 1902

61) Collins, U.S. Indian Agent — Collins 1903

62) Crandall, U.S. Indian Agent — Crandall 1904

63) Allen, U.S. Indian Agent — Allen 1905
Crandall, U.S. Indian Agent — Crandall 1905
Graham, U.S. Indian Agent — Graham 1905
Palin, Field Matron — Palin 1905

64) Allen, U.S. Indian Agent — Allen 1906
Crandall, U.S. Indian Agent — Crandall 1906a
Graham, U.S. Indian Agent — Graham 1906a

65) Crandall, U.S. Indian Agent — Crandall 1906b
Custer, U.S. Indian Agent — Custer 1906
Graham, U.S. Indian Agent — Graham 1906b

66) 1910 Census — Rogers 1915

SIXTEENTH CENTURY

Fired by the report of riches and gold of the Seven Cities of Cibola as "seen" by Fray Marcos de Niza in 1539, officials of the Spanish Empire were eager to gain further information about the Eastern Pueblos, with an eye toward colonization of the area. Between 1539 and 1541, Francisco Vásquez de Coronado led an expedition into the area, reporting on the condition, location, and related information about various pueblos. A major concern of the expedition was to determine the ability of each pueblo to raise a fighting force, apparently to establish the extent of possible resistance to colonization. As a result, the few population estimates that Coronado reports (as recorded by Pedro de Castañeda, a member of his expedition) usually give estimates of the number of men or warriors. His estimate of the total population for all pueblos combined is approximately 20,000 (Winship 1896:525). It is difficult to determine if this is a representative figure since Coronado clearly did not visit all the pueblos, nor may he have accounted for all those in existence at the time.

The next major expedition to the Eastern Pueblos was led by Antonio de Espejo. A major purpose of his campaign was not only to establish the number of souls at each pueblo for colonization but also to determine if it was worth the effort to "civilize" the Indians and convert them to Christianity. The estimates for pueblos that he does report are now widely recognized as greatly exaggerated and probably done to enhance the area as a desirable place for colonization (Bolton 1916). This has been established from a diary kept by one member of his expedition. Apparently Espejo kept no notes during the expedition, writing his report upon his return to Mexico. The diary of Diego Perez de Luxan, however, is known to have been kept daily. In it, he reports population figures, but, unfortunately, it is impossible to associate these figures with particular pueblos. These early Spanish explorers simply named towns or settlements as they encountered them with no regard for local names or names previously used by other explorers. As a result, unless they also provided detailed descriptions locating each pueblo, it is difficult to assign specific population estimates to individual settlements (Schroeder 1979). However, it is clear from Luxan's diary that the population for each pueblo ranged in the hundreds, not thousands as reported by Espejo (Hammond and Rey 1966).

The other population estimates for the 1500s are reported by Juan de Oñate, giving an overall figure of 60,000 individuals (Hammond and Rey 1938). This is the figure that is usually cited as a population estimate for the Pueblos (including the Hopi Pueblos) prior to European contact. Its accuracy is difficult to assess, but it is consistent with archaeologically based studies of the human carrying capacity of this region of the Southwest (Zubrow 1975; Kroeber 1939).

From these historical accounts and the archaeological record, it is clear that few large Pueblo settlements existed immediately prior to European contact. Populations usually were located in clusters of small settlements scattered throughout the areas best suited for agriculture.

SEVENTEENTH CENTURY

The seventeenth century saw the colonization of the Eastern Pueblos. By 1600, some missions already were being established. Between 1620 and 1626, Fray Alonso de Benavides (1630) came to the Pueblos as a major religious leader to help establish missions. Though it is difficult to determine, the few estimates that he provided may be inflated or may include a major pueblo with its surrounding smaller settlements (Hodge, Hammond, and Rey 1945). Benavides noted that famine and war already had caused some reduction of the population in the Jemez area by 1626. This also is suggested by the higher population estimate by Fray Geronimo de Zarate Salmeron for Jemez in 1621 (Reiter 1938; Schroeder 1979). Evidence of warfare and attacks by marauding tribes (particularly Apaches, Utes, and Navajos) occasionally was noted by contemporary observers throughout the period.

By far the best population estimates for the first two centuries of Spanish contact were those collected by Fray Bartolome Marquez in the year 1664. In a request to the Spanish government, Marquez sent a detailed listing of the Eastern Pueblos and their associated settlements, evaluating the number of additional missionaries he felt would be needed to tend the "souls" of the converted Indians. It is likely some depopulation from introduced diseases may already have occurred (Hackett 1937:108), though this is not adequately reported until the late eighteenth century. As far as we know, Marquez visited all the pueblos he reported and tried to provide an accurate accounting of the population (Scholes 1929).

Adding Marquez's estimates of population size from individual pueblos yields a total estimate of 16,442. This is approximately the same range for the total population size estimated over a hundred years earlier by Castañeda, suggesting a relatively stable overall Eastern Pueblo population size for this period. It is also possible widespread epidemics had not yet devastated these populations.

One of the most dramatic events in Pueblo history occurred in 1680—the start of the Pueblo Revolt (Hammond and Rey 1966). Throughout the seventeenth century, greatly increased missionary activity pressured the Pueblos to convert to Christianity and to abandon their traditional beliefs. Resentment toward the Spanish settlers, and in particular the missionaries, grew until a revolt (led by Popé of San Juan) occurred in 1680. Well over half of the missionaries and Spanish settlers in the Pueblo area were killed within a few days, the rest fleeing to El Paso. Not all pueblos participated in the revolt, but the entire Pueblo population was in a state of turmoil. Pueblos choosing not to participate fled to El Paso with the remaining Spanish and eventually established settlements in that area (Schroeder 1979).

For the next twelve years the Pueblos were free from Spanish rule, but in 1692 Diego de Vargas was sent on an expedition to reconquer this area. Many Indians were killed in retaliation for the Spanish deaths twelve years earlier.

Settlements were burned and many Indians taken captive. Others fled when news reached them of the Spanish return. Vargas frequently noted in his journal that pueblos were found recently abandoned. Many of the fleeing Indians joined other Indian tribes and conducted raids on the Spanish (Espinosa 1940). Once again, the Pueblo population was in a state of upheaval. Historical records document that at least ten earlier established Pueblo settlements were abandoned or destroyed in the aftermath of the Revolt (Table 1; also see Schroeder 1979). Only two pueblos, Ácoma and Isleta, can be unequivocally identified as occupying the same settlement before and after the Revolt.

The population estimates for 1680 apparently were collected just prior to the Revolt. Estimates for the rest of the seventeenth century are unreliable or simply not available (Hammond and Rey 1966). The Spanish preoccupation with regaining control over their colony and the fleeing of many Indians with the advance of the reconquering Spanish made reliable estimates impossible. Vargas provided some idea of the number of Indians he observed at each pueblo, but it is always described as the number of individuals baptized and present to reestablish the missions (Espinosa 1940.) It is obvious from these reports that the great majority of the population was not present or reported on. Also, the Indians fleeing to El Paso with the Spanish at the beginning of the Revolt did not return to repopulate the area but remained in settlements they had established in the El Paso area. Several new Pueblo settlements at Hopi also were established at the end of the seventeenth century (Simmons 1979).

EIGHTEENTH CENTURY

The return of the Spanish in 1692 did not mean a return to previously established population patterns for the Pueblos. Isolated revolts by individual settlements continued until about 1700. However, by 1706 (the next available population information), the Spanish once again had gained total administrative control over the Eastern Pueblos. An important part of the Spanish resettlement program for the indigenous population was the reestablishment of villages. This resettlement concentrated the Indian population into large pueblos rather than the former smaller, dispersed settlement clusters. The Spanish likely did this for two reasons. First, they felt it was easier to protect the Pueblo Indians from marauding tribes if there were fewer settlements to protect. Second, it was easier to administer and to control the area when the Indians were concentrated into larger settlements (Hackett 1937). This also required fewer missionaries. It is ironic, however, that the establishment of this new settlement pattern, seen by the Spanish as a benefit to the Indians, may very well have been a significant factor in promoting epidemic disease among the indigenous population.

Population figures for this time reflect the location of major churches and the surrounding *visita* pueblos of each mission. Census figures were commonly given for a church and its visita settlements combined, rather than for each individual pueblo. Since the location of the major churches with resident missionaries and the visitas associated with each church changed over time, overall population estimates by the missionaries are likely representative, while estimates for any given pueblo do not necessarily reflect the same settlement unit from year to year.

The eighteenth century also saw the establishment of a highly organized Spanish government located in Santa Fe. The Eastern Pueblo region of New Mexico was no longer a frontier but a well-established colony. With the advent of a stable government, more frequent and accurate census data were collected. It was now possible to provide an accurate count of the population rather than good guesses or estimates. Of course, each governor of the New Mexican territory had his own way of doing things, and each maintained different standards of accuracy. It does appear, however, that a census was attempted at least once every ten years, with additional information provided by missionaries or special observers.

NINETEENTH CENTURY

Spanish Rule

The nineteenth century saw a shift in governmental jurisdiction of the New Mexican territory and rule over the Eastern Pueblos. Census figures for the first half of the century are derived from both Spanish officials and American explorers in the area. Again, it should be noted that those having to administer the Pueblos in an official capacity seem to provide a more accurate accounting of the number of individuals per pueblo than the unsystematic, causal observations of explorers passing through the area.

American Rule

As a result of the Mexican-American War, the United States gained control of the New Mexican territory. A first priority of the American government was to make an accounting of all groups within its newly acquired territory. In conjunction with this project, Henry Schoolcraft was given the task of writing a history of the American Indian tribes in the United States. His book, *Historical and Statistical Information Respecting the History, Condition and Prospects of the Indian Tribes of the United States,* published in 1851, is an important historical document containing the firsthand observations Schoolcraft made of the various tribes he visited. Schoolcraft (1851) and John Calhoun, the first Indian agent to the Pueblos (Abel 1915), collected several censuses between 1847 and 1851 that are now available.

After the establishment of the U.S. government in the New Mexican territory, a series of Indian agents were assigned duty among the Pueblos. Their responsibilities were to administer government aid to the Indians (who were now technically wards of the federal government) by helping in the establishment and maintenance of Indian schools, conducting regular censuses, and reporting on the condition of the tribe on a yearly basis. Again, accuracy in the census information varied greatly among Indian agents. Some circumstances, such as the death of the agent, resulted in no census being taken. Often no money was allocated to hire enumerators, so the same figures would be repeated for several years (Robertson 1892:333). Figures presented in Table 1 represent only censuses actually taken in the year reported. In some cases, there are major discrepancies between the ten-year national census and the separate census figures reported by the Indian agents. For example, the 1890 census figures for some pueblos are relatively close, within a few individuals. Yet, for other pueblos, there are unaccountable discrepancies in the figures.

In evaluating the census figures for the American period, it is apparent that, although it is the most recent historical period considered in this study, it presents substantial problems. These problems were troubling enough to prompt Calhoun, in a letter dated December 28, 1850 (Abel 1915:28), to note:

> The taking of the census has troubled the Indians of several of the Pueblos during the present month, and as a matter of course, I have been greatly annoyed by their visits, and the expenditures necessarily incurred thereby.
> The Census [1849] as taken by Chs. Blummer, assistant Marshall, of the Pueblos of San Ildefonso, Pojoaque, Tesuque, and Nambe, exhibits a list of only *four hundred and seventeen* persons. In my letter No. 5, dated Octr. 4, 1849, you were informed that a census of 1847 put them down at *five hundred and ninety*. I have before me a memorandum from information given me by old citizens, one a native of this territory, who gave these Pueblos an average of over *three hundred* each. Mr. Blummer is capable and honest, and if the Census, as taken by him, is incorrect, it is because the Indians have concealed the truth. Let us pass over the estimates of visitors to these Pueblos, and compare the Census of 1847 with that of 1850 [taken in the year 1849]. The decrease in population is shown to be *one hundred and seventy three*. What has become of these Indians? We know of no special mortality that has fallen upon them for the last three years. Then, in my opinion, it follows that these Indians have deceived those who have been charged with the taking of the census, or many are renouncing their Catholicism and joining the nomadic, if not wild tribes who encircle this territory.

Even during this period, census figures usually reflected enrollment in mission churches and not necessarily the entire population.

While laments such as the one cited above are occasionally found in documents discussing population figures, the available information does have some utility in evaluating the condition of the Eastern Pueblos since 1540. It is apparent that there has been a trend of decreasing population in all the pueblos. Of the thirty-four Pueblo villages documented in Table 1, ten were destroyed or abandoned by the end of the Pueblo Revolt. Four additional pueblos were abandoned or "mexicanized" by 1838. The total population was roughly halved—

from approximately 16,000–20,000 individuals in the sixteenth, seventeenth, and mid-eighteenth centuries to roughly 7,800–10,000 individuals by the early twentieth century. Fluctuations in population size are evident on a pueblo by pueblo basis. However, catastrophic or steady declines in population are not readily apparent.

There also are historical inconsistencies in documenting who are "Indians." Often only men or adults or "baptized" individuals or individuals in residence at the time of the census are counted. By the nineteenth century, the official government policy of assimilation also helped to blur distinctions of Indians and non-Indians for census purposes.

DEPOPULATION TRENDS

The historic population figures for the Eastern Pueblos appear to document some decline in the population from the sixteenth to the twentieth centuries. However, an analysis of the rate of change in population size for the Pueblos reflects dramatic fluctuations in the population of these villages.

Cook and Borah (1971:73–118) devised a method to assess the rate of change in historic populations and to chart variations in this rate. This method is termed a coefficient of population movement, designated as ω. This coefficient is calculated as follows:

$$\omega = [(P_1 - P_2)/(t_1 - t_2) \times 100]/[(P_1)(P_2)]^{1/2}$$

where P_1 and t_1 represent the initial population estimate and date of the estimate, respectively, and P_2 and t_2 represent the subsequent population estimate and date (Cook and Borah 1971:90–91). Positive or negative values are assigned to ω, indicating population increases or decreases, respectively. This equation yields the percent change in population growth or decline averaged over the number of years between the two population estimates, thus the relative change in population size. Cook and Borah found that logarithmic values of ω provide an effective means of interpolating demographic trends, freed somewhat from the particular years for which historic estimates are available. This is important when available census estimates represent irregular time intervals, as in the case of the Eastern Pueblos. Direct comparisons of population estimates in such instances can be grossly misleading. This coefficient also accurately reflects population trends in both large-scale and small-scale populations. Cook and Borah (1971) were able to demonstrate consistent rates of decline in historic indigenous Mexican populations with this approach.

After applying this formula to the population estimates for individual pueblos in Table 1, dramatic reversals in the demographic trend between population declines and increases become evident in the course of only a few years. For example, among the larger Pueblo settlements, both Pecos (Table 2) and Zuñi (Table 3) show these fluctuations. Even Ácoma (Table 4), one of the two settlements which occupied the same physical location before and after the Pueblo Revolt, shows alternating population declines and increases with ac-

TABLE 2
Coefficient of Population Movement for Pecos Pueblo

Year	(Pop.)	to	Year	(Pop.)	Interval in Years	Direct ω	Log ω
1622	(2000)	–	1664	(1189)	42	− 1.252	0.098
1664	(1189)	–	1680	(2000)	16	+ 3.287	0.518
1680	(2000)	–	1692	(1500)	12	− 2.406	0.381
1692	(1500)	–	1694*	(736)	2	− 36.356	1.561
1694	(736)	–	1695*	(800)	1	+ 8.341	0.921
1695	(800)	–	1706	(1000)	11	+ 2.033	0.308
1706	(1000)	–	1730	(521)	24	− 2.765	0.442
1730	(521)	–	1749	(1000)	19	+ 3.493	0.543
1749	(1000)	–	1750*	(449)	1	− 82.230	1.915
1750	(449)	–	1760	(344)	10	− 2.672	0.427
1760	(344)	–	1776	(269)	16	− 1.541	0.188
1776	(269)	–	1779	(235)	3	− 4.508	0.654
1779	(235)	–	1789	(138)	10	− 5.386	0.731
1789	(138)	–	1790	(152)	1	+ 9.667	0.985
1790	(152)	–	1794	(180)	4	+ 4.232	0.627
1794	(180)	–	1799	(118)	5	− 8.508	0.930
1799	(118)	–	1800	(123)	1	+ 4.150	0.618
1800	(123)	–	1804	(125)	4	+ 0.403	0.395
1804	(125)	–	1805	(104)	1	− 18.418	1.265
1805	(104)	–	1808	(132)	3	+ 7.966	0.901
1808	(132)	–	1810*	(135)	2	+ 1.124	0.051
1810	(135)	–	1815	(40)	5	− 25.857	1.413
1815	(40)	–	1820	(58)	5	+ 7.474	0.874
1820	(59)	–	1823	(90)	3	+ 25.821	1.412
1823	(90)	–	1826	(40)	3	− 27.778	1.444
1826	(40)	–	1838	(17)	12	− 7.349	0.866

Both approximations and actual counts of individuals are included in the analysis. However, estimates which provided only the number of families were not used. Estimates by Spanish missionaries or government officials were used in preference to the casual guesses of explorers. Only one estimate from any given year was included, with preference given to figures provided by resident officials rather than general census figures.

*Estimates derived from Kessell (1979).

TABLE 3
Coefficient of Population Movement for Zuñi Pueblo

Year	(Pop.)	to	Year	(Pop.)	Interval in Years	Direct ω	Log ω
1664	(1200)	–	1680	(2500)	16	+ 4.691	0.696
1680	(2500)	–	1706	(1500)	26	– 1.986	0.298
1706	(1500)	–	1730	(800)	24	– 2.663	0.425
1730	(800)	–	1749	(2000)	19	+ 4.993	0.698
1749	(2000)	–	1750	(824)	1	– 91.607	1.962
1750	(824)	–	1760	(664)	10	– 2.163	0.335
1760	(664)	–	1776	(1617)	16	+ 5.748	0.760
1776	(1617)	–	1779	(1199)	3	– 10.007	1.000
1779	(1199)	–	1790	(1935)	11	+ 4.393	0.643
1790	(1935)	–	1798	(2716)	8	+ 4.258	0.629
1798	(2716)	–	1805	(1470)	7	– 8.908	0.950
1805	(1470)	–	1808	(1557)	3	+ 1.917	0.283
1808	(1557)	–	1809	(1598)	1	+ 2.599	0.415
1809	(1598)	–	1821	(1597)	12	– 0.005	2.301
1821	(1597)	–	1847	(2985)	36	+ 2.445	0.388
1847	(2985)	–	1849	(1200)	2	– 47.157	1.674
1849	(1200)	–	1851	(1500)	2	+ 11.180	1.048
1851	(1500)	–	1860	(1300)	9	– 1.591	0.202
1860	(1300)	–	1871	(1530)	11	+ 1.483	0.171
1871	(1530)	–	1874	(1500)	3	– 0.660	0.180
1874	(1500)	–	1880	(1608)	6	+ 1.159	0.064
1880	(1608)	–	1887	(1500)	7	– 0.993	0.003
1887	(1500)	–	1889	(1547)	2	+ 1.543	0.188
1889	(1547)	–	1895	(1600)	6	+ 0.561	0.251
1895	(1600)	–	1898	(1796)	3	+ 3.854	0.586
1898	(1796)	–	1899	(1422)	1	– 23.403	1.369
1899	(1422)	–	1900	(1523)	1	+ 6.863	0.837
1900	(1523)	–	1901	(1541)	1	+ 1.175	0.070
1901	(1541)	–	1902	(1540)	1	– 0.065	1.187
1902	(1540)	–	1903	(1547)	1	+ 0.454	0.343
1903	(1547)	–	1905	(1514)	2	– 1.078	0.033
1905	(1514)	–	1910	(1667)	5	+ 1.926	0.285

TABLE 4
Coefficient of Population Movement for Ácoma Pueblo

Year	(Pop.)	to	Year	(Pop.)	Interval in Years	Direct ω	Log ω
1583	(6000)	−	1598	(3000)	15	−4.714	0.673
1598	(3000)	−	1622	(2000)	24	−1.701	0.231
1622	(2000)	−	1664	(600)	42	−3.043	0.483
1664	(600)	−	1680	(1500)	16	+5.929	0.773
1680	(1500)	−	1706	(760)	26	−2.666	0.426
1706	(760)	−	1730	(600)	24	−0.987	0.006
1730	(600)	−	1749	(960)	19	+2.497	0.397
1749	(960)	−	1760	(1502)	11	+4.103	0.613
1760	(1502)	−	1776	(530)	16	−6.809	0.833
1776	(530)	−	1790	(820)	14	+3.142	0.497
1790	(820)	−	1798	(757)	8	−1.000	0.000
1798	(757)	−	1805	(731)	7	−0.499	0.302
1805	(731)	−	1808	(797)	3	+2.887	0.460
1808	(797)	−	1809	(816)	1	+2.356	0.372
1809	(816)	−	1821	(477)	12	−4.528	0.656
1821	(477)	−	1847	(750)	26	+1.756	0.245
1847	(750)	−	1851	(350)	4	−19.518	1.290
1851	(350)	−	1854	(1200)	3	+43.720	1.641
1854	(1200)	−	1860	(523)	6	−14.243	1.154
1860	(523)	−	1863	(499)	3	−1.566	0.195
1863	(499)	−	1871	(436)	8	−1.688	0.227
1871	(436)	−	1874	(500)	3	+4.569	0.660
1874	(500)	−	1889	(582)	15	+1.013	0.006
1889	(582)	−	1890	(597)	1	+2.545	0.406
1890	(597)	−	1895	(500)	5	−3.551	0.550
1895	(500)	−	1899	(1278)	4	+24.332	1.386
1899	(1278)	−	1900	(492)	1	−99.124	1.996
1900	(492)	−	1901	(650)	1	+27.939	1.446
1901	(650)	−	1902	(650)	1	0.000	0.000
1902	(650)	−	1904	(737)	2	+6.285	0.798
1904	(737)	−	1905	(739)	1	+0.271	0.567
1905	(739)	−	1910	(691)	5	−1.343	0.128

companying dramatic fluctuations in the rate of these changes. This pattern is true for the other pueblos documented in Table 1.

These population fluctuations may be reflecting enumeration inconsistencies as well as large-scale, frequent movement of Pueblo groups due to environmental, social, and political factors. Ten of the thirty-four pueblos documented in Table 1 were abandoned by 1711, the direct result of social upheavals during the Pueblo Revolt of 1680. By 1838, four more documented pueblos were abandoned or reverted to Spanish occupation exclusively. After the 1830s, population figures for the remaining twenty pueblos may represent large-scale movement of individuals from pueblo to pueblo, as well as a continual redefinition of "Indian" for census purposes. No consistent rate of depopulation can be demonstrated using just historic population estimates because the available data are confounded with other factors.

EPIDEMIC OUTBREAKS

Historians agree that epidemic disease periodically struck the Eastern Pueblo groups. It has not been possible to pinpoint precisely when epidemics first became a significant factor in the depopulation of Southwestern groups; however, the existence of some widespread diseases was documented as early as 1638 by Fray Juan de Prada (Hackett 1937:108). Epidemic disease likely arrived with, or shortly followed, first contact with the Spanish, as occurred with other Native American groups (Crosby 1972, 1976; Dobyns 1983).

Unfortunately, the historical incidence of epidemic disease is also poorly documented. A major smallpox epidemic, probably encompassing all the pueblos, occurred in 1781 (Bancroft 1888). However, reports from the nineteenth-century Indian agents indicate that sporadic outbreaks, particularly smallpox and influenza, occurred more frequently and with devastating effects on a pueblo to pueblo basis rather than as general epidemics. The pueblos are distinct settlements that are separated by hundreds of miles in some cases. Thus, it is not surprising that local epidemics could occur without widely affecting the rest of the population. One Indian agent (Walpole 1899:250) reports that agents made conscious efforts to keep affected Indians isolated from the rest of the community by restricting their attendance at traditional dances. A few widespread epidemics are reported for the Pueblos. The epidemic of 1781 reportedly killed 5,025 of the 9,104 Pueblo inhabitants counted in that year (Bancroft 1888).

Aberle and her co-workers (1940) published the only comprehensive study of historic Pueblo population dynamics, including epidemics, to date. They report on the "vital history" of San Juan Pueblo, noting that a total of seventeen epidemics were documented for San Juan between the 1780s and 1900. Despite efforts at inoculation as early as 1804 (Bloom 1924), epidemic outbreaks, usually of smallpox, occurred at ten to twenty-year intervals. Aberle, Watkins, and Pitney suggest that those susceptible to later epidemics were previously uninfected persons, the majority being children born since the last outbreak.

These periodic epidemic outbreaks observed at San Juan seem to follow the pattern of disease cycles noted by Kunstadter (1972) for small-scale populations.

An analysis of the population estimates for San Juan Pueblo shows the same dramatic shifts between population decline and increase as at the other pueblos (Table 5). However, there appears to be little relationship between epidemic outbreaks and declines in the growth rate of the population. Aberle, Watkins, and Pitney (1940:67–68) report a dramatic increase in the number of deaths and the magnitude of mortality associated with epidemic outbreaks. However, comparable declines in population estimates are not noted in the population figures for the years or periods immediately following epidemic outbreaks. Major epidemic outbreaks occurred in 1781, 1788–89, 1800, 1816, 1826–27, 1846–47, 1890–91, and 1899; yet, the population figures in subsequent years inconsistently reflect *both* declines and increases in the rate of change in the population (Table 5). This suggests that, while epidemics are altering the mortality profiles for the Eastern Pueblos and reducing the population, this pattern is not clearly reflected in the population estimates for individual pueblos.

POPULATION MOVEMENTS AND RESETTLEMENT

Dobyns (1983:310–11) suggests a widespread response to depopulation is evident among North American Indian groups, including the Pueblos. He cites the following as the major elements common to all such depopulation situations:

A. abandonment of settlements located in marginally productive environmental niches
B. migration to environments that were more productive in terms of the basic subsistence technology of the peoples involved
C. amalgamation of survivors of abandoned settlements into a diminished number of continuing or new ones, in an attempt to maintain a number of inhabitants culturally defined as proper by each group
D. amalgamation of survivors of diverse lineage and even ethnic origins into a diminished number of polities, resulting in:
    1) intermarriages, further diluting and erasing earlier ethnic distinctions
    2) adoption of locally determinant group languages, reducing linguistic diversity
    3) sometimes very rapid changes in many conventional understandings formerly shared, for the purpose of adjusting to the survival demands of quickly altering man-land ratios, colonial manipulation or domination, and so forth. (Dobyns 1983:311)

Dobyns concludes "there are enough clues in the scant written records of the protohistoric sixteenth century to indicate that Seneca village movements originated in epidemic population, just as they did *among the Pueblos*, the Venezuelan Achagua, and the Aricara [sic] and Pimans" (Dobyns 1983:314, emphasis

TABLE 5
Coefficient of Population Movement for San Juan Pueblo

Year	Interval (Pop.) to Year (Pop.)				Interval in Years	Direct ω	Log ω
1664	(*497)	−	1680	(300)	16	− 2.126	0.328
1680	(300)	−	1706	(340)	26	+ 0.482	0.317
1706	(340)	−	1730	(300)	24	− 0.522	0.282
1730	(300)	−	1749	(500)	19	+ 2.718	0.434
1749	(500)	−	1750	(261)	1	− 66.160	1.821
1750	(261)	−	1760	(316)	10	+ 1.915	0.282
1760	(316)	−	1776	(201)	16	− 2.852	0.455
1776	(201)	−	1779	(1014)	3	+ 60.028	1.778
1779	(1014)	−	1790	(275)	21	− 13.239	1.122
1790	(275)	−	1798	(262)	8	− 0.605	0.218
1798	(262)	−	1805	(194)	7	− 4.309	0.634
1805	(194)	−	1808	(201)	3	+ 1.182	0.073
1808	(201)	−	1809	(208)	1	+ 0.017	1.770
1809	(208)	−	1821	(232)	12	+ 0.910	0.041
1821	(232)	−	1847	(275)	26	+ 0.655	0.184
1847	(275)	−	1849	(500)	2	+ 30.339	1.482
1849	(500)	−	1851	(568)	2	+ 6.380	0.805
1851	(568)	−	1852	(400)	1	− 35.246	1.547
1852	(400)	−	1854	(500)	2	+ 11.180	1.048
1854	(500)	−	1860	(341)	6	− 6.418	0.807
1860	(341)	−	1863	(389)	3	+ 4.393	0.643
1863	(389)	−	1871	(426)	8	+ 1.136	0.055
1871	(426)	−	1874	(350)	3	− 6.651	0.817
1874	(350)	−	1879	(500)	5	+ 7.171	0.856
1879	(500)	−	1880	(408)	1	− 20.369	1.309
1880	(408)	−	1889	(373)	9	− 0.997	0.001
1889	(373)	−	1890	(374)	1	+ 0.278	0.556
1890	(374)	−	1895	(400)	5	+ 1.344	0.128
1895	(400)	−	1899	(378)	4	− 1.414	0.150
1899	(378)	−	1900	(379)	1	+ 0.264	0.578
1900	(379)	−	1901	(425)	1	+ 11.462	1.059
1901	(425)	−	1903	(402)	2	− 2.782	0.444
1903	(402)	−	1904	(419)	1	+ 2.071	0.316
1904	(419)	−	1910	(387)	6	− 1.324	0.122

*Population estimates for San Juan and Santa Clara combined. Half of original estimate used as population of San Juan.

added). He thus infers that epidemics are a universal cause underlying all historic Amerindian population shifts.

To the contrary, large-scale population movements apparently were a long-established demographic pattern for Pueblo groups. Archaeological studies reveal repeated settlement and abandonment of regions in response to changes in climate, social networks, and related shifts in resource availability (Berry 1982; Dickson 1975, 1979; Euler et al. 1979; Jorde 1977; Plog 1984; Powell 1983). For the Pueblos, then, population movements and resettlement did not "originate" with historic population as Dobyns claims. Such population movements already existed as a response to environmental and resource instability. Depopulation likely just heightened the frequency and incidence of these resettlements.

CONCLUSIONS

This study demonstrates several important characteristics of Eastern Pueblo historic population data. First, enumeration problems encountered throughout the historical period resulted in inconsistent, incomparable, often inaccurate population tabulations. Second, the rate of change in population size shows dramatic fluctuations, suggesting that the true rate of depopulation is masked by enumeration problems, social disruptions resulting from the Pueblo Revolt, indigenous warfare, and other factors. Third, epidemic outbreaks documented at San Juan Pueblo do not clearly coincide with substantial negative rates of change reducing the population. Again, other factors may mask the true impact of epidemics. Finally, large-scale population movements represent a long-established Pueblo demographic pattern that responds to inherent environmental instability. Epidemic depopulation, as well as the Pueblo Revolt, exacerbated, rather than initiated, such settlement shifts. Migration rates thus are confounded with overall population size and depopulation trends.

There is little question that, since the sixteenth century, the Eastern Pueblos have experienced a reduction in overall population size. Analysis of the available historic population estimates, however, shows dramatic swings in the magnitude and direction of these population trends. Unfortunately, this observed demographic pattern is confounded by various difficulties with the basic enumeration data available for these groups. While it is clear that significant depopulation occurred among the Pueblos due to direct and indirect contact with the Spanish, specific rates of population decline and recovery cannot be clearly documented spatially and temporally.

The observed fluctuating pattern of regional population increase and decline may be consistent with an ongoing process of population redistribution in response to the shifting resource availability that has been documented archaeologically in this region. Such population fluctuations may also be consistent with a recurrent pattern of epidemic outbreaks and recovery; however, this could not be demonstrated for San Juan Pueblo. Known epidemic outbreaks are not consistently associated with population declines.

The prehistoric pattern of population movements and periodic shifts in settlement patterns in response to an unstable desertic subsistence resource base likely continued throughout the historical period (Euler et al. 1979; Simmons 1979). Such shifts were altered and accelerated historically by devastating social disruptions, population reduction, and altered patterns and causes of mortality. Though it complicates our ability to evaluate the historic population dynamics of these groups, this long-established pattern of settlement shifts and demographic reorganization may have served to maintain Pueblo demographic viability by sustaining breeding cohorts and social integrity in the face of new biological and social disruptions. Demographic flexibility to adapt to an unpredictable environment may have provided a means for the Eastern Pueblos to persist despite depopulating epidemic disease, while other Native American groups were biologically and socially devastated.

REFERENCES CITED

Abel, A.H., ed., 1915, The Official Correspondence of John S. Calhoun, 1849–52. Washington, D.C.: U.S. Office of Indian Affairs.

Aberle, S.D., J.H. Watkins, and E.H. Pitney, 1940, The Vital History of San Juan Pueblo. Human Biology 12:141–87.

Adams, E., ed., 1954, Bishop Tamaron's Visitation of New Mexico, 1760. Vol. 15 of Publication in History. Albuquerque: Historical Society of New Mexico.

Adams, E., and F.A. Chavez, eds., 1956, The Missions of New Mexico, 1776. Albuquerque: University of New Mexico Press.

Allen, J.K., 1905, Report of School Superintendent in Charge of Pueblo, Aug. 19, 1904. Pp. 254–58 in Annual Report of the Commissioner of Indian Affairs . . . for the Year 1904, part 1. Washington, D.C.: U.S. Department of the Interior.

Allen, J.K., 1906, Report of Superintendent in Charge of Pueblo, Aug. 7, 1905. Pp. 260–64 in Annual Report of the Commissioner of Indian Affairs . . . for the Year 1905, part 1. Washington, D.C.: U.S. Department of the Interior.

Arny, W.F.M., 1872, Report No. 37, Office of Pueblo Indian Agency, Aug. 18, 1871. Pp. 380–95 in Annual Report of the Commissioner of Indian Affairs . . . for the Year 1871. Washington, D.C.: U.S. Department of the Interior.

Aschmann, H., 1967, The Central Desert of Baja, California: Demography and Ecology. Riverside, Calif.: Manessier.

Bancroft, H.H., 1888, The Works of H.H. Bancroft. Pp. 253–391 in vol. 17 of History of Arizona and New Mexico: 1530–1888. San Francisco: The History Co.

Bandelier, A., 1890, Final Report of Investigations Among the Indians of the Southwestern United States, Carried on Mainly in the Years from 1880 to 1885. Pp. 122–53 in Papers of the Archaeological Institute of America, American Series 4, vol. 1: Ethnographic. Cambridge, Mass.

Benevides, A. de, 1630, Memorial que Fray Ivan de Santander de la Orden de San Francisco. . . . Facsimile of Original Manuscript, Anthropology Department, Smithsonian Institution, Washington, D.C.

Berry, M., 1982, Time, Space and Transition in Anasazi Prehistory. Salt Lake City: University of Utah Press.

Bloom, L., 1913, New Mexico under Mexican Administration, 1821–1846. Old Santa Fe Genealogy and Biography 1:3–49, 131–75, 235–87.

Bloom, L., 1924, Early Vaccination in New Mexico. Publication no. 27. Albuquerque: Historical Society of New Mexico.

Bolton, H.E., 1916, Spanish Exploration in the Southwest, 1542–1700. New York: Charles Scribner's Sons.

Chavez, F.A., 1957, Archives of the Archdiocese of Santa Fe. Bibliographic Series, vol. 3. Washington, D.C.: Academy of American Franciscan History.

Collins, R.P., 1903, Report of School Superintendent in Charge of Pueblo, Aug. 5, 1902. Pp. 254–56 in Annual Report of the Commissioner of Indian Affairs . . . for the Year 1902, part 1. Washington, D.C.: U.S. Department of the Interior.

Colyer, V., 1869, Report of the Hon. Vincent Colyer, U.S. Special Indian Commissioner on the Tribes and Their Surroundings in Alaska Territory, From Personal Observation and Inspection in 1869. Pp. 975–1056 in House Executive Document, 41st Congress, 2nd Session. Washington, D.C.: U.S. Government Printing Office.

Cook, S., 1955, The Epidemic of 1830–1833 in California and Oregon. University of California Publications in American Archaeology and Ethnology 43:303–26.

Cook, S., 1973, The Significance of Disease in the Extinction of the New England Indians. Human Biology 45:485–508.

Cook, S., and W. Borah, 1971, Essays in Population History: Mexico and the Caribbean. Pp. 73–118 in vol. 1. Berkeley: University of California Press.

Coues, E., 1895, The Expeditions of Zebulon Montgomery Pike, 1805–07. New York: Francis B. Harper.

Crandall, C.J., 1902, Report of School at Santa Fe, New Mexico, Aug. 20, 1901. Pp. 549–52 in Annual Report of the Commissioner of Indian Affairs . . . for the Year 1901, part 1. Washington, D.C.: U.S. Department of the Interior.

Crandall, C.J., 1904, Report of School Superintendent in Charge of Pueblo, Aug. 17, 1903. Pp. 267–71 in Annual Report of the Commissioner of Indian Affairs . . . for the Year 1903. Washington, D.C.: U.S. Department of the Interior.

Crandall, C.J., 1905, Report of School Superintendent in Charge of Pueblo, Aug. 17, 1904. Pp. 258–62 in Annual Report of the Commissioner of Indian Affairs . . . for the Year 1904, part 1. Washington, D.C.: U.S. Department of the Interior.

Crandall, C.J., 1906a, Report of Superintendent in Charge of Pueblo Aug. 19, 1905. Pp. 270–75 in Annual Report of the Commissioner of Indian Affairs . . . for the Year 1905, part 1. Washington, D.C.: U.S. Department of the Interior.

Crandall, C.J., 1906b, Report of Superintendent of Santa Fe School, Aug. 17, 1906. Pp. 281–85 in Annual Report of the Commissioner of Indian Affairs . . . for the Year 1906. Washington, D.C.: U.S. Department of the Interior.

Custer, B., 1906, Report of Albuquerque School, Aug. 25, 1906. Pp. 275–76 in Annual Report of the Commissioner of Indian Affairs . . . for the Year 1906. Washington, D.C.: U.S. Department of the Interior.

Crosby, A., 1972, The Columbian Exchange: Biological and Cultural Consequences of 1492. Westport, Conn.: Greenwood Press.

Crosby, A., 1976, Virgin Soil Epidemics as a Factor in the Aboriginal Depopulation in America. William and Mary Quarterly 33:289–99.

Deetz, J., 1965, The Dynamics of Stylistic Change in Arikara Ceramics. Illinois Studies in Anthropology, no. 4. Urbana: University of Illinois Press.

Dickson, D.B., 1975, Settlement Pattern Stability and Change in the Middle Northern Rio Grande Region, New Mexico: A Test of Some Hypotheses. American Antiquity 40:159–71.

Dickson, D.B., 1979, Prehistoric Pueblo Settlement Patterns: The Arroyo Hondo,

New Mexico Site Survey. Arroyo Hondo Archaeological Series, vol. 2. Santa Fe: School of American Research Press.

Dobyns, H., 1966, Estimating Aboriginal American Population: An Appraisal of Techniques with a New Hemisphere Estimate. Current Anthropology 7:395–416.

Dobyns, H., 1983, Their Number Become Thinned: Native American Population Dynamics in Eastern North America. Knoxville: University of Tennessee Press.

Donaldson, T., 1893, Moqui Pueblo Indians of Arizona and Pueblo Indians of New Mexico. Extra Census Bulletin, 11th Census of the United States. Washington, D.C.: Bureau of the Census.

Dozier, E., 1970, The Pueblo Indians of North America. New York: Holt, Rinehart and Winston.

Ellis, F.H., 1964, A Reconstruction of the Basic Jemez Pattern of Social Organization, with Comparisons to Other Tanoan Social Structures. University of New Mexico Publication in Anthropology, no. 11. Albuquerque, N.M.

Espinosa, J.M., 1940, First Expedition of Vargas into New Mexico, 1692. Albuquerque: University of New Mexico Press.

Euler, R., G. Gumerman, T. Karlstrom, J. Dean, and R. Hevly, 1979, The Colorado Plateaus: Cultural Dynamics and Paleoenvironment. Science 205:1089–1101.

Graham, D.D., 1905, Report of School Superintendent in Charge of Zuni, Aug. 1, 1904. Pp. 263–64 in Annual Report of the Commissioner of Indian Affairs . . . for the Year 1904, part 1. Washington, D.C.: U.S. Department of the Interior.

Graham, D.D., 1906a, Report of Superintendent in Charge of Zuni Pueblo, Aug. 1, 1905. Pp. 275–77 in Annual Report of the Commissioner of Indian Affairs . . . for the Year 1905, part 1. Washington, D.C.: U.S. Department of the Interior.

Graham, D.D., 1906b, Report of Superintendent of Zuni School, Aug. 15, 1906. Pp. 285–86, 482 in Annual Report of the Commissioner of Indian Affairs . . . for the Year 1906. Washington, D.C.: U.S. Department of the Interior.

Gregg, J., 1844, Commerce of the Prairies: Or the Journal of a Santa Fe Trader, During Eight Expeditions Across the Great Western Prairies, and a Residence of Nearly Nine Years in Northern Mexico. New York: Langely.

Hackett, C., ed., 1937, Historical Documents Relating to New Mexico, Nueva Vizcaya and Approaches Thereto, to 1773 (collected by A. Bandelier and F. Bandelier), vol. 3. Papers of the Division of Historical Research, Publication no. 330. Washington, D.C.: Carnegie Institution.

Hammond, G., and A. Rey, 1929, Expedition into New Mexico Made by Antonio de Espejo 1582–1583, As Revealed in the Journal of Diego Perez de Luxan, A Member of the Party. Berkeley: The Quivira Society.

Hammond, G., and A. Rey, 1938, New Mexico in 1602: Juan de Montoya's Relation of the Discovery of New Mexico. Berkeley: The Quivira Society.

Hammond, G., and A. Rey, 1966, The Rediscovery of New Mexico, 1580–1594. Albuquerque: University of New Mexico Press.

Hodge, F.W., 1907, The Narrative of the Expedition of Coronado by Pedro de Castañeda. Pp. 275–387 in Spanish Explorers in the Southern United States (ed. by F.W. Hodge and T.H. Lewis). New York: Charles Scribner's Sons.

Hodge, F.W., ed., 1907–10, Handbook of American Indians North of Mexico. 2 vols. Bureau of American Ethnology, Bulletin no. 30. Washington, D.C.

Hodge, F.W., G. Hammond, and A. Rey, eds. and trans., 1945, Fray Alonso de Benevides's Revised Memorial of 1634. Albuquerque: University of New Mexico Press.

Jorde, L.B., 1977, Precipitation Cycles and Cultural Buffering in the Prehistoric

Southwest. Pp. 385–96 in For Theory Building in Archaeology (ed. by L. Binford). New York: Academic Press.

Kelly, H., 1940, Franciscan Missions of New Mexico, 1740–1760. New Mexico Historical Review 15:345–68.

Kessell, J.L., 1979, Kiva, Cross and Crown: The Pecos Indians and New Mexico 1540–1840. Washington, D.C.: National Park Service, U.S. Department of the Interior.

Kroeber, A., 1939, Cultural and Natural Areas of Native North America. Berkeley: University of California Press.

Kunstadter, P., 1972, Demography, Ecology, Social Structure and Settlement Patterns. Pp. 313–51 in The Structure of Human Populations (ed. by G.A. Harrison and A.J. Boyce) Oxford: Clarendon Press.

Lange, C., 1959, Cochiti. Austin: University of Texas Press.

Lange, C., and C. Riley, 1966, The Southwestern Journals of Adolph E. Bandelier, 1880–1882. Albuquerque: University of New Mexico Press.

McClure, W.P., 1889, Report of Pueblo Agency, Aug. 26, 1889. Pp. 262–64 in Annual Report of the Commissioner of Indian Affairs . . . for the Year 1889. Washington, D.C.: U.S. Department of the Interior.

Meline, J., 1867, Two Thousand Miles on Horseback. New York: Hurd and Houghton.

Mooney, J., 1928, The Aboriginal Population of America North of Mexico. Smithsonian Miscellaneous Collection 80:1–40.

Ortiz, A., ed., 1979, Handbook of North American Indians, vol. 9: Southwest. Washington, D.C.: Smithsonian Institution.

Palin, J., 1905, Report of Field Matron Among Zuni, July 25, 1904. P. 265 in Annual Report of the Commissioner of Indian Affairs . . . for the Year 1904, part 1. Washington, D.C.: U.S. Department of the Interior.

Plog, S., 1984, Regional Perspectives on the Western Anasazi. American Archaeology 4:162–70.

Powell, S., 1983, Mobility and Adaptation: The Anasazi of Black Mesa, Arizona. Carbondale: Southern Illinois University Press.

Prince, L.B., 1890, Report of the Governor of New Mexico to the Secretary of the Interior. Washington, D.C.: U.S. Department of the Interior.

Reiter, P., 1938, The Jemez Pueblo of Unshagi, New Mexico, part 1. University of New Mexico and School of American Research Monograph no. 5. Santa Fe: School of American Research.

Robertson, J.H., 1892, Report of Pueblo and Jicarilla Agency, Aug. 30, 1892. Pp. 333–38 in Annual Report of the Commissioner of Indian Affairs . . . for the Year 1892. Washington, D.C.: U.S. Department of the Interior.

Rogers, S., 1915, Indian Population in the United States and Alaska, 1910. Washington, D.C.: Bureau of the Census.

Romero, D., 1885, Report, The Pueblo Indian Agency, Sept. 10, 1885. Pp. 156–59 in Annual Report of the Commissioner of Indian Affairs . . . for the Year 1885. Washington, D.C.: U.S. Department of the Interior.

Sanchez, P., 1883, Report, The Pueblo Indian Agency, Aug. 8, 1883. Pp. 123–24 in Annual Report of the Commissioner of Indian Affairs . . . for the Year 1883. Washington, D.C.: U.S. Department of the Interior.

Sanchez, P., 1884, Report, The Pueblo Indian Agency, Aug. 8, 1884. Pp. 138–39 in Annual Report of the Commissioner of Indian Affairs . . . for the Year 1884. Washington, D.C.: U.S. Department of the Interior.

Sanchez-Albornoz, N., 1974, The Population of Latin America: A History. Berkeley: University of California Press.

Scholes, F., 1929, Documents for the History of the New Mexican Missions in the Seventeenth Century. New Mexico Historical Review 4:45–71.

Schoolcraft, H., 1851, Historical and Statistical Information Respecting the History, Condition and Prospects of the Indian Tribes of the United States. 6 vols. New York: Lippincott, Grambo, and Co.

Schroeder, A., 1979, Pueblos Abandoned in Historic Times. Pp. 236–54 in Handbook of North American Indians, vol. 9: Southwest (ed. by A. Ortiz). Washington, D.C.: Smithsonian Institution.

Segura, J., 1890, Report of Pueblo Agency, Aug. 25, 1890. Pp. 172–74 in Annual Report of the Commissioner of Indian Affairs . . . for the Year 1890. Washington, D.C.: U.S. Department of the Interior.

Segura, J., 1891, Report of Pueblo Agency, Aug. 26, 1891. Pp. 311–12 in Annual Report of the Commissioner of Indian Affairs . . . for the Year 1891, part 1. Washington, D.C.: U.S. Department of the Interior.

Simmons, M., 1979, History of Pueblo-Spanish Relations to 1821. Pp. 178–93 in Handbook of North American Indians, vol. 9: Southwest (ed. by A. Ortiz). Washington, D.C.: Smithsonian Institution.

Simpson, J.H., 1850, Report of the Secretary of War Communicating the Report of Lieutenant J.H. Simpson of an Expedition into the Navajo Country in 1849. House Executive Document no. 64, 31st Congress, 1st Session. Washington, D.C.: U.S. Government Printing Office.

Thomas, A., ed., 1932, Forgotten Frontiers, A Study of the Spanish Indian Policy of Don Juan Bautista de Anza, Governor of New Mexico, 1777–1787. Norman: University of Oklahoma Press.

Thomas, B., 1875, Report, Office of Pueblo Indian Agency, Sept. 8, 1875. Pp. 332–33 in Annual Report of the Commissioner of Indian Affairs . . . for the Year 1875. Washington, D.C.: U.S. Department of the Interior.

Thomas, B., 1876, Report, Office of Pueblo Indian Agency, Aug. 24, 1876. P. 111 in Annual Report of the Commissioner of Indian Affairs . . . for the Year 1876. Washington, D.C.: U.S. Department of the Interior.

Thomas, B., 1879, Report, Office of Pueblo Indian Agency, Aug. 14, 1879. Pp. 118–20 in Annual Report of the Commissioner of Indian Affairs . . . for the Year 1879. Washington, D.C.: U.S. Department of the Interior.

Thomas, B., 1881, Report, Pueblo and Jicarilla Apache Agencies, Sept. 1, 1881. Pp. 140–41 in Annual Report of the Commissioner of Indian Affairs . . . for the Year 1881. Washington, D.C.: U.S. Department of the Interior.

Thomas, B., 1882, Report, Pueblo and Jicarilla Apache Agencies, Sept. 1, 1882. Pp. 129–31 in Annual Report of the Commissioner of Indian Affairs . . . for the Year 1882. Washington, D.C.: U.S. Department of the Interior.

Twitchell, R., 1911–12, Leading Facts of New Mexican History. 2 vols. Cedar Rapids, Iowa: Torch Press.

Ubelaker, D., 1974, Reconstruction of Demographic Profiles from Ossuary Skeletal Samples. Smithsonian Contributions to Anthropology, no. 18. Washington, D.C.: Smithsonian Institution.

Ubelaker, D., 1976, The Sources and Methodology for Mooney's Estimates of North American Indian Populations. Pp. 243–92 in The Native Population of the Americas in 1492 (ed. by W. Denevan). Madison: University of Wisconsin Press.

Walpole, N.S., 1898, Report of Agent for Pueblo and Jicarilla Agency, Aug. 11, 1898. Pp. 206–11 in Annual Report of the Commissioner of Indian Affairs . . . for the Year 1898. Washington, D.C.: U.S. Department of the Interior.

Walpole, N.S., 1899, Report of Agent for Pueblo and Jicarilla Agency, Aug. 10, 1899. Pp. 245–55 in Annual Report of the Commissioner of Indian Affairs . . . for the Year 1899, part 1. Washington, D.C.: U.S. Department of the Interior.

Walpole, N.S., 1900, Report of Agent for Pueblo and Jicarilla Agency, Aug. 14, 1900. Pp. 292–97 in Annual Report of the Commissioner of Indian Affairs . . . for the Year 1900, part 1. Washington, D.C.: U.S. Department of the Interior.

Ward, J., 1865, Report No. 72, New Mexico Superintendency, June 30, 1864. Pp. 187–99 in Annual Report of the Commissioner of Indian Affairs . . . for the Year 1864. Washington, D.C.: U.S. Department of the Interior.

Ward, J., 1868, Report No. 55, New Mexico Superintendency, July 10, 1867. Pp. 210–13 in Annual Report of the Commissioner of Indian Affairs . . . for the Year 1867. Washington, D.C.: U.S. Department of the Interior.

Whipple, A.W., T. Ewbank, and W. Thomas, 1855, Report Upon the Indian Tribes. Pp. 11–13 in vol. 3, part 3, Pacific Railroad Report. Washington, D.C.: U.S. Department of the Interior.

Williams, M.C., 1887, Report, Pueblo Agency, Aug. 25, 1887. Pp. 179–80 in Annual Report of the Commissioner of Indian Affairs . . . for the Year 1887. Washington, D.C.: U.S. Department of the Interior.

Winship, G., 1896, The Coronado Expedition, 1540–42. 14th Annual Report of the U.S. Bureau of Ethnology. Washington, D.C.: U.S. Government Printing Office.

Zubrow, E., 1975, Prehistoric Carrying Capacity: A Model. Menlo Park, Calif.: Cummings.

INDIAN EXTINCTION IN THE MIDDLE
SANTA CRUZ RIVER VALLEY, ARIZONA

By HENRY F. DOBYNS[*]

THE MIDDLE Santa Cruz River Valley south from *Punta de Agua* to near the modern boundary between the United States and Mexico supported a large prehistoric population of northern Piman Indians. The number of ruins recorded in the area attests to the former density of Indian population, which was also documented to some extent in early Spanish records dealing with frontier affairs in northwestern New Spain. Yet, no native Piman Indian population remains in the middle river valley today. The only Indians currently living there are immigrant Papagos, Yaquis and a scattering of Indians from other tribes who inhabit migrant labor camps built by non-Indian farmers, primarily engaged in cotton production.[1] Nor has there been more than seasonal occupation by northern Piman Indians (a group which includes the contemporary Papagos) for over a century, except in immigrant settlements satellite to Anglo-American mining or farming enterprises.

The disappearance of the native inhabitants from most of the riverine and much of the upland area of southern Arizona opened many stretches of river, mountain springs, and the grass lands whose use they permitted, to Spanish and later to Mexican settlement. Gradually during the 18th century and rapidly during the final golden age of Spanish imperialism on the Sonoran frontier after Apache pacification, and even more quickly during the early years of Mexican independence when colonial regulations were swiftly relaxed, Spanish and then Mexican entrepreneurs moved in on lands and water resources vacated by the original northern Piman Indian occupants. In a discussion which remains the best yet published of Mexican land grants in south-central

---

[*] Department of Anthropology, Cornell University, Ithaca, New York.

1. Henry F. Dobyns, *Papagos in the Cotton Fields, 1950* (Tucson:Author, 1951).

163

Arizona, Mattison[2] attributed the native abandonment to raids by enemy Indians. Speaking of Tucson about 1846, he commented: (following Bancroft):[3] "On account of the frequent Apache raids the few remaining ranches in the Santa Cruz valley were abandoned in the last decade of the Mexican regime."[4] Referring to an earlier period under Spanish imperial rule, Mattison inferred that little is known of ranching then because ranchers lacked land titles. He concluded that such 18th century ranchers also had to retreat south of modern Arizona "on account of the Indian incursions." With regard to the northern Piman Indian settlements encountered by Spanish frontiersmen entering modern Arizona, Mattison wrote: "Indian attacks had caused most of the *rancherias* around the missions and the *visitas*, established by Father Kino and his successors in the 18th century, to be abandoned."[5]

Mattison and a host of writers of all kinds who have attributed the depopulation of northern Sonora and also New Mexico at various periods to long-sustained hostilities with enemy Apache Indian bands were correct in citing Apache raiding as *a* cause for the contraction of aboriginal Indian settlement. They erred, however, in assuming that warfare was the *only* or even the *principal* cause of territorial abandonment by the natives of New Spain's Sonoran frontier. The present paper seeks to bring together in a coherent analysis available evidence on the process of biological extinction of the aboriginal inhabitants of the middle Santa Cruz River Valley,[6] in order to demonstrate the fundamental importance of disease agents in that process. The area considered is cen-

---

2. R. H. Mattison, "Early Spanish and Mexican Settlements in Arizona," *New Mexico Historical Review*, 21:4 (Oct. 1946) pp. 273-327.

3. Hubert Howe Bancroft, *History of Arizona and New Mexico* (San Francisco: History Co., 1889).

4. Mattison, *op cit.*, p. 284.

5. *Ibid.*, p. 285.

6. Much of the data analyzed were collected while the author was Research Associate of the Arizona State Museum investigating Tubac history for the Arizona State Parks Board.

trally located in the region with which Mattison dealt, and was the key to wider land use, so that it constitutes an appropriate geographic sampling.

The last survivors of the native Indian population of the middle Santa Cruz River Valley, the inhabitants of Tumacacori, fled down river to San Xavier del Bac, an amalgamated community of northern Piman Indians which has survived to the present day by continually attracting migrants from other settlements.[7] Tumacacori provides, then, a suitable starting point for working backward through time so as to examine the evidence.

1. Tumacacori. The last settlement of sedentery, irrigation-agriculturalist northern Piman Indians in the middle Santa Cruz River Valley seems to have been abandoned during the latter part of December in 1848, or very soon thereafter. A U.S. military column en route to California found it inhabited toward the end of October of 1848.[8] Apaches raided both Tubac and Tumacacori in December of that year, killing nine persons at the former settlement of Mexicans and Manso Apaches, and even more individuals at the latter Indian amalgam settlement.[9] The Tumacacori Indians then abandoned their homes,[10] and fled to Bac, thus strengthening that community at a crucial time. Their absence from Tumacacori thereafter was noted[11] by a number of Forty-Niners following the southern route to the California gold fields the following year. A party of southern emigrants reached the abandoned buildings at Tumacacori on May 27, and a New Orleans journalist with the group thought it a ranch whose abandon-

---

7. Henry F. Dobyns, *Pioneering Christians Among the Perishing Indians of Tucson.* (Lima: Editorial Estudios Andinos, 1962) pp. 24, 27-29.

8. Henry F. Dobyns (Ed.), *Hepah, California! The Journal of Cave Johnson Couts from Monterey, Nuevo Leon, Mexico, to Los Angeles, California, during the years 1848-1849* (Tucson: Arizona Pioneers' Historical Society, 1961) pp. 57, 59, 61, 75 n. 14.

9. *El Sonorense,* February 21, 1849, p. 3, col. 1.

10. *Ibid.,* p. 1, col. 2. The copy of this newspaper in the Bancroft Library, University of California, Berkeley, was Bancroft's (1889:474-475) source for his statement cited by Mattison (1946:284) that Tumacacori was abandoned at this time after an Apache assault.

11. Although Mattison (*op. cit.,* p 293) thought the "time of abandonment" of Tumacacori "remains a matter for conjecture."

ment he placed in the previous February and attributed to a raid by fifty Apaches.[12] The peaches in the old Tumacacori Mission orchard were ripe by September 1, supplying passing migrants with delicious fruit.[13]

While an Apache attack precipitated the departure of the survivors at Tumacacori, it was merely the final straw in a long series of reverses. Tubac, three miles away and defensive partner of Tumacacori, had been partially depopulated during the fall by the gold rush to California from northwestern Mexico. When the Tubac population fell below what the Mexicans considered a safe size for resisting Apache attacks, they decamped to Tucson. While their migration augmented the size of Tucson, the increase merely restored the combined population to a previous level. It was not, in other words, a genuine increase over prior size. The Tumacacori increment at Bac had the same effect of maintaining viable settlement size by amalgamating previously independent villages. This was the ultimate such amalgamation of middle Santa Cruz River Valley settlements, and the final change in the demography of that region, so far as Indian occupation was concerned.

Tumacacori (Chukum Kavolik "Caliche Bend") had been an Indian mission staffed by Franciscan priests until the expulsion of foreign-born clergy from Mexico in 1827-1828. Its post-mission population may have fallen below the 103 enumerated there in 1796,[14] although the settlement had apparently stabilized at approximately 100 persons toward the end of the 18th century. Whatever their number, the refugees who fled Tumacacori to go to Bac in 1848 constituted the entire surviving native Indian population of the Middle Santa Cruz River Valley and beyond. No other native settlement remained occupied by that time, all having directly or indirectly contributed people to the Tumacacori population.

---

12. Ralph P. Bieber (Ed.), *Southern Trails to California in 1849* (Glendale: Arthur H. Clark, 1937) p. 209.

13. Mabelle Eppard Martin (Ed.), "From Texas to California in 1849, Diary of C. C. Cox," *Southwestern Historical Quarterly*, 29:2 (Oct.) p. 143.

14. Alfred Whiting, "Census of Tumacacori in 1796," *The Kiva*, 19:1 (Fall) pp. 1-12.

Prior to becoming a mission headquarters early in the 1770's when Franciscan missionaries who entered northern Piman territory in the summer of 1768 moved the former Jesuit mission there from Guebavi,[15] Tumacacori had been a visitation station of Guebavi since as early as 1742.[16] It was reported as inhabited by 150 persons in 1697.[17]

2. Tubac. The Tumacacori population had already received before the transfer of mission headquarters at least one infusion from another nearby aboriginal northern Piman settlement. The Mexican fort at Tubac was the successor to a royal post founded in Spanish colonial times in 1752 at an Indian village. Indians were recorded at Tubac[18] at least as early as 1726.[19] The Spanish post was founded as a counter measure to the Pima revolt against Spanish rule in November of 1751. The local populace fled during the revolt, and a Spanish officer with the punitive expedition recorded that forty Indians had returned to Tubac in April of 1752 after peace had been restored.[20] This was probably only part of the pre-revolt population. More natives likely returned later, but competition with the Spaniards for the Tubac site proved to be too much for the natives, and they moved to Tumacacori within a few years of the founding of the military post. On June 9, 1758, some Tubac Indians were recorded as resettled at Tumacacori,[21] and they had all moved before 1762.[22] What-

---

15. San Jose de Tumacacori (cited hereafter as "Tumacacori") Libro de Bautismos (cited as "B"), Libro de Casamientos (cited as "C"), and Libro de Entierros (cited as "E"). MS, Archive of the Bishop of Tucson. Copy in Arizona Pioneers' Historical Society.

16. Santos Angeles de Guebavi, Libro de Bautismos (cited hereafter as "Guebavi B") 7. Libro de Casamientos is cited as "Guebavi C," and Libro de Entierros as "Guebavi E." MS, Archive of the Bishop of Tucson. Copy in Arizona Pioneers' Historical Society

17. Harry J. Karns and Associates, *Unknown Arizona and Sonora, 1693-1721. Luz de Tierra Incognita by Captain Juan Mateo Mange* (Tucson: Arizona Silhouettes, 1954) p. 94.

18. Tjuivak "where something rotted"—Carl Lumholtz, *New Trails in Mexico* (New York: Charles Schribner's Sons, 1912) p. 385.

19. Alphonse Louis Pinart (collector), Libro de Bautismos del Partido de San Ygnacio de Caburica, in Coleccion de Pimeria Alta, Bancroft Library, University of California, Berkeley, p. 60 (Cited hereafter as "Pinart A").

20. Joseph Diaz del Carpio, Padron General de los Pueblos Cituados al Norte de esta Pimeria Alta. . . . Archivo General de Indias, Audiencia de Guadalajara 419, f. 93v-94 (Copy in Bancroft Library).

21. Guebavi B, 114.

22. Juan Nentvig, *Rudo Ensayo* (Tucson: Arizona Silhouettes, 1951) p. 141.

ever the size of the Tubac migration may have been, it was apparently little more than enough to maintain the size of the Tumacacori settlement.

3. Guebavi. Still, the reinforced Tumacacori population was evidently larger than the number of survivors at Guebavi (Ku Vaxia, "big spring"), since the Franciscans were motivated to relocate the mission headquarters. The native population at Guebavi had fallen to fifty by December 19, 1766,[23] despite numerous and repeated infusions of population from other northern Piman villages in the middle valley, and an earlier population of ninety to over 200 individuals estimated in 1699 and 1700 respectively.[24] Eighty persons were reported there in 1697.[25]

The impact of disease mortality upon local northern Piman Indian populations may be indicated by a brief analysis of the depopulation of Guebavi during one quarter-century period. The process of depopulation of this mission can be reconstructed during a twenty-four year period from the beginning of 1743 to the end of 1766. Records of baptisms and burials at Guebavi Mission are available from 1766 back to 1742 with a break in 1752-53 following the northern Piman revolt in November of 1751.[26]

In none of these twenty-four years did baptisms exceed burials. The disparity between seven recorded baptisms and 213 burials was 206. Adding this figure to the reported population of fifty at the end of 1766 yields a total of 256 persons alive at Guebavi at the beginning of 1743. In other words, if this reconstruction is correct, one northern Piman Indian survived in 1767 where five had lived only a quarter-century earlier in 1743. The rate of depopulation averaged approximately seven per cent annually. The actual rate fluctuated from zero to 19.9 per cent in 1751, with other peaks of 18.5

23. Nicolas de Lafora, *Relacion del Viaje que Hizo a Los Presidios Internos Situados en la Frontera de la America Septentrional Perteneciente al Rey de España* (Mexico: Editorial Pedro Robredo, 1939) p. 126.

24. Herbert E. Bolton, *Kino's Historical Memoir of Pimeria Alta* (Berkeley & Los Angeles: University of California Press, 1948) Vol. I, p. 204, 233.

25. Karns, *op. cit.*, p 94 .

26. Guebavi, B & E.

per cent in 1749, 15.3 per cent in 1766, and 12.2 per cent in 1762.

This computation is subject, of course, to several sources of bias, but does provide at least an approximation of reality. Baptismal figures may not truly represent the native birth-rate because of reluctance of Indian parents to have infants baptized. This seems unlikely, however, since northern Pimans had prior to this time typically sought baptism for their children, even carrying them a considerable distance to obtain it.[27] Burial records may be an underenumeration of actual deaths, but for the purposes to which the records have been put in estimating rate of depopulation, underenumeration of deaths would tend to balance any underenumeration of births. Lack of records of either type for two years of the twenty-four indicates an even greater actual disparity between the 1743 and the 1766 populations than was recorded, so the approximation offered here seems conservative. Determination of residence at Guebavi mission may be the most serious source of bias.

This possible source of error exists because Guebavi was absorbing population increments from other settlements from time to time which helped to maintain its size while its death rate far exceeded its birth rate. This process of amalgamation proceeded simultaneously at all the Spanish mission stations on the northern Piman Indian frontier because of Spanish pressure to consolidate settlements, biological depopulation, and to some extent for fear of Apache attacks. Biological decrease *interacted* with fear of enemy Indians and Spanish imperial policy to motivate northern Piman settlement amalgamation.

4. Ku Shu:tak. As Juan Bautista de Anza, commander of the Spanish fort at Tubac, returned northward from the City of Mexico with troops, supplies and colonists for an overland expedition to the California coast in 1775, he camped his pioneering host for the night of October 14-15 at a place

---

27. Francisco Xavier Alegre, *Historia de la Compañia de Jesus* (Mexico: J. M. Lara, 1841) V. II, p. 265.

called *Las Lagunas* (the lakes) on the middle Santa Cruz River.[28] None of the expedition's diarists mentioned an Indian population at these lakes and there indeed probably had been none there since before 1762, for the Jesuit writer Juan Nentvig[29] confused this place with Guebavi when he wrote about "Guebavi, in Pima Gusudac or Great Water." Before Nentvig, Juan Mateo Manje, while descending the Santa Cruz in 1699 came to "the settlement of Guebavi or Gusutaqui, which gets its title from another river which runs from east to west and joins it at this place."[30] The missionaries who advanced the Christian frontier north down the Santa Cruz in 1732 also used both native place names, calling their new mission The Holy Angels Gabriel and Rafael of "Guebavi, or Cusutaqui."[31]

Ku Shu:tak could not have been the same settlement as Ku Vaxia in aboriginal times. Linguistic analysis shows this: Guebavi or Guevavi in Spanish orthography is northern Piman Ku Vaxia in Lumholtz's English orthography, *Ku* being an augmentative[32] and *Vaxia* a water source such as a spring, waterhole or well,[33] although often translated into English with the general sense of *water*. Probably Nentvig's and Manje's Piman-speaking informants also rendered *vaxia* into Spanish as *agua*, thus misleading them. Lakes or streams in Piman place names are designated by another term for water, *shu:tak*[34] which refers in current everyday northern Piman speech to drinking water. The point of this brief analysis is that there was a prehistoric northern Piman settlement on the shores of what the Spaniards came to call "The Lakes" which survived into early historic times, but was often lumped with nearby *Ku Vaxia*. That two settlements

---

28. Herbert E. Bolton, *Anza's California Expeditions* (Berkeley: University of California Press, 1930) V. IV, p. 17.

29. Nentvig, *op. cit.*, p. 110.

30. Karns, *op. cit.*, p. 186.

31. George P. Hammond, "Pimeria Alta After Kino's Time," *New Mexico Historical Review*, IV :3 (July) p. 229.

32. Lumholtz, *op. cit.*, p. 379, 381.

33. *Ibid.*, p. 382.

34. ":" designates a "long" or "held" vowel.

actually existed is also shown in the distinction made by a
Jesuit missionary more familiar with the area than Nentvig.
On May 5 and 6, 1736, Ignacio X. Keller, S. J., baptized some
six individuals living at *Ku Shu:tak*. One more Indian from
the lakeside settlement was baptized on July 22, 1736.[35] Then
three more lake shore dwellers were baptized by this local
missionary on February 17, 1737,[36] five more on January 19,
1738,[37] and finally one on February 22 that year.[38] After that
time the lakeside settlement dropped from recorded history.
Probably its inhabitants migrated to nearby Big Spring (Guebavi) sometime in the early 1740's during the mission concentration program, and very likely a lingering tendency for
its natives to refer to themselves by this place name rather
than *Ku Vaxia* gave rise to the later Spanish misconception
that Guebavi was derived from *Ku Shu:tak*.

   5. Sopori. Another middle Santa Cruz River Valley settlement whose northern Piman inhabitants migrated to Guebavi
during the mid-18th century period of conversion to Christianity was Sopori, located on the creek of that name which
enters the Santa Cruz from the west. This village was a visitation station from Guebavi Mission prior to the 1751 revolt.
The burial of a native from Sopori was recorded in 1744.[39]
Between that time and August of 1747 part if not all the
Sopori Indians migrated to Guebavi. When another native
of Sopori was buried at Guebavi on August 17th, he was
identified by the officiating priest as "among those aggregated
[to the neophytes here] from the Sopori."[40] That the pre-
revolt migration did not entirely depopulate Sopori is suggested in a March 28, 1751, record of the baptism of an infant
"from the Sopori"[41] and the fact that a Spanish officer lead-

<hr>

35. Alphonse Louis Pinart (collector), Libro de Baptismos de los Pueblos de Santa
Maria Suamca. . . . desde 1732, Coleccion de Pimeria Alta, Bancroft Library, University
of California, Berkeley (Cited hereafter as "Pinart B") f. 16.

   36. Pinart B 20.

   37. *Ibid.*, 27.

   38. *Ibid.*, 29.

   39. Guebavi E 48.

   40. *Ibid.*, 51.

   41. Guebavi B 93.

ing a scouting party north into hostile territory reconnoitered Sopori after the 1751 Piman revolt, finding dead beasts there and tracks leading to Aribaca.[42] Sopori seems to have been re-occupied after the revolt, since a mestizo child was born there in 1754.[43] By 1757, however, the Guebavi missionary was baptizing children from Sopori "aggregated to Guebavi,"[44] and the settlement had been abandoned by its aboriginal populace by 1762.[45]

6. Upiatuban. Another *rancheria* resettled at Guebavi before 1749 according to a northern Piman chief. In a statement before Spanish military authorities, Captain General Luis Oapicagigua[46] claimed credit for persuading the natives of Upiatuban to congregate at Guebavi Mission, in extolling his unappreciated services to the missionaries engaged in changing the lifeways of recalcitrant northern Piman countrymen.

7. Konkuk. The northern Piman leader also claimed credit for convincing the people of a settlement he called *Concuc* to congregate at Guebavi at some date prior to 1749.

8. Calabazas. Various sites within a small area on the middle Santa Cruz River were occupied by Mexican settlers in the early 19th century, but there had been a prior northern Piman Indian aboriginal occupation. In 1806 the surviving Indians at Tumacacori Mission petitioned Spanish authorities for a grant of lands of the "abandoned pueblo" of Calabazas, to be used for stock range.[47] Because of the proximity of the place termed "Calabazas" in recent years to the terrace-top

---

42. Joseph Fontes, Diario de la marcha q. hizieron los Alferezes Dn Jph de fonttes y Dn Antto Olguin con la tropa de su cargo. Terrenate, 25 de diciembre de 1751. Archivo General de Indias, Audiencia de Guadalajara 419. Copy in Bancroft Library. f. 49.

43. Juan Maria Oliva, Pie de Lista de la Tropa que guarneze dho Presidio con expresion de sus clases, nombres, edades, servicios, su procederes: caballos, mulas que cada Yndividio tiene, con distinz.n de los buenos, medianos e inutiles. No. 2 Real Presidio de Tubac. 13 de Agosto de 1775. Archivo General de Indias, Audiencia de Guadalajara 515. Copy in Bancroft Library.

44. Guebavi B 110.

45. Nentvig, *op. cit.,* p. 141.

46. Luis Oapicagigua, Declaracion. San Ygnacio. 24 de marzo de 1752. Archivo General de Indias, Audiencia de Guadalajara 419, f. 189. Copy in Bancroft Library.

47. Mattison, *op. cit.,* p. 292.

early historic site excavated by Dr. Charles C. DiPeso[48] which he inferred was the northern Piman village called *San Cayetano* by the pioneer missionary explorer Eusebio F. Kino, S. J., it is here assumed that Calabazas and San Cayetano were the same, even though Kino in 1691 associated *San Cayetano* with the Piman place name *Tumagacori*.[49] Joseph Agustin de Campos in 1726 simply recorded baptizing Indian infants at "San Cayetano."[50] Whether or not DiPeso's "San Cayetano" was the same as "Calabazas," both clearly were depopulated and abandoned, probably within the 18th century, and the 1806 petition suggests that survivors ended up in the amalgamated Tumacacori population.

9. Toacuquita. Before the Indians of Calabazas moved, they received a sizable increment in population from yet another settlement on November 1, 1756. The missionary then at Guebavi recorded[51] baptizing on that day eighty "adults of the Rancheria of Doaquita today aggregated to the Calabasas." If there were eighty adult migrants, there should have been at least as many children (although under disease conditions then prevailing, there may not have been) suggesting an increment of about 160 persons at Calabazas in 1756, and indicating the extent of depopulation that was to occur in the middle Santa Cruz River Valley by the time only Tumacacori remained inhabited.

Missionaries from Guebavi had recorded people living at Toacuquita in 1750,[52] and in 1741.[53] The people of this settlement were probably mountain dwellers prior to their migration to Calabazas, since their village name begins with the Piman word *toak* for mountain.

There were several additional northern Piman Indian settlements in the middle Santa Cruz River Valley during pre-

---

48. Charles C. DiPeso, *The Upper Pima of San Cayetano del Tumacacori* (Dragoon: Amerind Foundation, 1956).
49. Bolton (1948) *op. cit.*, V. I, p. 119.
50. Pinart A 59.
51. Guebavi B 109.
52. *Ibid.*, 91.
53. *Ibid.*, 6.

historic and into historic times which were abandoned during the middle third of the 18th century as their dwindling populations amalgamated with the people in the places mentioned already. The date when the final inhabitants left these places for the surviving settlements cannot be set for lack of documentation, but their documented existence during the early contact period accentuates the demographic trend of depopulation and settlement consolidation.

10. Aquituni. People from this settlement between Sopori and Arivaca were met by missionaries from Guebavi at least as early as 1742, since they performed a marriage of natives from *Vupquituni,*[54] then. In 1748 the missionaries baptized children from *Aquituni.*[55] The aboriginal inhabitants abandoned Aquituni in the aftermath of the Piman Revolt, and it was not occupied when a Spanish scouting party passed through on December 27, 1751, en route from Sopori to Arivaca.[56] No record of its being reoccupied after the revolt has been found, so its population presumably was absorbed into the other settlements that did re-form after the pacification.

11. Xona. The priest who spent more time converting northern Piman Indians to Catholicism than any other man, Joseph Agustin de Campos, S. J., recorded on one of his trips northward from his San Ignacio Mission that on February 28, 1724, "A little above Guebavi where I was stopped, they brought me from *Xona*" a child to baptize.[57] Returning on March 11th, Campos baptized half a dozen individuals from this settlement.[58] Campos appears to have spoken Piman extremely well, and converted it into Spanish orthography better than any other Spaniard, so if he wrote *Xona,* there was a settlement with that name, and this term cannot be correlated with Concuc (*kon* or *kaun kuk,* "——standing"). The people of *Xona* appear to have migrated, probably

<hr>

54. Guebavi C 15.
55. Guebavi B 85.
56. Fontes *op. cit.,* f. 49.
57. Pinart A 45.
58. *Ibid.,* 48.

to Guebavi or to have died out prior to the arrival of resident missionaries in 1732.[59]

12. Bacarica. In 1699 the explorer-priest, Kino, counted forty northern Piman Indian houses in a *rancheria* he called San Luys del Bacoancos.[60] Two years earlier his military escort, Manje, reported ninety persons there.[61] On March 12, 1724, Kino's hardy collaborator Campos baptized fourteen Indians at *Bacarica*[62] which is here assumed, perhaps on insufficient grounds, to have been the same place. In 1726 Campos again baptized a person from this settlement.[63] Then it apparently dropped from written records, its population either extinct or amalgamated to some other.

13. The San Pedro River Valley. The pitiful remnant of northern Piman Indians who survived at Tumacacori Mission by the end of the 17th century represented not only the meager remains of a once flourishing Indian population of the middle Santa Cruz River Valley, but also a large number from the San Pedro River Valley to the east. It is impossible to identify which San Pedro River Valley aboriginal settlements contributed to the surviving populace since the Sobaipuri withdrawal from the San Pedro in 1762 caught the Spaniards so by surprise that most details went unrecorded. All that can be said here is that the Sobaipuris did contribute some persons to the middle Santa Cruz River Valley settlements in 1762 since there were approximately 400 refugees roaming among the various Santa Cruz Valley villages besides the 250 who settled at Tucson and some others settled at Santa Maria Soamca.[64]

14. The Desert Papagos. As the native riverine Indians perished in epidemics and endemic disease mortality and Apache raids, they were partially replaced in the Spanish

---

59. Hammond, *op. cit.*, p. 224, 229.

60. Bolton (1948) *op. cit.*, V. I, p. 204.

61. Karns, *op. cit.*, p. 94.

62. Pinart A 48–49.

63. *Ibid.*, 59.

64. Fancisco Elias Gonzales, Informe al Señor Gobernador Don Joseph Tienda de Cuerbo, 22 de Marzo de 1762. Archivo General de Indias, Audiencia de Guadalajara 511. Copy in Bancroft Library.

missions by Papago neophytes from the deserts. Underhill[65] noted that Apache attacks influenced modern Gila River Pima and Papago distribution greatly because "the desert Papagos seeped in" to take the place of their extinct relatives. It should be emphasized that disease mortality was much higher than war casualties. San Ignacio, Magdalena, Bac and Tucson received heavy increments of Papago converts during the 18th century, and the middle Santa Cruz River Valley missions were no exception. Many of the 103 residents of Tumacacori enumerated in 1796 were identified as Papagos.[66]

It is, therefore, necessary to keep in mind that the total depopulation of the middle Santa Cruz Valley wiped out not merely the local northern Piman population, but also additional contingents of unknown size from both the San Pedro River Valley to the east, and the semi-desert Papagueria to the west.

Extent of Depopulation

The native Indian population of the middle Santa Cruz River Valley vanished between roughly 1700 and 1850, the major reduction occurring by 1800. The extent of depopulation has been indicated in the preceding outline of the documented history of settlement amalgamation which contributed to the survival of just one of the enduring northern Piman villages on this river, Bac. At least a dozen settlements existed in the middle valley during the first quarter of the 18th century, but only one remained at the end of that century, even with reinforcements brought from the San Pedro River and the desert to the west beyond the immediate Santa Cruz valley.

This pattern of settlement amalgamation occurred in every part of northern Piman territory for which records are available. Fifteen or more San Pedro River Valley settle-

---

65. Ruth Murray, *Social Organization of the Papago Indians* (New York: Columbia University Press, 1939) p. 23.
66. Whiting, *op. cit.*

ments existing in 1700 provided the remnant that in 1762 reinforced Tucson, the middle Santa Cruz River Valley, and Santa Maria Suamca (whose population fled to Cocospera, Sonora, in 1768). Tucson and Bac were by 1800 the only lower Santa Cruz River Valley survivors of at least nine settlements there in 1700.[67] Cocospera was the only survivor of at least six 1700 settlements in the headwaters of the San Miguel River Valley. Four 1700 settlements in the Avra Valley had combined with others by 1800.

The rate of documented amalgamation was lower farther west, but this probably is a function of less documentation for that area, since the process clearly operated there. By 1749 Tubutama Mission contained resettled populations from at least five other settlements. Santa Teresa contained at least one other; Ati two others, Oquitoa one other,[68] Saric nine others of which three could muster over 1,200 persons in 1700.[69]

There were more aboriginal settlements in Papagueria in 1700, in other words, than there are villages and *rancherias* there today.

Estimation of Numbers. The decrease in settlement numbers just described can be translated at least approximately into population estimates. The northern Piman Indians seem to have considered a community of 200 to 300 persons as desirable under the conditions of life obtaining during the late 17th and early 18th centuries, and about 100 persons as absolute minimum. Underhill[70] worked out the 1850-60 population of Kuitatk, an amalgamated "defense" village in central Papago territory, at about 300. The forty houses Kino counted at Bacarica in 1699[71] suggest a population of 120 to 200 Indians (using conversion factors of three or five for average family size). Five northern Pimans per house was a ratio observed in 1697 at several settlements where both

---

67. Dobyns (1962) *op. cit.*, p. 27.
68. Oapicagigua, *op. cit.*, f. 188v.
69. Bolton (1948), *op. cit.*, V. I, p. 119, 275.
70. Underhill, *op. cit.*, p. 211.
71. Bolton (1948), *op. cit.*, V. I, p. 204.

houses and population were reported: Santa Catalina de
Kuitatkekam on the lower Santa Cruz River,[72] *Gu Oidak*[73]
and Quiburi on the San Pedro.[74] The northern San Pedro
River village had 5.4 persons per house, but others on that
stream had: 4.4 at *Jiaspi*,[75] 4.0 at *Haiwan Pit*[76] and 3.5 at
Cusac.[77] San Agustin de *A'ot* on the lower Santa Cruz had
4.2.[78]

The Jesuit missionary in charge of the visitation stations
among the Sobaipuris on the San Pedro River noted on April
2, 1743, that all the people at Vafcomarig (*Vav*-"rock,"[79]
Komalik-"flat"[80]) had joined those at *Baijcat* because of
Apache hostilities, as he put it. The combined settlement
contained 132 men and 138 women[81] or a total of 270 persons.
Since the priest seems to have counted adults only, the total
population could have been 500 to 600.

This historically recorded instance of settlement amalgamation on the San Pedro furnishes one index to the northern
Piman Indian view of the size below which a village population could not be allowed to fall, on the hostile Apache frontier. In 1735 the same missionary had counted fifty-six men
and fifty-six women at *Vav Komalik*,[82] a total of 112 individuals. The priest's terminology implied he listed only adults
so the total population may have been between 225 and 275.
There were eight years between 1735 and the 1743 record of
the amalgamation at *Baijcat* for the *Vav Komalik* population to fall. If depopulation was proceeding there at a rate
comparable to that in Guebavi Mission, a 1735 population
of 250 would have dropped to between 160 and 180 by 1743,
when amalgamation occurred.

---

72. Karns, *op. cit.*, p. 91.
73. *Ibid.*, p. 82.
74. *Ibid.*, p. 78.
75. *Ibid.*, p. 80.
76. *Ibid.*, p. 77.
77. *Ibid.*, p. 80.
78. *Ibid.*, p. 92.
79. Lumholtz, *op. cit.*, p. 386; Underhill, *op. cit.*, p. 219.
80. Underhill, *op. cit.*, p. 63.
81. Pinart B 14.
82. *Ibid.*

There is confirmation of this as the critical settlement size in northern Piman eyes in the number of Toacuquita migrants to Guebavi in 1756. That amalgamation brought eighty adults to Guebavi,[83] implying a total migration of 200 or more persons (using factors of 2.5 or higher to estimate total population from recorded adults). That the ideal settlement was even larger is indicated by the 250 Sobaipuris settling at Tucson in 1762,[84] combining with an existing population there. Since the *Toacuquita* amalgamation with the Guebavi Indians represented a presumably Spanish-influenced migration to a mission, the *Vav Komalik* consolidation with the *Baijcat* people, and the general Sobaipuri settlement at Tucson probably represent the most valid available measure of northern Piman Indian ideas of settlement ideal size and practice. In each case, the ideal fairly clearly exceeded 200 individuals by some margin, and practice seems to have been to amalgamate before total population dropped much below 200.

Early Contact Period Population. The recorded populations of northern Piman Indian communities around 1700 provides some further indication of their population prior to 18th century decline. In the middle Santa Cruz River Valley under discussion, Tumacacori had 150 people in 1697 and Bacarica had ninety in that year,[85] but forty houses in 1699, so that count may have under-enumerated, and Guebavi had ninety in 1699.[86] The average 1697-1699 population of these three settlements was 110 persons or more.

On the lower reaches of this stream, San Clemente and Santa Catalina Cuytoabagum (*Kui Toak ekam*) numbered 1,000 in November of 1699,[87] San Agustin 800 in 1697,[88] and Bac 900 in 1697.[89] The average population of these four set-

---

83. Guebavi B 109.
84. Elias Gonzales, *op. cit.*
85. Karns, *op. cit.*, p. 94.
86. Bolton (1948) *op. cit.*, V. I, p. 204.
87. Karns, *op. cit.*, p. 138.
88. *Ibid.*, p. 92 .
89. Excluding a 1,300 figure in 1699 because other settlements were probably represented in it (*ibid.*, p. 93, 137).

tlements appears to have been 675 persons. There also existed at that time four unnamed settlements between Bac and San Agustin, so the average population of all eight was at least 387 individuals without allowing any additional for the unnamed settlements.

On the lower San Pedro River, six settlements where the population was reported in 1697 had 120, 70, 500, 100, 80 and 380 persons,[90] for a total of 1,250 and an average of 208. On the upper San Pedro two riverine villages contained 500 and 100 in 1697,[91] and an upland settlement eighty, a total of 680 and an average of 226 for an ecological unit quite comparable to the middle Santa Cruz River Valley area where both riverine and upland settlements evidently contributed to the final few survivors.

These figures, regardless of whatever errors in sampling and reporting they might contain, clearly show—since they were reported by the same observers, whose biases should have at least been consistent—that northern Piman Indian settlement size varied by region along the streams used for irrigation, so it may not be possible to project averages for other regions to estimate the middle Santa Cruz Valley population. These figures also show a consistent pattern of a few large villages or towns of 500 population and over, and numerous smaller *rancherias* ranging in population from about seventy to 120 persons. It is very important to know whether the middle Santa Cruz River Valley population included residents of one town, or only *rancherias*. Tumacacori's 150 may have been the largest single center. The middle Santa Cruz River Valley may have lacked a more urban center. Assuming that to have been the case, one might utilize the average population figure of 110 persons obtained above for the known dozen settlements which existed in the area prior to 1700 to obtain a population estimate of 1,320 persons.

It is difficult to believe, on the other hand, that the mid-

90. *Ibid.,* p. 80, 82-83.
91. *Ibid.,* p. 77-78.

dle Santa Cruz River Valley lacked at least one town in pre-conquest times. The site excavated by DiPeso would seem to have been one such town. The size of the migration from *Toacuquita* to Calabazas in itself indicates that the mountain settlement was larger than Tumacacori. Assuming, then, that at least one town existed in this region, an average settlement size of 200 may be assumed as a conservative figure, being lower than the 208 for the lower or 226 for the upper San Pedro River, and much lower than the 387+ lower Santa Cruz average. If the twelve settlements known to have existed on the middle Santa Cruz River Valley and its hinterland in 1700 averaged 200 population, the total aboriginal populace of the region reached 2,400. This estimate accords with evidence presented above as the northern Piman view of ideal settlement size that brought on migration and amalgamation of communities.

Depopulation Ratio. Since it is known that only the fewer than 100 northern Piman Indian survivors at Tumacacori Mission remained in the middle Santa Cruz River Valley area in 1800, it is possible to estimate the extent of Indian depopulation in this area during the 18th century as 23/24ths of the 1700 population. Since this estimate does not take into account the Sobaipuri and Papago increments which entered the region to die during the 18th century, it must be considered a conservative estimate applying only to this immediate region. In other words, where more than twenty-four natives lived in 1700, only one remained alive in 1800. The depopulation ratio was over twenty-four to one.

DEMOGRAPHIC CONSEQUENCES OF EURO-AMERICAN CONTACT ON SELECTED AMERICAN INDIAN POPULATIONS AND THEIR RELATIONSHIP TO THE DEMOGRAPHIC TRANSITION

by

Cary W. Meister

ABSTRACT

The model or assumption that American Indian populations suffered a continuous decline from European contact to low point, or nadir, is followed by the Pueblo, Maricopa, Ute, and California Indians. The Gila River Pima and Navajo do not follow this pattern, however, so the "model of initial continuous decline to nadir" is not applicable to all American Indian soceities. Moreover, the history of Gila River Pima and Navajo population is different from what would be expected under the demographic transition theory, seriously questioning the validity of this concept.

Whenever Europeans or Euro-Americans have come into contact with American Indian populations, the result has often been significant and frequently rapid population decline (Dobyns 1966:410-414). Within this situation of overall population decline, the rate has differed from one ethnic group to another. Most studies that focus on the historical demography of American Indians imply or assume, however, that American Indian populations followed a course of continuous decline from contact until a low point, or nadir, was reached. The populations then are presumed to recover, stabilize, or become extinct. This assumption is what I shall call the "initial continuous decline to nadir" model. As a hypothesis it can be tested against population data from American Indian societies. Figure 1 presents the results of doing this for five groups of Indians of the western United States: Pueblo, Gila River Pima, Maricopa, aggregate California Indian population, and Ute. Figure 1 shows the population for each of these groups at selected dates as a percent of population at contact. Data on Navajo population trends are shown separately in Table 1, and Gila River Pima figures appear as Table 2.[1]

As indicated in Figure 1, the Pueblo, Maricopa, California Indians, and Ute do follow the model of initial continuous decline to nadir. The Gila River

Table 1
Navajo Population 1600-1961

Year	Population	Annual Growth Rate (%)
1600	< 4,000	
		> + 0.2
1800	> 6,000	
		< + 1.2
1860	12,000	
		− 0.9
1870	11,000	
		+ 2.2
1930	40,000	
		+ 2.7
1950	69,167	
		+ 2.4
1957	82,000	
		+ 3.2
1961	93,377	

Source: Johnston (1966:135).

Pima did not follow this pattern, however, having experienced two known periods of population decline — 1845 to 1882 and 1890 to 1895 — preceeded, separated, and followed by periods of population increase from 1700 to 1846, 1882 to 1890, and 1895 to 1972. The Gila River Pima are not the only population that fails to fit the model of initial continuous decline to nadir. As shown in Table 1, the Navajo minimum population occurred at the time of initial European contact or before. Navajos experienced only one brief period of decline between 1860 and 1870. Even at the end of that decline, Navajo population remained several times greater than it had been at contact.

These exceptions to the model of initial continuous decline to nadir make it very likely that more such cases will be found upon further analysis. Thus, one cannot assume that initial continuous decline to nadir characterized all American Indian populations.

The idea behind the model of initial continuous decline to nadir is that depopulation among American Indians was largely the result of lack of immunity to epidemic diseases such as measles, smallpox, influenza, and tuberculosis, which were introduced to the Americas from the Old World. Warfare is considered a factor of lesser importance, affecting only some populations, and to varying degrees. If not all American Indian populations experienced a continuous decline to nadir, however, then the low natural immunity of American Indians to introduced diseases was not entirely responsible for reducing these populations to their lowest point. It also means that an American Indian population, such as the Gila River Pima, could apparently recover from the effects of previously unknown diseases before the introduction of European medicine and increase at a respectable rate (0.15% annually) for its time, 1775 to 1846 (Meister 1975:429). At least

Table 2
Gila River Pima Population 1700-1972

Year	Population	Annual Growth Rate (%)
1700	3,000	
		+ 0.8
1775	5,300	
		+ 0.1
1846	5,875	
		. . .
1855	5,875	
		. . .
1858	5,875	
		- 1.4
1868	5,100	
		.- 0.5
1870	5,050	
		- 0.3
1882	4,875	
		+ 0:3
1887	4,950	
		+ 0.5
1890	5,025	
		- 0.5
1895	4,900	
		+ 0.6
1900	5,050	
		+ 0.7
1910	5,400	
		. . .
1915	6,045	
		+ 0.5
1920	6,200	
		+ 0.5
1930	6,510	
		+ 0.25
1940	6,690	
		. . .
1940*	6,440	
		- 0.2
1952*	6,325	
		+ 2.2
1960*	7,525	
		+ 1.6
1970*	8,800	
		+ 1.8
1972*	9,125	

Source: Meister (1975:429-430).

*Reservation population only. Before this date, figures include all Gila River and Salt River Pima, on or off-reservation.

NOTE: The term "Gila River Pima" here includes Pima residing on the Salt River Indian Reservation. Beginning with 1915, figures include Maricopa as well as Pima.

among the Gila River Pima, it appears that once a population with survivors possessing relatively greater immunity to previously unknown diseases replaced a population with low immunity to these diseases, factors other than low genetic immunity had to maintain an environment in which population decline could occur. The Pima are undoubtedly not unique, as the Navajo population trend shows.

In the main it was disease that caused the greatest decline in American Indian population, aided to a lesser extent by warfare. Yet, for many

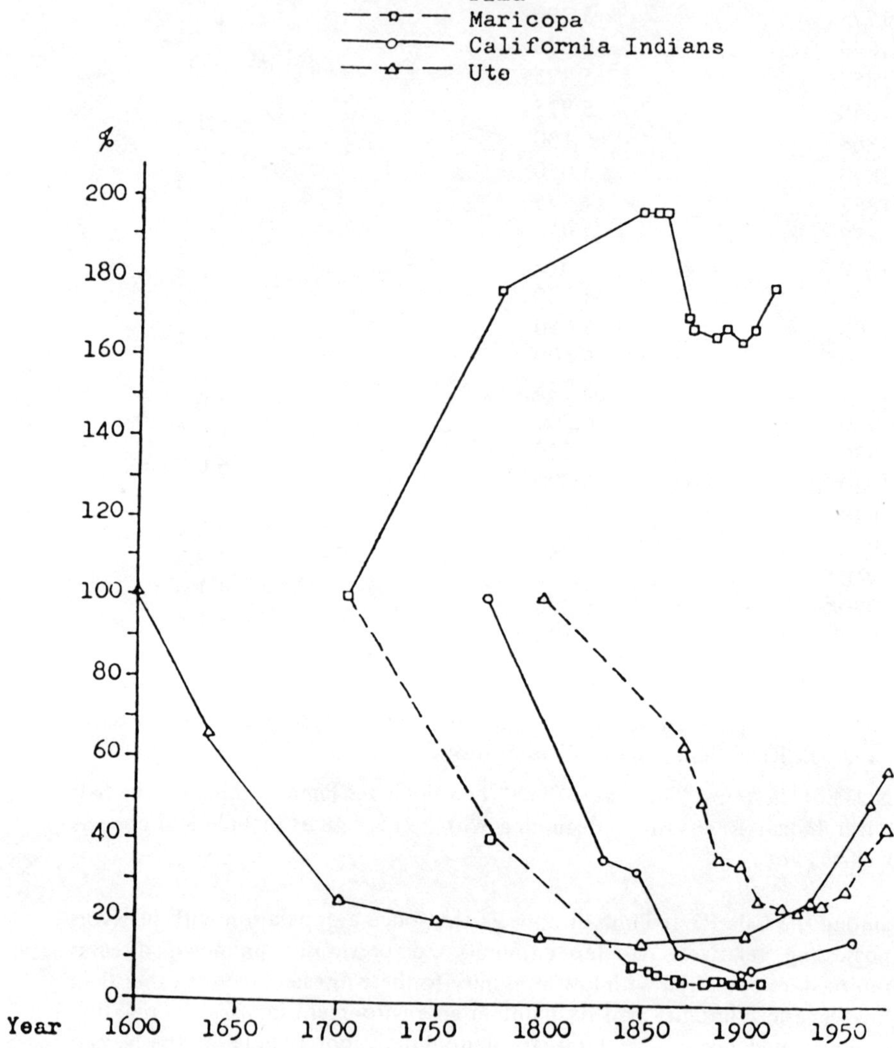

Fig. 1   Population as Percent of Population at Contact.

American Indian groups later population decline resulting from disease was made possible primarily because Indians had been driven from their land and robbed of their other resources, not that they lacked immunity to diseases of European origin. Merriam (1905:606) recognized this situation, stating that the factor behind California Indian depopulation was not

> . . . the number directly slain by the whites, or the number directly killed by whisky and disease, but a much more subtle and dreadful thing: it is the gradual but progressive and relentless confiscation of their lands and homes, in consequence of which they are forced to seek refuge in remote and barren localities, often far from water, usually with an impoverished supply of food, and not infrequently in places where the winter climate is too severe for their enfeebled constitutions.

Among the Gila River Pimas, from the beginning of Spanish exploration to 1775, migration of Piman-speaking refugees from other areas masked the actual birth and death rates. The population of the middle Gila River apparently increased to 177 percent of its size about 1700. By 1775, the Pima were relatively more immune to foreign diseases because of repeated exposures. Then population increased from 5,300 in 1775 to 5,875 in 1846 (Meister 1975:429). It remained stable until the 1860s, when Anglo-Americans started to settle at Florence upstream from the Pima. The Anglo-American farmers reduced the flow of the river to the extent that the Pima could no longer raise their summer maize crop. Thus, these irrigation farmers along the middle Gila River had to rely on their winter wheat crop for all of their food not gathered from desert plants or hunted. After a brief respite from want in the 1880s, when rains were more abundant and the river was fuller, the Pimas suffered even more severe water deprivation. Additional Anglo-American farmers had settled in the latter 1870s in the Safford Valley, even farther upstream on the Gila. They started irrigating more fields with Gila River water. This eliminated the Pima winter wheat crop. Thus, Pima agriculture was virtually destroyed, and Pima population declined further from 5,525 in 1890 to 5,375 in 1895 (Meister 1975:109-222, 429). With inadequate food, poor housing, and insufficient clothing, as well as tremendous stress caused by the destruction of a way of life, the weakened condition of the Pima made them easy prey for epidemic diseases which they could have resisted under better living conditions. The significance of this factor, deprivation of resources, is apparent even today in the age-adjusted death rate of American Indians, which is greater than that of the white United States population (Hill and Spector 1971:240).

That the Gila River Pima increased before the advent of modern medicine also has relevance to demographic theory. According to Wrong (1967:17-18), the demographic transition is "the dominant organizing idea or theory in the field of population studies since the discrediting of earlier efforts ... to formulate laws of population growth and change." Briefly stated, the demographic transition involves an evolutionary sequence of birth and death rates which vary so as to produce differing levels of population growth during three (or sometimes five) stages. In the three-stage version, populations are assumed to begin with high and essentially equal birth and death rates; hence, no population growth occurs. In the second stage, population rapidly increases because death rates are lower but birth rates remain high. In the third stage, birth and death rates are once again approximately equal, but at a much lower level than during the first stage.

Besides describing changes in birth and death rates, statements of the demographic transition (Stanford 1972:70-73; Thomlinson 1965:21-25; Wrong 1967:17-24) usually attempt to state factors which are believed to be responsible for the transition. In the first stage, it is assumed that the death rate was so high in populations without scientific medicine that the number of births could barely equal the number of deaths. The second stage begins when improved medical practices are introduced to a population. The third stage is reached with "industrialization" or "modernization." This is often as far as the discussion goes, but some have elaborated on the third stage to state that economic self-interest leads to fewer births. As upward social mobility becomes more possible and material goods increase in availability as a result of industrialization, families are reputed to decline in size because children require funds that could otherwise be devoted to increasing social status and acquiring material goods (Wrigley 1969:191).

The demographic transition has been rightly criticized both as a description of what occurred in Europe (Wrigley 1969; Wrong 1967:19-23), and as a "theory" with predictive value for other parts of the world. One of its weaknesses is that it inaccurately and incompletely describes changes in population that took place in Europe since the eighteenth century and then raises this inaccuracy to a generalization with the expectation or hope that the pattern will be repeated in other parts of the world. These are considered to be at earlier stages of the transition. Anthropologists should be especially suspicious of the demographic transition idea because it is presented as a universal evolutionary sequence. In many ways, the demographic transition concept is much like nineteenth century cultural evolutionary sequences, or what twentieth century antievolutionists believed were nineteenth century cultural evolutionary sequences. The demographic transition model proposes that all populations will go through all stages of the sequence. It is based on the history of European and Euro-American populations, and these populations are considered the most evolved or modern. In other words, Europe and North America set the model for the rest of the world. That other populations may take different directions is not conceded.

More specifically, Pima population history provides little support for the demographic transition idea. Let us examine the three stages of the demographic transition and see to what degree the Pima followed them. First, the initial stage consists of high and equal birth and death rates and hence stable population size. For the Pima, however, most of the time either births or deaths dominated, producing either increase or decline, and not stability. From 1858 to 1870, Pima deaths considerably outnumbered births, and decline occurred. From 1775 to 1858 Pima births outnumbered deaths, although immigration may have helped increase the population. From 1775 to 1846, the Pima annual growth rate was 0.15 percent. From 1882 to 1890, births outnumbered deaths, before Euro-American medical techniques other than some smallpox vaccination were in use. The annual Pima growth rate was 0.38 percent.

Looking at other populations, before the arrival of modern medicine among them, the Navajo increased throughout their known history, with one exception during a short period from 1860 to 1870 (Table 1). In other parts of the world, other populations have also apparently increased before the introduction of Euro-American medicine (Bowers 1971:30; Ho 1959:183-184; Kunstadter 1972:330, 348; Langer 1963; Wrigley 1969:168). According to research by Birdsell (1957), Dumond (1975), and Polgar (1971, 1972), the problem for hunting and gathering populations may not have been keeping the birth rate high enough to compensate for mortality, but rather keeping the number of births down. Sahlins (1972:141) and Woodburn (1968) have shown that hunters and gatherers were not always one step from starvation but rather often enjoyed sufficient food without seeking it every waking hour. Assuming a female reproductive period of 15 years, reduced to a mean of 12 because of maternal mortality, as well as two years between births, a woman could produce 6 children of which perhaps only 3 would live to reproduce. This, however, would still produce a 50 percent increase in population in one generation. Thus, with accidents and warfare relatively unimportant causes of death for hunters and gatherers, population size may have been limited mainly through the use of abortion and infanticide. Among the hunters and gatherers, the necessity for limiting the number of children may have been the inability of a mobile woman to care for more than one unweaned child at a time (Dumond 1975:718).

As a result of the above objections, one sees that the first stage of the demographic transition is a fiction devised by demographers who knew little about population before the eighteenth century in Europe. Inasmuch as they did not know what had occurred, it was safest for them to assume stability. The Pima and other American Indian populations show, however, that population increase occurred during what was supposed to be the first stage of the demographic transition. Nevertheless, even though Pima population increased before the introduction of modern medicine, it seems unlikely that the annual growth rate could have exceeded 1 percent (Wrigley 1969:205).

The second stage of the demographic transition model states that the death rate decreases when health advances, mainly the prevention or treatment of disease, are developed by a population or are introduced by another population. Among the Pima, however, population increase occurred before the introduction of scientific medicine. Although the 1775-1858 and 1882-1890 increases were followed by declines, the beginning of the continuous increase to the present of the Pima and Maricopa began about 1895. During the 1895-1910 period, the annual growth rate was 0.6 percent, and this was before much use of modern medicine among the Pima. The only such technique was smallpox vaccination. The Pima are not alone in this. Even in Europe, where the demographic transition supposedly took place, population increase cannot be attributed entirely to decreased mortality from medical advances. Other factors, such as the introduction of the potato as a staple crop (which led to earlier marriage and higher fertility), food imports from colonies, and emigration all played a part (Polgar 1972:207). Nevertheless, one can state that the greatest although not the only population increase among the Pima came during the 1950s when public health measures were intensified and medical care improved, so that certain causes of death were eliminated as significant. Presumably most if not all surviving United States Indian populations experienced this same change. For 1952 saw the start of drug therapy against tuberculosis and the use of antibiotics against pneumonia (Adair, Deuschle, and McDermott 1957:90). It thus would be better to revise the second stage of the demographic transition model to say that when modern medical treatment and sanitation are introduced, a population will experience its highest known annual growth rate.

The third stage of the demographic transition model has produced the most heated discussion among demographers, especially in relation to areas outside Europe and North America. Some demographers are amazed that those populations have not yet attained the third stage by reducing their fertility in order to compensate for the lowered mortality which has resulted from the introduction of public health programs. This situation is what has become known as the population explosion.

The Pima and Maricopa can shed some light on this situation. With an annual growth rate of 1.6 percent from 1960 to 1970 (Meister 1975:328), the reservation Pima (combined with a small number of Maricopa) are by no means in the proposed third stage of demographic transition. It is important to understand that the Pima and Maricopa are a "modernized" group integrated into the industrialized economy of the United States. Very few derive a living from subsistence farming because of the unavailability of water. The Pima (and Maricopa) rely largely on low and unstable wage income, lease income, and welfare (Munsell 1967:216-269). If the demographic transition concept is correct in ascribing declining birth rates to the possibility of upward social mobility, and not just integration into an industrialized economy, it is not surprising that the Pima and Maricopa have a high rate of population growth. Their position in the economy is such that for most, there is little real chance to acquire more than enough for daily needs. The Pima and Maricopa were cheated of their most valuable resource, the waters of the Gila River, and have little control over their remaining resources. Restrictions on tribally-initiated and tribally-run development are considerable, with already established non-Indian firms being encouraged to avail themselves of the tax advantages and captive labor force of the reservation.

Off-reservation, Pima and Maricopa face discrimination in hiring. Those few who do obtain employment paying a decent wage or salary are often expected to act like whites if they expect to be promoted or retained. Often they must shift their social associations from predominantly Indian to predominantly white. Thus, given the overall economic position of the Pima and Maricopa, limiting the number of children may not be advantageous and may even be disadvantageous. Munsell (1967) for the Salt River Pima-Maricopa, and Robbins (1968) for the Blackfeet, have shown that these two groups have ways of coping with the low end of the economy. When personal or family income is relatively high and stable, households tend to contain a nuclear family. When income is relatively low and unstable, however, families and other relatives move in together to form extended family households. Each member contributes some income or labor to the household, which functions as an economic unit. Thus, one person may have a car, another welfare income, another some lease income, while other members will engage in seasonal or part-time wage labor, which does not provide a stable income. Yet, by pooling resources the members of the household attempt to obtain a stable income. Still, it is a relatively low income in national economic terms.

In this environment, children may not be seen as a disadvantage. When someone falls on hard times, he or she must have relatives on whom to rely — brothers, sisters, sons, daughters, parents, even grandparents and grandchildren. If there are no children, one may have to rely on non-relatives, who owe their first priority to their relatives. If one has children, it is hoped that one of the children may somehow obtain a good living, in which case the parents hope not to be forgotten. Even though the children may not live with the parents, the parents may receive economic assistance from them. As Ward (1962:94) states,

> . . . without the thrust of growth there is no particular reason why people should want smaller families. Children may not die; they cannot be educated; meanwhile they work. A certain fatalism prevails. It is

only when hope and expansion begin that the choice of a smaller family makes sense.

One can be poor with two children or 10 children when it is not the number of children that puts a family in poverty but rather the family's role in an economy that has deprived it of its resources. Thus, the birth rate of the Pima and other populations of rapid growth should not be expected to decline until real economic opportunities are available. Only then will we know whether the third stage of the demographic transition will be realized, or whether it will join the first and second stages as a rejected hypothesis.

Acknowledgements

The research on which this paper is based was made possible in part by National Science Foundation Grant GS-30151. I would like to thank the following persons for their assistance: Dr. Henry F. Dobyns for his comments and criticism, especially concerning the Hispanic period of Piman history, and Dr. Joseph G. Jorgensen for his assistance in setting the context in which changes in American Indian population occurred. I am, however, responsible for any errors or discrepancies that may remain in this paper.

NOTES

1. The sources of the data in Figure 1 and Tables 1 and 2 are: (a) The Gila River Pima data are a compromise of the figures of Sauer (1935:5, Table I), Dobyns (1962, 1963, 1966:404), and Ezell (1961:16-21, 134) for the Hispanic period, and my own evaluation and analysis of government and non-government figures for the Anglo period (Meister 1975). The term "Gila River" Pima here includes Pima living on the Salt River Indian Reservation. After 1910 (Table 2), the Gila River Pima data also include Maricopa living on the Gila River and Salt River Indian Reservations. They are about 10% of the population. (b) The Maricopa data are from Mooney (1928:22) and Spier (1933:3) and Kroeber (1925:796, 799, 883) for the Hispanic period and again my own evaluations and estimates of government and non-government figures for the Anglo period (Meister 1975). The Pima and Maricopa data have been carefully evaluated and analyzed so as to produce reasoned estimates and do not represent raw figures. (c) The data for the Pueblo are estimates from Dozier (1970:130 *passim*) and are based primarily on Hispanic sources and the *Annual Report of the Commissioner of Indian Affairs*, but have been altered in conformance with Dozier's understanding of the forces affecting Pueblo population. (d) The Navajo data are from Johnston's (1966) exhaustive study of that population and are based on Spanish sources, the *Annual Report of the Commissioner of Indian Affairs*, and the Bureau of the Census. (e) Jorgensen (1972:37, 48, 91) has provided a fairly detailed series of figures for the Ute. These represent essentially the enrolled population. (f) For California, I have used mostly the estimates of Cook (1943) in *The Conflict between the California Indian and White Civilization*, but I have used Cook's (1964:72) later and larger figure for 1770. For 1905 and 1955, I have relied on Kroeber (1957:218, 221).

REFERENCES

Adair, John, Kurt Deuschle and Walsh McDermott
1957   "Patterns of Health and Disease Among the Navajos," in George F. Simpson and J. Milton Yinger (eds.) American Indians and American Life. *The Annals of the American Academy of Political and Social Science*, 311.

Birdsell, Joseph B.
1957   "Some Population Problems involving Pleistocene Man." *Cold Spring Harbor Symposia in Quantitative Biology*, 22:47-69.

Bowers, Nancy
1971   "Demographic Problems in Montane New Guinea," in Steven Polgar (ed.) *Culture and Population: A Collection of Current Studies.* Cambridge: Schenkman Pub. Co., for Carolina Population Center, University of North Carolina at Chapel Hill.

Cook, Sherburne F.
1943   *The Conflict Between the California Indian and White Civilization.* Berkeley: Ibero-Americana: 21-24.
1964   "The Aboriginal Population of Upper California." *Actas y Memorias del XXXV Congreso Internacional de Americanistas, Mexico, 1962,* 2:397-403. (Reprinted 1971 in R. F. Heizer and M. A. Whipple, Comps. and eds., *The California Indians: A Source Book.* Berkeley: University of California Press, pp. 66-72.)

Dobyns, Henry F.
1962   *Pioneering Christians Among the Perishing Indians of Tucson.* Lima: Editorial Estudios Andinos.
1963   "Indian Extinction in the Middle Santa Cruz River Valley, Arizona." *New Mexico Historical Review,* 38:163-181.
1966   "Estimating Aboriginal American Population, 1. An Appraisal of Techniques with a New Hemispheric Estimate." *Current Anthropology,* 7:395-416.

Dozier, Edward P.
1970   *The Pueblo Indians of North America.* New York: Holt, Rinehart and Winston.

Dumond, Don E.
1975   "The Limitation of Human Population: A Natural History." *Science,* 187:713-721.

Ezell, Paul H.
1961   *The Hispanic Acculturation of the Gila River Pimas.* American Anthropological Association Memoir 90.

Hill, Charles A., Jr., and Mozart I. Spector
1971   "Natality and Mortality of American Indians Compared with U. S. Whites and Nonwhites." *HSMHA Health Reports,* 86:229-246.

Ho Ping-ti
1959   *Studies on the Population of China, 1368-1953.* Cambridge: Harvard University Press.

Johnson, Denis Foster
1966   *An Analysis of Sources of Information on the Population of the Navajo.* Washington: Bureau of American Ethnology Bulletin 197.

Jorgensen, Joseph G.
1972   *The Sun Dance Religion: Power for the Powerless.* Chicago: University of Chicago Press.

Kroeber, Alfred L.
1925   *Handbook of the Indians of California.* Washington: Bureau of American Ethnology Bulletin 78.
1957   *California Indian Population About 1910. Ethnographic Interpretation 5.* Berkeley: University of California Publications in American Archaeology and Ethnology, 47(2).

Kunstadter, Peter
    1972 "Demography, Ecology, Social Structure, and Settlement Patterns," in G. A. Harrison and A. J. Boyce (eds.) *The Structure of Human Population*. Oxford: Clarendon Press.
Langer, William L.
    1963 "Europe's Initial Population Explosion." *American Historical Review*, 49:1-17.
Meister, Cary W.
    1975 History Demography of the Pima and Maricopa Indians of Arizona (USA), 1846-1974. Ph.D. dissertation, University of Michigan. Ann Arbor: Xerox University Microfilms.
Merriam, C. Hart
    1905 "The Indian Population of California." *American Anthropologist*, 7(n.s.):594-606.
Mooney, James
    1928 *The Aboriginal Population of America North of Mexico*. Washington: Smithsonian Miscellaneous Collections 80(7).
Munsell, Marvin
    1967 Land and Labor at Salt River: Household Organization in a Changing Economy. Ph.D. dissertation, University of Oregon. Ann Arbor: University Microfilms.
Polgar, Steven
    1961 "Culture, History, and Population Dynamics," in S. Polgar (ed.) *Culture and Population: A Collection of Current Studies*. Cambridge: Schenkman Pub. Co., for Carolina Population Center, University of North Carolina at Chapel Hill.
    1972 "Population History and Population Policies from an Anthropological Perspective." *Current Anthropology*, 13:203-211.
Robbins, Lynn A.
    1968 "Economics, Household Composition, and the Family Cycle: the Blackfeet Case," in June Helm (ed.) *Spanish-speaking People in the United States*. Seattle: Proceedings of the 1968 Annual Spring Meeting of the American Ethnological Society.
Sahlins, Marshall
    1972 *Stone Age Economics*. Chicago: Aldine-Atherton.
Sauer, Carl O.
    1935 *Aboriginal Population of Northwestern Mexico*. Berkeley: Ibero-Americana: 10.
Spier, Leslie
    1933 *Yuman Tribes of the Gila River*. Chicago: University of Chicago Press.
Stanford, Quentin H. (ed.)
    1972 *The World's Population: Problems of Growth*. Toronto and New York: Oxford University Press.
Thomlinson, Ralph
    1965 *Population Dynamics*. New York: Random House.
Ward, Barbara
    1962 *The Rich Nations and the Poor Nations*. New York: W. W. Norton.
Woodburn, James
    1968 "An Introduction to Hadza Ecology," in Richard B. Lee and Irven DeVore (eds.) *Man the Hunter*. Chicago: Aldine Publishing Co.
Wrigley, E. A.
    1969 *Population and History*. New York: McGraw-Hill.
Wrong, Dennis H.
    1967 *Population and Society*. New York: Random House, 3d edition.

CHAPTER NINE

Old World Diseases and the Dynamics of Indian and Jesuit Relations in Northwestern New Spain, 1520–1660

Daniel T. Reff (University of Oklahoma)

In the summer of 1591, Fathers Martín Pérez and Gonzalo de Tapia began the first permanent Jesuit mission in northern New Spain. The mission was founded along the banks of the Sinaloa River at San Felipe, which was at the time the northernmost Spanish settlement along the western slopes of the Sierra Madre Occidental. About the same time that Tapia and Pérez began working in Sinaloa, several Jesuits established a residence in Durango, several hundred miles southeast of San Felipe, along the eastern slopes of the Great Divide. From these humble beginnings, the Jesuits in a short span of about 80 years established missions throughout northwestern Mexico. In the process, over 500,000 natives were baptized, the majority of whom accepted the protection and supervision of the priests. Not to be denied further converts, the Jesuits advanced into Baja California and southern Arizona during the closing decade of the 17th century. Missionary efforts continued in both areas as well as in northwestern Mexico until 1767, when a bankrupt Charles III expelled the Jesuits from his overseas empire (Bannon 1955; Bolton 1936; Dunne 1940, 1944, 1948; Pérez de Ribas 1896, 1944; Polzer 1976; Shiels 1934; Spicer 1962).

Although the Jesuits clearly enjoyed remarkable success in northern New Spain, the reasons for this success are not altogether apparent. For many years it has been assumed that, aboriginally, most native groups in the Greater Southwest lived in small rancherías that lacked sophisticated economic and sociopolitical systems (Spicer 1962: 8–15). Against this backdrop the Jesuits have been cast in a role analogous to modern-day extension agents. Through the introduction of new crops, tools, cattle, and other innovations, the priests are said to have made possible for the first time in many areas native settlement in towns, permanent houses, intensive agriculture, craft production, and other advances in native economic and sociopolitical organization. Many researchers have suggested further that native recognition of Spanish technological and economic superiority played a dynamic role in acculturative processes (Bannon 1955; Bolton 1917; Dunne 1940, 1944; Fontana 1976; Hu-DeHart 1981; Spicer 1962: 58, 285–298, 1980: 19).

The traditional view of aboriginal culture and the dynamics of Jesuit and Indian relations have never been adequately scrutinized, particularly in light of historical evidence of Old World diseases and their impact on native populations during the 16th and 17th centuries. This chapter reviews extant evidence of disease and how epidemics of smallpox and other maladies affected mission and Indian relations. It is argued that Old World diseases undermined the structure and functioning of native societies prior to sustained contact with the Jesuits, and that native interest in and acceptance of missionization had little to do with the introduction of wheat, chickens, cattle, plows, or Jesuit knowledge of irrigation agriculture. Rather it is argued that native acceptance of missionization was largely influenced by the fact that the Jesuits pursued a policy of reconstituting native productive and organizational strategies that faltered or collapsed following exposure to introduced-diseases. From the point of view of the indigenous population of northern New Spain, acceptance of missionization was an opportunistic endeavor; the presumption that this opportunism was a function of native recognition of the inherent superiority of western civilization is not supported by empirical data.

EPIDEMICS IN THE GREATER SOUTHWEST 1519–1660

The idea that Old World diseases had a profound impact on native peoples during the historic period is not novel. For many years historians and anthropologists have recognized the probable importance of disease. However, with the exception of Sauer (1935), few researchers have acknowledged the relative abundance of historical data regarding disease episodes and their consequences in northern New Spain. The historical record indicates that Old World diseases first may have been introduced during Nuño de Guzmán's conquest of Nueva Galicia (1530–1531). Guzmán's expedition largely destroyed the fabric of Indian life in western Mexico (Sauer and Brand 1932). It was not primarily Guzmán's slave raiding and military exploits, however, that undermined the once populous and advanced cultures of northern Nayarit and southern Sinaloa. The numerous accounts of Guzmán's entrada suggest that the invaders also brought with them one or more devastating diseases. Indeed, we know from Guzmán's own *Memoria* that he was harboring *Plasmodium Malariae* (Carrera Stampa 1955: 40), and on at least one occasion during the Conquest, suffered an apparent relapse of quartan malaria (Bancroft 1886: 364). Guzmán, in fact, may have been the source of an infection that swept through his army in September of 1530, while it was encamped for the winter at Aztatlán, along the Río Acaponeta. The epidemic reportedly killed 8,000 of Guzmán's Indian allies, and left the province of Aztatlán largely depopulated (Carrera Stampa 1955: 154, 185). The symptoms mentioned by various eyewitnesses such as intense fever, chills, and bloody stools (Carrera Stampa 1955: 108–109, 138–139, 154) are all highly suggestive of dysentery (*Shigella* spp.), typhoid, and malaria (Ashburn 1947: 92; Cloudsley-Thompson 1976: 137; Kitchens 1949: 1017). Significantly, shortly after the epidemic subsided, Guzmán's army pushed into Sinaloa, where several participants in Guzmán's entrada (Carrera Stampa 1955: 125, 175) as well as many later observers (for example, Arregui 1946: 46; Cuidad Real 1976: II, 122; Mota y Escobar 1940: 85–86; Tello 1891: 611) commented on the large numbers of mosquitoes. In modern times, and most likely at the time of Guzmán's conquest, coastal Nayarit and Sinaloa were home to Anopheline *Albimanus*, a most efficient malaria vector (Faust 1949: 756).

The introduction of malaria, dysentery, and typhoid undoubtedly played a major role in the dramatic decline in the native population of northern Nayarit and southern Sinaloa during the decades immediately following Guzmán's conquest (Borah and Cook 1963; Sauer and Brand 1932). Acute infectious diseases also exacted a heavy toll. About 1534 to 1535, measles, which had raged for several years in southern and central Mexico (Ashburn 1947; Dobyns 1963; McNeill 1976), ravaged northern Nayarit and southern Sinaloa. According to Tello (1891: 251–255), measles and "bloody stools"—probably dysentery and typhoid that were introduced during Guzmán's entrada—killed 130,000 natives of the province of Culiacán, apparently along the Río San Lorenzo, Tamazula, Humaya, and Culiacán. Again from 1545 to 1548, an epidemic of what appears to have been typhus claimed hundreds of thousands of lives in southern Mexico and Nueva Galicia (Bancroft 1886: 529–530; Grijalva 1924: 213–214; Mendieta 1945: 174; Zinsser 1934: 194–195). After the epidemic subsided, from roughly 1548 to 1574, southern Mexico enjoyed a period of relative calm, excluding the interval from 1559 to 1564 when New Spain suffered from a major epidemic of what was probably, in part, influenza (Cook and Simpson 1948: 14; Grijalva 1924: 216; Ocaranza 1934: 84–85). Except for an epidemic characterized by sore throat ("hinchazones en la garganta") in 1551 (Tello 1891: 549), Nueva Galicia also seems to have been spared the ravages of disease. The chronicles of Baltasar Obregón (Hammond and Rey 1928) and Antonio Ruíz (AGN n.d.; Sauer 1932), specifically their comments about the size and complexity of native populations encountered during Ibarra's expedition (1564–1565), also suggest that northern Sinaloa and Sonora were not affected by Old World diseases.

While the third quarter of the 16th century may have been a time of relative calm, epidemiologically speaking, there were a number of developments during this period that contributed to the introduction and rapid spread of disease in northern New Spain. The most significant development was the discovery of vast silver deposits in and around Zacatecas in 1546. Shortly thereafter, muleteams and wagon trains began frequent journeys northward along what became the *Camino Real de la tierra adentro*, bringing men and supplies to Zacatecas (Bakewell 1971; Powell 1952). This movement of goods and people pre-dictably provided numerous opportunities for the northward spread of disease–opportunities that multiplied between 1550 and 1580 as new mines were opened to the north and east of Zacatecas at Fresnillo, Sombrete, Topia, Indehe, and Santa Barbara. The rapid expansion of the mining frontier led not only to commerce and communication between Nueva Vizcaya and southern Mexico, but to extensive trade and communication with Nueva Galicia. After 1565, muleteers began hauling large quantities of salt, fish, fruit, and other commodities from Chametla, Culiacán, and San Felipe to the burgeoning mining frontier on the eastern slopes of the Sierras. This commerce was conducted via the "Topia road," a mule trail that stretched for about 140 miles from the Villa of San Miguel to the Real of Topia, and then down the eastern slopes of the Sierras to Tepehuanes (West and Parsons 1941). Alternatively, fish and other commodities from Nayarit and Sinaloa were taken by muleteers southward along the camino real of the coast to Guadalajara. Here a thriving commercial center developed after 1560 that funneled west coast exports over the Sierras to Zacatecas or southward to Michoacán and Mexico City. Muleteams owned by residents of Mexico City, in turn, brought items like rope and cloth from the Capital to Guadalajara as well as to Compostela, Chametla, and San Miguel (Arregui 1946: 103–104; Cuidad Real 1976: II, 122; Mota y Escobar 1940; Navarro García 1967: 29–37; West 1949: 77, 79, 90; West and Parsons 1941).

The rapid expansion of the mining frontier led to an extensive trade and communication system that became "the routes of contagion" during the closing decades of the 16th and throughout the 17th and 18th centuries. Although it is difficult to determine precisely when disease agents first made their way northward along the camino reals of the coast and the interior, both roads apparently were functioning as conduits for the spread of disease from 1575 to 1581. At this time, typhus raged in southern Mexico, killing millions of Amerindians (Alegre 1956: 184–185; Bancroft 1886: 657–658; Florencio 1955: 257–270; Mendieta 1945: 174; Tello 1891: 623; Zinsser 1934: 256). Significantly, not long after typhus reached epidemic proportions in the south, it appeared in Zacatecas. In 1576 and 1577, "the Great Matlazahuatl" killed more than 2,000 native mine workers in Zacatecas (Bakewell 1971: 126–127). There is also indirect evidence that typhus subsequently spread farther northward to Spanish mining centers and Indian villages along the eastern slopes of the Sierras. Some disaster must have befallen Durango and southern Chihuahua between 1575 and 1579, because in 1579 Royal officials in Durango petitioned the King for the right to import 1000 Tlascaltec and other civilized Indians to increase the supply of Indian miner workers in Nueva Vizcaya (Mecham 1927: 231). Often requests of this nature or for new encomiendas were correlated with disease episodes (Friede 1967: 339; Griffen 1979: 100).

There are several additional lines of evidence that indicate that typhus and other Old World diseases affected native populations along the eastern slopes of the Sierras as well as in the mountains around Topia during the closing decades of the 1500s. Of particular interest are a wide range of behaviors, beliefs, and fears regarding disease that were present among the Zacateco, Irritila, Tepehuan, and Acaxee at the time of Jesuit contact (Alegre 1958: 74–94; DHM 1596: 30; DHM 1598: 51, 57; DHM 1601: 65; Pérez de Ribas 1944: III, 13–22). Indeed, shortly after the mission of Parras was founded among the Irritila and Zacateco, the Jesuits reported discovering a mass burial that logically may be attributed to an epidemic that occurred before the Jesuits began working in the Laguna region (Pérez de Ribas 1944: III, 263–264). Actually, a letter written by Father Juan Augustín de Espinosa that recounts the first Jesuit entrada into the Laguna region clearly indicates that Old World diseases, specifically smallpox, had affected the Zacateco and Irritila prior to 1590. In his letter, Espinosa recounts how he and a fellow Jesuit set out from Zacatecas for Cuencame in the summer of 1594. While Espinosa's companion, Father Gerónimo Ramírez, preached to the Zacateco at Cuencame, Espinosa went farther north to a pueblo at the base of the Cerro Gordo. Here the priest was visited by numerous caciques from the Laguna region and three from the Río Nazas, who asked Espinosa to visit their pueblos because their children were dying of smallpox. Espinosa acceded to their request and in one pueblo baptized 17 or 18 children who were sick and in danger of dying (Alegre 1956: 423–424; Pérez de Ribas 1944: III, 251–253). Significantly, Espinosa makes no mention in his letter of adults being ill. From what is known about smallpox (Dixon 1962), it is reasonably safe to assume that the Irritila and Zacateco of the Laguna region had been exposed to smallpox on a previous occasion, leaving those who survived—namely the adults encountered by Espinosa—with an active immunity to variola.

During the closing decades of the 16th century, northern Nayarit and southern Sinaloa apparently also suffered from typhus and other maladies (Tello 1891: 623, 692–694). Several early historians believed that by 1590 Old World diseases had contributed to a 90 percent reduction in the aboriginal population of Nueva Galicia (Bancroft 1886: 552–553). Unfortunately, we know little about what impact diseases such as smallpox had on native populations in northern Sinaloa and other areas farther to the north. Shortly after their arrival in Sinaloa in 1591, Fathers Tapia and Pérez wrote several letters describing native life that seem to indicate that Old World diseases did not have a profound or lasting impact on northern Sinaloa (AGN 1593; Shiels 1934: 109–113, 132–135). This situation changed dramatically, however, in 1593. An epidemic of smallpox and measles occurred at this time that claimed at least 1,000 of the Jesuits' new converts along the Río Sinaloa, Ocoroni, and Mocorito (AGN 1593, 1594; Pérez de Ribas 1944: I, 172–173). Significantly, many accounts seem to indicate that all age groups suffered equally during the epidemic, suggesting a lack of prior exposure to smallpox and measles. Moreover, one priest, Juan Bautista de Velasco, noted that many Indians complained to the Jesuits that it was only after the Jesuits came

to Sinaloa that the natives suffered from disease (AGN 1593: 41; Dunne 1940: 32; Alegre 1956: 392–393). On balance then, it would appear that northern Sinaloa had not suffered from Old World diseases prior to 1591.

The outbreaks of smallpox that occurred along both the eastern and western slopes of the Sierras in 1593 and 1594 were the first of many disease episodes during the Jesuits' tenure in northern New Spain. In the decades that followed, epidemics occurred at regular 5 to 7 year intervals. The annual reports and occasional correspondence of the Jesuits as well as the works of Pérez de Ribas indicate there were epidemics from 1601 to 1602, 1606 to 1607, 1612 to 1613, 1616 to 1617, and 1623 to 1625. This pattern reflects, in part, the appearance of a new generation of susceptibles, specifically children that lacked an active or passive immunity to disease. Another of Father Velasco's letters, from the year 1601, provides some support for this thesis. That year Sinaloa again suffered from what apparently, in part, was fulminating smallpox. According to Velasco (AGN 1601: 109), the *cocoliztli* had its greatest impact on children who had not yet reached juvenile age— presumably those who had been born since the epidemic of 1593. In the *anua* of 1602 we learn that the epidemic involved not only smallpox, but measles, typhus, sore throat ("garrotillo"), and several other unspecified diseases. Reportedly, almost everyone suffered from one or more illnesses, and large numbers of natives died along the Ocoroni, Sinaloa, Mocorito, and Río Culiacán (AGN 1602).

Like many disease episodes, the epidemic of 1601 to 1602 was preceded by several years of hunger, caused by drought and poor harvest. Poor harvests were reported again from 1604 to 1605, following heavy rains that destroyed mission and nonmission crops (AGN 1604). The ensuing hunger and malnutrition undoubtedly lowered native resistance to disease and set the stage for the third major epidemic to affect Sinaloa, as well as Durango and Chihuahua. The epidemic of 1606 to 1607 was truly widespread and, like many epidemics, it apparently originated in southern Mexico where several diseases raged from 1604 to 1607 (Alegre 1958: 144–146; Gibson 1964: 448). During the winter of 1606 to 1607, smallpox and several other maladies became widespread in Sinaloa and thousands of natives died, particularly along the Río Fuerte (Alegre 1958: 120; Pérez de Ribas 1944: I, 342–346). During the spring of 1607 at least several thousand additional converts and countless gentiles died in the Sierras among the Chicoratos, Cahuemetos (Pérez de Ribas 1944: I, 247; 1896: I, 218), Acaxee (Alegre 1958: 158–162; Pérez de Ribas 1944: III, 29, 49, 54–55, 79–84), and Tepehuan (Alegre 1958: 154). That same year, 1607, the Irritila and Zacateco of the Laguna region also were devastated by smallpox and other diseases (Alegre 1958: 151–153; DHM 1607: 86–87; DHM 1608; Dunne 1944: 109–117; Pérez de Ribas 1944: III, 269–285).

The epidemic of 1606 to 1607 was the first of many epidemics that are known to have affected mission communities on both the eastern and western slopes of the Sierra Madre and the

385

valleys and barrancas of the Topia region. Significantly, like many disease episodes, the epidemic predictably spread beyond the mission frontier, as is apparent from a letter written by Father Juan Fonte, describing the first Jesuit entrada among the southern Tarahumara. At the time of his visit, Fonte was working among the northern Tepehuan of Ocotlan, where he had been visited by several Tarahumara caciques who requested baptism and priests. Wishing to know more about the Tarahumara, Fonte traveled some 18 leagues beyond the Valley of San Pablo in November or December of 1607, visiting several Tarahumara rancherías in which he found a number of children who were sick and in danger of dying, including one child who was quite ill with smallpox (Pérez de Ribas 1944: III, 159–161). The fact that Fonte did not report that the child's parents or other adults and children had contracted the disease suggests that the southern Tarahumara had been exposed to smallpox on a previous occasion.

Fonte's experience among the Tarahumara was not unique. In 1612 to 1613 many natives in Sinaloa as well as among the Acaxee, Xixime, Tepehuan, and Laguneros (Irritila and Zacateco) suffered from typhus, smallpox, *cocoliztli*, influenza, and bloody stools, probably dysentery or typhoid (AGN 1612; AGN 1613; Alegre 1958: 234–235, 237–238, 244–245; Decorme 1941: II, 33–34; Pérez de Ribas 1944: I, 350; III, 66–67, 106–108). One or more of these diseases also must have spread beyond the mission frontier. Some acute or chronic infectious disease apparently was afflicting the Mayo when Father Pedro Méndez began working among them early in 1614. In a letter to his Superior, Méndez noted that during his first 15 days among the Mayo he baptized over 500 children and adults who died (Alegre 1958: 255; Pérez de Ribas 1944: II, 12–13). Later that same year, in December, Méndez again wrote to his Superior, noting that there had been numerous occasions when he made the rounds of his nine or so new missions, finding those people that had been baptized because they were sick or dying (AGN 1614: 22; Pérez de Ribas 1944: II, 21–23).

It is perhaps indicative of the extent to which maladies like typhus were spreading at this time that 350 Pima Bajo, an entire village, left their home in the Sierras in January of 1615 and traveled to San Felipe to ask for baptism (AGN 1615a; AGN 1615b; Pérez de Ribas 1944: I, 253–256). During the spring of the following year (1616) another group of 174 "Nebomes" came south, as did a third group late in 1616 (AGN 1615; AGN 1616). Although the Jesuits attributed this mass exodus to Nebome impatience for baptism, the Nebome, like other native peoples, apparently had suffered from Old World diseases and hoped that baptism might provide a measure of protection from and a cure for disease. Accordingly, three of the adults who came south in January of 1615 died en route and another reached San Felipe in a "death trance, . . . so leprous that there was not a part of his body, from his head to his feet, that was free of that plague" (Pérez de Ribas 1944: I, 255–256).

Not surprisingly, the Yaqui also suffered from diseases that outdistanced the northward moving mission frontier. In a letter describing his and Father Tomás Basilio's first entrada to the Yaqui, undertaken in the spring of 1617, Pérez de Ribas (HHB 1617) wrote that the two priests began their entrada at a time when the Yaqui were suffering from an epidemic of *cocoliztli* that had raged from a year among the Indians of Sinaloa. Pérez de Ribas went on to note that the two Jesuits baptized 1,600 infants, and 100 adults who were sick. Significantly, while many infants died, only some ("algunos") adults reportedly died, and still others regained their health. The apparent high case frequency and mortality rate for children as opposed to adults indicates that the Yaqui had suffered from the dreaded *cocoliztli* years before the first entrada by Pérez de Ribas and Basilio.

The epidemic that afflicted the Yaqui in 1617 was widespread and affected groups as distant as the Guasave and the Varohio. In his letter discussed above, Pérez de Ribas mentions that he and Basilio were visited by delegations of Varohios (Yhios), Baciroas, Tetaribes, Tehatas, Conicaris, Tepagues, and other groups who brought their sick children to the Río Yaqui to be baptized. According to Pérez de Ribas, the natives also visited and petitioned Father Diego de la Cruz on the Río Mayo to come to their lands to baptize. He did as the natives requested, and apparently found many who were ill, as Ribas noted that de la Cruz in one day baptized over 100 individuals (HHB 1617).

It is apparent from Pérez de Ribas's letter that fulminating smallpox or *cocoliztli* spread well up into the foothills of northern Sinaloa and southern Sonora in 1616 to 1617. This same area again suffered during the epidemic of 1623 to 1625. Like earlier disease episodes, the epidemic followed several years of great hunger caused by drought and poor harvests (AGN 1622; AGN 1623; Alegre 1958: 353). Coincident with this hunger were scattered outbreaks of disease that took on epidemic proportions in Sinaloa in October of 1623 (AGN 1625). The epidemic reportedly was the worst ever seen, and involved a variety of diseases, including smallpox, pneumonia ("dolor de costado"), typhus, and sore throat, possibly influenza or streptococcus (AGN 1623). Over the course of two years these maladies spread throughout Sinaloa and southern Sonora, up into the foothills and Sierras among the Acaxee and Xixime, over the Sierras among the Tepehuan, and from Zacatecas at least as far north as the mission of Parras (AGN 1623, 1624, 1625, 1626; Tello 1891: 779–780). According to Father Juan Lorencio, by the time the epidemic had run its course, over 8,600 natives died in Sinaloa alone (AGN 1625). This number, Lorencio noted, included only those who were baptized; there reportedly were many others who died during the epidemic whom the priests were unable to baptize. Included among these gentiles were many Chinipa, Pima Bajo, Eudeve, and Opata, including, apparently, the Opata cacique "Gran Sisibotari" from the Río Sahuaripa (AGN 1628: 345).

The devastation wrought by the epidemic of 1623 to 1625 contributed to a temporary slowing of mission expansion on both the eastern and western slopes of the Sierra Madre. It was not until the second half of the 1630s that the mission frontier again made significant advances, principally among the Opata and the Tarahumara. Predictably, the incorporation into the mission system of thousands of new converts ushered in a new and almost relentless wave of epidemics that were particularly destructive of the Opata and the Tarahumara, the first coming in 1636 to 1639. During these years, smallpox and *cocoliztli* raged among the Tepehuan and Tarahumara near Parral (AGN 1638) and destroyed nearly 20,000 Indians in New Mexico (Hackett 1937: 108). Some unidentified disease also claimed many lives among the Opata of the Sonora Valley (AGN 1639). Between 1645 and 1649 (AGN 1647, 1647a, 1647b, 1649; AHH 1666; Polzer 1972: 270; DHM 1645; Pérez de Ribas 1896: I, 304) and on numerous occasions during the 1650s (AGN 1653, 1653a, 1656; DHM 1652, 1653, 1658; Pérez de Ribas 1896: II, 498, 556) and 1660s (Alegre 1959: 266, 285; Decorme 1941: II, 33; DHM 1662, 1669), northern New Spain was beset with outbreaks of smallpox, "malicious" fevers (malaria or yellow fever?), bloody stools (dysentery or typhoid), sore throats, and other diseases. This situation did not change for at least another century. However, by 1678 the damage had already been done, and the native population of northern New Spain largely had been destroyed.

DEMOGRAPHIC CONSEQUENCES OF SPANISH-INTRODUCED DISEASE

Although the Jesuit materials clearly indicate that Old World diseases were a prominent feature of life in northern New Spain, the Jesuits seldom commented on case frequency and mortality rates during epidemics. The demographic consequences of Spanish-introduced disease are reflected, however, in a comparison of baptismal and census figures compiled by the Jesuits and other Spanish colonial officials. Not surprisingly, what the figures show is a dramatic decline in native population during the Jesuits' tenure in northern New Spain.

Among the Tepehuan, Zacateco, Irritila, and Acaxee, the decline was particularly rapid and pronounced. During the 1590s, when the Jesuits founded the mission of Parras, the Irritila and Zacateco of the Laguna region reportedly numbered 16,000 to 20,000 (Pérez de Ribas 1944: III, 293). As a consequence of disease, particularly the epidemics of 1607 and 1623 to 1625, only 1,569 Irritila and Zacateco survived in 1625 (Hackett 1926: 152–159). Similarly, between about 1593 to 1624 the Acaxee were reduced in number from approximately 14,000 (Pérez de Ribas 1944: III, 17) to less than 2,000 (Hackett 1926: 152–159). Census figures from 1625 also suggest that the Tepehuan lost 90 percent or more of their population by this date (Hackett 1926: 152–159). In 1638, Pérez de Ribas noted that there were more converts in one pueblo in Sinaloa than in all of the Tepehuan pueblos combined (Hackett 1937: 101–102), and that less than 10,000 of the 100,000 Laguneros, Tepehuan, Acaxee, and Xixime that had been baptized were still alive in 1638 (AHH 1638; Hackett 1937: 100).

The mission population along the west coast also underwent a significant reduction in size during the closing decade of the 16th and throughout the 17th century. Baptismal figures show that by 1624, about 106,000 natives had been baptized in Sinaloa

and southern Sonora (Dunne 1940: 218). Census figures for the same year show that the mission population numbered only around 67,000 (AGN 1624a); some 40,000 native converts, in effect, died between 1591 and 1624. In 1638, 18 years later, the Jesuits reported the total number of baptisms on the west coast reached 200,000 (AHH 1638; Hackett 1937: 100). Despite almost a 100 percent increase in baptisms since 1624, the mission population increased by only around 47 percent, to about 90,000 (AHH 1638; Hackett 1937: 97, 100).

Between 1591 and 1638, then, roughly two-thirds of the mission population of northwestern Mexico died; some 200,000 native converts in all. After the years 1636 to 1639, when a new wave of epidemics began in northern New Spain, an even larger percentage of native converts perished. This decline is reflected in a census conducted in 1678 by Father Juan Ortiz Zapata (AGN 1678). At the time of Zapata's census, the Jesuits had completed the reduction and missionization of all but a few native groups in northwestern Mexico. The total number of Indians that had been baptized since 1591 numbered over 500,000, as Pérez de Ribas (1896: II, 562) reported that the number of baptisms reached 400,000 as early as about 1654. Despite a significant increase in baptisms, the total mission population for all of northwestern Mexico declined from its previous high of 100,000 in 1638, to some 63,000 in 1678 (AGN 1678).

Census figures for individual groups and missions further testify to the destruction of the native population of northern New Spain during the 17th century. The Mayo and Yaqui, for instance, were each reported to have numbered around 30,000 at the time of missionization (Pérez de Ribas 1944: II, 24, 64). By 1678 the Mayo and Yaqui numbered 7,807 and 7,549, respectively (AGN 1678); a reduction in population of 75 percent. A comparison of baptismal and census figures for other Cáhita groups and the Pima Bajo also reveals a decline in population of 75 percent or more by 1678. Predictably, because many Opata and Tarahumara communities were exposed to Old World diseases at a later date, they retained a larger percentage of their population in 1678. However, as a consequence of epidemics in 1638 to 1639, 1645 to 1647, 1649, and 1652, already by 1653 the Opata numbered only about 25,000 (AGN 1653). By 1678 this number was further reduced by half, to approximately 13,500 (AGN 1678). The population of the Opatería continued to decline until approximately 1730. At this time the Opata numbered about 7,000 and the author of the anonymous *Estado de la Provincia de Sonora* commented that there were in all of Sonora only 12,132 adults—a mere fraction of the more than 70,000 souls recorded in "the ancient catalogs" (DHM 1730: 627).

The decline in native population documented above for the Opata and other groups pertains to mission converts. How many natives died from Old World diseases that spread in advance of the mission frontier we do not know. Groups such as the Irritila, Mayo, and Yaqui, however, suffered from smallpox and other maladies prior to sustained contact with the Jesuits. Probably many native groups lost between 25 to 40 percent of their populations prior to missionization. A decline in population of this magnitude is suggested, in part, by studies of virgin populations exposed to diseases such as smallpox (Ashburn 1947; Dixon 1962; Shurkin 1979). A premission reduction in population of 25 to 40 percent is also suggested by demographic observations made by Spanish explorers. In his chronicle of the Ibarra expedition (1564 to 1565), for instance, Obregón estimated that 15,000 men could be found along the lower Yaqui (Yaquimi; Hammond and Rey 1928: 257–258). If it is assumed that Obregón was referring to all able bodied men between the ages of 15 and 40—those who might be apportioned through *repartimientos* or assembled for military purposes—then it may be inferred on the basis of the 1930 Mexican census (see Cook and Simpson 1948: 25–26) that this cohort constituted approximately 30 percent of the Yaqui's total population, which would have been about 50,000 in 1564. This figure is 40 percent larger than the 30,000 Yaqui who were reported at the time of Jesuit contact.

CULTURAL CONSEQUENCES OF SPANISH-INTRODUCED DISEASE

The great loss of life and the suffering that many communities experienced during the 16th and 17th centuries predictably had a profound impact on the structure and functioning of native societies. The general character of the changes wrought by Spanish-introduced diseases is reflected in the incongruous descriptions of native life that were compiled by Spanish explorers, and later by the Jesuits. In the explorers' accounts, dating from 1530 to 1565 (Nuñez Cabeza de Vaca 1944; Di Peso 1974: IV; Hammond and Rey 1928, 1940; Hedrick and Riley 1974, 1976; Reff 1981; Riley 1976, 1982; Sauer 1932; Sauer and Brand 1932; Undreiner 1947), the Greater Southwest frequently is described in terms of large populations living in rancherias as well as in villages and towns. Through the use of a variety of agricultural techniques, including floodwater farming and canal irrigation, many settlements enjoyed crop surpluses and were said to be involved in extensive trade of salt, turquoise, shell, macaws, slaves, obsidian, copper, bison hides, coral, and a host of other basic commodities and luxury goods (Riley 1976). The explorers also mentioned or alluded to native elites, and noted that native settlements in a number of areas were integrated into sophisticated sociopolitical systems, or what the Spaniards termed "Kingdoms" (for example, Senora, Marata, Tototenac, Cibola). By comparison, the later Jesuits described the Greater Southwest in different terms. The priests made little or no mention of "Kingdoms," and frequently described native life in terms of small, economically and politically autonomous communities that lacked intensive agriculture, regular surpluses, extensive trade, and elites (Spicer 1962). The priests also reported, particularly the Jesuits, that many native groups were quite willing to accept mission tutelage—a response that differed markedly from the hostility directed toward the explorers.

Although it is true that we have been unable to identify or correlate many settlements and groups described by the explorers with those later discussed by the missionaries (Di Peso 1974: IV; Hedrick 1978; Reff 1981; Riley 1976; Sauer 1932; Undreiner 1947), this lack of continuity is precisely what would be expected, given the introduction of Old World diseases during the interlude separating the time of the explorers and the Jesuits. Infectious diseases would have had their greatest impact on large, nucleated settlements, prompting the abandonment of villages and towns and a proliferation of dispersed rancherias, an inference borne out by recent archaeological data from the Sonora Valley (Reff 1981). Disease-induced reductions in population and shifts in residence also would have had an impact on productive and organizational strategies. A community that lost 25 to 40 percent of its population in a short time would have great difficulty clearing, sowing, and harvesting agricultural fields; constructing and maintaining irrigation systems; organizing communal hunts; or preparing food for peak periods of consumption and scarcity. Without regular surpluses of food and other basic commodities, craft specialization would decline and local and long distance exchange would languish. The collapse of productive and organizational strategies likewise would undermine the status of elites empowered through differential access to or control of crop surpluses and trade. The status of religious specialists also would suffer because of the lack of experience in dealing with unprecedented suffering and loss of life. In point of fact, all aspects of native life would suffer from outbreaks of smallpox and other maladies. Given the uncertainty of life, native peoples also would be expected to show an interest in alternative behaviors and beliefs like those offered by the Jesuits.

Was it really "new" or "different" behaviors and beliefs, however, that prompted and sustained native acceptance of programs for reduction and missionization? In the past, many researchers have concluded that native interest in and acceptance of mission ways of life were prompted by a recognition of the benefits that accrued to missionization. Although this idea can be traced back in time at least to the works of a number of 18th century mission historians (for example, Alegre 1956–1960; Nentvig 1980; Treutlein 1949), it was Bolton who popularized the notion. In many of Bolton's works as well as those of his students (Bannon 1945, 1955; Dunne 1940, 1944), the missionaries are credited with the introduction of a variety of "innovations" that transformed the "barbarians" of northern New Spain into civilized Christians. This theme was clearly spelled out in one of Bolton's earliest works on the mission frontier, wherein he likened the mission to a "great industrial school," where besides learning good manners, agriculture, and self-government, "the women were taught to cook, sew, spin, and weave; the men to fell the forest, build, run the forge, tan leather, make ditches, tend cattle, and shear sheep" (Bolton 1917: 57). According to Bolton, once the missionaries taught the "erstwhile barbarians" the rudiments of civilization, they turned the wilderness of New Spain into a veritable bastion of progress, with imposing structures, fertile farms, and great stock ranches (Bolton 1917: 58).

The conclusions reached by Bolton in this early work were amplified in many of his later publications (1932, 1936), and have been generally accepted by modern anthropologists and historians. No less a scholar than Spicer has described the missionaries as "agricultural extension workers," and the mission as "a center for the diffusion of agricultural improvements" (Spicer 1962: 58). Purportedly native recognition of the technological and economic superiority of Spanish tools, crops, cattle, and other "innovations" prompted many communities to petition for baptism and missionization, and subsequently revolutionized aboriginal culture (Spicer 1963: 58, 292, 295–297; 1980: 32, 86).

The traditional model of culture change and contact is based on a number of assumptions of questionable validity. Implicitly, at least, it has been assumed that, aboriginally, most groups in the Greater Southwest lived in small rancherías, without permanent houses, sophisticated agricultural practices, regular surpluses, extensive trade, and some form of political organization that involved more than war captains or charismatic leaders. This characterization of aboriginal culture had been based largely on observations that postdate the founding of Jesuit missions in northern New Spain and on modern ethnographic fieldwork. As noted, it is contradicted by the exploration chronicles. Also, native populations that were not affected by Old World diseases prior to missionization frequently were described by the early missionaries as being far more numerous and complex than later historians and anthropologists have recognized. This is true, for instance, of the Cáhita and Guasave, who were described by Fathers Tapia and Pérez in 1593 in terms very different from those used by later Jesuits and modern researchers (AGN 1593; HHB 1633; Shiels 1934: 108–116).

The idea that Spanish or mission innovations were an important inducement for missionization, and that these innovations revolutionized native life, also lacks empirical support. Although the Jesuits seldom discussed the economic side of mission life (Bannon 1945: 194), there were several occasions when their interests were threatened by civil and ecclesiastical encroachment that prompted reports on the wealth and functioning of the missions. In 1638, Pérez de Ribas, who was at the time the Father Provincial, compiled one such report that was sent to Spain along with testimony taken from a number of civilians in Nueva Vizcaya (AHH 1638; Hackett 1937: 95–127). Some 20 years later, in 1657, Father Francisco Xavier de Faría prepared a much more detailed report on the status of the missions (AGN 1657). Significantly, both Jesuit reports as well as the testimony taken from civilians in 1638 clearly indicate that many Spanish or Jesuit "innovations" were of little consequence. All sources agree, for instance, that the Jesuit and their mission charges subsisted principally on maize, beans, squash, and other native cultigens (AGN 1657: 25–29; Hackett 1937: 97). It is also apparent that native, as opposed to Spanish, farming practices were employed by the Jesuits and their neophytes. In his report, Faría noted that the Jesuits had tried to use oxen and plows, but found that the oxen died from heat prostration and the plows created great dust storms (AGN 1657: 28). For a variety of reasons, but particularly because of the lack of suitable land and the heat, the Jesuits also had great difficulty growing wheat; most of the wheat that was consumed in the missions was in the form of communion wafers that were made from wheat raised on Spanish farms in the Valley of Santa Barbara and hauled to Sinaloa via Topia (AHH 1638; Hackett 1937: 98, 123, 125). Even in the late 1700s, after more than a century of experimentation, wheat was still difficult to raise in Sinaloa (Villa-Señor y Sánchez 1952: 383). More important is the fact that yields from maize were three to six times that of wheat (Nentvig 1980: 23; Treutlein 1949: 46). Not only was maize more productive, but it reportedly tasted better and was preferred over wheat by Indians as well as Sonorans and Mexican-born Spaniards (Treutlein 1949: 196).

In Faría's report, we learn that many other plants that the Jesuits had brought to the northern frontier were of little consequence during the early mission period. In 1657, for instance, there were only a few, scattered missions where the priests had been successful in establishing small orchards and vineyards. According to Faría, the "fruits" of the missions ordinarily were those that grew wild in the scrubland; most of the "wine" consumed in the missions was native (mescal), or was imported from Mexico (AGN 1657: 15, 25–29). The Jesuits also enjoyed limited success in their efforts to import artisans and farmers from Mexico to teach the Indians various trades. In 1638 the former Captain of the presidio and province of Sinaloa, Don Francisco de Bustamente, testified that the priests' houses and the churches in Sinaloa were built by the priests and the Indians, and that the priests had no other workmen or artisans (Hackett 1937: 94–117). This situation apparently changed only a little during the next 20 years. In Faría's report from 1657 he noted that, although the priests had endeavored to bring architects, mechanics, farmers, and others to the northern Frontier, there were only a small number of artisans scattered throughout the missions, such that one mission might have a carpenter, another a tailor, and so forth (AGN 1657: 15).

Of the many "innovations" introduced by the Jesuits and other Spaniards, cattle clearly had the most significant impact on aboriginal culture. The Jesuits introduced a large number and variety of domesticated animals (Bannon 1945: 195; Treutlein 1965: 177; Polzer 1972: 169), but it is doubtful that they constituted an "improvement" over deer and other wild game as a food resource. Many early observers, including the Jesuits, commented on the relative abundance of all types of wild game and fish in Sinaloa and Sonora (Hammond and Rey 1928: 87, 102, 257–259; Hedrick and Riley 1976: 45, 52; Pennington 1979: 207; Pérez de Ribas 1944: I, 134, II, 64, 123; Treutlein 1949: 106). There is little reason to believe that the number and variety of wild resources inhibited population growth and cultural development, or that they ever posed a threat to the economic well being of native peoples. The same cannot be said for cattle, which destroyed hundreds of thousands of acres of land in northwestern Mexico during historic and modern times. If cattle were, in fact, an "improvement" over wild

389

game, perhaps it was because cows, sheep, and goats were a more readily available source of nourishment during epidemics. Indeed, most epidemics in northern New Spain as well as in other areas of Mexico (Cooper 1965) occurred during the fall and winter, when large mammals such as deer were hunted aboriginally. As Pérez de Ribas (Hackett 1937: 100) pointed out, were it not for the cattle introduced by the Jesuits, the Indian otherwise would have died during times of sickness.

If it is true that Jesuit "innovations" were of little consequence, what exactly precipitated and sustained native acceptance of missionization? Although it is difficult to infer what was in the minds of native peoples, particularly given the absence of native commentaries, it nevertheless is apparent that many natives petitioned for missionaries and baptism, believing that baptism and the priests provided a protection from and a cure for disease (AGN 1639a; Alegre 1958: 470; Decorme 1941: 360–361). There is also good reason to believe that many natives were motivated by the realization that the Jesuits pursued a policy of reconstituting native adaptive strategies that faltered or collapsed in the wake of Spanish-introduced diseases.

Because the Jesuits received only modest alms from the *Patronato Real*, each priest had to implement economic and organizational strategies that provided income for his assigned mission and its outlying *visitas* (Treutlein 1939: 289). In most cases, the local missionary served in a managerial capacity, much as "big-men" do in prestate societies (Harris 1979). Accordingly, the Jesuits organized the division of Indian labor as well as the production, exchange, and redistribution of goods. Indians living within a mission community generally were required to work three days a week on communal or church lands. These lands provided surpluses that were redistributed by the local missionary among members of the mission community, usually during feasts and times of hunger arising from crop failures. For four months in 1656, for example, food shortages prompted the resident priests at Raum and Potam to distribute over 6,000 daily food rations (AGN 1657: 30). Alternatively, food surpluses were sold by the missionary and the profits gained were used to buy church ornaments or items such as chocolate and rosary beads that were redistributed among the missionaries' loyal following (AGN 1657: 32–36). Among that following were *alcaldes, fiscales,* and Indian governors who assisted the Jesuits in the administration of the mission community (Polzer 1976; Spicer 1962; Treutlein 1939).

Although it has been suggested that the mission community with its requisite economic and social organization was "a new phenomenon of Indian life" (Spicer 1962: 292), archaeological and historical data suggest that, in many important respects, it was not. Before the advent of Old World diseases, and later, of the Jesuits, many native peoples in northern New Spain were living in towns and villages as well as small rancherías. Neither the idea nor the reality of living in nucleated settlements and building substantial houses of adobe were new to groups like the Acaxee, Cáhita, Opata, Pima Bajo, or the Tarahumara. Archaeological evidence as well as the explorers' accounts also indicate that many native peoples were quite adept at floodwater and irrigation agriculture, and were familiar with the production and management of crop surpluses. Aboriginally, surpluses frequently seem to have been controlled by what Pérez de Ribas (1944: I, 133) and other Jesuits termed "principal caciques." Although anthropologists traditionally have characterized native sociopolitical organization in terms of egalitarian and politically independent communities, the "principal chiefs" among groups like the Mayo, Yaqui, and Opata had thousands of followers in numerous villages (AGN 1614; Pérez de Ribas 1944: II, 66–83, 131; AGN 1610, 1620; Dunne 1940: 112–128, 148). There is good evidence that many principal chiefs were paramount heads of chiefdoms similar to those that existed in the southeastern United States (Hudson 1976). Pérez de Ribas (1944: I, 133) noted that the principal chiefs alone decided matters of war and peace, and "were like heads and captains of families and rancherías." Pérez de Ribas also observed that the principal chief hosted important war rituals and had the largest fields, which were cultivated with the assistance of his subordinates. In an apparent reference to the principal chiefs of the Opata of the Sonora Valley, Castañeda, who was with Coronado, noted that "the dignitaries of the pueblos stand on some terraces which they have for this purpose and remain there for one hour, calling like town criers, instructing the people in what they are to do. . ." (Hammond and Rey 1940: 250). Interestingly, the "terraces" referred to by Castañeda may be equated with two "court-platform" structures that recently were identified during archaeological excavations at two large villages in the Sonora Valley—villages that were abandoned before the Jesuits arrived in the Sonora Valley (Pailes 1980; Reff 1981).

In conclusion, it is argued that many of the rights and responsibilities of the principal chiefs were assumed by the Jesuits after Old World diseases had undermined the structure and functioning of native societies, including native sociopolitical organizations. Just as native caciques and their subordinates once directed native life from the tops of ramadas (Beals 1943: 56) or earth platforms, so each day the priest or his assistants appeared at the door of the mission church, "instructing the people in what they are to do" (Bannon 1955: 61). Similarly, through the practice and advocacy of Catholicism, the Jesuits filled a void left by the death or failure of native religious leaders to chart a course through uncertain and inexplicable times. Although few natives appreciated or grasped the meaning of their new faith (Bannon 1955: 59), the Jesuits cannot be faulted in this regard for failing to "revolutionize" aboriginal culture. Indeed, perhaps their greatest legacy is that they recognized the worth of many aspects of native life. Were it not for Old World diseases that the Jesuits unwittingly fostered, their efforts to protect and preserve native peoples undoubtedly would have proved more fruitful.

Acknowledgments. I wish to thank Dr. Charles W. Polzer, S.J., for providing encouragement, support, and access to the extensive computer bibliography and microfilm collection of the Documentary Relations of the Southwest Project, Arizona State Museum, University of Arizona, Tucson. In searching for documentary evidence of disease and related information, I was aided immeasurably by the computer bibliographies and staff of the DRSW. Thanks also are due Nancy Ettlinger for reading and commenting on several drafts of this paper.

Note. This chapter originally focused on the probable impact of Old World diseases on the Opata and their relations with the Jesuits during the 1600s. Since 1980, I have analyzed historical documents and archaeological data from northwestern Mexico and the American Southwest that provide the empirical evidence of disease discussed in this paper. Because of space limitations, it has not been possible to describe in detail individual disease episodes or how many documentary sources cited can be dated, assigned authorship, or otherwise interpreted. These topics and issues are discussed in a more detailed and comprehensive analysis of the demographic and cultural consequences of disease in the Greater Southwest (Reff 1985).

DOCUMENT REFERENCES

AGN   (Archivo General de la Nacion, Mexico City)
n.d.   *Misiones 25.* Puntos sacados de las relaciones de Antonio Ruíz, P. Martín Pérez, P. Vincente del Aguila, P. Gaspar Varela, Juan de Grixalva, Capitan Martinez, y otras.
1593   *Misiones 25.* Anua del año de mil quinientos de noventa y tres.
1594   *Historia 15.* Memoryas Para la Historia de la Provincia de Synaloa. Anua del año de mil quinientos noventa y quatro.
1601   *Historia 15.* Memoryas Para la Historia de la Provincia de Synaloa. Carta del Padre Juan Bautista Velasco de el año de mil seiscientos uno.
1602   *Historia 15.* Memoryas Para la Historia de la Provincia de Synaloa. Anua del año de mil seiscientos y dos.
1604   *Historia 15.* Memoryas Para la Historia de la Provincia de Synaloa. Anua del año de mil seiscientos quatro.
1610   *Historia 15.* Memoryas Para la Historia de la Provincia de Synaloa. Anua del año de mil seiscientos quatro.
1612   *Historia 15.* Memoryas Para la Historia de la Provincia de Synaloa. Anua del año de mil seiscientos doze.
1613   *Historia 15.* Memoryas Para la Historia de la Provincia de Synaloa. Anua del año de mil seiscientos trece.
1614   *Historia 15.* Memoryas Para la Historia de la Provincia de Synaloa. Anua del año de mil seiscientos catorce.
1615   *Historia 15.* Memoryas Para la Historia de la Provincia de Synaloa. Anua del año de mil seiscientos quinze.
1615 a *Historia 316.* Carta de Diego Martínez de Hurdaide al virrey, 10 de Abril de 1615.
1615 b *Historia 15.* Memoryas Para la Historia de la Provincia de Synaloa. Carta del Padre Diego de Guzmán al Padre Provincial de Septiembre de mil seiscientos veinte y nuebe [sic. 1615].
1616   *Historia 15.* Memoryas Para la Historia de la Provincia de Synaloa. Carta del Padre Martín Pérez, del año de mil seiscientos diez y seis.
1620   *Historia 15.* Memoryas Para la Historia de la Provincia de Synaloa. Anua del año de mil seiscientos y veinte.
1622   *Misiones 25.* Carta Annua de la Provincia de la Compañia de Jesús en Nueva España.
1623   *Misiones 25.* Carta annua de la Provincia de la Compañia de Jesús de Nueva España.
1624   *Misiones 25.* Carta Annua de la Provincia de la Compañia de Jesús de Nueva España.
1624a *Fondo Cossio II–7.* Catalogo de la Gente que tienen los partidos de la Provincia de Cinaloa fecho en 12 de henero de 1624.
1625   *Misiones 25.* Carta Annua de la Provincia de la Compañia de Jesús de Nueva España.
1626   *Misiones 25.* Carta Annua de la Provincia de la Compañia de Jesús de Nueva España.
1628   *Historia 15.* Memoryas Para la Historia de la Provincia de Synaloa. Missiones de San Ygnacio en Mayo, Yaqui, Nevomes, Chinipas, y Sisibotaris.
1638   *Misiones 25.* Copia de una carta del Padre Gaspar de Contreras para el Padre Provincial, Santiago Papasquiaro, 5 August 1638.
1639   *Misiones 25.* Puntos de Anua de la nueba mission de San Francisco Jabier, año de 1639.
1639a *Misiones 25.* Puntos de Anua de la nueba mission de San Francisco Jabier, año de 1639.
1647   *Misiones 25.* Letras Annuas de la Provincia de la Compañia de Jesús de Mexico, año 1647.
1647a *Misiones 25.* Carta de Marcos del Rio al Padre Visitador Pedro Pantoja etc., Guasabus, 4 April 1647.
1647b *Misiones 26.* Annua del Pueblo de Santa Catalina de Tepeguanes.
1649   *Misiones 26.* Carta annua De la Provincia De la Compañia De Jesús de Mexico; Del año de 1648 y [1]649, Andres Rada, 10 July 1650.
1653   *Misiones 26.* Puntos de annua del año de 1653 del collegio y misiones de Cinaloa.
1653a *Historia 15.* Memoryas Para la Historia de la Provincia de Synaloa. Carta Annua de la Mission de San Ygnacio de los Rios de Hiaqui y Mayo: año de mil seiscientos cincquenta y tres.
1656   *Historia 15.* Memoryas Para la Historia de la Provincia de Synaloa. Anua de la Mission de San Ygnacio del Rio de Mayo y Hiaqui: año de mil seiscientos cincuenta y seis.
1657   *Historia 316.* Apologetico Defensorio y Puntual Manifesto que los Padres de la Compañia de Jesús, Missioneros de las Provincias de Sinaloa y Sonora, Francisco Xavier de Faría, November 1657.
1678   *Misiones 26.* Relación de los Missiones que la Compañia tiene en el Reyno y Provincias de la Nueva Viscaya en la Nueva España echa el año de 1678 con ocasion de la Visita General dellas que por orden del Padre Provincial Thomas Altamirano hizo el Padre Visitador Juan Hortiz Zapata de la misma Compañia.
AHH   (Archivo Historico de Hacienda, Mexico City)
1638   *Temporalidades 2009–1.* Memorial al Rey para que no se recenga la limosna de la missiones y consierva al

Senora Palafox en las relaciónes a la Compañia, 12 September 1638.

1666   *Temporalidades 1126–2*. Relación de lo sucedido en el pleito de la Compañia con los Religiossos de San Francisco.

DHM   (Documentos para la Historia de Mexico), Cuarta Serie, Tomo III. Mexico, 1857.

1596   Del Anua Del Año De 1596.

1598   Del Anua Del Año De 1598.

1601   Carta del Padre Nicolas de Arnaya dirigida Al Padre Provincial Franciso Baez el año de 1601.

1607   Del Anua Del Año De 1607.

1608   Carta del Padre Luis de Ahumada, dirigida al Padre Martín Pelaez, Provincial de la Compañia De Jesús el 13 de Noviembre de 1608.

1645   Relación de los sucedido en este reino de la Vizcaya desde el año de 1644 hasta el de 45 acerca de los alzimientos, danos, robos, hurtos, muertos y lugares despoblados de que se saco un traslado para remitir al padre Francisco Calderon, provincial de la provincia de Mexico de la Compañia de Jesús . . . Nicolas de Zepeda, San Miguel de las Bocas, Abril 28 de 1645, mas addendum de 11 de septiembre de 1645.

1652   Noticias de las Misiones sacados de la anua del Padre Jose Pascual; año de 1651.

1653   Carta que escribe el Padre Gaspar De Contreras al Padre Provincial Francisco Calderon el año de 1653.

1658   Puntos de Annua, Año 1658, Mission de Nebomes de N.P.S. Francisco de Borja.

1662   Puntos de anua de estos diez años que he asistido en este partido de San Pablo, de la Mision de Taramuras y Tepehuanes (de unas y otras hay), desde el año de 1652 hasta este de 1662 sumariamente lo que ha pasado cuanto a lo espiritual.

1669   Patrocinio del glorioso apostol de las Indias S. Francisco Javier en el reino de la Nueva Vizcaya, año de 1669.

1730   Estado de la provincia de Sonora, con el catalogo de sus pueblos, iglesias, lenguas diversas que en ella se hablan y leguas en que se dilata; con una breve descripcion de la Sonora jesuitica, segun se halla por el mes de Julio de este año de 1730, escrito por un padre misionero de la provincia de Jesús de Nueva España.

HHB   (Hubert H. Bancroft Collection, Bancroft Library, University of California, Berkeley)

1617   *Memorias Para la Historia de la Provincia de Sinaloa*. Carta del Padre Andres Pérez al Padre Provincial, Pueblo de Tesamo, 13 June 1617.

1633   *Mexican Manuscript 7*. Historia de las Missiones apostolicas, que los clerigos regulares de la Compañia de Jesús en echo en las indias occidentales del reyno de la Nueva Vizcaya, Juan de Albizuri.

Alegre 1956–1960
Arregui 1946
Ashburn 1947
Bakewell 1971
Bancroft 1886
Bannon 1945, 1955
Beals 1943
Bolton 1917, 1932, 1936
Borah and Cook 1963
Carrera Stampa 1955
Cloudsley-Thompson 1976
Cook and Simpson 1948
Cooper 1965
Cuidad Real 1976
Decorme 1941
Di Peso 1974
Dixon 1962
Dobyns 1963
Dunne 1940, 1944, 1948
Faust 1949
Florencia 1955
Fontana 1976
Friede 1967
Gibson 1964
Griffen 1979
Grijalva 1924
Hackett 1923, 1926, 1937
Hammond and Rey 1928, 1940
Harris 1979
Hedrick 1978
Hedrick and Riley 1974, 1976

Hu-DeHart 1981
Hudson 1976
Kitchens 1949
McNeill 1976
Mecham 1927
Mendieta 1945
Mota y Escobar 1940
Navarro García 1967
Nentvig 1980
Nuñez Cabeza de Vaca 1944
Ocaranza 1934
Pailes 1980
Pennington 1979
Pérez de Ribas 1896, 1944
Polzer 1972, 1976
Powell 1952
Reff 1981, 1985
Riley 1976, 1982
Sauer 1932, 1935
Sauer and Brand 1932
Shiels 1934
Shurkin 1979
Spicer 1962, 1980
Tello 1891
Treutlein 1939, 1949, 1965
Undreiner 1947
Villa-Señor y Sánchez 1952
West 1949
West and Parsons 1941
Zinsser 1934

References

Alegre, P. Francisco Xavier
    1956-   Historia de la provincia de la compañia de Jesús de Nueva España (1780). 4 Vols. New
    1960   edition by Ernest J. Burrus and Felix Zubillaga, editors. Rome: Bibliotheca Instituti Historici
            S. J.
Arregui, Domingo Lázaro de
    1946   Descripción de la Nueva Galicia (1621). New edition by Francois Chevalier. Sevilla:
            Escuela de Estudios Hispano Americanos de la Universidad de Sevilla.
Ashburn, P.M.
    1947   The Ranks of Death. New York: Coward-McCann.
Bakewell, P.J.
    1971   Silver Mining And Society In Colonial Mexico: Zacatecas 1546-1700. Cambridge:
            Cambridge University Press.
Bancroft, Hubert H.
    1886   The Works of Hubert Howe Bancroft. Vol. 10, History of Mexico, Covering the Years 1521-
            1600. San Francisco: The History Company.
Bannon, John F., S.J.
    1945   Pioneer Jesuit Missionaries on the Pacific Slope of New Spain. In Greater America, Essays
            In Honor of Herbert Eugene Bolton, pp. 181-197. Berkeley: University of California Press.
    1955   The Mission Frontier in Sonora, 1620-1687. Monograph Series 26. New York: United States
            Catholic Historical Society.
Beals, Ralph L.
    1943   The aboriginal culture of the Cáhita Indians. Ibero-Americana 19. Berkeley: University of
            California Press.
Bolton, Herbert E.
    1917   The mission as a frontier institution in the Spanish-American colonies. American Historical
            Review 23: 42-61.
    1932   The Padre on Horseback: A Sketch of Eusebio Francisco Kino, S.J. San Francisco: Sonora
            Press.
    1936   Rim of Christendom, A Biography of Eusebio Francisco Kino, Pacific Coast Pioneer. New
            York: Macmillan Company.
Borah, Woodrow W., and Sherburne F. Cook
    1963   The aboriginal population of central Mexico on the eve of the Spanish conquest. Ibero-
            Americana 45. Berkeley: University of California Press.
Carrera Stampa, Manuel, editor and annotator
    1955   Memoria de los servicios que habia hecho Nuño de Guzmán, desde que fue nombrado
            gobernador de Panuco en 1525. Mexico: José Porrua e Hijos.
Cloudsley-Thompson, J.L.
    1976   Insects and History. New York: St. Martin's Press.
Cook, Sherburne F., and Lesley B. Simpson
    1948   The population of central Mexico in the sixteenth century. Ibero-Americana 31. Berkeley:
            University of California Press.
Cooper, Donald B.
    1965   Epidemic Disease in Mexico City, 1761-1813. Austin: University of Texas Press.
Cuidad Real, Antonio de
    1976   Tratado Curioso y Docto de las Grandezas de la Nueva España. (Relación breve y
            verdadera de algunas cosas de las muchas que sucedieron al Padre Fray Alonso Ponce
            en las provincias de la Nueva España siendo Comisario General de aquellas partes). 2
            Vols. Josefine Garcias Quintana and Victor M. Castillo Farreras, editors and annotators.
            Mexico: Instituto de Investigaciones Históricas, Universidad Nacional Autónoma de
            México.

1

Decorme, Gerard, S.J.
    1941   <u>La obra de los Jesuítas Mexicanos durante la época colonial, 1572-1767</u>. 2 Vols. Mexico:
           Jose Porrua e Hijos.
De Peso, Charles C.
    1974   Casas Grandes, A Fallen Trading Center of the Gran Chichimeca. 8 Vols. <u>Amerind
           Foundation Publication</u> 9. Dragoon, Arizona: Amerind Foundation, and Flagstaff:
           Northland Press.
Dixon, C.W.
    1962   <u>Smallpox</u>. London: J. and A. Churchill.
Dobyns, Henry F.
    1963   Indian extinction in the middle Santa Cruz River Valley, Arizona. <u>New Mexico Historical
           Review</u> 38(2): 163-181.
Dunne, Peter M., S.J.
    1940   <u>Pioneer Black Robes on the West Coast</u>. Berkeley: University of California Press.
    1944   <u>Pioneer Jesuits in Northern Mexico</u>. Berkeley: University of California Press.
    1948   <u>Early Jesuit Missions in Tarahumara</u>. Berkeley: University of California Press.
Faust, Ernest Carroll
    1949   Malaria incidence in North America. In <u>Malariology</u>, edited by Mark F. Boyd, Vol. 1, pp.
           749-763. Philadelphia: W. B. Saunders.
Florencia, Francisco de, S.J.
    1955   <u>Historia de la provincia de la Compañía de Jesús de Nueva España (1964)</u>. Mexico:
           Editorial Academia Literaria.
Fontana, Bernard L.
    1976   The faces and forces of Pimería Alta. In <u>Voices from the Southwest, A Gathering in Honor
           of Lawrence Clark Powell</u>, edited by D. C. Dickinson, W. D. Laird, and M. F. Maxwell, pp.
           45-54. Flagstaff: Northland Press.
Friede, Juan
    1967   Demographic change in the mining community of Muzo after the plague of 1629. <u>Hispanic
           American Historical Review</u> 47:338-343.
Gibson, Charles
    1964   <u>The Aztecs Under Spanish Rule: A History of the Indians of the Valley of Mexico, 1519-
           1810</u>. Stanford: Stanford Uiversity Press.
Griffen, William B.
    1979   Indian Assimilation in the Franciscan Area of Nueva Vizcaya. <u>Anthropological Papers of the
           University of Arizona</u> 33. Tucson: University of Arizona Press.
Grijalva, Juan de
    1924   <u>Crónica de la orden de N.P.S. Augustin en las provincias de la Nueva España. . .de 1533
           hasta el de 1592 (1624)</u>. Mexico: Imprenta Victoria.
Hackett, Charles
    1923-   Historical Documents Relating to New Mexico, Nueva Vizcaya, and Approaches
    1937   Thereto, to 1773. Collected by Adolph F. A. Bandelier and Fanny R. Bandelier. 3 Vols.
           <u>Carnegie Institution of Washington Publication</u> 330. Washington.
Hammond, George, and Agapito Rey, editors, translators, and annotators
    1928   <u>Obregón's History of 16th Century Explorations in Western America</u>. Los Angeles: Wetzel.
    1940   Narratives of the Coronado Expedition, 1540-1542. <u>Coronado Cuarto Centennial
           Publication</u>. Vol. 2. Albuquerque: University of New Mexico Press.
Harris, Marvin
    1979   <u>Cultural Materialism and the Struggle for a Science of Culture</u>. New York: Random House.
Hedrick, Basil C.
    1978   The location of Corazones. In <u>Across the Chichimec Sea</u>, edited by Carroll L. Riley and B.
           Hedrick, pp. 228-232. Carbondale: University of Southern Illinois Press.
Hedrick, Basil C., and Carroll L. Riley, translators
    1974   The Journey of the Vaca Party. <u>University Museum Studies</u> 2. Carbondale: Southern Illinois
           University Museum.

2

1976   Documents Ancillary to the Vaca Journey. _University Museum Studies 5_. Carbondale: Southern Illinois University Museum.

Hu-DeHart, Evelyn
1981   _Missionaries, Miners, and Indians: Spanish Contact With the Yaqui Nation of Northwestern New Spain, 1533-1820_. Tucson: University of Arizona Press.

Hudson, Charles
1976   _The Southeastern Indians_. Knoxville: University of Tennessee Press.

Kitchens, S.F.
1949   Quartan Malaria. In _Malariology_ 2: 1017-1026. Philadelphia: W. B. Saunders.

McNeill, William H.
1976   _Plagues and Peoples_. Garden City: Anchor Press-Doubleday.

Mecham, John Lloyd
1927   _Francisco de Ibarra and Nueva Vizcaya_. Durham: Duke University Press.

Mendieta, Fray Gerónimo de
1945   _Historia Eclesiástica Indiana_. Mexico.

Mota y Escobar, Alonso de la
1940   _Descripción Geográfica de los Reinos de Nueva Galicia, Nueva Viscaya y Nuevo León (1605)_. Mexico: Editorial Pedro Robredo.

Navarro García, Luis
1967   _Sonora y Sinaloa en el siglo XVII_. Sevilla: Escuela de Estudios Hispano-Americanos.

Nentvig, Juan, S.J.
1980   _Rudo Ensayo: A Description of Sonora and Arizona in 1764_. Translated, clarified, and annotated by Alberto F. Pradeau and Robert R. Rasmussen. Tucson: University of Arizona Press.

Nuñez Cabeza de Vaca, Alvar
1944   _Relación de los naufragios y comentarios_. Tomo I. Colección de libros y documentos referentes a la historia de América. Madrid: Librería General de Victoriano Suarez (1906). Also in _Naufragios de Alvar Nuñez Cabeza de Vaca_. Páginas para la historia de Sinaloa y Sonora, Vol. 1, pp. 7-74. Mexico: Editorial Layac.

Ocaranza, Fernando
1934   _Historia de la Medicina en México_. Mexico.

Pailes, Richard A.
1980   The upper Rio Sonora Valley in prehistoric trade. In New Frontiers in the Archaeology and Ethnohistory of the Greater Southwest, edited by Carroll L. Riley and Basil C. Hedrick. _Transactions of the Illinois State Academy of Science_ 72: 20-39.

Pennington, Campbell W.
1979   _The Pima Bajo of Central Sonora, Mexico, Their Material Culture_, Vol. I. Salt Lake City: University of Utah Press.

Pérez de Ribas, Andrés
1896   _Crónica y historia religiosa de la provincia de la Compañia de Jesús de México en Nueva España_ (1655). 2 Vols. Mexico: Sagrado Corazón.
1944   _Historia de los triumphos de nuestra santa fee entre gentes las más bárbaras y fieras del nueve orbe_ (1645). 3 Vols. Edited by Luis Alvarez y Alvarez de Cadena. Mexico: Editorial Layac.

Polzer, Charles W., S.J.
1972   The Franciscan entrada into Sonora, 1645-1652, a Jesuit chronicle, _Arizona and the West_ 14(3): 253-278.
1976   _Rules and Precepts of the Jesuit Missions of Northwestern New Spain, 1600-1767_. Tucson: University of Arizona Press.

Powell, Philip Wayne
1952   _Soldiers, Indians, and Silver: The Northward Advance of New Spain, 1550-1600_. Berkeley: University of California Press.

3

Reff, Daniel T.
1981   The location of Corazones and Señora: archaeological evidence from the Rio Sonora Valley, Mexico. In The Protohistoric Period in the North American Southwest, A.D. 1450-1700, edited by David R. Wilcox and W. Bruce Masse, pp. 94-112. Arizona State Anthropological Research Papers 24. Tempe: Arizona State University.
1985   The Demographic and Cultural Consequences of Old World Diseases in the Greater Southwest, 1519-1660. MS, doctoral dissertation, University of Oklahoma, Norman.

Riley, Carroll L.
1976   Sixteenth Century Trade in the Greater Southwest. Southern Illinois University Museum Research Records 10. Carbondale: Southern Illinois University.
1982   The Frontier People: The Greater Southwest in the Protohistoric Period. Center for Archaeological Investigations Occasional Paper 1. Carbondale: Southern Illinois University.

Sauer, Carl O.
1932   The road to Cibola. Ibero-Americana 3. Berkeley: University of California Press.
1935   Aboriginal population of northwestern Mexico. Ibero-Americana 10. Berkeley: University of California Press.

Sauer, Carl O., and Donald D. Brand
1932   Aztatlán: prehistoric Mexican frontier on the Pacific Coast. Ibero-Americana 1. Berkeley: University of California Press.

Shiels, W. Eugene, S.J.
1934   Gonzalo de Tapia (1561-1594), Founder of the First Permanent Jesuit Mission in North America. New York: United States Catholic Historical Society.

Shurkin, Joel N.
1979   The Invisible Fire. New York: G. P. Putnam and Sons.

Spicer, Edward H.
1962   Cycles of Conquest: The Impact of Spain, Mexico, and the United States on Indians of the Southwest, 1533-1960. Tucson: University of Arizona Press.
1980   The Yaquis: A Cultural History. Tucson: University of Arizona Press.

Tello, Fray Antonio
1891   Libro segundo de la crónica miscelanea de la Santa Provincia de Xalisco. . . Guadalajara: La República Literaria.

Treutlein, Theodore E.
1939   The economic regime of the Jesuit missions in the eighteenth century. Pacific Historical Review 8:284-300.
1949   (Translator and annotator.) Sonora, A Description of the Province, by Ignaz Pfefferkorn. Albuquerque: University of New Mexico Press.
1965   (Translator and annotator.) Missionary in Sonora, The Travel Reports of Joseph Och, S.J., 1755-1767. San Francisco: California Historical Society.

Undreiner, George J.
1947   Fray Marcos de Niza and his journey to Cibola. The Americas 3: 415-486.

Villa-Señor y Sánchez, Joseph Antonio de
1952   Theatro Americano, descripción general de los reynos, y provincias de la Nueva-España, y sus jurisdicciones (1748). Mexico: Editora Nacional.

West, Robert C.
1949   The mining community in northern New Spain: the Parral mining district. Ibero-Americana 30: 131-147. Berkeley: University of California Press.

West, Robert C., and James J. Parsons
1941   The Topia road: a trans-sierran trail of colonial Mexico. The Geographical Review 31: 406-413.

Zinsser, Hans
1934   Rats, Lice, and History. Boston: Little, Brown.

4

CALIFORNIA

II. POPULATION DECLINE

HE MOST OBVIOUS and impressive result of white settlement upon the aborigines in California was the profound diminution in numbers suffered by the natives. Population decline is therefore the central phenomenon of our investigation and the point of origin from which any discussion of causative factors or subsidiary biological relationships must proceed.

The simple fact of this decline is so far beyond question as to need no emphasis. Its exact numerical course, on the other hand, is very difficult to compute. The methods employed to determine the initial factor, the aboriginal population, cannot be utilized except in very local instances, for we are dealing with an essentially dynamic rather than a static condition. Consequently, it is preferable to present no more than a general survey of the population decline in the region.

The aboriginal population, that is, the numbers of Indians at the beginning of the Spanish period, can be estimated with a reasonable degree of accuracy. Since, however, the analysis of the existing data together with discussion of methods constitutes a topic of investigation somewhat apart from the problem of interracial conflict, the material bearing on these matters has been incorporated as an appendix. This appendix presents the conclusion that in the year 1770 the native population in California, exclusive of the Modoc, Paiute, and Colorado River tribes, amounted to approximately 135,000.

During the next seventy years, or more exactly until 1834, the losses were confined to the missions and the territories subservient to them. There is no reason to suppose that the tribes outside mission influence suffered any diminution in this period. The tribes within the mission sphere were either aggregated completely in the mission establishments or suffered losses owing to the secondary disruptive effects of forcible missionization. The groups actually in the missions underwent a decline which can be determined with some accuracy and which has been discussed elsewhere.[1] The secondary losses can only be conjectured.

---

[1] S. F. Cook, *Population Trends among the California Mission Indians*, Univ. Calif. Publ., Ibero-Americana, No. 17 (Berkeley, 1940).

[3]

The mission losses, as indicated by the record of deaths, include, of course, gentiles and mission-born Indians. The index to statewide depletion is actually the total number of gentiles baptized minus the population living in the missions at the time of secularization. This

TABLE 1

POPULATION DECLINE

Year	Population	Source
1770	133,500	Appendix, p. 194.
1823	100,000	A. S. Taylor, *Indianology* (1864), Pt. I, p. 1.
1832	98,000	See text, p. 5.
1848	88,000	See text, p. 5.
1849	100,000	C. H. Merriam, "The Indian Population of California," *Amer. Anthro.*, n.s. (1905), 7:594–606.
1850	100,000	T. B. King, *Rept. to U. S. Govt.*, 1850. King says less than 100,000.
1851	73,000	J. D. Savage, in H. Dixon's "California Indians," MS, 1875. Savage gives 59,000 for northern and central California, to which may be added an estimated 14,000 for southern California.
1852	85,000	C. H. Merriam, *loc. cit.*
1856	61,600	T. J. Henley, *Repts., Commr. Indian Affairs*, 1856, p. 245.
1856	50,000	C. H. Merriam, *loc. cit.*
1860	35,000	*Ibid.*
1865	30,000	D. W. Cooley, *Repts., Commr. Indian Affairs*, 1865, p. 115.
1866	24,500	Supt. Maltby, letter to L. V. Bogy, *ibid.*, 1867, p. 133.
1867	21,000	L. V. Bogy, *ibid.*, p. 132.
1870	30,000	C. H. Merriam, *loc. cit.*
1870	20,000	E. S. Parker, *Repts., Commr. Indian Affairs*, 1870, p. 81.
1873	22,000	*Repts., Commr. Indian Affairs*, 1873, p. 344.
1880	20,500	C. H. Merriam, *loc. cit.*

in turn is contingent upon the assumption that withdrawals from the wild state for purposes of conversion constituted a dead loss. In other words, during seventy years there was no increase in population among the tribes in contact with the missions which would tend to restore the aboriginal number and to compensate the draining-off by conversion. This assumption seems reasonable in view of the apparent aboriginal equilibrium between birth and death rates existing prior to 1770. In fact, far from a restoration of losses, the whole trend appears to have been toward a decline among the unconverted remnant.

If the methods referred to previously are applied to the Bancroft transcripts, these records indicate approximately 54,000 gentile baptisms; but from this figure must be deducted the mission population at the end of the period of active missionization. The latter date was actually 1834, but for this purpose it is perhaps better to anticipate by two years and say 1832, at which time the mission records show a population of approximately 17,000. We may then take the difference, 37,000, to represent the decline from 1770 to 1832. The total native population in 1832, therefore, may be set at 98,000.

From 1832 to 1848 two disturbing processes were at work. The first was secularization, which very rapidly wrecked the missions economically and at least dispersed the neophytes. To what extent it was mere dispersal and to what extent actual loss of life or reproductive capacity was concerned it is impossible to say at the present juncture. Perhaps 5,000 would adequately cover the actual population reduction involved. The second process was the ever-increasing encroachment of the Mexican and American ranchers and agriculturists upon the non-Christian tribes, especially in the central valley and the northern Bay region. Here again we cannot assess accurately, but considering both prior and subsequent events, it would not be too liberal to postulate the loss of another 5,000. This would mean a native population of 88,000 in 1848.

The system of government now changed as the gold era began. The incursions of explorers, miners, and farmers began to take terrific toll of life among the Indians. The losses were very great, but we cannot be sure of figures until the 'sixties, at the end of which decade the Indians certainly numbered no more than 30,000. However, in the intervening time independent parties and government agents made a number of close estimates. No claim to perfection in their enumerations can be made, but in the aggregate a fairly clear picture is presented. Furthermore, the study made by Merriam[2] is doubtless quite reliable for this period even though his estimate of the aboriginal population seems too high. In table 1 appear the data from several independent estimates, Merriam's figures subsequent to 1848, and the censuses of the United States Bureau of Indian Affairs.

---

[2] C. H. Merriam, "The Indian Population of California," *Amer. Anthro.*, n.s. (1905), 7:594–606.

Despite minor discrepancies, it is apparent that the great decline began with the discovery of gold and the opening up of hitherto virgin territory, particularly in the foothill strip of the Sierra Nevada and the Eel, Trinity, and Klamath watersheds, and continued with the rapid extinction of the aborigines or their segregation on the reservations. Meanwhile the old mission population utterly disappeared, except for a few scattered individuals in the north and the desert peoples of the south. By 1870 all the surviving natives of northern and central California (except those east of the Sierra Nevada and the Cascade range) were on reservations or under government protection. The nonreservation Indians south of the Tehachapi, numbering perhaps 5,000, were living a semi-independent existence in the sterile mountains and deserts which offered little inducement to white settlement.

Subsequent to this time, conditions were more stable. The population continued to decline slowly until a minimum of approximately 15,000 was reached. Meanwhile there had been some interbreeding with the white stock. In recent decades there may have been a slight increase, for the United States census for 1930 lists 19,212 Indians in California. In other words, a leveling-off process has been apparent in the last two generations, and a more or less final equilibrium has been reached.

In assessing and evaluating the factors which contributed to decline of the aboriginal population certain difficulties arise. These involve primarily the problem of orderly investigation and presentation. The entire field is so vast and complex, its ramifications so wide and often obscure, that a sharp, clear segregation of individual components becomes not only difficult but perhaps undesirable. No phenomenon of this type ever depends upon a single factor or cause, or even upon a precisely distinguishable group of factors. Moreover, when such a factor appears to emerge as a concrete unit, one invariably discovers that it is related to other factors, these to still others, and so on almost without limit. Indeed, a philosophy of human ecology or environmental relations must of necessity concern itself with complexes rather than discrete units; it must attempt to see the picture as a whole rather than as individual strokes of the brush. Nevertheless, for the purpose of the analysis or the detailed study of a general situation, one is forced to consider specific phases and aspects of the problem as if they were independent, instead of interdependent as they actually are. Practical considerations of space and time demand a consecutive, rather than a simultaneous, treatment.

A preliminary attempt to organize our knowledge of the factors involved in population decline would first require a classification along certain broad lines. Since we are dealing with the impact of a new civilization, there must be concerned, at the beginning at least, the direct effect of pure physical contact between the two races. Two phases of this contact are distinguishable. The first involves the direct personal shock of conflict, which may take many forms varying from slight to extreme. For example, in this particular instance there is a range from mild exploration and conversion to a new religion with its accompanying modification of Indian daily life, through forced conversions, actual kidnaping, and punitive expeditions, to the direst state of slavery and massacres or wars of extermination. The second phase concerns the dislocation and disturbance of the finely adjusted native life with particular reference to displacement of sedentary populations and reduction of the natural food supply.

Following immediate contact, there occurs a long train of indirect consequences which affect every aspect of life. For convenience these may be grouped into four primary categories.

1. Dietary effects. Here we include changes in type of food, taste and distaste, deficiencies of various sorts leading to malnutrition, and often partial or complete starvation.

2. Disease. Apart from malnutrition may be distinguished epidemic diseases, usually newly introduced by the incoming race, together with venereal disease.

3. Social factors. Here must be considered a host of influences of the most diverse types, some of little consequence, others of the most profound significance. Thus there might be mentioned the question of forced or free labor with its economic ramifications, crime and punishment, urbanization, vagrancy, alcohol, and sex delinquencies.

4. Genetic factors. These do not follow so directly from the first interracial contact, but in subsequent years, during the period of adjustment, they possess great weight, since the nature of the final

equilibrium will be determined in large measure by the degree of interbreeding and by the character of the hybrids.

It is proposed to follow somewhat the lines suggested above, first considering the more concrete data and eventually discussing, so far as feasible, the bearing of the nonmaterial social and genetic aspects of the problem. However, it must be borne in mind that, when we speak of impact of civilizations or contact of races, we are using only the most general terms. Actually, we encounter a series of impacts and conflicts, each presenting different characteristics and involving different groups of individuals. In California, as has been mentioned in the introduction, the Indian was first confronted with the Spanish-Mexican civilization. The framework of that contact embodied two quite distinct elements. Of these, the first concerned the relation of whites to Indians after the latter, or at least many of them, had been incorporated in permanent establishments, the missions. The second involved the relation between the Spanish-Mexican secular—that is, military and civilian—groups and the wild Indians, a relation which, with some modification, continued into the American period.

Since the type of contact, together with the factors concerned, was quite different in the secular than in the clerical relationship, it is advisable to consider the two separately. Consequently, the discussion which follows is concerned only with the mission environment and its influence on the Indian.

The mission environment.—The mission status represents a type of interracial relationship which has been of frequent occurrence throughout Latin America but which has had few examples in English America. In motivation, it is unique in human history, since it was in large measure conditioned by the desire of the invading or dominant race to convert the other to a new way of thinking, that is to say, to a new religion. Economic and political factors were undoubtedly involved, but the driving force was provided by a group of men inspired primarily by religious, not material, zeal. The purposes were, consequently, not the deliberate social or military subjugation of the weaker race, although this may have been an inevitable by-product, but were those of religious conversion. Since the means to this end were inevitably material and practical, it was through their employment that the strictly biological and behavioristic effects were exerted during that period of contact when the strictly spiritual ends were being accomplished.

We have therefore to eliminate in this study the purely moral aspect of the problem. In the course of conversion it was considered essential to remove the native from his normal ecological niche and to transport him to a completely new environment. Indeed, an organized effort was made to eradicate in his mind many of the distinctive cultural traits which had been an integral part of himself and his ancestors for generations. As a result, in California a number of large groups of animals (using the term with no invidious connotations) were suddenly forced to make a really violent adaptation to a strange environment. Already delicately adjusted to the ancient habitat, they were obliged, in two or three generations, to accustom themselves, not only to new material surroundings, but to a whole series of quite profound cultural and psychological changes. Since the element of active physical conflict was largely absent, it is possible for us to analyze in some detail the economic, social, and cultural factors concerned in the unsuccessful effort of the Indian race to maintain itself under the particular external conditions imposed by the white man.

According to the classical conception, when the environment of a species changes, the species either undergoes certain parallel changes or "adaptations" which enable it to persist or, in default of such adaptations, it disappears. The rapidity and effectiveness of the adjustive process depend in turn upon a host of considerations involving the structure, functional activity, and genetic composition of the species. In general, the older, more exactly adapted and genetically stable the species, the less the facility with which it is capable of meeting changes. This is a very broad principle and must be applied with caution to such a complex type as *Homo sapiens,* but I think it may be held that the aboriginal California variety of the species belonged to the more stable, less flexible category. Consequently, one would expect the process of adjustment to be slow, difficult, and attended by great sacrifice on the part of the race as, indeed, it seems to have been.

During the course of adaptation, with most species, the intimate mechanism is not clear. In other words, what goes on in the group or the individual frequently escapes our observation, particularly when highly complex animals or man are involved. On the other hand, there are invariably manifestations that something is happening. These phenomena may be termed, for lack of a more descriptive word, "responses." In the invertebrates and lower vertebrates, such actions may be of the order of simple tropistic or neuromuscular acts. In the higher invertebrates and the vertebrates, such elementary activities may become increased in complexity to include conditioned reflexes, instinct, and all that the psychologist understands by "animal behavior." In man, the higher mental faculties of choice, judgment, and reason are superadded, with the result that purely observational or experimental analysis is extraordinarily difficult. Nevertheless, certain activities may be abstracted, so to speak, from the whole complex and mentioned, even though no complete discussion can be attempted.

In the animal and plant kingdoms in general, not only does the individual react or adjust to external changes, but there is also a very definite group response when the change is of sufficient extent to affect many individuals simultaneously. Group behavior, group function, or group physiology has been noted by natural historians from the most ancient times, but only recently has a competent scientific attack on the problem been developed. Students of the social life of animals have led the way and are opening up new fields as each year passes. Aside from simple description, their most valuable tool has been the analysis of population changes. An environmental change affects a group composed of individuals, and a fundamental characteristic of the individual is that he differs from all others in the group; thus one succumbs when another does not; one reproduces when another does not. By means of the sum of the effect on individuals the mass effect on the group may be ascertained.

To return to the situation of the mission Indian, it is possible to study the effect of the contact between Indians and whites by investigating the responses of the individuals and the group to the change in environment superinduced by that contact. Having set forth what those responses were, we may then attempt to discover the factors which gave rise to them, and, so far as feasible, attempt quantitative assessment.

Since no structural or functional adaptations could occur in the short space of two or three generations, the actual responses of the Indians to the mission system are restricted to visible activity by individuals or small groups and to population changes in the whole group. The visible activity with respect to the mission system could take but one of two forms: obvious opposition or acceptance. The positive aspect was manifested in an entirely unsensational manner, merely in carrying on the routine of daily life in the mission. The negative aspect, i.e., opposition, was made evident through either flight or rebellion. The extent of fugitivism and rebellion is then the key to the response of the individual, whereas population trends indicate the response of the group.

Population changes in the missions.—In a recent paper[2] the data bearing on this question have been examined and critically analyzed. The chief conclusions were set forth as follows (p. 48):

Primarily, as a result of consistent wholesale addition by conversion, the total population rose rapidly until approximately 1800. Thereafter the increase continued, but more slowly, up to an equilibrium point near 1820, subsequent to which a definite decline set in. These observed changes, which were based upon a large gentile immigration, mask the true situation with respect to the converted population. The latter was subject to a very great real diminution from the beginning. This is clear from the falling birth rate and the huge excess of deaths over births which was present throughout the mission era. Actually the critical and determining factor was the death rate, for it has been shown that the decline in gross or crude birth rate may be accounted for largely by the constantly increasing sex ratio (males to females). Since the latter was invariable at unity for children under ten, the change must have been due to a differential death rate between males and females during adolescence and maturity, which would result in a relative decline in the number of child-bearing women. The death rate as a whole was always remarkably high, even, for some as yet unexplained reason, at the very start of the missions. It tended definitely, however, to fall during the last thirty years and, at the existing rates of change, would probably have come into equilibrium with the birth rate ultimately. These aspects of the total death rate were due primarily to the state of the child death rate, since the adult death rate did not alter so materially in sixty-odd years.

The chief conclusion of a more general nature is that the Indian population, which presumably had been in a more or less steady equilibrium

---

[2] S. F. Cook, *op. cit.*

prior to missionization, underwent a profound upset as a result of that process, a process from which it was showing signs of recovery only at the time of secularization. The indications are, indeed, that several further generations would have been necessary to recast the race, as it were, and bring about that restoration of biotic equilibrium which eventually would have occurred.

Eliminating all detail and rounding off numerical values, the data upon which these conclusions were based are the following. The total mission population in 1770, 1780, 1790, 1800, 1810, 1820, 1830, 1834 respectively was: 100, 3,000, 7,400, 13,100, 18,800, 21,100, 18,100, 15,000. The sex ratio (male/female) in the decade 1770–1780 was normal, approximately 1; by 1834 it had risen to 1.35. The crude birth rate per thousand in 1780, 1800, 1820, 1830 was respectively 45, 40, 35, 32. At the same time the value of 540 children per 1,000 adult females remained constant throughout. For the total population the mean values for the death rate per thousand in the decades centering around 1778, 1788, 1798, 1808, 1818, 1828 were respectively 70, 70, 85, 83, 76, 70; for children 140, 145, 177, 167, 143, 102. Finally, the percentage of newly converted gentiles, which represents the proportion of immigration to the missions, expressed as number of gentile baptisms per thousand total baptisms was, for the years 1776, 1790, 1800, 1810, 1820, 1830, the following: 27, 12, 8.5, 6.0, 4.5, 2.5.

The group response of the natives to the mission environment was therefore a very marked decline in numbers, referable primarily to the high mortality rate and secondarily to a reduced birth rate and altered sex ratio.

III. DISEASE AND NUTRITION

I T IS NECESSARY now to consider what might have been the factors responsible for the observed changes. When any population undergoes a sudden and profound diminution, it is, of course, customary to investigate first the three most probable causes: war, famine, and pestilence. If these will not account for the decline, then search must be made for more obscure reasons, perhaps of an economic, social, or cultural nature. In the present instance, as far as the internal population of the mission is concerned, war may be excluded at the beginning, since the number of neophytes who died by violent means was negligible. Certain uprisings did occur and various recalcitrants, rebels, or criminals perished in fighting or by execution, but armed conflict on a large scale did not enter the picture. There remain, then, disease and starvation as effective factors which require extended consideration.

DISEASE

That disease was important cannot be doubted. Indeed, its existence would be postulated purely on the basis of the physical conditions: large numbers of natives brought together in contact with newcomers who were the carriers of numerous maladies to which the older population was unaccustomed and hence not immune. The result should be high incidence of the imported diseases and consequent high mortality, frequently reaching epidemic proportions. From the first entrance of the Europeans into the new world the aboriginal inhabitants suffered one sweeping epidemic after another, each segment of the population undergoing in turn a cycle of devastating pestilence followed by gradual immunization and recovery. Among the Indians of Lower California it has been estimated that disease was responsible for nearly one-half the observed reduction in population.[1] One might therefore assume that in the neighboring province of Upper California a similar decline occurred.

Mortality in the missions.—Since disease is the proximate cause of many deaths under all human conditions, we may begin with a con-

---

[1] S. F. Cook, *The Extent and Significance of Disease among the Indians of Baja California, 1697–1773,* Univ. Calif. Publ., Ibero-Americana, No. 12 (Berkeley, 1937).

[13]

sideration of the mortality figures in the missions.[2] Certain points merit
particular emphasis.

From the earliest birth records and also from the results of careful
extrapolation of the graph of the mission birth rate it appears highly
probable that the gentile, or wild Indian, birth rate was approximately
45–50 per thousand per year. Now there is no reason to suppose, on
any grounds whatever, that the premission or aboriginal population
was suffering a material decline in numbers. Therefore the premission
death rate must have equaled the birth rate. At least, it can have been
no higher. This would imply a death rate of, let us say, 50 per thousand.
But from the data it appears that the earliest mission death rate was
definitely greater: approximately 70 per thousand as a mean for the
decade 1774–1784, with the rate for the lowest year 54 per thousand.
Granting some statistical inaccuracy due to relatively small numbers
and possible errors of count and record, it is evident that the mortality
jumped during the process of missionization. Part of this increment,
but not all, was due to disease.

Throughout the life of the missions the mean death rate mounted
steadily, reaching a peak in the decade 1800–1810, then gradually declined so that at the end it was the same as, or perhaps slightly lower
than, at the beginning. The annual rates show, furthermore, a series
of marked fluctuations, reaching in 1806 a maximum of 170 deaths
per thousand. These annual fluctuations are of great significance because they indicate relatively rapid changes in death rate which can be
referred most plausibly to health conditions. No other factor—aside
from war, which did not exist, and natural calamities, of which there
were none—can induce such swift and reversible increases in mortality. The years of minimal mortality, if this argument is valid, represent the most healthy years, those in which major or minor epidemics
were absent. We may, then, draw an arbitrary line on the graph, con-
necting these minima, and say that the mortality shown above this
line certainly represents the effect of disease.

On the other hand, even in the best of times there was considerable
illness—endemic, residual, or chronic—which raised the death rate.

---

[2] The data are those used in Cook, *Population Trends* (1940), *ibid.*, No. 17. They were
derived in turn from the records of mission censuses in the Bancroft Library, Berkeley.

In fact, in the wild state itself a large proportion of the deaths was due to disease. But what we may term the "natural" component—the amount of illness to which any race is subject under the most ideal conditions—is included in the probable basic death rate of approximately 50 per thousand. The remainder may be called the "artificial" component: the excess over the wild or original mortality directly referable to the new conditions imposed by the unnatural environment, in this instance, the mission. The artificial component here is represented quantitatively in the difference between the minimum mission death rate, and the wild death rate.

Let it be noted particularly at this point that the artificial residual disease component is represented *in* this difference and not *by* it. If the latter expression were employed, the implication could be that the mortality involved was due entirely and exclusively to disease, whereas there is no evidence, at present at least, for assuming that this was so. There undoubtedly were numerous nondisease factors which, operating steadily over long periods, increased the mission death rate directly or indirectly. It is impossible to determine at the present juncture, or perhaps ever, the exact fraction of the difference which may be ascribed to the effects of bad health. Nevertheless, some numerical expression is highly desirable. A conservative, but purely arbitrary, estimate would be one-third, or, say, 35 per cent. Since we possess no rigid information like that available in studies of contemporary epidemiology and vital statistics, this value may be employed with the assurance that it does not too greatly misrepresent the actual situation.

We may, then, break down the data for each year as follows:

Causes of Death   *Death Rate*

Wild or natural incidence of disease and other causes . . . . . 50 per thousand
Mission or artificial incidence of
    disease and other causes . . . . Excess over 50 per thousand
   Endemic or residual disease plus
    other long-term causes . . . . Average of the minimum
                                        for the period minus 50
      Endemic or residual disease, 35 per cent
      Other causes, 65 per cent
   Epidemics plus local or temporary
       intensifications of endemics . . . . . . Excess over the average of the
                                       minimum for the period

Under ordinary circumstances, with a geographically stable population the decline over a certain period is simply the numerical difference between the total number of persons living at the beginning and end of the period. Here, however, we are dealing with an aggregation of individuals which arose *de novo* in the year 1769–1770, increased from zero to a maximum, and then diminished slightly until the end of the period in 1834. At this date the population, as a mission group, suddenly ceased to exist. The actual census figures for the period therefore show, not a diminution, but an augmentation from 0 to 14,910. It is necessary therefore to use the difference between the number of births and deaths to demonstrate what was happening to the population in the missions.[3] From the available data we find that from 1779 to 1833, there were 29,100 births and 62,600 deaths.[4] The excess of deaths over births was then 33,500, indicating an extremely rapid population decline.

If now, according to the suggestions made above, we arbitrarily set the most probable wild or natural birth and death rates each at 50 per thousand (see tabulation above), then for the number of persons involved there should have been 40,000 births and 40,000 deaths. The fact that only three-quarters of the predictable births actually occurred is referable to the low and declining birth rate (32 per thousand in 1833). Of the 62,600 deaths, 40,000 correspond to the expected wild or natural mortality, leaving 22,600 to be accounted for as due to the effect of mission life. If we utilize the periodic minimal death rates as set forth above and calculate for each year the difference between the minimum and 5 per cent of the population, we get the figures for the mortality due to endemic, residual disease and other causes. The total number of deaths for the 64-year period amounts to 11,300; 35 per cent of this total is 3,950.

The remainder, likewise 11,300, represents the results of epidemics or recurrent intensifications of commonly present illness. The total

---

[3] The increase, apart from births, was due to conversion of wild Indians, or really to immigration. There were approximately 83,400 Indians baptized, of whom only 29,100 were actually born under mission auspices, leaving 54,000 immigrants.

[4] The figures prior to 1779 involve relatively small numbers of persons, for whom the births cannot be calculated with much accuracy. It has seemed better, therefore, to omit the first decade entirely. Furthermore, in all calculations the numbers are rounded off to the nearest hundred since the last two digits have no statistical significance.

which may be definitely and directly attributed to disease is 15,250, or 45 per cent of the net population decrease. No claim is made to absolute accuracy, but if the underlying assumptions are in any measure correct, this value must indicate at least the order of magnitude of the disease effect.[8]

The time curve of the disease effect, in particular the nonepidemic component, is also of interest. If we examine the absolute numbers of deaths annually to be ascribed to this factor, we find a steady increase to a maximum in the decade 1800–1810, followed by a decline. Thus the course of the total death rate is quite closely approximated. It is probable that two closely related factors were operative: the high susceptibility of new immigrants and the selective action of the disease itself on the population. In the beginning, all or most of the mission inhabitants were nonimmune recent converts. As time went on, however, the number of converts in relation to the total mission population decreased, almost to the vanishing point in the years 1830–1834. On this basis alone one would expect the incidence of chronic disease to be at a maximum at first and to decline steadily. But the absolute number of new conversions increased consistently until about 1805, and then fell off rapidly. From 1770 to 1805, therefore, the number of susceptible newcomers increased more rapidly than the selected, partially immunized survivors of the old population. Subsequently the situation reversed itself, and from 1805 to 1834 the mission Indians as a group were consistently gaining resistance to the common imported diseases. Yet whenever a new disease, such as measles, smallpox, or cholera, arrived, it swept through the entire population irrespective of individual origin.

With these general conclusions derived from examination of the population records, we may turn to the contemporary documents for detail regarding certain other points.

Epidemics.—Of true epidemics carrying off hundreds or thousands in a few weeks or months there were remarkably few in Upper California. In fact, there was only one of really great extent, and perhaps

---

[8] With respect to disease Upper California seemed to resemble Lower California. Thus the estimated proportion of deaths attributable to disease in both regions was probably somewhere between 35 and 50 per cent. In both, epidemics and chronic or endemic ailments were of approximately equal weight as lethal factors.

two of moderate intensity. This situation contrasts forcibly with that in Lower California where at least five serious epidemics occurred within a comparable period of time.[*] Perhaps one might be tempted to fall into conventional ways and ascribe the relative immunity of California to the salubrity of its far-famed climate. At the same time one must remember that commerce with the outside world was very small, that the West Coast was for many years almost completely closed to immigration, and, finally, that a watchful military government together with a competent and vigilant clergy closed the door to every obvious source of infection.

The first notice of epidemic diseases in Upper California was contained in the works of Father Palóu who mentions one in the vicinity of Santa Clara in 1777:[7]

By the month of May of the same year (1777) the first baptisms took place, for as there had come upon the people a great epidemic, the Fathers were able to perform a great many baptisms by simply going through the villages. In this way they succeeded in sending a great many children (which died almost as soon as they were baptized) to Heaven.

However, no details are given of the territorial extent, the numbers affected, or the type of disease.

No other record of a real epidemic occurs until 1802, when the inhabitants of the missions from San Carlos to San Luis Obispo were affected by some respiratory ailment. The children were the victims, to the almost entire exclusion of adults.[8] The illness was variously

---

[*] All these were of insignificant proportions when compared with what took place on the mainland both in early days and more modern times. One need think only of the terrific scourges of the sixteenth century to appreciate the difference: smallpox, *matlazahuatl*, typhoid among the Aztecs killed literally millions. In 1779 and 1797 in Central Mexico smallpox alone must have accounted for half a million deaths. On the Atlantic Coast, in New England, prior to 1620, smallpox is estimated to have reduced the Indian population by 90 per cent.

[7] Francisco Palóu, *Life of Junípero Serra* (Mexico, 1787), translated by C. S. Williams (1913), p. 213. Also cf. Palóu, *Historical Memoirs of New California,* Bolton translation (Berkeley, 1926), IV:161.

[8] Carrillo to Arrillaga, Monterey, Jan. 20, 1802, Prov. St. Pap., 18:194; Carrillo to Arrillaga, Monterey, Feb. 27, 1802, *ibid.,* p. 190; Carrillo, Monterey "Diario," Feb. 28, 1802, *ibid.,* p. 193; the governor to the *comandante* of Monterey, Loreto, Apr. 9, 1802, Prov. Rec., 11:167; Carrillo to Arrillaga, Monterey, June 30, 1802, Prov. St. Pap., 18:170; "Informe de San Carlos," 1804, Arch. Mis. Pap. Orig., 1:306; Tapis to Arrillaga, Santa Bárbara, Mar. 1, 1805, Sta. Bárb. Arch., 6:28–35.

described as *"fuertes dolores de cabeza," "cerramiento de garganta,"* *"pulmonía y dolor de costado," "dolor de costado," "fuertes calenturas, toz y dolores de cabeza."* Clearly pneumonia and apparently diphtheria ·(*cerramiento de garganta*) are indicated. The greatest mortality was at Soledad with "many Christians and gentiles" and "more than seventy dead in that mission." "Great havoc" was also caused at Monterey and San Luis Obispo. At the peak of the epidemic at Soledad five or six died each day. Perhaps two to three hundred was the mortality at all the missions involved.

In 1806 occurred the first measles epidemic, by far the most serious witnessed in mission days. This was a clear example of a newly introduced malady attacking a fresh, unprotected population. Its mode of introduction is unknown (probably from Mexico by an incoming ship), but its spread was very rapid, and the damage very great among both children and adults. It was reported from San Francisco that from April 24 to June 27 the deaths had reached 234 in number, 163 adults and 71 children.[9] In Santa Bárbara during December, 44 neophytes died in 15 days.[10] The total mortality may be reckoned from the general censuses. In 1806 the deaths in excess of the mean of the years 1805 and 1807 were 1,800. If we allow 200 as being due to other causes, we may still ascribe 1,600 to measles. The total population for 1806 was given at 18,665, a decrease of 1,693 from the previous year. But in 1806 there were 1,572 baptisms. Hence the effective reduction was 3,265. Granting half this as being due to measles, we again have a mortality of about 1,600. Although the adults were hard hit, the children suffered most. The mean child death rate in 1806 for all the missions was 335 per thousand. In San Francisco alone it was 880, the population under ten years of age being almost completely wiped out.[11]

---

[9] Abella, in the *libro de misión* for San Francisco, June 27, 1806 (extracts by Savage in Bancroft Library).

[10] Carrillo to Arrillaga, Santa Bárbara, Dec. 31, 1806, Prov. St. Pap. Ben. Mil., 35:14.

[11] At about this time or a little earlier occurred a queer disease called *"el latido,"* which apparently was not widespread or particularly fatal. According to Bancroft (*California Pastoral* [*History of California*, vol. 34], p. 617), who took his information from Langsdorff, it began with pulsation in the lower belly followed by cramps and pain in the neck region. Cephas Bard (*Contribution to the History of Medicine in Southern California* [1894], p. 28) says it was "palpitation of the heart" but "was always referred to the epigastrium." Many guesses have been made as to what *"el latido"* really was, but its nature has never been ascertained satisfactorily.

For the next twenty years no outstanding epidemic occurred, although the diseases already present flared up occasionally. About 1827, however, there was a recrudescence of measles, which, although of moderate intensity, did not approach the severity of the first outbreak. From the census figures it may be estimated that the mission mortality amounted to several hundred, perhaps a thousand. The incidence was spotty, the child death rate, which reached 577 per thousand at San Juan Bautista and 524 at Santa Clara, being quite low elsewhere. At San Diego it was noted that the measles had caused "some" deaths among the white population and "more damage" among the Indians.[12] At San Buenaventura measles appeared at the end of 1827 and lasted till March, 1928. Many adults and children died, but "many more adults died of syphilis."[13]

By the end of the decade 1820–1830 California was coming into much closer contact with the outside world; probably associated with this increased external intercourse, several new diseases appeared, which at times became epidemic in their scope. Since the missions were secularized in 1834 and for practical purposes ceased to function, the effects of these recent introductions cannot be considered with respect to the missions themselves. They may, however, be mentioned. In 1833 for the first time there was an alarming amount of smallpox.[14] Scarlet fever may have been introduced along with other "contagious fevers,"[15] and it is certain that cholera reached menacing proportions in 1834.

Even though the missions were only lightly touched by large-scale epidemics, they suffered heavily from general illness and periodic semi-epidemics. Wholly aside from the evidence of the census reports discussed previously, we have many contemporary statements which tend to support this conclusion.

As early as 1787 it was recognized officially that there was much illness in the missions. Governor Pedro Fages wrote in that year regarding Mission San Antonio.

---

[12] Census, Aug. 26, 1827, St. Pap. Mis., 5:25.

[13] Ordaz, "Informe Anual," San Buenaventura, Dec. 31, 1828, Archb. Arch., 1:48.

[14] S. F. Cook, "Smallpox in Spanish and Mexican California, 1770–1845," *Bull. Hist. Med.* (1939), 7:153–191.

[15] G. D. Lyman, "The Scalpel under Three Flags in California," Calif. Hist. Soc., *Quarterly* (1925), 4:142.

It is this climate, in which are observed particularly extremes of heat and cold, which may be responsible for the frequent illness and deaths which have been experienced . . . [and concerning San Carlos] many and frequent are the deaths occurring among the neophytes."[16]

In 1794 Arrillaga pointed out that the increase in the size of the missions was more apparent than real, because "some of the missions are suffering from sicknesses which are causing considerable damage."[17] Two years later Borica commented that the bad state of the neophytes was partially due to the *"efluvios pestiferos* which spread from one to the other in their villages and the buildings where the unmarried men and women sleep."[18] It is thus clear that before the missions were twenty-five years old illness had become sufficiently noticeable to attract the attention of the governors.

Beginning in 1797 we have an incomplete series of annual reports from presidial commanders to the governor. These usually contained a statement on the community health. Thus for 1797 Grajera from San Diego said, "there have been no unusual or epidemic diseases."[19] Goycoechea reported from Santa Bárbara "many cases of typhoid and pneumonia . . . many have died of consumption, which misfortune is very common and principally among the Indians."[20] From San Francisco Argüello reported ". . . an epidemic among the neophytes of whom several died."[21] The following year there was an appearance of *"catarro"* at Santa Bárbara[22] which did not appear to be particularly fatal. Fatalities from dysentery, however, occurred at San Diego. Three years later "contagious fevers" are described from Los Angeles "which are doing great damage to the natives at San Gabriel and San Juan Capistrano."[23] In 1803 there were "unknown diseases which killed various Indians,"[24] followed by "colds and fevers"[25] in 1804 and "diarrhoea, vomiting, and other ailments such as belly ache and fever."

---

[16] Fages, "Informe general sobre misiones," St. Pap. Mis. and Col., 1:124.

[17] Arrillaga, "Informe," Sept. 9, 1794, St. Pap. Mis., 1:127.

[18] Borica, "Estado general de las misiones ... en 1795," Aug. 24, 1796, *ibid.*, 2:73.

[19] Grajera to Borica, June 30, 1797, St. Pap. Sac., 6:102.

[20] Goycoechea to Borica, Dec. 31, 1797, *ibid.*, p. 100.

[21] Argüello to Borica, Dec. 31, 1797, *ibid.*

[22] Borica to Goycoechea, Feb. 11, 1798, Prov. Rec., 4:99.

[23] Rodríguez, "Statement," San Diego, Jan. 10, 1801, Prov. St. Pap. Ben. Mil., 29:3.

[24] Argüello, "Informe," Dec. 31, 1803, St. Pap. Mis., 3:40.

[25] Carrillo, "Informe," June 30, 1804, *ibid.*, p. 50; also Prov. St. Pap. Ben. Mil., 34:12.

The year 1805 was a good one but nevertheless there appeared "severe constipation with fever and headache . . . from which several Indian children died";[26] also "consumption, bloody dysentery, and other unknown diseases among the neophytes from which they die with frequency."[27] In 1807 Argüello again stated that the "predominant diseases are syphilis, dysentery, and tuberculosis,"[28] which accounted for the extremely small increase in population. Fathers Miguel and Zalvidea in their reply to certain charges made against the missions affirmed that "the missions have three times as many sick as in other times," that the hospital at San Gabriel contained from three to four hundred patients and that

. . . granting that in all the missions there are many more patients than formerly, nevertheless it is certain that the Physician of Monterey said that in no other mission—even without having seen half the patients—were there so many as in this one.[29]

In subsequent years similar reports were made with monotonous regularity describing the death of the neophytes from consumption, dysentery, and pneumonia (or perhaps influenza). A few samples will suffice to establish the trend through the remainder of the mission era. In 1811 the president of the missions, Father Señan wrote: "The most dominant diseases are syphilis, tuberculosis, and dysenteries."[30] Again, regarding San Francisco:

The births scarcely correspond to a third part of the deaths, even in years when there is no epidemic. But in a year like 1806, when there was a simple epidemic of measles, more than three hundred died and twenty-three were born.

Six years later the succeeding president, Father Sarría, discussed the alarming population decrease which he said was going on "without there being recognizable any particular pest or epidemic apart from the regular diseases which are almost always present."[31]

Syphilis.—Without doubt the most important single component of

---

[26] Carrillo to Arrillaga, Santa Bárbara, June 30, 1805, *ibid.*, p. 27.
[27] Argüello to Arrillaga, San Francisco, Dec. 31, 1805, *ibid.*, p. 22.
[28] Argüello to Arrillaga, San Francisco, Dec. 31, 1807, *ibid.*, 37:38.
[29] Miguel and Zalvidea, San Gabriel, May 24, 1810, Sta. Bárb. Arch., 9:191–196.
[30] Señan, "Contestación al interrogatorio del ano 1811," *ibid.*, 7:112–216.
[31] Sarría, "Informe sobre frailes de California," November, 1817, *ibid.*, 3:39–93.

this entire disease complex was syphilis. Indeed, so widespread and so devastating in its effects was venereal disease that it merits extended consideration. Among the natives of Lower California, and in direct contrast with the inhabitants of the west coast of the mainland, syphilis was universal in its occurrence and extremely severe in its effects.[32] Upper California seems to have resembled Lower California rather than the mainland in this respect, although in the Franciscan missions of the north the disease may not have been so fatal, or its external manifestations so striking as in the older Jesuit missions of the southern peninsula. In both regions one might be inclined to discount the severity of the disease on grounds of exaggeration by those on the scene, were it not—and this is particularly true of Upper California—that there is absolute unanimity of opinion and emphasis on the part of priest and layman, soldier and civilian, contemporary reporter and later raconteur. After reviewing the evidence, one is impelled to the conclusion that venereal disease constituted one of the prime factors not only in the actual decline, but also in the moral and social disintegration of the population. These effects cannot be strictly assessed in numerical terms, but their weight can be appreciated if some of the evidence is reviewed.

Syphilis appeared in Upper California certainly within the first decade of settlement.[33] The conventional story, which may or may not have been true, attributed its introduction to the Anza expedition to Los Angeles in 1777. Thus Miguel and Zalvidea state that this "putrid and contagious disease had its beginning with the time Don Juan Bautista de Anza stopped at the mission San Gabriel with his expedition."[34] However, it may not be fair to lay the blame entirely on Anza's troops since there were numerous other means of introduction. The expeditionary force of Portolá in 1769 and other troops entering the country were without doubt heavily infected, not to speak of the early civilian settlers. Indeed, irrespective of the social status of the immigrants, it would have been a miracle had the country

---

[32] Cook, *Extent and Significance of Disease among the Indians of Baja California*, pp. 29 ff.

[33] In Lower California the disease was successfully excluded for at least forty years after the first mission was founded. Once introduced, however, it spread with extreme rapidity through the well-organized establishments.

[34] Miguel and Zalvidea, San Gabriel, Mar. 17, 1810, Sta. Bárb. Arch., 9:184–187.

escaped the pest.[35] Once introduced, the spread was an easy matter. The relations of the soldiers with the Indian women were notorious, despite the most energetic efforts of both officers and clergy to prevent immorality. In fact, the entire problem of sexual relations between the whites and the natives, although one which was regarded as very serious by the founders of the province, has apparently escaped detailed consideration by later historians, both Californian and American.

The very first expeditions were characterized by disorderly conduct with the Indian women on the part of the soldiers. The following significant excerpts are from the diary of Pedro Font in 1776.[36]

The extortions and outrages which the soldiers have perpetrated when in their journeys they have passed along the Channel, especially in the beginning (p. 252).

[The Channel Indians] are displeased with the Spaniards, because of [the latter's] taking away their fish and their food to provision themselves . . . now stealing their women and abusing them (p. 256).

The women [at San Luis Obispo] are affable and friendly . . . a reason why the soldiers were so disorderly with them when they remained in this vicinity for a time [i.e., during the halt of the Portolá expedition] (p. 271).

There were also numerous desertions, the soldiers going away to live among the natives and, of course, carrying their venereal disease to spread among their hosts. Thus Junípero Serra in his representation of 1773 asks a general pardon for all deserters:

. . . if any of them should yet be found scattered among the heathen, so that the danger of inquietude among the heathen and the perdition of the wretched wanderers and Christian renegades may be avoided. . . ."[37]

In 1773 a case of rape occurred in San Luis Obispo and in 1774 there were two cases at Monterey. By 1777 conditions had become bad in the south.[38] The soldiers at San Gabriel and San Juan Capistrano "go

---

[35] In 1798 Governor Borica wrote the viceroy (Prov. Rec., 6:92) that "there arrived at Monterey the new settlers for the town of Branciforte—destitute and some afflicted with syphilis."

[36] Fr. Pedro Font, *Diary of an Expedition to Monterey . . . 1775–1776,* translated by Bolton in *Anza's California Expeditions* (Berkeley, 1930), Vol. IV.

[37] Palóu, *New California,* Bolton transl., Vol. III.

[38] Ortega, San Diego, July 11, 1777, St. Pap. Sac., 8:31–52.

at night to the nearby villages to assault the heathen women." Four men confessed to several of these delinquencies, and the missionaries of San Juan Capistrano charged that the soldiers of the guard went so far as to beat the gentiles to make them disclose where their women were hidden. A few years later Governor Fages issued an order to the effect that:

The officers and men of these presidios are conducting and behaving themselves in the missions with a vicious license which is very prejudicial on account of the scandalous disorders which they commit with the gentile and Christian women. I adjure you to prevent the continuance of such dangerous behavior . . . inflicting severe penalties upon those who are guilty.[39]

The civilian settlers were no better. For instance, with respect to the founders of the city of San José:[40]

From that time (1782) the evil influence of the settlers began to be felt . . . the disgraceful conduct with regard to the heathen and bad example to the neophytes because of the brutality and violence exercised by these settlers on their women.

Even to the end of missionization complaints continued. In 1839 Inspector Hartnell remarked upon a certain white man "who had given venereal disease to many women of the mission."[41]

There is no need for further multiplication of instances. From those already given it will be clear that from the time the Spanish first set foot in California there was ample opportunity for the introduction of syphilis to the native population, not at one but at very many places. Indeed, since there were soldiers stationed at every mission, since the troops were continually moving around from one place to another, and since this military group was itself generously infected, the introduction may be regarded as wholesale and substantially universal.

Given the conditions of contact just outlined, a steady and rapid infiltration of venereal disease among the mission Indians was no more

---

[39] Fages to González, Monterey, July 1, 1785, *ibid.,* 2:43.

[40] Fr. Tomás de la Peña to the viceroy, "Detalles sobre la fundación ... el pueblo de San José," Colegio de San Fernando, July 27, 1798, St. Pap. Mis. and Col., 1:45.

[41] Hartnell, "Informe," San Antonio, Aug. 7, 1839, Hartnell "Diario," p. 37.

Other accounts will be found in the following: Prov. St. Pap., 9:107 (1789); *ibid.,* p. 121 (1789); *ibid.,* 10:151 ff. (1791); *ibid.,* 13:42 (1795); Prov. Rec., 4:145 (1796); Archb. Arch., 5:101 (1833). These by no means exhaust the list.

than might be expected. This undoubtedly occurred, but it apparently took a full generation for the situation to become really serious. It is noteworthy that in 1791, at least twenty years after the disease first arrived, Fages was able to contrast the "decadent condition" of the old missions (i.e., those in Baja California), which he ascribed to syphilis, with the "flourishing and progressive" state of the new ones.[42] However, Governor Borica, in his report for the year 1793–1794, mentions that there is much syphilis in the missions.[43] From this point on few statements of health conditions failed to mention syphilis. The precise extent of the malady with respect to numbers of persons involved is difficult to estimate; here, as in so many other instances, we are forced to rely upon the word of contemporary witnesses, who were much impressed but who may have been prone to some exaggeration. The following statements are pertinent and have a cumulative value even if their individual reliability may not be high:

Most Indian deaths are due to syphilis.[44]

The dominant diseases of the Indians are syphilis, of a very malignant type, and dysentery . . .[45]

The most dominant disease is syphilis, of which a considerable number die. . . .[46]

They are permeated to the marrow of their bones with venereal disease, such that many of the newly born show immediately this, the only patrimony they receive from their parents, and for which reason three-quarters of the infants die in their first or second year, and of the other quarter which survives, most fail to reach their twenty-fifth year.[47]

There are [in San Francisco] no good Indian boatmen—those who might be available are in great part attacked by syphilis . . .[48]

. . . according to his opinion the Indians are dying of syphilis; many have the lesions, and others have it internally . . .[49]

. . . That to the question he has been asked as to why the Indians die: he

---

[42] Fages, "Papel de varios puntos concernientes al Gobierno de la Peninsula de California," Feb. 26, 1791, Prov. St. Pap., 10:151.

[43] Borica, July 13, 1795, St. Pap. Mis., vol. 2.

[44] Carrillo, "Informe," Santa Bárbara, June 30, 1804, St. Pap. Mis., 3:50.

[45] "Contestación al interrogatorio del ano 1811," Sta. Bárb. Arch., 7:112–216.

[46] *Ibid.*

[47] *Ibid.*

[48] Abella to Argüello, San Francisco, Sept. 30, 1815, Archb. Arch., 2:102.

[49] Abella to Solá, San Francisco, July 31, 1817, *ibid.*, 3:146.

will reply, as a priest that he does not know, but as a physician he will say that they are very much contaminated and this malady syphilis is incurable among them.[50]

He speaks of a syphilitic Indian and says that in his opinion one of the reasons why they are practically all dying of this terrible malady is that the missions lack all medicines and there is no other physician than the Providence of God.[51]

. . . there are twenty-seven fugitives; of the others some are afflicted with chronic ailments and the rest mostly infected with the venereal virus.[52]

Perhaps as a result of the fine climate and small population epidemics and contagions are little known, except that among the neophytes venereal diseases are devouring them horribly . . .[53]

From these and many similar documents one receives the impression that syphilis among the mission Indians might be described as a totalitarian disease, universally incident. Perhaps this would be an extreme view. Perhaps there were some who were able to avoid the infection, but this must have been rare in communities so generally unsanitary, so crowded, and so characterized by sexual promiscuity as the missions. Even granting a fair number of exceptions, the mass effect of venereal disease upon the population must have been tremendous and must have made itself felt in a multitude of ways.

The number of those whose death was directly attributable to syphilis may not have been great, although there is some divergence of opinion concerning this point.[54] Some of the citations quoted previ-

---

[50] Abella to Solá, San Francisco, Jan. 29, 1817, *ibid.,* p. 125.

[51] Gil to Solá, 1818, *ibid.,* p. 43.

[52] "Informe de Santa Cruz," Dec. 31, 1825, Arch. Mis., 1:852.

[53] Victoria, "Informe general sobre California," Monterey, June 7, 1831, Dept. Rec., 9:132.

[54] There has been a certain amount of confusion in the minds of some modern historians regarding the precise effects of syphilis. Bancroft (*California Pastoral,* chap. 20) states that by 1805 syphilis "with scrofula and consumption" killed hundreds annually. Cephas Bard, a physician himself, ascribed the high mortality to such causes as "zymotic diseases, syphilis, tuberculosis and intemperance" (*op. cit.,* p. 12). Hittell (*History of California,* Vol. I) holds syphilis responsible for the very high death rate (p. 743) and then declares (p. 787) that "it had not among the Indians the terrible character which it has assumed amongst civilized peoples . . . nor was it until the introduction of spirituous liquors that it became aggravated into the deadly scourge which decimated and in some cases *almost of itself* exterminated whole tribes." Before the advent of spirituous liquors, he says, "the affected aborigines were able to continue their usual avocations without any great inconvenience . . ."; truly a remarkable situation, particularly since, until 1834, intoxication was held by the missionaries at a very low level indeed.

ously and various others which might be adduced seem to suggest many deaths from syphilis. But it is probable that often, when a syphilitic person succumbed for any more or less obscure cause, the demise was uncritically attributed to the venereal disease. However, many Indians may actually have died as a result of the disease itself. It is rather difficult to discount completely eye-witness accounts, even though they may be made by uninformed and possibly prejudiced individuals. Some credence must be given the repeated assertions that the Indians were *dying* from syphilis.

Though the direct mortality from this cause may not have been as high as might be implied by contemporary statements, the secondary effects were undoubtedly of great significance. A population thoroughly saturated with venereal disease will fall easier prey to other maladies, whether the latter be chronic or epidemic, and there can be no question that this increased susceptibility accounts for at least part of the virulence displayed by pneumonia, tuberculosis, and other ailments. If we allow for the debilitating action of syphilis, we may ascribe to it responsibility for much of the mortality included in the category of endemic or residual disease discussed above, together with their sporadically epidemic outbursts. It was pointed out that roughly 45 per cent of the net population decrease, or 15,250 deaths, might be attributed to disease. Of this number, no more than 3,000 can have been due to the measles and other swift, clearly recognizable epidemics. The remainder, say 12,250, were caused by the standard general maladies, consumption, dysentery, typhoid, and the like, including syphilis. To formulate the problem in concrete terms, we might refer between 1,000 and 5,000 of these deaths directly or indirectly to venereal disease. This would mean 1.5–8 per cent of the total mission deaths, 4.5–22 per cent of the effective population reduction, and 6.5–33 per cent of the reduction due to disease. Although these figures can in no wise be considered accurate in the mathematical sense, they probably fairly represent the scope of syphilis as a factor in destroying the mission-Indian population.

Although the primary and immediate effect of venereal disease was on the death rate, the question arises of its influence on the birth rate. The relationship here, if any, appears to be somewhat complex. As mentioned previously, although the crude birth rate steadily declined during the mission period, the fertility rate (i.e., the number of births per thousand women) remained very constant. This was obtained by relating the number of mission births to the number of adult women as given in the annual census reports. Now if syphilis, or any other factor, seriously reduced the actual conceiving or bearing capacity of the women, the fertility rate should have diminished in conformity. The observed facts were explained by means of the falling sex ratio. The latter, after some irregularities in the first decade, due probably to unequal conversion of the sexes, underwent a very steady and consistent increase until 1834. At that date the ratio of men to women was between the limits 1:35–1:50. Therefore, the relative number of women in the population decreased at substantially the same rate as the unadjusted number of births, a finding entirely consistent with the unchanging fertility rate. In view of these facts, we are almost forced to conclude that venereal disease did not reduce reproductive power among the mission Indians. Such a conclusion is of rather striking significance. It is at variance with general opinions, both contemporary and modern, since it implies that actual conception and delivery were not materially affected by widespread and severe incidence of syphilis. The additional explanation has been offered (based also upon the census records) that, since the sex ratio among newly born infants and children was invariably near 1:00, the shifting sex ratio among adults was due to a differential death rate, the women dying younger or in greater numbers than the men. Such an unequal mortality might be ascribed to a greater susceptibility among women to common ailments, to a possible difference in living conditions, or to a higher incidence and greater virulence of syphilis in women. If this last theory were true, then syphilis might be considered as having contributed, in a secondary and remote fashion, to the declining crude birth rate.

Though it is not possible to assess the importance of venereal disease, as opposed to other diseases, in its effect on crude birth rate, nevertheless we may form a general estimate of the significance of disease in this connection. As previously pointed out, the net diminution of population, as expressed in terms of excess of deaths over births was 33,600. As contrasted with the probable state of the population, had it not been missionized, it was computed that of this number there were 22,600 more deaths and 11,000 less births than there would have been in the aboriginal condition. Of these, 15,250 deaths were attributed directly to disease of all types. This, then, accounts for 45 per cent of the net population decrease. But if the indirect influence of venereal and other disease on the birth rate, through the differential sex mortality, be considered, the estimate must be revised upward. The birth deficiency of 11,000 amounts to approximately 30 per cent of the total. Purely arbitrarily, let us assume that one-half this deficiency may be ascribed to the effect just noted, whereas the other half was due to other causes. Then disease immediately and remotely may be held responsible for not 45 but 60 per cent of the net population decrease.

Environmental factors in disease.—We may regard disease as a basic factor in the contact relation between any two races or species, such as those with which we are here dealing. This is particularly true of new maladies introduced by the new, invading race with which the established race has had no experience. Yet, aside from the lack of immunity thus assumed, the intensity of the disease factor may and will be conditioned by subsidiary or secondary factors contingent upon the new environment. Although most of these, in the missions, cannot be discussed in detail at the present juncture, their existence merits at least cursory mention.

1. Sexual relations. This matter has already been touched upon in connection with the introduction and spread of venereal disease. It was pointed out that personal contact of this type was very common between whites and natives. It need only be added that, aside from the marital status, promiscuity was extensive among the Indians themselves. In fact, there was no obstacle whatever, except the unfortunately futile zeal of the missionaries, to the wholesale dissemination of the pest.

2. Aggregation. With respect to nonvenereal disease, contagion was enormously facilitated by the custom of gathering large numbers of Indians in one place. Under aboriginal conditions the native group was seldom larger than one hundred, and frequently less. In the missions several hundred or even one or two thousand were congregated

in a single set of buildings. They ate together, worked together, and even slept together, in close quarters. Once a microörganism was introduced, the chances for infection were vastly greater than under the gentile system.

3. Intercommunication. In contrast to the wild state, there was a great deal of moving around from one mission to the other, from the mission to the outlying villages, from the mission to the nearest presidio, and finally up and down the whole length of the coast. Infection could thus be transported with the greatest ease from one center of population to the other.

4. Change of climate. Although at the outset most mission inmates were natives of the adjacent territory, as the establishments expanded, many were brought in from considerable distances. As a rule, with the exception of those in the Salinas Valley, the missions were located on or near the coast, and were hence subject to the cool, damp, foggy seashore climate. Indians brought here from the hills and valleys of the drier and warmer interior would doubtless have to become acclimated in the purely literal sense. During the process they would be somewhat more prone to infection than normally. Even the Spanish were impressed by this fact. Again and again in their reports they ascribed the unhealthy state of the neophytes, particularly with reference to tuberculosis, to the climate and pointed out that the maximum illness appeared to coincide with the rainy season of late winter and spring. In a very general way, although no rigid correlation is possible, one may detect a higher mean death rate in those missions situated near the shore than in near-by establishments farther inland. A few specimen opinions concerning the role of the climate with respect to disease may be cited:

[The climate] is generally healthy, more for the Spaniards than for the innumerable heathen who inhabit it . . .[55]

According to observation this climate is remarkably extreme with respect to both cold and heat from which may result the frequent illness and death which we are wont to experience.[56]

Most of the summer there were heavy fogs and when they departed the

---

[55] Author unknown (probably Fages), "Relación del temperamento de 1785," Monterey, Dec. 31, 1785, Prov. Rec., 2:116.

[56] Fages, "Informe general sobre las misiones, 1787," St. Pap. Mis. and Col., 1:124.

sun shone with excessive heat, from which extremes, in my judgment, originated many ailments . . ."[57]

. . . but since April the north and northeast winds blew more frequently, very dry and sickly, causing severe bowel complaints and fevers . . ."[58]

5. Bad sanitation. Apart from the factor of simple crowding, the life in the missions must have been anything but sanitary. In the independent family huts adjoining the mission the Indians were probably no worse off than when living in their own villages. However, the large rooms or compounds, where the unmarried men or women slept, must have been breeding-places for disease. With little ventilation, no heat, no protection from dampness in the rainy season, with the occupants packed in as closely as was humanly possible, it would have been amazing if respiratory infections had not been rampant. Thus a survivor of the period wrote:[59]

The Indians in their wandering life as savages enjoyed good health . . . Afterward very harmful to them was enclosure within infected walls, according to the system adopted by the missionaries . . . The walls usually were a yard thick and lacked necessary ventilation: imagine the odor which would emanate from those never-washed bodies, without being able to change the air.

Perhaps the above is an overstatement, and certainly the missionaries repeatedly and earnestly repudiated the idea that unhealthful or unsanitary conditions obtained in the enclosures. But the facts cannot be denied that scores of persons were kept at night in general rooms and that few hygienic measures were taken for their protection.

The neophytes received their food from large containers daily. Complaints were made, perhaps without justification, that the kitchenware was not kept clean. However, we must remember that the cooking and scullerywork were performed by neophytes, and it is altogether too much to imagine that the strictest supervision could induce these semisavages to maintain modern standards of cleanliness. Despite attempts to localize its distribution, sewage was disposed of according to the methods now prevalent in rural Mexico, that is, anywhere and everywhere. The water supply usually came from small streams

[57] Goycoechea to Borica, Santa Bárbara, Dec. 31, 1797, St. Pap. Mis., 2:103.
[58] Carrillo to Arrillaga, Santa Bárbara, June 30, 1805, Prov. St. Pap. Ben. Mil., 34:27.
[59] Antonio M. Osio, "Historia de California," MS, 1878, p. 216.

(which might disappear in a very dry season), small ponds, or wells. A more perfect arrangement for the spread of gastrointestinal disorders could scarcely be devised.[60]

6. Poor diet. The significance of diet will be discussed at length in a subsequent section. At this point it will suffice to say that, if the diet was actually defective, its deficiency undoubtedly operated as a factor predisposing to infectious disease.

7. Lack of treatment. Considering that from 1776 to 1825 there was only one qualified physician in all California and that the missionaries had no particular medical training, it is not surprising that the neophytes received treatment only on the rarest occasions.[61]

Included in the mission regime, to be sure, was an infirmary or hospital, which served actually only as a space for sick Indians—where they might rest and be made comfortable, to a limited extent. But since there were no supplies or medicines, real treatment and nursing could not very well be given them. The following excerpts probably give a substantially just picture of mission hospitalization:

Each mission had its infirmary, which consisted of a porch and some straw mats where the Indians might recline. Sometimes the Fathers themselves prescribed medicines . . .[62]

In the Mission of San Luis, at the request of the Reverend Father Fray Luis Martínez, in a hospital which he has for his neophytes, in which I found about thirty patients, the greater part being women, I found tuberculosis and syphilis . . .[63]

Many times [each year] I took the female, and some male, patients of the mission [San Diego] to Agua Caliente . . . and stayed there bathing and treating them for two months.[64]

---

[60] In justice to the missionaries it must be stated that the military and civilian establishments were just as bad as the missions, perhaps worse. Furthermore, sanitary science as we know it was unheard of at that day. In spite of the criticism by the military, it is remarkable that the missionaries were able to accomplish as much as they did, considering the scanty means at their disposal.

[61] The only specific instance known to me of a physician's giving any but the most casual attention to the disease problems among the Indians is that of José Benites in 1804 and 1805. He made a rather careful survey and administered relief to many patients. Cf. S. F. Cook, "California's First Medical Survey," *California and Western Medicine* (1936), Vol. 45, No. 4.

[62] A. F. Coronel, "Cosas de California," MS, 1878, p. 224.

[63] Benites, quoted in Cook, "California's First Medical Survey."

[64] Apolinaria Lorenzana, "Memorias," MS, 1878, p. 48.

In San Gabriel, San Juan Capistrano and San Luis Rey they have built mortuaries in the hospitals for the better accommodation and administration of the sick. We say hospitals because, all the Fathers realizing that the Indians are rapidly disappearing, mainly from dysentery and syphilis, they have taken the most energetic measures to halt the rapid spread of the evil. In many of the missions these hospitals have been set up in proportion to the means available to the priests who are using such facilities as are at hand. In spite of all this it is observed with grief that the results are not commensurate with expectations.[65]

. . . lack of fundamental treatment by a physician, for there is none. In all the missions there is an apothecary shop but this resource, managed without knowledge or method, far from being of use may be of harm, in a word it is of no value . . .[66]

Summary.—To summarize, the mission Indians' lack of immunity to introduced infection and their possibly inferior physique predisposed them to whatever new diseases happened to attack them. The effect of these diseases, in terms of population decline, was undoubtedly greater under the mission system than it would have been in the wild or natural state. This in turn was at least partially due to the unfavorable factors which characterized the physical and social environment imposed by the missions.

NUTRITION

A faulty or insufficient diet over a short or a long period can affect the welfare of a population in three ways. It can render the group increasingly sensitive to bacterial infection or disease through lowered general resistance. It can be accompanied by specific deficiency diseases, such as the avitaminoses. Finally, it can kill by pure lack of quantity or direct starvation. Over several generations, where a relatively slow but consistent decrease in numbers is observed, acute starvation may be ruled out, except in very unusual individual cases. At the same time a condition of either quantitative or qualitative inadequacy may exist, the influence of which is felt only slowly and obscurely. A priori we have no right to assume any inadequacy to have been present in the mission population, for a poor diet is not in the same category as infectious disease, which is almost certain to be

---

[65] Anon., "Tabla estadística," Dec. 31, 1818, Sta. Bárb. Arch., 10:302.
[66] Victoria, "Informe general sobre California," Monterey, June 7, 1831.

present following racial contact of this sort. The mode of attack on the problem, in a broad sense, must be twofold, involving the questions: (1) What was the diet of the neophytes, and would it be considered by modern criteria adequate; and (2), is there any evidence, immediate or remote, that the population suffered from nutritional deficiency. To answer these questions, it is necessary to examine with care all available information pertaining to food supply.

The entire food supply of the neophytes was derived from three primary sources.

1. The largest and most important was the grain raised by the missions themselves. Although there was some variation from one mission to another, four basic materials were included, corn, wheat, barley, and beans, with the first two always predominating in quantity. There was absolutely no importation of these crops; hence the Indians' supply was strictly limited to what the missions could produce.

2. The missions supplied all animal food, in the form of beef, tallow, and lard, from their own resources.

3. To an undetermined extent the neophytes continued to utilize their primitive or wild food: acorns, small seeds, grasses, insects, shellfish and the like. These materials, however, were invariably used as a supplement rather than as a staple dietary component.

Mission diet.—There are two primary sources of knowledge relating to mission diet. The first consists of annual crop and livestock reports or censuses, the second of numerous statements by contemporary observers. The former is fundamental and merits detailed consideration.

Each mission submitted annually a statement of the quantity of staple foods produced, primarily wheat, corn, barley, and beans, together with a scattering of minor crops. The returns were in the form of *fanegas* sown and fanegas harvested in each crop. There was also submitted a census showing the number of cattle, sheep, goats, pigs, horses, and mules in possession of the mission at the end of each year. The crop reports are more valuable for present purposes than the livestock censuses, since they give a better index to total diet.[87]

[87] These reports, which formerly existed in the California Archives, were destroyed in the San Francisco fire of 1906. However, they had been previously copied and tabu-

The mission grain crop, which, as previously stated, formed the primary component of the diet, can be determined from the crop reports with considerable accuracy, since the annual harvest in fanegas is stated for each type of plant. The total, then, for a given period of time represents the maximum available to a single mission or all the missions for that period. In other words, it is impossible that the Indians could have received more corn or wheat than was produced or harvested by the missions.[68] Starting then with the gross harvest, we must first deduct the amount, for each year, which was used the following year as seed. This will give the net harvest—that which could be used for food purposes. As might be expected in any agricultural community, there were enormous variations from year to year owing to the innumerable factors which make for success or failure in a crop. Hence the net harvest for any one year in a mission, or even for any one year in all the missions, has little significance. Presumably— and this is borne out by many statements—on the one hand, in good years reserves were built up and, on the other hand, in poor years shortages were made up by gifts or loans from more fortunate missions. It is necessary therefore to base conclusions on averages of large numbers of missions and years.[69] This enables us to arrive at certain broad generalizations, although we are forced to concede the possibility of all sorts of local and individual exceptions.

The first column of table 2 gives the means for the annual net crop by missions; the net crops for presidios and pueblos are also included for comparison. These numbers in themselves are of secondary significance, because we wish to know how much food was provided for the neophytes rather than the total crop as such. It is, however, possible to obtain some idea of the diet if the volume of grain is expressed in terms of calories. From the population tables we may first determine

---

lated carefully by the workers under H. H. Bancroft. These tabulations or transcripts, made in the 1870's, are still available in the Bancroft Library of the University of California and may be considered essentially accurate copies of the originals.

[68] The question might be raised of the possibility of contributions from the military or civil establishments to the missions, but there is no record of such a contribution. Indeed, the trend was exclusively in the other direction. The missions supplied large amounts of grain to the presidios and perhaps some to the pueblos.

[69] It may be stated here that attempts to show correlations between annual crop variations and vital statistics have been uniformly unsuccessful.

TABLE 2

FOOD SUPPLY OF THE MISSION

(Each item represents the annual mean from 1783 to 1834)

Establishment	Mean annual crop in fanegas (net)	Mean quantity per person in fanegas (net)	Mean calories per person per day
Missions			
San Diego	2,875	2.18	955
San Luis Rey	5,685	3.49	1,530
San Juan Capistrano	2,905	3.81	1,670
San Gabriel	4,820	3.62	1,585
San Fernando	2,490	3.24	1,420
San Buenaventura	3,310	4.20	1,840
Santa Bárbara	2,600	2.55	1,115
Santa Ynéz	2,435	4.47	1,955
La Purísima	2,475	2.95	1,290
San Luis Obispo	1,890	3.21	1,405
San Miguel	1,540	1.98	865
San Antonio	1,580	1.63	715
La Soledad	1,705	3.51	1,535
San Carlos	1,885	4.10	1,790
San Juan Bautista	2,000	2.47	1,080
Santa Cruz	1,910	4.57	2,000
Santa Clara	3,070	2.67	1,165
San José	3,195	2.98	1,305
San Francisco	2,525	3.47	1,520
San Rafael	1,260*	....	.....
San Francisco Solano	1,316*	....	.....
Mean	2,680	3.21	1,405
Presidios			
San Diego	2,360	8.05	3,410
Santa Bárbara	850	2.48	1,015
Monterey	622	1.82	640
San Francisco	1,125	5.80	2,075
Mean	1,240	4.54	1,785
Pueblos			
Los Angeles	3,850	10.35	4,540
San José	2,455	14.95	6,550
Branciforte	610	13.68	6,000
Mean	2,305	12.99	5,700

* San Rafael, 16 years; Solano, 10 years. These missions were omitted in computing the average.

433

the annual grain production of each mission per person. These values
are given in the second column of table 2. It will be noted that there
is great variation among the missions, the range extending from 4.57
fanegas per person at Santa Cruz to 1.63 at San Antonio, the mean for
all the missions being 3.21 fanegas. The presidios show even greater
variations (8.05–1.82; mean, 4.54), whereas the pueblos are consistently
higher (14.95–10.35).

To convert these means to terms of calorific value, certain approximations must be made. The unit of one fanega may have been somewhat variable, depending upon local conditions and the complete lack
of standardized weights and measures. Nevertheless, taken over a
long time and in numerous localities, it may be considered equivalent
to 1.6 bushels. Under modern conditions, furthermore, the weight of
a bushel of any cereal crop varies, depending on the type of grain and
the conditions of preparation, moisture, and so on. Therefore it is impossible to assign an exact and accurate weight to a "bushel of wheat"
or a "bushel of corn." Thus a bushel of barley will weigh perhaps
46 to 50 pounds, husked corn 68 to 72 pounds, shelled corn 52 to 56
pounds, corn meal 48 to 50 pounds, wheat somewhere near 60 pounds
and beans also near 60 pounds. Converting and using mean values,
we should ascribe the following weights for a fanega of barley, corn,
wheat, and beans respectively: 77, 88, 96, 96 pounds. Not a great deal
would be gained by converting to pounds each individual crop item
in the mission reports (nearly 15,000 items). It is simpler to convert
the total annual crop per mission. The true factor, of course, lies somewhere between 75 and 100 pounds, but in view of the general uncertainty it is necessary to assign a purely arbitrary value. It seems
desirable to keep the inevitable error on the side of overestimate rather
than underestimate, in order that the mission diet may be presented
with the maximum liberality consistent with the facts as we know
them; hence it will be appropriate to regard a fanega of any crop as
containing 100 pounds.

The final approximation must come in assigning the calorific value
of a unit weight of these foods. Such a value varies considerably, depending on the plant species and also on its physical state. Thus the
Okey-Huntington tables give the following values (in calories per

pound):[70] whole wheat, 1,633; corn meal, 1,613; beans (dried red), 1,574. Most cereals therefore approximate 1,600 calories per pound. According to this estimate, the fanega has a calorific value of nearly 160,000. It is possible now to express the mission-Indian grain diet in terms of calories per person per day (third column in table 2). The range was from 2,000 in Santa Cruz to 715 in San Antonio, and the mean value for the nineteen old missions was 1,405. Before discussing the adequacy of this diet it is necessary to consider what deductions must be made.

It is very clear from the general information which has come down to us from the mission period as well as from contemporary sources that by no means all the produce of the missions was fed to the neophytes. Naturally, every possible pathway of leakage cannot be ascertained, but certainly there must have been included the food supplied to the missionary staff and the garrison, the supplies furnished the presidios, the grain exported in exchange for trade goods, and wastage due to accident and deterioration in the storehouses. Of these, the last source of loss, together with unidentifiable factors, cannot be evaluated at all. The grain exports are extremely difficult, if not impossible, to determine. The amounts consumed by non-Indians and those supplied to the presidios can be estimated within reasonable limits.

Every mission from the beginning had a garrison of several soldiers and their families, and the garrisons comprised from two to twelve men. The documentary series in the Bancroft Library contains numerous statements with respect to the number of persons in garrisons and the amounts of grain provided for their consumption. I have been able to tabulate 135 such statements from the years 1826–1833 in the missions San Francisco, San José, Santa Clara, Santa Cruz, and Solano. Since the garrison system was always very uniform and since the supplies necessary were always essentially the same regardless of geographical location or year, these 135 records may be considered a fair sample for all the missions throughout their existence. The mean

---

[70] *Okey-Huntington Allowances for Adequate Food at Low Cost*, California State Emergency Relief Administration, University of California (1933). The table of calories is taken from M. D. Rose, *Laboratory Handbook for Dietetics* (New York, 1937). Similar tables may be found in the standard texts on human nutrition.

number of garrison soldiers was 5.86 and the mean value of supplies per man per month was 0.975 fanegas, or 11.7 fanegas per year. For 5.86 men this amounts to 68.5 fanegas per year.

The quantities supplied to the presidios were more variable. In theory, each presidio grew enough crops to feed its own population and according to the data shown in table 2 this was actually the practice. Nevertheless, particularly in the last part of the mission period, the presidios were continually calling on the missions for supplies, which were provided on credit. It is significant that, even though the presidios raised as much corn and wheat per capita as did the missions, this quantity was regarded as inadequate for the white population of the former, although the missionaries seemed to feel that it represented an abundance for the Indian inhabitants of the latter.[71]

With respect to the actual quantities involved there are at hand in the documentary material of the Bancroft Library sixty-six statements in which the supplies furnished are listed and itemized. The period included is from 1808 to 1830, and nearly all the missions are represented. Although this sample is not as complete as might be desired,

---

[71] It is stated (Archb. Arch., 4[1]:24) that at San Diego in 1820 the annual need was 1,300 fanegas of corn and 286 of beans. For 1819, 1820, and 1821 the corn crop was respectively 2,531, 939, and 2,250 fanegas and the bean crop 304, 298, 274 fanegas. Nevertheless, the presidio in 1820 was asking for food from the four southern missions. Similarly, at Santa Bárbara in 1823 the annual requirement was placed at 1,100 fanegas of corn and 270 of wheat (*ibid.*, 4[2]:4). The production was 440 fanegas of wheat and 418 of corn.

In San Diego for 1778 the total food consumption of the "72 men of the presidio" (plus, of course, their families) was given as follows (St. Pap. Pres., 1:55) with the units converted approximately to pounds. (Numbers in parentheses give number of pounds per person annually.)

corn	58,500 (254)	crude sugar 2,330 (10.1)
beans	14,800 (65)	chili 1,500 (6.5)
lentils	1,150 (5.0)	meat 695 (3.0)
peas	1,300 (5.7)	flour 385 (1.7)
rice	860 (3.7)	biscuits 720 (3.1)
tallow	1,535 (6.7)	dried fish 240 (1.0)

In that year the presidio produced only 36,500 pounds of corn and 5,350 pounds of beans. For the balance, even at this early date, the presidio was dependent upon the missions and perhaps upon imports from Mexico. The establishment at the time had an approximate total white population of 230. The food supply per person for the year may thus be calculated. The result is approximately one pound per day per person, certainly an inadequate diet according to modern standards. Although it is probable that this strictly military ration was liberally supplemented by private sources of supply such as truck gardens, hunting, and fishing, these data are illuminating as showing what was regarded by the army as a reasonable base ration for white troops.

particularly for the earlier decades, it is reasonably comprehensive and may be utilized in default of any better data.[72] Examination of the sixty-six records indicates that the mean annual contribution of each mission to its presidio was 227.5 fanegas of grain.

Some foodstuffs were subministered to the ships which plied regularly with freight and passengers from San Blas and Acapulco to California. According to one record[73] the supplies of this sort from 1797 to 1804 amounted to a total of 250 fanegas (100 in 1799, 150 in 1804). If these years are representative, then throughout the entire period a rough proration would indicate 2 fanegas annually per mission.

Much greater were the quantities sold to foreign trading vessels. A fairly exact estimate might be made by collecting the miscellaneous items scattered through hundreds of thousands of documents in the Bancroft Library and elsewhere. But even if such a procedure were possible, any general averages computed on the basis of such data would not possess a high degree of validity. Foreign commerce, even of the smuggling or bootleg type, did not exist at all prior to 1815 or 1820. Hence no deductions from the mission produce figures could be made for the first fifty years. Subsequent to 1820, when trading increased greatly, the quantities of withdrawals for sale from the mission stores are largely conjectural. Though the records of general commerce are very numerous, they are usually in the form of customs receipts (i.e., imports rather than exports). Furthermore, the primary export items were hides and tallow rather than grains. In addition, it must be remembered that not only the missions sold such material,

---

[72] That this sample is satisfactory for the later period at least is demonstrated by the following calculation. The statements in the Bancroft Library list 19 contributions of the four missions—San Francisco, San José, Santa Clara, and Santa Cruz—for the decade 1821–1830 inclusive. According to these entries, the amount of cereal crops furnished the San Francisco Presidio was 4,420 fanegas. Interpolating on the basis of these figures, we get as the quantity supplied by the four missions in ten years (40 contributions) a total of 9,305 fanegas.

Now there is also a summary (Vallejo Docs., 20:251) of the monetary value of the credits advanced to this presidio in the same decade, amounting to $41,171 (41,171 pesos). We may safely assume that one-half the money was for cereal crops, the balance being for meat, fats, and manufactured goods. The prices for grains at this time were (Arch. Mis. [1824], 1:272): wheat, $2.00 per fanega; corn, $1.50 per fanega; and beans, $2.33 per fanega. Let us say, $2.00 per fanega as an average price. Then one-half the total sum, at this rate, would imply a purchase of 10,290 fanegas, which corresponds quite well with the estimate of 9,305 obtained by the first method.

[73] Subministrations to the ships, 1805(?), Sta. Bárb. Arch., 9:494.

but also the presidios and private individuals. Even Bancroft, who made a fairly complete survey of trade relations listing nearly every ship which touched at a California port from 1820 to 1845, nowhere gives data pertaining to the grain export of the missions. Consequently, in default of really adequate quantitative information, it is best to leave the question open and deduct nothing from the mean annual harvest of the missions, recognizing that, although some error is introduced by this omission, it is on the side of overestimating the food supply of the neophytes.[74]

The last cause of loss was deterioration and spoilage subsequent to the harvest. There are no data available concerning this point but it is safe to assume that at least a small part of each crop was thus eliminated.[75]

In sum, it is possible to deduct from the mean annual crop per mission 68.5 fanegas used for the garrison, 227.5 fanegas subministered to the presidios and perhaps 5 fanegas supplied to ships or sold in trade. Let us say, 300 fanegas in all. Deducting from the general mean in table 2 and converting units, the conclusion would be that the maximum dietary value of the grain crops to the neophytes was 1,205 calories per person per day. It must be emphasized that this is a maximum figure. It would be entirely in order to follow modern procedure

---

[74] Another factor involved is geographical location. The missions closest to the principal seaports (San Francisco, Monterey, and San Diego) probably disposed of more of their crops commercially than did those at remoter points.

One or two accounts at hand are suggestive. In 1823 (Arch. Mis., 1:580) a Russian ship put into San Francisco. There were sold to it 535 fanegas, 50 fanegas, and 500 fanegas of grain respectively from San Francisco, Santa Clara, and San José. If this rate applied generally to all the missions, the exports would have reached a tremendous volume (more than 300 fanegas annually per mission). Probably, therefore, this represents an exceptional transaction.

In the Vallejo Documents (1830) 1:213, there is a summary of the trading done in San Francisco from 1821 to 1830 inclusive. There were 32 ships involved and the value of the total imports amounted to $21,579. Since trading was almost entirely by barter, the exports may be assumed to have been of equivalent value. Now, wholly gratuitously, let us assume that one-third of the exports were cereals, and that one-half of these were from the missions. Further, let us assume that the average price per fanega was $2.00. Then the mission sales would have been 1,800 fanegas, or for the four Bay missions (including San Rafael but not Solano) 45 fanegas per year per mission. This estimate appears much too high.

[75] Father Durán (Archb. Arch., 3:71) reported from Santa Cruz in 1816 that between three and four hundred fanegas of corn could not be sent to the presidio because it spoiled on the ground owing to lack of transport. Such incidents may have occurred with some frequency.

and reduce by 10 per cent for domestic wastage and deterioration. Likewise, the assumed weight of grain per fanega is almost certainly 10 per cent too great. If these corrections are allowed, the calories per person per day would not exceed 1,000.

The principal type of animal food consumed by the mission Indians was beef, with perhaps some mutton and pork. An estimate of the quantities involved is difficult to obtain, since the mission records do not specify food consumption. There were, to be sure, annual livestock censuses through which one might arrive at an approximation of the maximum food supply as was done for the cereal crops. However, such a determination would have little, if any, significance; relatively few stock animals were consumed as food. The mission herds were enormous—adequate to supply meat bountifully to thousands of neophytes. However, a large proportion of the animals were slaughtered for hides and tallow, the principal export commodities, many of them were lost by theft, and many others strayed off the ranges or were killed by drought, frost, or wild animals. Even if these factors could be gauged in a semiquantitative manner, the results would be of doubtful value because the balance remaining for consumption as food could not be estimated without very large error. It is necessary therefore to rely upon the written statements of the missionaries.

The most comprehensive statement is that contained in a general report[76] for 1796 to the effect that of 50,000 head of cattle owned by the missions 6,000 were annually slaughtered for food. There were at the time thirteen missions with a total population of approximately 11,000. Six thousand cattle per year means 460 per mission per year or 9 per mission per week (18 every two weeks).

Other data of a numerical character are as follows.[77] In 1800 at Santa

------

[76] Salazar, "Informe," College of San Fernando, May 11, 1796, Sta. Bárb. Arch., 2:63–83.

[77] There are also semiquantitative records: "one piece per person per week" (Grajera, Mar. 2, 1799, Prov. St. Pap., 27:91); "cattle are killed during most months" (Argüello, Dec. 11, 1798, *ibid.*, p. 58); "meat for one or two days is given weekly" (Goycoechea, Dec. 14, 1798, *ibid.*, p. 70); "usually meat was given" (Perez, "Una vieja," MS, 1877); "every two weeks they slaughtered cattle" (Lorenzana, "Memorias," MS, 1878); "there was a daily ration of meat" (Coronel, "Cosas," MS, 1878); "a certain number were killed every week" (Solá, Apr. 3, 1818, Prov. Rec., 9:176–195). Furthermore, every missionary who expressed himself on the subject asserted that, as a universal procedure,

Bárbara 170 steers were slaughtered between January 1 and October 1.[78] At San Francisco in 1814 Langsdorff says that 50 to 60 steers a week were used.[79] Amador states that at San José 100 to 200 cattle were slaughtered every Saturday.[80] At San Diego, in 1814, the number killed every two weeks was 24.[81] If we reduce these estimates to the same basis as the first one (i.e., number killed per mission per week), the results are 4.4, 50–60, 100–200, and 12 respectively. Obviously the Langsdorff and Amador figures may be great exaggerations; at least, they are guesses. The three statements in which the missionaries themselves went on record show only 9, 4.4 and 12. In this connection it should be pointed out that the missionaries, perpetually on the defensive in matters of mission administration, were not likely to underestimate the food they gave to their Indian charges; furthermore, they were in a much better position than outsiders to know the actual number of beef slaughtered. We may, then, tentatively at least, accept the estimate of 9 animals per mission per week in 1796.

A modern range steer in good condition will weigh something over 1,000 pounds. The mission cattle were the old, unimproved Mexican and Spanish breed and moreover may not have been fed very heavily. Let us assume an average weight of 900 pounds. A dressed carcass today represents between 53 and 63 per cent of the total weight. Under mission conditions it is probable that not only the muscle and fat were utilized, but also much of the visceral material, such as heart, liver, and stomach. On the other hand, we should deduct the nonedible bones. A reasonable estimate would then be 60 per cent of the weight of the animal on the hoof or, say, 550 pounds. Nine animals per week would then amount to 4,950 pounds, or 710 pounds per day per mission. Since there were 13 missions in 1796, with a total population of 11,000, this means a daily individual allowance of 0.84 pounds of meat per day per person. In order to determine the exact calorific equivalent, it

---

numerous cattle were slaughtered for food. This was admitted, at least in principle, by all the military writers. There can therefore be no doubt whatever that meat, to a greater or lesser extent, was a fixed item in the mission dietary.

[78] Tapis and Cortes, Oct. 30, 1800, Sta. Bárb. Arch., 2:86–143.

[79] G. H. von Langsdorff, *Voyages and Travels in Various Parts of the World,* translated by T. C. Russell (1927), p. 151.

[80] J. M. Amador, "Memorias," MS, 1877, p. 102.

[81] Martín and Sánchez, 1811, Sta. Bárb. Arch., 3:27–37.

would be necessary to know the precise proportion of muscle, fat, liver, and so on which was eaten, as well as the type of cut. This is manifestly impossible to discover. The closest approximation is to assume a value of approximately 1,000 calories per pound, thus indicating an individual intake of 840 calories per day.

Aside from cereals and beef the missions produced small quantities of truck crops, principally legumes like lentils and peas. The total quantity of these may be determined from the annual reports. In the entire province from 1783 to 1833 there were produced in all 74,200 fanegas per year, allowing 5 per cent deduction for seed (see table 2), or 0.845 fanega per person per year. On a daily basis this is equivalent to .00023 fanega, or .00037 bushel per person. If the average weight of these crops is assumed to be approximately 60 pounds per bushel and the energy value to be 1,500 calories per pound, then the calories per day per person from this source amounted to 30.

There were perhaps other foodstuffs supplied in very small quantities by the missions. The invoices of ships and records of goods received by the missions show inconsiderable imports of chocolate, sugar, chili, vinegar, and various condiments. Some of these doubtless found their way to the infirmaries for the benefit of the sick, but the rank and file of the neophytes never saw them. There may have been other minor food items. Although there were few, if any, dairy cattle, and consequently there was no material supply of milk, butter, or cheese, there may have been some poultry. Such items can have been of little or no significance in energy production, yet they were undoubtedly valuable as accessory sources of food.

Wild Food.—Wholly apart from the mission economy itself, there was one food source available to the Indians, the aboriginal wild food. This consisted of scores of plants and animals, utilized according to season and location and in varying amounts by the Indians prior to missionization. In the aggregate these wild sources made up a fairly complete diet or, at least, one upon which a good many thousand persons had subsisted for generations. If the aboriginal food sources had remained entirely available to the neophytes, and if to this the mission dietary of grain and meat had been added, the Indians should have enjoyed an excellent nutritional environment. But the policy of the missions was opposed to the utilization of this supply. In theory—and the problem was subject to endless debate—it was felt that the material and spiritual welfare of the newly converted savages would be better served by keeping them confined strictly within the mission influence and by preventing any reversion to their old habits of life. This question of policy, with its social and religious implications, does not concern us here. The crux of the matter is that the neophytes were prevented from utilizing their aboriginal food sources, even though these were abundant.

However, no prohibition can ever be complete, and there were many exceptions to this rule. In the first place, mission policy by no means condemned the use of wild foods per se provided they could be obtained without detriment to the main objectives of the system. In the second place, whenever the mission production of foodstuffs fell below maintenance standards, as occasionally happened locally, the priests were compelled to allow their charges to find food wherever they could. This expedient was deliberately resorted to in the first decade, before agriculture and the stock industry had become fully established. Despite attempts to avoid such a predicament, conversion frequently outran cultivation. In the third place, throughout the entire history of the missions there was a continuous stream of fugitives leaving the establishments and subsequently returning, either voluntarily or by compulsion. The net result of all these factors seems to have been a steady flow into the missions of wild foods, in particular, seasonal herbs and tubers, acorns, and fish. It is manifestly impossible to gauge the extent of this importation in numerical terms; but it must have constituted a very material contribution, both in absolute quantity and as a source of vitamins and other nutritional elements.

Simply for the sake of comparison, there may be cited the dietary habits of the California Indians today. It has been shown that under modern conditions and after a century of so-called civilization, up to 10 per cent of the dietary regimen of the Sierra Nevada Indians still consists of wild food.[82] What may we then expect of the diet among

[82] S. F. Cook, *The Mechanism and Extent of Dietary Adaptation among Certain Groups of California and Nevada Indians,* Univ. Calif. Publ., Ibero-Americana, No. 18 (Berkeley, 1941).

similar people not one generation removed from their aboriginal surroundings? Considering the complete lack of concrete data, it may be permissible to base an estimate on the dietary in the missions upon our modern observations and to ascribe to wild sources approximately 10 per cent of the total, or, let us say, a statistical mean of 200 calories per person per day.[83]

Calorific value of the mission dietary.—To summarize the foregoing discussion, the average neophyte in the mission period received or obtained food having an energy value of 2,320 calories ($\pm$ 20 per cent) per day. It must be remembered that this figure represents the probable maximum diet and that the actual nourishment of any one individual at any particular time may have been much less. Indeed it has been suggested that a 20-per cent reduction in the estimate for grain intake would be legitimate. Moreover, the allowance of 840 calories per person per day from meat alone seems excessive. The actual energy value is therefore more likely to have been from 2,000 to 2,100 calories rather than the theoretical maximum of 2,320. Granting that our preliminary estimate is correct within reasonable limits, the question now arises whether this diet was adequate.

With respect to the number of calories included in the diet certain modern data may be used for comparison. It is considered that for the civilized white races the available food supplies should be sufficient to provide 3,300 calories "per man per day."[84] An allowance of 10 per

---

[83] A fairly clear statement of mission policy is contained in Lasuén's "Representación" of 1800 (Sta. Bárb. Arch., 2:172): "Even the most important tasks of the mission are left undone when there is not sufficient food for the workers. They are then permitted freedom to go out into the woods, but no one is forced to go. Nevertheless on such occasions sufficient provisions are bought and brought from other places to sustain all those, sick and well, who remain in the mission."

This statement is confirmed by several of the foreign visitors in the later mission era. F. W. Beechey records (*Voyage to the Pacific* [1831], 2:22): "If it should happen that there is a scarcity of provisions, either through failure in the crop, or damage of that which is in store . . . the Indians are sent off to the woods to provide for themselves, where, accustomed to hunt and fish, and game being very abundant, they find enough to subsist upon." Beechey (*ibid.*, p. 20) also describes a scene at San Francisco: ". . . others were grinding baked acorns to make into cakes, which constituted a large portion of their food. . . ." However, I find no other mention of acorns as an important dietary constituent.

[84] See Graham Lusk, *The Elements of the Science of Nutrition* (4th ed., 1928), pp. 756–758, for a discussion of the food supply to populations. The figures cited in the text are taken from Lusk.

cent is included for domestic wastage, making the required net intake 3,000 calories. In prewar Germany the value was 3,640 and in England 3,410. Our estimate of roughly 2,000 to 2,100 calories as the probable daily nourishment of the individual mission Indian appears therefore to be considerably below the optimum level. However, certain additional factors should be considered.

The estimates for modern civilized nations are based upon the supposition that the diet is wholly adequate with respect to quantity and quality. It is nevertheless possible for a population to exist with fair success on a maintenance diet of much lower level. Thus Lusk (*op. cit.,* p. 756) places the actual requirement of the people of prewar Germany at 2,285 calories per man per day, whereas the quantity used was 3,640 calories. Another factor is the character of the population with respect to size and age-sex composition. The Indian was, as a rule, somewhat smaller than the white man, perhaps sufficiently smaller to warrant a reduction in calorific necessity from 3,000 to 2,700. The age-sex factor is significant since the infant mortality of the mission group was high and the number of children consequently small. Furthermore, the sex ratio was high. The effect of these factors may be approximated by computing the dietary requirement. For this purpose we may use the values for the civilized white population of 2,000 calories for the average child up to fourteen years, 2,800 calories for a woman, and 3,600 calories for a man. The last two values are applicable to active, not sedentary, individuals, but it must be remembered that the mission Indians were active in the physical sense. This method yields 2,950 calories "per man per day" as compared with 3,000 for modern white races. Again, reducing by 10 per cent to account for average size difference, we get 2,655 calories. It therefore appears doubtful whether the probable maximum caloric supply of the mission Indians met the requirement for adequate diet in the quantitative sense and whether there was sufficient food for maintenance purposes.

Even if we were to concede the mission diet to have been quantitatively sufficient, there remains the question of the adequacy of its protein, mineral, and vitamin content.

As indicated previously, the food supply was predominantly grain. This means the presence of a moderate amount of plant protein. If the meat supplement was as extensive as the few data we possess seem to indicate, then we cannot regard the combination as being too low in total protein. Even if the meat supply was less than we have supposed, the population would still have had access to a maintenance level of the essential amino acids.

With regard to minerals doubts may arise. The grains and legumes would ensure sufficient phosphorus but perhaps might induce a calcium deficiency. However, calcium might have been obtained from other sources, such as the animal food. Moreover, there is some evidence that lime was incorporated with the cooked grain.[85] If so, it is unlikely that a serious calcium deficiency existed. Sodium chloride was, of course, present in the meat, although the grains contributed little. It is alleged by Governor Solá that the cereals were fed "without salt or any condiment."[86] A more explicit statement comes from Tapis and Cortes, two missionaries who were defending the system against charges of negligence and corruption. They assert:[87]

Neither salt nor lard is added to the *pozole,* for experience has shown us that they do not agree with most of them [the Indians] and to the minority with whom they agree neither one nor the other is denied, if they ask for them.

It is fairly clear therefore that salt was not regarded as a necessary dietary constituent and was not purveyed on an extensive scale. Whether an actual sodium chloride deficiency existed cannot be determined with certainty.

The adequacy of vitamins is similarly a matter of opinion. If the neophytes had been restricted rigidly to corn, wheat, beans, and beef, we might conclude that they received a fair supply of vitamins A and B_1, that vitamin C was low and that B_2 (or G) was doubtful. This would raise the possibility of the occurrence of scurvy and pellagra. However, there are no records which support this supposition. The Spanish and

---

[85] Coronel ("Cosas," p. 221) states that "el atole era maíz cocido con cal. ..." Furthermore, since the white population utilized extensively the *tortilla* which is invariably cooked with lime, it is highly improbable that the missionaries would neglect to include this substance in the standard dietary of the Indians.

[86] Solá to viceroy, Monterey, April 3, 1818, Prov. Rec., 9:176–195.

[87] Tapis and Cortes, Sta. Bárb. Arch., 2:86–143. Substantiating evidence comes from Lapérouse (*A Voyage Round the World* [translation, London, 1798], 2:215) who refers to "*atole* ... which is seasoned neither with salt nor butter."

Mexicans of the time were thoroughly familiar with scurvy and would have reported its presence.[88] Pellagra was of course unknown, but there is no definite, indirect evidence of its presence.[89] Furthermore, there were available small quantities of foodstuffs which would have no quantitative significance but which might have been of value as vitamin sources. A few cows supplied a little milk; there were some fresh vegetables in the mission gardens.[90] In the south a small citrus industry was established. In addition, the Indians must have procured a certain amount of wild green plant material. It is impossible to say to what extent these sources were utilized, but it is reasonable to assume that they did not provide the entire population with a completely balanced diet in the modern sense. On the other hand, there was probably enough material of this nature to prevent severe incidence of deficiency disease. Surveying the field a century afterward, one is apt to incline toward the belief that the accessory food factors were marginal and that the Indians as a whole lived continuously on the verge of clinical deficiency.

---

[88] Scurvy did occur seriously in the Portolá expedition of 1769 and at San Diego among the soldiers during the following winter; but there is no mention of its having attacked the natives.

[89] The only indication, and it is but an indication, that extensive deficiency diseases were present, lies in the descriptions of venereal disease. The frequent references to skin affections (pustules, sores, rashes, etc.), which ascribe the latter universally to syphilis, suggest the remote possibility that some of them may have been associated with dietary deficiencies. However, the descriptions are too general and inexact to use as diagnostic criteria.

[90] It is difficult to ascertain just how much fresh plant material was actually available. All observers testify that gardens existed generally and that a certain amount of fruit was raised. Opinion varied as to the actual production. Beechey (*op. cit.*, 2:37) states that "... beans, pease and other leguminous vegetables are in abundance, and fruit is plentiful." Choris, who saw California in 1816 with the Katzebue expedition, says (see A. C. Mahr, *The Visit of the Rurik in San Francisco in 1816* [1932], p. 93): "In their free time the Indians work in gardens that are given them; they raise therein onions, garlic, canteloupes, watermelons, pumpkins, and fruit trees. The products belong to them. . . ." However, Vancouver, writing at an earlier date, thought otherwise. With respect to San Francisco he says: (*A Voyage of Discovery to the North Pacific Ocean* [London, 1801], p. 23): "[The garden] contained about four acres . . . and produced some fig, peach, apple, and other fruit trees, but afforded a very scanty supply of useful vegetables." Of Santa Clara he writes (p. 33): "The extent of it, like the garden at San Francisco, appeared unequal to the consumption of the European residents"; and of San Carlos (p. 62): "With these advantages it generally produces a great abundance of the several kitchen vegetables and some fruit." However, owing to sales to passing ships ". . . the productions of this and the only other garden at San Carlos were nearly exhausted."

The foregoing discussion is based upon purely statistical considerations and refers only to general conditions. There are, however, certain purely individual and local data which have definite significance.

Contemporary accounts.—Among those interested persons who commented at that time on the status of the mission Indians or in later years wrote down their impressions, there existed two divergent schools of opinion. One held that the Indians were satisfactorily fed, the other maintained the opposite. Naturally, opinions were highly colored by current political and social controversies, such as the perennial contest for power between the missionaries and soldiers. Sometimes personal considerations—racial or religious prejudice, political or business ambitions, or pure like and dislike—entered the picture. It is therefore unwise to rely completely upon the unsupported opinion of any one individual, no matter how superlative his ability or integrity.

On the positive side we find the great missionary presidents, Serra and Lasuén, who were beyond any question fully convinced that everything necessary was supplied to their converts. Thus Lasuén[91] avers:

Besides their three meals . . . they are rarely denied anything that they come to ask for in order to eat. . . . This . . . is done according to the means of each mission. This is not uniform but every effort is expended on the neophytes. It is not to be denied that among the missionaries there are some more and some less solicitous and liberal regarding the convenience of their spiritual children just as there are good fathers of families. . . .

The inference here is plain that, although it was the intention to give the neophytes all they wanted, it was not always within the means of the missions to do so.

Tapis and Cortes contend as follows:[92]

That this food is sufficient to sustain them and enable them to withstand their work . . . may be observed by anyone who is possessed of eyes and wishes to see.

. . . He may observe that certain neophytes who raise chickens do not feed them on their wild seeds . . . but on the *pozole* left over after eating all they want. Besides this daily consumption of provisions, during the

---

[91] "Representación," San Carlos, Nov. 12, 1800, Sta. Bárb. Arch., 2:154–240.
[92] *Loc. cit.*

wheat harvest the fourth part of an *almud* is given daily to those engaged in the harvest. The same practice is pursued on Sundays and during Lent as well as on the principal holidays of the year.[93]

Eulalia Perez,[94] who spent her youth in San Diego, states that breakfast consisted of chocolate with *atole* of corn with bread on holidays; on other days usually *pozole* and meat. At noon there were *pozole* and meat with greens, and at night *atole* with meat or at times pure *atole*. She goes on to describe her experiences in carrying refreshment to the workers in the fields. "This refreshment was made from water with vinegar and sugar or with lemon and sugar, so that the Indians should not become sick." The custom of giving fruit juices as a beverage seems to have had a rather wide vogue, particularly toward the end of the mission period.

Amador in his recollections describes all the meals as consisting of *atole* (a gruel made by boiling ground corn, wheat, or barley) and *pozole* (a cooked mixture of barley, beans, corn, pigs' feet, squash and chili).[95] He also says that "the Indians at San José never went hungry." Coronel thus describes the diet:[96]

Food was given three times a day.... It consisted of beans and corn or wheat cooked together, which was called *pozole;* sometimes *atole* and meat were given in the morning. . . . To the married men were given weekly a ration of grain, that is corn, wheat and beans, and daily a ration of fresh or dried meat, generally fish.

---

[93] Regarding actual quantities given the neophytes, there are two statements which are worthy of mention. Romero ("Memorias," MS, 1878, p. 19), who worked as a servant for eleven years at San Fernando, says that each married man was given 3 *cuartillas* of grain a week and each unmarried man 2 *cuartillas*. Since a *cuartilla* equals 6 pounds and since each family had on the average one child, the net grain ration would have been equivalent to 1,320 calories per day per person for families and 2,740 calories for single men. However, the latter were expected to distribute their ration among relatives. Hence the result is approximately the same.

Tapis and Cortes (Sta. Bárb. Arch., 2:86–143) state that each neophyte who ate at the general mission mess received about three-quarters of an *almud* in the form of *atole* or *pozole*. Since an *almud* is approximately 800 cubic centimeters or 1.6 pounds of corn or wheat, this would imply an equivalent of 1,930 calories. But since Tapis and Cortes estimate that one-quarter of the neophytes were always absent from any particular meal, the average equivalent would be 1,450 calories.

These values come definitely within the range predicated on the basis of general crop statistics.

[94] "Una vieja," MS, 1877, pp. 17–18.

[95] J. M. Amador, "Memorias," p. 102.

[96] A. F. Coronel, "Cosas," p. 221.

Langsdorff in 1818 described the mission diet as follows:[97]

The principal food of the Indians is a thick soup composed of meat, vegetables and pulse. Because of the scarcity of fish here [San Francisco] the missionaries obtained a special dispensation from the Pope allowing the eating of meat on fast days. The food is apportioned three times a day . . . in large ladlefuls. At meal times . . . each family sends a vessel to the kitchen and is served as many measures as there are members. I was present once at the time the soup was served, and it appeared incomprehensible to me how anyone could consume so much nourishing food three times a day. . . . Besides this meal, bread, Indian corn, peas, beans and other kinds of pulse are distributed in abundance, without any stated or regular allowance.

The above quotations and many other similar accounts give the impression of abundance and liberality, of easy-going pastoral richness, an impression which has crept into the secondary literature and colored many of the more popular and less critical works on early California. With this in mind, it is only reasonable to present the opposite side of the picture.

He charged the Ministers of that mission of San Francisco to exercise greater care with the cleanliness of the great copper tanks or kettles from which the *atole* and *pozole* are given to the neophytes. The latter [*atole*, etc.] are composed some days of wheat and others of peas . . . with none of the corn or wheat bread known as tortillas.[98]

In 1806 the crops failed at San Diego[99] and there was scarcely enough food to maintain the neophytes. In 1819 the crops were destroyed[100] at Santa Ynéz, and the missionary feared there would be a famine. In the same year the Bay region suffered.[101] The minister at San Francisco reported that the stock were dying and the crops poor. He undertook to plant crops in the region of San José "to alleviate the great misery in which these unfortunate neophytes find themselves."

Until 1779 at San Diego the neophytes were left at their native villages because there was no food at San Diego.[102] Of four hundred converts only twenty were living at the mission. By 1787 about one-

<hr>

[97] *Op. cit.,* p. 51.
[98] Solá to the viceroy, Monterey, Apr. 3, 1818, Prov. Rec., 9:178.
[99] Rodríguez to Arrillaga, San Diego, June 20, 1806, Prov. St. Pap., 19:140.
[100] Uria to De la Guerra, Santa Ynéz, Apr. 26, 1819, De la Guerra Docs., 5:263.
[101] Cabot to Solá, San Francisco, Oct. 30, 1819, Archb. Arch., 3:116.
[102] Fages, "Informe," 1787, St. Pap. Mis. Col., 1:129.

half were at the mission, and the crops were large enough so that "they all can be fed."

In 1821 Father Prefect Payeras wrote Governor Solá, referring to San Francisco, that "this mission can supply nothing because for the last three or four months the neophytes have had nothing to eat."[103]

The following three opinions were expressed by the military commanders of the presidios in 1798 in answer to a questionnaire submitted by the governor:

...I consider the quantity [of food] so small that in the course of the year it does not amount to 22 fanegas of grain per individual, and it is likewise observed that it is insufficient for their sustenance and much less to resist the arduous strain of the labors in which they are employed.[104]

Although sufficient to sustain life it [the ration] cannot suffice for him who works from morning till night.[105]

Without being prompted by pity, but only using common sense, I deem this food insufficient with which solely to maintain themselves and to resist the hardships to which they are subjected.[106]

At about the same time the governor wrote the viceroy that conditions at San Francisco had improved and that the Indians "now get three hot meals a day."[107] This was owing to the efforts of Fray José María Fernández, who opposed the methods of his colleague, Fray Landaeta. Apparently under the Landaeta regime they did not get three meals a day.

In 1826 Father Zalvidea wrote that "these unfortunate Indians lack fat...beans and corn."[108] At the other end of the colony Argüello complained that "the soldiers are in no wise different from the Indians and the worst is that they are all feeling starvation. May God intercede in all this!"[109]

The multiplication of further instances is unnecessary. It will be

---

[103] Payeras to Solá, San Francisco, Aug. 5, 1821, Archb. Arch., 4:76.

[104] Sal, Monterey, December 15, 1798, Prov. St. Pap., 17:63. Note that the opinion of Sal is not borne out by his figures; 22 fanegas per person per year amounts to 5 pounds per day, a far greater quantity than the missions could have provided. Possibly some error is involved in the original or in the Bancroft transcript.

[105] Grajera, San Diego, March 2, 1799, *ibid.*, p. 191.

[106] F. Goycoechea, Santa Bárbara, Dec. 14, 1798, *ibid.*, p. 70.

[107] Borica to the viceroy, Monterey, July 1, 1798, Prov. Rec., 6:97.

[108] Zalvidea to Echeandía, San Juan Capistrano, July 15, 1826, Archb. Arch., 5:25.

[109] Argüello to De la Guerra, San Francisco, Apr. 21, 1820, De la Guerra Docs., 4:136.

clear that there was no unanimity of opinion concerning mission diet. This divergence may be partly, but not entirely, explained on the grounds of personal ignorance, political bias, or religious prejudice. The truth seems to lie, as it so often does, between the extremes. There is no doubt that the missions intended to produce and to give the neophytes what would be regarded today as a fairly adequate ration. This policy was carried out in general through the years; there were, however, many local exceptions. Evidently considerable want and suffering were caused by crop failure, indifference and neglect on the part of certain missionaries, and numerous other factors. Thus in the aggregate the quantity and quality of the diet fell below the theoretical standard set up by the missionary administration. On the other hand, the evidence does not warrant the contention that the neophytes were subjected to conditions of really acute malnutrition or starvation over more than brief intervals of time.

To return now to the primary question concerning the significance of food in the population decline, we are again obliged to adopt a middle ground. It cannot be stated categorically that the whole group suffered direct losses from starvation. Nor, despite the doubtful adequacy of the vitamin and mineral intake, is there unimpeachable evidence that immediate damage was done by an acute lack of any accessory factor. Conversely, it does not appear that the neophytes universally and consistently received entirely adequate and nutritionally complete food. The tremendous incidence of disease, especially continuous, nonepidemic disease, suggests a level of nutrition probably insufficient for ordinary maintenance and certainly below the optimum necessary to provide a high resistance to infection. The low resistance implicit in a high-disease incidence and mortality is in definite conformity with the only moderate caloric intake and marginal vitamin supply which undoubtedly existed. A suboptimal diet may therefore be regarded as one factor which operated indirectly to check any population increase through its tendency to predispose to disease. It is, of course, manifestly impossible to assign any numerical value to the relative significance of such a factor.

IV. NEGATIVE RESPONSES TO THE MISSION ENVIRONMENT

THE POPULATION CHANGES induced by disease and perhaps by faulty diet must be regarded as purely mass effects operating on the aggregate without respect to individuals. To be sure, illness is a personal matter, and the total mortality must be viewed as the sum of the individual deaths. Yet these processes contain an element of inevitability. A man becomes infected when he comes in contact with the appropriate bacteria; he survives if his innate resistance is sufficiently high, he dies if he is constitutionally unable to cope with the disease or if external conditions over which he has no immediate control are such as to render his recovery impossible. He himself has no latitude for response; his fate is in a certain sense predetermined.

On the other hand, there are many factors which may be racially and personally unfavorable, which in the long run and including many persons may affect the numbers and vitality of a population but which are not directly and necessarily lethal to one single person. In a very broad sense some of these factors may be regarded as stimuli, capable of evoking a response in the individual. Then his response (or lack of it), its manner and extent will determine his status with respect to the environment of which such factors are an integral part. Further, if the responses of a sufficient number of persons are of the same type, the biological status of the whole group may be affected. It is difficult and probably unnecessary to attempt any sharp differentiation between individual and group responses of this pattern. The primary thesis is that, if enough separate units are observed to behave in a definite manner in the face of a given set of conditions, then we may think of such behavior in terms of group reaction. Furthermore, the factors which give rise to this particular type of group behavior may be conceived as operating first on the individual to induce his response. The final group response, or in ecological terms "adaptation," will then represent the statistical trend of the aggregate, and the latter may be affected at any time by changes in the nature and intensity of the stimulating factors.

[56]

452

Individual human responses may take very different forms. There may be first utter indifference, then mild like or dislike, stronger like or dislike, until there is some overt act. Aside from a few written opinions we have no means of assessing the reaction of the individual Indian to the mission system until the stage of action is reached. But action, as far as the Indian was concerned, was pretty definitely circumscribed. If his feeling was one of indifference or satisfaction, he would remain a neophyte and live and die unnoticed in the historical annals. If the reverse were true, he might pursue a sullen and discontented existence, indulging perhaps in a certain passive resistance to the system. In this event his unhappiness might be reflected in a thousand little ways which, although quite apparent to an observer on the spot, would not cause sufficient excitement to warrant official attention or comment. Nevertheless, if a large number of fellow neophytes shared his attitude, the result would be seen in the material and moral degeneration of the entire system. Since the system, even before secularization, was in this condition, it cannot be doubted that a great deal of general discontent was present, perhaps more than is obvious from the written record of the times. Now if the negative response evinced in a mild form by mere passive resistance became intensified to the point of physical action, there were only two possible lines of procedure. The Indian might exhibit one of the two universal modes of response to an unfavorable environment, flight. He might leave the missionary environment bodily and betake himself elsewhere. On the other hand, he might attempt the other mode of response, active, physical resistance, which would necessarily take the form of armed rebellion and warfare. Either mode of response could be embarked upon by an individual or by a group of any dimensions.

We have therefore to examine the extent to which the Indians gave evidence of negative individual and group responses to the mission environment by these two tangible methods. Subsequently we have to consider the factors inherent in that environment which could give rise to such extreme behavior.

Fugitivism.—Apostasy began as soon as conversions began, although it was some years before official notice was taken of it. By 1781, however, Junípero Serra[1] was able to list fifteen persons whom he described as being "confirmed apostates." Subsequent to that date no year passed without some mention of fugitives in the official correspondence. The problem became continuously more acute as more and more neophytes ran away, until secularization converted practically all the mission population into fugitives.

Generally speaking, and regardless of original motive, there were two categories of fugitives, temporary and permanent. The criterion between the two categories is whether or not a person was dropped from the mission rolls. On many occasions, undoubtedly thousands, neophytes ran away. Of these, a very large proportion returned to the fold after absences varying from a few days to several years. Some of these, probably the majority, came back of their own volition. Perhaps they went out only for the purpose of a temporary vacation; perhaps they changed their minds with reference to the desirability of the wild as opposed to the mission environment. The reasons leading to such voluntary return are as manifold as human nature. Others, quite a large number, were forcibly brought back by the many expeditions, large and small, which went out for this exact purpose. There was a residue, however, of determined souls who ran away, stayed away, and eluded all attempts to recapture them. After an indeterminate period, which may be estimated as approximately two years, they were given up for lost and dropped from the records as standing members of the mission community. These formed the group of permanent fugitives.

The number of permanent fugitives has been already estimated in a previous publication.[2] As explained there, the clue lies in the difference between the mission population as calculated from baptism-death data, and that stated in the annual censuses, the so-called "unaccounted depletion." It was shown that this source of loss represented about 4 per cent of the total losses (i.e., 96 per cent were by death) and that up to 1831 the cumulative desertions were 3,464. In 1832, 1833, and 1834 the desertions increased very greatly, bringing the final total to 5,428. This figure has significance as an index of response as discussed above. It means specifically that up to 1831 the mission environment had

---

[1] "Padrón," San Carlos, Dec. 22, 1781, St. Pap. Ben. Mil., 3:27.
[2] S. F. Cook, *Population Trends among the California Mission Indians,* Univ. Calif. Publ., Ibero-Americana, No. 17 (Berkeley, 1940), pp. 27–28.

affected the neophyte population so adversely that out of about 81,000 individuals (the actual total baptisms were 81,586) 3,400, that is, one out of every twenty-four, resorted actively and successfully to flight. If we eliminate from the total baptisms those who because of infancy, senility, illness, or death were physically unable to escape, the ratio will be very much higher. But to gauge the true extent of this response we must consider those who attempted escape and subsequently gave up the attempt or failed. The only evidence of a quantitative nature pertaining to this matter consists of a series of reports or notes scattered at random through the documentary material. I have collected such items as I have been able to find and have embodied them in table 3. The source of each item is on record but has not been appended to the table. In addition, in table 4 will be found the only specific and complete data covering a single year.

Although the data contained in table 3 constitute a rather inadequate sample, certain deductions can be made. As a mere approximation, let us take the entries in the table in which specific numbers of fugitives are given and compute the proportion of the mission population represented. The numbers which are listed as "caught" may be used for this purpose with the full realization that those caught by no means represent all who ran away. The mean value is 8.3 per cent. If the mean is restricted to those fugitives not labeled "caught" or "returned" the result is almost the same: 9.8 per cent. Now there exists a statement[3] giving the total number of fugitives for each of fifteen out of the nineteen missions up to the year 1817 (see table 4). From the censuses incorporated in the Bancroft compilation of vital statistics it may be calculated that the percentage of fugitives per mission, based on cumulative baptisms up to that year, ranges from 0.1 to 15.6, with a mean of 5.95. The total number was 3,205, but that represents all fugitives, permanent and temporary, up to the end of 1817. The two groups may be segregated within this total by the method outlined above, since the permanently missing persons were dropped from the census rolls; the discrepancy between the cumulative baptisms minus cumulative deaths on the one hand and the current existing population on the other represents the permanent fugitives. This value, for the nineteen

---

[3] "Estado," 1817, St. Pap. Mis., 4:44.

TABLE 3

FUGITIVES FROM VARIOUS MISSIONS, 1781–1829

No.	Year	Mission	Number of fugitives	Remarks	Percentage of the mission population
1	1782	San Carlos........	15	All adults.........	2.9
2	1782	San Diego........	2	....	0.29
3	1782	San Carlos........	...	"Several".........	...
4	1783	San Diego........	2–4	....	0.4
5	1786	San Buenaventura.	...	"Frequent"........	...
6	1787	San Buenaventura.	...	"Several".........	...
7	1787	San Diego........	30	More than 30 caught	3.3
8	1787	San Carlos........	...	Several caught......	...
9	1793	San Francisco.....	21	....	3.0
10	1795	San Francisco.....	280	....	32.1
11	1796	San Francisco.....	21	Caught...........	...
12	1796	San Francisco.....	150	....	19.0
13	1796	Santa Clara.......	41	....	2.9
14	1796	San Francisco.....	200	....	25.3
15	1797	San José..........	83	Caught...........	...
16	1798	Santa Cruz.......	138	80 adults, 58 children	27.4
17	1798	Santa Cruz.......	90	Caught...........	17.9
18	1798	San Francisco.....	48	Returned voluntarily	7.4
19	1799	San Carlos........	50	Caught...........	7.0
20	1800	Santa Clara.......	21	Caught...........	1.7
21	1804	Santa Clara.......	32	Caught...........	2.6
22	1805	San Gabriel.......	40	....	2.5
23	1805	San Juan Bautista.	200	....	16.9
24	1805	San Francisco.....	13	Caught...........	1.1
25	1806	San Francisco.....	10	Caught...........	0.9
26	1806	Santa Clara.......	48	Caught...........	3.4
27	1807	San Francisco.....	62	....	6.7
28	1813	San Buenaventura.	2	....	0.2
29	1816	Soledad..........	19	....	3.8
30	1816	San Fernando.....	...	Fugitives increasing.	...
31	1816	San Francisco.....	6	Caught...........	0.5
32	1816	San Juan Bautista.	12	All male..........	2.1
33	1816	San Buenaventura.	1	....	0.07
34	1816	Santa Cruz.......	40	Returned voluntarily	11.2
35	1819	San Francisco.....	...	"All" ran away temporarily.........	...
36	1819	San Juan Bautista.	47	....	7.1
37	1819	San José..........	15	....	0.9
38	1820	San Francisco.....	30	....	2.4
39	1824	Santa Bárbara....	453	Fled after rebellion..	49.1
40	1824	Santa Bárbara....	163	Caught...........	...
41	1825	Santa Cruz.......	27	....	6.3
42	1826	Solano	13	....	4.5

missions in 1817, was 1,596. The probable total fugitives for the nineteen missions in 1817 (based on 3,205 for 15 missions) was 4,060. Then the temporary fugitives at the time of the 1817 count amounted to 2,464. Since the entire population of the missions at that time was 20,427, the percentage of current fugitives would have been 12.1, a value which

TABLE 4
Total Number of Fugitives up to 1817

Mission	Number of fugitives	Percentage of cumulative baptisms
San Diego	316	7.5
San Juan Capistrano	254	7.1
San Gabriel	473	8.6
San Fernando	5	0.2
San Buenaventura	27	0.8
Santa Bárbara	595	15.1
La Purísima	52	1.8
San Luis Obispo	136	6.1
San Antonio	167	4.3
San Carlos	431	15.6
San Juan Bautista	174	8.0
Santa Cruz	60	5.8
Santa Clara	310	4.9
San José	3	0.1
San Francisco	202	3.8

checks reasonably well with that of 8.3–9.8 derived from the data in table 3. As a compromise, 10 per cent will not be far from the actual value.

The extent of fugitivism may be better appreciated if we translate the existing data into different modes of expression. It should be consistently remembered that the act of escape was the culmination of the response; it was the final gesture, arising from an urge which in many instances may have been frustrated. As suggested previously, a large share of the population was not in a physical condition appropriate to the arduous necessities accompanying the process of running away. Many persons were too young, too decrepit, too ill to attempt it. A great many more found themselves inhibited by the moral suasion or physical pressure exercised by the missionaries. Others were swayed by fear of the punishment which was often meted out to recovered apostates or by the desire for certain rewards, perquisites, and inducements held out to the faithful. As the years went on, many had been raised from childhood in the mission and had no haven of refuge outside to which to flee, even had they so desired. Escape was a serious and dangerous procedure fraught with innumerable perils and uncertainties. Numerous must have been the primitive Hamlets who preferred to bear those evils which they had, rather than fly to others they knew not of. And yet, in the face of all this, at any particular time approximately one person out of ten was undertaking to escape the mission environment. The escape response therefore constituted a biological phenomenon of very deep significance. It passes definitely from the category of the isolated individual and becomes a group movement, a mass tendency which was held in check only by the severest measures on the part of the dominant race.

Here we begin to observe an example of the action and interaction, the mutual interplay of factors, which so frequently arises at the point of contact of two species, races, or cultures. The escape response must be regarded as basic, the primary reaction to the inherent conditions of missionization. Once this process started, however, the situation changed because certain new problems were thereby engendered. First, from the moral and religious point of view the effect was very bad, since it advertised the fact that, so far as the neophytes were concerned, the mission system was not a success and that conversion to Christianity was not a force sufficiently powerful to hold the converts. Thus a bad influence was brought to bear upon the remaining, faithful Christians as well as upon the gentiles. Second, the material effect was disturbing through the disruption of mission administration and reduction in the necessary labor supply. Third, social problems were created among the troops and civilians by the presence of idle and impoverished Indians in their midst. Fourth, the only too acute danger existed that certain of the fugitives would inflame anti-Spanish sentiment among the gentiles, to the extent of armed uprising and attack. A very hazardous state of affairs thus came into being, one which could not be tolerated by the whites.

In responding to this new situation, which they themselves had created, the clerico-military administration had three courses open to them, all of which they pursued at one time or another: (1) by various means to prevent escape; (2) to punish those who escaped and were caught; (3) to send out armed forces to capture runaways and return them to their missions. However, the effect of the first two of these procedures was to intensify the original escape complex by adding new factors which exerted an unfavorable influence on the converted Indians. Physical restraint and confinement, as well as punishment of a corporal or any other nature, would render more violent the desire to get away on the part of a previous fugitive and would crystallize the urge in others who as yet had not gone the whole distance in this type of response. Moreover, it led to abuses on the part of individual soldiers and clergymen which were in no wise contemplated by the mission founders. This was followed by more widespread apostasy and thus a vicious circle was established. The final stages were witnessed after secularization, when the control and restraint of the church fathers was removed and the entire mission system went to pieces with terrific rapidity.

The third procedure operated somewhat differently but to the same end. Since many fugitives went to the wilderness and were harbored by unconverted gentiles, the expeditions necessarily followed them thither. This resulted in a rude awakening for the savages. They saw armed parties come among them and drag off the Christians to a fate which must have seemed like slavery. Their first impressions of the white men, therefore, can scarcely have been favorable. This in turn predisposed them against conversion. Consequently, when many of them in the later days were brought by strong moral pressure or even physical force to the missions, the desire to escape was already present in the minds of many of them, even before they saw their new environment. Obviously, this tendency to escape became increasingly intensified, the more such neophytes were brought under mission auspices.

A great deal could be written concerning the details of administrative policy toward fugitivism and the methods used to combat it, but such extensive consideration, although of historical interest, does not appear necessary at the present juncture. The primary thesis is clear: fugitivism as the first active response of the neophytes to the mission environment was of such wide scope as to constitute a mass reaction to certain elements in that environment.

Rebellion.—The second mode of response was active resistance. Customarily among the animals—apart from sex or food competition between individuals—physical combat is the last resort when flight or escape is prevented. It must be regarded as the extreme response, to be utilized when all else has failed, a response the appearance of which requires a stimulus of maximal intensity. The analogy of the animal can, of course, not be pressed too far, since the response of the animal is always with reference to other individuals. One cannot conceive of a wolf or a lion attempting to bite or claw a set of circumstances or a complex of environmental factors as he would a tangible enemy of his own or some other species. Nevertheless, there are points of similarity. The human being would not attempt to take physical action against a political or economic system, but he might do so against a person whom he regarded as being responsible for that system. Furthermore, a group of human beings, unable to flee from such an environment, might pool their individual responses and organize a joint effort against the system through resistance to those persons or groups who were regarded as upholding it. Active resistance or rebellion therefore becomes a group response rather than one in which individual units are concerned. It is naturally not essential that the entire population be involved, although in extreme examples it may be. What is necessary is that the stimulus become sufficiently intense to pass the threshold of reaction of several individuals simultaneously, so that the response of all occurs at the same time. If the stimulus—be it of whatever nature, physical, economic, social, or moral—arises suddenly and with great force, the response will be equally quick and strong. But if the stimulus, as represented in the general environment, is relatively constant and perhaps at a low level of intensity over long intervals of time, there will be no large-scale group response. The response will then take the milder form of attempted flight rather than resistance. Occasionally, however, and apparently almost at random in the statistical sense, the threshold of reaction will be passed simultaneously in a number of persons, and, if the number is great enough, there will be a sudden and seemingly inexplicable local outburst of active physical rebellion. Thus we may explain the periodic uprisings which disturbed the even tenor of mission days. For rebellion was not a continuous performance, as was apostasy, but appeared now and then, on a few occasions when the cumulative influence of mission environment reached a point where some small group of neophytes could no longer find release in flight and could no longer restrain the antipathy which they felt toward the mission routine.[4]

Many of the so-called uprisings or rebellions noted by the missionaries or subsequent historians were little more than personal quarrels or family feuds, such as might arise in any community. Frequently they spent their force in a single homicide or other act of violence. Several cases of attacks on priests are on record, of which the most noteworthy was the murder of Father Quintana at Santa Cruz. But these cannot be regarded as revolts, fundamentally, against the system. Frequently also small struggles took place between mission Indians and adjacent heathen or between heathen and the Spanish, in which certain neophytes participated. These likewise must be left out of consideration. It should be noted, however, that, whenever a strictly internal uprising did occur, the tendency of the rebels was to enlist the sympathy and material support of any available gentiles. This was clearly true in the first noteworthy insurrection, in 1775 at San Diego.[5] This affair is significant in numerous respects. In addition to its extent—for several hundred Indians were concerned and the material damage inflicted was great—its effect on the Spanish was profound, so that it colored their entire Indian policy in subsequent years. Al-

---

[4] It should be emphasized that no moral or ethical connotations are here intended. The mission Indians for present purposes are to be considered in the light of organisms only, and their behavior is to be investigated by the same methods as would be employed with an entirely nonrational species of animal. Whether missionization was good or bad for them, or whether civilization for them was desirable on spiritual or cultural grounds, is completely aside from the question.

[5] For details concerning this famous revolt any of the standard works may be consulted (e.g., Bancroft, Hittell, Engelhardt). For contemporary records Palóu, *New California*, 4:37–38, may be mentioned, as well as Ortega, "Account of Insurrection," Nov. 30, 1775, St. Pap. Ben. Mil., 1:1, Carrillo, "Evidence taken," 1776, Prov. St. Pap., 1:221 ff., and Rivera y Moncada, "Statements," June 18, 1776, St. Pap. Ben. Mil., 1:22.

though it occurred only six years after the arrival of the first expedition of Portolá and Serra and the founding of the mission, it was a distinct reaction to missionization on the part of converts. The latter at the time had not been aggregated into the mission establishment proper but, owing to lack of accommodations, were permitted to remain in their own villages. The full force of the mission environment had therefore by no means affected them. Nevertheless eight Christian villages participated, as well as an indeterminate number of heathen villages. As a matter of fact, aside from having gone through the formal process of religious conversion, the Christians differed in no essential respect from the heathen. The reasons offered for their action were very simple but illuminating. According to the testimony recorded by Rivera y Moncada the neophytes revolted because the fathers baptized them, and they wanted to kill the fathers and soldiers "in order to live as they did before."

The rapidity and intensity of this San Diego response designates these Yuman Indians as being endowed not only with considerable energy and drive, but also with unusual perspicacity in recognizing the hidden dangers of missionization, racially speaking, even before they had acquired any degree of practical experience with it. Indeed this tribe was always troublesome. In direct nonconformity with conventional mission policy the administration was compelled indefinitely to allow them to a very marked extent to live in their own villages. They were never tractable as laborers. Beyond the distance of one day's march they remained unconquered and predominantly unconverted through mission history, and after 1834 they caused enormous trouble by repeated attacks on white settlements.

In 1785 an attempt was made to murder the missionaries at San Gabriel,[6] and the following year there was an abortive conspiracy at San Diego.[7] Trouble broke out in 1794 at San Luis Obispo which was termed an "uprising" (*levantamiento*).[8] Further minor disturbances continued for several years, often in conjunction with the stock-raiding activities of the surrounding gentiles, but nothing of real significance

---

[6] Fages, Dec. 5, 1785, Prov. Rec., 2:131.

[7] Zuñiga to Fages, San Diego, August 15, 1786. Prov. St. Pap., 6:35.

[8] Arrillaga, 1794, *ibid.*, 12:187.

happened until the Purísima rebellion* in 1824. Early in March of this year the neophytes at Santa Ynéz, Purísima, and Santa Bárbara initiated a well-organized revolt. At Santa Ynéz and Purísima they took over the missions with some loss of life and much property damage. However, troops were immediately dispatched, and the insurrection was crushed after a brisk battle in which the Indians incurred numerous casualties. The survivors, to the number of hundreds, fled in a body to the valley and were recovered with the greatest difficulty. This is the only instance where the converted Indians, north of Los Angeles, organized and carried out a really serious rebellion. Although the proximate reasons advanced by the culprits were inadequate and even fantastic, there is no doubt that the ultimate cause lay in years of dissatisfaction and discontent, which increased steadily and finally exploded in open warfare.

To summarize, there were no more than two really important examples of active physical resistance by the Indians, and in both these the outcome was complete failure. In this respect, the contrast is indeed significant between the aborigines of California and those of the Southwest, like the Yuma and Apache.

Contemporary opinion.—That the neophytes were not all completely happy and contented in their new environment was entirely obvious to those who lived with them and watched over them.[10] Indeed the failure of the converts to appreciate the efforts made on their behalf

---

* The documentary material concerning this affair is voluminous. The political and ecclesiastical background as well as the military events have been adequately treated by Bancroft and other historians.

[10] Exceptions to this statement are to be found in the early reports of missionaries during the first years of conversion. Since the original neophytes came in on a voluntary basis, and since the routine of the mission had not yet been established in full force, there probably was a higher degree of contentment in the early years than afterward. It must be remembered also that the first accounts of mission work are likely to be optimistic and enthusiastic.

Some individuals in later years made similar statements. The following excerpt from Benjamin Morrow (*A Narrative of Four Voyages* [1832], p. 212) shows to what absurd extremes some persons could go, for there is no single phrase or expression in the quotation which is not essentially false: "These converted Indians have a very smart, active, friendly, and good-natured demeanor. Their features are handsome and well proportioned; their countenances are cheerful and interesting; and they are generally a very industrious, ingenious and cleanly people. The sins of lying and stealing are held by them in the utmost abhorrence, and they look upon them as two of the most heinous crimes of which a man can be guilty, murder alone excepted."

was a continual source of perplexity and sadness to the missionaries. Likewise, the soldiers and civilians, long after the missions had disappeared, could not understand why the natives failed to adopt their new mode of life with enthusiasm and to thrive under it. The problem also drew comment from strangers who chanced to visit the territory as explorers or traders. Finally, the Indians themselves on a few occasions expressed their own ideas. It is of interest to set forth some of these comments and opinions, not because they throw much light on the underlying factors, but because they constitute an excellent example of the operation of the human mind when confronted with a problem in human behavior or biology and of the doubtful value of personal testimony relating to a rather abstract proposition. With respect, then, to the question: Why did the Indians seek escape from mission life, the following answers may be cited as illustrative of contemporary thought.

1. Opinion of White Men.

Notwithstanding all this, an irresistible desire for freedom sometimes breaks out in individuals. This may probably be referred to the national character. Their attachment to a wandering life, their love of alternate exercise in fishing and hunting and entire indolence, seem in their eyes to overbalance all the advantages they enjoy at the mission, which to us appear very great.[11]

. . . after they [the Indians] became acquainted with the nature of the institution and felt themselves under restraint, many absconded. Even now, notwithstanding the difficulty of escaping, desertions are of frequent occurrence, owing probably, in some cases, to the fear of punishment—in others to the deserters having been originally inveigled into the mission by the converted Indians or neophytes . . . in other cases again to the fickleness of their own disposition.[12]

Parmi les Indiens, dont la plus grande partie paraissent si soumis, il y en a qui connaissent tout le prix de la liberté, et qui cherchent à se la procurer par la fuite. Ils réussissent facilement a s'évader, mais ils sont souvent repris ... et, sans considérer que ces hommes n'ont fait qu'user du

---

[11] G. H. von Langsdorff, *Voyages and Travels in Various Parts of the World*, translation by T. C. Russell (1927), pt. 2, p. 171.

[12] F. W. Beechey, *Narrative of a Voyage to the Pacific and Bering's Strait* (London, 1831), 2:170–171.

droit le plus naturel, ils sont ordinairement traités en criminels et mis en fers impitoyablement."[13]

And if they alleged, as proof of cruelty, the number of Indians who have fled ... I had the satisfaction of replying that they were already coming back and that they assured me that none had gone for fear of work, nor of punishment, but because of fear of the disease, contagious and mortal, which was actually prevalent in the mission at the time; also on account of their natural preference for the wilderness."[14]

Let the more intelligent Indians be asked why they run away and they will reply: "The same things happen to us as to every son of Adam. Naturally we want our liberty and want to go to hunt for women ..."[15]

The neophytes during their period of probation see mission life as it is. They are not compelled to stay but most wish to do so and become baptized. Thereafter, however, they are prone to run away for no other reason than "innate fickleness."[16]

... they go astray for no other reason than that they are Indians."[17]

2. Indian Opinion.

[A certain Indian of San Antonio ran away] because he wanted to live away from the mission. He did not get a bit of land to farm and also he could not stand the oppression under which they live, and the many floggings they are given.[18]

[Many Indians have run away saying they are now a] free nation. They cry with one voice: We are free and will not obey or work.[19]

[Some Indians came to San Carlos saying that many were running away from San Francisco Solano] because the Indians do not like Father Altimira.[20]

The following items constitute the testimony of certain Indians who escaped but were caught. On their return each was asked to state why

[13] Auguste Bernard du Hautcilly, *Voyage autour du Monde* (Paris, 1835), 2:5. Most Frenchmen who visited California were unfavorably impressed by the aspects of compulsion characteristic of the mission system.

[14] F. de Lasuén, "Representación," San Carlos, Nov. 12, 1800, Sta. Bárb. Arch., 2:206.

[15] R. Abella to Solá, San Francisco, Jan. 29, 1817, Archb. Arch. 3(1):125.

[16] Paraphrase of statement of E. Tapis to Arrillaga, Santa Bárbara, Mar. 1, 1805, Sta. Bárb. Arch., 6:28.

[17] J. Cabot to De la Guerra, San Miguel, Mar. 6, 1818, De la Guerra Docs., 7:89.

[18] Echeandía to alcalde of Monterey, Monterey, Jan. 17, 1831, Dept. Rec., 9:81.

[19] Portilla to Figueroa, San Luis Rey, Dec. 20, 1834, St. Pap. Mis., 9:49.

[20] Sarría to Argüello, San Carlos, Oct. 18, 1823, Archb. Arch., 4(2):86.

he absconded. The arabic numerals below indicate the individual reasons given:

1. He had been flogged for leaving without permission.
2. The same reason.
3. The same reason. Also, he ran away because he was hungry.
4. He had been put in jail for getting drunk.
5. He had run away previously and had been flogged three times.
6. He was hungry. He absconded previously and, when he returned voluntarily, he was given twenty-five lashes.[21]
7. He was frightened at seeing how his friends were always being flogged.
8. Because . . . of the great hunger he felt.[22]
9. When he wept over the death of his wife and children, he was ordered whipped five times by Father Antonio Danti.
10. He became sick.
11. His wife and one son died.
12. Because of hunger; also, he was put in the stocks while sick.
13. He wanted to go back to his country.
14. His wife, one son, and two brothers died.
15. His wife and a son had run away to their country, and at the mission he was beaten a great deal.
16. Because of a blow with a club.
17. They beat him when he wept for a dead brother.
18. He went to see his mother.
19. His mother, two brothers, and three nephews died, all of hunger, and he ran away so that he would not also die.
20. Lorenzo went away.
21. His father died.
22. Being bad, they whipped him.
23. His wife sinned with a rancher, and the priest beat him for not taking care of her.
24. They made him work all day without giving him or his family anything to eat. Then, when he went out one day to find food, Father Danti flogged him.
25. His wife and two sons died, and he had no one to look after.
26. His little niece died of hunger.
27. He was very hungry.

---

[21] Nos. 1–6 inclusive are from a letter by Gutiérrez at Monterey, March 7, 1836, Prov. St. Pap. Ben. Mil., 81:44. Note that these incidents occurred after secularization when the mission (San Antonio) was in charge of an administrator.

[22] Nos. 7–8 from a *relación* by Argüello *et al.*, San Francisco, Aug. 9, 1797, Prov. St. Pap., 16:71. These Indians were new converts and ran away in a body shortly after conversion. They also participated in armed resistance to parties sent out to bring them back.

28. After going one day to the presidio to find food, when he returned, Father Danti refused him his ration, saying to go to the hills and eat hay.

29. When his son was sick, they would give the boy no food, and he died of hunger.

30. Twice, when he went out to hunt food or to fish, Father Danti had him whipped.[28]

Much of the above-cited Indian testimony will obviously be heavily discounted. Several of the accusations are absurd, and many of the reasons advanced are trivial and irrational. Yet they ring true to the primitive psychology of the Indian, as most persons who have had dealings with this and similar races will admit, and they merit at least a fair examination.

If we examine the opinions expressed by competent white observers, we find that they exhibit a uniform trend. They all ascribe Indian aversion to mission life to love of liberty, distaste for their surroundings, longing for their native home, or revolt against all forms of restraint or compulsion. In other words, the white man, thinking of the Indians as a group, conceives their responses in terms of pure abstractions. These abstractions are those in which his own thoughts are likely to be cast. In the early nineteenth century the rights of man and human liberty were dominant among politico-social ideas. Hence the emphasis laid on them by the white commentators.

The Indian neophyte, on the other hand, possessed no such philosophical background nor such a ready-made system of concepts to which he might refer his condition and his actions. The new convert had no comprehension of liberty as opposed to servitude or slavery because he had known only one type of social status and had no basis for comparison with anything else. Furthermore, aside from small family or tribal affairs he had never encountered a situation which demanded expression in terms of abstract social concepts. Consequently, when called upon to give an account of his reasons for a specific line of conduct, he was totally unable to go beyond the concrete events of daily life. We must, therefore, regard Indian testimony as rationalization of underlying discontent in terms of sharp personal experience with definite environmental factors. Viewed in this light,

---

[28] Nos. 9–30 were with the same group as Nos. 7–8. Argüello, "Relación," San Francisco, Aug. 12, 1797, *ibid.*, p. 74.

Indian testimony makes sense. Moreover, it is no longer incompatible with the testimony of the white man. Both groups approach the same solution of the problem, but they approach it by different pathways and in different modes of expression. Where the Frenchman or the American assigns love of liberty as the cause for flight or resistance, the Indian says he ran away because he was put in jail. Where the white man talks about slavery, the Indian says he objected to being made to work by some individual, for instance, some particular father in the mission.

From the statements given here and many more which might be adduced certain factors emerge as possessing definite weight in the mission environment. The most important, and yet by far the most difficult to assess, is that called loss of liberty, by which is meant the restriction of the Indians' freedom of action, particularly with respect to the freedom they had previously enjoyed. Under the missions they were under no greater physical restraint or social compulsion than many civilized groups today; yet with their background the loss of personal license was a severe blow. Perhaps the best analogy is not that of slavery, which implies rigorous physical exactions, but captivity.

Since it is not feasible to attempt analysis of the whole general concept of what we might call captivity, it is necessary to limit discussion to those more material aspects which can be treated from an objective, or at least semiobjective, point of view. The environmental factors concerned which are sufficiently concrete to warrant discussion here relate to such tangible aspects of mission life as aggregation or crowding, bodily confinement in restricted areas, reaction to the type of food furnished, forced labor, delinquency and its punishment, restricted sex relations, and certain cultural factors such as religious beliefs and language. To put these factors in terms of liberty or freedom, they relate to restriction of freedom in space, restriction in diet, restriction in type of physical activity, restriction of sex relations, and restriction of social and intellectual expression. Be it remembered that the word "restriction" as here used does not necessarily imply a reduction or diminution in the scope of any of these categories but rather implies their redirection in new and unaccustomed channels.

RESPONSES BASED ON SPATIAL RESTRICTIONS

The initial act of contact between the mission organization and the Indian was one involving spatial relationships. The process of conversion itself took the native from one region, the ancient environment, and placed him in another. Thenceforward he was restricted rigidly to the latter. Now his reaction to the new environment, his entire frame of mind concerning it, would necessarily be modified by the manner in which he was brought into the fold. If he came gladly and willingly, then he would be predisposed in its favor. If he were driven to conversion against his desires, then he would be prone thereafter to dislike or hate the system under which he was obliged to live. Compulsory migration, or in the term of the times "forced conversion," becomes the initial factor of restrictions imposed in space.

Resistance to compulsory conversion.—At the outset it must be stated unequivocally that neither the plans of the Franciscan hierarchy nor those of the political government of New Spain contemplated conversion of the heathen on any other than a voluntary basis. Hence it is not at all surprising that the theory endorsed by Serra, Palóu, Lasuén, and the other early missionaries and the routine actually practiced by them employed no other means of conversion. Any pressure was restricted to legitimate moral suasion, spiritual arguments, and social or economic inducements extended without recourse to threats or physical compulsion.

The method of kindliness and persuasion sufficed to bring in large numbers of heathen during the first twenty years of the missions. In 1787 Captain Goycoechea of Santa Bárbara, a bitter enemy of the missions, was able to say, ". . . we still do not solicit heathen, only receive those who voluntarily offer themselves for baptism."[24] The motives which prompted these voluntary conversions were undoubtedly various. In the light of centuries of experience the missionaries very skillfully played upon every conceivable natural desire. They emphasized the externals of their religion—the ceremony, the music, the processions. They also sought to make mission life as attractive as possible by holding out the inducements of clothing, shelter, and food. Accord-

---

[24] Goycoechea to Fages, Santa Bárbara, June 27, 1787, *ibid.*, 7:58.

ing to any moral or ethical standards, these methods were entirely proper and laudable.[25] However, inevitably, after the adjacent natives had been assimilated in their entirety and it became imperative to broaden the field of conversion, mild methods gradually became inadequate. Instead of waiting for the heathen to come in (Serra was obliged to wait months for his first converts at San Diego), the fathers began to go out after them. These expeditions took the form, in the beginning, of peaceful little trips to neighboring villages, where perhaps the local chieftains could be persuaded to undergo baptism. Frequently neophytes were sent out to proselyte among the heathen brethren; occasionally soldiers were employed for the same purpose. Obviously, troubles arose; some gentiles were recalcitrant, some were even hostile. This in turn called for stronger methods. Mild, sober exposition of the beauties of Christianity and the charms of mission life no longer sufficed. Meanwhile the grim threat of the military had long been in the background. It was entirely natural that the missionaries, when simple persuasion began to lose its power, should turn to the soldiers for support. The latter, jealous of the missions and seeking to advance the political power of the state, were only too willing to co-operate. The entrance of the military into the active field of proselyting ended the era of true voluntary conversion. The terms *conquista* and *reducción* lost completely their original spiritual connotation and came to signify little more than the subjugation of the natives in the strictly material sense.

The shift in practice and its accompanying alteration in policy occurred during the decade 1790–1800, principally under Governor Borica. As early as 1787 Governor Fages reported:[26]

We find that the gentiles who are gathered in these missions are regularly those which inhabit their vicinity and that on passing six or seven

---

[25] The opinion of the laity was that the mundane inducements were more potent than the spiritual. Thus Beechey, who was generally quite fair in his estimates, says (*op. cit.,* 2:23), "When these establishments were first founded, the Indians flocked to them in great numbers for the clothing with which the neophytes were supplied. . . ."

Jesús J. Vallejo, a violent partisan of the missions, states ("Reminiscencias," p. 27): "I am of the opinion that most of the Indians abandoned their savage life animated more by the desire to improve their social condition than impelled by religious sentiments. . . ."

[26] "Report on the Missions," 1787, St. Pap. Mis. Col., 1:150.

leagues distance from their native heath they either will not be baptized or will not remain long in the mission.

He went on to say that it was impossible to reach these natives because of the labor involved in getting them and recovering them when they ran away.

In 1794 the governor was memorialized by the missionaries of San Francisco.[27] They wished permission to hunt new mission sites north of the Bay and reported that neophytes had been sent by boat to the Bay islands, "para que conquistaran Gentiles." Subsequently the governor refused such requests, commenting as follows:[28]

The zeal of the Religious for the salvation of souls stimulates them to attract to our religion by all methods the unhappy heathen who live in darkness and so they use whatever means they judge appropriate although some of these methods are fruitless. There is no doubt in view of what has just happened to the Christian Indians whom they sent by sea to catechize [heathen] that in the future they should abstain from such conquests and impressments.

The following year the governor wrote that guards would be furnished missionaries to confess or baptize Indians who could not get to the mission but "never to capture fugitives or above all gentiles."[29] Again in 1798 orders were issued to the effect that gentiles must be handled carefully and not be brought by force to the mission.[30]

It is clear from the tenor of the official correspondence, as well as from much other evidence, that the missionaries near San Francisco were recruiting heavily by means of private parties and expeditions from the Costanoans and the Coast Miwok. The great increase in baptisms shown in the San Francisco baptism records at about this time substantiates such a presumption. Several hundred were baptized, so many, in fact, and from such a distance, that purely voluntary conversion could not be assumed even if we did not possess voluminous evidence of definite physical resistance on the part of the gentiles.[31]

---

[27] Fernández to Borica, San Francisco, Nov. 30, 1794, Prov. St. Pap., 12:28.

[28] Borica, Monterey, Dec. 3, 1795, Prov. Rec., 5:31.

[29] Borica to the *comandante* at San Francisco, Monterey, June 9, 1796, *ibid.*, p. 86.

[30] Argüello to Borica, San Francisco, Mar. 30, 1798, Prov. St. Pap., 17:97.

[31] As an example, the "Raimundo affair" of 1797 may be mentioned. Raimundo was a mission Indian who went out with a party of neophytes in search of fugitives and new converts. The party was cut to pieces in the East Bay region by gentiles.

By 1810 extensive expeditions in search of fugitives were established policy. At the same time many prisoners were taken and brought back to the missions. Often some of these were criminals and raiders and were treated as prisoners of war. Others were innocent of wrongdoing but were caught in the general net. Frequently they were released, but the temptation was strong to baptize them and retain them as neophytes. As time went on, the friction between wild Indians and whites increased, until toward the end of the mission period all pretense of voluntary conversion was discarded and expeditions to the interior were frankly for the purpose of military subjugation and forced conversion. It is not feasible to cite specifically all available data bearing on this matter. The following samples of events and opinions should suffice to establish the general validity of the contention that large numbers of gentiles, subsequent to 1800, were converted by coercion.[32]

1805. Luis Peralta went on a punitive expedition from Santa Clara.[33] After he had caught up with the Indians the latter began to fight. He fired on them and killed "five of the bums (*gandules*)." The survivors fled to the brush, where he attacked again and killed five more. The Spanish then "beat the bush" and captured "twenty-five head (*piezas*)," all women. The prisoners were then brought to Santa Clara for conversion.

1806. After a rumored conspiracy at Santa Clara, Gervasio Argüello went out to catch the culprits. He brought back forty-two Christians and forty-seven gentiles.[34]

1806. The governor's instructions to presidial commanders contained the statement concerning the Indians: "By frequent expeditions on

---

[32] Much detail will be found in the works of H. H. Bancroft and Father Zephyrin Englehardt (*Missions and Missionaries*). The former inclines to be unsympathetic with the missionaries; the latter is a strong proponent of the mission system. Although he does not deny the facts, Englehardt seeks to justify the activities of the fathers on the ground that their intentions and motives were above reproach but that their policy of conciliation was nullified by a hostile and often brutal military element. It must be admitted that he presents a strong case for the clergy.

[33] Peralta, "Diario," 1805, Prov. St. Pap., 19:33. The contemptuous tone which characterizes his references to the Indians is very typical of the soldiers and civilians subsequent to 1800.

[34] Arrillaga to *comandante* of San Francisco, Monterey, July 17, 1806, Prov. Rec., 12:266.

the part of the Commanders we might be able to achieve their total conquest or reduction."[35]

1816. Father L. A. Martínez made an expedition to the tulares. Although the "fruit of his expedition" was only five persons, the incident called forth comment by the prefect, Father Sárría, who protested vigorously forced conversions made with the aid of troopers.[36]

1819. Father Amoros reported that they had just baptized in San Rafael one hundred Indians from the region of Tamales, "the remnants who had survived the conquests of San Francisco Mission."[37]

1823. Amoros reported:[38] "It seems that the Guiluc nation is remaining quiet. The gentiles brought by Sergeant Herrera were baptized and are very contented." However, since the seventeen men from Livantolomi did not wish to come, he advised a small expedition to collect them.

1823. The following account represents what was probably an extreme example, but it is sufficiently graphic in detail to merit reproduction in full. This is contained in a personal letter from Father Altimira to the prefect.[39] He had uncovered excesses committed by a group of Indians from San José who had been permitted to go out hunting gentiles for conversion. The gentiles from the rancheria Lybaitos deposed as follows:

Several days ago there came here an Indian from San José called Ildefonso with many mission Indians armed with bows, spears, and 2 guns, saying that they had come to hunt fugitives. They went to Ululatos and the Indian Ildefonso told them that they must come to San José and be made Chrisians, that Farther Narciso [Durán] was summoning them, and if they did not respond, the Father from San Francisco would come to get them, and they would suffer much because they would be severely chastised. The Ululatos, Christians and gentiles, resisted, saying they did not want to, whereupon they [the San José Indians] held them [the Ululatos] up, robbed them, and beat them. We [the Lybaitos] being afraid, ran away and escaped. They then went to the rancheria of the Chemo-

---

[35] Arrillaga, San Diego, Dec. 22, 1806, Prov. St. Pap., 19:109.

[36] Martínez to Solá, San Luis Obispo, May 30, 1816, Archb. Arch., 3(1):33, and Sarría to Solá, *ibid.,* p. 119.

[37] Amoros to Solá, San Rafael, Sept. 26, 1819, *ibid.,* 3(2):111.

[38] Amoros to Argüello, San Rafael, April 10, 1823, *ibid.,* 4(2):84.

[39] Altimira to Señan, San Francisco, July 10, 1823, *ibid.,* p. 21.

coytos, fought, killed five men, and wounded one other. Afterward they went to another rancheria, called Sucuntos, and killed all the people[*sic*]. They carried off many gentiles by force and shipped them away. They went to another rancheria on an island called Ompimes, and then we saw no more of them. They were here three days and nights. Your Christians, Ululatos, Suisunes, and the gentiles unbound each other and set out for the Tulares, for which reason they are here. All of us are fatigued and dispersed.

Altimira then protested strongly against such measures and exhorted the prefect to correct the situation. He mentioned Father Amoros and, referring to Father Durán, said:

It is already an old scandal the way he operates in this matter. A thousand times I have heard mentioned his outrageous and arbitrary sorties, in which he goes out, or sends a large body of neophytes.

The following opinions of contemporary observers are significant and representative.

Ein Soldat ging noch weiter und beschwerte sich gegen uns dass der Komandant ihnen nicht erlauben wollte, sich dort drüben Menschen einzufangen um sie, wie in den Missionen, für sich arbeiten zu lassen.[40]

Empero esto se salvará con conoser que California tiene incalculable numero de Indos selvaticos y estos cubrian las bajas y aun aumentaban el numero anual de cada mision porque con frequencia ó se prestaban voluntariamente a recibir el bautismo y quedaban en la mision ó se hasian espediciones militares en las cuales se conducian porcion de Indios que se obligaban a ser Cristianos y a quedar agregados por total a las comunidades establecias.[41]

The Indians were captured by the military who went into the interior in pursuit of them, detachments of soldiers being frequently sent out from the Presidio and other military posts in the Department on these expeditions to bring the wild Indians into the missions to be civilized and converted to Christianity. Sometimes two or three hundred would be brought in at a time, men, women, and children. They were immediately turned over to the padres at the different missions.[42]

The Indians who were brought into the fold of the missions were either induced through persuasion, by force, or enticed by presents.[43]

---

[40] Adelbert Chamisso, "Diary, 1816," in A. C. Mahr, *The Visit of the Rurik* (1932), p. 34.

[41] Juan Bandini, "Apuntos para la historia de la Alta California," MS, 1847, p. 100.

[42] William H. Davis, "Glimpses of the Past," MS, 1878, p. 6.

[43] Charles Wilkes, *Narrative of the United States Exploring Expedition* (1844), V:183.

Referring to parties of neophytes who were permitted to spend vacations in their home territory, Beechey says:[a]

> On these occasions the padres desire them to induce as many of their unconverted brethren as possible to accompany them back to the mission, of course implying that this is to be done only by persuasion; but the boat being furnished with a cannon and musketry, and in every respect equipped for war, it too often happens that the neophytes and the *gente de razón*, who superintend the direction of the boat, avail themselves of their superiority, with the desire of ingratiating themselves with their masters, and of receiving a reward. There are, besides, repeated acts of aggression which it is necessary to punish, all of which furnish proselytes. Women and children are generally the first objects of capture, as their husbands and parents sometimes voluntarily follow them into captivity [p. 23].
>
> The expenses of the late expedition fell heavy upon the mission, and I was glad to find that the padre thought it was paying very dear for so few converts, as in all probability it will lessen his desire to undertake another expedition; and the poor Indians will be spared the horrors of being butchered by their own countrymen, or dragged from their homes into perpetual captivity [p. 31].
>
> As for the various methods employed for the purpose of bringing proselytes to the mission, there are several reports, of which some were not very creditable to the institution: nevertheless, on the whole I am of opinion that the priests are innocent, from a conviction that they are ignorant of the means employed by those who are under them [p. 17].

From the above-cited evidence and from much more which might be adduced, it appears incontrovertible that mission policy under the pressure of various uncontrollable circumstances, underwent a profound change whereby conversion, instead of being entirely voluntary, was, with a few exceptions, a compulsory procedure. As suggested before, this forced translocation of large numbers of Indians could not fail to engender in many of them a conscious antipathy to their new environment, an antipathy which found an outlet in apostasy, fugitivism, and physical resistance. Particularly is this true of the converts made during the second half of the mission period. Not only were the newly baptized gentiles affected by this factor, but the "old Christians" as well. The latter, who had been born in the missions or who had been voluntarily converted years previously, were inevitably impressed by the treatment afforded other members of their race.

---

[a] F. W. Beechey, *op. cit.*, Vol. 2.

This must have been true despite the fact that the neophytes themselves were often the actual agents of coercion. Great masses of sullen, discontented newcomers, introduced against their will, were certain to modify the entire mission atmosphere and to contaminate with the virus of their hatred many racial brethren who otherwise would have been at least partially satisfied with their lot.

Homesickness.—We may now turn to another aspect of what has been designated restriction in space, an aspect which is very closely related to and associated with the factor of forced conversion and which, for lack of a more precise term, may be called "homesickness."

Homesickness was one of the most subtle and elusive of the imponderables in the Indian–mission complex, and yet perhaps one of the most universal. The word is used here in its broadest sense: the nostalgic urge which drives a human being toward some place, group of persons, or mode of life with which he has been familiar—an urge which, unsatisfied, gives rise to profound mental and physical disturbances. It is not necessary to assume that this feeling was at all times acute. Indeed, it may well have been absent in many neophytes, particularly those born in or brought at an early age to the missions. In many others the memories of early days and old friends or places doubtless grew dim and indistinct with the passage of time, until the longing fell below the level of the conscious and was revived only occasionally in connection with some incident or word which called up half-forgotten associations.

The evidence for the existence of widespread homesickness is presumptive rather than explicit, intuitive rather than objective. There is very little in the written documents covering the matter; the missionaries and soldiers were by no means psychoanalysts and, furthermore, had relatively little interest in the private emotions of the Indians. There are, to be sure, numerous scattered remarks by the clergymen with reference to the eagerness and desire of the neophytes to get out into the country again, away from the mission, but as a rule they did not specifically emphasize the factor of nostalgia. However, there are a few reports having a direct bearing on the problem which may be cited as illustrations.

In the autumn of 1823 numerous neophytes were moved from San

Francisco and San Rafael to fill up the new mission at Solano. There was a good deal of difficulty in persuading some of these to go, particularly those who originated on "the coast of Bodega" and other places in Marin County.[45] At the same time there was an agreement that certain neophytes at San José who did want to go might do so "because they are natives of the region around the new mission."[46] It is very clear that members of each tribe wished to be situated as close as possible to the ancestral home.

An interesting point is raised by W. H. Davis concerning the Indians who were Christianized in the later mission years:[47]

> Sometimes two or three hundred would be brought in at a time, men, women, and children ... After they had become adapted to their new condition, their influence on the new arrivals of Indians brought in was very marked, and they yielded much more readily to the civilizing influences exerted upon them than those first captured.

Evidently the presence of old friends and acquaintances or of any fellow tribesmen made life much more bearable under the strange new conditions.

Lasuén relates the following anecdote as characterizing the Indian temperament. After describing how the neophytes continually begged leave to hunt and fish because they were hungry, he goes on:[48]

On one of these occasions to some of those greedy people who requested permission to go to the woods I answered with certain annoyance: "Well, you make me realize now that, although you were given a steer, a mutton, and a fanega of grain every day, you would, despite all this, long for your woods and your shores." Then the keenest-witted Indian of those who had heard me replied, somewhat shamefacedly, "It is so Father, as you say, it is so."

Finally, the following graphic, although probably overdrawn, description by Katzebue may be quoted:[49]

---

[45] Sarría to Argüello, San Juan Bautista and San Carlos, Sept. 5 and 12, 1823, Archb. Arch., 4(2):56, 70.

[46] Altimira to Argüello, San Francisco, Oct. 4, 1823, *ibid.*, p. 25.

[47] W. H. Davis, "Glimpses of the Past," p. 6.

[48] Lasuén, "Representación," San Carlos, Nov. 12, 1800, Sta. Bárb. Arch., 2:174.

[49] Otto von Katzebue, in A. C. Mahr, *op. cit.*, p. 61. The reports of Chamisso and Choris, both of whom were with the Katzebue expedition, relate the same incident in almost the same words. Either the affair was one which made a great impression on all three travelers or else there was close collaboration in writing the three accounts.

Twice in the year they receive permission to return to their native homes. This short time is the happiest period of their existence; and I myself have seen them going home in crowds, with loud rejoicings. The sick, who can not undertake the journey, at least accompany their happy countrymen to the shore where they embark and there sit for days together mournfully gazing on the distant summits of the mountains which surround their homes; they often sit in this situation for several days, without taking any food, so much does the sight of their lost home affect these new Christians. Every time some of those who have the permission run away, and they would probably all do it, were they not deterred by their fears of the soldiers. . . .

Suggestive statements, hints, and inferences might be gleaned in much greater number from the documentary collections, but those given above may be accepted as adequate indication that homesickness existed among the mission Indians and may have been significant among the factors conducive to fugitivism.

Whatever the weight of this factor in the entire mission environment, it is certain to have operated less intensively among the earlier converts from territory adjacent to the missions than among those brought in later from distant regions. Each mission started with a group of neophytes who actually lived at or very near the mission site, and these subsequently continued to live literally in their home territory. Since the converts came from the same or closely related villages they all spoke the same language, had more or less the same cultural background, and understood each other thoroughly. As the radius of conversion lengthened with the years, however, people were brought in from a great distance. They came from different terrain, spoke a distinct language, and were thrown into a well-developed community of indifferent and possibly hostile strangers. Among such Indians the desire to return to their old country was vastly stronger than among those who had been raised almost on mission property itself. The missions around the Bay illustrate this principle quite clearly, particularly the mission of San Francisco. From 1770 to 1790 the converts were drawn exclusively from the peninsula, down as far as San Mateo. During these two decades fugitivism was not serious, because the Indians, if they did run away, went no farther than a few miles' or a few hours' travel from the mission. In the 'nineties the East Bay was overrun, and the Bolbones and Sacalanes, with other Costanoan tribe-lets, were carried wholesale to San Francisco. Precisely at this time escape in masses began. Repeatedly the apostates from this mission are specified as being Sacalanes or similar tribesmen, thus indicating that the foreigners from the *otra banda* were dissatisfied with existence as mission Christians. In the next decade, 1800–1810, large numbers of Valley and Delta Yokuts, Miwok, and Wintun, as well as Marin County Miwok, appeared at the San Francisco mission. These gave even more trouble and rendered the fugitive problem acute as long as the missions lasted. It cannot be maintained that simple yearning for the ancient habitat was the dominating reason for this augmentation of apostasy, but it must have been of some significance among the Yokuts, Wintun, and Miwok who were brought into the missions.

As indicated, the drive toward the escape-response became inten-sified (among all the neophytes) following the conversion of large numbers of distant gentiles. Now this intensification gave rise in turn to counterresponses on the part of the dominant white civilization which were of importance to both races. No longer was it possible to await with some confidence the return of neophytes who wandered off into the woods and the fields for a few days or who went over the hill to visit their gentile relatives and friends. No longer could a cor-poral with a few men go out in the morning and round up the forget-ful ones before evening. It now became necessary, if the mission system was to be held intact and the proper discipline and morale were to be maintained, to send out large, elaborate, and expensive expeditions comprising scores of soldiers, who would penetrate far into the interior and conduct real campaigns. In other words, we have here the imme-diate cause of the great expeditions which began shortly after 1800 and lasted till 1845. The effect of these was threefold: (1) they recap-tured many or most of the runaways; (2) they captured and brought back many new converts; (3) they antagonized the interior tribes and disrupted their whole natural existence. The results now became cumulative. The "forced" conversion of numerous new gentiles rein-tensified the powerful desire to escape already existing among those who had been "voluntarily" converted, and the further increase of apostasy induced more expeditions. Moreover, the rough treatment given the heathen decreased the possibility of their peaceful conversion and magnified their physical, or even military, resistance. This situation in turn carried with it a train of evils such as robbery, murder, and stock-raiding, which eventually became intolerable to whites and Indians alike; these evils, even if no other factors had intervened, would ultimately have spelled the doom of the entire mission regime. We see here, therefore, another example of that action and reaction which is so likely to characterize a racial or cultural contact: missionization → restriction in space (and many other causes) → flight or escape → pursuit, recapture and new conversion → intensification of the restriction → increased escape → more extensive and violent pursuit → . . . etc. Provided no other factors act to modify the chain of events, the final result is inevitably open warfare and the physical (not spiritual) conquest of one race by the other.

Revolt against overaggregation.—A third factor in the space-relation complex pertains to the population density or state of aggregation. It has been known for many years and recognized by naturalists as an established empirical fact that most animal species show favorable or adverse responses, either as individuals or groups or both, depending upon how many individual units are gathered together in a limited volume or area. The range of phenomena concerned is very wide, extending from a colony of bacteria or protozoa in a test tube to populations of large mammals. Naturally, the secondary factors involved— such as reproductive habits, available food, presence of predators or parasites, and so forth—are extremely variable, and the situation of one species is never exactly duplicated by that of another. In recent years the whole problem of space, density, and crowding with respect to individual and group welfare has been attacked from an experimental and quantitative standpoint. As a result, the importance of the purely spatial element has been established beyond question. One need mention in this connection no more than the work of Allee on goldfish and various invertebrates, Park on flour beetles, Gause on protozoa, Pearl on fruit flies, and Retzlaff on mice, to appreciate the extent of this trend of investigation.[50] Quite uniformly it has been proved that

---

[50] It is manifestly impossible to cite the entire literature in this field. Complete bibliographies will be found in the standard ecological texts and the monographs of Shelford, Chapman, and Elton. More specific references, as well as extended discussions of crowd-

for every population in any habitat whatever there is an optimum number of individuals. If the number is too great, the reproduction rate falls off and mortality from all sorts of causes increases. If the number is small, there tends to be an increase to the optimum.

Human beings are no exception to the general rule. Sociologists and historians can point to innumerable instances of overaggregation or overpopulation of a given restricted region, and our modern cities constitute a proving ground and laboratory for studies in human population density. In studying the responses of the California Indians we must therefore take cognizance of the shift in grouping which occurred during the process of missionization. In the aboriginal state, as has been repeatedly stressed by Kroeber and his colleagues, the coastal and valley Indians were spaced very exactly in conformity with the food supply. In regions of prolific sustenance the general density of population was high, whereas in barren areas it was low. Condensations of population were found along rivers, in coast lowlands, and in small fertile valleys. In the missions were likewise large aggregations within restricted territories. There was also satisfactory equilibrium with available food supply, since this could be adjusted through agriculture to any population level. The difference between the two habitats lay in density, not with reference to an extensive region or territory, but with reference to the numbers congregated for living purposes in a single small spot. In the native environment the actual number of individuals living in close physical contact was defined by the village or rancheria, and the latter was always strictly limited in extent. According to our present information, the village population never exceeded 200 (Channel Chumash), infrequently reached 100–150 (Valley Yokuts), and as a rule was below 100. Among many tribes not more than 30–50 constituted the habitat unit, a value which might decrease to the limits of one or two families. Wherever, for reasons of concentrated food resources, a large population could be supported, the whole aggregate exhibited a decided centripetal tend-

---

ing and aggregation, are given by W. C. Allee in his works: *Animal Aggregations, a Study in General Sociology* (Chicago, 1931); "Recent Studies in Mass Physiology," *Biological Reviews,* 9 (1934):1–48; and *The Social Life of Animals* (Chicago, 1938). Finally, all papers of consequence which have appeared since 1920–1925 have been abstracted in *Biological Abstracts* and *Berichte über die wissenschaftliche Biologie.*

ency, that is, it broke up into groups of uniform small dimensions, all of which might be close together, while each kept its territorial and social integrity. Indeed, this trend toward disaggregation, toward establishment of numerous units of 100 or less individuals, was a fundamental trait of the primitive social structure and must have represented a powerful species urge.

The tendency in the missions was in the opposite direction, toward forcing the Indians into larger and larger aggregates. As compared with the normal group of 30–100, the mission population averaged 500–600 and frequently was much greater. Aggregates of over 1,000 were common and occasionally a population of 2,000 and more was reached. This centrifugal mission trend naturally conflicted violently with the innate Indian centripetal preference, generating controversy, not only between missionaries and neophytes, but between two schools of Spanish opinion. The issue was not drawn, to be sure, in modern biological terms. The converts simply expressed repeatedly a desire to "live in their rancherias," in which matter they were supported by certain civilians and ecclesiastics. But the weight of missionary authority was against it.

The arguments against leaving the Indians scattered in their native homes after baptism were numerous and, from the standpoint of the missionary, unquestionably cogent. They were well summarized by Lasuén in 1802 and are worth repeating here. Lasuén pointed out:[51]

1. Wherever tried, the method had not worked. He cited the Colorado River disaster of 1783, although it might be answered that the causes of that fiasco were to be found elsewhere. He also pointed to the bad conditions in San Diego and the Dominican missions of Lower California. However, in this instance the missionaries really had little choice in the matter, for the Yumans of the regions flatly refused to come into the missions and nothing effective could be done to compel them.

2. The neophytes would revert to their original barbarous customs, which was undoubtedly true.

3. The neophytes would forget their catechisms and tend to apostacize from the Christian religion. This was also quite true and is a

---

[51] Lasuén to the guardian, Santa Clara, June 16, 1802, Prov. St. Pap., 18:269.

rather sad commentary upon the depth and sincerity of the process of conversion.

4. All the Christians now under the direct supervision of the missions would run away to the rancherias again and this would mean tremendous religious and economic loss. As a matter of fact, Lasuén might well have stated in so many words that it would have disrupted, in the material sense, the entire mission system. This argument is in itself a powerful bit of evidence of the existence of a centripetal drive on the part of the Indian communities which had to be counteracted in order to hold the missions together.

5. It would be necessary to baptize each rancheria *in toto,* for the existence side by side of gentiles and new converts would breed much friction and trouble.

We find thus a direct collision between two forces, each characteristic of, and inherent in, its own type of civilization: the disintegrative predisposition of the Indian culture and the integrative or fusing tendency of the white mission-military culture. The two are mutually exclusive; no compromise is possible. The weaker culture or race must give way and surrender to the stronger, to the probable detriment of the former.

The effects of this involuntary condensation of population were no doubt manifold. There must have been a general mental or psychological factor operative, which found expression in attempts of individuals to get away from the central aggregation or perhaps in a mass resistance to centralizing measures. However, we have no way of assessing or evaluating the extent and quality of such a factor. As a more concrete effect, the increased susceptibility to epidemics has already been mentioned, for it is obvious that the chances of spread of infections were enormously enhanced by bringing so many persons into close physical relationship. In much the same way the spread of ideas was facilitated. Purely by the laws of probability, if there is a group of $10x$ persons in a single physical aggregate, the chance of random contact between individuals is greater than if the same number of persons occur in 10 groups of x units each. Thus the condensation of population increases the possibility that an idea, say of escape, will travel through the whole population or that a conspiracy to revolt or to take some other joint action may be brought to fruition. There might well have been also an intensification of day-to-day wear and tear on the nervous system of the individual neophyte since, with the denser immediate population, he came in contact with a greater number of his fellow Indians than he ever did in his natural state. This in turn would have meant more stimuli per unit of time, more mental and emotional activity, and more quarrels and hates, as well as more friendships. On the whole, the entire tempo of his existence was accelerated by the mere physical presence of so many of his fellow men. A broadening of the field of stimulation is likely to be followed by a corresponding intensification of response, and it is probably safe to consider that apostasy and resistance would have been noticeably less in the missions, had the neophytes been segregated in relatively small groups.

This quickening of central nervous activity was particularly effective in the later converts who were brought in as adults from outlying tribes. The sudden transition from the settled, customary existence in a small rancheria to life amid the almost urban conditions of a large mission establishment must have come as a deep mental shock to this class of Indian. Not particularly facile and adaptable as a race, the converts must have found it extremely difficult to make the change. It is not surprising, therefore, that the immediate flight response was most highly developed among the latecomers and that the majority of the fugitives were among those most recently converted.

Resistance to confinement.—Before leaving the problem of spatial relationships one rather minor aspect of the problem merits mention. This relates to the enclosure of individuals within extremely narrow confines, i.e., incarceration. Imprisonment in the missions consisted of two types: jailing for civil or criminal offenses and shutting up in buildings for social or moral reasons. Concerning the former little need be said. In all cultural societies it frequently becomes necessary to curtail the liberty of the criminal, and mission society was no exception. But the number of persons involved was not great.

The other type of confinement was probably of greater biological and psychological significance. It affected not simply the socially maladjusted individual, but the solid citizen, the whole sober and working community. Reference is made to the widespread custom of shutting up and locking in every night large numbers of both females and males. There has been much bitter controversy respecting this practice by both friends and enemies of the missions, a controversy based primarily on humanitarian considerations. The idea of wholesale confinement was repugnant to numerous soldiers and civilians who were not otherwise noted for their gentleness and charity in dealing with Indians. The missionaries themselves regretted its necessity but supported it on grounds of pure administrative expediency in the control of community morals. It must be admitted that they advanced some extremely strong arguments. However, from the standpoint of this discussion the effects of the measure are of more consequence than its justification. Descriptions of the *monjerio,* or women's sleeping quarters, vary little. That given by Father Tapis of Santa Bárbara may be considered accurate and typical.[52]

The room of the single women is 17 *varas* [a *vara* equals roughly a yard] long by 7 wide, is of brick and has a high, wide window for light and ventilation. It has its sewer for corporeal necessities during the night. Along the walls is a platform, 20 *varas* long by 2¼ wide, with two stairways of brick and mortar at the ends for those who want to ascend and sleep upstairs. In the evening they have a fire for heat and every night they are given a tallow candle to illuminate the room.

Lasuén's description is almost the same.[53]

It is 17 *varas* long, more than 6 in width and of equal height; walls of one and one-half *adobes,* plastered with mortar [*mezcla*] and whitewashed, a strong and well-made movable platform [for bedstead] along both sides and a seat [*testera*] of more than one *vara* in height and two in width, three large windows with bars on one side and four loopholes on the other. Its toilet facilities are separate and everything made of good timber covered with planks and a roof of tiles.

Accusations were made that conditions in these rooms, as well as in those of the unmarried men, deteriorated in certain missions in such a way as to become nearly unbearable. The lack of ventilation and the odor were stressed particularly by certain political opponents of the missionaries. Although these charges were doubtless grossly exag-

---

[52] Oct. 30, 1800, Sta. Bárb. Arch., 2:99–100.
[53] "Representación," 1800, *ibid.,* p. 181.

gerated, there must have been some residue of fact. Assuming the *vara* to be equivalent to an English yard, then, according to Tapis, the floor area would have equaled nearly 1,100 square feet. The sleeping platforms along the walls, 17 by 2¼ varas (Tapis must have erred in giving 20 varas as the length), would have provided approximately 700 square feet. Although we have no precise data, it is probable that in the medium and larger missions at least fifty to one hundred women must have slept here. The smaller estimate yields a probable space of 14 square feet, or an area 7 by 2 feet, for each person. There can be no doubt that the women were packed in tightly, and that accumulation of filth was unavoidable. But let us ignore the possible physical effect of such crowding, the disturbances of rest, the spread of infection, and the inadequate ventilation. There still remains the mental and emotional strain caused in a group of adolescents and young men or women who were used to the utmost freedom of personal movement in their native state. It is unbelievable that they should not have resented years of being confined and locked in every night in a manner which was so alien to their tradition and their nature.

To summarize some of the foregoing discussion it may be stated that, apart from demographic changes, the missionized Indians responded to their environment primarily by numerous individual attempts to escape from it, or to resist it, in the physical sense. One group of factors which was at least partially responsible for the observed response was associated with the spatial restrictions imposed by the missions. In particular one may distinguish within this group: (1) emotional or material resistance to any type of compulsory conversion; (2) the emotional tendency to return to the familiar ancestral habitat which we have termed "homesickness"; (3) a revolt against over-aggregation in the missions which ran counter to a centripetal drive on the part of the Indians or urge to reëstablish the pristine, lower population density; and (4) a probable resistance to any confinement, especially to the custom of mass incarceration of both sexes at night. Further resolution of the components in this group of factors might be achieved if an exhaustive study were attempted.

V. LABOR, SEX, AND PUNISHMENT

LABOR

IN HIS REPORT on the state of the missions for 1795–1796 Governor Borica assigned as one of the causes for the bad condition of the neophytes "the labor which until recently they have performed ... without regard to their feeble constitutions."[1] Others also have repeatedly expressed or implied the idea that manual labor was one of the outstanding factors in the downfall of the mission Indians. Some examination of this theory is therefore desirable.

The labor problem, as it pertains to the neophytes, presents two aspects, the first relating to the extent and severity of the effort undergone and the second to the degree of compulsion exercised by the authorities. In other words, was the actual physical exertion detrimental to the Indians and was the compulsion of sufficient severity to induce a generally unfavorable response on their part?

Concerning the type, amount, and hours of labor in the missions we have several statements which are definitely reliable. During the early years of Borica's tenure as governor there was a good deal of agitation with respect to the condition of the neophytes. In the course of the controversy lengthy statements were issued by the four presidial commanders, and detailed rejoinders were submitted by the clergy, in particular the "Reply" of Tapis and Cortes and the great "Representación" of Lasuén. Among the matters discussed was labor, a very clear picture of which may be obtained from these documents. It must be remembered that as a group the soldiers were unfriendly to the missions, whereas the clergymen naturally were attempting to put up a strong defense of their institution. Some of these statements merit quotation *in extenso* since they constitute the basic source material on the question.

At the San Gabriel, San Juan Capistrano, and San Luis missions the number of hours of work in which the neophytes are employed is regulated. They begin their labors at six in the morning and work until almost sunset. In this one, the San Diego Mission, a certain excess of hours has been noted. . . . The Indian women are employed in every masculine oc-

---

[1] June 30, 1797, St. Pap. Mis., 2:98.

cupation, precisely as the men, but those in an advanced stage of pregnancy, those who are nursing, and the old women are assigned to carrying wood, and the children are used to frighten away birds from the gardens and orchards and to perform other light tasks.[2]

The time that the Indians regularly go to work is an hour or more after sunrise until close to noon and after two in the afternoon until almost sunset. Those who work by piecework (*tareas*) quit more or less early, according to when they finish. . . . The Indian women who are pregnant are put to work at the *metate* to grind *atole*, flour, etc.; the work of those who are nursing is not reduced as I am informed by those not in this condition. All those who are considered useful participate in hauling adobes, rock, bricks, and the like for construction. The small children are employed in driving the birds away from the vegetable gardens and orchards and other light tasks, according to their age and sex.[3]

The customary time that the Indians work in the missions, excepting piecework during the winter, is daily, in the summer until nine o'clock, unless some indispensable work presents itself such as freeing the season's grain from mildew or guarding adobes and tiles. I have seen several Indian women with children at the breast carrying adobes, also some pregnant but not in an advanced stage. The children are assigned to clearing the gardens, that is, pulling grass and weeds and other work that they are capable of enduring. Only the old people who are not strong enough for any task are exempted from work.[4]

In winter they work scarcely three hours in the morning and another equal period in the afternoon: in the summer about four hours now and then, leaving the trivial and light tasks to the pregnant Indian women, those nursing, the old people and the children.[5]

The customary hour for ringing the bell to go out to work is more than an hour after sunrise. At the stroke of the bell the people gather slowly in the quadrangle (with the exception of those doing piecework) and they jointly divide the duties of the day. After the tasks are distributed, many return to their homes and leave of their own volition to begin their work, which is unquestionably two hours after sunrise, and which terminates at the hour when the priests eat. It is absolutely certain that they never work more than one hour and a half in the afternoon, because it never occurs that Indians are found at work at the conclusion of the Divine Office, which is performed when the sun is midway to the horizon and lasts three-quarters of an hour, unless they are engaged in planting, weeding, culti-

[2] Grajera to Borica, San Diego, March 21, 1799, Prov. St. Pap., 17:191.
[3] Goycoechea to Borica, Santa Bárbara, Dec. 14, 1798, *ibid.*, p. 70.
[4] Sal to Borica, Monterey, Dec. 15, 1798, *ibid.*, p. 63.
[5] Argüello to Borica, San Francisco, Dec. 11, 1798, *ibid.*, p. 58.

vating or harvesting grain. On such occasions they are delayed somewhat as their fields are rather more distant. Then, however, they are excused from vespers.

In order that the so-called "great labor" that the commandant ascribes to the piecework system may be understood, we shall explain this clearly and distinctly. To the women no other piecework is given than that of grinding, and each grinds two *almudes* of wheat per day for *atole,* and when it is for bread eight and sometimes nine women grind seven *almudes* of soaked wheat. The men are given a piecework contract; nine men making 360 adobes two *tercias* long and one wide, which, divided among nine men makes 40 adobes a person. The soil is soft and water is close at hand. Those engaged in this piecework never work after eleven o'clock, neither on Saturdays, and often even not on Fridays because they had advanced the work during the early days of the week. Those who make tiles operate by piecework. Sixteen young men and, at times, an equal number of fairly old men who happen to be in the village, are designated. All these people, together with two women who haul sand and cow dung to them, make 500 tiles a day . . . These Indians finish the task at eleven, and even at that they have always advanced Saturday work so that they have the day free for going out or to rest.[*]

Then follows a description of weaving and spinning, also a discussion in acrimonious vein of the hardships suffered by neophytes who are loaned as laborers to the presidio.

The pregnant Indian women have never been, we repeat, have never been, assigned to the *metate* for grinding *atole,* flour, and other arduous tasks. And so that this may never happen they are very careful to advise us when they find themselves in a state of gestation so that their names may be entered on the register we have of the pregnant women. They are employed in finishing wool, pounding oak bark for the tannery, and accompanied by other women who assist them, cleaning wheat on the threshing floor after threshing . . . Sometimes they are employed in the garden and orchard pulling up weeds and grass. . . . After parturition they remain at home all the time they wish and when they feel that they may be of use or possess inclination to work they present themselves with the others whose duty it is to supply the *pozolera* with wood, having as associates in this task the old men who are able to work. During the wheat harvest the women who are nursing prepare the meal for *atole,* each one being given an *almud* of wheat which they grind on the *metate.* All the women who

---

[*] Reply of Tapis and Cortes to Goycoechea's statements, Santa Bárbara, Oct. 30, 1800, Sta. Bárb. Arch., 2:86–143. This is probably the most specific and detailed firsthand account of mission labor we possess. Lasuén's discussion is as authoritative, but is less concrete and much more prolix and argumentative.

are considered useful participate in carrying adobes, when the cart assigned to this work does not suffice . . . These same women also take part in the conveyance of brick and tile, and very rarely rock, the latter being small and for the purpose of leveling off the foundations. The hauling of other construction material is the duty of the ox-driver and his oxen and the mule-driver and his mules. Of the children, nine years of age and over, some are employed in combing wool for the looms and passing the shuttles to the weavers, others in watching the tiles and bricks so that the animals do not tread on them, others in chasing the birds away, but most of them in diverting themselves with their childish games.

In spite of individual differences arising from personal experiences or political bias all observers, not only those cited above but others as well, are agreed with respect to certain essential points. There can be no doubt that the standard working week consisted of from 5 to 6 days at 6 to 8 hours per day, let us say, 30 to 40 hours per week. Nowhere do we find any claims that more than 40 hours were required, except under extreme provocation. The actual tasks were those characteristic of rather primitive agriculture and strictly home industry. Much of this work would be classed today as light labor. It is very significant that even the bitterest opponents of the missions never accused the clergy of giving the Indians work which might cause either excessive fatigue through extremely long hours or physical injury through intense exertion and occupational hazard. The worst they could do was the charge that pregnant women were too severely treated. There is no doubt that by modern standards the work was very reasonable both as to hours and nature. One need only compare the mission labor condition as set forth in the excerpts quoted with modern civilized labor conditions such as are encountered by the average farmer or worker in heavy industry. We may conclude immediately therefore that, as far as the adult neophyte was concerned, he was not obliged to perform labor which could in any way be injurious physically in either the individual or racial sense.

The only possible exceptions were the pregnant women and the children. Respecting the latter, all presidial commanders are in agreement that nothing more arduous was required of them than a little gardening and bird chasing. Overburden of pregnant women would be a serious charge, were it not for the fact that because of the low birth rate, as well as for religious reasons, the missionaries were exceedingly anxious for pregnancies and deliveries to be successful and would be most unlikely to jeopardize the issue. Finally, it must be remembered that in the California "Arcadia" no one did any really strenuous work, and what would be regarded by the Spanish white population as onerous labor would have been considered quite ordinary by the average American of the period. The purely physical effects of manual labor may therefore be dismissed as a factor effective in the racial disintegration of the mission Indian.

The mental and moral aspects of labor, however, belong in an entirely different category. The compulsion placed on the Indian, the restriction upon his daily activity through obligatory physical effort is important. But it is not the whole story. His reaction to labor itself, in the abstract, must be considered, since mental or bodily exertion of the type demanded by white civilization was completely new to him. It constituted an environmental factor, of the nonmaterial type, with which he had never come in contact and which therefore required an emotional and intellectual readjustment or adaptation very difficult for him to make. Labor, with its associated complex system of rewards and penalties, has perhaps constituted a more serious obstacle to the racial reorientation of the Indian than brutal but quite comprehensible physical conflict. We may focus attention on the aspect of compulsion in labor among the mission Indians, keeping continually in the background the idea that labor in any form was alien to their disposition, their social heritage, and their biological environment.

Despite innumerable lamentations, apologies, and justifications, there can be no serious denial that the mission system, in its economics, was built upon forced labor. Any coöperative system of support, any organization which is economically self-sustaining, as were the missions, must of necessity be founded upon the productive toil of its members. This very necessity is the primary compulsion, but if the corporate members are of sufficient intelligence, the compulsion becomes rationalized and there is an appearance of willingness and volition. On the other hand, if the mass is stupid and ignorant, then the hierarchy of authority at the top must exercise force, moral or physical, to obtain the essential effort on the part of the mass. Compulsion then becomes personal, and we begin to speak of "forced labor." Thus in its essence the mission system predicated forced labor by the neophytes. Understanding all this, the missionary fathers did their utmost to enlighten the neophytes, but with little success. The next step was moral suasion, and it must be admitted that, in general, such measures were adequate. When, however, they failed, physical means became necessary,[7] for the economic discipline of the community had to be maintained at all costs. It was very natural that many neophytes, not in the least comprehending the ideals of the Church and its servants or the complexities of administrative theory, should regard necessary "forced labor" as directed personally at themselves and should rebel against it. On the other hand, it is noteworthy that of all the complaints and grievances of the neophytes, relatively few were directed against the work itself.

One certain adjunct to the mission labor system, and one which was repeatedly deplored by the priests, was the diversion of workers to the presidios and other army posts. Abuses grew up here which did not affect the main body of neophytes seriously but which became enormously magnified in their moral implications. It was at first contemplated that the construction and care of military establishments should devolve upon the army itself, but the soldiers were few and the officers negligent. Military effort was directed mainly toward garrisoning and protecting the missions. It was also a great temptation to the not overly industrious soldiers to tap the great reservoir of substantially free Indian labor. Hence a system soon came into effect whereby the clergy loaned their charges for work in the presidios as manual laborers and as domestic servants. It was fully understood that all such services should be paid for, the Indians to receive a fair wage, payable in money or commodities. Not only neophytes might be permitted to work at the presidios but gentiles as well, provided they came voluntarily and were paid in full.

---

[7] The term slavery has been uncritically applied to the mission social system. It should be pointed out that there was no implication of personal ownership whatever. Furthermore, in theory always, and in practice usually, the fruit of Indian labor was devoted to the welfare and improvement of the Indian himself. Any selfish enrichment of the mission was incidental and contrary to the tenets of the Church. The system was much closer to socialism or communism, in the Marxian sense, than slavery.

The wages were not high but perhaps were adequate. The daily wage rate was 1½ *reales* a day,[8] in 1787. This amounts to about six American cents. In addition, food and clothing were furnished. An appreciable number of Indians was involved. In 1790 Governor Fages used about 70 in Monterey over a period of six months. The workers were employed in groups, each group remaining some two months at the presidio.[9] From 1786 to 1789 inclusive a total of 1,184 pesos was contributed by the company at Santa Bárbara[10] as compensation for Indian helpers. This amounts to an average of 396 pesos annually, or at 1½ *reales* a day, 2,110 man days per year and, assuming a five-day week, 8 men continuously at work. In 1794 Sal reported[11] that 78 men were working at San Francisco: 40 neophytes and 38 gentiles. The same year Arrillaga stated that at Santa Bárbara the pay was 1½ *reales* per day plus an *almud* of maize per week.[12] At Monterey the remuneration was a strip of cotton cloth and a blanket per month. Very shortly afterward complaints began to arise that the stated pay was not forthcoming. Borica wrote to this effect[13] to the *comandante* of San José in 1795 and in 1804 the viceroy himself directed the governor to pay the Indians from San Juan Bautista who, in 1800, worked at Monterey.[14] Tapis and Cortes, as well as Lasuén, were very bitter concerning the failure of the soldiers to compensate the neophytes, and in 1825 the guardian, Fr. López, set forth a long argument to the effect that the missions were feeding the colony by Indian labor.[15] He also maintained that the neophytes had not been paid since 1810, fifteen years previously. There is thus no doubt that subsequent to 1790 the attempt to pay for Indian labor was abandoned and the work was done under unmitigated compulsion.[16]

---

[8] Fages to Lasuén, Monterey, July 10, 1787, Prov. Rec., 3:63.

[9] Fages to Castro, a series of letters, April to September, 1790, Dept. St. Pap. San José, 1:28–40.

[10] Goycoechea, Santa Bárbara, Dec. 30, 1792, Prov. St. Pap., 12:61.

[11] Sal to Arrillaga, San Francisco, Apr. 30, 1794, *ibid.*, p. 73.

[12] Arrillaga to Sal, Monterey, May 7, 1794, Prov. Rec., 2:147.

[13] Borica, Monterey, Dec. 23, 1795, *ibid.*, 4:241.

[14] Iturrigaray to Arrillaga, Mexico, 1804, Prov. St. Pap., 19:7–8.

[15] López to Alaman, Mexico, July 5, 1825, Archb. Arch., 3(2):141–148.

[16] In justice to the military it should be stated that they themselves were grossly underpaid, months and years often elapsing during which they received no compensation whatever.

Although, as with normal mission labor, that which was performed for the military was not over-severe physically, yet it no doubt served to intensify the aversion with which all labor was regarded by the Indians. It was a particularly offensive example of compulsory activity which was incessantly kept before the eyes of the Indians. The latter, who found it sufficiently difficult to comprehend why they should be required to work for their own economic advantage in the mission, were completely at a loss to see any justification for their being obliged to donate the sweat of their brow to the soldiers. As the guardian López put it, "The Indians are complaining bitterly at having to work that the soldiers may eat . . ."[17] Furthermore, the unjustifiable forced labor at the presidios probably served to create greater dislike for the draft upon their services at the missions, which was socially more or less reasonable. Since the neophytes were incapable of drawing fine distinctions, their tendency would be to charge the responsibility for abuses to those in direct authority over them, that is, to the missionaries.

Turning now to a more fundamental aspect of the labor problem, we observe that the California tribes shared with other Indians the characteristic, or the vice, of whole-hearted aversion to physical labor. Whether the labor was compulsory or voluntary, the Indian—at least at the time of his first contact with the white man—preferred not to perform it. Hence he has been universally termed lazy and indolent. Now there is very little to be gained by applying opprobrious epithets to a race or a group without analyzing, at least in a cursory fashion, the reasons for such inherent traits as call forth the epithets.[18]

In their wild state the Indians underwent extensive physical exertion. Even in California, where life was easier than in the eastern

---

[17] See fn. 15.

[18] A very restrained description of mission-Indian work habits is the following, taken from Lasuén's "Representación": ". . . besides those who have escaped or are away on leave, the sick and their caretakers. Those who are well are prone to offer some indisposition as a pretext, knowing that they are generally believed and that even in case of doubt the missionary always excuses them from work. Nobody hurries them; they sit down, they lie down and often leave to return whenever they see fit. When they work by the job [*tarea*] they are permitted to leave it unfinished and others, generally the majority, are urged not to exceed it. These *tareas* are customarily very moderate so that without more than the time necessary for common work and with only a little less indolence or with fair activity many are able to finish a whole day's work in the morning, and in three or four days that of a whole week to obtain recompense and have the rest of the time free."

forests or on the central plains, much hard work was devoted to the obtaining of food, whether through fishing and hunting or by gathering acorns, nuts, and other plant materials. The processes involved in preparing the food were likewise laborious and tedious. Furthermore, the building of shelters and the manufacture of clothing, utensils, and weapons demanded much time and effort. No Indian group ever survived a year in a state of complete indolence and inactivity. Indeed, among numerous tribes extraordinary exertions and hardships were necessary for simple survival. It is therefore inaccurate to assume that the Indian disliked to work simply because muscular exercise was involved. He disliked it because of the conditions under which it was performed. The whole basis of the aboriginal labor system was the idea of intermittent effort rather than steady, consistent exertion. This, in turn, was associated with the facts that, first, the food supply was highly seasonal and, second, no preparative measures were required. The fish ran at a certain time, the acorns were ripe in a definite month. Hence the native worked hard to accumulate these materials when they were available. He strove mightily and without stint for a brief period. Then he rested and loafed until his environment demanded another expenditure of energy. Even the women, upon whom devolved the domestic tasks, operated on much the same basis. Hence there was developed a tremendously powerful tradition of labor only when necessity demanded. There was no concept of continuous effort over a long period of time, directed toward a consistent production of commodities or an end to be achieved in the relatively distant future. In a sense the Indian style and method of labor was admirably adapted to his environment and to the needs of his way of life.

Now, place him in a so-called civilized environment, surrounded by a race with an utterly different tradition, that of the value of labor performed throughout the year. In order to conform to the new type of culture he is forced—in the widest sense—to alter his inherited method of work. Whether in a mission, on a reservation, or as an independent agent he is obliged to work every day, a certain number of hours, at tasks the immediate value of which are obscure to him. Since he sees no direct necessity for ploughing the wheat field or weeding the vegetable garden, he feels no internal compulsion to perform these tasks. He is thus regarded as lazy and improvident, and pressure is brought to bear from without. Since he cannot appreciate the value of the work, it becomes irksome to him, and he resents the pressure which forces him to do it. In other words, he tends to carry over into the new environment the habits of thought and the methods of labor which served him adequately under aboriginal conditions. As a result, not only the external compulsion but the labor itself acts as a stimulus which generates negative or adverse responses.

At this point a vicious cycle, similar to those already discussed, begins to form. In response to disinclination toward the new type of labor and to either impersonal economic compulsion or personal moral and physical pressure, the mission Indian takes one of two courses. He exercises passive resistance by stalling or "soldiering" on the job or by malingering and inventing all sorts of excuses for not working. Alternatively, he avails himself of the flight mechanism and runs away. No matter which course he adopts, he is regarded by the white race, clerical and secular alike, as indolent, improvident, and exasperatingly oblivious to his true economic welfare. To correct this failure in racial, social, and environmental adjustment, the missionaries, soldiers, and civilians respond by doing exactly the worst possible thing under the circumstances; increasing the extent and severity of the pressure, which in turn forces a little more labor from the Indian but also intensifies his own trend toward refusal to work or toward escape.

Thus we see in seventy years of mission experience an irreconcilable conflict between the inborn, almost instinctive tendency of the Indian to work in his ancient way and the necessities of the European and American economic system. Although, urged by compulsion of various categories, the Indian did perform a great deal of labor, this native, original tendency was substantially unaltered. Its tenacity was demonstrated by the fact that, when all compulsion was withdrawn at secularization but the opportunity for volitional labor and self-support was provided, the neophytes reverted in a body to their ancestral methods and disintegrated completely as an economic unit. As individuals, they either returned to the wild life among the heathen or subsisted miserably upon the thin charity of the white men, indulging in manual labor only to ward off acute, absolute starvation.

Apart from the strictly mission enterprise, as well as including it, the California Indian race proved itself a total failure as far as the labor system was concerned. From the point of view of population changes the race was doomed to severe depletion, if not extinction, in free competition with the whites simply because it could not sufficiently rapidly and successfully adapt itself to the labor system basic to white economy. This in turn is referable to the inherent attitude of the Indian toward consistent, long-continued physical exertion, an attitude built up through generations of adjustment to the wild environment, not to any genetically ingrained moral turpitude or reprehensible intellectual backwardness.

DEMOGRAPHIC CHANGE IN NORTHWESTERN
NEW SPAIN

The process of Spanish colonization in Northwestern New Spain, here roughly defined as Sonora and the Californias, set into motion a complex set of factors that contributed to demographic change; absolute population decline among the Indian groups involved, the growth of a largely mestizo settler population, and a number of different types of social and economic interactions between the two populations. Scholars in recent years have debated the causes and the nature of change. Alfred Crosby established a framework for the debate in his provocative book entitled *The Columbian Exchange,* which discusses, as the sub-title implies, the consequences of interaction between the Old and New Worlds after 1492.[1] In a recent study Henry Dobyns elaborated on one of Crosby's principal themes, the introduction and impact of Euro-Asiatic diseases, and prepared a chronology of epidemics between the sixteenth and early twentieth centuries that affected Native American populations. Dobyns applied his "epidemic mortality" model to Florida and calculated both a high contact population and the rate of population loss due to each of the major epidemics. The model when applied to all of North America has major implications for our understanding of the course of Native American history.[2] In a recent bibliographic article historical demographer Shelia Johansson cast doubt on the high contact population estimates and the degree of demographic collapse.[3]

A second approach which has not really taken the form of a debate is the dichotomy between the course of demographic change in the densely populated areas of "high civilization" in the core areas of Mesoamerica

[1] Alfred Crosby, *The Columbian Exchange: Biological and Cultural Consequences of 1492* (Westport: Greenwood Press, 1972).

[2] Henry Dobyns, *Their Number Became Thinned: Native American Population Dynamics In Eastern North America* (Knoxville: University of Tennessee Press, 1983).

[3] Shelia Johansson, "The Demographic History of the Native Peoples of North America: A Selective Bibliography," *Yearbook Of Physical Anthropology* 25 (1982), 133-152.

462

and the Andean region on the one hand, and the relatively sparsely settled areas on the fringes of the areas of "high civilization". Scholars have studied the question of demographic change in both areas, but few have systematically compared them.[4] Furthermore, most in-depth research has focused on the Indian population, and few have examined long-term trends in the settler population.

This present essay will attempt to briefly summarize patterns of demographic change in three areas within Northwestern New Spain; the Pimería Alta region of northern Sonora, Baja California, and northern Alta California. Attention will be given to both the Indian and non-Indian populations, but considerations of space will limit the analysis to gross generalizations. The Pimería Alta shall be the first area examined.

THE PIMERÍA ALTA

The Jesuits opened the Sonora mission frontier in 1620, but the missions did not develop in isolation. Miners discovered placer and hard rock deposits, and cattle ranches and farms developed to supply the mines.[5] The Jesuits had established missions on the fringe of the region later known as the Pimería Alta in the 1640s, but it was not until 1687 that Eusebio Kino established the first mission among the Upper Pima. The need to consolidate areas already occupied and shortages of missionaries prevented expansion of the mission frontier.

[4] For examples of studies of Meso-America see Sherburne Cook and Woodrow Borah, *Essays In Population History*, 3 volumes (Berkeley and Los Angeles: University of California Press, 1971-1979); and for Peru Noble David Cook, *Demographic Collapse Indian Peru, 1520-1620* (Cambridge: Cambridge University Press, 1981). For more general overviews see Nicholas Sanchez Albornoz, *The Population of Latin America A History* (Berkeley and Los Angeles: University of California Press, 1974); and two useful collections of essays: William Denevan, editor, *The Population of the Americas in 1492* (Madison: University of Wisconsin Press, 1976), and David Robinson, editor, *Studies in Spanish American Population History* (Boulder: Westview Press, 1981). The "Spanish Borderlands" has been the Latin American frontier region most closely studied. Sherburne Cook identified the different factors that contributed to Indian depopulation in Alta California in *The Conflict Between The California Indian And White Civilization* (Berkeley and Los Angeles: University of California Press, 1976), and in volume three of *Essays in Population History*, Cook co-authored a detailed study of the sacramental registers of eight of the Alta California missions. Henry Dobyns has a useful 1963 article entitled "Indian Extinction In The Middle Santa Cruz Valley, Arizona," *New Mexico Historical Review* 38 (1963), 163-181; and a longer monograph entitled *Spanish Colonial Tucson: A Demographic History* (Tucson: University of Arizona Press, 1976). In an unpublished PhD dissertation Mardith Schuetz studied the five San Antonio, Texas missions in some detail: "The Indians of the San Antonio Missions, 1718-1821," PhD Dissertation, University of Texas, Austin, 1980. These titles in no way exhaust the list, but are representative.

[5] James Hastings ably summarizes the colonization of Sonora in an article entitled "People of Reason And Others: The Colonization of Sonora to 1767," *Arizona and the West*, 3 (1961). 321-340.

The fragmentary baptismal registers from Cucurpe mission, located just south of the first Pimería Alta missions, enables a partial reconstruction of the frontier population of the 1680s. The first register records a total of 448 baptisms of Indians, most likely Eudeve, five non-Indian children, twelve Seri/Tepoca from the fringes of Spanish Sonora, two Yaqui from southern Sonora, and two gentiles (non-Christian Indians), most likely Upper Pima. The second register for the "Hiaquis [Yaqui] and servants of the settlers" recorded the baptism of 78 Indian children, five non-Indian children, four Opata from central Sonora, one Nevome, five Seri, one Pima, and fourteen Yaqui children. In the 1680s a small settler population with a predominantly Yaqui labor force occupied the valleys just south of the territory occupied by the Upper Pima. Although no missions as yet existed in the Pimería Alta, there were contacts between the Spanish and mission Indians on the one hand, and Upper Pima on the other.[6]

The same pattern of settlement spread into the Pimería Alta after 1687. As the Jesuits established missions and "pacified" the region, non-Indian settlers established mining camps in the Altar Valley in the 1730s and 1740s, and in the Cieneguilla mining district off and on for seventy years after 1771. In the first years of the Cieneguilla rush, for example, as many as 7,000 people lived in the mining district, making it one of the larger population centers in the province. A number of farming communities developed in the second half of the eighteenth century to supply the mines; Santa Ana, San Lorenzo, and Terrenate. Small communities arose and died around the different presidio sites in the region; Terrenate, Altar, Santa Cruz, Tubac, and Tucson. During the course of the eighteenth century the settler population in the Pimería Alta grew in separate communities, but also penetrated the Indian villages and in some instances marginalized the Indians in their own villages as occurred in southern Sonora. By the 1790s, for example, Imuris, a former *vista* (subsidiary settlement) of San Ignacio mission, had been depopulated of Indians, and was a small farming hamlet. The Franciscan stationed at San Ignacio continued to claim lands there. Individual Spaniards also established ranches in the region. In the 1730s, for example, three ranches existed on the Santa Cruz River between Soamca and Guevavi missions.[7] In 1821, the non-Indian population in the Pimería Alta was 7,900 ± 600.[8]

The population of the Pimería Alta mission was an open population in

<hr>

[6] Ms. Cucurpe Mission Baptismal Registers, Magdalena Parish Archive, Magdalena de Kino, Sonora.

[7] Robert H. Jackson, "Demographic and Social Change in Northwestern New Spain: A Comparative Analysis of the Pimería Alta and Baja California Missions." unpublished Master's Thesis, University of Arizona, 1982, chapter 6.

[8] *Ibid.*, p. 159.

the sense that the missionaries repopulated the missions with gentile Pápago from the deserts west of the missions. Small numbers of other Indians settled in the missions voluntarily or otherwise; Yumans and other Colorado River groups, Yaqui, Opata, Seri, and Apache.[9] The repopulation of the missions serves to give the impression of relative fluctuations in numbers, but the evidence clearly indicates an actual decline in population. Writing in 1716, the Jesuit, Luis Velarde, wrote that,

> . . . despite the illnesses and epidemics that have consumed many people, there are about ten thousand souls [in the Pimería Alta] of both sexes.[10]

The application of the family reconstitution methodology to the extant sacramental registers from the Pimería Alta missions provides the basis for a more detailed explanation of the causes of population loss. A fifty year sample from San Jose de Tumacacori mission for the years 1773-1825 gives the following results. Women married young—around age fifteen—and on average had three children during a mean period of childbearing of seven years terminated by premature death. There were, however, exceptions. María Pilara Arcayos, for example, bore ten children between 1773 and 1785, and outlived five husbands. Of a sample of 123 children born at the mission, 93% died before reaching age ten.[11]

Indian women proved capable of bearing children, but premature death, due in part to complications from childbirth, limited the number of live births. High infant and child mortality rates wiped out any potential population growth through natural reproduction. High death rates can be attributed to a number of factors: the inability of young mothers to properly care for their children—loss of the knowledge to do so, the impact of the full range of childhood diseases, poor nutrition, and deaths during epidemics. The populations of the Pimería Alta missions, then, failed to reproduce in sufficient numbers to make up for high mortality—not enough children survived to make much of an impact on the continued survival of the populations.

What contributed to the high mortality? Both epidemic and endemic diseases were by all accounts major if not the most important factors, but we must explore what elements contributed to the high level of susceptibility to disease of the Indian populations. Some have argued that isolation of America from the Eurasian disease pool left the New World populations

---

[9] *Ibid.*, p. 47.

[10] Luis Gonzalez R., editor, *Etnología Y Mision En La Pimería Alta, 1715-1740,* (México, D. F.: Universidad Nacional Autónoma de México, 1977), p. 82.

[11] Ms San José de Tumacacori Mission Baptismal, Burial, and Marriage Registers, Diocese of Tucson Chancery Archive, Tucson, Arizona.

with little or no natural immunities to combat such new diseases as smallpox and measles. This is, however, by itself too simple an explanation. Many factors can affect the working of the immune system, diet, stress, etc., and any discussion of epidemics must take into account population density and the quality of housing, the quality of diet, weather, and even levels of stress—a recent article has shown how stress can weaken the immune system and leave an individual more susceptible to disease.[12] Authors Laudenslager and Reite deal with modern day situations, but their findings can be applied to historic mission populations. High mortality certainly produced the stressful situations that the two authors talk about, but the whole process of cultural change in the missions was also stressful, although the degree of change and the violence of the process varied from mission to mission and region to region.

In attempting to restructure Indian society the missionaries initiated major changes, although the degree of change was greatest in the Californias. For example, both the sexual division of labor and the rhythm of labor changed in the mission economy. Whereas women had previously performed most of the menial tasks, the burden was now shifted to the men. To maintain the new labor regime the missionaries introduced the use of corporal punishment, common enough in Europe but alien to Indian culture. Other aspects of cultural change also created stress. Even the separation of the sexes when unmarried must be considered.

New housing and clothing, although not quite the same phenomena as stress, also created health problems. Poor or non-existent sanitation in dormitories and other permanent forms of mission housing created hazards, and such dwellings could not be periodically burned to kill vermin. Furthermore, cold and damp habitation, reported at some missions, promoted respiratory ailments. Contaminated water carried parasites. Improperly washed woolen clothes also harbored parasites. All of these elements, basic to the missionary program, created stress that adversely affected the immunological system, and directly contributed to the process of population loss.

The question of stress must be placed into some kind of historical perspective. European populations experienced high death rates in the seventeenth, eighteenth, and early nineteenth centuries. Smallpox, for example, killed 10-15% of children each year, and roughly half the children died

[12] Mark Laudenslager and Martin Reite, "Losses and Separations: Immunological Consequences and Health Implications," forthcoming in P. Shaver, editor, *Review of Personality and Social Psychology volume 5: Special Issue on Emotions, Relationships, and Health,* (Beverly Hills: Sage, 1984). I would like to thank Shelia Johansson for calling my attention to this article.

before reaching age ten.[13] Indian populations in the missions experienced higher infant and child mortality rates, and also higher mortality among adults. I would argue that one of the major differences between the European and mission populations was the degree of stress and the general standard of living. This is not to say that Europeans, especially rural peasants and the urban poor lived ideal lives, but the process of cultural change was an extremely traumatic experience for many. The whole mission enterprise was a major factor in the process of demographic collapse, and the creation of communities with higher population densities helped facilitate the spread of disease.

One twist must be added to the explanation of demographic change in northern Sonora. The open frontier and development of mining and ranching communities provided opportunities for seasonal and permanent work away from the missions. Indians could pass culturally as *castas,* and intermarried with Indians (ethnic mingling) and non-Indians (miscegenation). Mission records document few such marriages—not all couples sought the benefits of church marriage, but censuses do record instances of mixed pairings. Furthermore, missionaries, at least during the Franciscan period, assigned children the ethnicity of their fathers, so that Pimans were "Pima" even if biologically "mestizo".[14]

Mestizaje raises the question of how "Pima" were the Pimans living in the missions. The missionaries stationed at Caborca and San Xavier del Bac missions, located on the edge of the Papaguería, continued to recruit numbers of gentile Papago up to 1820 and even after, and maintained relatively large populations. In 1820, for example, the two missions and three visitas counted populations of 366 and 310 respectively. The other missions, on the other hand, had much smaller populations that may have been Indian only in name. In the same year, Saric had a population of only 18, San Ignacio with one visita—47, and Tubutama with one visita—37.[15]

Estimating population levels at the opening of the mission frontier in the 1680s and the degree of population loss is a matter of educated guess work. Sauer's estimate of 30,000 for the Pimería Alta can be adjusted upward to 32,000. I arrived at a figure of some 9,100 (this guestimate may be too low) living in the missions and the Papaguería in 1800, including the Gila Pima.[16] The original riverine Pima population, the groups that occupied the

[13] Michael Flinn, *The European Demographic System, 1500-1820* (Baltimore: The Johns Hopkins University Press, 1981), summarizes European vital statistics from family reconstitutions.
[14] Jackson, "Demographic and Social Change . . . ." pp. 103-108.
[15] *Ibid.,* p. 178.
[16] *Ibid.,* p. 57.

river valleys in the 1680s, was for all intents and purposes extinct. The Pápago and Gila Pima survived because they managed to remain outside of the missions.

BAJA CALIFORNIA

The Baja California missions prove to be both an interesting and important case study of demographic collapse because of the relative isolation of the Indian population from such factors as war and miscegenation, and because the non-Indian population remained small and settled in areas that had already lost most of its Indian population. The largest concentrations of non-Indian settlement were at Loreto Presidio, the "capital" of Baja California, and in the southernmost section of the peninsula below modern La Paz where several marginal mining camps existed beginning in the 1740s and 1750s and relatively abundant water allowed agriculture to flourish. In 1808, for example, 1,593 non-Indians lived in the peninsula, 33% at Loreto and 62% in the south.[17] The combined Indian populations of Loreto and the missions in the southern region in the same year was about 190—8% of the total mission population.[18]

The populations of the Baja California missions were basically closed populations. Once the missionaries recruited the gentile population from the hinterland of a given mission there was no source of additional recruits. With birth rates generally failing to match death rates, the populations inevitably declined. Spanish officials recognized the problem and at several points in the eighteenth century ordered reconcentrations of peoples to ensure sufficient labor at those establishments with greater agricultural potential. José de Gálvez ordered the most ambitious resettlements in 1768 with disastrous results.[19]

Epidemic disease had a devastating impact on the Baja California Indians. The record shows the outbreak of an epidemic on average every four years during the course of the eighteenth and early nineteenth centuries.[20] San Francisco de Borja mission, established in 1762, proves to be a case that clearly demonstrates the impact of these epidemics on a mission population. The number of Indians grew between 1762 and 1768 as the result of the

---

[17] *Ibid.*, p. 192.

[18] Robert H. Jackson, "Epidemic Disease and Population Decline in the Baja California Missions, 1697-1834," *Southern California Quarterly* 63 (1981), 308-346.

[19] *Ibid.*, pp. 321-322.

[20] *Ibid.*, p. 316.

recruitment of large numbers of gentiles, but then experienced net loss in population after 1769 as the number of recruits declined. Mission population dropped from 1,640 in 1768 to 192 in 1808.[21] Sixty-seven percent of the net loss in numbers occurred in major epidemic years.

The Indian populations also experienced high infant and child mortality. A family reconstitution for Mulegé mission, established in 1705, for the years 1771-1821, gives a figure of 94% mortality before reaching age ten (derived from a sample of 143 children born at the mission, 76% of all births recorded during the period). Mean age at first marriage for women was thirteen, and the period of childbearing 6½ years. A mere 12% of the children born after 1771 lived to marry. Most failed to live long enough to produce children.[22]

The eighteenth century was not a complete disaster for all of the Indians living in the Baja California missions. The population of San Francisco Xavier mission, established in 1699, actually grew through natural reproduction between 1738 and 1768. In the former year 298 Indians lived at the mission and its visitas, 380 in 1755, 448 in 1762, and 482 in 1768. The removal of population in 1768 and epidemics between 1769 and 1782, probably introduced as a consequence of increased contact between Sinaloa-Sonora and the Californias after the Jesuit expulsion in 1768 and the mounting of the 1769 "sacred expedition" to Alta California, combined to disrupt the balance between fertility and mortality, and initiated a period of population loss. There were the numbers 212 mission inhabitants in 1771, 169 in 1782, and 82 in 1808.[23]

The population of a second mission, Guadalupe, established in 1720, also showed signs of recovery in the last Jesuit years. In 1744, the population stood at 701, dropped to 472 in 1755, but then grew to 524 in 1762 and 544 in 1768. The same fate as San Francisco Xavier's, however, overcame the Indians living at Guadalupe—resettlement and epidemics. In 1771, 140 Indians remained at the mission, and 74 in 1794 when civil officials ordered the mission closed and the survivors moved to Mulege and Comondu missions.[24]

The Indian population of Baja California thus declined during the course of the eighteenth century but at varying rates. In 1755, an estimated 22,674

---

[21] Robert H. Jackson, "Demographic Patterns in the Missions of Central Baja California," to appear in the forthcoming *Journal of California and Great Basin Anthropology.*

[22] *Ibid.*

[23] *Ibid.*

[24] *Ibid.*

Indians remained in the peninsula, 21,000 in 1762, 12,300 in 1773, 9,300 in 1782, and 5,900 in 1800.[25] In 1847, a mere 1,200 Indians lived in Baja California.[26]

NORTHERN ALTA CALIFORNIA

Non-Indian settlements, pueblos and presidios that became population centers, developed alongside of the missions, but, as occurred at the Villa de Branciforte established in 1797, limited markets dominated by the missions contributed to the economic stagnation of the pueblos. A subsistence standard of living or service in the military remained the only alternatives for non-Indian settlers.[27] It was only with the development of trade and the break-up of the missions in the 1820s and 1830s that prospects for the settlers improved. In the case of the Villa de Branciforte the improved economy manifested itself in population growth [see figure 1]. In 1808, population stood at 32, but grew to 294 in 1845.[28] In 1836, the population of the jurisdiction of Monterey, the capital of Alta California, totaled 1,131, including 572 living on ranches in the Salinas and Pajaro Valleys.[29]

Although there were several exceptions, the populations of the northern Alta California missions were generally open populations. Death rates were consistently higher than birth rates, and the missionaries only maintained or expanded population levels by recruiting gentiles from increasing distances from the mission centers. Missionaries stationed at Santa Cruz mission, for example, recruited from the area of modern Santa Cruz County, the immediate hinterland of the mission, the southern Santa Clara Valley and Pacheco Pass area, and finally brought in Yokuts from the Central Valley.[30] Needless to say, population levels fluctuated with the success of the recruitment of gentile Indians. Two case studies will serve to demonstrate my point: San Antonio mission, established in 1771, and San Juan Bautista mission, established in 1797.

San Antonio, the third mission in Alta California, offers an interesting demographic pattern [see Table 2]. Between 1771 and 1810 Franciscans

[25] Jackson, "Demographic and Social Change. . . ." p. 65.

[26] *Ibid.*, p. 155, note 107.

[27] Robert H. Jackson, "An Introduction to the Historical Demography of Santa Cruz Mission and the Villa de Branciforte, 1791-1846," unpublished manuscript.

[28] *Ibid.*, pp. 49, 53-54.

[29] *Ibid.*, pp. 51-52.

[30] Robert H. Jackson, "Disease and Demographic Patterns at Santa Cruz Mission, Alta California," forthcoming *Journal of California and Great Basin Anthropology.*

TABLE I: BAPTISMS, BURIALS, AND POPULATION AT SAN ANTONIO MISSION

Year	Gentile Baptisms	Natal Baptisms	Burials	Excess of Baptisms	Excess of Burials	Population
1771	19	0	3	16		
1772	16	0	3	13		
1773	126	5	2	129		
1774	23	7	8	22		178
1775	146	10	77	79		259
1776	64	12	22	54		343
1777	46	10	46	10		
1778	27	11	17	21		346
1779	59	20	11	68		415
1780	70	27	14	83		502
1781	51	21	38	34		540
1782	60	24	25	59		
1783	107	26	34	99		582
1784	88	40	46	82		774
1785	114	40	77	77		850
1786	86	47	67	66		886
1787	38	42	30	50		979
1788	47	62	45	64		1028
1789	12	64	34	42		1064
1790	14	70	60	24		1092
1791	24	47	109		38	1083
1792	13	62	51	24		1074
1793	30	67	41	56		1142
1794	20	49	41	28		1159
1795	13	35	48	0	0	1150
1796	28	30	51	7		1168
1797	40	37	50	27		1176
1798	29	44	84		11	1123
1799	55	39	89	5		1097
1800	27	65	79	13		1114
1801	23	44	70		3	1097
1802	78	40	135		17	1152
1803	135	49	82	102		1158
1804	93	27	96	24		1203
1805	137	69	94	112		1296
1806	22	47	153		84	1217
1807	4	52	113		57	1140

TABLE I: *Continued*

Year	Gentile Baptisms	Natal Baptisms	Burials	Excess of Baptisms	Excess of Burials	Population
1808	4	40	78		34	1108
1809	9	65	68	6		1114
1810	29	38	59	8		1122
1811	0	59	79		20	1103
1812	6	53	69		10	1093
1813	0	55	73		18	1074
1814	0	47	78		31	1044
1815	0	45	82		37	1008
1816	0	57	82		25	985
1817	0	41	64		23	962
1818	0	33	75		42	922
1819	0	47	67		20	902
1820	0	37	61		24	878
1821	0	37	40		3	875
1822	0	37	78		41	834
1823	0	43	60		17	817
1824	0	35	45		10	806
1825	0	42	48		6	801
1826	0	34	83		49	751
1827	0	39	53		14	744
1828	0	22	54		32	710
1829	1	24	31		6	704
1830	1	22	46		23	681
1831	0	21	41		20	661
1832	0	17	38		21	640
1833	0	20	57		37	
1834	13	17	61		31	
1835	5	15	35		15	526
1836	16	17	48		15	
1837	9	11	32		12	
1838	23	9	34		2	
1839	0	14	53		39	
1840	0	10	26		16	
1841						150

FIGURE 1
Population of the Villa de Branciforte

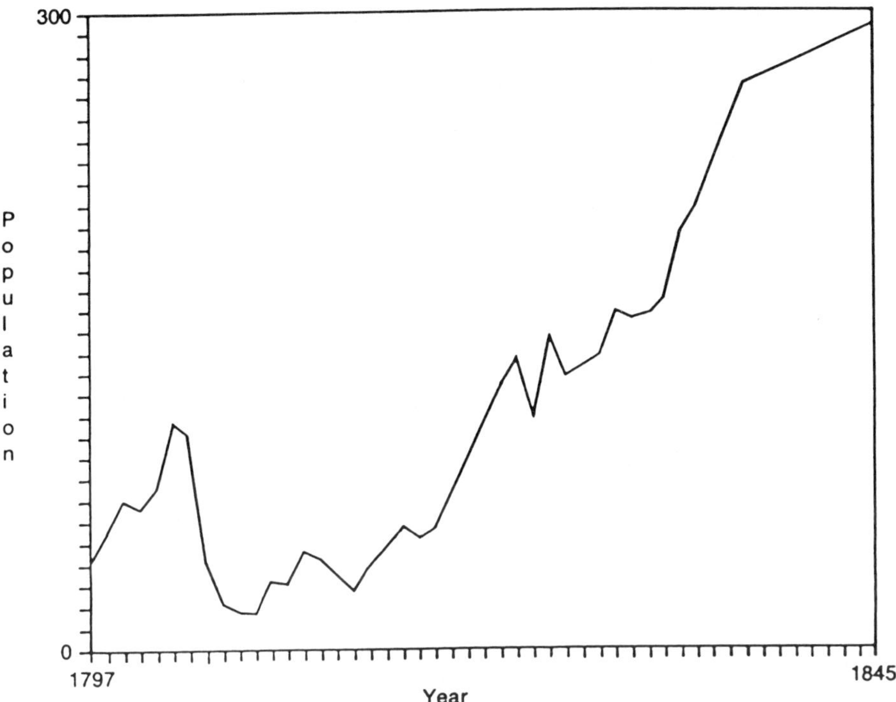

stationed there baptized 2,026 gentiles and recorded the baptism of 1,354 children born at the mission. Burials totaled 2,270 leaving a net gain in population of 1,110. In 1810, the population of the mission was 1,122, a decline from 1,296 in 1805. After 1811, however, the number of gentiles recruited dropped to 74 with none at all between 1811 and 1829. 960 births were recorded during the period and 1,727 burials, giving a net loss in population of 693. Total population stood at 878 in 1820, 681 in 1830, and 150 in 1841 [see figure 2]. Based on the difference between baptisms and burials, 473 Indians should have remained at the mission, indicating that some 323 Indians escaped from the mission following secularization.[31] Interestingly, a large percentage of total baptisms (52%) were of children born at the mission, which is different from patterns observed at other

[31] Ms. San Antonio Mission Baptismal and Burial Registers, Diocese of Monterey Chancery Archive, Monterey, California (hereinafter cited as DMCA); and Zephyrin Englehardt, O.F.M., *San Antonio de Pádua. The Mission In The Sierras* (Ramona: Ballena Press, 1972), pp. 93-94. I tested Engelhardt's population figures against a sample of contemporary censuses.

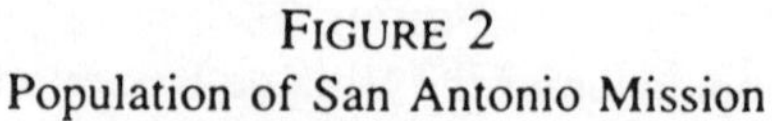

FIGURE 2
Population of San Antonio Mission

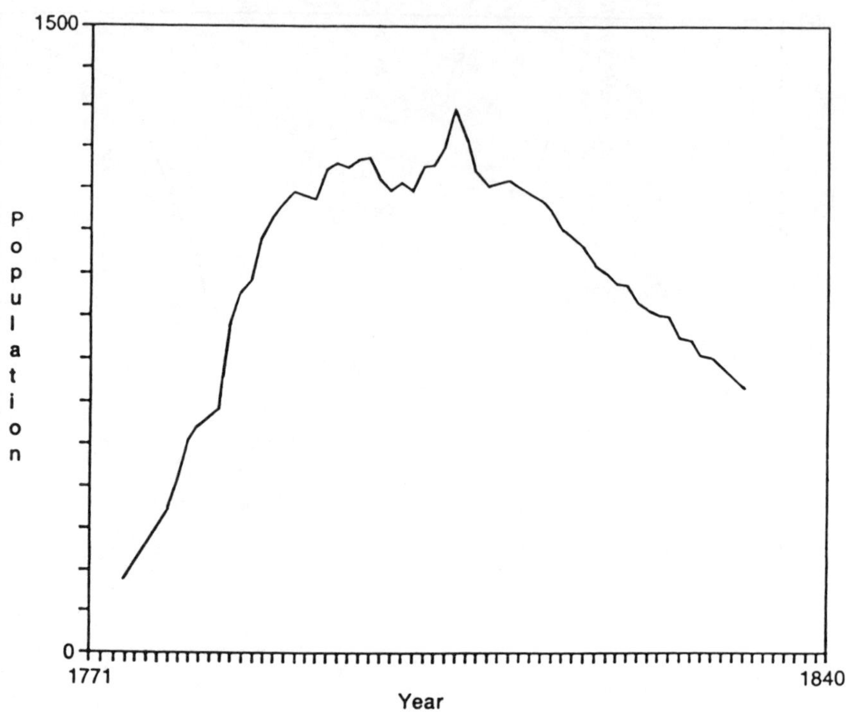

missions in the same region. The pattern can be attributed to the small size of the aboriginal population and the successful completion of gentile recruitment by 1810. After 1810, the mission population became a closed population, and declined in total numbers.

San Juan Bautista had a different pattern from that observed at San Antonio, and some of the data poses a problem of interpretation [see figure 3 and Table 2]. Between 1797 and 1807, Franciscans stationed at the mission baptized 1,492 gentiles and 306 mission-born infants. Burials totaled 796, leaving a net gain in population of 1,002. In 1807, total population stood at 1,072, down from 1,112 in 1805. Between 1808 and 1816, the number of gentiles baptized dropped to 38, there were 256 births, and 594 burials resulting in a net loss of population of 300. In 1809 the population stood at 902, but was only 700 in 1810. Since the registers suggest that 846 Indians should have been at the mission in 1810, 146 people are unaccounted for. It is possible that the loss represented large scale flight, or the removal of people from San Juan Bautista to other missions. In 1816, the

Figure 3
Population of San Juan Bautista Mission

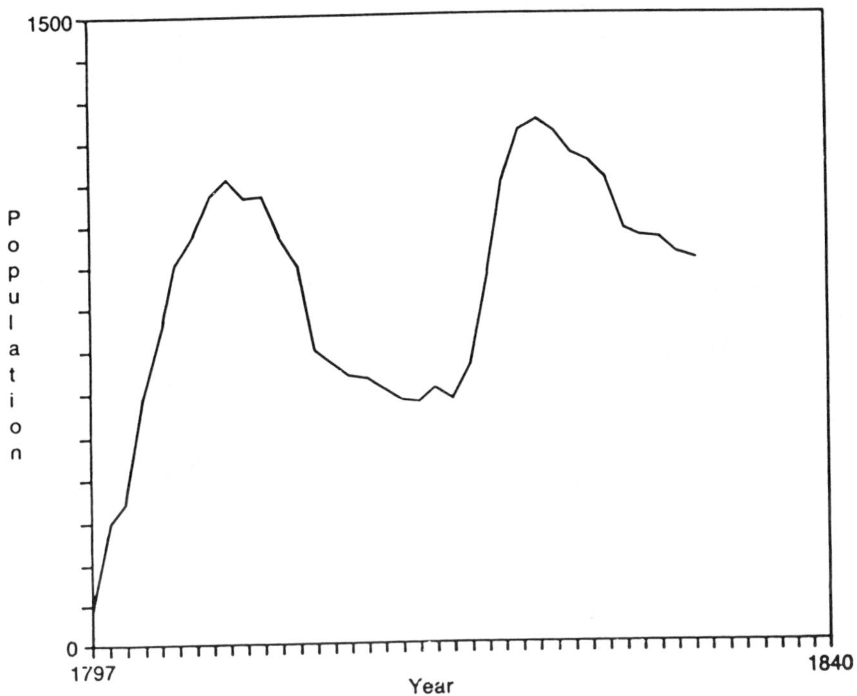

population was 575. Over the next seven years, 1817-1823, the missionaries baptized 877 gentiles, mostly Yokuts from the Central Valley, and noted 349 births. Deaths totaled 524. for a net gain of 702. In the latter year the population was 1,248. After 1824, however, the number of recruits dropped to 251, there were 686 births and 1,480 burials, a net loss of 543. The number of inhabitants was 964 in 1830 and 916 in 1832.[32] Again, because of the relatively small size of the aboriginal population in the San Benito Valley, the percentage of gentile baptisms was smaller in relation to total baptisms. The difference between the two missions, however, was the recruitment of large numbers of Yokuts from the Central Valley after 1816, and especially in the years 1819 to 1823. At San Antonio, on the other hand, few Yokuts entered the mission during the 1830s.

The relative geographic isolation of northern Alta California from the rest of New Spain shielded the region from most epidemics. Only three and

[32] Ms. San Juan Bautista Mission Baptismal and Burial Registers, DMCA; and Zephyrin Engelhardt, O.F.M., *San Juan Bautista: A School of Church Music* (Santa Barbara: Mission Santa Barbara, 1931).

TABLE II: BAPTISMS, BURIALS, AND POPULATION RECORDED AT SAN JUAN BAUTISTA MISSION

Year	Gentile Baptisms	Natal Baptisms	Burials	Excess of Baptisms	Excess of Burials	Population
1797	84	3	7	80		85
1798	173	8	10	171		296
1799	58	20	33	45		347
1800	285	19	15	289		586
1801	151	17	33	135		723
1802	225	26	84	167		910
1803	116	42	103	56		976
1804	166	21	109	78		1073
1805	143	63	108	98		1112
1806	22	30	199		147	1068
1807	69	57	95	31		1072
1808	1	25	93		67	980
1809	0	25	78		53	902
1810	1	28	85		56	700
1811	4	27	63		32	666
1812	0	31	59		28	638
1813	11	33	52		8	633
1814	1	20	47		26	607
1815	2	34	62		26	580
1816	18	33	55		4	575
1817	29	40	35	34		608
1818	7	24	52		21	582
1819	107	40	69	78		660
1820	171	64	36	199		843
1821	296	64	102	258		1098
1822	206	64	142	128		1222
1823	61	53	88	26		1248
1824	26	56	114		32	1221
1825	12	31	101		58	1166
1826	45	35	90		10	1146
1827	18	32	81		31	1108
1828	55	25	227		147	986
1829	12	33	58		13	969
1830	22	28	49	1		964
1831	7	28	81		46	928
1832	20	35	69		14	916
1833	6	43	95		46	

TABLE II: *Continued*

Year	Gentile Baptisms	Natal Baptisms	Burials	Excess of Baptisms	Excess of Burials	Population
1834	1	40	61		20	
1835	1	47	64		16	
1836	1	40	54		13	
1837	6	38	68		24	
1838	6	68	159		85	
1839	5	50	55	0	0	
1840	8	57	54	11		

possibly four attacked the mission populations. There is conclusive evidence for measles outbreaks in 1806 and 1828 and smallpox in 1838, with a possible fourth outbreak of smallpox in 1802. Other factors, then, caused the high mortality at the missions. The creation of communities with high population densities generated problems of sanitation, and dysentery was a major problem. Close contact also facilitated the spread of contagious diseases. Other ailments included fevers, respiratory maladies, and even syphilis. The stress factor as discussed above played an important role in the process, and different evidence points to the stress provoking changes outlined earlier in this essay. Furthermore, the types of endemic diseases that plagued the Indian populations fit into the stress model. Syphilis generally debilitated, but several Indians at Santa Cruz mission reportedly died of what would have been advanced cases of the disease.[33]

Secularization in the mid-1830s accelerated the dissolution of the mission populations. The breakdown of the mission regime between 1835 and 1840 enabled a mass flight of Indians who either returned to the Central Valley or went to work on the ranches granted to the non-Indian settlers. A comparison of data from the registers and population counts from 1840 allows us to make a fairly accurate estimate of the numbers of Indians who left the missions. As already seen in the case of San Antonio mission, some 323 Indians left, 50% of 1832 population levels. The following sample of data from five missions—Santa Cruz and the San Francisco Bay missions excluding San Francisco—shall compare 1832 and 1840 population levels with estimates of the number of Indians who left. The data for San Jose mission shows that in 1834 the Franciscans baptized 892 gentiles, and

---

[33] Jackson, "Disease and Demographic Patterns . . ."

continued to baptize gentiles after secularization. It is not clear, however, if the new converts lived at the mission or went to work on the ranches. For the sake of argument we shall use the low estimate of the number of Indians who left after secularization. The results are as follows. In 1832, the population of the five missions stood at 5,364; in 1840 at 2,005. An estimated 2,383 Indians left the missions, 44% of 1832 population levels.[34] The incipient *Californio* elite inherited not only the material goods of the missions, but also received one of their major resources—a large labor force.

The degree of ethnic mingling in the missions and dissolution of the mission populations after secularization prevents an accurate estimate of the degree of population loss among the local Indian populations, the Ohlone/Costanoan and other groups. In the case of Santa Cruz we know that a mere 3% of the population in 1834-1835 had originated in the Santa Cruz area or had been born at the mission. For all intents and purposes the Awaswas Ohlone were extinct.[35] The situation was different at the other missions in northern Alta California. At San Jose, for example, the local population recruited into the mission, as many as 1,300 people, was probably absorbed into the more than 5,000 Indians brought to the mission from the Central Valley.[36] My own conclusion is that by 1840 the local populations were either extinct or had been assimilated into the mass of the last groups recruited into the mission. Only detailed reconstruction from the mission registers will resolve the question. Anglo-American colonization of California only completed the process begun in the missions.

CONCLUSIONS:
THE LARGER HISTORICAL CONTEXT

Two strands of demographic change can be observed in Northwestern New Spain; demographic collapse among the Indian groups brought into the missions, which concurs with Dobyn's general findings on Indian population loss, and the growth of a largely "mestizo" non-Indian population. Of the three areas discussed in this essay, however, only Sonora developed a market economy in the eighteenth century, which stimulated the growth of the settler population.

One theme discussed in this essay has been the role of stress associated with cultural change in weakening the immune system and increasing the susceptibility of the Indians to different types of disease. There really is no way to know if the Indians continued to lack natural immunities to the new diseases or if the stress factor inhibited or prevented the development of immunities.

[34] *Ibid.*
[35] *Ibid.*
[36] *Ibid.*

One historical fact, however, sheds some light on the question. The Indian populations of Mesoamerica and the Andean region recovered after initial demographic collapse, whereas those discussed here did not. Some scholars have argued that smaller populations were more thoroughly disrupted by the process of demographic collapse, which in turn precluded recovery. Such an argument has attraction, but does not account for the continued survival of two Indian groups in northern New Spain, the Yaqui of southern Sonora and the Pueblos of New Mexico. A cultural explanation, then, would seem to have as much validity as a purely biological one.

The Spanish operated from a position of relative strength in the Californias and the Pimería Alta, and more successfully destroyed aboriginal cultural patterns, especially religious practices. A Dominican missionary stationed in northern Baja California, Luis Sales, described in detail the measures taken to disrupt religious practices, especially dances, and to discredit traditional religious leaders.[37] The Yaqui and Pueblos, however, maintained a stronger position vis a vis the Spanish because of the form that the "conquest" took, and their geographic isolation, and thus retained much of their culture and religion, even if in modified form.[38] Groups in Mesoamerica and the Andean region survived despite the trauma of conquest, exploitation, and demographic collapse as did the Yaqui and Pueblo Indians,[39] and these groups retained much of their religion and social organization in modified or covert forms.[40] The Indians living in the missions of Northwestern New Spain, especially in the Californias, failed in the "collective enterprise of survival." One major reason, but by far not the only one, was the destruction in the missions of the social relationships and religion, the dances and other collective practices that reenforced social relationships, which enabled the Indians in other regions to survive the stress of the "colonial enterprise."

University of California　　　　　　　　　　　　ROBERT H. JACKSON
Berkeley, California

[37] Luis Sales, O.P., *Observations On California, 1772-1790,* translated and edited by Charles Rudkin (Los Angeles: Dawson's Bookshop, 1956), especially letter one.

[38] Archaeologists who excavated Quarai pueblo in eastern New Mexico in the 1950s, for example, found a Kiva in the convento of the seventeenth century Franciscan mission. The archaeologists argued that the Kiva had been built following or during the construction of the convento. Edward Spicer outlined the elements of Yaqui religion in *The Yaquis: A Cultural History* (Tucson: University of Arizona Press, 1980).

[39] For a discussion of the nature of exploitation of the Indians in Central Mexico see Charles Gibson, *The Aztecs Under Spanish Rule A History Of The Indians Of The Valley Of Mexico, 1519-1810* (Stanford: Stanford University Press, 1964).

[40] Two new studies deal with changes in religion and social organization: Karen Spalding, *Huarochiri. An Indian Society Under Inca and Spanish Rule* (Stanford: Stanford University Press, 1984); and Nancy Farriss, *Mayan Society Under Colonial Rule: The Collective Enterprise of Survival* (Princeton: Princeton University Press, 1984).